The History and Theory of English Contract Law

The History and Theory of English Contract Law

By

THOMAS ATKINS STREET, A.M., LL.B.

BeardBooks
Washington, DC

Copyright 1906 by Edward Thompson Company

Reprinted 1999 Beard Books, Washington, D.C.

Printed in the United States of America

ISBN 1-893122-24-7

PART I

GENERAL HISTORY AND GENERAL PRINCIPLES OF CONTRACT

PREFACE

In this, the second volume of THE FOUNDATIONS OF LEGAL LIABILITY, the author has undertaken to work out along historical and evolutionary lines the fundamental principles of our law of contract. The same method has been here pursued that was followed in the writing of the first volume, and the same general aim has been kept in view. Nevertheless, the result is appreciably different. The former volume is, within its limits, a rounded treatise on the subject of torts; the present volume is more in the nature of a preliminary study of the law of contract than a rounded treatise on that subject.

In the former volume we were able to preserve a very satisfactory balance between matter of pure legal history and matter expository of legal principles. In this volume we have been forced to lay more stress on matter of pure legal history than on matter expository of the existing state of the law. The reason for this is to be found in certain grave difficulties which were encountered at the very threshold of these inquiries into the law of contract. The existence of these made it necessary that some preliminary work of a very searching nature should be done. The author accordingly set about the doing of this preliminary work, and the result is the book that is now before the reader. It was thought better to deal fully and exhaustively with the root principles in our law of contract rather than to attempt a systematic presentation of the whole subject. Legal theory in the field of contract was found not to be ripe for that rounded scientific synthesis which, it is to be hoped, will some day appear.

The volume now before us is divided into four parts and is supplemented by an appendix. The first part deals with the history and general principles of our contract law. The second is devoted to the history and theory of the law of bailment. The third is concerned with the history and principles of the law of bills and notes. In the fourth part an attempt has been made to expound the genesis and theory of our law of representation, or agency, as it manifests itself in the relations of principal and agent and of master and servant. This last portion of the volume deals with principles which belong in part to the law of torts. The reason why a topic belonging to tort law has been put at the end of the present volume will become apparent when the reader comes to consider the close affinity of the law of representation in the respective fields of contract and tort. In fact, the two bodies of legal truth are manifestations of the same general principles, and it was found to be utterly impracticable to separate the two branches of legal doctrine.

In the Appendix we have printed the Negotiable Instruments Law, with notes and comments. In point of logical and historical sequence, this matter belongs at the end of our treatment of the law of bills and notes, but for the sake of appearances we have relegated it to the Appendix. This statute occupies a unique position among modern statutory enactments. It is the culmination of that process of development which the law of bills and notes has been undergoing since the common-law courts assumed to apply the principles of the law merchant; and it is a sort of statutory interpretation of past history in this field. It thus has a natural and necessary place at the end of any historical treatment of the law of bills and notes. Our notes and comments on the statute are merely intended to show its connection with the past, to explain a few points of difficulty connected with it, and, further, to direct the reader's attention to the cases in which the meaning of a few provisions of the statute has been judicially considered since the statute went into effect. We have also taken this occasion to direct attention to certain excellent articles, bearing on the interpretation of the statute, which have grown out of the Ames-Brewster controversy.

And now a few words in regard to some of the results which have been accomplished by the labor thus expended. In the opening chapters a full account is given of the early history of contract, and the genesis of the ideas which underlie this branch of the law is fully explained. It cannot be expected that these chapters will have the interest for the general reader, or even for the professional reader, that other parts of the book will have. Nevertheless they contain important truths which the intelligent student cannot by any means afford to overlook.

Beginning with chapter three, the appearance and development of the simple parol contract is carefully traced. The general effect of the recognition of this form of engagement receives attention, and in chapter six an account is given of the origin and nature of the bilateral contract (mutual promises). In chapter seven we have sought to exhibit in a true and accurate way the double basis of our simple contract law. We have shown that the English law of simple contract is unshakably planted on two main ideas — the conception of debt and the conception of obligation resulting from promise. Particular pains have been taken to bring the conception of debt into the prominence which it deserves and requires.

After having, in several successive chapters, dealt with certain important principles bearing on the doctrine of consideration, we come next, in chapters ten and eleven, to consider the peculiar and difficult subject of accord and satisfaction. We have, it is thought, succeeded in giving a rational and consistent account of this subject from beginning to end. The subject is very important because of its bearing on the doctrine of consideration and because of its direct antithesis to the theory of the bilateral contract.

In chapter twelve we enter somewhat fully upon the question of the scope of the bilateral contract. We have here fully demonstrated that this form of contract is not based on consideration in the sense of detriment to the promisee, as is generally supposed, but that it is based on consent. This truth is not merely of academic interest. It plainly has the profoundest bearing upon the theory of our contract law, and the recognition of it enables us for the first time to give a rational account of the important class of cases of which *Scotson v. Pegg* is the type. When the bilateral contract is rightly understood it will be found to embody the most beautiful notion of contractual obligation ever evolved by the wit of man. Though not founded on consideration in the sense of detriment to the promisee, the bilateral contract is yet underlaid by the good sense which characterizes the doctrine of consideration. A promise is given for a promise, and the agreement contemplates that performance shall be given for performance. The doctrine of consideration has here proved a salutary safeguard against too great an extension of contractual liability. We respectfully invite the considered judgment of legal scholars on the value of the work which we have done in clearing up the theory of this most delicate and flexible species of contract.

No less important, in our opinion, than the discovery of the nature of the bilateral contract, is the work which has herein been done in connection with the subject of quasi-contract. This matter comprises chapters twenty-one to twenty-five, inclusive, of the present volume. The key to the theory of quasi-contract is to be found in the distinction between duties in the nature of debt and obligations in the nature of assumpsit. It is at this point that the importance of the distinction between the conception of the debt and the conception of the assumptual promise, which is dwelt upon with such emphasis in the earlier part of the book, becomes fully manifest. Advertence to this distinction, it will be found, renders the subject of quasi-contract at once intelligible and consistent.

Concerning the work done in the second, third, and fourth parts of this book nothing special need be said, as the treatment and the subject-matter of these parts will largely be found to be self-explanatory. We only wish to add that all has been done with equal care and in the same spirit of absolute fidelity to truth.

We entered upon the writing of THE FOUNDATIONS OF LEGAL LIABILITY with a perfectly open mind. We have not at any time in the progress of this work entertained any view or opinion which we were not willing and even glad to sacrifice as wider and better information led to sounder views. Notwithstanding the pains we have taken and the careful recension that every part of this work has several times received at our hands, we have no doubt fallen into errors. These we shall be glad to admit and correct as enlarged knowledge leads us to a better perception of truth.

While thus admitting the possibility and even inevitableness of a certain amount of error in the writing of so extensive a treatise as that of which the present volume forms a part, we feel bound in justice to refer to one or two circumstances connected with the writing of this treatise which ought, it seems, to have some weight when one comes to consider the value of the various conclusions which the author has reached.

First we will mention the circumstance that THE FOUNDATIONS OF LEGAL LIABILITY takes account of facts found in the fields of both tort and contract. As every student of legal theory is well aware, the field of legal liability is a natural unit. The subject of tort cannot be understood without a knowledge of contract, and the theory of contract cannot be understood without a knowledge of the principles of tort. It is evident that the mere fact that account has been taken of both tort and contract in the same work supplies a certain safeguard against hasty and narrow generalization. There has been no time in the progress of this work when we have not corrected our conclusions in one department by conclusions which had been reached in the other. The value of this check will be seen to be very real when it is further suggested that the whole work was written as a unit, and every part of it was carefully worked over by the author just before publication, in the light of all the knowledge which he had theretofore gained.

Second among the factors which ought to give weight to the conclusions which have been reached in this work, may be mentioned this circumstance: Every part of it has been written in obedience to the modern spirit of historical and scientific inquiry. Every topic treated has been separately dealt with, both in its entirety and in its continuity. The author has in no instance taken the pen in hand to write on any particular theme until he had first made himself conversant, so far as within human limitations he could, with all the available material, from the first utterance of the common law to the latest important decisions of our courts. The largeness of view incident to this method of procedure has been of great value in enabling the writer to place the correct interpretation upon the facts which were thus subjected to scrutiny. We have often had occasion to observe the grievous errors into which the most eminent of scholars have from time to time fallen merely because of the narrowness of view incident to the study of decisions of a particular period to the exclusion of decisions from other epochs.

We now come to speak of a feature of this work as to the value and propriety of which there may reasonably be expected to be some difference of opinion. We refer to the use which has been made of quotations, chiefly, of course, quotations from judicial opinions. The casual reader might suppose that the freedom with which such quotations have been introduced is to be taken as evidence of a lack of mastery of detail on the part of the author. How far such a criticism may be justified, we leave for others to say. Our own point of view may be indicated in a very few words. Of late years much stress has been deservedly laid in all branches of historical inquiry upon the original sources. The source-book has come to have a value and a significance heretofore unknown. This spirit of deference to the original springs of knowledge the author has of course imbibed to a considerable extent, and indeed, this entire treatise is the fruit of an effort to get at the original sources of our law. To one so imbued, the terse, the pointed, and ofttimes profound observations which fall from the judges acting in their official capacity come to have a peculiar value and significance. They are at once a fruit of the past and a germ of future doctrine. The time and occasion when a particular principle is enunciated are also often worthy of note. Consideration of these facts has caused us to use great care in culling from the most important cases in every period suggestive words from the opinions of the judges who have taken part in the decisions. We have generally preferred to reproduce the exact words, giving the proper credit by marks of quotation. There is commonly found some note of individuality in the language of the different judges from whom we have quoted, that amply compensates for any defects of style. It would often have been easy for the author to appropriate and reproduce the thoughts of the judges whose reasoning in particular cases has appeared to him to have peculiar value. But he has consistently refrained from so doing. Only a cheap and superficial credit could accrue from such procedure, and the loss to the student would be considerable. It is best to let the lights of the law shine directly upon the reader, with the least possible interference from intervening media.

Not to prolong these words unduly, we hasten to that part of our preface which it is a pleasure no less than a duty to write. We refer, of course, to the matter of the acknowledgment of indebtedness to the writings of other scholars. The epoch-marking work of Professors Pollock and Maitland on the History of English Law (before the time of Edward I) has laid us under the heaviest obligation. The conclusions reached by these scholars have often supplied a necessary starting point in tracing the history of legal doctrine into modern times.

Of individual writers, Professor Ames has perhaps taught us more than any other author. Even where our final conclusions have differed widely from his, as notably in regard to the nature of the bilateral contract and in regard to the nature of the bill of exchange, we have found his views to be stimulating and suggestive. It is needless to say that the History of Assumpsit by this author was of very great assistance in working out the earlier stages in the history of the doctrine of consideration.

In our chapter on the dependence of mutual promises, the discerning reader will find the impress of Professor Langdell's essay on Dependent and Independent Covenants and Promises, which forms a considerable part of his book on contracts. To this piece of work the chapter in question owes a large part of whatever merit it may possess. The essay of Professor Langdell is in fact so original and even brilliant that no writer could subsequently deal with the same topic without reflecting and perhaps even reproducing, to a greater or less extent, the thoughts of his predecessor. We have merely to add that our brief chapter on this subject was written only after a thorough re-examination of the authorities.

Our indebtedness to the authors of various articles in the Harvard Law Review and Law Quarterly Review is considerable; but the fact that we have invariably referred in the footnotes, to such articles in these and other periodicals as have been of assistance to us in the progress of this work, renders any detailed acknowledgment in this place unnecessary.

In conclusion we have to add that in unfolding the principles of the common law we have from time to time found it convenient and instructive to refer to principles of the Roman, or civil, law. We make no pretense to any special knowledge of this system of law, and hence we lay no claims whatever to originality in this field. On points of Roman law we have usually been content to accept without question the conclusions of such competent writers as Mr. W. A. Hunter and Prof. Rudolph Sohm.

CONTENTS

PART I

GENERAL HISTORY AND GENERAL PRINCIPLES OF CONTRACT.

CHAPTER I

EARLY HISTORY OF ENGLISH CONTRACT LAW.

	PAGE
Age of Glanvill	1
The Real Contracts	3
Formal Contracts	7
Jurisdiction of Ecclesiastical Courts	11
Bractonian Epoch	14

CHAPTER II

EARLY HISTORY OF ENGLISH CONTRACT LAW.—*Continued.*

The Innominate Contract	21

CHAPTER III

EARLY HISTORY OF CONSIDERATION.

Genesis of the Conception of Consideration	29

CHAPTER IV

EARLY HISTORY OF CONSIDERATION.—*Continued.*

The Nude Pact	36
Term 'Consideration' Established in Usage	39
Consideration in the Law of Conveyance	40

CHAPTER V

READJUSTMENT.

Suretyship and Guaranty	46
The Bailments	47
Contract of Hiring	48
The Mandate	48

CHAPTER VI

ORIGIN AND NATURE OF THE BILATERAL CONTRACT.

	PAGE
Unilateral and Bilateral Modes of Engagement	52
First Recognition of the Bilateral Contract	55
Consideration in the Bilateral Contract	57

CHAPTER VII

THE DEBT AND THE ASSUMPSIT.

The Early Assumptual Considerations	61
Implied Promise to Pay Debt	62

CHAPTER VIII

CONSIDERATION.

Types of Consideration	67
Benefit to Promisor Not a Good Consideration	68
Adequacy of the Consideration	69
Legality and Competency of Consideration	73
Forbearance to Prosecute Invalid Claim	76

CHAPTER IX

THE CONSIDERATION AND THE PROMISE.

Rewards	81
Consideration Moved by Previous Request	83

CHAPTER X

ACCORD AND SATISFACTION.

Accord Must Be Executed	89

CHAPTER XI

ACCORD AND SATISFACTION.—*Continued.*

Part Payment of Debt	96

CHAPTER XII

SCOPE OF THE BILATERAL CONTRACT.

Consensual Nature of Bilateral Contract	107
Promise of Performance of Existing Obligation	112
Unilateral Promise Given for Performance of Existing Obligation Invalid	112

	PAGE
Mutual Promises in Furtherance of Performance of Existing Obligation Valid	116

CHAPTER XIII
SCOPE OF BILATERAL CONTRACT.—*Continued.*

Novation	122
Novation by Change or Substitution of Contract	126
Composition with Creditors	130

CHAPTER XIV
DEPENDENCE OF MUTUAL PROMISES.

Dependence of Mutual Covenants	134
Dependence of Mutual Promises	135

CHAPTER XV
CONTRACT LAW IN MANSFIELD'S DAY.

The Written Promise	141
Moral Obligation as a Consideration	143

CHAPTER XVI
LEGAL OBLIGATION AS A CONSIDERATION.

Promise Supported by Legal Duty	147
The Implied Promise	149

CHAPTER XVII
CONSIDERATION AND THE RIGHT OF ACTION.

Right of Stranger to Sue on Contract Made for His Benefit	152

CHAPTER XVIII
LEGALITY OF CONTRACT.

Illegality Fatal to All Forms of Contract	162
Contract in Restraint of Trade	164
Wagers	165

CHAPTER XIX
THE STATUTE OF FRAUDS.

Origin of the Statute	168
Purpose and Method of the Statute	169

	PAGE
The Statute Affects Only Simple Contracts	171
Dispenses with No Common-law Requirement	173
Interpretation of the Statute	174
Violation of Statute Renders Contract Voidable but Not Void	177
The Agreement or Memorandum	178
The Signing	181

CHAPTER XX

THE STATUTE OF FRAUDS.—*Continued.*

Collateral Liability of Personal Representatives and of Guarantors and Sureties	183
Promise to Indemnify	186
Promises Supported by Consideration of Marriage	190
Contracts for Sale of Land	193
Contracts Not Performable Within One Year	193
Sales of Goods	194
Place of Statute of Frauds in Modern Contract Law	195

CHAPTER XXI

DUTIES IN NATURE OF DEBT.

Quasi-contracts and Implied Promises	199
Judgments, Customary and Statutory Duties	206

CHAPTER XXII

DUTIES IN NATURE OF DEBT.—*Continued.*

Benefit Conferred under Mistake of Fact	211
Duty to Compensate for Chattels or Service Wrongfully Appropriated	215

CHAPTER XXIII

DUTIES IN NATURE OF DEBT.—*Continued.*

Benefits Conferred under Unenforceable Contract	220
Original Contract Materially Modified	221
Full Performance Prevented by Default of Defendant	222
Performance Prevented by Act of God or Rule of Law	223
Nonperformance Attributable to Default of Plaintiff	225

CHAPTER XXIV

DUTIES IN NATURE OF DEBT.—*Continued.*

Money Paid under Undue Pressure	228
Money Paid to Defendant's Use	232

CONTENTS. xv

CHAPTER XXV
OBLIGATIONS IN NATURE OF ASSUMPSIT.

	PAGE
Various Types of Quasi-assumptual Obligations	235
The Equitable Estoppel	241

PART II

HISTORY AND THEORY OF LAW OF BAILMENT.

CHAPTER XXVI
EARLY LAW OF BAILMENT.

History of Bailments Prior to End of Seventeenth Century.......... 251

CHAPTER XXVII
MODERN LAW OF BAILMENT.

The Case of Coggs v. Bernard	270
Classification of Bailments	271
The Deposit	274
Special Deposit with Bank	276
The Finder of Lost Goods	278
The Mandate	278

CHAPTER XXVIII
MODERN LAW OF BAILMENT.—Continued.

The Commodate	281
Pledge	283
Letting for Hire	284
Procuring of Service	288
Bailment for Custody	289

CHAPTER XXIX
MODERN LAW OF BAILMENT.—Continued.

The Innkeeper	294
The Bailment for Carriage	298
Exceptions to Liability of Common Carrier	300
Postmaster	306

CHAPTER XXX
OWNERSHIP AND POSSESSION.

	PAGE
Severance of Ownership and Possession Essential to Bailment	308
Special Property of Bailee	311
Right of Bailee as Against Stranger	314

PART III
HISTORY AND PRINCIPLES OF LAW OF BILLS AND NOTES.

CHAPTER XXXI
BILLS AND NOTES.

General Observations	323
The *Lex Mercatoria*	324

CHAPTER XXXII
BILLS AND NOTES.—*Continued.*

Early History of Bills of Exchange	335

CHAPTER XXXIII
BILLS AND NOTES.—*Continued.*

Adaptation of Bills to Common-law Theory of Contract	343
Custom of Merchants Accepted as a Source of Legal Duty	347
Extension of the Custom to Transactions Other than Those Between Merchants	350

CHAPTER XXXIV
BILLS AND NOTES.—*Continued.*

Early Bill of Exchange Not Transferable	354
The Bill of Exchange Becomes Transferable	359

CHAPTER XXXV
BILLS AND NOTES.—*Continued.*

The Promissory Note	363
Inland Bill Comes to Be Within Custom of Merchants	369
Note Payable to Bearer	370

CHAPTER XXXVI
BILLS AND NOTES.—*Continued.*

	PAGE
Marius on Bills of Exchange	373
Liability of Indorser	376
Rapid Development of the Law of Commercial Paper	378

CHAPTER XXXVII
BILLS AND NOTES.—*Continued.*

Is the Bill of Exchange a Specialty?	381
Promissory Note Held Not to Be Within the Law Merchant	383
Statute of 3 & 4 Anne Makes Notes Negotiable	385
Effect of Statute on Notes Not Containing Words of Negotiability	386
Bills and Notes Are not Specialty Contracts	387
Note Given for Precedent Debt Treated as Conditional Payment	389
Recital of Value Received	391

CHAPTER XXXVIII
BILLS AND NOTES.—*Continued.*

The Innocent Purchaser	393
The Currency of the Bill	395
The Promise to Accept	399
Virtual Acceptance	401
Bill Payable to Fictitious Party	403
Notice of Defects. Circumstances Giving Rise to Imputation of Fraud	404

CHAPTER XXXIX
BILLS AND NOTES.—*Continued.*

Common-law Principles Ingrafted upon the Law Merchant	409
Warranties Incident to Transfer of Commercial Paper	411
Characteristics of Law Merchant and Method of Growth	416

CHAPTER XL
TRANSFERABLE SECURITIES.

Transferable Bonds, Coupons, and Debentures	419

PART IV
HISTORY AND THEORY OF LAW OF REPRESENTATION.

CHAPTER XLI
REPRESENTATION.

	PAGE
General Observations	429
Principle of Representation Not Found in Roman Law	433
Representation in Old English Law	437

CHAPTER XLII
REPRESENTATION.— *Continued.*

Responsibility for Commanded Acts	442
Immunity of Servant Acting at Instance of Master	444
Early Law of Representation in Contract	446
State of the Law of Representation from Sixteenth to Eighteenth Century	448

CHAPTER XLIII
MODERN LAW OF REPRESENTATION.

Representation in Relation of Master and Servant	456
Liability of Master for Negligent Act of Servant Done in Course of Employment	457
Fellow-servant Doctrine	470

CHAPTER XLIV
REPRESENTATION IN MODERN CONTRACT LAW.

Right to Delegate	475
Undisclosed Principal	477
Power of Agent Acting within Scope of Apparent Authority	480
Ratification	487
Death	491

APPENDIX.

THE NEGOTIABLE INSTRUMENTS LAW	495

FOUNDATIONS OF LEGAL LIABILITY

CHAPTER I

EARLY HISTORY OF ENGLISH CONTRACT LAW.

Age of Glanvill.

A SKETCH of the history of the common-law principles of contract may well begin with the age of Glanvill; for English contract law had no distinct or conscious existence before the king's court began, in that period of the twelfth century, to gather up the heterogeneous customs of the local courts and to weld them into that body of universal custom which we know as the common law. There was no common law before there was a common court. What Glanvill has to say about contracts is the first satisfactory information we have concerning the subject.

Naturally the first question that presents itself is this: What was the first contract known to the common law? About this there is no room for any difference of opinion. The first contract with which we are to deal — the first known to the common law of England — is the real contract. In quite modern times the term 'bailment' has been applied to this contract. In the present connection we shall speak of it as the real contract, or contract *re*. This is the term used in the Roman law, upon which Glanvill largely drew for his terminology, and the use of this expression indicates the fact that in this form of engagement the legal duty is predicated upon the delivery of a chattel (*res*). The particular real transactions which gave rise to contractual duties in Glanvill's time will be presently noticed. It will be perceived that the chief duty incident to them was the duty, on the part of the bailee, of returning the chattel or its value to the original owner. This duty was called a debt and the action of debt was used

Chapter I

Beginning of English Common Law.

Contract *re* the first contract known to the law.

The debt.

Volume II

for its enforcement. We observe then that the early real contract or simple debt was founded directly on legal duty and did not derive its obligatory force from any word or promise of either party.[1] The conclusion that the simple debt, or real contract of bailment, is the most ancient contractual obligation known to our law is amply established by the known facts of legal history, but it is also borne out by *a priori* considerations of the nature and needs of the society in which contract law originated.[2]

Antiquity of barter. Probably the earliest of human transactions is that of barter. This is completed by mutual delivery of the articles respectively exchanged, and there is nothing left to impose an obligation on either party. The next step is the loan, in which a chattel is delivered by one party to the other to be *The loan.* used by him and then returned specifically or in kind. In this transaction a trust is reposed in the borrower and the law consequently imposes on him the duty to return to the lender that which is his. The duty incident to the deposit, pawn, and hiring of a chattel, originates in the same way and is charac-*The bargain and sale.* teristic of the same stage of legal growth. The contract of bargain and sale represents a much maturer stage of development.

In modern times the suggestion of contract almost inevitably brings to the mind the idea of the obligation of promise. To us the binding force of the executory promise is almost a fundamental perception in legal thinking. The obligation of the contract is conceived as a distinct legal entity. In American law, at least, it reposes under the protection of constitutional provisions, along with land, chattels, and other kinds of property, tangible and intangible.

Nothing is more surprising than the extreme slowness with which this conception was evolved. So far from being

---

[1] In Edgcomb *v.* Dee, (1670) Vaugh. 101, it is said that debts by simple contract (i. e. real contract) were the first and would probably be the last debts in the world, and that contracts by writing (i. e. formal contracts) were of later introduction.

[2] See A Treatise on the Action of Debt, by Lord Chief Baron Gilbert, at end of Gilbert's Cases in Law and Equity, 358 *et seq.*

an original and primary perception it is really a highly abstract notion which an immature jurisprudence cannot entertain. The history of English contract law is in a measure the history of a transition from the conception of contractual duty imposed by law to that of contractual obligation resulting from promise.

The Real Contracts.

The simple real contracts enumerated by Glanvill[3] are the *mutuum, commodatum, depositum, locatum* (or *locatio-conductio*), *vadium* (or *pignus*), and the *emptio-venditio* (bargain and sale). The *mutuum* involved a loan of chattels consumable in use and therefore returnable only in kind by number, weight, or measure. The *commodatum* was the loan of an article to be specifically returned. The *depositum* involved the delivery of a chattel for gratuitous safe-keeping. The *locatum*, as he calls it, consisted in letting a chattel out to hire for compensation; while the *vadium* was what we call pledge or pawn.

Of the bare loan of chattels consumable in use and returnable only in kind (*mutuum*) Glanvill has little to say. By such a transaction the title in the property lent evidently passes upon its delivery to the borrower, and the latter is consequently liable absolutely for the return of its value in like material or in money. In the case of the gratuitous loan of a chattel for temporary use (*commodatum*) the title does not pass. The thing remains the property of the lender, and when the borrower is through with it he is bound to return the identical chattel if it be in existence.[4]

According to Glanvill, if the chattel were lost or destroyed the borrower was held liable for its value though he were free from negligence. Only one concession seems to have been made in his favor. Having obtained possession with the consent of the owner, he could not be treated as a thief.

The deposit, or placing of a chattel for gratuitous safe-keeping (*depositum*), is only noticed by Glanvill along with

[3] Glanvill, Bk. X.   [4] Glanvill, Bk. X. ch. 13.

the *mutuum, commodatum,* and other just foundations of debts (*justæ causæ debendi*). Indeed, its importance would hardly require separate treatment. That it is clearly within the theory of the other real contracts is obvious.

<small>Pledge.</small>

The lender, especially of money, according to Glanvill, was not apt to part with his goods without exacting security. Hence the prominence given to the contract of pledge (*vadium*).[5] The thing pledged might be either personalty or realty. In both cases the procedure for the enforcement of the creditor's right against the thing pledged was substantially the same. If the loan was not secured by a pledge the lender was likely to exact personal security.[6]

<small>The surety.</small>

<small>The hiring and bargain and sale.</small>

Concerning the *locatum* and *emptio-venditio* a few words of explanation are necessary — for it is a somewhat curious thing to see the contract of hiring and the contract of bargain and sale treated as real contracts. In the Roman law these agreements (*locatio-conductio* and *emptio-venditio*) were consensual contracts, that is, they derived their validity solely from the consent of the contracting parties. In the English law of the twelfth century no such category of contracts existed. The contracts of hiring and bargain and sale consequently had to be classed as real contracts or be treated as anomalies. The former alternative was adopted, and though the character of these two contracts had to be somewhat changed before this could be done, the law of contract was thereby brought into approximate symmetry.

<small>Roman consensual contract becomes real contract in English law.</small>

<small>Scope of the consensual contract.</small>

The extent to which the scope of these contracts was narrowed in the process of turning a Roman consensual agreement into an English real contract is easily perceived. The contract of hiring (*locatio*) included in Roman law not only the consummated delivery by which a chattel is put into the custody of the hirer, but also the executory consensual agreement by which one party binds himself to let another have the use of a thing for a consideration, as well as all contracts for the finished result of labor (*locatio-conductio operis*) and

---

[5] Glanvill, Bk. X. chs. 3–6.   [6] Glanvill, Bk. X. ch. 3.

contracts for personal service in general (*locatio-conductio operarum*).⁷

The English law had no room for so broad a conception as this. Consequently in recognizing the location, our law required a real transaction, i. e., the actual delivery of a chattel, before it could raise the legal duty. In other words, the contract of hiring was restricted to those cases where a chattel was let for hire. By using the term *locatum* instead of the familiar *locatio*, Glanvill perhaps intended to indicate this difference in the scope of the Roman and English contracts.

<small>Change effected by narrowing scope of contract.</small>

In the bargain and sale we find a similar transformation of a Roman consensual agreement (*emptio-venditio*) into an English real contract. In order to effect this it was only necessary to require as a condition precedent to the passage of title either that the chattel sold should be actually delivered to the purchaser or that the purchaser should actually pay the price agreed upon. If either of these acts were done, the bargain was complete. The purchaser, having paid the price, could maintain detinue for the chattel; the seller having delivered the thing sold could maintain debt for the agreed price. Glanvill says that the payment of part of the purchase money was equally as effective as the payment of all, and this is consistent with the principle underlying the formation of the contract. In harmony with the conception of the bargain and sale as a real contract the principle was recognized that the risk of loss was upon the person having possession.⁸

<small>Conditions of validity of bargain and sale.</small>

Glanvill may well have been puzzled to understand the true function of the earnest. It did not have the same effect as part payment, for the passage of earnest did not complete the sale and make it irrevocable as did part payment. Where only earnest was given to bind the bargain, the purchaser might recede from the contract, but forfeited the earnest. If the seller, having received earnest, wished to go back on the trade, Glanvill thought he should be made to suffer, but was unable to say just what penalty should be imposed upon him.

<small>Function of the earnest.</small>

---

⁷ See Sohm, Institutes of Roman Law, Ledlie's Trans., 2d ed., 419.
⁸ Glanvill, Bk. X. ch. 14.

6 FOUNDATIONS OF LEGAL LIABILITY.

Forfeiture of double earnest.

In Bracton's day it had become settled that, in such case, the seller should forfeit double the earnest, thus surrendering what he had received and its equivalent.[9]

Giving of earnest a collateral bargain.

The analogy between the earnest as thus conceived and the wager of early Roman law (*sacramentum*) will not escape the reader. However, we are told by high modern authority that the earnest was a distinct payment for the seller's forbearance to sell or deliver the thing to any one else.[1] The giving of earnest therefore operated as a collateral agreement. The fact that a contract in which earnest was given acquired something of a religious sanction in the middle ages perhaps made the king's court more loath to recognize it as sufficient to make the contract legally and fully binding in a court of law.

Earnest does not make real contract.

Superficially it would seem that the passage of earnest was enough to make the contract of bargain and sale a true contract *re*. But this could not easily be allowed, for the earnest was not the subject of the contract nor a part of it; and the principle was very tenacious that a contractual duty could be raised only upon a real transaction.

The difficulty, however, was finally surmounted by legislative intervention on the part of Edward I. The *Carta Mercatoria* (1303) declared: "Every contract between the said merchants and any persons whencesoever they may come, touching any kind of merchandise, shall be firm and stable, so that neither of the said merchants shall be able to retract or resile from the said contract when once God's penny shall have been given and received between the parties to the contract."[2]

Earnest in mercantile law.

In the eyes of the law merchant, the giving of earnest thus came to be a sufficient formality to make the contract binding.[3]

---

[9] Bracton, 62a.

[1] 2 Poll. & Mait. Hist. Eng. Law, 2d ed., 208.

[2] See Select Pleas in Manorial Courts, Fair of S. Ives, edited by F. W. Maitland, p. 133.

[3] Fleta had pointed out that among the merchants a more advanced view was being entertained and that the giving of earnest was coming to be much more seriously taken than formerly. (See Fleta, 127.) According to him, the seller who had received the *arrha* must deliver the thing sold or forfeit five shillings for every farthing. To the growing feeling that giving earnest was a sufficient vestment to turn an otherwise nude pact into a binding agreement, the *Carta Mercatoria* gave the royal sanction.

Only at a much later day did this principle become recognized as a common-law rule of general application.[4]

Though Glanvill does, as a matter of fact, treat the real contracts which we have enumerated with comparative fullness, he nevertheless assigns, as a reason for not being more elaborate, the circumstance that the local courts had jurisdiction over the simple debt. Litigation incident to the real contracts consequently reached the king's court only in rare cases.

Formal Contracts.

One important simple contract known to Glanvill could not be classed among real contracts. This was suretyship, a form of engagement which is ancient and which has a special history of its own. It is probably coeval with the *fides facta,* or pledge of faith, and certainly dates from the time when the giving of credit first came to be common. It has been surmised that the duty of paying *wergild* and *bote* first gave occasion for the extension of credit.[5] Where the sum due was greater than the party buying off the feud could raise, he was allowed to give security and pay it by instalments. This was done among the Franks by a ceremony. The debtor passed a *festuca,* or rod, to the creditor, who handed it to the surety (*plegius*). Such surety took the place of the earlier hostage and was personally liable for the debt. In the twelfth century the engagement of the surety had largely lost its formal elements. Glanvill does not give details as to the way in which the obligation of the surety was created. Probably the repetition of a recognized formula, such as gave validity to the Roman stipulation, was enough.

[4] "If the bargain be that you shall give me ten pounds for my horse, and you do give me one penny in earnest, which I do accept, this is a perfect bargain; you shall have the horse by an action on the case [sic? detinue was the proper remedy] and I shall have the money by an action of debt." Noy Maxims, ch. 42, p. 87.

Blackstone, possibly misled by the way in which part payment and something in earnest to bind the bargain were treated in the Statute of Frauds as being *in pari materia,* shows some confusion and treats the giving of earnest as being part payment or part delivery. But at any rate, according to him, "the property in the goods was absolutely bound by it." 2 Bl. Com. 447.

[5] 2 Poll. & Mait. Hist. Eng. Law, 2d ed., 187.

Volume II

The surety a debtor.

Certainly a writing was not necessary, much less a seal.⁶ The obligation of the surety constituted a simple debt and was enforced, like the real contracts, by the action of debt, but it obviously was not based upon a real transaction.

The specialties.

In addition to the simple contracts *re* and the simple formal contract of suretyship, the law of Glanvill's day was coming to know a formal sealed contract. This was the sealed evidence of indebtedness, the *carta,* or obligation, as it was called. It will be observed that there are two formal sealed contracts which have become prominent in English law. These are (1) the sealed obligation of indebtedness, and (2) the covenant (also under seal). They are both specialties. The sealed obligation is the older. Its obligatory character seems to have been gradually stamped upon it by the exigencies of the law of evidence. The process by which this was done can be made out with reasonable certainty.

Written obligation of indebtedness.

Glanvill tells us that, in his day, a debt could be established by "proper witness, by duel, or by a charter." ⁷ The duel as a mode of proof in debt became obsolete at such an early date that we know of no instance in which it was ever resorted to. The proof by witness (*secta*) was adapted only to pure contracts *re,* where a chattel had been delivered by the plaintiff to the defendant. Accordingly, where a money debt resulted from a loan or sale, it was common, even in Glanvill's time, to prove the existence of the debt by a writing, that is, by an instrument (*carta*) under the seal of the debtor.

The seal becomes conclusive.

In a day when the judicial means of establishing disputed facts were crude, it is not strange that a mysterious sanctity should attach to a writing bearing a defendant's seal. Accordingly we find that, if the defendant could not impeach the instrument by a denial of the seal, he was bound by its admissions and was held to performance according to the tenor of the document.⁸ The early courts thus enforced the deed, or

---

⁶ See, for sketch of the history of the contract of suretyship, Holmes, Common Law, pp. 247–250, 260, 264, 280. Also 2 Poll. & Mait. Hist. Eng. Law, 2d ed., pp. 186-188.

⁷ Glanvill, Bk. X. ch. 12.

⁸ "Ubi sigillum suum esse publice recognoverit in curia, cartam illam præcise tenetur warrantizare." *Ib.*

sealed obligation, upon principles of estoppel. Having solemnly affixed his seal, the debtor was not permitted to dispute it.[9]

In course of time it was inevitable that the sealed evidence of indebtedness should become an obligation in itself. This indeed happened. Possibly in Bracton's language we see traces of this tendency towards a *realization* of the formal sealed contract.[1] But at any rate, a hundred years after Bracton wrote, the sealed obligation had become a contract in itself.[2] By an entirely natural process the sealed obligation, having first served as evidence of indebtedness, thus came to be looked upon as being itself the foundation of the action. In other words, the sealed obligation had become a specialty.

Owing to the peculiar sanctity attached to the use of the seal, and owing to the unusual character of the written instrument as a species of evidence, the specialty has always been considered as of a higher nature than the simple contract. Consequently where one delivers an obligation for a simple debt already owing, the latter is merged in the former and ceases to be a separate ground of action.[3]

The other formal sealed contract, the covenant, belongs to a later period than the age of Glanvill. "The king's courts," says he, "do not intermeddle with contracts founded merely on private agreement (*privatas conventiones*)."[4] In other

---

[9] Of course it was always permissible for the debtor to impeach the sealed evidence of indebtedness by showing that the seal attached to it was not his. Says Glanvill: "He may deny or controvert it in two ways: thus, he may acknowledge in court the seal to be his own but deny that the charter was made either by him or with his consent, or that of his ancestor; or he may absolutely deny both the seal and the charter." Bk. X. ch. 12.

[1] Per scripturam vero obligatur quis, ut si quis scripserit alicui se debere, sive pecunia numerata sit sive non, obligatur ex scriptura, nec habebit exceptionem pecuniæ non numeratæ contra scripturam, quia scripsit se debere." Bracton, 100b.
See also Bracton and Azo, Selden Soc., vol. 8, p. 156, note. In Bracton's time and for long afterwards the terms obligation and *scriptura* ('writing) meant an obligation under seal.

[2] "L'obligation est contract en lui meme." Bellewe's Cases, tit. *Contract* (8 Rich. II.).
To same effect see *ib.*, p. 255: "In debt upon an obligation the defendant cannot plead that he owes nothing to the plaintiff. He must answer to the deed by a plea of *non est factum*."

[3] Brooke Abr., tit. *Contract,* pl. 29 (29 Hen. VIII.).

[4] Glanvill, Bk. X. ch. 18.

words, mere promises, whether sealed or unsealed, created no legal obligation unless they were made of record; that is, unless they were put into the form of a recognizance. In the latter case they ceased to be private and became judicial covenants.[5] The real contract, the simple contract of suretyship, and the sealed obligation of indebtedness (which was itself merely a formalized debt) were therefore the only contracts recognized and enforced by the common law in the twelfth century.

Gradual shifting of contract law to the idea of obligation of promise.

Though as we have now seen the conception of debt in our early law was nearly coextensive with the idea of obligation incurred by means of a real contract or transaction *re*, it did not remain so. It was indeed inevitable that in the end the idea of obligation incurred by the agreement of the parties should take its place beside and finally overshadow the idea of duty incurred by the delivery of a chattel. The recognition of the sealed obligation undoubtedly tended to educate the mind into a broader conception of the debt. The peculiar character of the contract of suretyship contributed to the same end. Being of purely formal origin, it could not be classed as a contract *re*. Yet it constituted a simple debt, and having lost all vestiges of formality, it either had to be treated as anomalous or the conception of debt had to be modified. The latter alternative was pursued, and from this period onward suretyship takes its place with other simple contracts and, like them, is supported in one epoch by *quid pro quo*, in another by consideration. It is obvious that even in Glanvill's day the more subtle notion was struggling for recognition. His use of the term *justa causa debendi* as descriptive of the common basis of all debts shows that the mind of this writer

---

[5] In another connection Glanvill, noting the fact that private agreements to deliver a chattel in future pledge to secure a debt created on the faith of such promise, are not binding, says: "The King's Court is not in the habit of giving protection to or warranting private agreements of this description, concerning the giving or accepting things in pledge, or others of this kind, made out of court, or even in any other court than that of the King. If, therefore, such compacts are not observed, the King's Court does not interfere: and hence it is not bound to answer concerning the right of different creditors, as prior or subsequent, or respecting their privileges." Glanvill, Bk. X. ch. 8.

had framed an abstract conception of the simple debt which would no longer comport with the older and narrower conception.

Jurisdiction of Ecclesiastical Courts.

In studying English contract law in the age of Glanvill we are struck by the circumstance that the common law had finally and positively refused recognition to the promise supported merely by the good faith (*interposita fide*) of the promisor. The creditor who had not taken the precaution to exact a pawn (*pignus*) or require a surety (*plegius*) had to prove the delivery of a chattel under such circumstances that the law imposed a legal duty (real contract). Relief for a mere violation of faith could be obtained only in the court Christian, which had power to impose penance or enjoin satisfaction.[6] Important questions are thus suggested for solution. What was the exact extent of the jurisdiction of the spiritual courts in the field of contract? To what extent did the possession of this jurisdiction cause the king's court to refuse recognition to agreements which otherwise might have found their way through these courts into the English common law?

In course of time it came to pass that the jurisdiction of the spiritual courts over matters of contract wasted away. The very fact that these courts had jurisdiction over a particular form of engagement caused the king's court to refuse recognition to it. This leads us to say a few words about the formal pledge of faith as recognized and enforced in the ecclesiastical courts.[7]

In the time of Glanvill (there is no sure ground before his day) the mediæval canon law began to take on some shape, and classical Roman law was being disinterred throughout Europe. About the latter Glanvill had evidently learned something from Vacarius and the Italian glossators. Bracton, a century later, had learned much more and consequently showed deeper traces of the influence of Justinian's system. The ecclesiastical or canon law gradually gained a foothold in the

---

[6] Glanvill, Bk. X. ch. 12.   [7] Glanvill, Bk. X. ch. 12.

field of contract by sanctioning the old formal agreement by pledge of faith. The nature of this promise is well described by Messrs. Pollock and Maitland as follows:

"It may look like an oath. We may think that it implicitly contains all the essentials of an oath; but no relic or book or other thing is sworn upon and no express words of imprecation are used. A gage is given; that gage is *fides;* that *fides* is the giver's Christianity; he pawns his hope of salvation. . . . A man's Christianity is realized; it becomes a thing, an object to be given and returned. . . . When a man makes a vow to God he will place his faith upon an altar and will find sureties who are to have coercive power over him. But more, when he makes a promise to another man he will sometimes offer God as his surety. . . . When we obtain details of the ceremony by which faith is 'made' or 'given' or 'pledged,' we often find that the manual act takes place, not between the promisor and promisee, but between the promisor and a third person who is sometimes expressly called a *fideiussor*. He is generally one whose station gives him coercive power over the promisor; he is the bishop of the diocese or the sheriff of the county. He does not accept any legal liability for the promise; but he holds the promisor's faith in his hands and can constrain him to redeem it by ecclesiastical censure or temporal distress. . . . It may well be that sometimes the promisor put his faith directly into the hands of the promisee, and in this form the ceremony would become fused with that mutual grasp of hands," a formal engagement which may have had a somewhat different origin.[8]

The pledge of faith viewed as a pledge of one's Christianity brought the ceremony within the cognizance of the ecclesiastical courts. The great struggle between Henry II and Thomas à Becket in the twelfth century involved chiefly the question of the extent of the jurisdiction of the temporal and spiritual courts. The king would have stripped the ecclesiastics of all jurisdiction in pleas of debt, whether the

---

[8] 2 Poll. & Mait. Hist. Eng. Law, 2d ed., 191.

EARLY HISTORY OF CONTRACT.   13

creation of the debt was accompanied by a pledge of faith or not.[9]

From this radical position, which virtually deprived the ecclesiastical tribunals of all jurisdiction over breaches of oath and breaches of faith, the king was compelled to recede. Glanvill, a few years later, stated that a breach or violation of faith belonged to the courts Christian; but he added that, by statute, the ecclesiastical courts could not use this power to oust the king's jurisdiction over debts of the laity or their tenements.[1]

The writ of prohibition afforded the means by which the temporal courts laced up the ecclesiastics straitly within the limits of their proper jurisdiction, and the reports of the proceedings of the courts in Bracton's day show that this writ was continually "buzzing about the ears of the ecclesiastical judges." The latter retaliated from time to time with their ready spiritual weapons, and Northampton, for instance, was once laid under an interdict because its mayor had enforced a prohibition.[2]

The controversy was kept up far into the fourteenth century. By the royal document known as *Circumspecte Agatis*, which came in time to be treated as having the authoritative force of a statute, the king undertook to define for his judges, for whose guidance it was drawn up, the limits of the rival jurisdictions. The bishops' courts were not to be interfered with in spiritual matters, and it was taken as settled that defamation and laying violent hands upon a clerk were subjects of ecclesiastical jurisdiction. Some of the copies of this document include breaches of faith in the same category, so long as spiritual correction and not the collection of money was the object of the suit. The controversy dragged on. In the

---

[9] See Constitutions of Clarendon (1164), "Placita de debitis, quae fide interposita debentur, vel absque interpositione fidei, sint in justitia regis."

[1] "Judex ipse ecclesiasticus licet super crimine tali possit cognoscere et convicto penitentiam vel satisfactionem injungere; placita tamen de debitis laicorum vel de tenementis in Curia Christianitatis per Assisam regni, ratione fidei interpositae, tractare vel terminare non potest." The statute referred to is, of course, the Constitutions of Clarendon. Glanvill, Bk. X. ch. 12.

[2] 2 Poll. & Mait. Hist. Eng. Law, 2d ed., 200.

Volume II

The end of the controversy.

end the ecclesiastical jurisdiction in the field of contract was limited to testamentary and matrimonial causes and other merely spiritual matters (*mere spiritualia*). It is interesting to observe one formal requirement which was always necessary before the pledge of faith was recognized as giving rise to obligation. This was the hand-shake.[3] This formality became a distinguishing characteristic of the contract cognizable by the court Christian. The acceptance of this formality as being a sufficient *vestment* in the spiritual forum was probably a sufficient reason why the king's court should regard this form of contract with disdain, or, at least, should refuse it recognition. In Blackstone's day men sometimes shook hands over a bargain.[4] Even to-day this method is sometimes used to give the sanction of honor to promises which parties recognize as having no legal validity.

Agreement by pledge of faith repudiated by common-law courts.

The history of the effort of the formal pledge of faith to gain its place among English contracts is thus exceedingly interesting. That it never crossed the threshold was largely due to the fact that it was too closely identified with a court whose conceptions, procedure, and jurisdiction were an object of peculiar jealousy to the judges in the king's courts.

Bractonian Epoch.

Bracton contributes little to English law of contract.

Passing on from the age of Glanvill to the next century, the student will be surprised to find that Bracton, the author of the most finished treatise on English law prior to Blackstone's Commentaries, contributed little or nothing to our theory of contracts. What he wrote on the subject of obligation is hopelessly out of harmony with contract law as it then existed. Still less does it give an idea of what that branch of the law was afterwards to become. In late years the part of his treatise which is devoted to contracts has attracted much attention, but, as has been said, no part of it is more poorly done.[5] The mistake of Bracton was that, finding English contract law as stated in Glanvill to be meagre in

---

[3] See 2 Poll. & Mait. Hist. Eng. Law, 2d ed., 202.
[4] 2 Bl. Com. 448.

[5] Salmond, Essays in Jurisprudence, p. 174; 2 Poll. & Mait. Hist. Eng. Law, 2d ed., 194.

substance and unshapely in form, he attempted to make it conform to the theory of the civil law of contract as expounded by the Italian legists. With Glanvill and Azo before him, Bracton appropriated the substance of the English writer and copied so much from the other as was not wholly inconsistent with it. There is no experience behind what he says, and it is therefore of little practical value. The lesson to be learned from it, say Messrs. Pollock and Maitland, is that at the end of Henry III's reign no general doctrine of contract had been worked out by the royal courts.[6]

Chapter I

Influence of the Italian legists.

Concerning only two contracts does Bracton speak at much length. These are the contracts of sale and of hiring, which, as we have seen, were consensual contracts in Roman law, but which in Glanvill were treated as real contracts. This character they of course retain in Bracton's pages.[7]

Hiring and bargain and sale.

Bracton is fuller than Glanvill in his statement of the duties incident to the real contracts, and does not hesitate to use the texts of the civilians to fill in *lacunæ* where Glanvill, with greater fidelity to the actual state of English law, had refrained from speculation.[8] What Bracton lays down as law

Law of bailment.

---

[6] 2 Poll. & Mait. Hist. Eng. Law, 2d ed., 194.
On this subject see Bracton and His Relation to Roman Law, Güterbock, translated by Brinton Coxe, ch. 18; also Bracton and Azo (Selden Soc. Pub., vol. 8), 142 *et seq.*

[7] These two contracts he treats under the title "Acquiring Control" (i. e., ownership, *dominium*). Bracton, 61b, 62, 62b.

[8] The entire passage in which Bracton treats of the pure real contracts is as follows:
"§ 1. Re autem contrahitur obligatio veluti in mutui datione, quae consistit in rebus, quae pondere, numero, mensura sunt; pondere, sicut in rebus quae ponderantur, numero, sicut pecunia numerata: pondere, aere, argento et auro; mensura sicut in vino, oleo, frumento, quae res autem in appendendo, numerando, metiendo in hoc dantur ut statim fiant accipientium. Quia mutuum proprie dicitur id quod ex meo fit tuum, et quandoque non eaedem res sed aliae eiusdem naturae redduntur creditori.
"Hiis autem, cui res aliqua utenda datur, re obligatur, quae commodata est; sed magna differentia est inter mutuum et commodatum, quia, is, qui rem commodatam accepit, ad ipsam restituendam tenetur vel ejus precium, si forte incendio, ruina, naufragio aut latronum vel hostium incursu, consumpta fuerit vel deperdita, substracta vel ablata. Et qui rem utendam accepit, non sufficit ad rei custodiam, quod talem deligentiam adhibeat, qualem suis rebus propriis adhibere solet, si alius eam diligentius potuit custodire. Ad vim autem majorem vel casus fortuitos non tenetur quis, nisi culpa sua intervenerit, ut si rem sibi commodatam domi secum detulerit cum peregre profectus fuerit et illam incursu

concerning the duties of the respective parties to real contracts reposed in his pages for approximately four hundred and fifty years, exerting little or no influence upon the decisions of the courts in this field. Finally, at the beginning of the eighteenth century, this ancient learning was disentombed by Lord Holt, who made it a part of our law of bailment.[9]

The formal contract. Curiously un-English is Bracton's talk about the formal contract of stipulation. The ancient formal Roman contract, *stipulatio,* had, of course, long been obsolete, but the civilian school from which Bracton derived what he knew of Roman law still talked of the principles underlying the stipulation as being practically applicable in the law of contract. The sealed obligation, the covenant, which was now coming into notice, and the engagement of the surety, were formal English contracts which furnished some analogy to the stipulation, and it was these which Bracton probably had in mind when he reproduced the Roman learning. But little that he has to say on this subject was co-ordinated with actual transactions in every-day life. When he tells us that the stipulation is a formal verbal contract entered into by question and answer, as if one says, *Dost thou promise? I promise; will you give? I will give,* etc.,[1] we are not to understand that the recital of such formulas, without more, necessarily resulted in the formation of a contract enforceable in the king's court in the thirteenth century. The chief formal contract in English law was the sealed

hostium vel praedonum, vel naufragio amiserit, non est dubium, quin ad rei restitutionem teneatur. Commodata autem res dicitur ad commodum data, et proprie dicitur commodata cum nulla mercede accepta res utenda data. Gratuitum enim esse debet commodatum, et si merces intervenerit potius dici debet locatio et conductio quam commodatum.

"Is apud quem res deponitur, re obligatur, et de ea re, quam accepit, restituenda tenetur et etiam ad id, si quid in re deposita dolo commiserit. Culpae autem nomine non tenetur, sc. desidiae vel negligentiae, quia, qui negligenti amico rem custodiendam tradit, sibi ipsi et propriae fatuitati hoc debet imputare. Creditor, qui pignus accepit, re obligatur, et ad illam restituendam tenetur; et cum hujusmodi res in pignus data sit utriusque gratia sc. debitoris, quo magis ei pecunia crederetur data sit, et creditoris, quo magis ei in tuto sit creditum, sufficit ad illius rei custodiam diligentiam exactam adhibere, quam si praestiterit et rem casu amiserit, securus esse possit, nec impedietur creditum petere." Bracton, 99, 99*b.*

[9] Coggs v. Bernard, 2 Ld. Raym. 909.

[1] Bracton, 99, 100.

writing, and where the engagement was put under seal no particular phraseology was or could be required.

In Glanvill's day, as we have seen, no attention was paid in the king's courts to the covenant. In Bracton's pages we are informed that the king's court would sometimes take jurisdiction to enforce a covenant as a matter of favor.[2] This marks the first recognition by the royal court of a form of agreement which was subsequently to attain much prominence.

The word 'covenant' is an inaccurate transliteration of the Latin word *conventio* and is applied to an undertaking or agreement to do some act or give some thing to the covenantee. It first appeared in connection with leases of real property. By the time of Henry III, the covenant had become the popular foundation on which to levy a fine. The term 'covenant,' it will be observed, is theoretically as broad as the modern conception of executory contract. It is applicable to any agreement to do or refrain from doing a particular act. Bracton said there were as many kinds of covenants as there are things to be contracted about, and with a wise nod he suggests this as a reason why the high and mighty court of the king could not afford to undertake to enforce them. The Statute of Wales recites that contracts of covenant are infinite in number and consequently are impossible of enumeration.[3]

Chapter 1

The covenant.

Nature of the covenant.

---

[2] The language of Bracton on this point is as follows: "Iudicialis etiam esse poterit stipulatio vel conventionalis. Iudicialis, quae iussu iudicis fit vel praetoris. Conventionalis, quae ex conventione utriusque partis concipitur, nec iussu iudicis vel praetoris, et quarum totidem sunt genera quot paene rerum contrahendarum. De quibus omnibus omnino curia regis se non intromittit, nisi aliquando de gratia." Bracton, 100.

Whereupon Professor Maitland gives us the following note: "When writing of judicial stipulations he is perhaps thinking of recognizances, for, though these contracts are recorded in writing, they are not sealed by the parties; they are already becoming common. Again, when the essoiner pledges his faith for the appearance of the essoinee, this may be regarded as a judicial stipulation. It would be needless to say that the last clause of this passage is not from the Institutes. The King's Court will not trouble itself about 'conventional stipulations'— that is, about contracts made outside the court and by mere word of mouth. Bracton, who has been looking at Glanvill, Bk. X. ch. 8, does not deny that the extra-judicial 'stipulation' (parol agreement) is binding. The King's Court will sometimes enforce it as a matter of grace, but it is not bound to do so." Bracton and Azo, 152.

[3] Stat. of Realm, vol. 1, p. 66. See also 2 Poll. & Mait. Hist. Eng. Law, 2d ed., 218.

18   FOUNDATIONS OF LEGAL LIABILITY.

Volume II

The covenant formalized.

The covenant, like the modern assumptual promise, embodies the idea of contractual duty arising out of the agreement of the contracting parties. The conception was therefore admirably adapted to future developments in contract law. Its promising career was, however, cut short and its importance greatly lessened by reason of the fact that the covenant was soon turned into a formal contract. This resulted from the requirement that the covenant should be evidenced by a deed. In other words, the covenant, like the other specialty already noticed, must be under seal.

Reasons for this step.

This requirement was perhaps partially due to a mere caprice of legal history, but undoubtedly the chief reason for requiring the covenant to be sealed is that at the time when the question of the validity of the parol covenant arose, there was practically no judicial machinery for sifting the truth of oral testimony. The courts were therefore loath to sanction so broad a contract. Besides, admitting the validity of the parol covenant, there was no conception such as the later doctrine of consideration, to serve as a test of liability. The covenant evidently could not be given absolutely free rein. It is therefore not surprising that, by the end of the reign of Edward I, it had become an established rule in the king's court that the only enforceable covenant is that which is in writing.[4]

Bearing of the event on future of English contract law.

It is curious and perhaps in a measure profitable to speculate for a moment on the course of future development in English contract law, if the parol covenant had been recognized. In that event our courts would certainly have adopted substantially the whole of the Roman law of obligation. The need for the formulation of such a doctrine as that of consideration would not have been felt. Nor would our lawyers have been forced to go afield into the law of torts and shape the action on the case upon an assumpit to the curious purpose

---

[4] 2 Poll. & Mait. Hist. Eng. Law, 2d ed., 219.

These writers show that there was quite a long period of uncertainty on the question whether the covenant must be under seal. As early as 1234-35 an action was dismissed because the plaintiff had no deed. Later authorities from the same century indicate that the rule was then not altogether established. 2 Poll. & Mait. Hist. Eng. Law, 2d ed., 218, note.

of redressing a grievance arising from a failure to perform a parol agreement. They would have found the entire theory of contracts already worked out in some detail by the civilians. How much legal theory would have lost by such a mischance can hardly be imagined.

The reader will perceive that the two specialty contracts to which attention has now been directed are not based upon consideration. They derive their obligatory force solely from their form. The sealed debt is binding because the admission of indebtedness, being under seal, is taken as conclusive. The covenant is likewise binding because the promise is proved by the seal of the covenantor. No doubt both kinds of specialties usually arise out of transactions in which something of value passes, and it has been wisely conjectured that during the formative period of our law the king's court would not have bestirred itself to enforce a sealed promise if its gratuitous character had been openly revealed. In regard to covenant it may be pointed out that it was originally a subsidiary agreement connected with and consequently supported by some other transaction, such as the sale or lease of land. This may account for the circumstance that a recompense or equivalent was not deemed necessary to give it validity. However this may be, the general principle was settled at an early day that a specialty is good without a consideration or any other similar element.[5]

In modern times the notion that something must always be given for a promise in order to make it binding has become so deeply imbedded in legal consciousness that our judges have sought to bring the specialty contract within the doctrine by declaring that the seal raises a presumption of consideration. This fancy has been indulged for more than three hundred years.[6] But it is as erroneous as it is superfluous.

At the close of the Bractonian epoch the situation can be summed up in a few words. The key to the contract law of the period is found in the conception of the duty originating

---

[5] See Anson on Contracts, p. 49; Leake on Contracts, p. 76; Clark on Contracts, pp. 82, 72.

[6] The idea appears in Sharington v. Strotton, (1566) 1 Plowd. 298.

> **Volume II**
>
> Contract law at end of Bractonian period.

in the transactions involving things. Real contracts (the contracts *re* of the Roman law) occupy nearly the entire horizon of legal thought so far as the law of obligation is concerned. The real contracts which Bracton knew were the bailments, *commodatum, pignus, depositum,* the *mutuum* (which is a contract *re,* but not a bailment), and the contracts of sale and letting to hire. Both of the latter contracts were consensual agreements in Roman law and had been turned into real contracts only by limiting their original scope. In addition to the real contracts there were the formal contracts. The undertaking of the surety had once been properly formal; but it had now come to repose for its validity upon the passage of a *quid pro quo,* like other simple contracts (debts), or upon the duty imposed directly by law, as where one became bail for another in court. The sealed obligation and the covenant (also under seal) were the only formal contracts which were to persist as such.

> The unilateral duty characteristic of early contract law.

The reader will observe that the various contracts to which attention has been directed are illustrations of unilateral duties. Such was to remain the character of English contracts for many generations. To be sure, mutual covenants might be entered into by the two parties, but the duties respectively imposed were independent; in other words, separate contracts. Furthermore, in enforcing contracts of bargain and sale by means of the actions of debt and detinue, the courts were not unconsciously giving effect to bilateral engagements. The duties of the buyer and seller are in a sense connected with each other, but in early theory they were separate and distinct grants.

CHAPTER II

EARLY HISTORY OF ENGLISH CONTRACT LAW (CONTINUED).

The Innominate Contract.

WE now come to consider that stage in the evolution of contract law which follows the recognition of the real contract. If progress be made along natural lines it is obvious that contracts which are not perfect real contracts, but which are analogous to them, should next obtain recognition. This leads us to consider the place of the innominate real contract and the history of its gradual recognition in English law. We shall find that while the course of development was tedious it was nevertheless along the same lines that had been pursued in Roman law when the latter was passing through a similar stage. Reference to the history of the innominate contract in that system will therefore throw some light upon an obscure and hitherto untold chapter in our English law of contracts. The fact that English law was not directly influenced at this point by the maturer Roman law makes the analogy not only helpful but really instructive.

Chapter II

Analogy from Roman law.

The duty imposed by law in the real contract arises, as we have seen, upon the delivery of a chattel. Now if, in the place of the delivery of a *res*, we substitute the *doing of any act*, we have the conception which underlies the innominate real contract. The recognition of the innominate real contract is manifestly made possible by a broadening of the conception underlying the real contract.

Conception underlying innominate real contract.

The recognition of the innominate real contract in Roman law was brought about by the equitable intervention of the pretor. In his court one who had performed a promise was allowed to sue for redress upon the failure of the other party to perform his counter-promise. The action was specially framed in case (*actio in factum præscriptis verbis*), and the

Innominate contract in Roman law.

22 FOUNDATIONS OF LEGAL LIABILITY.

Volume II

liability of the defendant was based solely on the ground of performance by the plaintiff.[1]

Paulus's formula.

Paulus summed up the innominate contracts in a well-known formula. Either, says he, I give something to you, in order that you may give something to me; or I give something to you that you may do some act for me; or, I do an act for you that you may give something to me; or, I do an act for you that you may do an act for me. (*Do tibi ut des; do ut facias; facio ut des; facio ut facias*).[2] These categories can probably be reduced to two, as *facio* necessarily includes *do;* and others might be added, as refraining from acting is fully as adequate to support an innominate real contract as acting (*facio ut non facias; non facio ut facias; non facio ne facias*).[3]

The analogy of these engagements to the real contract on the one hand and to the modern bilateral contract on the other is highly instructive, but we do not here pause to trace it out.[4] In the mature Roman jurisprudence the innominate real contracts were included in the broad conception of contractual duty arising solely from agreement. In the modern English law they are identified with unilateral contracts supported by the executed consideration.

Let us now inquire how far the innominate contract was recognized in the early common law.[5] Naturally it was first

---

[1] Sohm, Institutes of Roman Law, Ledlie's Trans., 2d ed., 397, 398; Hunter, Roman Law, 3d ed., 532.

[2] D. 19, 5, 5.

[3] Hunter, Roman Law, 3d ed., 540, 541.

[4] See Hunter, Roman Law, 3d ed., 540 *et seq.*

[5] Bracton strives to give the innominate contracts some sort of recognition, but how foreign the conception was to the English law at this period may be gathered from the circumstance that he treats them strangely out of place, under the head of conditional grants. Bracton, however, recognized the fact that such agreements were binding only *sub modo,* as a plaintiff who had performed his part could only recover the thing given for the promise or the expenses incurred upon the faith of it. "Istae donationes consistunt sub modo et obligant contrahentes, ita quod si dedero vel fecero, tu teneris ad dandum vel faciendum, secundum quod convenit; sed tamen ut repetere possim quod dedi, si tu non vis facere quod promisisti, si ad hoc tantum agere possunt quod tu facias, nisi aliter convenerit ab initio. Poterit enim huic donationi sub modo adici conditio ab initio, ut si dicam, et si non dederis vel non feceris, quod convenit, quod ego repetere possum quod dedi, vel impensas factas circa rem quas feci, aliter non." Bracton. 19.

recognized in connection with agreements for the performance of personal service. In Glanvill and Bracton, as we have seen, the *locatum* included only the letting of things to hire and did not extend, as did the Roman *locatio,* to contracts of personal service (*locatio operis rei* and *locatio operarum*). There are no early precedents of servants bringing the action of debt to recover compensation for personal services rendered.[6] Even taken with the explanation that the local courts possibly gave redress in such cases, this is sufficiently surprising. But it was not long before the performance of personal service was recognized as being a just foundation for a debt. The references made to such right of action in the year books takes this principle for granted.[7] The historians of our early law hazard the guess that even in the latter part of the reign of Edward I, the king's court would have put services rendered on the same footing with goods sold and delivered;[8] in other words, that they would have placed the doing of service in the same category with the delivery of a chattel which constituted the *quid pro quo* of other simple debts. After the passage of the Statutes of Laborers special remedies under the statute were given to the employer and he was deprived of the right to wage his law as against the servant's claim for compensation. Actions of debt for the recovery of hire consequently remained uncommon, the proper remedy being that given by the statute.[9]

Chapter II

Personal service.

Debt unusual remedy for servant.

With the exception of debts incurred for personal service, the innominate real contracts were slow to get secure footing. In 1422, a creditor recovered judgment and had execution issued against his debtor. A third person thereupon promised the creditor to pay the debt if the latter would release the execution of record. This the creditor accordingly did. Subsequently he brought an action of debt on this promise. It was held that he could not recover. The promise, in the view of the court, was *nudum pactum ex quo non oritur actio.*[1]

Slow development of innominate contract.

[6] 2 Poll. & Mait. Hist. Eng. Law, 2d ed., 211.
[7] Y. B. 40 Edw. III. 24, pl. 27.
[8] 2 Poll. & Mait. Hist. Eng. Law, 2d ed., 211.
[9] Y. B. 11 Hen. IV. 33, pl. 62; Y. B. 39 Hen. VI. 18, pl. 24.
[1] Y. B. 9 Hen. V. 14, pl. 23.

In 1428 an attempt was made to obtain recognition of the validity of an innominate contract in an action on the case for a deceit. The agreement was in the form *facio ut facias*. The defendant, being the father of a marriageable girl, promised that, if the plaintiff would marry her, he would enfeoff them of certain lands and tenements. The marriage was accordingly solemnized. It was held by Paston, J., that the defendant was not liable, on the ground that no *quid pro quo* had passed to him. It could not yet be perceived that the act of marrying the defendant's daughter might be so treated. The *quid pro quo* must still be a material thing.²

About thirty years later (1459) a very similar agreement in the form *facio ut des* was debated in the Common Pleas. The plaintiff and defendant made an agreement to the effect that the former should marry the defendant's daughter Alice and that the defendant should pay him a sum of money. The plaintiff performed by marrying the girl and then sought to recover the sum promised him by her father. Two of the judges thought the action maintainable, two thought that it was not, while the fifth was of opinion that only the ecclesiastical court had jurisdiction. The reasoning of Moile and Danvers, JJ., is instructive, for it shows that they fully grasped the idea of the validity of a promise given for an act done upon faith of such promise. Said Danvers: "If I tell a man if he will carry twenty quarters of wheat of my master Prisot's to G. he shall have 40 s. and thereupon he carry them, he shall have his action of debt." Likewise Moile: "If I say to a surgeon that if he will cure J. safe and sound, I will pay him 100 s., and he does restore J. to health, he may have an action of debt against me, and yet the thing is done for another." He further said that, though the person for whom such an act is done, has not *quid pro quo* in a technical sense, still it is such in effect.³

The foregoing language shows that the conception which underlies the innominate real contract, namely, that of a promise being made binding by the doing of any act, was clearly

---

² Y. B. 7 Hen. VI. 1, pl. 3.   ³ Y. B. 37 Hen. VI. 8, pl. 18.

grasped. At a later day this idea was accepted without question.[4] But it was only after the invention of the new contractual remedy, assumpsit, that English remedial law was equal to the task of enforcing all innominate contracts. The action of debt was an impossible remedy upon innominate contracts in the form *do ut facias* and *facio ut facias*, for in these the promise is to do some act other than to make a payment of money, and debt could be used only when there was a duty to pay an ascertained sum of money or deliver a specific amount of ponderable or measurable chattels.

Inadequacy of debt as a remedy upon innominate contracts.

As has already been observed, Glanvill casually used the phrase *justa causa debendi* to indicate the common element lying at the foundation of the various debts. But it was late in the fourteenth century before any serious attempt was made to generalize the many "causes of owing" and to name the element common to all true debts. Taking no account of the exceptional contract by specialty, it is obvious that the common element in the various debts was that the debtor had received something from the creditor which he was bound to return or pay for. This element finally came to be known as the *quid pro quo*, an ungainly phrase which was unknown even to mediæval Latinity save in this particular connection.[5]

Origin of term quid pro quo.

---

[4] In Y. B. 39 Hen. VI. 18, pl. 24, the plaintiff sued in debt for a sum of money promised him for going to Rome and obtaining a papal bull. The right of action was not questioned and the point argued was whether the defendant was entitled to wage his law. In Rogers *v.* Snow, (1572) Dalison 94, the plaintiff suing in assumpsit upon a contract in the form *facio ut des*, was defeated because his count did not allege with sufficient distinctness, performance on his part; but it was assumed that the action could be maintained if the plaintiff had performed. "If I promise a man 20 s. if he will go to York in my behalf, an action on the case lies upon this promise, but he must allege performance on his part. This the court conceded."

[5] Just when the term *quid pro quo* first came into use is not fixed with certainty. It was undoubtedly a familiar expression at the beginning of the reign of Edward IV.; for in the case before the Common Pleas in 1459 to which reference has already been made, two of the judges used the term in its accepted sense. Y. B. 37 Hen. VI. 8, pl. 18.

Instances of an earlier use of the expression *quid pro quo* have been pointed out, but in connections where the term possessed no technical significance. Possibly the earliest mention of it is in Y. B. 39 Edw. III. 18, but the term is not there used in connection with contract. See article by Mr. J. W. Salmond in 3 L. Quar. Rev. 168.

Quid pro quo primarily a physical object.

The *quid pro quo* was primarily a material or physical object, and it constituted the recompense or equivalent acquired by the debtor. Upon the passage of the *quid pro quo* the law raised that real contractual duty peculiar to the debt and with which the reader is now familiar. It may be helpful to conceive of the *quid pro quo* as a form of consideration. But as we shall presently see, consideration was not directly or indirectly evolved out of the older conception. So far as it goes, the old doctrine of *quid pro quo* in debt corresponds with what we, in modern times, call 'consideration' in the same class of cases. But the notion underlying *quid pro quo* was not elastic and it was impossible for it to exert any sensible influence upon the development of our law of contracts. If a powerful force had not operated from another direction our law of contract would apparently have remained in the straight-jacket supplied by the action of debt.

Notion inelastic.

In the law of bargain and sale the actions of debt and its twin sister detinue did indeed show some flexibility and here a close approach was made to the recognition of the obligatory force of the parol agreement. It will be remembered that in the early sale no legal duty was raised in the time of Glanvill and Bracton unless the chattel sold was actually delivered or the purchase price was paid. Where either of these acts was performed, debt or detinue lay to enforce the legal duty imposed on the other party. It was therefore contrary to principle to allow either the seller or buyer to maintain an action until he had himself complied with the terms of the sale.

Extension in law of sales.

But as the bargain and sale is really a consensual agreement it was hard to keep it within the limits of the theory of real contract supplied by our early law. Consequently a tendency to break away from the old doctrine was soon manifested. In 1347, Thorpe said that where an obligation was delivered for the price of goods purchased, the seller could maintain debt and the purchaser detinue.[6] The delivery of the obligation thus served to give color of reality to the transaction. Where no such bond was given, neither action should

---

[6] Y. B. 21 Edw. III. 12, pl. 2.

in strict theory have been allowed, but in 1441 it was said by Fortescue, C. J., that in case of the present sale of a horse, the property was in the purchaser without the payment of the price or delivery of the animal, and that consequently the seller could maintain debt for the purchase money, and the buyer, detinue for the animal.[7]

Title passes upon agreement of sale without payment.

Very properly this view of the sale was not taken in those bargains where it was agreed expressly or by implication that payment of the purchase price should be made simultaneously with the delivery of possession. In such case no title passed until the purchase price was paid.[8]

In a case reported by Dyer an action of detinue was brought on what was termed an absolute contract for eighty quarters of wheat. The following distinction was drawn: When the day of payment is specified, the contract is good immediately and an action (i. e., detinue for the chattels) lies upon it immediately without payment; but if the time of payment be not specified, the money is due at once and the contract is made void by the failure of the purchaser to pay. Thus, if a man buy of a draper twenty yards of cloth, the bargain is void if the purchaser does not pay the price agreed upon forthwith; but if the day of payment be appointed by agreement of the parties, in that case one shall have his action of debt and the other an action of detinue.[9] In other words, the giving of credit did not suspend the right of the purchaser to have possession. The bargain and sale had evidently come to be considered as being made up of two reciprocal grants.[1] It had thus lost the distinguishing features of a real contract. But this episode in the law of sales was exceptional. The proprietary action of debt was hampered by procedural de-

Bargain and sale ceases to be pure real contract.

---

[7] Y. B. 20 Hen. VI. 34, pl. 4; Y. B. 21 Hen. VI. 55, pl. 12; Y. B. 37 Hen. VI. 8, pl. 18; Y. B. 39 Hen. VI. 18, pl. 24.
[8] Y. B. 17 Edw. IV. 1, pl. 2.
[9] Dyer, 29b.
[1] Said Vaughan, C. J., in Edgcomb v. Dee, Vaugh. 101: "Contracts of debt are reciprocal grants. A man may sell his horse for present money at a day to come, and the buyer may, the day being come, seize the horse, for he hath property then in him; which is the reason that actions in the debet and also in the detinet are actions of property; but no man hath property by a breach of promise but must be repaired in damages."

fects harmful to its usefulness and fatal to its future growth. An anomalous extension of the law of sale might give the mediæval lawyer a glimpse at the conception of the obligation of promise. It could not supply him with a general theory.

A glance at the state of English contract law at the close of the fifteenth century will suggest to the reader that this branch of the law had about reached the limit of its development along the old lines. The pure real contracts, the contract of suretyship, the bargain and sale, and contract of hiring in their more extended scope, and the innominate contracts, so far as these were or could be enforced by means of existing remedies, bounded the field of simple contractual liability. The covenant and sealed obligation were formal contracts and not capable of much change. Undertakings of record, such as the recognizance and judgment, undoubtedly imposed duties properly to be classed as contractual duties, since they might be enforced by debt, but they require no extended comment. The narrow horizon of contract law in that world was due more to the inelastic nature of the ancient contractual remedies, debt and detinue, than to any other fact. The time was now at hand when they were to be in great part superseded.

CHAPTER III

EARLY HISTORY OF CONSIDERATION.

AS we have elsewhere pointed out,[1] trespass on the case is the original and proper remedy where the cause of action is founded upon misfeasance in the performance of any undertaking or promise. Case having become a recognized remedy for the negligent misfeasance of agreements actually undertaken, it was natural that pressure should be exerted to induce the courts to go a step further and to hold a promisor liable in damages for a refusal or negligent failure to enter upon performance. The efforts made in this direction during the fifteenth century are easily traced.

Chapter III

Liability for negligent misfeasance.

In 1400 an action was brought against a carpenter for his failure to build a house for the plaintiff, as he had agreed to do, within a stipulated time. The objection was made that a covenant was alleged and no writing shown. The action was dismissed on that ground, but one of the judges said that if the writ had alleged that the work had been begun and subsequently stopped through negligence the action might be maintained.[2] Exactly the same case came up nine years later with the same result.[3] Brooke, writing about a hundred years later, points out that the undertakings sued on in these cases were *nuda pacta*.[4] But this objection was not taken at the time, as the element of consideration had not then been differentiated.

Nonfeasance of parol promise not actionable.

In 1424 another notable attempt to hold a defendant liable for the nonperformance of a parol agreement was made in an

---

[1] See vol. 3, *Action on the Case*.
[2] Watton v. Brinth, Y. B. 2 Hen. IV. 3, pl. 9.
[3] Y. B. 11 Hen. IV. 33, pl. 60.
In Y. B. 20 Hen. VI. 34, pl. 4, it was said that where a carpenter agrees to build a house of certain proportions, which he does, but in a negligent manner, an action on the case will lie for the damage, because the covenant being fulfilled no other remedy is available. Negligent misfeasance was, of course, at the root of this doctrine.
[4] Brooke Abr., *Accion sur Case*, pl. 40.

Unsuccessful attempts to gain recognition for validity of simple promise.

action on the case against a millwright.[5] For the defendant it was pointed out that this was merely an action for the nonfeasance of a covenant and that the promise was not proved by a writing under seal. Martin, J., who was against the action, remarked that if it could be maintained, trespass would lie for any breach of covenant. Several dicta were thrown out by the judges suggesting particular cases where the action would lie. These are not very instructive. The case went over to another day and the questions raised were left unsettled. One weakness in the plaintiff's case was probably fatal. He did not allege that a specific sum was to be paid for the building of the mill. Consequently, if the defendant had performed his agreement to build he could not have maintained an action of debt for his recompense, and it was not fair to insist that he should be liable for not building the mill under these circumstances. The decision justifies Brooke in the conclusion that " if it be not expressed what he is to have for his work, it is a nude pact, *unde non oritur actio*." [6] The cases noted above fall perceptibly short of giving recognition to the idea of the binding force of a simple promise.[7] Another link in legal theory is still necessary. To supply this we must take up another thread, viz., the conception which underlay the action for a deceit. By tracing its history we shall discover the true genesis of the doctrine of consideration and learn how simple promises first became actionable as such.

[5] Y. B. 3 Hen. VI. 36, pl. 33.
[6] Brooke Abr., *Accion sur Case*, pl. 7.
This case has been much commented on in modern times in connection with the subject of actionability of executory agreements. See History of Assumpsit by Professor Ames, 2 Harv. L. Rev. 11; Holmes, Common Law, 267, 285; Hare on Contracts, 161, 162. Sir Wm. Jones in his Essay on Bailments, Am. ed. (1806), p. 63, uses this case as authority for the position that a mandatary is bound by his assumption or agreement to act as such, but this conclusion is not warranted.
[7] In 1435 Paston, J., and Juyn,

C. J., concurred in holding that a defendant was liable for failure to perform a parol promise to procure a release. Y. B. 14 Hen. VI. 18, pl. 58. The decision would seem to furnish the desired precedent in favor of the validity of the simple promise, but it was premature, and apparently exerted no influence on subsequent decisions. The *ratio decidendi* was defective, inasmuch as the court followed the analogy of cases wherein persons plying a public calling are held for damages resulting from their refusal to supply service. Clearly the situations are not within the same principle.

GENESIS OF CONSIDERATION. 31

Prior to the passage of the Statute of Westminster II, the old common-law action of deceit had a very narrow scope, and it appears to have been limited to cases where the plaintiff suffered damage by a deception practiced upon a court or in connection with litigation, as, for instance, where an action was fraudulently or collusively conducted by an unauthorized person.[8] The action of deceit was, however, apparently stimulated by that provision of the statute which authorized the framing of writs *in consimili casu* and its scope was accordingly soon extended.

Confining our attention to cases bearing on the law of contract, we find a suggestive case argued at length in 1432. It was alleged that an agreement had been made between the plaintiff and defendant whereby the latter was to purchase a certain estate for the plaintiff. The defendant, however, deceitfully colluding, as was alleged, with a stranger, "had disclosed plaintiff's evidence" and had purchased the premises for him instead of for the plaintiff. The court was of the opinion that the defendant was liable in an action on the case for deceit.[9] Collusion with the stranger seems to have been taken as the gist of the action, but the fact was remarked upon that the position of the defendant was analogous to that of one guilty of a misfeasance in carrying his agreement into effect.

In 1441 a very instructive case was argued in the Exchequer Chamber. The plaintiff alleged that he had bargained with the defendant, for a certain sum paid, to enfeoff him of certain premises within a stated period. The weakness of the reasoning on which the preceding case was decided was made apparent by an observation of Ascough, J.: "If the defendant had retained the land in his own hands without feoffment made, then the plaintiff would have only a writ of covenant [if he had a specialty]; and I submit that the law is the same where the defendant makes a feoffment to a stranger." The majority of the court showed a decided in-

Chapter III

Original scope of the action of deceit.

Extended scope of the action of deceit.

---

[8] See 2 Poll. & Mait. Hist. Eng. Law, 535.
[9] Brooke Abr., *Accion sur Case*, pl. 108; Y. B. 11 Hen. VI. 18, pl. 10; Y. B. 11 Hen. VI. 24, pl. 1; Y. B. 11 Hen. VI. 55, pl. 26.

Volume II

The deceitful promise to enfeoff.

clination to sustain the action, but the case was adjourned.[1] By the end of the century it was settled that an action on the case for deceit would lie where one who agreed to enfeoff A enfeoffed a stranger instead.[2] Doubtless in all of the cases where this rule was applied the plaintiff had parted with the purchase money at the time the defendant agreed to convey.

Ex post facto fraud.

Where the plaintiff had suffered such a detriment in fact, there could be little impropriety in allowing the promisee to maintain an action for the deceit. To be sure, the fraud involved was of an *ex post facto* nature, since no distinction could be drawn between cases where the defendant at the time of obtaining the money actually intended to repudiate his promise and those where such intention was subsequently formed. Still the rule adopted was calculated to further the ends of justice and was not fatally repugnant to sound theory.

Emergence of the idea of the obligation of promise.

However prominent the idea of tortious deceit may have been in these decisions, it is clear that such actions could not be maintained without sanctioning the idea of the legal obligation as incident to the giving of a promise. One who gets a thing of value on the faith of a promise to do a particular act may be declared guilty of a legal fraud upon failing to perform the promise. But the court which enforces this liability is, at the same time, giving damages for the breach of a simple promise supported by an executed consideration.

Promise given for executed consideration becomes actionable.

The final establishment of the principle that the failure to perform a simple promise is actionable where the promisee has parted with a thing of value on the faith of the promise, belongs to the opening years of the sixteenth century. A case from 1505 marks the culmination of legal theory on this point. The plaintiff had purchased and paid for a quantity of barley

---

[1] Y. B. 20 Hen. VI. 34, pl. 4.

[2] The steps by which this principle was established are noted by Professor Ames, 2 Harv. L. Rev. 12, 13, citing Y. B. 16 Edw. IV. 9, pl. 7; Y. B. 2 Hen. VII. 12, pl. 15 (1487); Y. B. 3 Hen. VII. 14, pl. 20 (1488). In the last case Brian, C. J., said: "If an agreement is made between you and me that you shall make me a title to so much land and you enfeoff another of the same land, shall not I have an action on the case?" (implying the affirmative) and the court agreed with him: for, adds the reporter, when he proceeds to enfeoff another than the one agreed, it is a great misfeasance.

GENESIS OF CONSIDERATION. 33

to be delivered at a certain place on a day named. The vendor did not perform, and the vendee, who was a brewer, was forced to buy other barley at an increased price. Thereupon he brought an action of assumpsit. The action of debt could not be maintained because the barley was not separated so as to be capable of identification, and hence no property had passed. The elaborate summary of the law given by Frowike, C. J., in sustaining the action shows that liability in assumpsit was predicated on the fact that money had been paid or other thing of value given by the plaintiff for the promise.[3]

Chapter III

Frowike's summary.

---

[3] Mich. Term, 21 Hen. VII., Kielw. 77, 78.
For Frowike's summary of the law as then understood see Keilw. 77a–78. The case was adjourned. See Dyer 22b, where Fitzjames, J., says it was decided in accordance with Frowike's opinion. At any rate the doctrine of the case was never afterwards questioned. At a previous debate on this case, reported in Y. B. 20 Hen. VII. 8, 18, Frowike, C. J., seems to have stood alone, Kingsmil, Fisher, Vavisor, and Fineux, JJ., being of the contrary opinion. The victory of Frowike was truly a triumph.

The most instructive part of Frowike's opinion is as follows:

"If a man sells to me one of his horses in his stable and further agrees to deliver to me the horse by a certain day, I shall not take the horse without delivery; but if he sells to me one of his horses in his stable for a certain sum paid down, I may take the horse, since it belongs to me, without delivery; and in both cases, if he aliens or converts the horse to his own use, so that I cannot have my bargain, I shall have an action on the case against him by reason of the payment of the money. And also if I sell ten acres of land, parcel of my manor, and then make a feoffment of the manor, you shall have good action against me on your case because of the receipt of your money, and in this case you have no other remedy against me. Also if I sell you certain land and further agree to enfeoff you by a certain day, and do not do it, you shall have a good action on the case, and this has been decided. So if I sell to you twenty oaks from my woodland for money paid, and then I sell the wood, action on the case lies. . . . And if I agree with a carpenter to build [me] a house and pay him £20 to complete it by a certain day and he does not build the house by the time stipulated, then I shall have an action on the case by reason of the payment of my money; and yet it sounds only in covenant, and without the payment of the money in this case there is no remedy. Still if he builds the house and does the work defectively, action on the case lies. Also for the nonfeasance, if the money be paid, action on the case lies. So it seems to me in the case at bar the payment of the money is the basis of the action on the case, and this without any transmutation of the property."

Compare with the foregoing the following note of a decision in Y. B. 21 Hen. VII. 41. pl. 66: "If one covenants to build me a house by a certain day and does nothing towards it, I may have an action on the case for this nonfeasance [sic?] as well as if he had done it amiss; for I am endamaged thereby; and Fineux, C. J., held this for law,

3

34 FOUNDATIONS OF LEGAL LIABILITY.

Volume II

Forbearance as a consideration.

After this it could only be a question of a very few years until it should be recognized that the doing of any act by the promisee is a sufficient detriment to support a promise given to procure the doing of that act. In *Estrigge v. Owles* (1587),[4] it was held that indulgence to a debtor and forbearance *per paululum tempus* to enforce the claim against him might be a good consideration. As was said by the court a few years later: "This forbearance is a good consideration, although it cannot be any benefit to him who makes the promise, yet because it is a damage to the creditor to forbear his suit and duty."[5] A remedy had at last been found in which effect could be given to all innominate contracts whatsoever.

Attitude of the court of equity.

The Court of Chancery indirectly had something to do with forcing the law judges to recognize the validity of the simple promise, and the part so played by it must not be overlooked. Indeed, the attitude of the chancellor served as an admonition to the law judges that they must go in and occupy the field covered by the simple promise, otherwise the court of equity would take this jurisdiction upon itself. The uneasiness felt by the law judges on this point was voiced by Fairfax, J., in 1481, who insisted that the action on the case should be extended so as to obviate the necessity of suitors

And so it is if one bargains with me that I shall have his land to me and my heirs for £20 and that he will make the estate to me. If I pay him the £20 and he refuses to make the estate to me according to his covenant, I shall have an action on the case."

[4] 3 Leon. 200. See also Gill v. Harewood, 1 Leon. 61, where the consideration was that the plaintiff *per parvum tempus deferret diem solutionis*.

[5] Banes' Case, (1612) 9 Coke 94. Here an executor having assets was charged upon a promise to pay the debt of his testator made in consideration of forbearance. Compare Smith v. Jones, Owen 133, Yelv. 184; Mapes v. Sidney, Cro. Jac. 683.

In the latter case the creditor agreed to forbear, in consideration of which the defendant promised to pay £80. The plaintiff alleged that he had forborne *per magnum tempus*. The court held that the suit would lie, as it was inferred that the agreement meant total forbearance. See also Finer v. Jeffry, Style 57; Pooly v. Gilberd, ('1613) 2 Bulst. 41; Woolaston v. Webb, (1611) Hob. 18; Flight v. Gresh, (1625) Hutton 77; Cowlin v. Cook, Latch 151; Beven v. Cowling, Popham 183; Best v. Jolly, 1 Sid. 38; Goodwin v. Willoughby, Popham 177. Also the cases of Semple v. Pink, (1847) 1 Exch. 74, and Oldershaw v. King, 2 H. & N. 399, 517.

going into chancery.⁶ In 1506, Fineux, J., who had disagreed with Frowike, C. J., two years before,⁷ remarked that since an action on the case (assumpsit) would lie for the nonfeasance of a simple promise, there was no need to sue a subpoena.⁸

That the Chancery Court did anticipate the law courts in giving redress for the breach of a simple promise has been pointed out more than once.⁹ But after the law courts took the matter in hand, the equitable jurisdiction over parol contracts withered away. In the Diversity of Courts (Chauncerie), which belongs to about 1525, we are told that a man could have a remedy in that court for covenants made without specialty, if the party had sufficient proof of the covenants, since he was without remedy at common law. The Court of Chancery, however, like the court of law, paid no attention to a purely gratuitous promise. Upon the *nudum pactum* there was "no more help in chancery than there is at common law."¹

⁶ Y. B. 21 Edw. IV. 23, pl. 6.
⁷ Y. B. 20 Hen. VII. 8, pl. 18.
⁸ Y. B. 21 Hen. VII. 41, pl. 66.
⁹ Judge Holmes in 1 L. Quar. Rev. 173, and Professor Ames in 2 Harv. L. Rev. 14, 15, call attention to some of the cases where relief was given in equity on parol contracts. The chancery court was actuated by the same motive that subsequently led the common-law courts to take the identical step, viz., a desire to restore a defrauded person to the situation in which he was before the breach. One case, e. g., Appilgarth v. Sergeantson, (1438) 1 Cal. Chan. 41, will illustrate this. This was a suit brought by a female complainant against a defendant who had obtained her money on a promise of marriage and had deceitfully married another. This was very like the case in the law courts against one who, after a contract to enfeoff, conveyed land to another. Other similar cases where equity gave such relief are cited by Mr. S. R. Bird in Antiquary, vol. 4 p. 185, vol. 5, p. 38. See 8 Harv. L. Rev. 256.
¹ Cary, 5.

CHAPTER IV

EARLY HISTORY OF CONSIDERATION (CONTINUED).

Volume II

Mutual promises not yet recognized as valid contract.

FROM the failure of Frowike to make any reference to the bilateral contract of mutual promises in his summary of the law of assumpsit, it is manifest that this form of engagement had not yet been recognized and that the only simple promises which were now binding in law were those supported by an executed consideration. This inference is corroborated by an abundance of other evidence from the same period. The language of St. Germain, which is quoted further on, is pertinent here.[1] Likewise, as we shall see, in the great case of *Sharington v. Strotton* (1566)[2] much was said about actionable assumpsits, but not one of the illustrations there given affords an instance of a contract of mutual promises. Brooke, digesting the case from 11 Henry IV,[3] observed (*cir.* 1576) that "the action upon the case upon assumpsit shall be brought *for that the defendant, for a certain sum of money to him paid, did promise.*"[4]

Reference to the authorities cited above shows that the term *nudum pactum* had long been familiar to our lawyers. No maxim is older than that which declares that no cause of action can arise from a nude pact. *Ex nudo pacto non oritur actio.*

Nudum pactum in Roman law.

In the Roman law the *pactum* was a formless consensual agreement and could not support an action for affirmative relief, though it might supply the subject-matter of a good defense (*exceptio*).[5] The mediæval civilian jurists broke down the distinction between the contract and *pactum*, and it

---

[1] See *post*, p. 39.
[2] 1 Plowd. 302.
[3] 33, pl. 60.

[4] Brooke Abr., *Accion sur Case*, pl. 40.
[5] Sohm, Inst., Ledlie's Trans., 2d ed., 429.

GENESIS OF CONSIDERATION.   37

came to be the generally accepted doctrine among them that
any agreement was enforceable provided it was based upon an
adequate *causa,* or cause.⁶ Hence the term *nudum pactum*
was used by the civilians of any agreement or promise which
was unsupported by an adequate cause in the sense of the civil
law.⁷

The early English lawyers naturally used the term *nudum
pactum* to indicate those engagements on which debt would
not lie because of the absence of a *quid pro quo.* After assumpsit appeared they also naturally at once applied it to those
promises which were ineffective because of the absence of
that element which was to go by the name of consideration.
This meaning was fixed upon the term *nudum pactum* in English law as early as the beginning of the sixteenth century.

But while a term was thus ready at hand to indicate the
agreement which was rendered non-actionable by the absence
of consideration, some difficulty was found in choosing the
name for this positive factor whose presence was thus seen
to be necessary to make the promise binding. The term *quid
pro quo* was exceedingly awkward, and besides, usage had
associated this term exclusively with the debt.

The term 'cause' (Latin *causa,* French *cause*) doubtless
just missed being adopted as the name of the element which
gave validity to the parol contract, but it was too wide a notion, and had associations with the civil law which would have
made it confusing. *Causa* or *cause* is the nearest Continental
analogue of our 'consideration.'⁸ But the two conceptions are

Chapter IV

Nude pact in English law.

Origin of term 'consideration.'

Distinction between 'consideration' and *causa.*

---

⁶ See 3 L. Quar. Rev. 177; Stair's Inst. 1, 10, 7; Molina, De Justitia, Disput. 257.

⁷ *Nudum pactum* was defined by the civilians as follows: "Nudum pactum est ubi nulla subest causa praeter conventionem; sed ubi subest causa fit obligatio, et parit actionem;" and again, "Nuda pactio est tenuis et destituta tam nomine proprio quam mutatione rerum et factorum, manens in simplici paciscentium colloquio." See 16 Vin. Abr., tit. *Nudum Pactum,* also Sharington v. Strotton, 1 Plowd. 309.

⁸ Sir F. Pollock, in Appendix (F) to his work on Contracts, has a note on *cause* which is very instructive. He observes that in the Civil Code of Lower Canada the English *consideration* is used as a synonym for *cause.* The Roman theory, says he, whether in its classical or modern shape falls short of the completeness and common sense of our own, but only one step seems wanting.

Volume II
The cause of French law.

radically different. *Cause* is much the wider notion; as a deliberate intention of bestowing a bounty may be an adequate *cause* for supporting an agreement, but can never be an adequate consideration at common law except in conveyances founded on love and affection. But there was a considerable period when the term 'cause' was used synonymously with the term 'consideration.'⁹

English usage at close of year-book period.

St. Germain's Dialogue of the Doctor and Student contains a chapter on the subject of contracts which is exceedingly instructive in several particulars. The second dialogue, which was printed in English in 1530 and had probably appeared — or at least was written — several years sooner, shows conclusively that the term *nudum pactum* had become fixed in

If the Roman lawyers, or the civilians in modern times, had ever fairly asked themselves what were the common elements in the various sets of facts which under the name of *causa* made various kinds of contracts actionable, they could scarcely have failed to extract something equivalent to our consideration. The fact that they did not take that step is much more difficult to account for than the fact, if it be a fact, that we did.

In Rogron's *Codes Français Expliqués* (Paris, 1836), p. 209, the expression *sans cause* is expounded as follows: "La cause est ce qui détermine l'engagement que prend une partie dans un contrat; il ne faut pas la confondre avec la cause implicite du contrat, autrement le *motif* qui porte à contracter. La cause de l'engagement d'une partie est le fait ou la promesse de l'autre partie; elle peut aussi consister dans une pure libéralité de la part de l'une des parties: ainsi, lorsque je m'oblige à payer mille francs à Paul, pour tels services que son père m'a rendus, la cause déterminante du contrat, ce sont les services qui m'ont été rendus, le *motif* qui m'a porté à contracter, c'est le désir de m'acquitter envers lui des services de son père; si celui-ci ne m'a jamais rendu les services dont il a été parlé dans l'acte, le contrat est sans cause. Je m'oblige à donner mille francs a Paul pour qu'il suive une affaire pendante devant le tribunal de la Seine; la cause déterminante est la promesse de Paul qu'il suivra mon affaire; si elle est jugée irrévocablement au moment où nous avons stipulé, le contrat est sans cause. Autre exemple: je vous vends ma maison, la cause de la vente est, d'un côté, la maison elle-même, de l'autre, le prix. Enfin je donne, dans la forme des dispositions entre vifs, ma maison a Paul, qui l'accepte: ma libéralité est ici la seule cause du contrat."

See further, article on History of Contract in 3 L. Quar. Rev. 176-178, by J. W. Salmond.

⁹ In Calthorpe's Case, 3 Dyer 336*b*, we find one of the earliest attempts to define consideration. It is used as synonymous with cause, but is distinguished from *quid pro quo*. " A consideration is a cause or meritorious occasion requiring a mutual recompense in fact or law. Contracts and bargains have a *quid pro quo*."

Termes de la Ley defines consideration as the material cause or *quid pro quo* of a contract without which it will not be effectual or binding.

meaning and was applied to cases where consideration was absent. The same authority shows that usage had not yet settled upon consideration as the proper name for the element which rendered simple agreements effective. On the contrary, other terms were competing with it.[1] 'Consideration' was,

^{Chapter IV}

^{Other terms compete with term 'consideration.'}

[1] Thus St. Germain uses the following expressions: Recompense (four times), cause (three times), a certain consideration (twice), consideration of worldly profit (once), cause (in sense of a desire to maintain the cause of learning or service of God, once), *quid pro quo* (once), goods or some other profit (once), thing assigned for a promise (once), new charge (i. e., detriment, once), and charge by reason of the promise (once).

The most important parts of the chapter in question are as follows:

STUDENT (discoursing on the law of England): "And a *nude* contract is, when a man maketh a bargain, or a sale of his goods or lands, without any recompense appointed for it; as if I say to another, I sell thee all my land, or else my goods, and nothing is assigned that the other shall give or pay for it, this is a nude contract, and, as I take it, it is void in the law and conscience. And a nude or naked promise is, where a man promiseth another to give him certain money such a day, or to build an house, or to do him such certain service, and nothing is assigned for the money, for the building, nor for the service; these be called naked promises, because there is nothing assigned why they should be made; and I think no action lieth in those cases, though they be not performed. Also if I promise to another to keep him such certain goods safely to such a time, and after I refuse to take them, there lieth no action against me for it. But if I take them, and after they be lost or impaired through my negligent keeping, there an action lieth. . . . And therefore, after divers that be learned in the laws of the realm, all promises shall be taken in this manner; that is to say, If he to whom the promise is made have a charge by reason of the promise, which he hath also performed, then in that case he shall have an action for that thing that was promised, though he that made the promise have no worldly profit by it. And if a man say to another, heal such a poor man of his disease, or, make an highway, and I will give thee thus much, and if he do it, I think an action lieth at the common law; and moreover, though the thing that he should do be all spiritual, yet if he perform it, I think an action lieth at the common law. As if a man say to another, fast for me all the next Lent, and I will give thee twenty pounds, and he performeth it, I think an action lieth at the common law. And likewise if a man say to another, marry my daughter, and I will give thee twenty pounds; upon this promise an action lieth, if he marry his daughter. And in this case he cannot discharge the promise though he thought not to be bound thereby; for it is a good contract, and he may have *quid pro quo*, that is to say, the preferment of his daughter for his money. But in those promises made to an university, or such other as thou hast remembered before, with such causes as thou hast showed, that is to say, to the honor of God, or to the increase of learning, or such other like, where the party to whom the promise was made is bound to no new charge by reason of the promise made to him, but as he was bound to before; there they think that no action lieth

^{St. Germain on law of parol contract.}

however, soon adopted as the exclusive and proper designation of the element in question.² The term was somewhat familiar, since it had already been used in the law of real property. Fortunately the meaning there attached to it was not so technical as to prevent its subsequent transportation into the field of contract. To this field let us now for a moment turn.

Consideration in the Law of Conveyance.

Consideration unnecessary to pass title.

It is sometimes said that a consideration is necessary to be acknowledged or proved in order to pass title to real estate. But as a statement of a common-law principle and without explanation this is a mistake. In common-law conveyances no consideration was necessary in order to pass a title. A simple gift of lands to a person and his heirs accompanied by livery of seisin was all that was necessary to pass a fee simple. The courts of law did not deem any consideration necessary, but if a man voluntarily gave land to another and put him in possession the conveyance was complete and irrevocable, just as a gift of money or goods made without any consideration is and ever has been quite beyond the power of the giver to recall, if accompanied by delivery. A feoffment with livery of seisin or the delivery of a deed bearing the grantor's seal was always sufficient at common law to pass the legal title.³

Equity jurisdiction over uses.

This principle of law was modified by the growth of chancery jurisdiction over uses. It will be recalled that the court of equity began to enforce uses against the holders of legal title in the latter years of the fourteenth century, first at the

---

against him, though he perform not his promise, for it is no contract, and so his own conscience must be his judge whether he intended to be bound by his promise or not." Dial. II., ch. 24.

² In 1557, in an action on the case, the plaintiff declared that the defendant, in consideration that the son of the plaintiff would marry the defendant's daughter, assumed and promised to pay him 400 marcs. Joscelin v. Shelton, 3 Leon. 4, Benloe 57, Moo. K. B. 13. This is said to be the first instance where, in assumpsit, the promise sued on was alleged to have been given 'in consideration' of the act done on the faith of it. 2 Harv. L. Rev. 17, 18.

³ Green v. Thomas, 11 Me. 321. Perkins tells us that the requisites of a deed are writing, sealing, and delivering. Perk. Prof. Book, § 117. The Statute of Frauds, 29 Chas. II., of course added another — signing. The statute of 13 Eliz. against fraudulent conveyances introduced still another factor.

GENESIS OF CONSIDERATION. 41

instance of the clergy and later at the instance of the laity. The fact that these uses could be alienated by will and otherwise dealt with in many respects as chattels caused them to become very common. Chancery was powerless to touch the legal estate, but operated on the feoffee and compelled him to administer the estate vested in him for the benefit of the *cestui que use*. It frequently happened that persons made feoffments of land or conveyed by deed to a grantee to hold to the use of the feoffer or grantor himself, and at about the beginning of the sixteenth century, that is, at a time just contemporary with the extension of assumpsit to parol agreements, the courts of equity reached the conclusion that where a person made a feoffment to a stranger without any consideration passing and without any declaration showing to whose use the feoffment was made, the use resulted to the feoffer himself.[4] The language of Perkins on this point is based on a case decided in 1522, and evidently the principle was not an old one. Says he: "And if a tenant in fee simple of land, do at this day enfeoff a stranger thereof, without any consideration, the feoffee is seized to the use of the feoffor and his heirs; for the law in this case doth not make any consideration."[5]

Chapter IV

Consideration necessary to pass use in equity.

The resulting use.

---

[4] See 2 Bl. Com., 327 *et seq.*; Williams on Real Prop., 156 *et seq.*

[5] Perk. Prof. Book, § 533; Y. B. 14 Hen. VIII. 5, pl. 5.

Had it not been for the statute of *Quia Emptores* (1290), which had the effect of making the feoffee to hold, not of the feoffor, but of the person of whom the feoffor himself held, there would have been an obvious difficulty in reaching this conclusion; for the fact that the feoffee would otherwise have held *of the feoffor* would have tended to rebut the presumption that the feoffee was to hold also for the use of the feoffor. This circumstance caused some of the older lawyers and judges to infer that the requirement of a consideration in these cases dates from that statute (18 Edw. I.), but this is an obvious mistake. Thus, in Villers *v.* Beamont, 2 Dyer 146*b*, the learned counsel say: "Before the statute of *Quia Emptores Terrarum* if a man made a deed of feoffment without any cause or consideration, the feoffee should have it to his own use because it was a tenure between the feoffor and feoffee; but since that statute, if no consideration be expressed, nor any money paid besides, it shall be intended to be to the use of the feoffor." Perkins, §§ 529–533, seems to be the authority on which the above statement was made, but even the excellent Perkins cannot be accepted as correct in this instance. It is clear that the requirement of a consideration in order to pass the use could not have dated *from* the statute in question, and in fact could have had no existence before equity assumed jurisdiction over uses.

42   FOUNDATIONS OF LEGAL LIABILITY.

Volume II

Love and affection sufficient to support use.

The case in which the law "made a consideration," as Perkins expresses it, was where the feoffment was to one of the same blood. Love and affection had been held sufficient to vest the use as early as 1504, when it was said that a grant to a brother was made on "good consideration, for the elder brother is bound by the law of nature to aid and comfort his younger brother, as the father is likewise bound to his sons." Apparently no earlier use of the word 'consideration' in the year books is to be found.[6]

Effect of Statute of Uses.

The Statute of Uses[7] had the effect of vesting the legal title in the beneficiary, and from that time the common-law courts treated the beneficial estate as a legal estate. Hence the rule that a consideration is necessary in order to pass the title to a stranger, now made its appearance in the law courts.[8] Equity, as we thus perceive, was responsible for the addition of the fourth requisite, consideration, into a deed in addition to the three elements enumerated by Perkins.[9]

---

[6] Y. B. 20 Hen. VII. 10b, pl. 20.

[7] 27 Hen. VIII. ch. 10.

[8] Before the statute, if an estate was made to a stranger and his heirs without any consideration, the feoffor was held, in equity, to have the use, for want of any consideration to pass it to the feoffee; after the statute, the feoffor, having the use, was deemed in lawful seisin and possession. "Consequently by such a feoffment, although livery of seisin be duly made to A, yet no permanent estate will pass to him; for the moment he obtains the estate he holds it to the use of the feoffor; and the same instant comes the statute and gives to the feoffor who has the use, the seisin and possession. The feoffor therefore instantly gets back all that he gave; and the use is said to result to himself." Williams on Real Prop., 158.

A distinction, however, is to be noted in the case where there was an express declaration that the use was to be for the feoffee. In 1535 it was held by all the judges in the Common Bench that if one enfeoffed a stranger without any consideration, but expressly stated in the deed that the feoffee should hold to his own use there was no resulting trust. Benloe 16, pl. 20. See also 2 Bl. Com. 332.

[9] Blackstone accordingly enumerates good and sufficient consideration among the essential requisites of a deed. 2 Bl. Com. 296.

Another aspect of consideration came up in connection with the subject of uses during this period. In 1501 it was decided that an heir of the feoffee took the estate charged with the use. Keilw. 42; 2 Bl. Com. 328. In a short time the same rule was extended to persons not paying a consideration and to those who take with notice. 2 Bl. Com. 328; Keilw. 43b, 45b; Bacon on Uses 312. By 1537 this rule was well established. Bury v. Bokenham, 1 Dyer 8, 10a; Constable's Case, 1 Dyer 102; Wilkes v. Lenson, 2 Dyer 169; Assaby v. Manners, 2 Dyer 235a; Page v. Moulton, 3 Dyer 206b. In Y. B. 22 Edw. IV. 6, pl. 18, Hussey, C. J., had de-

In 1566, the celebrated case of *Sharington v. Strotton* [1] was argued and determined in the Court of the King's Bench. It raised the question whether love and affection for persons of one's own blood is a sufficient consideration to sustain a covenant to stand seized to the use of such kinsman. The arguments of counsel, as polished up by Plowden in his report of the case, are truly remarkable performances.

It will be observed that the covenant to stand seized to uses, like the bargain and sale of land and the lease and release, is a mode of conveyance which derives its force from the Statute of Uses; and it has always been admitted that these conveyances must be supported by a consideration. The exceptional character of the covenant to stand seized has always been apparent. Blackstone tells us that by this conveyance "a man seized of lands covenants in consideration of blood or marriage that he will stand seized of the same to the use of his child, wife, or kinsman, for life, in tail, or in fee. Here the statute executes at once the estate; for the party intended to be benefited, having thus acquired the use, is thereby put at once into corporal possession of the land, without ever seeing it, by a kind of parliamentary magic. But this conveyance can only operate when made upon such weighty and interesting considerations as those of blood or marriage." [2]

Sharington v. Strotton established this rather exceptional principle in our law. The argument by Fleetwood and Wray against the sufficiency of the consideration of love and affection to raise the use made it altogether clear that if value and recompense to the owner, or even detriment to the covenantee, was to be taken as a test of consideration, then the consideration was not sufficient. It was admitted that the use might be raised without the owner parting with the possession of the property, but in order to make the possession to be to the use of another they insisted that it was necessary for something

clared the earlier rule as follows: "If one enfeoffs another in trust and the latter dies, his heir being in by descent, no subpœna lies against him."

[1] 1 Plowd. 298.
[2] 2 Bl. Com. 337. See *Wallis v. Wallis*, 4 Mass. 135; *Jackson v. Sebring*, 16 Johns. (N.Y.) 515; *Cheney v. Watkins*, 1 Har. & J. (Md.) 532.

to be done which imports in itself a good and sufficient consideration. They then proceeded to show that the love and affection entertained by the covenantor for the covenantees was only a motive, or cause, as distinguished from consideration, "and the consideration ought to be to him that is seized of the land, for if he has no recompense, there is no cause why the use of the land should pass."

Bromley and an apprentice, doubtless Plowden himself, argued in favor of the validity of the conveyance, deriving the principle for which they contended from the law of nature. They insisted that, as the covenantor, in providing for those of his own name and blood, had followed a fundamental instinct or had taken nature for his guide, this should be a sufficient consideration in law.[3]

As if feeling the technical weakness of this reasoning, counsel then strove to show that no consideration at all was necessary to support the covenant. In this connection the learning as to the validity of deeds not based on a consideration was reviewed: "For every deed imports in itself a consideration, viz., the will of him that made it, and therefore where the agreement is by deed, it shall never be called a *nudum pactum.*" In an effort to make it appear that determination of mind to do an act, and deliberation in fixing the

---

[3] In the course of the eloquent argument of the apprentice the following novel but strangely beautiful language was used: "In the Old Testament God prohibits marriage within the Levitical degrees, which was upon no other consideration than to increase love; for God, who knows the nature and affections of men better than man himself, saw that love grew by nature between cousins and those who are near in blood, and being desirous to enlarge that love further, he prohibited certain degrees within which it was not lawful for any to marry, to the intent that they should marry into other families, and thereby bind their lineages together in love, so that love might be increased, which God desires above all other things. And this prohibition he made upon divine policy, for love was sufficiently implanted by nature in those who are near to each other in blood, and there was no need to make it greater than nature had made it, but to marry elsewhere begets other love in other families, whereby love is propagated and increased. . . . From whence we see that by the law of nature, and by the law of the realm, and by the law of God (which in intent approves them both), brotherly love and advancement of one's blood is taken to be of great effect, and seems to be a sufficient consideration to raise a use in land." Sharington *v.* Strotton, 1 Plowd. 306.

mental purpose, are the chief elements which consideration is intended to establish, it was said: "There are two ways of making contracts or agreements for lands or chattels. The one is by words, which is the inferior method; the other is by writing, which is the superior. And because words are oftentimes spoken by men unadvisedly and without deliberation, the law has provided that a contract by words shall not bind without consideration."

After lengthy deliberation the court decided that the covenant was effective, and in reply to the naïve request of the apprentice, May it please your Lordship to show us for our learning the causes of your judgment, Catline, C. J., said: "It seems to us that the affection of the said Andrew for the provision of the heirs male which he should beget, and his desire that the land should continue in the blood and name of Baynton, and the brotherly love which he bore to his brothers, are sufficient consideration to raise the uses in the land. And where you said in your argument *naturæ vis maxima*, I say *natura bis maxima*, and it is the greatest consideration that can be to raise a use." [4]

It is obvious that the meaning given by the court to consideration in this case was vastly broader than the meaning which it had acquired in assumpsit. Love and affection is a consideration only in the sense of motive, cause, or reason.[5] It will be observed that love and affection is not an assumptual consideration. It is associated with conveyance, not with promises. Accordingly no further account will be taken of it in connection with the theory of our contract law.

<small>Chapter IV</small>

<small>Consideration of love and affection upheld.</small>

<small>Exceptional nature of this form of consideration.</small>

---

[4] Sharington v. Strotton, 1 Plowd. 309.
  Marriage as a Consideration.— During this period marriage was frequently held to be a sufficient consideration to support a conveyance of real property and to support a covenant to stand seized. Assaby v. Manners, (1565) 2 Dyer 235a.
  It had been held sufficient to support assumpsit several years prior to this case. Joscelin v. Shelton, 3 Leon. 4, Benloe 57, Moo. K. B. 13; Brooke Abr., *Accion sur Case*, pl. 108.

[5] A covenant to stand seized cannot be supported by the consideration of love and affection for an illegitimate child. Blount v. Blount, 2 Law Repos. (4 N. Car.) 587; Gerrarde v. Worseley, 3 Dyer 374a.

CHAPTER V

READJUSTMENT.

<small>Volume II</small>

AS the conception of the obligation of promise became dominant in contract law, the whole subject underwent more or less readjustment, and various forms of engagement previously known to the law shifted their position. Some of the old contracts, like suretyship, hiring, and the bargain and sale, fitted into the new system of ideas much more readily than into the old. In some of them, such as the true real contracts, the new conception did not at all points supersede the old. But in all forms of engagement, promise acquired new significance as the source of legal obligation, and the presence of consideration or mutuality of promise came to be recognized as the chief characteristic of simple contracts. Concerning the transition which the contract of suretyship now underwent, a few words will here be helpful.

<small>Promise acquires new significance.</small>

Suretyship.

We have already seen that suretyship was originally a contract entered into by means of a formal ceremony involving the delivery of the *festuca,* or staff, supposed to be symbolic of the power which the surety had over the individual for whom he bound himself. It was the only simple contract known to our early law which was not a contract *re.*

<small>Suretyship not a contract *re.*</small>

In a system of law in which the delivery of a chattel was conceived as being almost the sole source of contractual liability, the undertaking of the surety was felt to be exceptional. The result was that the early courts, after having for a time looked askance at this form of simple contract, began in the reign of Edward III to require that the undertaking of the surety should be evidenced by a deed or sealed writing. As late as 1314, the action of debt seems to have been brought

<small>Sealed writing becomes essential in contract of suretyship.</small>

against a surety who had not bound himself by a sealed instrument.¹ In 1343 it was doubted whether it should not be proved, like the covenant, by a specialty;² and later it was assumed as a matter of course that the surety could only be bound by a sealed writing.³

In suretyship, the surety becomes bound for a benefit accruing to another, and it was considered an indispensable requisite that he should be the principal and only debtor. One *quid pro quo* could not originate two separate obligations. There could not be "a double debt upon a single loan,"⁴ and, if the person who got the *quid pro quo* became bound, the other did not.⁵

When assumpsit appeared the whole law of suretyship was simplified and extended. The liability of a surety could now be substituted for that of another and he could be held either with or without his principal. In the law of assumpsit it is not material to whom the benefit accrues, if only the promisee parts with something or incurs a risk for the promise.

Nor is it necessary, in assumpsit, that the surety should be primarily or jointly liable. Thus, if A advances money to B on the faith of C's promise to repay if B, the principal debtor, should not, this is a good assumpsit though such a promise would not create a debt. The recognition of this principle at the end of the second decade of the sixteenth century was the beginning of the law of guaranty.⁶

Turning our attention for a moment to the most ancient branch of our simple contract law, the purely real contracts

---

Chapter V

Surety principal debtor.

Recognition of the parol guaranty.

The bailments.

---

¹ Y. B. 7 Edw. II. 242.
² Y. B. 18 Edw. III. 13, pl. 7.
³ Y. B. 44 Edw. III. 21, pl. 23.
⁴ Marriot *v.* Lister, 2 Wils. C. Pl. 142.
⁵ There is, of course, a form of obligation in which, although a benefit accrues to a third person, the one who makes the contract is primarily liable. This situation is to be distinguished from suretyship. Thus, as said by Moile in 1459, If I say to a surgeon, cure J and I will

pay you 100 s. and the surgeon does so, I am bound for the money. Here the act being done at my request is in contemplation of law done for me. In other words, I get the benefit. Y. B. 37 Hen. VI. 9, pl. 18; Stonehouse *v.* Bodvil, T. Raym. 67; Bret *v.* J. S., Cro. Eliz. 755; Haines *v.* Finch, Aleyn 6.
⁶ Y. B. 12 Hen. VIII. 11, pl. 3; Browne *v.* Garborough, (1568) Cro. Eliz. 63.

of Glanvill's day, we find that in large part they have been bodily transferred to the field of assumptual law. The most important of them, viz., the *commodatum, depositum,* and *pignus,* have been assigned a position and given a name (bailments), which points to their real origin and differentiates them from other simple contracts. The *mutuum,* which is a loan of chattels to be consumed and returned in like kind and quantity, has no such special place in the law, belonging, like other contracts based upon consent and consideration, to the body of assumptual law.

The contract of hiring, as we have elsewhere seen, includes two sorts of transactions, viz., hirings in some way involving chattels, and hirings of labor or service purely. Only the first of these could find a place among real contracts, and the early common law accordingly recognized none other. Both sorts of engagements were included in the Roman *locatio;* for in that system the *locatio* was a consensual contract. Now in modern English contract law the real contract of hiring, namely, the letting of chattels for hire or hiring of service to be done upon or about chattels, takes its place among the recognized bailments. Hiring of labor and service, however, like the *mutuum,* forms a part of assumptual law and neither requires, nor perhaps admits, of separate classification.

And now a few words must be said about the place of the mandate. The Roman contract of *mandatum* is an agreement whereby one party undertakes to execute gratuitously a commission received from another.[7] The civil law had no difficulty in recognizing a contractual obligation on the part of the mandatary, for in that system agreement alone is under certain conditions recognized as a sufficient basis for a contractual obligation. But obviously there is no place in English law for so broad a notion of contractual liability. In our system there must be either a debt, to the creation of which the delivery of a *quid pro quo* is essential; or there must be an assumpsit, to support which either an actual consideration or mutuality of promise is necessary.

[7] Sohm, Inst., Ledlie's trans., 2d ed., 422.

The principle that no liability attaches at common law upon the nonfeasance of a gratuitous commission by the person who promises to do the gratuitous act is illustrated in *Elsee v. Gatward* (1793).[8] It appeared that the defendant, a carpenter, had promised to repair a house for the plaintiff before a given day, but omitted to do so, whereby the walls of plaintiff's house were damaged. A count in the declaration which stated these facts was held to be bad because it did not show a consideration for the promise.

Chapter V

Nonfeasance of gratuitous commission not actionable.

The principle is illustrated still better in *Thorne v. Deas* (1809).[9] In this case it appeared that the plaintiff and defendant were joint owners of a brig. The defendant voluntarily promised the plaintiff to get the vessel insured in their joint interest, but he neglected to do so and the vessel was lost. Thereupon the plaintiff brought an action to recover so much as he would have received from a policy of insurance if the insurance had been effected. It was held that he could not recover.

Where the mandatary, instead of omitting altogether to do the thing which he promises to do, actually enters upon the performance of the mandate and does it amiss, a different rule prevails. In *Thorne v. Deas,* Judge Kent observed: "By the common law, a mandatary, or one who undertakes to do an act for another, without reward, is not answerable for omitting to do the act, and is only responsible when he attempts to do it and does it amiss. In other words, he is responsible for a misfeasance, but not for a nonfeasance, even though special damages are averred."

Misfeasance in performance of mandate actionable.

Now, while it is admitted that the mandatary who enters upon performance may become liable if he is guilty of a misfeasance, the authorities are not clear upon the question as to just when such liability arises. Certainly not all misfeasances by mandataries which result in damage are actionable. Upon principle the distinction appears to be this: The mandatary is liable for a misfeasance of the mandate, if the right of action can be brought within the principle of actions for negligence, but not otherwise. The action is grounded strictly upon neg-

Qualification.

---

[8] 5 T. R. 143.   [9] 4 Johns. (N. Y.) 84.

4

Negligent injury to person or property the ground of the action.

ligence, and hence is subject to the limitations of the right of action for negligence. In the first volume of this treatise it was made clear that the right of action for negligence is limited to situations where damage is negligently done to person or property. It follows that the right of action for misfeasance on the part of a mandatary is limited to situations where his misfeasance results in physical hurt or in damage to property. If I deliver my liquors to a man to convey from one place to another and he is to do it for nothing, he will be liable for breaking one of the casks if he is chargeable with negligence.[1] So a carrier of passengers is liable for a negligent injury to a passenger, although the latter is being conveyed without compensation.[2]

Misfeasance on part of carpenter.

The two following decisions are worthy of note. In *Elsee v. Gatward* (1793),[3] one of the counts of the declaration alleged that the plaintiff had employed the defendant, a carpenter, to make repairs upon a house, using the old material. It was not alleged that he was to be paid for the work. The carpenter entered upon performance of the work, and instead of using the old material, as had been agreed, used new material, thereby increasing the expense. It was held that the count showed a good cause of action. The decision was right, because the defendant had used up the plaintiff's new material without authority.

Doctrine of Wilkinson v. Coverdale untenable.

In *Wilkinson v. Coverdale* (1793),[4] the plaintiff sought to recover of one who had promised without consideration to effect insurance on a house belonging to the plaintiff. In taking out the policy in performance of the mandate the defendant negligently failed to have a clause inserted which would have protected from the loss which actually happened. Lord Kenyon allowed the case to go to the jury, on the theory that the negligent performance of the promise might result in liability. The jury, however, found against the plaintiff on

---

[1] Coggs v. Bernard, 2 Ld. Raym. 909.

[2] Steamboat New World v. King, 16 How. (U. S.) 469; Rose v. Des Moines Valley R. Co., 39 Iowa 246; Todd v. Old Colony, etc., R. Co., 3 Allen (Mass.) 18; Flint, etc., R. Co. v. Weir, 37 Mich. 111; Annas v. Milwaukee, etc., R. Co., 67 Wis. 46.

[3] 5 T. R. 143.

[4] 1 Esp. 75.

READJUSTMENT. 51

the ground that no promise on the part of the defendant to take out the insurance was proved. Nothing further was heard of the case. This ruling of Lord Kenyon at Nisi Prius is clearly untenable. There was no infliction of hurt or damage such as would have supplied a cause of action for negligence, and there was no consideration such as would support a contractual obligation.

Chapter V

CHAPTER VI

ORIGIN AND NATURE OF THE BILATERAL CONTRACT.

<small>Volume II</small>

THE recognition of the bilateral contract of mutual promises is an event second only in importance to the recognition of the validity of the promise supported by the executed consideration. The exceptional character of this form of engagement has not been sufficiently appreciated. We must now bring its appearance into the proper historical perspective and examine somewhat into its nature. We must begin, however, with a clear perception of the difference between the unilateral and bilateral modes of engagement.

Unilateral and Bilateral Modes of Engagement.

<small>Unilateral contract.</small>

Most negotiations which lead to the formation of a contract begin with an offer, or, as it is termed in the civil law. pollicitation. The form in which the offer is put or the circumstances in which the parties are placed may be such that performance of the condition of the offer is all that is required of the person to whom the offer is made. Actual fulfilment of the condition of the offer, in such a case, is evidence of the promisee's assent, and the performance turns the offer into a binding promise or unilateral contract. The promisee has now done all that can be required of him, and nothing remains but for the promisor to perform. Thus, as was said in *Morton v. Burn* (1837),[1] if A says to B, " if you will furnish goods to C I will guarantee the payment." B is not bound to furnish the goods, but if he does furnish them A can be sued on the guaranty.

<small>Performance of offer a condition precedent to existence of contract.</small>

In *Train v. Gold* (1827),[2] Wilde, J., illustrated the same principle, saying, " If A promises B a sum of money if he will do a particular act, and B does the act, the promise thereupon

---

[1] 7 Ad. & El. 19, 34 E. C. L. 18.   [2] 5 Pick. ('Mass.) 380.

NATURE OF BILATERAL CONTRACT.

becomes binding although B, at the time of the promise, does not engage to do the act. In the intermediate time the obligation of the contract or promise is suspended; for until the performance of the condition of the promise, there is no consideration and the promise is *nudum pactum;* but on the performance of the condition by the promisee, it is clothed with a valid consideration which relates back to the promise, and it then becomes obligatory." In technical strictness we should say that the performance of the condition turns what was before a mere offer into a binding promise.

The objection to this form of contracting is found in the fact that it involves risk and uncertainty for both parties. The position of the promisor is uncertain because it is optional with the promisee whether he will fulfil the required condition or not; and until a decision is made the promisor must hold himself in readiness to comply. The position of the person to whom the offer is made is insecure, because the offer is not binding on the promisor and can be withdrawn at any time before its condition is fulfilled.

From this it results that in most cases a person who sets afoot negotiations leading up to a contract, instead of agreeing to be bound if the other party will perform and leaving him free to act as he chooses, will so frame his offer as to require an immediate and reciprocal engagement and decline to be bound if it is not given. Where the negotiations take this course the result is the formation of a bilateral contract.

From what has been said it appears that in unilateral engagements the contractual relation does not begin until one party performs the act which constitutes the consideration for the promise of the other.[3] Consequently in this contract only one of the parties is under a legal obligation. The contract is therefore one-sided, though the consent of both parties is essential. On the other hand, in the bilateral engagement the contractual obligation has its inception when the mutual prom-

Chapter VI

Defect of the unilateral mode of engagement.

Bilateral contract.

Distinction between unilateral and bilateral contracts.

---

[3] In suits upon unilateral contracts, it is only where the defendant has had the benefit of the consideration for which he bargained that he can be held bound. Woods, J., in Richardson *v.* Hardwick, 106 U. S. 255.

ises are given, and both parties are mutually bound to each other from that time.

It is sometimes a delicate matter to determine whether the result of the negotiations is a binding engagement, and, if so, what sort. The offer may be made in one *mode* and accepted in another. In every case it is of course merely a question of interpretation to determine the true intention of the parties. The difficulty that may be encountered in determining the mode of a contract is illustrated in *Cooke v. Oxley* (1790).[4] Oxley wished to sell Cooke certain tobacco at a stipulated price, and Cooke requested Oxley to give him till four P. M. of that day to agree or dissent, which Oxley granted. At the appointed time Cooke agreed to the bargain and informed Oxley of his decision, but the latter declined to perform. The court looked at this situation solely from the standpoint of a bilateral contract made at the time of the conference. In this aspect it was impossible to hold Oxley as bound from that time, because Cooke was not bound. Consequently, it was said, Oxley's agreement was *nudum pactum*. The doctrine of this case is not now accepted as sound; and the reason is that the situation here disclosed is that of an offer turned into a binding contract of sale by acceptance according to the terms of the offer. Oxley might, to be sure, have withdrawn his offer, but no such withdrawal was alleged.[5]

A further cause of confusion in discriminating between unilateral and bilateral contracts is the fact that, in many cases, before one can get into court on a bilateral agreement, it is necessary for him to perform his part of the engagement, a circumstance which leaves the subsisting obligation one-sided. But we should guard against applying the term 'unilateral' to the original relation. The *mode* of a contract, that is, whether it be unilateral or bilateral, is determined by the situation existing at the time the contract is made.

[4] 3 T. R. 653.
[5] See Anson on Contracts, § 34; Langdell on **Contracts**, § 10.

First Recognition of the Bilateral Contract.

There are one or two cases from near the middle of the sixteenth century which give effect to bilateral contracts *sub silentio*.[6] But it was not until 1588 that this form of engagement obtained a secure footing in the law. Its validity was then placed on the ground that one promise is a good consideration for another. "A promise against a promise," it was said, "will maintain an action."[7] Since that day it has been customary, in declaring on bilateral contracts, to lay one promise as having been made in consideration of the other.[8]

Appearance of bilateral contract.

---

[6] In Pecke v. Redman, (1555) 2 Dyer 113a, an agreement had been made between plaintiff and defendant whereby the latter agreed to deliver to the former 20 quarters of barley per annum for a stipulated price, during the joint lives of the parties. The plaintiff brought assumpsit upon a breach and recovered damages.
  Andrew v. Boughey, (1551) 1 Dyer 75a, was somewhat similar, but part of the purchase price had been paid down at the time the contract was made.
  Norwood v. Read, (1558) 1 Plowd. 180, involved a contract by which the defendant, for 40 s. in hand paid, agreed to deliver 50 quarters of wheat at the price of £33, to be paid on delivery. The contract was held good. The 40 s. seems to have operated as earnest to bind the bargain.

[7] Strangborough v. Warner, (1588) 4 Leon. 3.

[8] Gower v. Capper, (1597) Cro. Eliz. 543; Wichals v. Johns, (1599) Cro. Eliz. 703; Bettisworth v. Campion, (1608) Yelv. 134.
  In Wichals v. Johns it was alleged that in consideration that the plaintiff at the request of the defendant had promised to pay £120 to one R, to whom the defendant was indebted, the defendant assumed he would pay to the plaintiff this £120 when he should be required. After verdict for the plaintiff Popham and Clench held this good, "for there is a mutual promise, the one to the other: So that if the plaintiff doth not pay to R, the defendant may have his action against him. So also the defendant shall be charged as to him, and a promise against a promise is a good consideration." In Bettisworth v. Campion, the promise to sell all the iron made at a particular furnace was declared upon as being made in consideration of the defendant's promise to pay at a specified rate for the iron, and it was said that the consideration on each part was the mutual promise, the one to the other.
  In Rogers v. Snow, Dalison 94, judgment was stayed in what might appear to be a case of mutual promises because the plaintiff did not allege performance on his part. But the contract was clearly unilateral, being an innominate engagement in the form *facio ut des*. The brother of the defendant was indebted to the plaintiff in the sum of £300. It was agreed by the defendant that if the plaintiff would accept the bond of the debtor without surety and forbear for a stated period to sue upon it, he (the defendant) would then pay, etc. No counter-promise on the part of the plaintiff to accept the bond and to forbear was stated.

Need for recognition of bilateral contract.

It is startling to think what would have been the result if our law of contract, having reached the point of recognizing all promises given for an executed consideration, had ceased to develop. The theory of the law was then ample for all transactions where one party is ready to do the act or give the thing which constitutes the consideration for the promise of the other party. But how narrow is the conception of contract which stops here is apparent when we consider how few are the important transactions of life in which one of the parties is ready to perform. The act to be done on one part cannot be done in a moment of time, and the compensation to be paid on the other will not be paid until the service stipulated for is actually rendered. Here, then, we see the necessity for the recognition of the bilateral engagement.

If the judges had not given countenance to mutual promises, legislation would finally have been forced to intervene to give validity to contracts based upon agreement. Only one feasible course would probably have suggested itself to the mind of the legislator, viz., to give validity to contracts in writing. This would substantially have rounded out the theory of our contract law on the archaic basis of form. The sealed evidence of indebtedness is a formal contract: so with the covenant; and such would have been the contract in writing. The unilateral contract can also, it will be perceived,

Effect of this event on course of legal history.

be treated as a formal or quasi-formal contract; for it derives its validity from the act of performance, by one party, of the consideration which binds the other party to his promise. But when the bilateral contract appeared on the scene it completely changed the aspect of things, and reacted with great power upon the general conception of contractual obligation. The result is that in modern times we have completely lost sight of the fact that consideration may be treated as a matter of form as well as of substance.

But our law of contract was not destined to develop along lines of form. The bilateral contract came and with it all notion of vestments fell away from our idea of obligation; men could now think and talk of intention to bind. Presently the sealed instrument is becoming obsolete, and survives only as a kind of fossil from an earlier period. The new contract runs into every channel of action, and in its wide freedom is thought to lay open the door to fraud and imposition. Soon the legislative arm, which under different conditions might have been invoked to extend the power to contract, is compelled now to intervene to check it.[9] When Lord Mansfield and his fellow judges, in 1765,[1] favored the recognition of the written agreement as another kind of formal contract, they were speaking to a deaf world. The need for any extension of contractual liability had passed.

Chapter VI

Extension of law of contract.

It is commonly assumed that in the bilateral contract the mutual promises are considerations for each other in the sense that the word 'consideration' bears when one speaks of the ordinary unilateral promise. But this is a mistake. The bilateral contract is not based upon consideration in the sense of detriment, but is based solely upon consent, and when we say that mutual promises are considerations for each other we use the term 'consideration' in the broad sense of reason, cause, or equivalent. While it is true that the bilateral contract is based on agreement and not upon consideration it should be remembered that the mutual promises are given for each other. The promise and the counter-promise draw their vitality from one source, the *consensus* of the parties, and one promise is given in consideration of the fact and because of the fact that the other promise is given. The use of the term 'consideration' in this sense is a linguistic necessity.

Consideration in the bilateral contract.

Not the least noteworthy fact in connection with the recognition of the bilateral contract is found in the circumstance that the exceptional character of the consideration in mutual promises was not noticed. Detriment did not then stand out in such bold relief as it does to-day. Besides, as Manwood had shown two years before, there was at least one recognized form of assumptual consideration in which there was no present detriment. What, then, was the impropriety of admitting another? The conclusion that the consideration in mutual promises is exceptional does not imply that there is anything

Exceptional character of the consideration in bilateral contract escapes notice.

[9] Statute of Frauds and Perjuries, 29 Chas. II. (1677).
[1] Pillans *v.* Van Mierop, 3 Burr. 1663.

unsound or anomalous about the bilateral contract. Having gained recognition by whatever fiction or by whatever straining of the conception of consideration, the bilateral consensual agreement stands on equal footing with any other recognized form of engagement and is perhaps the most important of all.

Consensual contracts in Roman law.

The recognition of the validity of mutual promises brought into our law a purely consensual contract. It has generally been supposed that the common law does not recognize any such engagement. The perdurance of this error is a striking monument to vicious methods of investigation. As the civil law is commonly thought to be the exclusive possessor of the conception of contractural obligation as resulting from the *consensus* or agreement of the parties, it is necessary to compare for a moment the Roman consensual contracts with our contract of mutual promises.

In the Roman system of law the consensual contract, based on agreement merely, was of late development, and when finally sanctioned it was recognized as being valid only in four situations, viz., where the contract in question was one of buying and selling, letting and hiring, partnership, and gratuitous commission (*mandatum*).[2] Though the Roman consensual contracts were few in number, there can be no doubt their scope was wide enough to include all transactions common in primitive communities, and the state of society must necessarily be somewhat advanced where other consensual contracts press for recognition. This stage was, however, soon reached in Roman law, and other contracts based likewise on agreement gained recognition. These were called pacts, and their character as obligatory contracts was, as might be expected, at first denied. No relief could at first be had upon them in an affirmative action. But presently the pretor, that great personage who, like the English chancellor, operated *ab extra* to change the complexion of the legal system, let it be known in his edict that he would grant equitable actions upon pacts which had not matured into contracts, provided they were

The pact.

[2] Sohm, Inst., Ledlie's trans., 2d ed., 415-422.

NATURE OF BILATERAL CONTRACT. 59

founded upon sufficient cause.³ By this means the earlier limitation upon consensual contracts was broken down and was never again re-established in Roman law or in systems deriving from it.

Now it will be seen that the English bilateral contract has a much wider scope than the four Roman consensual contracts; for, instead of determining the validity of the consensual agreement by the nature or subject-matter of the contract, the common law determines its validity by mutuality of promise. In the English system no need could therefore ever be felt for the further recognition of consensual *pacta*, as happened in the Roman law. The significance and the importance of the advent of the consensual contracts in Roman law have been ably expounded by Professor Maine.⁴

The recognition of mutual promises in the common law was certainly not less significant or important. The exercise of the will of the two parties to the contract in making their respective promises was now capable of being separated from other elements and made the subject of legal contemplation. The formality of performance, by one party, of the act which constituted the consideration for the other's promise, a formality which is necessarily incident to the formation of every unilateral contract, was now disregarded. Form was thus altogether eliminated from the conception of the simple contract, and from that time external acts became significant merely as symbols of internal volition.

The consensual contract cannot be enforced without recognizing the obligation of contract in a very different sense from that in which the English lawyers had been accustomed to think of it. The conception of the tie or *nexus*, or, as the Romans called it, the *vinculum juris*, in contract law was thus clearly, for the first time, brought home to English legal consciousness. It was a fitting consequence of this change that the actionable assumpsit should now gradually attain to the dignity of being called a contract. Prior to this period the

---

³ Sohm, Inst., Ledlie's trans., 2d ed., 429-431; Maine's Ancient Law, 326 *et seq.*

⁴ Ancient Law, ch. 9.

Chapter VI

Scope of English bilateral contract.

Significance of recognition of bilateral contract.

The conception of obligation.

term 'contract' meant no more and no less than an obligation actionable in debt. Parol executory agreements were called assumpsits, promises, agreements, undertakings; in fact, anything but contracts.[5]

Beauty of this conception of contractual obligation. The conception of contractual obligation embodied in the bilateral contract is, to our mind, the most beautiful notion that ever appeared in contract law. Though not founded upon consideration in the sense of detriment to the promisee, the bilateral contract is yet underlaid by the good sense which characterizes the doctrine of consideration. A promise is given for a promise, and the agreement contemplates that performance shall be given for performance. The doctrine of consideration has here proved a salutary safeguard against too great extension. The common law has thus escaped the laxity which resulted in the civil law when the limits of the four consensual contracts were broken down.

---

[5] Norwood v. Read, (1558) 1 Plowd. 180; Slade's Case, (1602) 4 Coke 94, 94b. In Sidenham v. Worlington, (1585) 2 Leon. 224, the court was at great pains to show that the assumpsit is not a contract.

Let the reader note the definitions of assumpsit and contract given in *Termes de la Ley:* "*Assumpsit* is a voluntary promise made by word, by which a man assumes and takes upon him to perform or pay anything to another. This word contains in it any verbal promise made upon consideration." "*Contract* is a bargain or covenant between two parties, where one thing is given for another, which is called *quid pro quo.*"

CHAPTER VII

THE DEBT AND THE ASSUMPSIT.

NEAR the middle of the sixteenth century an event occurred which, though apparently insignificant in itself, was nevertheless fraught with great possibilities for the future of our contract law. This was the recognition of existing legal duty as a sufficient 'consideration' to support an express promise. Thus, if one made a promise to his creditor to pay a debt owing by him, the creditor was permitted to sue in assumpsit upon this express promise. He could thus evade the necessity of bringing the more cumbersome action of debt and he thereby deprived the debtor of the right to wage his law. *Assumpsit upon promise to pay a debt.*

Brooke, in reporting a case from the year 1535, makes an observation which shows that at the time his Abridgment was compiled the point had been determined. Says he: "If one who is indebted to me promises to pay before Michaelmas, I may have an action of debt on the contract or an action on the case upon the promise [assumpsit]; and the point of view is different, for debt does not lie upon a promise."[1] *Origin of indebitatus assumpsit.*

In *Manwood v. Burston* (1586),[2] three considerations were enumerated as being sufficient to support assumpsit: "1. A *The assumptual considerations.*

---

[1] Brooke Abr., *Accion sur Cuse*, pl. 5. Brooke is abridging Y. B. 27 Hen. VIII. 24, pl. 3, but the observation above quoted is not found in that case. The principle was evidently of later origin; but as Brooke died in 1558, the date when the point was decided cannot be far from the middle of the century.

The same writer has a note of a case from 1542 which recognizes the idea that a promise to pay an existing debt will support assumpsit. Brooke Abr., *Accion sur Case*, pl. 105 (33 Hen. VIII.).

[2] 2 Leon. 203. In this action Manwood, Chief Baron of the Exchequer, was the plaintiff and appeared *in propria persona*. The enumeration of the different considerations above quoted appears in his argument before the judges in the Exchequer Chamber. He had evidently thought the matter out very fully.

In arguing this case Manwood pointed out the great advantage to

debt precedent; 2. Where he to whom a promise is made is damnified by doing anything, or spends his labor at the instance of the promisor, although no benefit cometh to the promisor. . . . 3. A present consideration." These three forms of consideration are really reducible to two, viz., precedent debt and detriment to the promisee.

Assumpsit upon promise to pay sealed debt.

In the early actions upon a promise to pay a debt it was necessary to show that the promise was made after the debt was created.[3] At first no difficulty was perceived in allowing recovery or an assumpsit to pay a debt evidenced by a sealed obligation, as was done in *Ashbrooke v. Snape* (1591).[4] But this was unnecessary. The wager of law was not available against a debt evidenced by a sealed instrument, and hence there was no real need for thus extending assumpsit. Accordingly this case was not followed.

The implied promise to pay a debt.

In *Slade's Case* (1602)[5] the question was raised whether the action of assumpsit could be maintained upon a simple debt without proof of a subsequent express promise. The argument in *Norwood v. Read* (1558)[6] had contained the suggestion that "every contract executory is an assumpsit in itself." This view was now accepted, and, after full argument before all the judges of England and barons of the Exchequer, it was held in the King's Bench that assumpsit will lie upon any simple debt without proof of a promise. This holding proceeds on the idea that the creation of a simple debt

the plaintiff of allowing him to sue on the assumpsit instead of forcing him to bring debt. In suing on the promise it is not necessary, said he, "to show any certainty of the contract or other circumstance or how or in what manner the debt did accrue or begin." It was only necessary to allege the existence of the debt and that in consideration thereof the defendant promised. One of the worst pitfalls for the pleader in debt was the danger that he might not describe the circumstances with accuracy or state correctly the sum due; for if one sued for a debt of £20 and only succeeded in showing that the defendant owed him a less sum he could no more recover than he could get judgment for an ox when he had sued for a horse. 3 Bl. Com. 154.

[3] "For if he promises at the time of the contract, then debt lies on this [promise] and not assumpsit; but if he promises after the contract then action lies on the assumpsit." Dalison 84, pl. 35, 14 Eliz.

[4] Cro. Eliz. 240.
[5] 4 Coke 92b.
[6] 1 Plowd. 180.

DEBT AND ASSUMPSIT. 63

can be viewed in a double aspect, viz., (1) as originating a contractual duty on which debt will lie, and (2) as importing a promise on which assumpsit can be maintained.[7]

It will be noted that prior to this decision the express promise to pay a debt, made after the creation of the debt, was considered as being supported by the consideration of the legal duty to pay the precedent debt. The necessity for appealing to this exceptional sort of consideration arose from the fact that when a man promises to pay an existing debt he incurs no present detriment, and hence consideration in the ordinary sense is absent.[8] *Slade's Case* abrogated the need for relying

Chapter VII

Consideration of legal duty.

---

[7] It was said: "Every contract executory imports in itself an assumpsit, for when one agrees to pay money, or to deliver anything, thereby he assumes or promises to pay, or deliver it, and therefore when one sells any goods to another and agrees to deliver them at a day to come, and the other in consideration thereof agrees to pay so much money at such a day, in that case both parties may have an action of debt, or an action on the case on assumpsit; for the mutual executory agreement of both parties imports in itself reciprocal actions upon the case as well as actions of debt." 4 Coke 94. In connection with this decision it is interesting to note that, as Professor Ames has pointed out, 2 Harv. L. Rev. 17, it was a victory for the King's Bench. This court had no jurisdiction by original writ in case of debt and it is not surprising that the judges in this department were quite willing to extend assumpsit, which was a branch of case, so as to permit them to entertain this remedy in suits upon debts. The doctrine that assumpsit might be maintained upon an implied promise to pay a debt therefore originated in the King's Bench. The decisions of this court were for a while reversed in the Exchequer Chamber, but the innovation prevailed. Edwards *v.* Burre,

(1573) Dalison 104; Hinson *v.* Burridge, Moo. K. B. 701; Turges *v.* Beacher, Moo. K. B. 694; Paramour *v.* Payne, Moo. K. B. 703; Maylard *v.* Kester, Moo. K. B. 711.

[8] The exceptional character of the consideration which supports a promise to pay an existing debt is shown in Hodge *v.* Vavisour, (1616) 3 Bulst. 222. The defendant being indebted to the plaintiff for certain goods, afterwards and in consideration thereof, as the declaration alleged, did assume and promise to pay the same at one year. For non-payment at the time stated, an action of assumpsit was brought. After verdict and judgment for plaintiff, it was moved in arrest of judgment that the promise was not binding. It was insisted for the defendant that the allegation, "*quod postea in consideratione inde,* the defendant did assume and promise," was bad, because it showed a past consideration, which is not good to support a promise. The proper remedy, it was said, was debt. But this contention was dismissed by the court and it was held that the promise was grounded upon a good consideration. Haughton, J., observed, "the defendant is clogged with the debt continually and therefore this is a good consideration to raise a promise." Croke, J., said: "If a man owes another so much for certain goods

upon the consideration of legal duty, for the promise which was now implied is raised by implication of law at the very moment the debt is created. Hence such implied promise is supported by the consideration (*quid pro quo*) which originates the debt. Accordingly this exceptional type of consideration, of which only a momentary glimpse has been caught, disappeared almost entirely from view. Prior to *Slade's Case* an implied consideration was used to support an actual promise; now the law raised an implied promise upon a real consideration.

Slade's Case marks an important epoch in the history of English contract law, but no event in legal history is more likely to be misinterpreted. Indeed, after having considered the matter from different points of view during several years which have been occupied with this work, the writer is prepared to say that *Slade's Case* and the events which followed in its train are calculated to give rise to an inference on a most important point which is exactly opposed to the true state of facts. Truly the case may be said to throw a false light upon a large part of modern contract law. It is therefore of the utmost importance that the real significance of the decision should not escape us. To this end we must here lay the proper emphasis upon the distinction between the conception of contractual obligation which underlies the common-law debt and that conception of contractual obligation which is found in the assumptual promise.

An idea, we take it, almost universally prevails to the effect that our law of contract is underlaid by some single conception. It must all have its root, so we imagine, in one general notion of liability. The conception of the obligation of promise is of course supposed to supply the notion which lies at the root of this great branch of the law. However it may have been in ages past, all contract law is now considered reducible to this one head. The obligation of promise is looked upon as a sort of menstruum in which all other forms

and he demands him when he will pay him for them, who answers at such a time, and the other agrees unto it, this is good; and the law will here imply a tacit consideration by the law annexed unto it."

of contractual obligation have gradually dissolved. But this is all wrong. The instinct for generalization has plainly overleaped the truth at this point. This is merely a fruit of that unnatural yet necessary extension of the action of assumpsit which resulted from the procedural defects of the action of debt.

Our law of contract is unshakably planted upon two conceptions instead of one. The idea of contractual duty imposed by law, which was the first conception of contract revealed in the common law, eternally abides. It has not been supplanted; it has only been in a measure obscured by the modern conception of the obligation of promise.

Double basis of English contract law.

It is true that the action of debt was swallowed up in the action of assumpsit, and *Slade's Case* marks the point at which this event occurred. But — and here is the whole import of that decision — the point involved was one of remedy purely. It was necessary that simple contract law should be entirely freed from the meshes of the action of debt. The only way to accomplish this was for the courts to hold that upon the creation of a simple debt the law raises an implied promise such as will support assumpsit. The step was taken. The result was that the action of debt as a remedy upon simple contracts practically disappeared, its place being taken by indebitatus assumpsit. But though the action disappeared, the conception of liability which underlies the debt did not. The supersession of the action of debt resulted of necessity in an occultation of the conception of liability which underlies the debt, but it did not destroy that conception.

Permanence of the conception of debt.

Still, from *Slade's Case* until this good day there has been more or less confusion in the minds of legal thinkers between the conceptions of contractual duty imposed by law and the conception of the obligation of promise. The older notion has been almost entirely overlooked. Men have talked about the implied promise, which is nominally the foundation of the action of indebitatus assumpsit, until they have actually come to think that the same conception of liability is here presented to view as in the ordinary engagement by actual promise. But the distinction is fundamental and must be preserved.

Confusion between the conception of debt and the idea of the obligation of promise.

5

As we shall hereafter perceive, the sole clue to a proper understanding of the quasi-contracts is found in the ancient and indestructible conception of contractual duty imposed by law. A thing to be constantly borne in mind by the student of modern contract law is that in dealing with the mysterious implied promise, he is really in contact with the simple debt in disguise. The implied promise is purely a remedial fiction. *Slade's Case,* we say, sheds a false light on the subsequent history of contract, because it so easily gives rise to the misleading inference that the conception of the debt has been superseded and extinguished by the notion of the obligation of promise.

CHAPTER VIII.

CONSIDERATION.

WITH the death of Elizabeth (1603), the formative period in the history of consideration came to a close and English contract law was ready to enter upon its modern career. It will be noted that several forms of consideration had now appeared. First in importance is that detriment to the promisee (1505) which is necessary to give validity to the simple unilateral promise. This is the original norm of the assumptual consideration and is the type into which all other forms of consideration are commonly but erroneously supposed to be resolvable.[1] Next in importance is the consideration of mutual promises (1588). Least notable of the three different types of the assumptual consideration is the consideration of legal duty or precedent debt (*cir.* 1550).

<small>Chapter VIII</small>

<small>End of formative period.</small>

<small>Types of consideration.</small>

It is not possible by any valid process to resolve these different sorts of consideration into one. No present detriment to the promisee is found either in the consideration of legal duty or in mutual promises. In the one case the detriment is past, having been incurred when the debt was created. In the other there is a contemplated detriment to both parties, i. e., future performance of the respective promises; but the contract is valid from the time the mutual promises are made. It is indispensable to consideration in the sense of detriment that the detriment should concur with the promise.

<small>These not resolvable into any one head.</small>

Of the recompense, or benefit, to the grantor of real property, which is necessary to pass the use in equity to a stranger; and of love and affection, which is sufficient to support a covenant to stand seized to the use of one closely related by blood or marriage, we take no further account, as these are not assumptual considerations.

[1] Langdell on Contracts, §64; Two Theories of Consideration, 12 Harv. L. Rev. 515.

68   FOUNDATIONS OF LEGAL LIABILITY.

Volume II

Benefit to promisor not a good consideration.

We now proceed to consider certain principles pertaining to the subject of consideration which have an importance apart from any relation of time or of history and which are necessary to be mastered at this juncture.

First to be noted is the principle that a mere benefit to the promisor is not a sufficient consideration to support a promise. This proposition was explicitly stated by Professor Langdell a quarter of a century ago,[2] and subsequent research has abundantly justified his conclusion. The idea that a benefit to the promisor may be a sufficient consideration has, however, been very persistent. In *Stone v. Wythipol* (1588),[3] Coke, who was of counsel, observed: " Every consideration that doth charge the defendant in assumpsit must be to the benefit of the defendant, or charge of the plaintiff, and no case can be put out of this rule." The same idea appears in the elaborate definition of consideration given by Lush, J., in *Currie v. Misa* (1875).[4] " A valuable consideration in the sense of the law," says he, " may consist either in some right, interest, profit, or benefit accruing to the one party, or some forbearance, detriment, loss, or responsibility, given, suffered, or undertaken by the other."

Persistence of notion to contrary.

Heritage from debt.

Good reason for the impression that a benefit to the promisor may be a good consideration is found in the fact that the element which constitutes detriment to the promisee also usually represents a benefit to the promisor. Benefit looks big to the eyes of the layman, and it is in terms of benefit that one would naturally at first conceive of consideration. The idea is doubtless a heritage from debt, for it is of the essence of debt that the *quid pro quo* should accrue as a benefit to the debtor.

Detriment to promisee essence of consideration.

The principle, however, must be considered established that the element which alone gives efficacy to the assumptual promise is detriment to the promisee. Any number of cases can be cited wherein it has been held that detriment to the promisee, unaccompanied by any benefit to the promisor, will

---

[2] Langdell on Contracts, § 64.
[3] Cro. Eliz. 126.
[4] L. R. 10 Exch. 162. In Scotson v. Pegg, 6 H. & N. 295, Martin, B., said "any act done whereby a contracting party receives a benefit is a good consideration for a promise from him."

CONSIDERATION. 69

support a promise, but not one can be cited where a benefit to the promisor, unaccompanied by a detriment to the promisee, has been held to be sufficient to support a unilateral promise.[5]

Upon the proposition above stated cases like *Foakes v. Beer* (1884)[6] supply crucial and conclusive proof. But of this we shall speak later.

Adequacy of Consideration.

The subject of adequacy of consideration can be dismissed in a few words. Strictly speaking, the adequacy of a consideration is not a question for judicial determination at all. That is a thing for the parties to settle. The law merely requires that there should be some consideration of which legal notice can be taken, but the size or extent of that detriment as compared with the thing which is promised is wholly immaterial. Upon this point legal theory has never wavered.[7] There is a saying, current in the common law from the earliest

Chapter VIII

Adequacy of the consideration a question for the parties

---

[5] The foregoing statement has been made after a careful examination of the article by Prof. E. H. Bennett, Is Mere Gain to Promisor a Good Consideration? (10 Harv. L. Rev. 257). This learned writer has here collated the cases which lend countenance to the view that benefit to the promisor is capable of supporting a promise where detriment to the promisee is altogether absent. But it will be found that the contracts involved in those cases are either instances of promises supported by the consideration of legal duty or they are bilateral agreements. Both of these types of engagement are somewhat exceptional and will be specially dealt with further on in this work. The decisions referred to do not, we submit, have any bearing on the proposition to which we have committed ourselves in the text, viz., that benefit to the promisor is incompetent to support the ordinary unilateral promise.

[6] 9 App. Cas. 605.

[7] It has been said that an agreement for the mere exchange of money is the one case where the consideration on one side must be coextensive with the consideration on the other. This principle confessedly has very limited scope, because it can only apply to agreements for the present payment of money on request; for the payment of any sum, however small, is a sufficient consideration theoretically for the payment of any larger sum at a future time. Again, present agreements for the exchange of specific pieces of money, such as of a gold coin for bills, would be valid though their respective values should not correspond, for here the kind and quality of the money would become of essence in the contract. See Langdell on Contracts, § 55; *Schnell v. Nell*, 17 Ind. 29; *Bailey v. Day*, 26 Me. 88.

time, to the effect that a peppercorn can be a consideration for the release of £100. In 1840 it was said in the Exchequer Chamber that the surrender of a piece of paper void in law as an evidence of indebtedness is sufficient to support a guaranty of £10,000.[8] These dicta represent the theoretical vanishing point of consideration as regards the question of adequacy.

In *Sturlyn v. Albany* (1587),[9] it was said, "when a thing is to be done by the plaintiff, be it never so small, this is a sufficient consideration to ground an action;" and in the days of the Commonwealth, Rolle, C. J., said, "a little consideration will serve to ground a promise upon."[1]

Size of the detriment immaterial. Where the *animus contrahendi* is present it is difficult to imagine an act or detriment so insignificant as to be incapable of being a consideration. Anything of possible value in the eye of the law is sufficient; and for the purpose of determining this, the law looks, or should look, through the eyes of the parties themselves. Every consideration is, for all purposes, the full legal equivalent of the promise for which it is given; and where the diverse appetites of the parties concur in saying there is such equivalence, the courts do not allow it to be gainsaid.[2]

Intention of parties. Passing from the subject of adequacy to the more important question as to when and how an act, forbearance, loss, risk, or other detriment, acquires the quality of being a consideration, we observe that the intention of the parties as exhibited in the contract, and their mode of dealing with the act or detriment in question, ought to determine whether or not it bears the character of being a consideration for the promise. Judge Holmes has wisely said, "It appears to me that it has not always been sufficiently borne in mind that the same thing may be a consideration or not as it is dealt with by the

---

[8] Brooks v. Haigh, 10 Ad. & El. 323, 309, 37 E. C. L. 115, 108.
[9] Cro. Eliz. 67.
[1] Bunniworth v. Gibbs, Style 419.
[2] "The value of all things contracted for," says Hobbes, "is measured by the appetite of the contractors; and therefore the just value is that which they be contented to give." Leviathan, pt. I., c. 15, quoted by Sir F. Pollock, Contracts (6th ed.), p. 172.

CONSIDERATION. 71

parties. . . . It is hard to see the propriety of erecting any detriment which an instrument may disclose or provide for into a consideration unless the parties have dealt with it on that footing."[3]

Chapter VIII

To illustrate this, suppose A says to B, " Meet me at the jeweler's to-morrow at eleven A. M. and I will give you a watch." B says, " Very well, I will do so." This agreement discloses on its face a detriment to B in that he is required to go to the jeweler's, yet it is obvious that there is no *animus contrahendi*. The parties do not stamp that detriment with legal character. Suppose, however, B gives the conversation a different turn by saying, " That will cause me trouble; I promise to go only on condition that you make a binding agreement to give me the watch for going." A says in reply, " I consent to that also." In this case, *going to the jeweler's* is stamped with the quality of being a consideration by the mode in which the parties deal with it.

In this connection it will be found that the courts have shown a very natural bias in favor of sustaining honest agreements, and when they find an element present which fills the bill they sometimes treat it as a consideration, though the parties may not have done so. The fact that the parties do not happen to treat an act of detriment as a consideration in a particular case is not, therefore, always conclusive that the act or detriment in question is not a sufficient consideration to support the promise in that case.

Bias of courts towards sustaining validity of agreements.

In *Taylor v. Manners* (1865),[4] it was held that the payment by a debtor of the probate and legacy duty on a debt owing to the estate was a sufficient consideration to support a release of the debt by the residuary legatees; and it was so held notwithstanding the fact that the transaction was in intention purely gratuitous. *Wilkinson v. Oliveira* (1835)[5]

---

[3] Common Law, p. 292.

" The mere presence of some incident to a contract which might under certain circumstances be upheld as a consideration for a promise does not necessarily make it the consideration for the promise in that contract. To give it that effect it must have been offered by one party and accepted by the other as one element of the contract." Brown, J., Fire Ins. Assoc. v. Wickham, 141 U. S. 579.

[4] L. R. 1 Ch. 48.

[5] 1 Bing. N. Cas. 490, 27 E. C. L. 468.

Volume II

The nominal consideration.

illustrates the same proneness on the part of the courts to treat an act as a consideration which might appear to have been originally gratuitous. As has been observed,⁶ on the other hand, a manifest intention on the part of the parties to treat a particular act or detriment, however insignificant, as a consideration is conclusive of its character as such. A nominal consideration is good enough if it is treated by the parties as a consideration. This proposition is merely another form of saying that the adequacy of consideration is for the parties to determine and not the court. In *Thomas v. Thomas* (1842),⁷ certain executors, being moved by a desire to carry out the wishes of the deceased, let a dwelling to a widow, in consideration that she should pay a nominal sum per annum as ground rent, and the contract was sustained.

Abandonment of vicious habit.

The disposition of the courts to treat as a consideration that which the parties have dealt with as such, is illustrated in a very late line of decisions to the effect that the abandonment of a vicious habit by the promisee may be sufficient to support a promise. Thus, in *Talbott v. Stemmons* (1889) ⁸ the testator promised to leave his grandson a certain sum provided the latter would never take another chew of tobacco. The promise was held binding on the ground that the abandonment of the habit was a detriment in law, although doubtless a benefit to the plaintiff in fact. The same principle was applied in *Hamer v. Sidway* (1891),⁹ by the Court of Appeals of New York;¹ and in *Dunton v. Dunton* (1892),² the Supreme Court of Victoria enforced a promise to pay a monthly stipend to a woman, provided she would conduct herself with sobriety and in an orderly and virtuous manner.

Leading virtuous life.

This decision manifestly puts a new aspect on cases like *Binnington v. Wallis* (1821),³ and *Beaumont v. Reeve* (1846),⁴ where unsuccessful attempts were made to maintain an action upon a promise to pay an annuity to the plaintiff,

---

⁶ Pollock on Contracts, p. 171.
⁷ 2 Q. B. 851, 42 E. C. L. 945.
⁸ 89 Ky. 222.
⁹ 124 N. Y. 538.
¹ The doubt suggested by Professor Hare as to the validity of these agreements can therefore no longer be entertained. See Hare on Contracts, p. 225.
² 18 Vict. L. R. 114.
³ 4 B. & Ald. 650, 6 E. C. L. 639.
⁴ 8 Q. B. 483, 55 E. C. L. 483.

formerly mistress of the promisor. In those cases it was held that the moral obligation resting on the promisor to provide for the plaintiff was not a good consideration. That point was undoubtedly well taken. But now that a consideration for the promise is found, not in the moral obligation of the promisor, but in the detriment which the promisee incurs in shaping her conduct according to the condition of the promise, the result in cases like those referred to should be different.

Legality and Competency of Consideration.

A consideration which is sufficient in other respects may be bad because it is illegal or incompetent. The illegal consideration consists of any act or forbearance which is contrary to law. A promise to pay a sum of money to one having charge of an arrested person, provided he will let such person go at large contrary to law, is not binding.[5]

An action cannot be maintained by the publisher of a libel who has been mulcted in damages, in a suit growing out of the libel, on a promise of indemnity given by a person who induced the publication of the libel.[6] The printer of libelous matter cannot even recover his wages of the person who employed him to do the printing.[7] A note given in consideration of a forbearance to prosecute the maker on a charge of false pretenses cannot be enforced, because the consideration of the note is the compounding of a felony.[8]

The general principle is that no act or forbearance which is for any reason unlawful or contrary to public policy can be recognized as a consideration for a binding promise.[9] It has been held that a contract which involves, to the knowledge of both parties, a breach on the part of one of them, of an existing contract with a third person, cannot be enforced.[1]

---

[5] Fetherston v. Hutchinson, Cro. Eliz. 199.
[6] Shackell v. Rosier, 2 Bing. N. Cas. 634, 20 E. C. L. 438; Lea v. Collins, 4 Sneed (Tenn.) 393.
[7] Poplett v. Stockdale, 2 C. & P. 198, 12 E. C. L. 87.
[8] Clubb v. Hutson, 18 C. B. N. S. 414, 114 E. C. L. 414. See also Bell v. Wood, 1 Bay (S. Car.) 240; Plumer v. Smith, 5 N. H. 553.
[9] Harrington v. Victoria Graving Dock Co., 3 Q. B. D. 549.
[1] Moody v. Newmark, 121 Cal. 446.

Promise to indemnify against consequences of unlawful act.

A promise to indemnify a man if he will commit a trespass is invalid,[2] unless the agent is ignorant of the trespassory character of the act which he is called upon to do.[3] The qualification just stated is well illustrated in *Battersey's Case* (1623).[4] It appeared that one H had arrested another and brought him to the plaintiff's inn. Upon H's promise to save the plaintiff harmless the latter was induced to take charge of the prisoner and keep him in custody. It subsequently developed that the arrest was illegal, and the injured party recovered damages of the plaintiff. The plaintiff then sued H on his promise to indemnify. It was objected that the consideration for the promise was bad because the imprisonment was unlawful. But it was held that the plaintiff was not chargeable with notice of that fact and that the promise was good. "If I request one man to enter into another's ground and in my name to drive out the beasts and impound them, and promise to save him harmless, this is a good assumpsit and yet the act is tortious; but where the act appears in itself to be unlawful, there it is otherwise, as if I request you to beat another and promise to save you harmless, this assumpsit is not good."

The incompetent consideration.

The incompetent consideration[5] consists of the doing of some act which the actor is under a legal obligation to do.

---

[2] Babcock *v.* Terry, 97 Mass. 482; Cumpston *v.* Lambert, 18 Ohio 81.

[3] Avery *v.* Halsey, 14 Pick. (Mass.) 174; Coventry *v.* Barton, 17 Johns. (N. Y.) 142; Stone *v.* Hooker, 9 Cow. (N. Y.) 154; Ives *v.* Jones, 3 Ired. L. (25 N. Car.) 538.

The principle is well established that a promise of indemnity to an officer who is charged with the execution of legal process is valid where it turns out that the goods levied upon by him were not the goods of the defendant in execution. Arundel *v.* Gardiner, Cro. Jac. 652; Elliston *v.* Berryman, 15 Q. B. 205, 69 E. C. L. 205; Robertson *v.* Broadfoot, 11 U. C. Q. B. 407.

[4] Winch 48.

[5] The reader will note that the term 'incompetent consideration' is first used by us. Judges and legal writers are accustomed to say that contracts based upon this sort of consideration are bad because of the absence of consideration, that is, for the absence of such a consideration as the law recognizes as sufficient. Inasmuch as there is an actual detriment here such as would ordinarily be accepted as a good consideration, it seems better to say that the consideration is merely incompetent.

CONSIDERATION. 75

The doing of such an act is not a good consideration, because it is no detriment to the man who does it. On the contrary, it is a benefit to him, inasmuch as it releases him from a legal obligation.

Chapter VIII

The most familiar illustration of the incompetent consideration is found in cases where, in consideration of the payment of part of a debt, the creditor promises to forego as to the remainder. As we shall hereafter see, this promise is not binding.

Similarly, a promise to forbear for a specified time as to the residue of a debt given in consideration of part payment of a debt already due is invalid; and, as is well known, such an agreement will not release a surety.[6] It is held that a promise to convey land[7] or make a quit-claim[8] is nugatory where the only consideration is the payment of a lawful debt.

Doing of act which one is legally bound to do.

In *Schneider v. Heinsheimer* (1899),[9] B, being under contract to execute a bill of sale to A, refused to do so except upon condition that A would settle a certain claim. The promise to settle the claim was held not binding. In *Gaar v. Green* (1896),[1] a purchaser of machinery was bound by contract to execute notes for the purchase price thereof, and refused to do so except upon condition that the seller would agree to do certain things about the machinery, and the promise so obtained was held to be invalid.

In both England and America it has long been established as a rule of law that where seamen have shipped under articles stipulating for the payment of particular wages, a promise to pay them larger wages, made in order to induce them to do their duty in performance of their original contract, is void. In the first case involving this point (1791),[2] the ruling was based on grounds of public policy; but in the second (1809)[3]

Promise to increase wages of sailors.

---

[6] Holliday v. Poole, 77 Ga. 159; Potter v. Green, 6 Allen (Mass.) 442; Warren v. Hodge, 121 Mass. 106; Liening v. Gould, 13 Cal. 598; Parmelee v. Thompson, 45 N. Y. 58.
[7] Phœnix Ins. Co. v. Rink, 110 Ill. 538.
[8] Tucker v. Bartle, 85 Mo. 114.
[9] 26 Misc. (N. Y.) 11.
[1] 6 N. Dak. 48.
[2] Harris v. Watson, Peake N. P. (ed. 1795) 72.
[3] Stilk v. Myrick, 2 Campb. 317. To the same effect see Frazer v. Hatton, 2 C. B. N. S. 512, 89 E.

Lord Ellenborough put the decision on the ground of want of consideration.

Peck v. Requa (1859)[4] is the only case which countenances the idea that the doing of an act which one is legally bound to do can be a consideration for a promise given to induce the doing of that act. This decision is the result of a pure judicial oversight. It appeared that the plaintiff was under contract with the defendant to resign an office in a corporation. The plaintiff, however, refused to comply with this contract, and in order to induce him to carry it out, the defendant executed and delivered to the plaintiff the promissory note upon which suit was brought. The plaintiff thereupon resigned the office. It was held that he could recover on the note. The consideration was clearly incompetent[5] and the decision must consequently be considered erroneous.

The detriment disclosed in cases like *Talbott v. Stemmons* (1889)[6] and *Dunton v. Dunton* (1892),[7] referred to above, comes very near to being an incompetent consideration, but it is not. It may very well be that a man is under a moral duty to quit a vicious habit or to live a decent life, but the law reecognizes no such legal duty. Consequently one who quits a vicious habit or lives a decent life can recover on the promise which induced such course of conduct.

Forbearance to Prosecute Invalid Claim.

For more than two hundred years the opinion prevailed that forbearance to prosecute an invalid claim is under all circumstances an incompetent consideration; or, as the authorities say, is no consideration at all. " Forbearance, where

C. L. 512; Harris *v.* Carter, 3 El. & Bl. 559, 77 E. C. L. 559.
  Public policy was also assigned as one of the reasons for a similar holding in New York. Bartlett *v.* Wyman, 14 Johns. (N. Y.) 260. In this case the promise was given to prevent the sailors from taking the illegal step of abandoning the ship.
  [4] 13 Gray (Mass.) 407.
  [5] The fallacy of the decision is found in the assumption that the plaintiff had the right to retain the office if he chose to do so and stand a suit for damages for a breach of the original contract. He did not have the right to do so; he was merely in a position to follow that course if he wished. A man may have the power, but he has no legal right to break his contract.
  [6] 89 Ky. 222.
  [7] 18 Vict. L. R. 114.

CONSIDERATION. 77

originally there is no cause of action, is no consideration to raise an assumpsit." [8]

In *Stone v. Wythipol* (1588),[9] it appeared that the plaintiff had a claim against B for merchandise sold to him, the claim, however, being unenforceable by reason of B's minority. After B's death, his executor promised the plaintiff to secure or pay the claim provided the plaintiff would forbear to institute suit thereon for a specified period. It was held that the promise was bad.[1] In *Manning's Case* (1600),[2] it was held that a promise by an heir, to whom no assets have descended, to pay a debt of his ancestor is unenforceable where such promise is given for a forbearance to sue.[3] In *Loyd v. Lee* (1717),[4] it was ruled that where a married woman executes a promissory note, a promise given, after discoverture, to pay the note is invalid where the only consideration for such promise is forbearance to sue.

The principle in question was applied in *Edwards v. Baugh* (1843),[5] wherein it was held that a declaration upon a promise given in consideration of a forbearance to sue was bad where such declaration merely alleged a dispute between the plaintiff and defendant over the existence of a debt, but failed to show that the debt was actually due. In *Wade v. Simeon* (1846),[6] it was held that forbearance after the actual institution of a suit is upon the same footing as forbearance before suit is brought. In both situations the forbearance is an incompetent consideration if the claim in respect to which the forbearance is granted is ungrounded.

In the case last referred to, Tindal, C. J., explained the principle on which these decisions rest, in the following words: "It is almost *contra bonos mores*, and certainly contrary to all the principles of natural justice, that a man should insti-

Chapter VIII

Illustrations of early doctrine.

Forbearance after institution of suit upon invalid claim.

---

[8] Loyd v. Lee (1717), 1 Stra. 94.
[9] Cro. Eliz. 126.
[1] To the same effect, Smith v. Jones (1610), Yelv. 184; Tooley v. Windham (1590), Cro. Eliz. 206; Davis v. Wright, 1 Vent. 120; Rosyer v. Langdale, Style 248; Jones v. Ashburnham (1804), 4 East 455. Compare Goodwin v. Willoughby, Popham 177; Woolaston v. Webb, Hob. 18.
[2] Rolle Abr. 28, pl. 57.
[3] Compare Barber v. Fox, 1 Vent. 159.
[4] 1 Stra. 94.
[5] 11 M. & W. 641.
[6] 2 C. B. 548, 52 E. C. L. 548.

tute proceedings against another, when he is conscious that he has no good cause of action. In order to constitute a binding promise, the plaintiff must show a good consideration, something beneficial to the defendant, or detrimental to the plaintiff. Detrimental to the plaintiff it cannot be, if he has no cause of action; and beneficial to the defendant it cannot be; for, in contemplation of law, the defense upon such an admitted state of facts must be successful, and the defendant will recover costs, which must be assumed to be a full compensation for all the legal damage he may sustain. The consideration therefore altogether fails." [7]

Modification of doctrine.

Dismissal of suit brought in good faith to enforce doubtful claim.

In *Longridge v. Dorville* (1821),[8] a principle was recognized which was destined to modify very materially the rule applied in the line of cases above considered. It was there held that if a claim is doubtful in law and fact and legal proceedings have been instituted upon it in good faith, a promise given in consideration of a surcease of such proceedings is good. The facts were these: A ship called the Carolina Matilda in sailing down the river Thames on a voyage to Norway ran foul of another ship, called the Zenobia. The owners of the Zenobia at once libeled the Carolina Matilda and arrested her at Gravesend. Thereupon the representatives of the owners of this ship, in order that she might be released and proceed on her voyage, promised to pay such damages, not exceeding £180, as had been actually sustained by the Zenobia, the exact amount to be ascertained upon the making of repairs. The legal proceedings against the Carolina Matilda and her owners were then dismissed. The damages to the Zenobia having subsequently been ascertained, the defendant's representatives of the Carolina Matilda were called upon to make good their promise to indemnify, but refused to do so. Upon suit being brought it was insisted for them that at the time of the collision the Carolina Matilda had a regular Trinity-house pilot aboard; that in consequence her owners were not as a matter of law legally liable for the damage done to

[7] Wade *v.* Simeon, 2 C. B. 563, 52 E. C. L. 563.
[8] 5 B. & Ald. 117, 7 E. C. L. 43.

the Zenobia; and that the promise to indemnify to the extent of that damage was not enforceable. But it was held that the giving up of a right of action which was being prosecuted in good faith upon a really doubtful claim was a sufficient consideration.

<small>Chapter VIII</small>

The same principle was applied forty years later in a case where a compromise of a disputed claim was effected prior to the institution of suit. It is enough, so it was held, if the claim be based on reasonable grounds and be pressed in good faith. Where these conditions concur, a forbearance to institute an intended suit is a good consideration.[9]

<small>Claim based on reasonable grounds and pressed in good faith.</small>

In *Callisher v. Bischoffsheim* (1870),[1] it appeared that the plaintiff in good faith believed that he had a valid claim against the government of Honduras and was on the point of instituting proceedings to enforce its payment. Thereupon in consideration that the plaintiff would forbear for a specified time to institute proceedings upon the claim, the defendant promised to deliver to the plaintiff certain debentures of the Honduras Railway. In a suit upon this promise it was held that the plaintiff's forbearance to institute suit for the period agreed upon was a good consideration, although the claim upon which he was about to sue was wholly without foundation. "Every day a compromise is effected on the ground that the party making it has a chance of succeeding in it, and if he *bona fide* believes he has a fair chance of success, he has a reasonable ground for suing, and his forbearance to sue will constitute a good consideration. When such a person forbears to sue he gives up what he believes to be a right of action, and the other party gets an advantage, and, instead of being annoyed with an action, he escapes from the vexations incident to it. . . . It would be another matter if a person made a claim which he knew to be unfounded."[2]

One decided merit of the modern doctrine is that in many

---

[9] Cook v. Wright (1861), 1 B. & S. 559, 101 E. C. L. 559.
[1] L. R. 5 Q. B. 449.
[2] Cockburn, C. J., in Callisher v. Bischoffsheim, L. R. 5 Q. B. 452. The weight of modern decisions is in favor of this view both in England and America. Forbearance to Sue, by E. H. Bennett, 10 Harv. L. Rev. 113. See also 1 Am. and Eng. Encyc. of Law, 2d ed., 711–714.

cases it simplifies the issue. Formerly when an action was brought upon a promise given for a forbearance to sue, the court necessarily had to pass upon two questions. It first had to determine whether the contract sued on was actually made, and then it had to consider the question whether the original cause of action was maintainable. This circumstance stripped the plaintiff of all benefit that might otherwise accrue from the adjustment, and greatly increased the burden of litigation. Now the making of the agreement is treated as eliminating all question of the merit of the previous claim, provided there is no fraud or bad faith and provided the claim is not clearly illegal.

CHAPTER IX

THE CONSIDERATION AND THE PROMISE.

BETWEEN the consideration and the promise there must be a causal relation. The consideration must draw the promise from the promisor, and the promise must be the inducement which causes the promisee to incur the detriment which constitutes the consideration. The two factors must be so far mutual that each may be looked upon in a way as being both the cause and the effect of the other. "The consideration and the promise ought to go together." [1] There could never have been any real doubt about the existence of such a principle, for it inhered in the very conception from which consideration was developed. The thing or money which was given to the unfaithful promisor in the early assumpsit was given for the promise and was the ground on which the action of deceit was maintained.

Nevertheless the principle in question has not always been consistently maintained. This leads us to consider two classes of cases in which it has been violated.

Chapter IX

Consideration and promise to go together.

Rewards.

In *Williams v. Carwardine* (1833),[2] it appeared that a reward had been offered for information leading to the discovery of the perpetrator of a murder. The plaintiff gave the information when she believed herself to be dying and in order "to ease her conscience." Having recovered from the illness, she sued for the reward and obtained judgment. There seems to have been no evidence showing that she even knew of the offer when the disclosure was made. Judgment

Information given without knowledge of offer.

---

[1] Docket *v.* Voyel ('1602), Cro. Eliz. 885. [2] 4 B. & Ad. 621, 24 E. C. L. 126.

was given on the ground that the offer was a general promise to pay the sum to any one giving the information required, and that the contract was made perfect by performance regardless of qualifications.

Knowledge of offer unnecessary.

Under the authority of this case it is held in England and in some of the American States that knowledge of the fact that the offer of reward has been made is not necessary in order to enable the person who complies with the terms of the offer to recover the reward.[3] The conclusion cannot be sustained in point of principle, for where there is no knowledge of the offer it is impossible to say that the person complying with the terms of the offer is induced to act by the promise.

Contrary doctrine.

More than one American court independently reached a different conclusion from that reached in *Williams v. Carwardine* only a few years after that case was decided and before the profession had become familiar with it.[4] In *Stamper v. Temple* (1845),[5] which is a well-considered case, Judge Turley pertinently inquired how there could be any contract when the act was done in ignorance of the offer. It was accordingly there held that in the absence of such knowledge no recovery could be had. The same conclusion was reached in New York in *Fitch v. Snedaker* (1868).[6] The principles of contract on which the right to recover a reward is based are correctly stated in the Massachusetts cases.[7]

The statutory right to reward.

It may not unreasonably be held, in case of public rewards offered under the authority of law, that any person who complies with the offer is entitled to the reward without regard to his knowledge of the offer. And so it has been decided in the state of Kentucky.[8] But here the right to the reward is a statutory right and need not be placed altogether on grounds

---

[3] Gibbons *v.* Proctor ('1892), L. T. 594; Eagle *v.* Smith, 4 Houst. (Del.) 293; Dawkins *v.* Sappington, 26 Ind. 199.

[4] Lee *v.* Flemingsburg, 7 Dana (Ky.) 28.

[5] 6 Humph. (Tenn.) 113.

[6] 38 N. Y. 248. See to same effect, Williams *v.* West Chicago St. R. Co., 191 Ill. 610; Howland *v.* Lounds, 51 N. Y. 604; Wilson *v.* Stump, 103 Cal. 255.

[7] Symmes *v.* Frazier, 6 Mass. 344; Wentworth *v.* Day, 3 Met. (Mass.) 352; Loring *v.* Boston, 7 Met. (Mass.) 411.

[8] Auditor *v.* Ballard, 9 Bush (Ky.) 572.

CONSIDERATION AND PROMISE. 83

of contract. The performance of the condition of the offer creates a sort of statutory debt.

Chapter IX

Consideration Moved by Previous Request.

From the principle that the promise and the consideration must concur, it follows that a past consideration is not good. Here it is necessary to distinguish between the past consideration and the executed consideration. The term 'executed consideration' is used to indicate that consideration which is executed for the promise and by virtue of which the promise is made good. The term 'past consideration' is used exclusively for that consideration which has no efficacy because of the fact that the act done or detriment suffered by the promisee was accomplished before the promise was given. Some writers unfortunately use the term 'executed consideration' in the sense of past consideration. A consideration executed for a promise makes it good; but, as was long ago said by Rolle, a consideration totally past is void.[9] St. Germain's Doctor propounds to the Student of the common law the following question: "What hold they if a promise be made for a thing past, as, I promise thee forty pounds for that thou hast builded me such a house, lieth an action there?" To which the answer is made, "They suppose nay."[1]

Past consideration invalid.

Distinguished from executed consideration.

We now come to consider a qualification of this general principle which was recognized in the sixteenth century and was consistently upheld for more than a hundred and fifty years. Though the doctrine in question is obsolete, the episode is instructive.

A past consideration, it was held, is sufficient to support a promise if that consideration appears to have been executed upon a previous request. *Hunt v. Bate* (1568)[2] seems to be the first case in which the distinction subsequently recognized was drawn. There a plaintiff, who out of mere kindness had

Consideration moved by previous request.

---

[9] 1 Rolle Abr. 11, pl. 1. "Consideration may be executory or executed; it must not be past." Anson on Contracts, 93*.

[1] Dial. II., ch. 24.
[2] 3 Dyer, 272a, 1 Rolle Abr. 11 (Q), pls. 2. 3; *Riggs v. Bullingham* (1568), Cro. Eliz. 715.

gone bail for his neighbor's servant, sued the master upon a subsequent promise to hold him harmless. The action was declared not to be maintainable. But at the same time a promise to pay twenty pounds, in consideration that the plaintiff at the special instance of the defendant had previously taken to wife the cousin of the defendant, was declared to be good.[3] In *Sidenham v. Worlington* (1585),[4] the latter principle was recognized and applied.

The right to recover on a promise supported by a consideration previously executed upon request was thus established in the law. The course of justice was thereby subserved and the judges fancied that the rule in question was an evasion rather than a subversion of the general principle; for whatever technical difficulty was presented they met by a fiction. The past consideration, so it was said, continued until the making of the promise,[5] or the promise when made related back to the previous request and was coupled with it.[6]

The principle was perhaps not bad in itself, but it was inadequate. An express promise made subsequently to the conferring of the benefit was absolutely necessary to be alleged and proved in order to maintain the action;[7] whereas there are many cases in which benefits are conferred upon request and ought to be paid for, whether any promise is made

---

[3] 3 Dyer 272a.

[4] 2 Leon. 224. Walmsley, for the defendant, argued that the consideration stated would not sustain the promise, because, said he, "the consideration and promise did not concur and go together; for the consideration was long before executed, so as now it cannot be intended that the promise was for the same consideration. As if one giveth me a horse, and a month after I promise him £10 for the said horse, he shall never have debt for the £10 nor assumpsit upon that promise; for there it is neither contract nor consideration, because the same is executed." In the same connection it was argued by Windham that "if one selleth a horse unto another and at another day he will warrant him to be sound of limb and member it is a void warrant, for that such warranty ought to have been made or given at such time as the horse was sold."

[5] Langdell on Contracts, § 92.

[6] Lampleigh v. Brathwait (1615), Hob. 105, Moo. K. B. 866. See Bosden v. Thinne. Yelv. 40.

[7] Hayes v. Warren (1732), 2 Stra. 933. In this case the declaration was "for work and labor done by the plaintiff for the defendant, in consideration whereof he promised to pay." It was objected, and the objection was sustained, that this was a past consideration and no request was alleged.

or not. The recognition of implied promises and the consequent extension of general assumpsit which took place in the seventeenth century supplied ample means for enforcing liability for benefits conferred, in all cases where the ends of justice were thereby subserved.

This development of law consequently supplied a competing principle much broader and more efficacious than the old, for it is manifestly better that the law should determine on fixed principles the actionability of transactions where no promise is in fact made at the very time the consideration passes, than that those who part with their labor or property should be remitted to the doubtful contingency of being able to prove a subsequent promise. With the extension of general assumpsit, therefore, the idea that a promise may be supported by a consideration previously executed on request gradually disappeared;[8] and the law now is that the subsequent promise has no vitality *per se*. It is admissible in evidence as tending to show that the benefit was not expected to be gratuitous,[9] but it will not create a liability where the law would not enforce the duty to compensate apart from such promise.

During the ascendancy of Mansfield as chief justice of the King's Bench the ghost of the old doctrine began again to stalk abroad and was, to some extent, at the basis of the doctrine of moral obligation as a consideration which was sanctioned by that judge. But in 1778, while he was yet presiding in the King's Bench, the House of Lords in *Rann v. Hughes* (1797),[1] refused to hold an executor liable *de bonis propriis* upon an express promise to pay a debt of his testator, on the ground that where there is no legal obligation and no new consideration, such as forbearance, the promise is *nudum pactum*. In other words, an express promise upon a past consideration can give no right of action other than that which

---

[8] Professor Langdell is authority for the statement that the courts of England have not recognized the principle in question since Hayes *v.* Warren (1732), 2 Stra. 933. See to the same effect, Anson on Contracts, 96*.

[9] Paynter *v.* Williams, 1 Cromp. & M. 810; Kennedy *v.* Broun, 13 C. B. N. S. 677, 106 E. C. L. 677. Compare observations of Bowen, L. J., in Stewart *v.* Casey, (1892) 1 ch. 115, 116.

[1] 7 T. R. 346, note *a*.

the law itself would imply, and no right of action whatever exists unless the law would imply a promise on the facts of the past transaction.

In *Hopkins v. Logan* (1839),[2] Maule, B., said: "An executed [i e., past] consideration is no consideration for any other promise than that which the law would imply; if it were, there would be two coexisting promises on one consideration." In *Roscorla v. Thomas* (1842),[3] the case put by Windham, in arguing *Sidenham v. Worlington* (ante), arose. The seller of a horse, after the trade had been concluded, warranted the animal to be sound and free from vice. It was held that an action would not lie on this warranty, for the reason stated by Maule in *Hopkins v. Logan*. Consequently the past consideration is not now sanctioned in England in any form,[4] and

---

[2] 5 M. & W. 241.

[3] 3 Q. B. 234, 43 E. C. L. 713. In 1837 the Supreme Court of North Carolina enunciated the principle subsequently laid down in Roscorla v. Thomas, 3 Q. B. 234, 43 E. C. L. 713, holding, in Hatchell v. Odom, 2 Dev. & B. L. (19 N. Car.) 302, that a promise made by the vendor of a slave, upon the slave being discovered to be unsound, either to cure him or refund the price, was void for want of consideration, there being neither a warranty of soundness nor a fraud in the sale.

[4] Bradford v. Roulston, 8 Ir. C. L. 468, decided in 1858 by the Irish Exchequer, recognized the old doctrine and sustained an action on an express promise made under circumstances where none would have been implied by law. It was therefore out of harmony with the trend of judicial opinion as shown in Roscorla v. Thomas and subsequent cases. Professor Langdell (Contracts, § 93) criticises Bradford v. Roulston, saying that the court treated the question purely as one of authority, gave too little weight to Roscorla v. Thomas, and attached too much importance to cases which had received no judicial recognition for a century and a quarter. This criticism is justified, but nevertheless the opinion in Bradford v. Roulston is an instructive one by reason of the large array of authorities cited. Among other things Pigot, C. B., said: "Where a past consideration — that is, a thing previously done by the plaintiff at the request of the defendant — is one from which the law implies a promise, an express promise different from, or in addition to, that which the law implies, is *nudum pactum*, on the ground that the whole consideration is exhausted by the promise which the law implies. Among those authorities are Brown v. Crump, 1 Marsh. 567, 4 E. C. L. 348; Granger v. Collins, 6 M. & W. 458; Hopkins v. Logan, 5 M. & W. 241; Roscorla v. Thomas, 3 Q. B. 234, 43 E. C. L. 713. And this principle of law was recognized and approved in Kaye v. Dutton, 7 M. & G. 807, 49 E. C. L. 807, 8 Scott N. R. 495, by Tindal, C. J., and also in all the stages of Elderton v. Emmens, 4 C. B. 479, 56 E. C. L. 479, 6 C. B. 160, 60 E. C. L. 160, 4 H. L. Cas. 624. This is in exact conformity with the opinion of

this is certainly the true common-law doctrine.[5] The American courts have not, on the whole, as yet reached the clear and consistent principle which is to be deduced from the English authorities. Here there are many comparatively modern decisions in which it is expressly held that a promise will be enforced if supported by a consideration previously executed upon request.[6] But when we come to analyze these cases it will be found that the circumstances are generally such that the law would of its own force impose a duty to compensate for the benefit conferred, regardless of the subsequent promise. Whatever anomaly is involved in these decisions results from the currency of the idea that moral obligation may be a good consideration. Of this notion we shall have something to say later.

Chapter IX

American authorities.

Rolle, expressed at the end of his report of Hodge v. Vavisor, 1 Rolle 413, and it is involved in the decision of Docket v. Voyel, Cro. Eliz. 885. But it has also been held, in a long series of decided cases, that where there is a past consideration, consisting of a previous act done at the request of the defendant, it will support a subsequent promise; the promise being treated as coupled with the previous request. The leading authority for this proposition is Lampleigh v. Brathwait, Hob. 105, 1 Smith Lead. Cas. (8th Am. ed.) 268. It has been so laid down in a great number of ancient authorities. . . . But in Roscorla v. Thomas, 3 Q. B. 234, 43 E. C. L. 713, Lord Denman intimated an opinion which, in one construction of the language, would seem to lay down, as a general rule of law, that a past or executed consideration will support no promise save one which the law would imply from it; that proposition importing, not merely that where a promise would be implied by law, and would therefore exhaust the consideration, no other express promise will be sustained by the same past consideration, but further, that no promise at all will be sustained by such consideration, unless a promise would be implied from it by law, and then only such promise as would be so implied."

[5] Anson on Contracts, 100*.
[6] Pool v. Horner, 64 Md. 131; Gleason v. Dyke, 22 Pick. (Mass.) 393; Wilson v. Edmonds, 24 N. H. 517; Goulding v. Davidson, 26 N. Y. 609; Holden v. Banes, 140 Pa. St. 63; Boothe v. Fitzpatrick, 36 Vt. 681. See Allen v. Bryson, 67 Iowa 596.

CHAPTER X

ACCORD AND SATISFACTION.

<small>Volume II</small>

IN this and the succeeding chapter we shall deal with the law of accord and satisfaction. The subject has an importance in the theory of contract which is altogether out of proportion to its apparent scope.

<small>Principle of accord and satisfaction.</small>

The general principle underlying the accord is simple and of exceedingly narrow compass. It is this: where there is a subsisting unilateral obligation by which A is legally bound to do for B a particular act, for instance, to pay money, to deliver a chattel, or to satisfy an unliquidated claim for damages, A, instead of doing the act legally due from him, may, with the consent of the creditor, do some other act or deliver some other thing than that which he is obligated to render, and this will operate to satisfy the existing obligation. Every element of a perfect contract is here present. The parties agree, and the doing of an act other than that which is due supplies a consideration for the undertaking of the creditor to surrender or forego the original claim. Accordingly all decisions in any way touching this matter proceed upon the tacit or express assumption that such a transaction is valid.

<small>Accord as an alternative of the formal release.</small>

The accord supplies one of the two means by which, at common law, a unilateral debt, obligation, or claim could be satisfied without performance. The other means was, of course, by a release under seal.[1] Where the original obligation was not under seal, or, if under seal, stipulated for the payment of money, an accord and satisfaction had equal validity with the sealed release.[2]

<small>Antiquity of the accord.</small>

The accord is very ancient. It was recognized long before the action of assumpsit appeared. Britton, writing during the reign of Edward I, notices the accord as a good defense

---

[1] Pinnel's Case, 5 Coke 117a. [2] Peytoe's Case, 9 Coke 79a.

ACCORD AND SATISFACTION.   89

to an action of trespass. Says he: "The defendants may say that the parties made accord of this trespass; and if the plaintiff deny it, let the truth be inquired by the country. And if the plaintiffs will not agree to the accord, let the defendants be awarded quit and the plaintiffs in mercy."[3]

While the general principle underlying the accord is so simple as to require no explanation, we find associated with it two other principles which are so peculiar as to justify one in speaking of them as the two greatest mysteries of the common law. The first of these is the rule that the accord must be executed. To illustrate: Suppose A is indebted to B in a certain sum, and they make a bilateral agreement whereby A agrees to deliver and B agrees to accept, at a stated day in the future, a specified amount of wheat in satisfaction of the debt. Here is a flawless bilateral engagement and yet it is not valid. The accord must be actually executed before it can operate as a satisfaction. The other rule to which we allude is that the payment of part of a debt already due cannot operate as a satisfaction of the whole, although the creditor accepts it as such.[4] All that is of importance in the law of accord and satisfaction will be developed in tracing the history of these two most remarkable rules.

Accord Must Be Executed.

The principle that in order to be binding an accord must be executed is to be explained on historical grounds. It is a fossil that has come down to us from a previous legal formation, and though it does not harmonize altogether with modern contract law and has apparently overstayed its time, it yet remains in our law substantially unimpaired.

A moment's consideration will show that the mere agree-

---

[3] Britton, Bk. I., 52*b*. An instance from 1341 is found in Y. B. 15 Edw. III. (Rolls ed.) 84, pl. 31.

[4] Said Sir George Jessel, M.R., in Couldery *v.* Bartrum, 19 Ch. D. 394: "According to English common law a creditor might accept anything in satisfaction of his debt except a less amount of money. He might take a horse, or a canary, or a tomtit if he chose, and that was accord and satisfaction; but, by a most extraordinary peculiarity of the English common law, he could not take 19s. 6d. in the pound; that was *nudum pactum.* . . . That was one of the mysteries of English common law."

ment of accord, unaccompanied by the delivery of the thing which the debtor agrees to give and which the creditor agrees to accept, is a consensual bilateral agreement. It creates no debt and there is no executed consideration which would support the promise of the creditor to abstain from enforcing his claim. Now when the accord was first recognized, the action of assumpsit had not appeared and the recognition of the bilateral agreement was three hundred years in the future. It followed that the accord would in that early period support no action; and this species of engagement could therefore never appear in court except in the form of a defense to an action brought by the creditor on the original claim. This peculiar limitation has served to keep in obscurity the distinction which the accord bears of being one of the oldest simple contracts known to the law.

The early authorities are explicit upon the point that the only accord which is valid is that which has been carried into effect. Accord without satisfaction is not good.[5] "Upon an accord the thing that is promised in recompense must be paid or delivered in hand, for upon an accord there lieth no action."[6] "In every accord it behooves of necessity to have payment of the compensation; otherwise it avails not; for if dispute arises between you and me over divers trespasses and there is an agreement between us that I shall pay you money by way of compensation, and I tender to you the said money and you refuse to receive it, this accord is void. But if you receive the money, then this is good satisfaction. Moreover, for the nonpayment of the money you shall never have any action whatever."[7] The reason assigned in the case wherein the above language was used is that a mere parol agreement was inoperative at common law. "By our law words without

---

[5] Fitz. Abr., *Accorde*, pls. 1–5; Brooke Abr., *Accord and Concord*, pls. 3, 6, 7, 8.

[6] Doctor & Stud., Dial. II., ch. 24.

[7] Pigot. J. (1475), in Y. B. 16 Edw. IV. 8, pl. 5. All the court, save Littleton, agreed that this was a correct statement of the law. Littleton would have applied the same rule to the accord as to the arbitrament. To the same effect see Y. B. 17 Edw. IV. 8, pl. 6; Y. B. 6 Hen. VII. 11. pl. 8; Andrews *v.* Boughey, 1 Dyer 75a; Onely *v.* Kent, 3 Dyer 355b; Richards *v.* Bartlet, 1 Leon. 19; Peyfoe's Case, 9 Coke 79b.

ACCORD AND SATISFACTION.   91

reason (*sans reason*) shall bind no one."[8] The unexecuted accord was *nudum pactum*. A different rule prevailed in arbitrament, "for the arbitrators are a sort of judges appointed by the parties themselves,"[9] and their adjudication creates a duty in the nature of a debt like the judgment of a court. The very term 'satisfaction' is used in the phrase 'accord and satisfaction' to convey the idea of an accord rendered effective by actual performance.

During the period covered by the first stage of the action of assumpsit, the principle which required the accord to be executed could not be departed from, for, as we have seen, during this period the only binding parol engagement was the unilateral promise supported by the executed consideration. When, however, the bilateral contract was recognized (1588) the situation was changed, for the law now gave effect to mutual promises. Hence in point of abstract theory there was no reason why the old rule denying the efficacy of the executory accord should longer be followed. Accordingly we find a decision at the beginning of the seventeenth century to the effect that an executory accord may be good.[1] But judicial utterance on this point was not clear enough to become effective in later decisions.

The question whether the advent of the bilateral contract had abrogated the rule requiring the accord to be executed was not directly considered until *Case v. Barber* (1681).[2] An executory accord was there pleaded to an action brought by the creditor on the original claim. Defendant's counsel admitted that in pre-bilateral days, the accord was required to be executed in order to be valid; but he insisted that "of late it hath been held that upon mutual promises an action lies, and consequently, there being equal remedy on both sides, an accord may be pleaded without execution." The court agreed that this reasoning was unanswerable, saying, "for the reason

Chapter X

Executory accord theoretically valid in modern law.

Validity recognized.

---

[8] Genny, J., in Y. B. 16 Edw. IV. 9, pl. 5.
[9] *Ibid.*
[1] Goring *v.* Goring (1602), Yelv. 10. A debtor's promise to pay part of the debt was here held binding;

"for," said the court, "the plaintiff agreeing to take £150 for £205 is a promise on his part, and so one promise against another."
[2] T. Raym. 450.

92   FOUNDATIONS OF LEGAL LIABILITY.

of the law being changed, the law is thereby changed; and anciently remedy was not given for mutual promises, which now is given." Judgment was, however, given for the plaintiff for other reasons.

Old rule maintained

A few years later the same question was presented again in *Allen v. Harris* (1696),³ where, A being under contract to supply a waistcoat to B, it was agreed that A should pay B twenty shillings in discharge of this obligation, and the plaintiff agreed to accept it. Subsequently, upon trover being brought for the waistcoat, and the executory accord pleaded, counsel for the defendant referred to *Case v. Barber* and relied upon its reasoning. This, however, was not accepted, the court saying: " Upon accord no remedy lies. And the books are so numerous that an accord ought to be executed, that it is now impossible to overthrow all the books. But if it had been a new point, it might be worthy of consideration."

A rule which in former ages had been inevitable because of the immature development of contract law was thus fastened upon our law of contract in its maturity. The fight against the doctrine thus established by *Allen v. Harris* was kept up far into modern times, but unsuccessfully. Thus in *James v. David* (1793)⁴ a courageous attempt was made by Lane, counsel for the defendant, to get the court to recognize the validity of an executory accord based on mutual promises. But Lord Kenyon said: "I am sorry that the agreement disclosed in the plea is not a conclusive answer to the action; but as no satisfaction is pleaded the plaintiff is entitled to judgment." The principle in question was recognized in *Reeves v. Hearne* (1836),⁵ and in *Bayley v. Homan* (1837).⁶ In *Gabriel v. Dresser* (1855)⁷ another lively tilt occurred between court and counsel, but with the same result.

Unsuccessful efforts to impeach the ancient rule.

Doctrine supposed to be grounded on public policy.

The historical explanation herein given of the origin of the rule that an accord must be executed renders superfluous such an explanation as that suggested by the court in *Lynn v.*

³ 1 Ld. Raym. 122. See also Wickham *v.* Taylor, T. Jones 168.
⁴ 5 T. R. 141.
⁵ 1 M. & W. 323.
⁶ 3 Bing. N. Cas. 915, 32 E. C. L. 379.
⁷ 15 C. B. 622, 80 E. C. L. 622.

Bruce (1794),[8] where Eyre, C. J., said, "*Interest reipublicæ ut sit finis litium,* accord executed is satisfaction; accord executory is only substituting one cause of action in the room of another, which might go on to any extent." The idea embodied in this statement tends, no doubt, to harmonize the principle with modern conceptions and in a measure explains the reason for its retention in modern law; but it does not supply us with the real reason for its origin.

It may cause some surprise that a rule originating in so remote a period and so contrary to the spirit of modern contract law should, in common-law jurisdictions, still stand practically unimpaired. Hard-headed common sense has no doubt contributed largely to this result. Agreements in accord and compromise nearly always embody concessions to the debtor. These concessions are given in order to secure performance and not that the creditor may merely obtain ground for another lawsuit. The gist of the whole transaction is that the creditor is compensated for his concession by obtaining actual performance. Contemplated performance, therefore, and not a new counter-promise is the inducement which draws the promise from the creditor to forego his original claim. When the debtor belies this hope and fails or refuses to execute the act which constitutes the ground of the accord, it is not unjust that the creditor should be allowed to sue him on the original claim. It is not always the debtor who is in default. But inasmuch as the law adopts the principle that both parties must be bound or neither, the debtor who keeps faith and makes a tender, in conformity with the terms of the executory accord, is at the mercy of his creditor and has no redress where the latter refuses to abide his agreement.

Though the weight of authority in England is clearly to the effect that an accord by mutual promises is not effective, there is much apparent and some real conflict.

The instinctive perception of the theoretical soundness of the bilateral agreement of accord has certainly been a power-

---

[8] 2 H. Bl. 319. This explanation is, however, much older than Lynn *v.* Bruce. It is found in Peytoe's Case, 9 Coke 79*b*.

Volume II

Disturbing influence.

ful disturbing factor in modern times. In *Crowther v. Farrer* (1850),[9] a creditor agreed to stop prosecution of two lawsuits and in consideration thereof the defendant promised to pay a certain amount of money. The plaintiff forbore to prosecute the suits further and, upon alleging performance on his part, was permitted to recover on the promise made by the defendant. On motion in arrest of judgment, the judges were clearly of opinion that the declaration would have been bad on special demurrer, but allowed judgment to stand; because, while the agreement was strictly a bilateral one, stopping the litigation was an act which was capable of being treated as an executed consideration. Said Coleridge, J.: "The declaration discloses a mutual agreement binding each party to the other, supposing the other to have performed his part." This decision cannot be considered as authority for the bald proposition that an executory accord is binding.

Note given in satisfaction of claim.

If a debtor delivers to the creditor his promissory note payable at a future date and the creditor accepts it in satisfaction of the debt, it will so operate, at least conditionally.[1] The accord is here in a measure executory because the creditor gets only a promise of future payment, but the present delivery of the note is a circumstance sufficient to enable the court to treat this accord as being executed. The note is a different thing from that which the debtor is legally bound to render, and its delivery operates with the same effect as would the delivery of any other chattel.

At one point only has the ancient rule, requiring that the accord shall be executed in order to be effective, been really impeached. Executory agreements for the composition of debts entered into by the debtor and his several creditors are binding. This was established in *Good v. Cheesman* (1831).[2]

---

[9] 15 Q. B. 677, 69 E. C. L. 677.

[1] *Sard v. Rhodes*, 1 M. & W. 153; *Sibree v. Tripp*, 15 M. & W. 23; *McLane v. Piaggio*, 24 Fla. 72; *Moon v. Martin*, 122 Ind. 211; *Peace v. Stennet*, 4 J. J. Marsh. (Ky.) 440; *Foster v. Collins*, 6 Heisk. (Tenn.) 1.

[2] 2 B. & Ad. 328. See also *Boyd v. Hind*, 1 H. & N. 938; *Flockton v. Hall*, 14 Q. B. 380, 68 E. C. L. 380; *Slater v. Jones*, L. R. 8 Exch. 186; *Barclay v. New South Wales Bank* (1880), 5 App. Cas. 374.

In *Heathcote v. Crookshanks* (1787), 2 T. R. 24, the contrary doctrine had been announced.

ACCORD AND SATISFACTION.   95

It is to be observed, however, that the principle recognizing the validity of executory agreements for the composition of debts is not given full effect, for it has been held that if the debtor fails to do anything which by the terms of the agreement is imposed upon him he cannot claim the benefit of it, and the several creditors can subsequently sue upon their entire debts. The agreement is rather a conditional than absolute discharge. In *Evans v. Powis* (1847),[3] it appeared that an executory agreement for the composition of debts required the debtor to pay fifty per cent of the indebtedness in certain instalments on certain days. After the time for the payment of these instalments had passed, a creditor sued for the whole. It was held that a plea setting up the agreement of composition was bad which failed to show payment or tender of payment at the precise times agreed upon.

The reasoning on which the validity of composition agreements is to be sustained will be considered later.

In America it is generally laid down that an accord must be executed before it can operate as a satisfaction.[4] But here, as in England, a perception of the theoretical validity of mutual promises has caused more or less recognition to be given to the executory accord. A rule that does not square with true theory must needs cause trouble in the application of it.

Chapter X

Composition of debts.

American rule.

---

[3] 1 Exch. 601.
[4] Pope v. Tunstall, 2 Ark. 209; Holton v. Noble, 83 Cal. 7; Williams v. Stanton, 1 Root (Conn.) 426; Francis v. Deming, 59 Conn. 108; Sanford v. Abrams, 24 Fla. 181; Hall v. Smith, 10 Iowa 48; Ogilvie v. Hallam, 58 Iowa 714; Bigelow v. Baldwin, 1 Gray (Mass.) 245; Herrmann v. Orcutt, 152 Mass. 405; Barnes v. Lloyd, 1 How. (Miss.) 584; Burgess v. Denison Paper Mfg. Co., 79 Me. 266.
In Colorado and Texas the courts have upheld executory accords. To what extent the civil law may have contributed to the acceptance of this doctrine in those states is not clear. Whitsett v. Clayton, 5 Colo. 476; Gulf, etc., R. Co. v. Harriett, 80 Tex. 73. See also Schweider v. Lang, 29 Minn. 254.
In New York, the early case of Coit v. Houston, 3 Johns. Cas. (N. Y.) 243, which followed the dictum in Case v. Barber (1681), T. Raym. 450, to the effect that an accord executory may be binding, has been overruled. Tilton v. Alcott, 16 Barb. (N. Y.) 598; Kromer v. Heim, 75 N. Y. 574.

CHAPTER XI

ACCORD AND SATISFACTION (CONTINUED).

Part Payment of a Debt.

<small>Volume II</small>

<small>Question stated.</small> THE typical accord and satisfaction contemplates the doing of some act or the delivery of some thing which the debtor is not already bound to render. The horse, the hawk, or the robe, to use the classical illustration, is given in satisfaction of a money debt or in satisfaction of some claim for unliquidated damages. The situation now to be considered is that in which the debtor pays part of a subsisting debt with the understanding that such payment is to be received in satisfaction of the whole. Creditors often find it to their interest to make such terms with doubtful debtors, and they sometimes assent to such arrangements out of a spirit of generosity. The question which now arises is whether or not a part payment made with such an understanding satisfies the debt. Here it will be noted the accord is executed, and the only question is as to the sufficiency or competency of the satisfaction as a matter of law.

<small>Part payment a good satisfaction.</small> The first thought of the common law on this point was that such an arrangement is binding, and this seems sensible enough. In 1455 it was said by one of the judges: " If one be indebted to me in £40 and I take from him 12*d*. in satisfaction of the £40, in this case I shall be barred of the remainder." [1] Forty years later Fineux, J., observed that in his opinion " there is no difference between an accord and satisfaction in money and in a horse; for notwithstanding the sum is less than that in demand, still when the creditor has received it by his own agreement it is as good a satisfaction as anything else." [2] But in this case the learned Brian, C. J., ex-

---

[1] Y. B. 33 Hen. VI. 48*a*, pl. 32. Compare Y. B. 15 Edw. III. (Rolls ed.) 84, pl. 32.

[2] Y. B. 10 Hen. VII. 4, pl. 4.

ACCORD AND SATISFACTION.   97

pressed a different opinion. His idea was that as a matter of pure arithmetic it was not possible for a smaller sum of money to satisfy a debt for a larger sum. "The payment of £10 cannot be payment of £20. But if it were a horse, which horse is paid according to the concord, that is a good satisfaction; for it is not manifest whether the horse is worth more or less than the sum in demand; and notwithstanding the horse may be worth only a penny, this is not material, for such fact does not appear."[3] To the profitable Perkins, summing up the decisions at the close of the year-book period (1532), the clear weight of authority seemed to be in favor of the validity of such an accord.[4]

As time went on Brian's arithmetical view obtained currency and finally prevailed. In 1562, all the judges agreed that if one is indebted to J. S. in £100 and the debtee makes an acquittance whereby he acknowledges the receipt of £20 in full satisfaction, the release is not effectual unless it is under seal.[5]

In *Anonymous* (1588),[6] it appeared that the defendant was indebted to the plaintiff in the sum of £10, falling due at the following Christmas. Upon communication between them it was agreed that the defendant should, upon the day of the maturity of the debt, pay to the plaintiff £5 in full satisfaction, and that as to the other he should be acquitted of it. The judges unanimously agreed that the agreement was not binding on the creditor, " for £5 cannot be a satisfaction for £10." But it was also held that where the debtor promises to pay the

Chapter XI

This doctrine repudiated.

---

[3] Brian, C. J., in Y. B. 10 Hen. VII. 4, pl. 4.

[4] "If a man be bound in one hundred pounds to pay one hundred marks to the obligee, etc., and the obligee accept of ten pounds from the obligor, in satisfaction of the hundred marks, it is a good performance of the condition; and yet some have said the contrary, because ten pounds cannot be satisfaction for one hundred marks, etc. But that is not material in this case, because the obligee is content therewith, etc. And if the obligee had received a horse, or a gold or silver ring, or a quarter of wheat, or a cup, etc., of the obligor, in satisfaction for the hundred marks, it had been a good performance of the condition of what value soever the horse, or, etc., had been." Perk. Prof. Book, § 749.

[5] Dalison 49, pl. 13. To the same effect see Anonymous (1588), 4 Leon. 81; Richards *v* Bartlet (1583), 1 Leon. 19.

[6] 4 Leon. 81.

7

98 FOUNDATIONS OF LEGAL LIABILITY.

£5 before the maturity of the whole debt, the **agreement is binding.**

The classical authority on this branch of the subject of accord is found in *Pinnel's Case* (1601),[7] wherein it appeared that the debtor had paid something like £5 in full satisfaction of a debt of £8 not yet due. The judges agreed that payment of part before the maturity of the obligation might operate as a satisfaction of the whole; " for, peradventure, parcel of it before the day would be more beneficial than the whole at the day, and the value of the satisfaction is not material."

It will be noted that payment was not here made in accordance with the terms of the contract and in part performance of it; but, by the mutual consent of the parties, upon sufficient consideration, the terms of the obligation were varied by the payment of the money before it was due.

It was further said: " If I am bound to pay you £10 at Westminster and you request me to pay you £5 at the day at York and you will accept it in full satisfaction of the whole £10, it is a good satisfaction for the whole; for the expense to pay it at York is sufficient satisfaction." The law, then, was clearly with the defendant on the question of satisfaction; but for defective pleading judgment was given for the plaintiff.

In this case it was also resolved by the court that " by no possibility a lesser sum can be a satisfaction to the plaintiff for a greater sum." Coke adopted this principle in his Commentary on Littleton, saying: " It is apparent that a lesser sum of money cannot be a satisfaction of a greater."[8] This proposition, it may be observed, is a part of the *ratio decidendi* and in no proper sense can it be spoken of as a mere dictum.

No specific allusion was made in *Pinnel's Case* to the doctrine of consideration, and the resolution that payment of part cannot be satisfaction of the whole was not expressly put on the ground of the want of a consideration for the promise to forego the residue. From this it has been inferred that the proposition in question is based solely on the notion of mathematical inadequacy and is merely a survival of a bit of formal

---

[7] 5 Coke 117a.   [8] Co. Litt. 212b.

ACCORD AND SATISFACTION.

logic of the mediæval lawyer.[9] But this is a mistake. Mathematical sense does in a way sanction the proposition that part cannot be a satisfaction of the whole, but the proposition in question is much better supported on the ground whereon the modern decisions place it; namely, on the ground that there is no good consideration for the promise of the creditor to forego the excess.

Coke's statement that a lesser sum of money cannot be a satisfaction for a greater sum could, it seems to us, only come from a soil where the doctrine of consideration was beginning to flourish. If there is no connection between the two it is certainly strange that in the generations preceding the development of the doctrine of consideration, a rule different from that now announced should have prevailed.

But the articulation between the doctrine of consideration and the rule in *Pinnel's Case* is not left to mere inference. In *Richards v. Bartlet* (1583),[1] it was held that a promise to accept part in satisfaction of all is not binding; "because here is not any consideration set forth in bar by reason whereof the plaintiff [the creditor] should discharge the defendant of this matter; for no profit, but damage, comes to the plaintiff by this new agreement, and the defendant [the debtor] is not put to any labor or charge by it." In *Fitch v. Sutton* (1804),[2] Lord Ellenborough was called upon to consider the validity

Chapter XI

Bearing of doctrine of consideration on this question.

---

[9] This view is taken in Two Theories of Consideration, 12 Harv. L. Rev. 522.
Professor Ames's position, as set forth in the article referred to, is briefly this: The doing of any act (not unlawful or against public policy) is such a detriment to the actor as will support the promise of another given in consideration of that act. The payment of part of a debt is an act and is therefore a good consideration for the promise of the creditor to forego the residue of his debt. Hence, Lord Ellenborough was wrong when he said, in Fitch *v.* Sutton, 5 East 230, that the rule declared in Pinnel's Case, 5 Coke 117*a*, was to be supported on the ground of the absence of consideration. This idea, says Professor Ames, was an incorrect after-thought brought in to support a rule which was no longer to be supported on the mediæval notion of mathematical inadequacy. In this view the doctrine of Pinnel's Case is an anachronism and should not be maintained. We admit that payment of part of a debt is an act and that such act furnishes a consideration for the promise to forego the residue. The point, however, is that the consideration is incompetent.

[1] 1 Leon. 19.
[2] 5 East 230.

of a release for a debt given upon payment of part. "It is impossible," said he, "to contend that acceptance of £17 is an extinguishment of a debt of £50. There must be some consideration for the relinquishment of the residue; ... otherwise the agreement is *nudum pactum.*"

<small>Consideration here is incompetent.</small>

The point which we would impress in regard to the situation now before us is, not that consideration is absent, but that the act which is sought to be set up as a consideration lacks legal capacity to be a consideration. The consideration is incompetent; and this because the act done does not involve a legal detriment to the promisee.

<small>Doctrine of Pinnel's Case prevails.</small>

In modern times the rule laid down in *Pinnel's Case* has been reluctantly accepted as law, for notwithstanding a natural bias in favor of sustaining settlements made in good faith, the courts have been unable to escape its logic. In *Cumber v. Wane* (1717),³ the creditor had accepted the defendant's promissory note for £5 in satisfaction of a debt of £15. It was held that this was no satisfaction, and judgment was given for the whole debt. The court unfortunately put this decision on the ground that, in order to operate as a satisfaction, the thing given or done must not appear to be unreasonable. It had been said in *Pinnel's Case* that it is only necessary that the satisfaction may be beneficial in some aspect, and it has always been accepted as law that the reasonableness of the satisfaction is a thing with which the court has nothing to do. *Cumber v. Wane* has therefore been deservedly criticised. Furthermore, the decision on the particular facts of the case is now overruled.

<small>Negotiable security a good satisfaction.</small>

In *Sard v. Rhodes* (1836),⁴ it was held that the acceptance of a negotiable security could be pleaded in satisfaction of a simple contract debt for a like amount. This decision prepared the way for *Sibree v. Tripp* (1846),⁵ wherein it was decided that a negotiable instrument for less than the amount of a liquidated debt can operate to satisfy it. *Cumber v. Wane* was criticised and an effort was made to distinguish that case on the ground that it did not affirmatively appear from the

---

³ 1 Stra. 426, 1 Smith Lead. Cas. (8th Am. ed.) 633.

⁴ 1 M. & W. 153.

⁵ 15 M. & W. 23.

report of that case [6] that the promissory note was negotiable. Efforts so to reconcile *Cumber v. Wane* are now abandoned.[7]

Lynn v. Bruce (1794),[8] presented the following state of facts: A debtor promised to pay £73 on a debt of £105 and the creditor agreed to accept it in satisfaction of the whole. The debtor failed to keep his promise and was sued on the promise to pay the £73. The plaintiff could not recover for two reasons. In the first place there was no consideration for his promise to accept the £73 in satisfaction of the debt, and in the second place the accord remained in the form of mutual promises.

In *Foster v. Dawber* (1851),[9] it was held that the holder of a bill of exchange or promissory note may waive and discharge his rights by parol without any consideration. Baron Parke stated, as a reason for this, that no person is liable on such a contract except through the law merchant, and that with the introduction of that body of law was introduced the rule of the civil law that there may be a release and discharge from a debt by express words, although unaccompanied by satisfaction or any solemn instrument. This novel ruling is based upon an incorrect idea of the nature of the law merchant, and the decision must be considered unsound. In America no such rule as that sanctioned in *Foster v. Dawber* is countenanced, and the parol discharge of a negotiable instrument without consideration is unknown. Of course if the note or bill is surrendered this operates as an executed gift.[1] Furthermore, voluntary surrender or destruction of the evidence of indebted-

---

[6] 1 Stra. 426.
[7] See Lord Blackburn's opinion in Foakes v. Beer, 9 App. Cas. 605.
[8] 2 H. Bl. 317.
Professor Ames makes what to our mind is a mistaken criticism of Lynn v. Bruce. Perceiving that the executory accord ought in theory to be recognized as binding, and believing that the proposition that part cannot be satisfaction for the whole of a debt is not a consequence of the absence of consideration, but is merely a result of the mathematical view to which we have referred, this writer concludes that Lynn v. Bruce is wrong. See 13 Harv. L. Rev. 38, 39. It is approved by other writers on the theory of contract. Langdell, Contracts, §89; Harriman, Contracts, 65; Leake, Contracts, 2d ed., 619; Pollock, Contracts, 6th ed., 176; Anson, Contracts, 89.
[9] 6 Exch. 839.
[1] Slade v. Mutrie, 156 Mass. 19.

102   FOUNDATIONS OF LEGAL LIABILITY.

ness puts it out of the power of the plaintiff to produce the best evidence of his claim, and this is enough to defeat his subsequent action.[2]

When *Foster v. Dawber* was decided, it was thought in some quarters to have made a breach in the doctrine of accord and satisfaction and to have opened the way for giving effect to all parol releases whether upon consideration or not.[3]

This expectation was not realized; for in the case of *Foakes v. Beer* (1884),[4] the House of Lords, being called upon for the first time to consider the validity of the payment and acceptance of part of a debt in satisfaction of the whole, carefully went over the entire ground and adhered to the ancient doctrine.

House of Lords accepts principle of Pinnel's Case.

In this case, a creditor by judgment for £2090 19s. agreed that she would not "take any proceedings whatever on the judgment" provided the debtor would pay £150 in every half year "until the whole of the said sum of £2090 19s. shall have been fully paid and satisfied." The debtor performed his undertaking and then the question was raised whether the plaintiff in the judgment could have execution for the interest. It was held that she could. The decision was put upon the ground of the want of a sufficient consideration.[4]* The consideration in such cases is incompetent. No act which does not involve some detriment to the promisee is a sufficient consideration according to our law. "A man is under a moral and

---

[2] Silvers *v.* Reynolds, 17 N. J. L. 275.

[3] See article on Accord and Satisfaction, in the Law Magazine and Review (London, May, 1863), printed with editorial comment in 3 Am. L. Reg. N. S. 65. Said this writer: "This decision looks like the precursor of the total overthrow of the rule; for it is inconceivable that the same court will continue, for any length of time, to hold an agreement to accept part of a sum of money in discharge of the whole to be a satisfaction, if put in the form of a promissory note or bill of exchange, but not if put in any other form of a contract, even though it be followed by actual payment or execution." See, to same effect, opinion of Monro, J., in Hope *v.* Johnston, 11 Rich. L. (S. Car.), 139, 140.

[4] 9 App. Cas. 605.

[4]* Judicial decision in America has followed the rule declared in Pinnel's Case, 5 Coke 117a, and applied in Foakes *v.* Beer. There are a few exceptions, as will appear from reference to the following cases: Clayton *v.* Clark, 74 Miss. 499; Brenner *v.* Herr, 8 Pa. St. 106; Shelton *v.* Jackson, 20 Tex. Civ. App. 443.

legal obligation to pay his just debts. It cannot therefore be stated as an abstract proposition that he suffers any detriment from the discharge of that duty." [5]

Chapter XI

Now notwithstanding the doctrine of *Pinnel's Case* continues to prevail, no rule of law has been the subject of more constant animadversion. It is a favorite diversion among dissenting judges and others, to whom the reason for the rule does not appeal, to collect and repeat the many hard things that have been said about it.[6]

Popular prejudice against the rule.

There are several reasons for this prejudice. In the first place, we all have a natural bias in favor of honest compromises whether there be any consideration or not. Human sympathy is much more likely to go out to the debtor than to the creditor, and when the latter has pledged himself to acquit the other upon payment of part it seems not unjust to hold him to the promise. In the second place, the release of an entire debt upon payment of part bears a very close analogy to an executed gift. A debt can undoubtedly be the subject of a gift as well as any other species of property. If the debt be evidenced by a note or written instrument there should be actual delivery, and where it is in form of a naked chose, a

Reason for this prejudice.

---

[5] Alderson, J., in Jones *v.* Waite, 5 Bing. N. Cas. 341, 35 E. C. L. 130.

In contemplation of law the performance is no new detriment to the debtor, but on the contrary is beneficial to him, inasmuch as it discharges him from an existing legal obligation. Sir F. Pollock, 17 L. Quar. Rev. 419.

[6] A number of such dicta are collated by Professor Ames in 12 Harv. L. Rev. 525. An illustration of this talk is found in the dissenting opinion of Munro, J., in Hope *v.* Johnston, 11 Rich. L. (S. Car.) 138, 139. Said he: "It might well be doubted, if a doctrine so utterly absurd, and standing as it confessedly does in humiliating contrast to the common sense of mankind, would, at any period in the world's history, have been permitted to occupy a place in the jurisprudence of any nation not absolutely barbarous. But that it should have been permitted for centuries to occupy a place in the jurisprudence of one of the most enlightened nations of the earth, and in a system too which is termed *par excellence* the perfection of human reason, almost surpasses belief."

Similar expressions are found in Kellogg *v.* Richards, 14 Wend. (N. Y.) 116; Harper *v.* Graham, 20 Ohio 115; Brooks *v.* White, 2 Met. (Mass.) 283; Clayton *v.* Clark, 74 Miss. 499; Smith *v.* Ballou, 1 R. I. 496; Works *v.* Hershey, 35 Iowa 342; Seymore *v.* Goodrich, 80 Va. 304.

written assignment by way of gift may be considered needful.[7] This being so, it may be said that our law should also recognize the present gift of the balance of a debt upon payment of part. If the debtor should pay the whole debt and the creditor return part by way of bounty no difficulty could of course arise.

But the ordinary payment of part of a debt in satisfaction of the whole is not a true gift, although it closely resembles one, and its validity cannot therefore be determined by the principle applicable to gifts. The similarity of this transaction to a gift has, however, been used to circumvent the rule in some instances. Thus, in *Thomas v. Heathorn* (1824),[8] Mr. Justice Holroyd suggested that where it is proved under the general issue that a smaller sum was given in satisfaction of a greater, the jury might treat such transaction as having the same legal effect as if the whole was paid down and a portion given back as God's penny. But, as has been observed by Lord Blackburn in *Foakes v. Beer* (1884),[9] this is artificial and unsatisfactory.

In our judgment the principal reason why this obstinate questioning of the old rule continues is to be found in the long prevalent but certainly erroneous notion that a benefit to the promisor is a sufficient consideration to support a promise. There can be no doubt of the fact that it is often to the advantage of the creditor to compromise with his debtor; for perchance he would otherwise get nothing. All men of business recognize the truth that prompt payment of part may be more beneficial to them than it would be to insist on their right and enforce payment of the whole. Consequently if benefit to the promisor were alone sufficient to support a promise, the transaction under consideration would be binding. Lord Mansfield is reported to have said on one occasion: "If a party choose to take a smaller sum why should he not do it?" and Buller, approving the suggestion, remarks that there are cir-

---

[7] See 2 Kent Com. 439; Sanborn v. Goodhue, 28 N. H. 48; Bond v. Bunting, 78 Pa. St. 210.
[8] 2 B. & C. 477, 9 E. C. L. 152.
[9] 9 App. Cas. 618.

cumstances under which such an agreement might not only be fair, but advantageous.[1]

True, but this is irrelevant. Benefit to the promisor, as we have elsewhere stated, is incapable of supporting a promise. And these very decisions which perpetuate the doctrine of *Pinnel's Case* furnish cumulative evidence of the truth of that proposition. The learned J. W. Smith was in error when he intimated in his note to *Cumber v. Wane* that a benefit or possibility of benefit to the creditor would make a good consideration for the acceptance of part of a debt in satisfaction of the whole.[2] What is required is a detriment to the promisee, not a benefit to the promisor. Even so learned a person as Lord Blackburn fell into the same error in *Foakes v. Beer,* and, while admitting that the doctrine of *Pinnel's Case* is fully established in the law, he expressed the opinion that it was originally a mistake.[3] But this misgiving is without any sound basis.

Agreements for the composition of debts with creditors furnish a real exception to the rule that part payment of a debt cannot work a satisfaction of the whole. When this question first arose in *Fitch v. Sutton* (1804),[4] it was answered in the negative, no reason being apparent why the rule which applies to agreements made between a debtor and one creditor should not also be applied where there are several

Chapter XI

Composition with creditors.

---

[1] Stock *v.* Mawson, 1 B. & P. 290.

[2] 1 Smith Lead. Cas. (8th Am. ed.) 639. Said he: "If there be any benefit, or even any legal possibility of benefit, to the creditor thrown in, that additional weight will turn the scale and render the consideration sufficient to support the agreement."

Concerning this benefit or possibility of benefit of which Mr. Smith speaks, Lord Selborne observed in Foakes v. Beer: "[It] is not that sort of benefit which a creditor may derive from getting payment of part of the money due him from a debtor who might otherwise keep him at arm's length or possibly become insolvent; but is some benefit, actual or contingent, of a kind which might in law be a good and valuable consideration for any other sort of agreement not under seal." 9 App. Cas. 614. This simply means that what is required is not a benefit to the creditor at all, but a detriment to the promisee.

[3] Ld. Blackburn, 9 App. Cas. 622.

[4] 5 East 230. The earlier case of Heathcote *v.* Crookshanks, (1787) 2 T. R. 24, involved the validity of executory agreement of composition. In Fitch *v.* Sutton, 5 East 230, the agreement had been carried into effect and **the part payment had been made.**

Volume II

creditors. Nevertheless the distinction is now settled and the principle that composition agreements are valid has not been questioned since *Good v. Cheesman* (1831).[5] The reasoning on which this apparent violation of principle is to be justified will be considered further on.

The collateral payment.

It remains to note a rather fine distinction originating in the head of Coke whereby effect might conceivably be given to agreements for the acceptance of part of a debt in satisfaction of the whole. In *Bagge v. Slade* (1614),[6] the learned chief justice said: "If a man be bound to another by a bill in £1000 and he pays unto him £500 in discharge of this bill, the which he accepts accordingly and doth upon this assume and promise to deliver up unto him his said bill of £1000, this £500 is no satisfaction of the £1000; but yet this is good and sufficient to make a good promise, and upon a good consideration, because he hath paid money, £500, and he hath no remedy for this again."

The idea here is that the £500 is not paid in satisfaction of the debt, but for a collateral act, i. e., the surrender of the bill.[7] *Reynolds v. Pinhowe* (1594)[8] may perhaps be explained upon the principle above stated. There £4 was paid on a judgment for £5, with the understanding that the creditor would acknowledge satisfaction of record. The agreement was held to be binding. The decision was, however, actually put on the erroneous ground that it was a benefit to the creditor to get his money without further trouble. The suggestion made by Coke has not proved fruitful and we do not believe it to be good law at this day. The distinction is too artificial.[9]

---

[5] 2 B. & Ad. 328, 22 E. C. L. 89.
[6] 3 Bulst. 162.
[7] As early as 1581, it had been decided in a case between Coke and Hewet that where an agreement was made between a debtor and creditor by which the former promised to pay part and the latter agreed thereupon to deliver the obligation, this was good. Reported by Tanfield in Greenleaf *v.* Barker, Cro. Eliz. 194, 1 Leon. 238.

[8] Cro. Eliz. 429.
[9] Professors Langdell and Ames, in our opinion, give too much credit to Bagge *v.* Slade and Reynolds *v.* Pinhowe. Langdell on Contracts, §§ 88, 54. Two Theories of Consideration, by J. B. Ames, 12 Harv. L. Rev. 523; also note by Professor Ames, 11 Harv. L. Rev. 330, 331.

CHAPTER XII

SCOPE OF THE BILATERAL CONTRACT.

THE point has now been reached in the prosecution of these studies where it becomes necessary for us again to take up the subject of the bilateral contract. We have already indicated that this contract is not directly based upon consideration in the sense of detriment, but is based upon consent. This conclusion represents a decided departure from current views and has only been adopted by us after mature deliberation. The present chapter will contain cumulative evidence on this important point, and the attentive reader will soon perceive that the bilateral contract has a flexibility and power which it could not possibly possess if it were based upon consideration in the sense of detriment. We begin with a word of criticism on that view of the bilateral contract which looks upon it as an engagement founded upon consideration in the ordinary sense. *[Bilateral contract based upon consent.]*

At the outset it may be noted that the efforts of legal scholars to work out a theory of the bilateral contract along the ancient lines have proved unfruitful. Much has been written in recent years by very able scholars about the bilateral contract, but the different ones who have dealt with the subject have done little else but devour each other.[1] On the constructive side little has so far been accomplished.[2] *[Unsatisfactory state of legal theory.]*

---

[1] Modern criticism has been mainly destructive. See especially, Successive Promises of Same Performance, by Prof. Samuel Williston, 8 Harv. L. Rev. 27; Two Theories of Consideration, by Prof. J. B. Ames, 12 Harv. L. Rev. 515, 13 Harv. L. Rev. 29; Mutual Promises as a Consideration, by Prof. C. C. Langdell, 14 Harv. L. Rev. 496; What Is a Promise in Law, by C. D. Ashley, 16 Harv. L. Rev. 319; Notes on Consideration, by Prof. J. H. Beale, 17 Harv. L. Rev. 71.

[2] Professor Ames's articles on Two Theories of Consideration are exceptionally strong in the constructive aspect; but we think he builds on wrong lines. He has here put forth very powerful efforts to show that the bilateral contract is based upon consideration in the sense of detriment. If this distinguished scholar had right-

FOUNDATIONS OF LEGAL LIABILITY.

Volume II

First theory.

There are only two theories on which the proposition that the bilateral contract is based upon consideration in the sense of detriment can be supported. Apparently the most plausible is the theory that each party incurs a detriment in assuming or promising to do, give, or forbear, and that this detriment is a consideration for the other promise.

In order to sustain this view, it is necessary to assume that the promise creates a legal obligation, for there can be no detriment where the promise is not binding. The proposition in question, therefore, exhibits the weakness of reasoning in a circle, and the further fact that it cannot be sustained by reasoning not vitiated by this fallacy, is fatal to its soundness.[3] The legal obligation is the result of the agreement, and hence it cannot be said to be the detriment which makes the mutual promises binding. Legal obligation cannot be treated as the cause of itself. The law adds it when the parties to the contract give consent as evidenced by their mutual promises.

Objections

That it is not the legal obligation of one promise which constitutes the consideration for the other promise is indubitably shown by cases where no obligation exists, or can be enforced, against one party and yet nevertheless the other is held liable. Thus, an adult may be held liable on an agreement to marry made with an infant, a principle which of course also applies to all contracts between infants and persons *sui juris*.[4] Contracts within the statute of frauds may be enforced against a party whose signature the writing bears, though it may not be enforced against the other.[5] So, in the case where a married man engages to marry a woman ignorant of the fact that he is married, the man is liable in damages

---

ly interpreted the materials which he so diligently gathered, he would have set all things right. He barely missed the true clue.

Professor Williston's paper is valuable as showing the weakness of existing theories. In his endeavor to reconstruct the definition of consideration he met insuperable difficulties. If he had been a little more radical he would have had better success.

[3] This criticism was first extended to all bilateral agreements by Professor Williston, 8 Harv. L. Rev. 35, and notwithstanding the able paper from Professor Langdell in 14 Harv. L. Rev. 496, it is, we submit, a sound criticism and touches a vital point.

[4] Holt. *v* Clarencieux, 2 Stra. 937.
[5] Laythoarp *v.* Bryant, 2 Bing. N. Cas. 735, 29 E. C. L. 469.

upon breach of the contract, although performance on his part is obviously impossible.⁶

The proposition that the obligation incident to making the promise is the detriment which constitutes the consideration for the counter-promise is clearly untenable.

A second theory has been advanced by Professor Ames. Perceiving the unsoundness of the view above referred to and yet believing that the two respective promises in the bilateral contract are considerations for each other in the ordinary sense of detriment to the promisee, this distinguished scholar would have us believe that the detriment is found in the mere physical effort put forth by each party in making his promise. The mere making of a promise, says he, is a detriment *per se*, in that it involves the doing of an act which the promisor is not under obligation to do. The act of giving the promise is the only thing that either does, and this act must be the consideration for the other promise.⁷

No, we insist: it is not the mere act of making one promise which makes the other binding. The mutuality of the promises gives validity to both. The law simply here recognizes a consensual contract, the only condition being the requirement of mutuality.⁸ The soundness of the position here assumed will, we think, be fully manifest when we come to consider certain decisions which are presently to be dealt with.

Chapter XII

Second theory.

Detriment found in mere making of the promise.

View of present writer.

⁶ Wild *v.* Harris, 7 C. B. 999, 62 E. C. L. 999.

⁷ 13 Harv. L. Rev. 31, 32. Mr. C. D. Ashley has perceived the weakness of Professor Ames's theory, as will appear from a perusal of his article. What Is a Promise in Law, 16 Harv. L. Rev. 319.

⁸ Professor Langdell seems to have felt, but he did not admit, a quarter of a century ago, that the bilateral contract is founded on agreement. Langdell on Contracts, (1879) §§ 103, 148. He uses the term 'consensual contract' (§ 149) but says (§ 103): "It should, perhaps, be added that in strictness there are no consensual contracts in our law, as a promise which has nothing else to make it binding must have a consideration. Still, those contracts which can be enforced only by an action of assumpsit, though they are not purely consensual, are substantially so; and they may therefore properly be termed consensual by way of distinguishing them from other contracts." No, certainly; contracts on which assumpsit alone lies are not *purely* consensual. Some of them are consensual and some of them are not, but all bilateral agreements are consensual.

110   FOUNDATIONS OF LEGAL LIABILITY.

Bearing of consideration.   Although the bilateral contract is not founded upon consideration in the sense of detriment to the promisee, the doctrine of consideration has, as we have already intimated, a very important bearing on this form of engagement. This will be readily perceived when attention is directed to what may be called the content of the respective promises in the bilateral contract. In order that one promise should be able to support another it must have a certain substantiality. This quality appears to be determined by the following sensible rule, that is to say, the promise in question must appear to be for the doing of some act which if actually performed would be a good consideration for a binding unilateral promise. The principle in question may be stated in another way, thus: a promise to do an act, to deliver a thing, or to forbear the exercise of some right, which act, thing, or forbearance is capable of being a consideration for an enforceable unilateral contract, will be upheld, provided it be given for another similar promise to do, give, or forbear; and all that need be shown is that one promise was given as an inducement for the other.

Abstract character of thing promised.   For the purpose of testing the validity of the promise the law does not inquire whether, in the particular instance, there may or may not be some obstacle which renders actual performance impossible and thereby makes a breach certain. It only requires that the act, thing, or forbearance in question should, when stripped of its accidents in the particular case, be competent matter for the consideration of a unilateral promise. Thus, the promise of a married man to marry a woman ignorant of his status is binding on him, though he labors, in the particular case, under disability to perform.[9] The act which he promises to do, i. e., to marry, is, in the abstract, a sufficient consideration to sustain a promise given for such an act; and this is enough. The fact that he labors under a disability to perform that act is irrelevant.

The best illustration of the principle stated in the preceding paragraph is found in wagers. These contracts are held

---

[9] Wild v. Harris, 7 C. B. 999, 62 E. C. L. 999; Coover v. Davenport, 1 Heisk. (Tenn.) 368.

… to be good as a matter of common-law principle, even though the event on which the wager depends appears to have taken place before the making of the wager.¹ These contracts appear at first blush to exhibit a fatal weakness. There seems to be an unreality about the 'consideration' for the losing promise, and some writers have therefore considered that the decisions holding wagers on past events to be good at common law are unsound.²

Chapter XII. The wager.

The reason why it could be held at common law that wagers on past events are binding is that the wager, like all other bilateral contracts, is based on agreement. It conforms to the test we have propounded in the circumstance that the money or thing promised is a sufficient consideration to support a unilateral contract, although in the particular case a contingency will transpire or has already transpired which excuses one party from making the payment.³

Consensual nature of this contract.

It would seem to follow from the way in which we have stated the test of the sufficiency of the two respective promises in the bilateral contract, that an agreement which is good when put into the form of a bilateral engagement would also be good when put into the unilateral form. A contract good in one mode should also apparently be valid in the other. But this is not true. The bilateral contract is of wider scope than the unilateral contract. There are certain contracts which are valid when put into the bilateral form, but invalid when the undertaking is unilateral. The difficulty caused by

Bilateral contract of broader scope than unilateral contract.

---

¹ March v. Pigot, 5 Burr. 2802; Jones v. Randall, 1 Cowp. 37; Da Costa v. Jones, 2 Cowp. 729.

But of course if the bet appears to be in furtherance of an object which is contrary to public policy it is void. Allen v. Hearn, 1 T. R. 57.

² Langdell on Contracts § 89.

³ Metaphysical reasons have been adduced to show that the wager on future uncertain events is as weak from the legal standpoint as wagers on events that have already happened. Thus, as was once said by Judge Holmes: If wagers on past events are unsound, "it is hard to see how wagers on any future event, except a miracle, could be sustained. For if the happening or not happening of any event is subject to the law of causation, the only uncertainty about it is our foresight, not in its happening." Holmes's Common Law, 305. The courts have therefore been guilty of no inconsistency or violation of principle in placing both kinds of wagers on the same basis.

the existence of the cases which recognize this has been very great. The phenomenon is certainly inexplicable under the theory hitherto accepted, that the bilateral contract is founded upon consideration to the same extent and in the same way as the unilateral contract. But the difficulty disappears when that theory is put aside and the true relation between consideration and the bilateral contract is discovered.

Promise of Performance of Existing Obligation.

Suppose A is bound by contract with B to do the act x, and that C, being for some reason also interested in the performance of the act x, says to A, "Do the act x and I will pay you so much." Two courses are open to A. (1) He may refrain from giving C a counter-promise to do the act x. Indeed, C's offer may be such as neither to invite nor require a counter-promise. Now, if without giving a counter-promise, A proceeds to do the act x, and then claims the money which C has promised, he cannot recover. In this case A, it will be noted, sues upon a unilateral obligation. (2) The negotiations between A and C in the situation above imagined may, however, take a different turn. If when C makes his offer A should reply, "So be it; if you promise so much, I promise on my part to do the act x," the engagement takes the bilateral form. If A then proceeds to perform the act x, and brings suit upon the promise made by C, he can recover.

The distinction here noted between the effects of the unilateral and bilateral forms of engagement savors somewhat of the artificial, not to say paradoxical, and the reader may well reserve his judgment until the authorities which establish so remarkable a distinction are produced.

UNILATERAL PROMISE GIVEN FOR PERFORMANCE OF EXISTING OBLIGATION INVALID.

The reason why the unilateral promise above imagined is not binding on C is that the consideration for that promise is an incompetent consideration. The doing of an act which a man is already under obligation to do is incompetent to support a promise, for the reason that such an act is no detriment to the one who performs it.[4] This principle has already been expounded, and the following decisions in which unilateral promises, such as is imagined above, have been held to be invalid, merely furnish cumulative evidence of the existence of the principle referred to.

In *Reynolds v. Nugent* (1865)[5] one Nugent had agreed to enter the military service for a bounty of $100. He was on the point of refusing to perform his agreement, when Reynolds offered him $250 more to enlist, which Nugent then did. It was held that the promise to pay the additional $250 was without consideration. In *Hanks v. Barron* (1895),[6] it was held that a bond whose sole consideration was the payment by the obligee of a debt owing to a third person is void. In *Johnson v. Sellers* (1858),[7] it was held that an offer made to induce a person to carry out his contract with a third person is not rendered valid by performance of the condition of the offer, for such a performance cannot be a consideration for a promise.

In *Merrick v. Giddings* (1882),[8] it was held, upon facts which need not be stated in detail, that "if A is under a legal obligation to B to do a certain act for B, a promise by C, a third party, to A, in consideration of A's performance of that act, is not binding, because such performance of an act the necessary element of detriment to the promisee is wanting." Afterthoughts on Consideration, 17 L. Quar. Rev. 419.

Promise given in consideration of performance of legal duty.

---

[4] Sir Frederick Pollock demonstrates that performance of an act which one is obligated to do cannot be a consideration for a unilateral promise, as follows: "Andrew's performance of his binding promise to Peter does not appear capable of being a consideration for a new promise by John to Andrew; not because it cannot be beneficial to John, for this it may very well be, but because in contemplation of law the performance is no new detriment to Andrew, but on the contrary is beneficial to him, inasmuch as it discharges him of an existing obligation. Therefore

[5] 25 Ind. 328. See also Ritenour v. Mathews, 42 Ind. 7, 14; Ford v. Garner, 15 Ind. 298.

[6] 95 Tenn. 275. It is said in Havana Press Drill Co. v. Ashurst, 148 Ill. 115, and in Robinson v. Jewett, 116 N. Y. 40, that the performance of an existing obligation cannot be a consideration.

[7] 33 Ala. 265. There is a similar dictum in Ecker v. McAllister, 54 Md. 362, 45 Md. 290.

[8] 1 Mackey (D. C.) 394.

114   FOUNDATIONS OF LEGAL LIABILITY.

which A was already bound, though not to C, to do, is **not** a valuable consideration."

The only authority which is in any way opposed to the doctrine above stated is found in the English case of *Shadwell v. Shadwell* (1860).[9] Upon examination of this decision two things become apparent, namely — first, that the case did not turn upon the point now under consideration; and secondly, that in so far as it gives rise to an inference contrary to the doctrine of the American cases referred to above it is unsound. The facts were as follows: The plaintiff, one Lancelot Shadwell, was a young barrister. He became engaged to a young lady and informed his wealthy uncle, Charles Shadwell, of that fact. Thereupon the uncle wrote to him a note in these words: "My dear Lancey,— I am glad to hear of your intended marriage with Ellen Nicholl; and as I promised to assist you at starting, I am happy to tell you that I will pay you £150 yearly during my life and until your annual income derived from your profession of a Chancery barrister shall amount to 600 guineas, of which your own admission will be the only evidence that I shall receive or require. Your ever affectionate uncle, Charles Shadwell." The marriage subsequently took place and the promise made by Charles Shadwell was kept during his life. After his death, however, the executors were advised that the promise was not binding, and refused to pay the yearly instalment of £150. Lancelot Shadwell thereupon brought suit, alleging among other things that his income had not passed the 600-guinea mark.

The Court of Common Bench held that the plaintiff could recover. The idea on which the court proceeded was that this letter showed that at some time in the past when Lancelot Shadwell was not yet engaged to Ellen Nicholl, the uncle had promised him to aid him at starting if he should marry. Thereupon the plaintiff, relying upon that promise, assumed the responsibility of marriage. This letter, it was said, in addition to containing an admission of the past promise merely defined what the amount of the yearly assistance would be.

[9] 9 C. B. N. S. 159, 99 E. C. L. 159.

It may be that this construction was a little strained. The court undoubtedly desired to sustain the promise, as it appeared to reflect the real wishes of the testator, and there was nothing to show that the arrangement ought to be upset. At any rate the court saw fit to put the construction which we have indicated upon the letter, and they accordingly sustained the promise. It should be remarked, however, that Byles, J., who was an able and acute judge, dissented, on the ground that the promise was of mere bounty and was understood by the plaintiff to be such. There was no intention on the part of the parties, so this judge thought, to enter into a contractual relation.

Promise of mere bounty not enforceable.

From what has been stated it appears that however questionable *Shadwell v. Shadwell* may be in respect of the application of legal principles to the facts proved, there is nothing anomalous about it and nothing which has any bearing on the question of the validity of a promise given for the performance of an act which another is bound to perform. The question simply was whether the promise given by the testator before Lancelot Shadwell had engaged himself to Ellen Nicholl, which promise was the inducement for the engagement and subsequent marriage, was sufficiently shown and defined by the letter which was written after the engagement was actually announced.

There is, however, another aspect of the case. Suppose the letter in question be interpreted not as an admission of a prior promise which was the inducement for the engagement, but as a present promise made by the uncle in order to induce his nephew to go on and marry as he was already bound in law to do by reason of the existing engagement. In this view, which is not the view taken of the case by the judges who decided it, precisely the same question arises as that involved in the American cases above noted, and in this view it must be said that the promise was bad because the consideration was incompetent.

Another view.

The promise in this case it will be observed was of a purely unilateral nature, since the nephew was not expected to give and did not give a promise to the uncle to go on and fulfil his engagement with Ellen Nicholl. This point is sometimes overlooked, and hence the case has been from time to time erroneously treated as authority for the same principle as that embodied in *Scotson v. Pegg* (*post*), in which the contract was bilateral.

The case of *Shadwell v. Shadwell*. it may be remarked in passing, has caused no end of difficulty to legal scholars. The consensus of scholarship nowadays is to the effect that the decision is erroneous, and the view taken by Byles, J., dissenting, is supposed to be the correct one.[1] Properly viewed the case is intelligible; but in the aspect in which it is intelligible it has no bearing on the question of the validity of a promise given to secure the performance of an existing obligation.

MUTUAL PROMISES IN FURTHERANCE OF PERFORMANCE OF EXISTING OBLIGATION VALID.

We are now to consider the situation imagined in (2) *ante*, wherein the engagement which is made in furtherance of the performance of an existing obligation takes the form of mutual promises. *Scotson v. Pegg* (1861)[2] is the leading authority.

The facts in this case were of the following nature: Scotson had on his ship a cargo of coal which by the terms of affreightment he was bound to deliver to the original freighter or to his order. This party transferred the bills of lading to Pegg, and Scotson thus became bound to deliver the cargo to Pegg. Scotson and Pegg then made an agreement whereby the former promised to deliver the cargo to Pegg. and the latter in consideration of this promise agreed to unload and discharge the cargo at the rate of forty-nine tons per day. Scotson thereupon put his ship in readiness to be unladen, but

---

[1] Langdell on Contracts, §§ 54. 68, 84; Anson on Contracts, p. 91; Holmes, Common Law, p. 292; Successive Promises of Same Performance, 8 Harv. L. Rev. 27; Pollock on Contracts, p. 179, also 6th ed., p. 175. This writer, after having vainly endeavored to reconcile the case, finally commits himself to its unsoundness. Afterthoughts on Consideration, 17 L. Quar. Rev 420.

[2] 6 H. & N. 295.

Pegg failed to discharge the cargo at the rate agreed upon; by reason whereof the unlading of the ship was delayed and Scotson incurred damage. In an action of assumpsit the defendant pleaded that the promise on Scotson's part to deliver the cargo to the defendant was a promise to do a thing which he was already under contract to do, and that consequently such promise was not a sufficient consideration to support the defendant's promise, for breach of which the action was brought. But it was held by the Court of Exchequer that the agreement between Scotson and Pegg, which, it will be observed, was in the form of a bilateral engagement,[3] was binding.[4]

There is American authority to the same effect. The best-considered case on this point is *Abbott v. Doane* (1895).[5] Here A said, in substance, to B: "I will give you my note for five hundred dollars, provided you will agree to pay off a debt you owe C." B accepted the offer and the agreement was carried out. When A's note fell due, he refused to pay it, and defended on the ground that there was no consideration. The action was, however, sustained.[6]

In *Green v. Kelley* (1892),[7] A, being surety upon a note for B, promised to take it up according to its tenor by paying C, the creditor, and in consideration thereof, B promised to pay A the amount of the note and secure it by a mortgage. This was held good.

In *Grant v. Duluth, etc., R. Co.* (1895),[8] A made a con-

Chapter XII

Bilateral contract valid.

American authorities

---

[3] For some unaccountable reason, Professors Williston and Langdell labor under the impression that Scotson v. Pegg was a unilateral contract. 8 Harv. L. Rev. 33, 14 Harv. L. Rev. 500; Langdell on Contracts, § 84. Professor Ames falls into the same error. 13 Harv. L. Rev. 29, 30.

There can be no mistake as to its real character. As said by Sir Wm. Anson (Contracts, 8th ed., p. 91): "Scotson promised to deliver Pegg a cargo of coal then on board Scotson's ship, and Pegg promised in return to unload it at a certain rate of speed." If this does not make a bilateral contract, what does? Performance by one party does not change the *mode* of a contract.

[4] In *Chichester v. Cobb*, (1866) 14 L. T. N. S. 433, the doctrine of Scotson v. Pegg was followed by the Court of Queen's Bench.

[5] 163 Mass. 433.

[6] To the same effect, Day v. Gardner, 42 N. J. Eq. 199 ('semble); Monnahan v. Judd, 165 Mass. 93 (semble).

[7] 64 Vt. 309.

[8] 61 Minn. 395.

tract with B by which B agreed to perform certain work. B let a subcontract to C, by which C agreed to perform a part of this work. After C had partly performed the work, B defaulted in paying him for his labor. Thereupon C refused to proceed, upon which A made an agreement with C by which C agreed to complete his contract with B on the understanding that A would pay him extra compensation over and above what B had agreed to pay him. It was held that the contract between A and C was binding.

<small>Explanation of the validity of the bilateral contract here.</small>

To the mind of the writer the distinction to which these cases point is entirely sound. The bilateral contract, being based upon consent and not directly upon consideration, is naturally a more flexible instrument than is the unilateral form of engagement. The mutual promises in cases similar to *Scotson v. Pegg* are good because each person promises to do an act which, considered without reference to the particular facts of that case, would be a consideration for a unilateral promise. In determining the validity of these mutual promises no account is taken of the fact that in the particular case one of the parties is under a legal obligation to a third person to do that act. The abstract character of the act promised is, as we have already seen, the feature which is considered in determining the validity of mutual promises. It is not surprising to find that those who cling to the accepted theory of the bilateral contract should meet with difficulty in trying to account for cases like *Scotson v. Pegg*.

<small>Paradox of promise and performance.</small>

Professor Pollock, in the first edition of his work on contracts, and Professor Langdell in his book published at about the same time, pointed out that it followed from this and similar decisions, that a promise can sometimes be a consideration when the actual performance of the thing promised would not be a consideration.[9] If it had merely been said that

---

[9] Langdell on Contracts ('1880), § 84; Pollock on Contracts (1st ed.) 158. After Sir William Anson (Contracts, 1st ed., p. 80) criticised the reasoning on which this proposition was based, Sir Frederick Pollock discreetly withdrew his approval of the doctrine. Pollock on Contracts, 6th ed., p. 175. See also 14 Harv. L. Rev. 499, note, where this shifting of opinion is noted. But in After-

SCOPE OF BILATERAL CONTRACT. 119

mutual promises may be binding where performance of the thing promised would not be a sufficient consideration to support a unilateral contract, no exception could be taken to the statement. But as it stands the proposition is an unintelligible and misleading paradox.

The whole trouble has its root in the notion that mutual promises are considerations for each other in the same sense that performance of an act is a consideration for the unilateral promise given for that act. The enormous amount of confusion caused at this point by the failure to apprehend the true nature of the bilateral contract can only be appreciated by one who has endeavored to unravel the mazes of the conflicting views. An idea of its extent may be gathered from a perusal of the papers referred to below.[1]

In view of the confusion which exists in regard to the matter now under discussion it is not surprising that the courts should sometimes fall into error; and in truth there are a few cases in which it has been held that bilateral engagements such as was presented in *Scotson v. Pegg* are invalid.[2] This re-

Chapter XII

Conflicting authority.

---

thoughts on Consideration (1901), 17 L. Quar. Rev. 419–421, where the same writer publishes, by anticipation, the chapter on Consideration as recast for a new edition of his work on contracts, the old view, that a promise to do an act may be a consideration while actual performance would not, reappears in all its vigor.

[1] Professor Williston thinks that promises like that sued on in Scotson *v.* Pegg, 6 H. & N. 295, should be held to be bad. 8 Harv. L. Rev. 27–38. Professor Ames thinks they should be held good, but gives a bad reason — i. e., the promise is a consideration. 13 Harv. L. Rev. 29. So thinks Professor Langdell (14 Harv. L. Rev. 496 *et seq.*) and Sir Frederick Pollock, for reasons little different from the others. 17 L. Quar. Rev. 421.

Professor Williston's article was a valuable contribution because it exposed weakness in accepted views. The article of Prof. Langdell in 14 Harv. L. Rev. 496 was a reply to Prof. Williston's paper. Like so many others, Prof. Williston was caught in the meshes of the verbal formula that each of the two mutual promises is a consideration for the other.

[2] Ford *v.* Garner, 15 Ind. 298; Harris *v.* Cassady, 107 Ind. 158; Gordon *v.* Gordon, 56 N. H. 171.

These cases cannot be considered of much authority. In the last two cases the point referred to was not necessary to the decision. In Ford *v.* Garner, 15 Ind. 298, it appeared that A and B were sureties for C. They entered into a bilateral contract with C whereby they promised to effect insurance on the life of her son for her benefit, or, in case of his death before such insurance was effected, that they would pay her a certain sum; in consideration of which promise she agreed that the debt owing by her, and on which they were sureties, should be paid

sults from an improper application of the principle which has been worked out in regard to the unilateral contract. The idea underlying these decisions is that the doing of a thing which a man is already under contract to do cannot be a good consideration and that a promise to do such an act cannot stand on any higher ground. The reasoning is all right, but it overlooks the fact that a consideration in the sense of detriment is not necessary to make mutual promises binding. The surprise one feels upon coming into contact with these decisions is not that they should exist, but that they should be so few in number. In dealing with this problem the courts have had to feel for the true principle by a sort of legal instinct, and if haply they have sometimes missed the point one cannot wonder.

Before dismissing this subject it should be observed that the doctrine of *Scotson v. Pegg*[3] does not apply where the promise given by one of the parties to a bilateral contract is a promise to discharge a statutory or official duty. The discharge of a statutory duty is viewed in a different light from the discharge of a contract obligation, and it is clear that on grounds of public policy neither a promise to do one's official or statutory duty nor the performance of such duty can support a counter-promise.[4] But if something be done

Qualification of doctrine.

out of certain money presently to be collected by her. It was held that her promise to pay the debt already owing imposed no additional obligation upon her, and that consequently the promise on the part of A and B to effect insurance on the life of her son, or in lieu to pay her a stipulated sum, was not binding.

The case of Arend v. Smith, 151 N. Y. 502, was superficially somewhat similar to Abbott v. Doane, 163 Mass. 433, and is generally supposed to be authority for a contrary doctrine, but it seems not to be so. There the promise upon which suit was brought appeared to be merely the promise of an accommodation. It was apparent that there was no *animus contrahendi*, and the court therefore decided the case on the ground that the promise was gratuitous. That the debtor acted on the hope engendered by the promise was immaterial.

[3] 6 H. & N. 295.

[4] Newton v. Chicago, etc., R. Co., 66 Iowa 422; Putnam v. Woodbury, 68 Me. 58; Gilmore v. Lewis, 12 Ohio 281; Robb v. Mann, 11 Pa. St. 300.

In Wimer v. Worth Tp., 104 Pa. St. 319, A contracted with B to support her during life and to bury her at death. B afterwards became a charge on the poor-district of W township. The overseers of the poor of said township took a bond

SCOPE OF BILATERAL CONTRACT. 121

over and above the measure of duty imposed by law the promise may be good.[5] In *Morrell v. Quarles* (1860)[6] it appeared that one Bell, after the commission of a crime in the state of Alabama, had fled to the state of Louisiana. The defendant Quarles thereupon offered a reward of one thousand dollars for his apprehension. The plaintiff, a police officer in New Orleans, knowing of the defendant's offer, arrested Bell in that city and turned him over to the proper authorities. In an action to recover the reward it was insisted for the defendant that the plaintiff, as an officer of the law in Louisiana, had done no more than his duty in arresting the fugitive, and that consequently he could not recover. This argument was held to be untenable, and judgment was given for the plaintiff. The result might have been different if it had been shown that police officers in Louisiana were required by the law of that state to arrest fugitives from a sister state.

Chapter XII

---

from A for a certain sum payable in instalments, and in consideration thereof executed to A a release from his obligation to support B. The overseers supported B during her life, and buried her at death, and A paid to them a sufficient sum to reimburse them for such expenses. It was held that the overseers only fulfilled the duty imposed on them by law, and that a promise by A in excess of what he owed to B and in excess of the actual expenditure of the overseers, was unenforceable.

[5] England v. Davidson, 11 Ad. & El. 856, 39 E. C. L. 254; Harris v. More, 70 Cal. 502; Davis v. Munson, 43 Vt. 676; Reif v. Paige, 55 Wis. 496.

[6] 35 Ala. 544. Compare Means v. Hendershott, 24 Iowa 78; Warner v. Grace, 14 Minn. 487; Russell v. Stewart, 44 Vt. 170.

CHAPTER XIII

SCOPE OF THE BILATERAL CONTRACT (CONTINUED).

Volume II

Distinct type.

IF we have thus far written about the bilateral contract to any purpose, the reader has learned that this form of engagement radically differs from other assumptual obligations and that separate account must be taken of it in any work which treats of the theory of our contract law. While it is neither possible nor desirable within the limits of this work to go extensively into the subject, we nevertheless propose at this juncture to deal briefly with a few important matters pertaining to it, our object being to give a more adequate idea of the nature and scope of this most remarkable species of contract.

Novation.

Forms of novation.

The agreement of novation consists of a bilateral agreement for the substitution of one obligation for another, and may take place either by the substitution of a new for an old party, or by the substitution of a new agreement between the same parties, or by a change of parties and agreement at the same time.[1]

Novation an executory accord.

The term 'novation' is adopted from the Roman law, but the recognition of the contract itself is not due to any importation of foreign ideas; it follows as a natural and necessary consequence from the admission of the validity of mutual promises. In its essence the novation is an executory accord, and the principle underlying it is at war with the hoary rule that the executory accord is invalid. Some of the most difficult problems in o r contract law arise from this antinomy.

In pre-bilateral days the novation was of course a legal impossibility. A colloquy between court and counsel from 1433 shows that the English judges clearly perceived the im-

---

[1] 21 Am. and Eng. Encyc. of Law, 2d ed., 660.

possibility of giving effect to even the simplest form of novation in the state of law then existing. The situation imagined was this: A owes B twenty pounds and B owes C a like amount. By agreement among the three B discharges A and is himself in turn discharged by C, and the latter accepts A as his debtor instead of B. Here there is a simple shifting of the parties. Rolf, as counsel, insisted that such an agreement was binding. But all the judges were of a contrary opinion. Cotesmere, J., said that though all three were of one accord that A should pay the money to C, this was only a *nudum pactum;* that B was not in any manner discharged of his debt and that C had no right of action against A.[2] At that time, as Professor Ames has rightly observed, the debtor B could be discharged only by a release under seal or by an executed accord. Furthermore, as assumpsit was then unknown, debt was the only remedy available against the new debtor, A. But this action would not lie because no *quid pro quo* had passed.[3]

With the appearance of the bilateral contract these difficulties disappeared. In *Flewellin v. Rave* (1610),[4] the case appeared to be this: A was indebted to C in a certain sum of money and B was indebted to A. It was agreed among the three that B in discharge of his debt to A should discharge the debt of A to C by paying and delivering unto the latter certain goods and commodities which he (B) then had in his hands and possession, the same being properly the goods and commodities of A. It was held that the agreement was good and that C could maintain an action against B upon the failure of the latter to comply with the new contract.

No doubt as to the validity of a simple contract of novation by which one debtor is substituted for another has ever been entertained in modern times. All that is requisite is that

Chapter XIII

Novation invalid in early law.

Novation becomes valid with recognition of bilateral contract.

---

[2] William Andrew *v.* Administrator, Y. B. 11 Hen. VI. 38*b*, pl. 30.
We are indebted to Professor Ames for the reference to this interesting debate. See Novation, by J. B. Ames, 6 Harv. L. Rev. 184, where the passage in question is given in full.

[3] The point insisted on by Rolf was that mere words of grant could create a debt where there was a pre-existing duty. But this was too radical. Before mere words of grant can create a debt the grant must be evidenced by a sealed instrument.

[4] 1 Bulst. 68.

the several parties affected by the novation should consent to the present discharge of the old obligor and to the assumption of the indebtedness by the new.[5] In *Roe v. Haugh* (1697),[6] it appeared that B was indebted to C in the sum of £42 and that A, in consideration that C would accept A as his debtor for the £42 instead of B, undertook and promised C to pay him the said £42, and that C, trusting to A's promise, accepted A as his debtor. The defect in the declaration was that it did not aver that B was discharged. After judgment for the plaintiff it was moved in arrest that this defect was fatal. Three judges in Exchequer Chamber thought the point was well taken, but four thought the judgment ought to stand. "This being after verdict, they should do what they could to help it; to which end they would not consider it only as a promise on the part of C, for as such it would not bind him except B was discharged; but they would construe it to be a mutual promise, viz., that C promised to A to pay the debt of B, and A on the other side promised to discharge B; so that though B be not actually discharged, yet if A sues him he subjects himself to an action for the breach of his promise."

Discharge by necessary implication.

The court thus gave a qualified recognition to the notion of discharge by necessary implication. In *Tatlock v. Harris* (1789),[7] Buller, J., stated the rule as to novation by change of debtor thus: "If A owes B £100 and B owes C £100 and the three meet and it is agreed between them that A shall pay C the £100, B's debt is extinguished and C may recover that sum against A." In other words the mere agreement among the parties concerned, that the new promisor shall pay the old debt, discharges the old debtor by necessary implication. But this dictum is too broad; for it is established that an actual agreement to discharge the debtor must be shown. Furthermore, the discharge of the debtor must be such as to operate to release him *eo instanti*.[8] The creditor must in effect say

Actual agreement for discharge must be shown.

---

[5] Caswell *v.* Fellows, 110 Mass. 52. See also Pugh *v.* Barnes, 108 Ala. 167.
[6] 12 Mod. 133, 1 Salk. 29.
[7] 3 T. R. 180.
[8] Cochrane *v.* Green, 9 C. B. N. S. 448, 99 E. C. L. 448.

SCOPE OF BILATERAL CONTRACT.

to the other parties, "I take you, *Robert*, as my debtor and discharge *James*."[9]

Two reasons are assigned for this rule. If the discharge does not take place the instant the agreement is made, but is only to occur when the new promisor actually pays the debt, we have a true instance of an executory accord which, as we have elsewhere learned, is ineffectual.

Discharge must be a present discharge.

Again, it is said, the discharge of the old debtor is the consideration for the promise of the person who assumes the debt. Consequently if the old debtor is not discharged the new promise is supposed to be ineffectual for want of consideration.[1]

The most common form of novation is that in which one debtor is substituted for another. *Lyth v. Ault* (1852)[2] shows that a valid novation can take place upon the mere discharge of one or more of several debtors without the substitution of another in his or their place. In that case it appeared that a debt had been contracted to the plaintiff, Lyth, by two partners, Ault and Wood. Upon dissolution of the firm, it was agreed among the three that the defendant Wood should become solely and separately liable to the plaintiff for the balance due on the debt, and that the defendant Ault should then and there be discharged of all liability.[3] It was held that the agreement was binding.[4] "The parties have a right to substitute a liability different from that upon which the original debt was founded." Stress was laid by all of the judges in this case on the fact that the sole liability of one debtor may conceivably be a better or more desirable security than the joint liability of two or more; but this suggestion

Novation upon discharge of one of several debtors.

---

[9] Coxon *v.* Chadley, 3 B. & C. 591, 10 E. C. L. 191. See Commercial Bank *v.* Jones, (1893) A. C. 313.
[1] Liversidge *v.* Broadbent, 4 H. & N. 603.
[2] 7 Exch. 669.
[3] To the same effect, Morris Canal, etc., Co. *v.* Van Vorst. 21 N. J. L. 100, 119; Ludington *v.* Bell, 77 N. Y. 138.

In Early *v.* Burt, 68 Iowa 716, the contrary was casually held, but no authorities were cited and the decision was placed on the ground that a promise to pay what one owes is no consideration.
[4] Pollock, C. B., in Lyth *v.* Ault, 7 Exch. 672.

is altogether aside from the point at issue, and goes upon the erroneous notion that a mere benefit to the creditor may be a good consideration for his discharge of one of the debtors.

Novation by Change or Substitution of Contract.

The most difficult branch of novation is that which pertains to the making of changes in the original obligation, or the substitution of one agreement for another, as between the same parties, for it is here that we come most directly into conflict with the principles underlying accord and satisfaction. The following observations will serve to show how the principle of the bilateral contract as it manifests itself in the law of novation operates to limit, and at points even to subvert, the law of accord.

Conflict with doctrine of accord and satisfaction.

It is fundamental in the law of contract that the power which binds can unbind. Consequently if two parties to an agreement desire to rescind or alter the contract or to substitute an entirely new one in its place they are free to do so. This principle evidently conflicts with that which declares the executory accord to be invalid. Reconciliation of the two is impossible.

Rescission; substitution.

Hence a sort of compromise between the two principles has been effected. The principle that the accord must be executed has been permitted to hold its place throughout the field of unilateral duties and obligations; while the principle of novation is given effect in cases where a bilateral engagement as yet unperformed by either party is changed or abrogated by mutual consent and a new agreement substituted in its place.

Compromise.

In *Taylor v. Hilary* (1835),[5] a case whose facts need not be stated in detail, it was said: "Before the breach of the first agreement a new agreement is entered into, varying the contract in an essential part, [viz., as to] the time of payment. The latter then is a substituted contract and is an answer to an action upon the former. The plea is not a plea of accord

---

[5] 1 C. M. & R. 741; 5 Tyrw. 373.

and satisfaction and does not therefore require an averment of performance."

<small>Chapter XIII</small>

The result of the matter is that while the simple executory accord is nugatory, what we may call a double executory accord is good. As long as there are mutual obligations, those obligations by mutual consent can be abrogated or changed, or new obligations can be substituted in their place.

<small>Distinction stated.</small>

In *Collyer v. Moulton* (1868),[6] the distinction was not inaptly stated in the following words: "So long and so far as the contract remains executory and before breach it may be annulled by agreement of all parties; but when it has been broken and a right of action has accrued, the debt or damages can only be released for a consideration." To be more accurate, one should say that as long as there are mutual obligations, either before or after breach by one of the parties, a new consensual agreement altering or abrogating those obligations is valid; but after one party has performed and the obligation has become wholly one-sided, that obligation cannot be changed or abrogated except in conformity with the principles of accord and satisfaction. Where there are mutual executory obligations the agreement to annul on one side is said to be supported by the consideration of the agreement to annul on the other. To use the popular formula, the mutual promises are considerations for each other.

The following are concrete illustrations of the distinction just stated: If A owes B a hundred dollars and they mutually agree that upon a certain day in the future A shall bring a horse and deliver the same and that B shall thereupon receive the animal in lieu of the money and in full satisfaction of the debt, the agreement is invalid because the accord is executory. But if A and B are mutually bound by a bilateral agreement, the one to build a house, for instance, within a specified time, and the other to pay therefor a certain sum when the work is finished, and they agree to rescind or modify the contract or to substitute another in its place, this agreement is binding. And it is immaterial whether the new agreement is made be-

<small>Illustration.</small>

[6] 9 R. I. 90.

Novation of pre-existing bilateral contract.

fore or after a breach by one of the parties so long as there are subsisting mutual obligations.

An early and in a way a leading American authority sustaining the validity of agreements novating a pre-existing bilateral contract is found in *Lattimore v. Harsen* (1817).[7] It there appeared that one Harsen, a contractor, had agreed to open up a certain cart-way for a sum of money to be paid by Lattimore. After entering upon performance, Harsen became dissatisfied and determined to quit the work. Thereupon Lattimore released him from his contract and agreed that if Harsen would go on and complete the work, he would pay him by the day and compensate him for the materials supplied. This agreement was held good. The court concluded that the new contract abrogated the first. In a similar case in Massachusetts[8] the court said that the old contract had been waived. Other cases in which bilateral agreements made upon pre-existing bilateral contracts have been held binding are cited below.[9]

Qualifications.

Now notwithstanding the fact that a bilateral contract substituted for a pre-existing bilateral contract is unquestionably good, the principle is not to be blindly applied. For instance, if the procurance of the new contract appears to have resulted from anything like coercion or bad faith, such new agreement ought not to be enforced. One party to an executory contract, seeing that the other party will be subjected to great and perhaps irremediable damage by a failure promptly to fulfil the contract, may withhold performance merely to secure greater compensation. Wherever this vice is found to infect the new contract, considerations of common honesty and of public policy are sufficient to defeat it.[1]

---

[7] 14 Johns. (N. Y.) 330.
[8] Munroe *v.* Perkins. 9 Pick. (Mass.) 298.
[9] Stoudenmeier *v.* Williamson, 29 Ala. 558; Connelly *v.* Devoe, 37 Conn. 570; Rogers *v.* Rogers, 139 Mass. 440; Endriss *v.* Belle Isle Ice Co., 49 Mich. 279; Goebel *v.* Linn, 47 Mich. 489; Moore *v.* Detroit Locomotive Works, 14 Mich. 266; Osborne *v.* O'Reilly, 42 N. J. Eq. 467; Lawrence *v.* Davey, 28 Vt. 264.

[1] This very just criticism has been made on Goebel *v.* Linn, 47 Mich. 489. See Lingenfelder *v.* Wainwright Brewing Co., 103 Mo. 578, 594; also 8 Harv. L. Rev. 31.

SCOPE OF BILATERAL CONTRACT. 129

There is a line of decisions which superficially appear to be altogether inconsistent with the *Lattimore v. Harsen* and kindred cases. But perhaps the conflict is more apparent than real. It must be admitted that the subject is not free from difficulty; but in our opinion the cases to which we refer point to precisely the same distinction as that which was dealt with in the preceding chapter. It was there shown that where A is under contract to do a particular act for B, a new promise by A to C to do the same act is good provided the new contract takes the bilateral form, but not otherwise. The only difference in the situation now being considered is that the new agreement is between the same parties as the old. But, as we shall see, this does not alter the principle.

Adapting the distinction in question to the present situation we can state it thus: If there is a subsisting contract between A and B by which the latter is bound to do the act x, and B refuses to perform, a promise given by A to induce B to perform is invalid if such new agreement takes the unilateral form, but it is valid if it takes the bilateral form.

To illustrate: A employs B to build a sawmill for an agreed compensation. B soon finds that he has made a losing contract and refuses to go on with the work. A thereupon, as an inducement, tells B that if he will proceed and complete the work as he had originally contracted to do, he (A) will pay him an additional sum over and above the contract price. B thereupon builds the mill and sues for the additional compensaion. He cannot recover.[2]

In *Lingenfelder v. Wainwright Brewing Co.* (1890)[3] it appeared that an architect was engaged about the erection of a brewery. Upon discovering that the contract for the erection of the refrigerating plant had been awarded to a business rival he refused to proceed with his contract. The brewery company was in great haste to have the plant finished, and in order to induce the architect to resume work, agreed to pay

Chapter XIII

Promise given to secure performance of pre-existing obligation.

(1) Unilateral promise invalid.

---

[2] Festerman v. Parker, 10 Ired. L. (32 N. Car.) 474.
To the same effect, McCarty v. Hampton Bldg. Assoc., 61 Iowa 287; Ayres v. Chicago, etc., R. Co., 52 Iowa 478; King v. Duluth, etc., R. Co., 61 Minn. 482; Vanderbilt v. Schreyer, 91 N. Y. 392; Erb v. Brown, 69 Pa. St. 216.

[3] 103 Mo. 578.

him a commission of five per cent upon the cost of the refrigerating plant. Thereupon the architect proceeded to carry out his contract. It was held that the promise to pay the additional compensation was unenforceable.

Rationale of this principle. The idea underlying cases like these is that of a promise given to secure performance of an existing contractual obligation which is not abrogated or changed. The new promise is not given for a counter-promise of the defaulting party to go ahead and perform, but is given for performance. Hence the engagement of the party who makes the offer of additional compensation is in the form of a unilateral contract. That promise must therefore be supported by a consideration in the sense of detriment. But the doing of what one is under legal obligation to do is an incompetent consideration and hence the promise to pay the additional compensation is not binding.

Bilateral contract valid. Where, however, the new agreement takes the form of mutual promises, this seems necessarily to involve an abrogation or waiver of the old contract and the substitution of the new in its place. Both parties acquire rights against the other by reason of their mutual promises from the time the new agreement is made, and hence the promises on the part of both are good. Perhaps after all, the safest and simplest way of stating the rule is to say that where a new bilateral agreement is substituted for the old and the respective rights under it are mutually waived, the new agreement is valid.

Composition with Creditors.

The delicacy and flexibility of the bilateral contract as an instrument for effectuating the intention of contracting parties is beautifully shown in those decisions which support the validity of agreements for the composition of debts.

Composition defined. The composition with creditors is defined to be an agreement between a debtor and his several creditors whereby the latter agree with the debtor, and mutually among themselves, to receive, and the debtor agrees to pay, a certain part or pro-

SCOPE OF BILATERAL CONTRACT. 131

portion of the demands due the several creditors in discharge of the whole of such demands.⁴

<small>Chapter XIII</small>

As we have elsewhere learned, such an agreement between a debtor and a single creditor is invalid. So long as it is unperformed it is subject to the rule which declares executory accords to be invalid; and after performance the agreement is not binding because of incompetency of the consideration. It certainly seems curious that a different rule should prevail where there are more than one creditor, yet the validity of the composition in such case has not been doubted since *Good v. Cheesman* (1831).⁵

<small>Difficulty presented by such agreements.</small>

The secret of this apparent deviation from principle is found in the fact that the mutual promises of the several creditors among themselves, whereby each agrees to refrain from pressing the debtor for the full amount of such creditor's claim, constitutes a good bilateral contract as among the creditors and the debtor incidentally reaps the benefit of it. A contract which, as between the debtor and a single creditor, would be ineffectual is supported by the good bilateral agreement with which it happens to be inseparably associated.⁶

<small>Explanation of its validity.</small>

---

⁴ See 6 Am. and Eng. Encyc. of Law (2d ed.) 377.

In most agreements of this sort the discharge of the debtor is expressly conditioned upon performance on his part. Hence if he does not pay the amount agreed upon by way of composition or if he fails to pay at the time stipulated, the creditors can enforce their original claims to the full extent. Rosling *v.* Muggeridge, 16 M. & W. 181; Constable *v.* Andrew, 2 Cromp. & M. 298; Leake *v.* Young, 5 El. & Bl. 955, 85 E. C. L. 955; Mullin *v.* Martin, 23 Mo. App. 537; Penniman *v.* Elliott, 27 Barb. (N. Y.) 315; Cobleigh *v.* Pierce, 32 Vt. 788.

⁵ 2 B. & Ad. 335, 22 E. C. L. 91; Boyd *v.* Hind, 1 H. & N. 938; Evans *v.* Powis, 1 Exch. 601; Mallalieu *v.* Hodgson, 16 Q. B. 689, 71 E. C. L. 689; Pfleger *v.* Browne, 28 Beav. 391; Norman *v.* Thompson, 4 Exch. 756.

⁶ Several other explanations of the validity of the agreement for the composition of debts have been suggested, but they are more or less unsatisfactory. Anson on Contracts (Huffcut's ed.), 108, note.

CHAPTER XIV

DEPENDENCE OF MUTUAL PROMISES.

Volume II

Question stated.

THE doctrine of the dependence of mutual covenants and mutual promises forms an interesting and instructive chapter in the history of the bilateral contract. The question for discussion is this: When are mutual promises independent of each other, so that a plaintiff may recover upon the promise made to him without having himself performed the act or paid the money promised by him; and when are the mutual promises dependent upon each other, so that a plaintiff must allege performance or readiness to perform as a prerequisite of the right to recover? In other words, when is performance by the plaintiff, of his promise, a condition, concurrent or precedent, to the right of recovery on the counter-promise?

The covenant an analogue of the parol promise.

It is to be observed that the covenant is an exact analogue of the parol promise on which assumpsit lies. The covenant is based upon the formality of a seal, while the normal parol promise is based upon consideration. A further difference is found in the fact that one particular portion of the field which, in theory, belongs to covenant was appropriated by another action (debt) long before the covenant appeared. This was where the duty imposed by the covenant was to pay a sum certain of money. Such a covenant was the same as the sealed obligation and there was no reason why the writ of covenant should be used to enforce such a duty. The older remedy was available and consequently debt was the proper action. With this exception the scope of assumpsit and covenant is the same. Hence, they both can appear either in the unilateral or bilateral form. Conversely, all bilateral contracts must consist either of mutual parol promises or of mutual covenants; for if one person covenants and the other promises, we have, not a bilateral contract, but two unilateral contracts.

DEPENDENCE OF MUTUAL PROMISES. 133

A contract cannot be in part a simple contract and in part a specialty.¹

Again, mutual promises never give rise to a debt. The fundamental conception which underlies debt is that of a unilateral duty; for a debt can only be created, as we have already seen, by the actual receipt of a *quid pro quo*. Debt normally and necessarily therefore imports that one side of the contract has been performed. Hence a unilateral duty which constitutes a debt can never be part of a bilateral contract, but always constitutes, by itself, a unilateral contract or obligation.²

It is true that in the later period of the development of the action of debt, it was conceived that a bargain and sale might result in the creation of two duties (debts), that of the seller to deliver and that of the buyer to pay the price. We have already seen, however, that the bargain and sale was something of an anomaly in early contract law. Besides, the two duties were in theory separate independent unilateral duties and did not together make a true bilateral contract.³ When the bargain and sale had been made each party had a perfect right of action against the other, and this fact was taken to be a sufficient reason why nonperformance of the counter-duty should not be treated as a good defense. For instance, if the seller sued for the purchase price it was no defense that the plaintiff had not delivered the thing sold, for the defendant had his own separate action for its recovery.⁴ Slowly and even with some difficulty the seller was protected by allowing him to hold possession until the price was paid, if the terms of the bargain permitted such construction; but the general rule that the 'reciprocal grants' which made up the contract of bargain and sale constituted separate unilateral duties, remained unimpaired.

Chapter XIV

Covenant and parol promise distinguished from the debt.

Independence of reciprocal duties resulting from bargain and sale.

---

¹ Langdell on Contracts, § 184.
² Langdell on Contracts, § 112.
³ See Parol Contracts Prior to Assumpsit, by Professor Ames, 8 Harv. L. Rev. 259.

⁴ The reader will find traces of the old learning on this subject in Pordage *v.* Cole, 1 Saund. 319*d*, and the notes appended thereto.

Dependence of Mutual Covenants.

Mutual covenants treated as independent,

From what has been said it is manifest that before the recognition of mutual promises at the end of the sixteenth century, the bilateral contract always had to take the form of mutual covenants, and the courts, for some reason, took exactly the same view as regards the dependence of the duty raised by covenant as of that raised by the creation of a debt. Consequently, where there were two reciprocal covenants, one party could sue and recover damages for the nonperformance of his opponent's covenant regardless of whether he had himself performed the duty incumbent upon him.

unless expressly made mutually dependent.

If, however, by the terms of the covenants, one was made dependent upon the other, the intention of the contracting parties could not be disregarded. It therefore always became a question of interpretation whether, in a particular instance, performance by one party was a condition precedent to his recovery against the other. Fine distinctions were taken. Thus, if a covenant was made 'for' or 'in consideration of' performance, as distinguished from being made for or in consideration of the other covenant, performance was held to be a condition precedent; otherwise not. Thus, in *Brocas's Case*[5]

Distinctions.

there were mutual covenants between the lord and his copyholder by which the former agreed to assure the freehold to the copyholder and his heirs; and the copyholder " in consideration of the same performed," covenanted to pay a sum of money. It was the opinion of the whole court that " the said copyholder is not tied to pay the said sum, before the assurance made, and the covenant performed. But if the words had been ' in consideration of the said covenant to be performed,' then he is bounden to pay the money presently, and to have his remedy over by covenant.' [6]

Inadequacy of doctrine.

The distinction was sometimes very subtle and the result attained fell entirely short of adequately protecting parties to contracts. In many cases the remedy over would be entirely inadequate, owing to the insolvency of one of the parties or

---

[5] 3 Leon. 210.
[6] See also *Thorp v. Thorp*, 12 Mod. 455.

to some other reason. Every consideration of justice demanded that nonperformance on the part of the party plaintiff should be available in defense, but it was not so. The dependence of one covenant upon the other could only be established by the words of the contract without the aid of any presumption.

Dependence of Mutual Promises.

When the simple bilateral contract was established it was at once held without hesitation that one party could recover on the promise of the other without showing performance on his own part. This was in entire conformity with the rule applied in covenant and in harmony with the theory which underlay debt   Thus, in *Nichols v. Raynbred* (1614),[7] Nichols brought an assumpsit declaring that " in consideration that Nichols promised to deliver the defendant to his own use a cow, the defendant promised to deliver him fifty shillings." Judgment was given for the plaintiff, notwithstanding the declaration did not aver the delivery of the cow; " because it is promise for promise."

In *Bettisworth v. Campion* (1608),[8] there was a contract by which the plaintiff agreed to let the defendant have all the iron, the product of his furnace, at a stipulated rate. Suit was brought to recover part of the purchase money in arrear. The plaintiff failed to allege that he had supplied the defendant with all the output of his furnace. This was held to be immaterial, in arrest of judgment, on the ground that the consideration of the defendant's promise to pay was the counter-promise that the defendant should have all, and that performance was not a condition precedent to the right to maintain the action. In *Gower v. Capper* (1597)[9] the action was grounded on one of two mutual promises and judgment was given for the plaintiff without argument, notwithstanding the defendant had pleaded nonperformance on the part of the plaintiff. " A promise against a promise is a sufficient ground for an action."

[7] Hob. 88.   [8] Yelv. 133.   [9] Cro. Eliz. 543.

The solution of the problem is not as easy as it might superficially appear. Two courses were open to the courts. They could follow the rule which had been applied in the field of covenant; and this is what they did, as we have just seen. On the other hand, they might have followed the rule which was applied in case of unilateral promises supported by the executed consideration. *Rogers v. Snow* (1572)[1] is of the latter type. This was an action upon a unilateral promise, and it was held that the plaintiff must allege performance. "If I promise a man twenty shillings for going to York, in an action upon this promise, he must allege performance on his part."

A moment's consideration will show that this latter rule would have worked but little better as applied to mutual promises, than the other rule which was in fact adopted. In the contract of mutual promises it often happens that the acts respectively promised are to be done at the same time, and where this is so it is quite as hard on the plaintiff to require him to perform as a condition precedent to a recovery, as it is on the defendant to require him to perform notwithstanding the plaintiff has failed to perform. Mutual dependence is as bad as mutual independence as a universal working rule. On the question of the dependence of the promises the bilateral contract evidently presents special difficulties of its own.

The doctrine of the mutual independence of promises having proved unsatisfactory, the courts naturally broke away from it, and in so doing first steered of course towards the doctrine of mutual dependence. Thus, in 1704, Holt, C. J., in a case where the contract contemplated simultaneous performance by both parties, said, "If either party would sue upon this agreement, the plaintiff for not paying or the defendant for not transferring, the one must aver and prove a transfer or a tender; . . . and though there be mutual promises, yet if one thing be the consideration of the other, there a performance is necessary to be averred, unless a certain day be appointed for performance. If I sell you my horse for

---

[1] Dalison 94.

ten pounds, if you will have the horse I must have the money; or if I will have the money you must have the horse." [2]

This decision left the law on the subject of the dependence of promises in as bad a fix as ever. In escaping Scylla Lord Holt had fallen into Charybdis. He had, it is true, impaired the doctrine of mutual independence of covenants and promises, but he applied the new notion of mutual dependence to contracts where the two acts are performable at the same instant as well as to cases where one act is to be performed before the other.

A way to escape from the trouble was pointed out in *Turnor v. Goodwin* (1713),[3] where the defendant had agreed to pay a certain sum of money for the assignment of the judgment. Parker, C. J. (afterwards Lord Macclesfield) said: "Here are no words that expressly show the priority of the act. The defendant would have assigning to be *first assigning* and the plaintiff would have it *assigning thereupon,* that is, after payment. . . . We are all of opinion that there is one way that will solve all these difficulties, and that is, that this assignment shall neither precede nor wait, but shall accompany the payment, and both to be done at the same time." And as regards tender, he added: "The defendant [having promised to pay upon the assigning] ought to find out the plaintiff to tender him the money and at the same time to demand an assignment; and then if the plaintiff refuse, the defendant will be excused. He is not to tender the money absolutely, because he is not bound to pay it absolutely; but he is to tender it *sub modo,* on the same terms he is to pay it." This ruling was subsequently cited and applied in *Merrit v. Rane* (1721),[4] where the contract provided for the transfer of certain stock at a stipulated price.

A means having been thus found to effectuate the obvious intention of the parties, as well as to accomplish the ends of justice, it remained for Lord Mansfield subsequently to give shape and consistency to the law of the whole subject and to

Chapter XIV

Difficult dilemma.

Solution of the trouble.

---

[2] Callonel *v.* Briggs, 1 Salk. 112.
See the earlier opinion of this judge in Thorp *v.* Thorp (1701), 12 Mod. 455.

[3] Fortescue 145, 10 Mod. 153.
[4] 1 Stra. 458.

138   FOUNDATIONS OF LEGAL LIABILITY.

place it upon a firm and satisfactory basis. This was finally done in *Kingston v. Preston* (1772).⁵ In delivering the judgment of the court in this case Lord Mansfield summed up the law as follows: "There are three kinds of covenants: 1. Such as are called mutual and independent, where either party may recover damages from the other, for the injury he may have received by a breach of the covenants in his favor, and where it is no excuse for the defendant to allege a breach of the covenants on the part of the plaintiff. 2. There are covenants which are conditions and dependent, in which the performance of one depends on the prior performance of another; and, therefore, till this prior condition is performed, the other party is not liable to an action on his covenant. 3. There is also a third sort of covenants, which are mutual conditions to be performed at the same time; and in these, if one party was ready, and offered to perform his part, and the other neglected or refused, to perform his, he who was ready and offered, has fulfilled his engagement, and may maintain an action for the default of the other; though it is not certain that either is obliged to do the first act."

His lordship then proceeded to say, that the dependence or independence of covenants was to be collected from the evident sense and meaning of the parties, and that, however transposed they might be in the deed, their precedence must depend on the order of time in which the intent of the transaction requires their performance.⁶

The facts involved in *Kingston v. Preston* brought the case within the second class specified by Lord Mansfield, and his language was mere dictum on the question of mutual dependence. But the reasoning was sound, and the end accomplished by adopting the view thus sanctioned by him was so just that his statement of the law has not been subsequently questioned. In *Goodisson v. Nunn* (1792),⁷ the agreement was for the sale and purchase of an estate. Buller, J., reviewed and approved the decisions from Mansfield's time, saying that if

---
⁵ (13 Geo. III.) Referred to in Jones *v.* Barkley, 2 Dougl. 689.
⁶ See Jones *v.* Barkley, 2 Dougl. 684.
⁷ 4 T. R. 761.

DEPENDENCE OF MUTUAL PROMISES. 139

there had been no modern decisions he would not have hesitated to make a new precedent in opposition to the ancient rule. Lord Kenyon expressed himself to the same effect. It was accordingly held that the plaintiff could not recover against the purchaser without showing readiness to perform on his part.

In *Morton v. Lamb* (1797),[8] the contract of sale specified a time and place for delivery of the chattels sold, but did not specify a time and place for payment. Lord Kenyon said there could be no doubt that the parties intended that payment should be made at the time of delivery. Consequently it was held that a declaration which showed that the seller (plaintiff) carried the corn at the proper time to the designated place and was ready to deliver but refused to do so because the defendant would not pay the price, was good. His lordship cited Lord Holt's decision in *Callonel v. Briggs*,[9] to the effect that where two concurrent acts are to be done, the party who sues the other for nonperformance must aver that he has performed, or was ready to perform, his part of the contract.

In *Rawson v. Johnson* (1801),[1] there was a contract for the sale of malt, and the purchaser brought an action to recover damages for the failure of the defendants to deliver. It was objected that the plaintiff only averred a readiness and willingness to pay for the malt in question and did not state an actual tender of the price agreed upon. Lord Kenyon said: "No doubt can be entertained how this case should be decided; one man agrees to do a certain act in consideration of another man doing another act; the acts are to be done at the same time and place; one of the parties goes there intending to do his part and the other stays away altogether; the former is obliged to bring this action for this breach. . . . Would it be any answer to say that he ought to have pleaded a tender of the money? . . . Under this averment the plaintiffs must have proved that they were prepared to tender and pay the money, if the defendant had been ready to have **received it** and to have delivered the goods; but it cannot be

Chapter XIV

Readiness to perform sufficient in case of concurrent condition.

---

[8] 7 T. R. 121.　　[9] 1 Salk. 113.　　[1] 1 East 112.

necessary in order to entitle them to maintain their action, that they should have gone through the useless ceremony of laying the money down in order to take it up again."

With these decisions the idea that mutual covenants and mutual promises were independent unless expressly made dependent upon each other disappeared from the law. The old decisions are therefore no longer authority, but their true place in the law has not always been recognized and the principle applied in them has sometimes given trouble even in modern times.

From what has been said it appears that in the end two very just and entirely distinct principles have been worked out by the courts as applicable to the two different situations, viz.: (1) where the mutual promises are not to be performed simultaneously; and (2) where they are both to be performed at the same time. The principle applied in the first class of cases is that of general dependence; that is, the act to be first performed is treated as a condition precedent to recovery by the person whose duty it is to perform that act.

The principle applied in the other class of cases is that the two promises are mutual concurrent conditions. Neither party is required to do the act or part with the thing promised by him until the other is also ready to perform and does perform the act required of him. It results in the application of this rule, that the plaintiff is not required to allege that he has actually delivered the thing or done the act required by him, but that he has conditionally tendered performance, where this is practicable; or has been ready to perform. If the case is one where a tender is required or is feasible, the court becomes a stake-holder for the other party in the event the tender turns out to have been well made.

CHAPTER XV

CONTRACT LAW IN MANSFIELD'S DAY.

LORD MANSFIELD became Chief Justice of the King's Bench in 1756, a position which he retained till 1788. He was Scotch by extraction and, being better versed than his predecessors in the civil law, showed a decided bias for the legal conceptions of that system. His genuine learning and great ability together with his wonderful personality enabled him to effect, without opposition from the other judges, most radical changes. He left a very deep mark in our law of contract, but he came too late to revolutionize it or put it on a different basis. Let us examine the innovations accomplished or attempted by him.

The Written Promise.

In *Pillans v. Van Mierop* (1765)[1] his lordship and his associates held that a bill of exchange is good without a consideration. His idea was that this quality was derived from the law merchant. But he further suggested that any contract which by a rule of law is required to be put in writing and which conforms to that requirement is valid without regard to the presence of a consideration. Said he: "I take it that the ancient notion about the want of consideration was for the sake of evidence only, for when it is reduced into writing, as in covenants, specialties, bonds, etc., there was no objection to the want of consideration, and the statute of frauds proceeded upon the same principle." Wilmot, J., agreed with this suggestion and unearthed the old learning of the civil law concerning *nudum pactum*, which was of course more or less irrelevant to the subject of *nudum pactum* in the common law.

If this view had prevailed we should have in English law three classes of contracts: (1) specialties, (2) contracts sup-

[1] 3 Burr. 1663.

ported by a consideration, and (3) contracts in writing. Sir Frederick Pollock thinks that if this notion had occurred a century or two earlier to a judge of anything like Mansfield's ability, the English law of contract might have been shaped along the same lines as those of the law of Scotland.[2] This is doubtful, however.[3]

At any rate, Lord Mansfield's suggestion came too late and was barren of results.[4] It only served to challenge attention to the point in question, and a few years later a judgment was delivered (1778) in the House of Lords in which Skynner, L. C. B., used the memorable words: "It is undoubtedly true that every man is by the law of nature bound to fulfil his engagements. It is equally true that the law of this country supplies no means nor affords any remedy to compel the performance of an agreement made without sufficient consideration; such agreement is *nudum pactum ex quo non oritur actio;* and whatsoever may be the sense of this maxim in the

---

[2] Pollock on Contracts, 169.

[3] Substantially the same view of the function and purpose of consideration had been presented in the argument of Sharington *v.* Strotton, 1 Plowd. 298, 302, where it was said: "But the common law requires that there should be a new cause whereof the country may have intelligence or knowledge for the trial of it, if need be, so that it is necessary for the public weal." It is needless to say that this notion is altogether erroneous.

[4] Mansfield's opinion that contracts in writing (under the law merchant) require no consideration, evidently made impression on Blackstone, whose Commentaries were published ('1767) a short while after Pillans *v.* Van Mierop was decided. Says he: "As this rule [i. e., the requirement of a consideration] was principally established to avoid the inconvenience that would arise from setting up mere verbal promises, for which no good reason could be assigned, it therefore does not hold in some cases, where such promise is authentically proved by written documents. For if a man enters into a voluntary bond, or gives a promissory note, he shall not be allowed to aver the want of a consideration in order to evade the payment: for every bond, from the solemnity of the instrument, and every note, from the subscription of the drawer, carries with it an internal evidence of a good consideration. Courts of justice will therefore support them both, as against the contractor himself." 2 Bl. Com. 445.

Williamson *v.* Losh, Chitty on Bills, 9th ed., 75, note x, was decided (1775) under the influence of the notion advanced in Pillans *v.* Van Mierop, 3 Burr. 1663, and was one of the cases whose *ratio decidendi* was overruled by Rann *v.* Hughes, 7 T. R. 346, note a. In this case assumpsit was maintained against an executor on a promissory note in these words: "I, John Losh, for the love and affection that I have for Jane Tiffin, my wife's sister's daughter, do promise that

civil law, it is in the last-mentioned sense only that it is to be understood in our law." [5]

From whatever direction we approach this case of *Rann v. Hughes*, whether by retracing our steps from the present day or by traveling more tediously over the three preceding centuries, it must appear to mark an epoch in the history of the development of English contract law. The fact that it does mark an epoch is easily lost to the modern reader, because it is in such complete harmony with accepted views.

Moral Obligation as a Consideration.

Another idea which first came into prominence in Mansfield's day, and which caused much confusion in the law of contracts for a half century, was that of moral obligation. Mansfield seems to have thought that a promise to do what the promisor is already under a moral obligation to do is binding. He was no doubt largely influenced by the old cases in which it was held that a promise based upon a consideration previously executed upon request is good.

In *Hawkes v. Saunders* (1782),[6] which was an action against an executrix in her own right to recover a legacy which she had promised to pay to plaintiff "in consideration of sufficient assets being in her hands." Lord Mansfield said: "Where a man is under a legal or equitable obligation to pay, the law implies a promise, though none was ever actually made. *A fortiori*, a legal or equitable duty is a sufficient consideration for an actual promise. Where a man is under a moral obligation which no court of law or equity can enforce, and promises, the honesty and rectitude of the thing

---

my executors, administrators, or assigns shall pay to her the sum of £100 of money, one year after my decease, and a caldron and a clock, a wainscot chest, and a bed and bed-clothes, seven pudden-dishes: as witness my hand this 16th day of February, 1763."

[5] *Rann v. Hughes*, 7 T. R. 346, note a.

It will be noted that this case did not involve exactly the same point as that involved in *Pillans v. Van Mierop*, 3 Burr. 1665, inasmuch as the earlier case involved a contract which was required to be in writing under the law merchant; while the later case involved a contract that was required to be in writing under the statute of frauds. But evidently the same principle was involved.

[6] 1 Cowp. 289.

is a consideration; as if a man promise to pay a just debt, the recovery of which is barred by the statute of limitations; or, if a man, after he comes of age, promises to pay a meritorious debt contracted during his minority, but not for necessaries; or, if a bankrupt in affluent circumstances, after his certificate, promises to pay the whole of his debts; or, if a man promise to perform a secret trust, or a trust void for want of writing by the statute of frauds. In such and many other instances, though the promise gives a compulsory remedy where there was none before either in law or equity, yet as the promise is only to do what an honest man ought to do, the ties of conscience upon an upright mind are a sufficient consideration." [7]

Such was the origin of the so-called moral consideration. It by no means follows that these decisions of Lord Mansfield were incorrect, and we shall later examine them in another aspect. The idea that moral duty, however, is enough of itself to support a promise could not endure. After the advent of Lord Kenyon an attempt was made in the case of *Deeks v. Strutt* (1794)[8] to hold a personal representative liable on an implied promise to pay a legacy "in consideration of sufficient assets." Liability was denied, Lord Kenyon remarking on the pernicious consequences likely to follow the extension of notions lately current. This decision has generally been taken as having overruled *Atkins v. Hill* and *Hawkes v. Saunders,* but in those cases express promises were proved.[9]

The efficacy of the moral consideration was, however, recognized for many years after Mansfield's death. Probably the most radical applications of it were in *Lee v. Muggeridge* (1813),[1] where a woman was held liable on a promise made after discoverture to pay a debt contracted while she was a *feme covert;* and in *Barnes v. Hedley* (1809),[2] where usurious securities had been given for a loan. Under the Statute

---

[7] See Atkins *v.* Hill, 1 Cowp. 284.
[8] 5 T. R. 690.
[9] See article by E. H. Bennett, 10 Harv. L. Rev. 258.

[1] 5 Taunt. 46, 1 E. C. L. 14.
[2] 2 Taunt. 184.

CONSIDERATION OF MORAL DUTY. 145

of 9 Anne, c. 16, this rendered the whole debt utterly void. Subsequently the evidence of the debt was destroyed and a promise was made by the borrower to repay the principal with legal interest. It was held that this promise was enforceable.

An analogous ruling was made in *Flight v. Reed* (1863),[3] where bills of exchange were given by the defendant to the plaintiff to secure the repayment of money lent at usurious interest while the usury laws were in force. After the repeal of the usury laws by 17 and 18 Vict., c. 90, the bills were renewed upon consideration of the past loan, and the defendant was held liable.

Lord Mansfield applied the doctrine of moral consideration to the promise of a discharged bankrupt in *Trueman v. Fenton* (1777),[4] going partly, to be sure, on a few previous but not decisive cases looking in the same direction. The validity of a promise, made after attaining majority, ratifying a debt incurred during infancy was recognized until the passage of the Infants' Relief Act.[5] Promises to pay debts barred by the statute of limitations are still good. The features common to these cases, as said by Sir William Anson, are that in each of them the parties agree; " in each, one of the parties has got all that he bargained for, while the other cannot obtain what he was promised, either because he has dealt with one who was incapable of contracting, or because a technical rule of law forbids the agreement to be enforced. If the party who has received the benefit which he expected from the agreement afterwards acquires capacity to contract; or if the rule of law is repealed, as in the case of the usury acts; or, as in the case of the statute of limitations, admits of a waiver by the person whom it protects, then a new promise based upon the consideration already received is binding. The cases thus regarded seem a plain and reasonable exception to the general rule that a past consideration will not support a promise." [6] The doctrine of moral obligation as a consideration probably contributed somewhat to the solution of these

Chapter XV

Promise to pay money lent at usury.

Promise of discharged bankrupt.

Promise to pay debt barred by limitations.

[3] 1 H. & C. 703.
[4] 2 Cowp. 544.
[5] 37 & 38 Vict., c. 62.
[6] Anson on Contracts, 104.

10

cases, but it is not necessary to place them on such ground.

<small>Doctrine of moral consideration criticised and limited.</small>

In a learned note to *Wennall v. Adney* (1802),[7] Messrs. Bosanquet and Puller, in 1802, examined the then recent doctrine of moral consideration and showed that Lord Mansfield's generalization had been wider than the authorities on which it was based. They therefore concluded that an antecedent moral obligation was not of itself sufficient to sustain a promise. In *Littlefield v. Shee* (1831),[8] Lord Tenterden observed that the doctrine that a moral obligation is a sufficient consideration for a subsequent promise is one that should be received with some limitation; and in 1838, judgment against a married woman on her promise to pay for goods furnished her by the plaintiff during coverture was not allowed. Denman, C. J., put the decision in this case on the ground that the debt was the debt of her husband, and no moral obligation was shown.[9]

<small>Doctrine of moral consideration repudiated.</small>

Finally, in *Eastwood v. Kenyon* (1840),[1] the conclusion reached by Messrs. Bosanquet and Puller was declared to be sound, viz., that a moral obligation cannot give an original cause of action if the obligation on which it is founded never could have been enforced at law though not barred by any legal maxim or statute provision. *Lee v. Muggeridge* was therefore overruled, and the right of a guardian who had advanced money in behalf of his ward (without her request) to recover on her promise made after reaching majority, to pay therefor, was denied.[2] Since that decision the doctrine of moral obligation has found no support in any quarter.

---

[7] 3 B. & P. 247.
[8] 2 B. & Ad. 811, 22 E. C. L. 187.
[9] Meyer v. Haworth, 8 Ad. & El. 467, 35 E. C. L. 442.
[1] 11 Ad. & El. 438, 39 E. C. L. 137.
[2] The Supreme Court of Massachusetts in Mills v. Wyman, (1825) 3 Pick. (Mass.) 207, anticipated Eastwood v. Kenyon by several years, repudiating the idea that a moral obligation can support a promise. There a son of full age, having ceased to be a member of his father's family, fell sick among strangers and, being poor and in distress, was relieved by the plaintiff. Subsequently the father wrote to plaintiff and promised to reimburse him, but it was held that an action on the promise could not be sustained.

CHAPTER XVI

LEGAL OBLIGATION AS A CONSIDERATION.

IN a previous chapter [1] we noted the appearance, in the sixteenth century, of that exceptional form of consideration which supported the promise to pay a precedent debt. This was the consideration of legal duty. In the same connection we also explained why, after this sort of consideration had served a temporary purpose and had materially assisted in bridging a serious chasm in our remedial law, it dropped almost entirely out of sight. No more was heard of it until Mansfield's day, and, as might be imagined, its reappearance was accompanied, as before, by a further extension of contractual liability, and rights of action came to be recognized which had been unknown before.

Hawkes v. Saunders (1775),[2] a case which has already been referred to, is an illustration of this. The plaintiff there recovered on a promise made by an executor to pay a legacy. Mansfield said plainly that where one is under legal or equitable obligation the law implies a promise, and that *a fortiori* legal or equitable duty is a sufficient consideration. Buller industriously fished up a lot of cases from the old books, whose language, at least, supported this view.[3]

The conception underlying this and similar decisions is at the root of not a little modern law, though unfortunately these cases were, as we have already seen, implicated with the notion of moral consideration and were in a degree discredited by the connection. The idea embodied in *Hawkes v. Saunders* is that where a person is charged by law or by contract with

---

[1] Ch. VII., *ante*.
[2] 1 Cowp. 289.
[3] Stone *v.* Withipool, Latch 21; Wells *v.* Wells, 1 Vent. 41; Reech *v.* Kennegal, 1 Ves. 125; Trewinian *v.* Howell, Cro. Eliz. 91; Atkins *v.* Hill, 1 Cowp. 284. See Buller, J., in Hawkes *v.* Saunders, 1 Cowp. 291.

the duty of doing a particular act, an express promise made to the party entitled to performance will be enforced.

This doctrine has been applied in several situations.[4] Thus, it has been held that where a devisee of land is charged by the testator with the payment of a pecuniary legacy to a third person, and such devisee expressly promises the legatee to pay the same, the legatee can maintain an action on this promise;[5] and it is generally recognized that a creditor of a deceased person can recover on a note given by the personal representative for a debt owing by the decedent, especially where there are assets.[6]

It is commonly said that the existence of assets is the consideration which supports such a promise, but it is obviously the existing legal duty resting on the executor to use the assets for that purpose which gives validity to his personal promise.[7]

If a depositor in a bank issues a check thereon and the bank expressly promises to the holder to pay the check to him, the latter can maintain an action on this promise though the consideration moved from the person who made the deposit in the bank; and where the promise to pay the third party is put into the form of a promissory note, the payee of the note can recover on it without question if it be delivered to such payee.[8]

The law of insurance supplies innumerable instances where the consideration, i. e., the premium paid, moves from the insured, but the promise evidenced by the policy binds the insurer to make payment to a third person. In all jurisdictions the beneficiary in these cases is permitted to recover in an action at law, and in two only was this end accomplished by statute.[9]

---

[4] Clark v. Herring, 5 Binn. (Pa.) 33; Swasey v. Little, 7 Pick. (Mass.) 299.

[5] Beecker v. Beecker, 7 Johns. (N. Y.) 99; Van Orden v. Van Orden, 10 Johns. (N. Y.) 30; Pelletreau v. Rathbone, 18 Johns. (N. Y.) 428.

[6] Williams on Executors, vol. 3, p. 1673 (Rand & Talcott); Daniell on Negotiable Instruments, § 263.

[7] Snead v. Coleman, 7 Gratt. (Va.) 300; Boyd v. Johnston, 89 Tenn. 284.

[8] Fanning v. Russell, 94 Ill. 386; Hatton v. Jones, 78 Ind. 466; Eaton v. Libbey, 165 Mass. 218.

[9] In England, by 45 & 46 Vict., c. 75, § 11; in Massachusetts, by Stat. 1887, ch. 214, § 73; 1894, ch. 225. In Massachusetts judicial decision allows direct recovery by a

It has sometimes been supposed that the fact that a stranger to the consideration may maintain an action on negotiable instruments and policies of insurance is due to a mysterious quality derived solely from the law merchant. But this explanation is unnecessary and misleading; for this quality is, as we see, by no means limited to those contracts.

Chapter XVI

Where it is held, as in the foregoing cases, that the existence of legal obligation is sufficient to sustain an express promise to the beneficiary, it is only a short step to the conclusion that where the legal obligation exists, the express promise is irrelevant and need not be proved. Thus, it is now universally held that when a legacy is given and is directed to be paid by the person to whom the land is devised, an acceptance of the devise charges the devisee with the payment of the legacy and he becomes personally bound to pay it, although he makes no express promise and though the land devised is of less value than the legacy. In these cases a promise is implied in fact from the circumstance of accepting the devise.[1]

Implied promise.

Dispensing with proof of an actual promise in these cases where the legal obligation already rests on the defendant is exactly analogous to the process by which actual subsequent promises became irrelevant in the early history of indebitatus assumpsit. It is obvious that where existing legal obligation is held to be a sufficient consideration to sustain a promise in fact, the only argument against raising an implied promise on the same liability is that of policy and convenience. Lord

Analogy from former period.

mortgagee on a fire policy taken out for his benefit by the mortgagor. Palmer Sav. Bank v. Insurance Co. of North America, 166 Mass. 189.

[1] Harland v. Person, 93 Ala. 273; Williams v. Nichol, 47 Ark. 254; Olmstead v. Brush, 27 Conn. 530; Zimmer v. Sennott, 134 Ill. 505; Porter v. Jackson, 95 Ind. 210; Bacon v. Woodward, 12 Gray (Mass.) 382; Prentice v. Brimhall, 123 Mass. 293; Wiggin v. Wiggin, 43 N. H. 561; Brown v. Knapp, 79 N. Y.

136; Fuller v. McEwen, 17 Ohio St. 288.

Even in England this principle has had some recognition. See Ewer v. Jones, 2 Ld. Raym. 937, 2 Salk. 415, where Lord Holt said that if money be devised to be paid out of certain land the legatee may have an action of debt. This dictum has met with approval. See Braithwaite v. Skinner, 5 M. & W. 313; Webb v. Jiggs, 4 M. & S. 119.

Kenyon adverted to this in holding that the law would not imply a promise to pay a legacy as against an executor with assets,² a decision which would have been reactionary and unsound if no other remedy had existed.

There is still another limited class of cases illustrating the principle that legal obligation may render valid a unilateral promise imperfect for lack of a consideration in the sense of detriment. These cases are usually cited in support of the principle that a promise to pay one for doing voluntarily an act which the promisor was himself legally bound to do is actionable. The first decision to this effect is found in *Watson v. Turner* (1767),³ in which case the overseers of the poor promised to pay the bill of a medical attendant who, without any previous request from the overseers, attended a pauper taken suddenly ill and cured her. They were held liable on the promise. The doctrine of moral consideration had not then been advanced, and as pointed out by Selwyn,⁴ this decision may well be put upon the ground that the legal obligation resting on the overseers to care for the poor is sufficient to sustain the promise. Buller, however, who sympathized thoroughly with Mansfield's views on the subject of consideration, subsequently put the case on the ground of moral obligation.⁵ This suggestion was subsequently accepted as the true one; for, in *Atkins v. Banwell* (1802),⁶ the court refused to imply a promise in a similar case, where no express one was shown, thus showing that legal obligation could not well be the basis of such a promise as was proved in the previous case. By this time it was coming to be well recognized that where legal obligation exists the law will imply a promise and indebitatus assumpsit will lie. It is needless to add that in so far as these decisions recognize legal obligation, or legal duty, as a consideration they are sound enough. This consideration is exceptional and peculiar, but it has a real and secure place in common-law doctrine. Moral obligation, on

---

² Deeks *v.* Strutt, 5 T. R. 690.
³ Bull. N. P. 147a, Selwyn N. P. 53, note 4.
⁴ Nisi Prius, 13th ed., 66.
⁵ Bull. N. P. 147a.
⁶ 2 East 505.

[Margin notes: Promise to pay for act which promisor was bound to do. Obligation of overseers of poor to compensate one who attends pauper.]

the other hand, is an entirely spurious type of consideration.

In *Wing v. Mill* (1817)[7] and in *Paynter v. Williams* (1833)[8] actions were sustained by parish authorities where paupers were attended, against the authorities of the parish of their settlement. In the earlier of these cases a promise was proved, but in the later one a promise was implied, as of fact, on the very slender circumstance that the defendant parish had been paying an allowance for the maintenance of the deceased pauper.

[7] 1 B. & Ald. 105.   [8] 1 Cromp. & M. 810.

CHAPTER XVII

CONSIDERATION AND THE RIGHT OF ACTION.

Volume II

IT will be observed that the principle considered in the preceding chapter is sufficiently broad to include all cases where after a contractual obligation in favor of a stranger has been incurred, the party who is bound to perform such duty subsequently makes an express promise to the stranger and thus brings him into some sort of privity with the contract. This rule, consequently, to a certain degree directly impinges upon another important rule of the common law, the scope and bearing of which we must now consider.

Stranger to consideration has no right of action on the promise.

The principle that the consideration must be a detriment moving from the promisee is consistently applied in the common law by holding that the right to maintain an action of assumpsit on the contract resides in the person from whom the consideration moves. The recognition of this principle in a court of common law carried with it the further consequence that no person other than the one from whom the consideration moved could maintain any action at all. This corollary, to a man trained in common-law ways of thinking, was self-evident and needed no argument to sustain it. A person for whose benefit a contract is made, if he is a stranger to the consideration, cannot maintain an action upon it.[1]

Let us consider the course of decision on this subject. In

---

[1] Com. Dig., *Action upon the Case upon Assumpsit* (E).

Professor Langdell has put the English common-law view in the following clear and vigorous language: "This latter proposition is so plain upon its face that it is difficult to make it plainer by argument. A binding promise vests in the promisee, and in him alone, a right to compel performance of the promise, and it is by virtue of this right that an action is maintained upon the promise. In the case of a promise made to one person for the benefit of another, there is no doubt that the promisee can maintain an action, not only in his own name, but for his own benefit. If, therefore, the person for whose benefit the promise was made could also sue on it, the consequence would be that the promisor would be liable to two actions. In truth, a bind-

Bourne v. Mason (1660),² the right of a stranger to the consideration to maintain assumpsit was denied. Only one limitation on this principle was ever subsequently recognized by the English courts. Privity of blood between the person from whom the consideration moves and the beneficiary was for a while held to be sufficient to enable such person to sue.³

This exception, after being denied in *Norris v. Pine* (1671),⁴ was approved in *Dutton v. Poole* (1677),⁵ on the same reasoning that had been decisive in favor of the efficacy of the consideration of love and affection in *Sharington v. Strotton*. Said Scroggs, C. J.: There is such "apparent consideration of affection from the father to his children, for whom nature obliges him to provide, that the consideration and promise to the father may well extend to the children." ⁶

The general principle that a stranger to the consideration

Chapter XVII

Exception in favor of blood.

---

ing promise to A to pay $100 to B confers no right upon B in law or equity. It confers an authority upon the promisor to pay the money to B, but that authority may be revoked by A at any moment." Langdell on Contracts, § 62.

It should be added that the term 'promisee' is here used to indicate the promisee in law, that is, the one from whom the consideration moves. Such promisee does not always coincide with the promisee in fact. See the remarks in connection with the case of Edmundson *v.* Penny, 1 Pa. St. 334, *post*.

² 1 Vent. 6. It appeared that P was the debtor to both A and B in different sums. C was the debtor of P. It was agreed by A, B, and P that B should sue P's debtor, C, and upon recovery should pay P's debt to A. B recovered against C, but did not pay A. The latter thereupon brought suit against B. It was held that only P could sue B, as the consideration moved from him.

In Anonymous, (1646) Style 6, A and B entered into a contract by mutual promises to contribute a specified sum as a portion for their intermarried children. It was held that the right of action was vested respectively in A and B and not in the children. The recovery, however, it was said, would inure to the benefit of the married couple.

³ Sprat *v.* Agar (1658), in King's Bench, referred to in Bourne *v.* Mason, 1 Vent. 6. See, to the same effect, Anonymous, also referred to in the same case.

In Sprat *v.* Agar, A promised B that if the latter's daughter would marry A's son, he would settle certain lands upon them. It was adjudged that an action could be maintained by the son in right of his wife, as the consideration moved from her. In the other case the promise was made to a father to pay his daughter a certain sum upon a consideration moving from the father. It was held that action could be maintained by the daughter because of privity of blood between her and the person from whom the consideration moved.

⁴ Cited in Dutton *v.* Poole, 2 **Lev.** 211.

⁵ 2 Lev. 211, 1 Vent. 318.

⁶ 2 Lev. 211.

cannot recover on a promise made for his benefit was strengthened by *Crow v. Rogers* (1727),[7] and *Price v. Easton* (1833).[8] Finally, in the last century, when a case similar to that of *Dutton v. Poole* again came before the courts the principle on which it was decided was declared untenable. It was thus established in England that the rule limiting the right to bring assumpsit to the person from whom the consideration moves is subject to no exception whatever.[9]

In this connection it should be observed that the promisee in legal contemplation is the person who furnishes the consideration. Accordingly such promisee is the party who must sue. The promisee in law is therefore not to be confounded with the person to whom the promise is communicated or with the beneficiary. If a promise is made to C to do something for him on a consideration moving from D, the latter is the promisee in contemplation of law though he is not the promisee in fact, and the right of action on the promise is vested in him. In other words, the consideration may draw the legal promise to it, but the promise alone cannot draw the right of action to the promisee in fact, where the consideration moves from another source.

This principle is illustrated in *Edmundson v. Penny* (1845),[1] where Chief Justice Gibson said: "The plaintiff must unite in his person both the promise and the consideration of it; and if the action, in such a case, cannot be sustained on the foundation of the consideration by drawing the promise to it, it cannot be sustained at all."[2] The same principle

---

[7] 1 Stra. 592.
[8] 4 B. & Ad. 433, 24 E. C. L. 96.
[9] Tweddle v. Atkinson, (1861) 1 B. & S. 393, 101 E. C. L. 393.
[1] 1 Pa. St. 335.
[2] In this case the defendant had promised to pay Penny a sum for service to be rendered by one McCandless. The learned Chief Justice said further: "Whatever may be the conflict of opinion in the earlier cases, it is now settled that a parol promise to one for the benefit of another, can support an action on it only by him from whom the consideration moved, or who was the meritorious cause of it. . . . In the case before us, the suit, though marked to the use of Mr. McCandless, who rendered the services, is strictly an action at law to which equitable parties are strangers as regards the title to recover, though not to the debt or damages when recovered; and as between Penny and Edmundson, it stands as an action on a promise without consideration. As a promise to Penny, the contract does not stand on the foot of a moral obligation, for Ed-

THE RIGHT OF ACTION.   155

was recognized in the case of *Warren v. Batchelder* (1844).³   Chapter XVII

While the foregoing principle must be accepted as embodying the common-law doctrine of the relation between the consideration and the right of action, it should not escape attention that at various times some of the ablest English judges have shown a disposition to disregard it and to recognize the right of the stranger to sue on a contract made for his benefit. In the time of the Commonwealth, Rolle, C. J., thought there could be no question of such right. Accordingly, in a case where a father gave goods to his son provided he would pay twenty pounds to another, it was held that an action could be maintained against the son by the person entitled to the money.⁴ The idea that a third person for whose benefit a contract was made should be permitted to sue, although he was not in privity with the consideration, also commended itself to no less personages than Lords Holt and Mansfield. In *Yard v. Eland* (1698),⁵ Lord Holt said that on a promise not under seal, made by A to B for a good consideration, to pay B's debt to C, C may sue. Lord Mansfield said, a hundred years later,⁶ that he could not conceive how a doubt could be entertained as to *Dutton v. Poole*.⁷ These utterances are clearly out of harmony with the general trend of opinion. Such obstinate questionings, however, have an import which will presently become apparent.

Idea that stranger should be permitted to sue finds favor with eminent judges.

The reason for the rule that none but those in privity with the consideration can maintain an action on the promise is found in the original conception underlying assumpsit. This remedy, as we have already seen, was founded on the notion

Historical explanation.

---

mundson was under no obligation to compensate Penny for the services of McCandless, and . . . it must be taken for a promise to McCandless himself. . . . But how would McCandless declare, when he does not appear on the face of the paper to be a formal party to it? Simply by laying the promise according to the legal effect of it, as a verbal one made immediately to himself." Edmundson *v.* Penny, 1 Pa. St. 335.

³ 15 N. H. 129.
⁴ Starkey *v.* Mill, (1651) Style 296.
⁵ 1 Ld. Raym. 368.
⁶ Martyn *v.* Hind, (1776) 2 Cowp. 437, 443.
⁷ 1 Vent. 318, 332, 2 Lev. 211.

In Rokwood's Case, Cro. Eliz. 163, younger sons were allowed to bring an action for the amount the heir had promised his father to pay them.

of giving redress for damages incurred by the nonfulfilment of a deceitful promise. Only the person who suffered the detriment or damage in question could therefore bring suit upon breach of the promise. This rule was clearly a procedural one and was peculiar to the action of assumpsit. The statement of the rule that the stranger to the consideration cannot maintain assumpsit does not imply that the promisor owes no legal duty to the person for whose benefit the contract is made. Quite the contrary. The contractual duty exists, and unless we suffer ourselves to become entangled in a verbal quibble, we must admit that the duty is one owing to such third person. The remedy by the action of assumpsit, then, is not as broad as the limits of contractual liability. In other words, we are here confronted with one of those deficiencies in remedial law which are inevitable under the common-law system of actions.

The statement of the reason whereon the rule with which we are dealing is based suggests two possible courses by which its effect may be evaded. If in the development of the remedy of assumpsit it should at any point break over the original limitation and should become coextensive with contractual duty, the stranger to the consideration to whom performance is due should be permitted to sue on the promise. The same result would necessarily follow if the action of assumpsit should be altogether abolished and the single civil action on the facts of the case be substituted in its place.

Both these alternatives have been pursued. The first alternative proved only partially successful. In the form of indebitatus, the action of assumpsit is certainly as broad as legal duty, and in this form the remedy could possibly be perverted so as to permit a third person to sue on all contracts made for his benefit. The courts, however, have rightly hesitated at this point. There is no question that if A delivers to B money to be turned over to C, the latter may sue in indebitatus for money had and received or for money paid to his use.[8] But if no money is delivered and B merely promises to pay money to C on a consideration moving from A, the result is different.

[8] Hall *v.* Marston, 17 Mass. 575.

THE RIGHT OF ACTION. 157

The action here must be in special assumpsit on the contract, and indebitatus does not properly lie.

The Massachusetts case of *Brewer v. Dyer* (1851),[9] supplies an instance where indebitatus was improperly used for this purpose. In that case the court said that the right of action was to be sustained upon the broad ground that "the law, operating on the act of the parties, creates the duty, establishes the privity, and implies the promise and obligation on which the action is founded." The Massachusetts court has, it may be observed, since receded from this position, and the doctrine of that case has been overruled.[1]

The course of decision in this state shows that the extension of indebitatus assumpsit afforded no satisfactory solution of the trouble. The decision in *Brewer v. Dyer* evidently imposed a greater strain upon the action of assumpsit than it could well bear. We observe in passing, that Massachusetts has not adopted the new system of procedure.[2]

Turning to the state of New York we find that here, as in Massachusetts, there was some early recognition of the right of the third person to sue.[3] The doctrine was placed upon the insecure authority of *Dutton v. Pool*.[4] The question was not, however, presented for elaborate consideration until the important and leading case of *Lawrence v. Fox* (1859)[5] arose. The right of the third person to sue on a contract made for his benefit was by that case fully established. This decision constitutes a new point of departure in American contract law, and, as said in 1876 by the Supreme Court of the United States,[6] the doctrine there laid down now prevails in the greater number of the American states.

The reason why the New York court could advance where the Massachusetts court has been compelled to beat a retreat

Chapter XVII

Perversion of indebitatus.

Modern American doctrine.

---

[9] 7 Cush. (Mass.) 337.
[1] Marston v. Bigelow, 150 Mass. 45.
[2] As to the extent of the changes in procedure made in Massachusetts, see Mass. Acts 1851, ch. 233, and Public Statutes 1882, ch. 167; also Hepburn on Development of Code Pleading (1897), §§ 165-167.

[3] Schemerhorn v. Vanderheyden, (1806) 1 Johns. (N. Y.) 140.
[4] 1 Vent. 318, 332.
[5] 20 N. Y. 268.
[6] Hendrick v. Lindsay, 93 U. S. 143. See also the note on Right of Third Party to Sue on Contract Made for His Benefit, in 25 L. R. A. 257.

158   FOUNDATIONS OF LEGAL LIABILITY.

Explanation found in abolition of actions.

is manifest. In 1848, forms of action had been abolished in New York and complete theoretical equilibrium between remedial law and contractual liability was thus established. The procedural difficulty no longer remained. To a mind trained under the new procedure, the conclusion reached in *Lawrence v. Fox* is just as logical and just as inevitable as the contrary conclusion reached in jurisdictions where the forms of action are still in existence.

If our reasoning is sound upon the question now under discussion it would seem to follow that the English courts also should recognize the right of a stranger to sue upon a contract made for his benefit, now that forms of action have been abolished by the Judicature Acts. The English courts, nevertheless, refuse to sanction the action. The reason is not far to seek. In the first place, the law on this point had been definitely settled long before assumpsit was abolished, and the conclusion thus reached being, as was supposed, logical and rational, was not easily to be shaken.

Position of English courts.

Explanation of this attitude.

Again, it will be observed that in our view the difficulty is resolvable into a question of procedure. It is easy, however, to take refuge behind the proposition that the difficulty is not one of procedure, but of contractual liability. Thus Lindley, J., once said that if an agreement is made between A and B that B shall pay a sum of money to C, the inability of C to sue is due not to any defect of remedy. "It is," said he, "a mere question of contract."[7]

Is the problem one of procedure merely?

The difficulty of working out the rights of the beneficiary under the old system of procedure or under theory conforming to it has proved to be very great. Inasmuch as the person with whom the contract is made or who furnishes the consideration undoubtedly has a right to sue in case of breach, it would seem feasible to work out the rights of the beneficiary through him; but, as trenchantly said by Lord Coleridge in *West v. Houghton* (1879),[8] the beneficiary has no means of compelling such party either to institute suit against the delinquent or to turn over the fruits of the action when recov-

Difficulty presented by English doctrine.

[7] *In re* Rotherham Alum, etc., Co., 25 Ch. D. 103, 111.
[8] 4 C. P. D. 197.

ered. Hence it is sometimes held, as in that case, that at law the actual party to the contract, i. e., the person supplying the consideration, can recover only nominal damages.[9]

The court of equity has sometimes given protection to the stranger to the consideration by working his rights out under one of the parties to the promise.[1] But if Lindley, J., was correct in the position assumed in the case above referred to, the third person has no better right in equity than at law.

In applying the modern doctrine that the stranger to the consideration may sue upon a contract made for his benefit, the American courts have in a sense acted unconsciously. Being trained in the atmosphere of the new procedure, they have been forced to sustain the right of action, but they have not, it must be said, clearly perceived the ground on which their action is to be upheld. We consequently find that our courts are usually content to take hold of any plausible theory which seems to be adequate to the decision of each particular case, failing to look deep enough to see the underlying principle. The theories of 'agency,' 'trust,' and 'property rights' have served this purpose.

The test most frequently proposed is that found in an intention on the part of the contracting parties to bestow a benefit on the stranger. "The contract," it is said, "must be made for his benefit as its object, and he must be the party intended to be benefited."[2] But, as Professor Williston has clearly shown,[3] this test is, like the others, inadequate; for in many cases the interest of one of the contracting parties is much more obviously intended to be protected than the interest of the third party. Such is the case where one contracting party exacts of the other a promise to assume and pay a debt.

Another phenomenon illustrates the failure of the American courts fully to grasp the true reason for permitting the stranger to sue. This is found in the fact that *Lawrence v.*

---

[9] Compare Burbank *v.* Gould, 15 Me. 118.
[1] Lloyd's *v.* Harper, 16 Ch. D. 290; Gandy *v.* Gandy, 30 Ch. D. 57.
[2] Simson *v.* Brown, 68 N. Y. 355.
[3] See the article on Contracts for Benefit of a Third Person, by Prof. Samuel Williston, 15 Harv. L. Rev. 786, 787.

Fox has been followed in states where the old forms of action remain, while in still other jurisdictions, it seems, as in England, the old doctrine prevails notwithstanding the introduction of the new procedure. It will be found that on the whole the code states have been quickest to respond and these have become the chief protagonists of what is now known as the American doctrine.[4] That the courts of those common-law states where the question has remained open should yield to the influence of the movement set afoot by the leading New York case cannot appear strange when we consider the weight given in American jurisdictions to decisions made in sister states, and when we further take into consideration the constant effort on the part of the courts to break through the limitations of the action of special assumpsit.

The controversy over the right of a stranger to the consideration to sue upon a promise made for his benefit involves perhaps the most momentous issue raised in the law of contract since the decision of *Slade's Case*.[5] The fact that the battle is still going on renders it of surpassing interest. On the one side is the theory on which assumpsit was originally based. On the other is the consciousness that the legal remedy upon a simple contract should be as broad as the contractual obligation. Around these two standards the contending forces are marshaled. It is not difficult, we believe, to indicate the side to which victory inclines. The common-law theorist may in a few words dispose of the right of the stranger to sue upon a contract made for his benefit. Legal evolution is, however, against him. The introduction of the

---

[4] It should in these states be said that the action which the stranger is permitted to maintain on the promise made for his benefit is not an action of assumpsit on the contract, but an action on the case in the nature of assumpsit.

For a general view of the growth of the code system see Hepburn, Historical Development of Code Pleading in America and England ('1897). The so-called 'code states' are New York, Missouri, California, Kentucky, Iowa, Minnesota, Indiana, Ohio, Oregon, Washington, Nebraska, Wisconsin, Kansas, Nevada, North Dakota, South Dakota, Idaho, Montana, Arizona, North Carolina, South Carolina, Arkansas, Wyoming, Utah, Colorado, Connecticut, and Oklahoma.

[5] 4 Coke 94.

civil action as the sufficient remedy in all cases where the facts show legal liability has determined the issue.[6]

In closing this discussion concerning the problem of the right of a stranger to the consideration to maintain an action on an assumptual contract, we suggest that in the end it will perhaps be found best to take the view that the obligation on which such stranger is permitted to sue is not an assumptual obligation created by the contract, but is an obligation in the nature of an assumpsit created by law on the facts of the case. In other words, we here perceive a manifestation of the notion underlying one branch of the law of quasi-contract. In this view the subject of the right of the stranger to sue should be dealt with in connection with those quasi-contractual obligations which form the subject of discussion in Chapter XXV (*post*). The reader may at least be advised, after reading that chapter, again to direct his attention to the discussion which has been given in the present chapter.

---

[6] An idea of the present state of the conflict may be gotten from the excellent article by Prof. Williston, Contracts for the Benefit of a Third Person, 15 Harv. L. Rev. 767, and from 7 Am. and Eng. Encyc. of Law, 2d ed., 104–109.

CHAPTER XVIII

LEGALITY OF CONTRACT.

Volume II

The law creates the obligation.

IN discussing the principles of contract we no doubt often use language which if taken literally would seem to indicate that the parties create the obligation themselves. This is not true. The obligation of a contract results from an act of the law. Acting upon the elements which the parties supply, the law itself adds the bond (*vinculum juris*) which ties one party to the other. As a final step the law must sanction the engagement and give its approval before there can be any true contract.

Contract must be lawful.

It is self-evident that such sanction cannot be given where the engagement in question is subversive of the law itself or tends to weaken the foundations of human society. The law will not permit any of its creatures to be used for its own destruction. The machinery for the administration of justice cannot be used to promote an iniquitous or unlawful purpose. From this it results that one fundamental condition must always be fulfilled before any contract can exist or be enforced, namely, the condition that the engagement be such that the law can recognize and clothe it with obligation. It must not be illegal.

Illegality fatal to all forms of contract.

Illegality is a weakness that cannot be cured by form. The sealed obligation of indebtedness, the deed, the covenant, the recognizance, the judgment of record — contracts which the common law has come to regard with something of superstitious reverence because, generally speaking, form is unimpeachable — all vanish like mist before the destructive breath of this agent, and when infected by it they are as frail as the assumptual promise. The defect may be found in the matter of consideration, in the promise as expressed in the agreement, or it may be found in the purpose which the agreement, though legal in expression, is intended to accomplish. If it lurks in any element, or subsists only in the purpose or intention of the parties, it is fatal to the validity of the contract. But in this connection it is to be borne in mind that while some contracts are rendered wholly void by the presence of illegality, other contracts are rendered void only in part. If the legal surgeon can pare off the chancre infecting a part of the contract and leave the remainder sound and enforceable this will be done.

Chapter XVIII

The subject of illegality as affecting the validity of contracts is necessarily of great compass and of deepest importance. It can be fully and satisfactorily handled only in a treatise intended to set forth the substantive law of contracts. The truth here to be impressed is that the requirement of legality qualifies the whole body of contract law. The principle which underlies it is necessarily contemporary with the first recognition of contractual liability. There has been no period since contract law reached the stage of consciousness, when the maxim *ex turpi causa non oritur actio* was not recognized. A contract based upon an unlawful consideration or designed to promote an unlawful object is and always has been void *ab initio* " by the common law, by the civil law, moral law, and all laws whatsoever. . . . You shall not stipulate for iniquity. . . . No polluted hand shall touch the pure fountains of justice. Whoever is a party to an unlawful contract, if he hath once paid the money stipulated to be paid in pursuance thereof, he shall not have the help of a court to fetch it back again. You shall not have a right of action when you come into a court of justice in this unclean manner to recover it back. *Procul, O procul, este profani.*" [1]

Ex turpi causa non oritur actio.

Agreements in violation of the laws against champerty and maintenance were probably the first class of contracts which were held to be void because of illegality. Such agreements tended to the abuse of legal process. Both champerty and maintenance were indictable offenses, and where such agreements were found to infect any cause of action, the guilty

Champerty and maintenance.

---

[1] Language of Lord Chief Justice Wilmot in Collins *v.* Blantern, 2 Wils. C. Pl. 341, 1 Smith Lead. Cas. (8th Am. ed.) 715.

parties were punished by fine as well as by the dismissal of the suit.² Maintenance is a broader term than champerty and does not often appear in contracts. It was defined by Lord Abinger in *Findon v. Parker* (1843),³ as a term applied to cases where a man improperly and for the purpose of stirring up litigation encourages others to bring actions or make defenses which they have no right to make; and it has been held that an engagement of indemnity to protect an informer against costs incurred in attempting to enforce a statutory penalty is within this definition.⁴

Champerty, itself a form of maintenance, applies to agreements by which one who maintains another is to have part of the land, or debt in suit, as recompense for his assistance. It is said to be the most odious form of maintenance.⁵ It often takes the form of a promise to supply evidence or bear the expenses of a suit in consideration of receiving a part of the recovery.⁶

One of the earliest of the illegal agreements to attract the attention and call forth the denunciation of the courts was the engagement in restraint of trade. "The immortal immorality" of Hull in passing upon the validity of such a contract is often referred to.⁷ The occasion which called forth his denunciation is worth noticing. Debt was brought upon a sealed obligation containing a provision that if a man did not exercise his craft of dyer within a certain town where he had carried on business, for six months, then the obligation should be void. Hull vigorously denounced the agreement, saying: "The condition is against the common law, and, *per Dieu*, if the plaintiff were here, he should go to prison until he pay a fine to the king."⁸ This case shows that at that time (1414) all agreements in restraint of trade were considered absolutely void and unlawful.

² Com. Dig., *Maintenance*, A1.
³ 11 M. & W. 682.
⁴ Bradlaugh v. Newdegate, 11 Q. B. D. 5. See also Harris v. Brisco, 17 Q. B. D. 504.
⁵ Com. Dig., *Maintenance*, A2.
⁶ Stanley v. Jones, 7 Bing. 369, 20 E. C. L. 165; James v. Kerr, 40 Ch. D. 458.
⁷ See National. Enameling, etc., Co. v. Haberman, 120 Fed. Rep. 416.
⁸ Y. B. 2 Hen. V. 5, pl. 26.

In the course of the centuries the rule has been gradually modified to suit the modern needs of the commercial society,[1] and now the doctrine is that whether the covenant be general or particular its validity is alike determined by the question whether it is reasonable and is based upon good consideration.[2]

Chapter XVIII
Modern rule.

The history of the law concerning wagers probably affords the most interesting illustration of the struggle of a vicious contract to hold its position against the policy of the law. It will be remembered that the wager as a valid form of contract made its appearance only after the recognition of mutual promises. Neither debt nor indebitatus assumpsit would ever lie for money won at play. Lord Holt once emphatically said that there is no way in the world to recover money won at play but by special assumpsit.[3]

The wager.

It being seen that the wager fell strictly within the theory of assumpsit, the contract was recognized as being good. It is defined as being a promise to give money or money's worth upon the determination or ascertainment of an uncertain event. The normal wager is that made up of mutual promises, but it can be unilateral, as where one pays down a sum of money for a promise by the other party to pay a specified sum upon the happening of a certain contingency. There are a number of wagers or aleatory contracts which are recognized as being good to this day. Some confusion has arisen from the fact that the term has become a vehicle of reproach, being gradually restricted to contracts of a gambling or sporting nature. Insurance contracts are aleatory and are therefore wagers, but, subject to the requirement that the party insured have an insurable interest, they are recognized as valid and are not usually thought of as being of the same legal nature as the bet upon a horse race or other idle wager.

Wager a good assumpsit.

Insurance.

The validity of the wager being once recognized it speed-

---

[1] See language of Lord St. Leonards in Egerton v. Brownlow, 4 H. L. Cas. 237.

[2] Nordenfelt v. Maxim-Nordenfelt Guns, etc., Co., (1894) A. C. 535, 548.

See also Lord Macclesfield's opinion in Mitchel v. Reynolds, 1 P. Wms. 181, 1 Smith Lead. Cas. (8th Am. ed.) 756.

[3] Walker v. Walker, Holt K. B. 328, 5 Mod. 13, Comb. 303; Hard's Case, 1 Salk. 23; Bovey v. Castleman, 1 Ld. Raym. 69; Smith v. Airey, 2 Ld. Raym. 1034, Holt K. B. 329.

166   FOUNDATIONS OF LEGAL LIABILITY.

Volume II

The idle wager.

ily attained obtrusive prominence. Lord Mansfield seems to have been specially indulgent of litigation brought to enforce the payment of trivial and idle bets. In *Jones v. Randall* (1774),[4] he sustained an action to recover money won by wager laid upon the result of a lawsuit. In *March v. Pigot* (1771),[5] two licentious characters, addicted to the turf, laid wagers on the lives of their respective fathers, the one who should first lose his father and thereby come to an estate being bound to pay the amount agreed upon to the other. It happened that the father of one of them was actually dead at the time the bet was made. His lordship held that this was immaterial and held the defendant liable. However, he did hold that a wager on the result of an election was void, being calculated to promote corruption in voting.[6]

Wager on election invalid.

A climax was reached in the wager laid upon the sex of the Chevelier d'Eon. The trial of the suit before Mansfield and a jury raised a great noise and scandal throughout Europe. Subsequently the case was brought before the whole bench and the judges declared that such wagers were impertinent and that the courts would not sit as the arbiter of them.[7]

Wager on sex of Chevalier d'Eon.

Thenceforth the courts began to exercise their wits to defeat wagers in all possible cases. Not being able to declare all idle betting to be immoral and contrary to public policy, they endeavored to engraft as many exceptions as possible upon the principle which declared wagers valid. They repented too late of the folly of their predecessors in giving any kind of recognition to this sort of agreement. Curious results followed. A wager on the future amount of hop duty was held void as tending to disclose to the world the amount of the public revenue.[8] In a case where rival carriagemen laid a wager that a certain person would go to the assembly room in the carriage of one rather than the other, it was suggested that the wager was bad as tending to subject one of the public to the inconvenience of being harassed by rival

Courts begin to discountenance wagers.

[4] 1 Cowp. 37.
[5] 5 Burr. 2804.
[6] Allen *v.* Hearn, 1 T. R. 57.
[7] DaCosta *v.* Jones, 2 Cowp. 729.

See Campbell's Lives of the Chief Justices, Am. ed. (1899), vol. 4, pp. 138–143.
[8] Atherfold *v.* Beard, 2 T. R. 610.

coachmen.⁹ A bet on the duration of the life of Napoleon was held to be bad because it tended on one side to weaken the patriotism of an Englishman; on the other, to encourage the idea of assassinating a foreign ruler and so to provoke retaliation upon the English sovereign.¹

All these reasons were as idle as the various bets which gave occasion for them. The courts were tired of them and felt, as Bailey, J., said in the last case, that it would be a good rule to postpone the trial of actions on idle wagers until the docket should be cleared of other matters and the court should thus be idle too. Finally legislative action has been brought into play and gambling contracts are now made void by statute. This legislation has effectually assisted the courts in establishing the principle, towards which decisions were already fast tending, that all idle bets are demoralizing and against the policy of the law.

⁹ Eltham *v.* Kingsman, 1 B. & Ald. 683.
¹ Gilbert *v.* Sykes, 16 East 150.

CHAPTER XIX

THE STATUTE OF FRAUDS.

<small>Authorship of the statute.</small>

ABSENCE of legislative interference is a feature which characterizes in a striking way the account thus far given of the development of English contract law. We come now to consider a notable instance of such interference. We refer to the Statute of Frauds (1677),[1] an enactment by which certain simple contracts are required to be in writing.

At the time when the statute was passed, it was known to be of great importance and subsequent dispute has arisen as to the person or persons most entitled to the honor of having framed it or assisted in its passage. At one time its authorship was attributed to Lord Hale. Lord Mansfield, however, on one occasion remarked upon the improbability of this, saying that the act was not passed until after the death of the learned Lord Chief Justice.[2] Lord Mansfield added that the statute "was brought in in the common way and not upon any reference to the judges."[3] In the same connection he is reported further to have said: "I can never conceive, for the reasons I formerly mentioned, that this statute was

---

[1] 29 Chas. II., ch. 3.
[2] Lord Hale died Dec. 25th, 1676 (28 Chas. II.).
Mr. John F. Baker, of New York, speaking on the question of the authorship of the Statute of Frauds, says:
"The Statute of Frauds must have been prepared as early as 1673, for at the first session of that year it was introduced into Parliament; and after that it went before several committees, and was discussed at several sessions previous to its passage in the spring of 1677. . . . After a careful investigation of the question, I think the conclusion will not escape the mind of the student that Sir Matthew Hale was the master-spirit in formulating the statute, and that he prepared the bulk of that instrument; that Sir Leoline Jenkins, an able authority in probate law, drew the sections as to wills; that Lord Guilford took some part in preparing the statute; and that Lord Nottingham not only drew the sections in relation to trusts and devises, but was conspicuously active in piloting the bill through Parliament." 2 Harv. L. Rev. 42.
[3] Windham v. Chetwynd, 1 Burr. 414, 418.

drawn by Lord Hale, any farther than by perhaps leaving some loose notes behind him, which were afterwards unskilfully digested."[4] Lord Ellenborough had occasion, in *Wain v. Warlters* (1804),[5] to give to the language used a technical interpretation, and justified himself by referring the verbiage to Hale as the reputed author of the statute. But Lord Mansfield's conjecture was doubtless correct.

<small>Chapter XIX</small>

Lord Nottingham said that the bill "had its first rise" in himself and that he brought it into the House of Lords, where it received some new touches at the hands of the judges and civilians.[6] It is doubtful whether this rather vague claim was intended to include the honor of authorship, and that question can hardly be said to be fully settled. The names of Lord Keeper Guilford and Sir Leoline Jenkins, an eminent civilian, have been associated with the name of Lord Hale as joint producers of the statute.[7]

It was certainly not passed without the sanction of the legal profession. Though, as Lord Mansfield said, it may not have been brought in upon a reference to the judges, several were called in to assist the committee in the House of Lords,[8] and in the House of Commons all the members who were "of the long robe" are said to have been present upon its passage.[9]

<small>Statute generally approved by legal profession.</small>

Purpose and Method of the Statute.

The preamble of the statute informs us that it was enacted "for prevention of many fraudulent practices which are commonly endeavored to be upheld by perjury and subornation of perjury." It may strike the mind as a little curious that the legislative body should thus have proceeded by indirection to remedy this evil. "An Act for the Prevention of Frauds and Perjuries," as its title runs, would certainly lead one to expect additional safeguards to be thrown around the proce-

<small>Preamble.</small>

---

[4] Wyndham v. Chetwynd, 1 W. Bl. 97.
[5] 5 East 17.
[6] Ash v. Abdy, (1678) 3 Swanst. 664.
[7] Gilbert, Rep. in Eq. 171; Smith on Contracts, 74.
[8] 13 Lord's Journ. 20, 45.
[9] 5 Common's Journ. 410.

170   FOUNDATIONS OF LEGAL LIABILITY.

<small>Volume II</small>

dure in the courts or heavier penalties to be imposed upon the crime against which the enactment was leveled. Not so; the course pursued was to take numerous agreements out of the body of litigable transactions. With the policy of the statute we are not at this juncture particularly concerned. It cannot escape observation, however, that the method of reaching the evil aimed at was very indirect and ran curiously counter to the previous development of English contract law.

<small>Statute follows unnatural lines.</small>

The almost infinite amount of litigation which has resulted from the enactment known as the Statute of Frauds shows that it was poorly drafted and altogether failed to pursue natural lines of cleavage in our law. No one seam of legal thought was consistently followed. Of the six classes of engagements enumerated in the fourth and seventeenth sections, no two adopt the same basis of classification, nor, with the exception of the first and second, are they conceived from the same point of view. Absence of benefit to the promisor, as in the guaranty; the nature of the consideration (whether land or hereditaments); the time of performance; and the price of the subject-matter of the contract (in § 17) are all used as separate bases for the requirement of a writing. Time and again have judges lamented the lack of skill exhibited in framing the statute and the looseness of the language used in describing the different contracts intended to be brought within it.[1]

<small>Subsequent legislation and judicial sense approve the statute.</small>

But notwithstanding all the difficulties of interpretation which the statute has presented, and notwithstanding the oblique and wholly unscientific way in which the statute cuts into the symmetry of our contract law, it is safe to say that no enactment has ever received more universal commendation. It may be conceded that much of the encomium showered

---

[1] Lord Mansfield, speaking of the clause regulating testamentary power, said that the statute was not meant to check this power, but only to guard against frauds. "In theory it seems a strong guard; in practice it may be some guard. But I believe more fair wills have been destroyed for the want of observing its restrictions than fraudulent wills obstructed by its caution. In all my experience in the Court of Delegates I never knew a fraudulent will but what was legally attested, and I have heard the same from many learned civilians." Wyndham v. Chetwynd, 1 W. Bl. 100.

upon it has been misplaced and in many cases perfunctory; since the courts have been most eulogistic when compelled to apologize for the gross injustice which the application of the statute has sometimes occasioned.[2] On the whole it has apparently vindicated its right to be, and there is probably no jurisdiction applying the common law in any form where the provisions of this statute, especially section four, are not in some way in force. Subsequent legislation as well as judicial sense has therefore in the main approved it.

The Statute Affects Only Simple Contracts.

Let us now examine the language of the statute in order to see how far it extends into contract law and how it operates. Section 4 is as follows: "No action shall be brought whereby to charge any executor or administrator upon any special promise to answer damages out of his own estate; or whereby to charge the defendant upon any special promise to answer for the debt, default, or miscarriages of another person; or to charge any person upon any agreement made upon consideration of marriage; or upon any contract or sale of lands, tenements, or hereditaments, or any interest in or concerning them; or upon any agreement that is not to be performed within the space of one year from the making thereof; unless the agreement upon which such action shall be brought, or some memorandum or note thereof, shall be in writing, and signed by the party to be charged therewith, or some other person thereunto by him lawfully authorized."

Section 17 is in these words: "No contract for the sale of any goods, wares, and merchandises for the price of ten pounds or upwards shall be allowed to be good, except the buyer shall accept part of the goods so sold, and actually receive the same, or give something in earnest to bind the bargain, or in part payment; or that some note or memoran-

[2] Lord Nottingham, not an altogether disinterested witness as to its merits, used to say of the statute, that every line was worth a subsidy. Upon this Mr. J. W. Smith facetiously and truthfully observes, "every line has cost a subsidy, for it is universally admitted that no enactment of any legislature ever became the subject of so much litigation." Smith on Contracts, 75.

dum in writing of the said bargain be made and signed by the parties to be charged by such contract, or their agents thereunto lawfully authorized."

We first observe that the statute gives no express intimation whether it is to apply to formal sealed contracts as well as to simple contracts. If it be interpreted as running into the whole field of contract law, then sealed obligations must be signed as well as sealed, something not required by the common law. A deed is a writing sealed and delivered, but not necessarily signed. Blackstone was of the opinion that the statute restored the old Saxon form of signing and superadded it to sealing and delivery in the case of a deed.[3]

Statute does not apply to sealed contracts.

This view seems not to be the true one, however; for the reason on which the statute was based could hardly apply in the case of sealed instruments. Accordingly by modern authority the statute applies only to simple contracts.[4] In other words, it was intended to operate only upon those contracts where the contractual obligation results from promise.

Implied promises not within the statute.

Not only this; it extends only to express promises and to contracts which are in fact entered into by the consent (agreement) of the respective parties. Implied promises are evidently not within the statute in any aspect. The term 'special promise' in the first two clauses of section four have been

---

[3] 2 Bl. Com. 306.
Preston, in his edition of Sheppard's Touchstone, p. 56, note 24, expressed the opinion that Blackstone was in error.

[4] Cooch v. Goodman, 2 Q. B. 580, 42 E. C. L. 817; Aveline v. Whisson, 4 M. & G. 801, 43 E. C. L. 414.

In Cherry v. Heming, 4 Exch. 631, Rolfe, B., said: "I am strongly inclined to think that the statute does not extend to deeds, because its requirements would be satisfied by the parties putting their mark to the writing. The object of the statute was to prevent matters of importance from resting on the frail testimony of memory alone. Before the Norman time, signature rendered the instrument authentic.

Sealing was introduced because the people in general could not write. Then there arose a distinction between what was sealed and what was not sealed, and that went on until society became more advanced, when the statute ultimately said that certain instruments must be authenticated by signature. That means, that such instruments are not to rest on parol testimony only, and it was not intended to touch those which were already authenticated by a ceremony of a higher nature than a signature or a mark."

In most of the American states signature to deeds of conveyance is expressly required, and in all it is uniformly practiced. Wash. Real Prop., 4th ed., 553.

STATUTE OF FRAUDS. 173

expressly held to mean an express promise as distinguished from such as is implied.[5] The term 'agreement' in the other clauses certainly seems just as clearly to import an express contract as the term 'special promise' in the first two clauses. Indeed, when we remember that a promise is never implied, either in fact or in law, except upon an executed consideration, that is, where one party has received a benefit for which he must pay, it is plain that implied contracts are wholly aside from the purpose and intent, as well as without the language of the enactment.

Chapter XIX

Dispenses with No Common-law Requirement.

The next question that arises is: Does the statute dispense with any of the common-law requisites of the simple contract? The three well-known elements of the normal simple contract are consent, promise, and consideration. Obviously the statute did not mean to dispense with consent or promise, for its sole purpose was to secure better proof of both. It did this by requiring that the agreement, or a sufficient memorandum of it, be reduced to writing. The question whether the Statute of Frauds dispensed with the requirement of consideration and thereby turned contracts conforming with its provisions into purely formal contracts did not arise for a hundred years after its passage. The legal profession tacitly assumed that the statute dispensed with nothing previously required by the common law and merely superadded another requirement to the old. In 1765, Lord Mansfield advanced an idea then entirely new, viz., that contracts within the Statute of Frauds are sufficiently proved by a writing in conformity with its provisions, and that no proof of a consideration is necessary in such contracts.[6]

Statute does not dispense with requirement of consideration.

The House of Lords, however, soon put a quietus upon

---

[5] Goodwin v. Gilbert, 9 Mass. 510; Pike v. Brown, 7 Cush. (Mass.) 133; Allen v. Pryor, 3 A. K. Marsh. (Ky.) 305.

[6] Pillans v. Van Mierop, 3 Burr. 1663.

This suggestion was made in a case where it was actually decided that in contracts subject to the law merchant no proof of consideration is necessary. Hence upon the question of the effect of the Statute of Frauds it was purely dictum.

this notion; for in the case of *Rann v. Hughes* (1797),[7] to which we have elsewhere alluded, Lord Chief Baron Skynner used these often-quoted words: " All contracts are by the law of England distinguished into agreements by specialty and agreements by parol, nor is there any such third class, as some of the counsel have endeavored to maintain, as contracts in writing. If they be merely written and not specialties, they are parol, and a consideration must be proved. But it is said that the Statute of Frauds has taken away the necessity of any consideration in this case." After reading the statute, his lordship added that the words were merely negative. " This does not prove," said he, " that the agreement was still not liable to be tried and judged of as all other agreements merely in writing are by the common law, and does not prove the converse of the proposition that when in writing the party must be at all events liable."[8]

Interpretation of the Statute.

Coming to the question of the interpretation of the language of this statute, we are at the outset confronted by a great and obvious difficulty. The contracts embraced within it are various and the rule applicable in construing the statute as applied to one class is inappropriate in other connections. A court construing the statute favorably in applying it to a contract within the first or second clause, might well be disposed to construe it strictly in disposing of a contract under the fourth or fifth clause. This accounts for some of the conflict as regards the principles of interpretation to be applied, but there is still real conflict due to changes in legal temperament and to the supposed exigencies of justice.

As was natural, the judges were at first disposed to a liberal interpretation, and applied it to cases obviously within its meaning regardless of the ultimate result. The statute was remedial and ought, it was said, to be favorably construed

---

[7] 7 T. R. 346, note a.
[8] In Wain *v.* Warlters, 5 East 10, Lord Ellenborough said: " The statute never meant to enforce any promise which was before invalid merely because it was put in writing."

in order to further the object and intention of the legislature. Its words were not to be strained so as to take particular cases out of the operation of the statute.

<small>Chapter XIX</small>

Lord Mansfield took a different view and was inclined to take cases out of its operation which were within its letter where justice so required.[9] Wilmot, J., agreed with him. Contemplating the results that might follow from applying the provisions of the statute to sales made by auction, the latter said that had the Statute of Frauds been always carried into execution according to the letter, it would have done ten times more mischief by protecting fraud than it has done good by preventing fraud.[1] He accordingly suggested that sales by auction being transacted openly before many people were not within the purview of the statute, since it was meant to prevent mischiefs incident to private and clandestine sales.

<small>Lord Mansfield's attitude.</small>

This suggestion was afterwards put aside by Lord Ellenborough, who was unwilling to dispense with the statutory requirement of the written evidence merely because the quantum of parol evidence was such as to remove the danger of perjury. At the same time a way was found out of that particular difficulty by holding that the auctioneer by virtue of his position is the agent of both seller and buyer for the purpose of making the required memorandum of the sale.[2]

On the whole, the decisions seem to evince a disposition on the part of the courts to construe the statute strictly and thus limit its application to as few cases as possible, a feature possibly more characteristic of the later decisions, but not confined to them. For instance, it is held in *Harrison v. Cage* (1697),[3] that mutual promises to marry are not, within the

<small>Modern attitude of the courts.</small>

---

[9] On one occasion his lordship said: "The object of the legislature was a wise one and what the legislature meant is the rule both at law and in equity. The key to the construction of the act is the intent of the legislature; and, therefore, many cases, though seemingly within the letter, have been let out of it; more instances have indeed occurred in courts of equity than in law, but the rule is the same in both. For instance, where a man admits the contract to have been made it is out of the statute; for here there can be no perjury. Again . . . if the contract is executed, it is never set aside." Simon *v.* Metivier, 1 W. Bl. 599, 3 Burr. 1921, Bull. N. P. 280.

[1] 1 W. Bl. 601.

[2] Hinde *v.* Whitehouse, ('1860) 7 East 558.

[3] 1 Ld. Raym. 386.

language of the third clause of section four, "an agreement made in consideration of marriage"; though it had previously been expressedly held that such promises were "directly within the words and not out of the intent of the statute."[4]

Interpretation of fifth clause of section 4.

The disposition to construe the statute closely is strikingly manifest in the interpretation placed upon the fifth clause, which embraces contracts not to be performed within one year. It is now settled that agreements to be performed on contingent events which may happen within a year are not within the statute. Thus a verbal promise to pay on the return of a ship is good though the ship does not return for two years.[5] Likewise damages may be recovered for the breach of an agreement to leave money by will, though the promisor lives for many years and the contract is not reduced to writing.[6]

Another class of cases has established the rule that a contract which may be performed on one side within a year is not within the statute, although on the other side it is not to be performed within a year.[7] This clause of the statute in question is therefore judicially read "not to be performed *on either side* within a year."

General provisions.

The observations just made will serve to warn the reader how very cautious one should be in pronouncing an opinion upon any part of the statute. With this admonition we pass to the consideration of certain features impressed by the statute alike upon all contracts within its compass. Three points are here to be noted.

1. Contracts within the statute are not avoided by a failure to comply with its regulations, but are only rendered unenforceable.

2. The agreement, or a sufficient memorandum thereof, must be reduced to writing.

---

[4] Philpott v. Wallet, 3 Lev. 65.
[5] Anonymous, 1 Salk. 280.
[6] Fenton v. Emblers, 3 Burr. 1281.
[7] Donellan v. Read, 3 B. & Ad. 899, 23 E. C. L. 215; Cherry v. Heming, 4 Exch. 631. See also Piper v. Fosher, 121 Ind. 407; Smalley v. Greene, 52 Iowa 241. *Contra*, Whipple v. Parker, 29 Mich. 369.

3. This writing must be signed by the party to be charged or his agent.

Violation of Statute Renders Contract Voidable but Not Void.

The fourth section declares that unless its requirements be fulfilled, " no action shall be brought." The seventeenth section declares that no such contract " shall be allowed to be good." The interpretation of the former of these expressions has long been settled beyond question. Where parties have entered into a contract within section four without complying with its provisions, the obligation exists in legal theory, but no action can be maintained upon it, because it is incapable of proof. The contract is therefore not void, and is only voidable in the sense that it is not capable of being enforced. The statute operates only upon the remedy and operates upon it only as a rule of procedure.[8]

The language used in section seventeen would indicate a substantial difference in legal interpretation, and for a time it was thought that contracts within section seventeen might be held void upon failure to comply with its provisions. Its meaning has been, however, determined otherwise. The two sections are to be construed *in pari materia*. The purpose to be effected is the same in both cases. Consequently it is now said that "allowed to be good" means good for the purpose of a recovery under it. In other words, it has the same effect as "no action shall be brought," in the fourth section.[9] In England the question was set entirely at rest by the language of the Sale of Goods Act,[1] which re-enacted the seventeenth section of the Statute of Frauds, changing the phraseology of this provision to " shall not be enforceable by

Contracts violative of statute voidable only.

---

[8] Leroux *v.* Brown, 12 C. B. 801, 74 E. C. L. 801; Britain *v.* Rossiter, 11 Q. B. D. 123; Maddison *v.* Alderson, 8 App. Cas. 488; Townsend *v.* Hargraves, 118 Mass. 334; Bird *v.* Munroe, 66 Me. 344.

[9] See the opinion of Lord Blackburn in Maddison *v.* Alderson, 8 App. Cas. 467, 488. In Carrington *v.* Roots, 2 M. & W. 248, and in Reade *v.* Lamb, 6 Exch. 130, it was ruled that the language of both sections meant substantially the same, viz., that the contract would be void if not in writing, but this view had to be given up. Leroux *v.* Brown, 12 C. B. 801, 74 E. C. L. 801. See further, Townsend *v.* Hargraves, 118 Mass. 325.

[1] 56 & 57 Vict., c. 71, § 4.

action," in order to make it more clearly conform in meaning with section four of the Statute of Frauds.

Leroux v. Brown (1852)[2] illustrates in a striking manner the result reached by treating the statute as operating only upon the procedural right rather than as destroying the obligation of the contract altogether. The apparent paradox involved in the reasoning on which the decision was based lends it much interest. The plaintiff sued upon a contract within the statute, which was made in France and not reduced to writing, there being no such requirement in the French law. Under the rules of private international law, the validity of a contract so far as regards its formation is determined by the *lex loci contractus*. All matters pertaining merely to remedy and procedure are governed by the *lex fori*. It is obvious that if the fourth section of the statute should be construed as totally avoiding the contract under the law of England, the plaintiff could recover, for it was valid under French law and its invalidity under English law would be immaterial. If, however, the statute merely affected the mode of proof, the result would be otherwise. Leroux's counsel, though he was suing in an English court, accordingly labored to show that the contract was void by English law. In this he was unsuccessful and his action was therefore defeated.[3]

The Agreement or Memorandum.

The final clause of section four, which is general, applying equally to all contracts within that section, requires that the *agreement,* or some note or memorandum thereof, be in writing. The judicial construction placed upon the word 'agreement' affected the law of simple contracts more radically than any other feature of the statute. In *Wain v. Warlters* (1804),[4] it was declared that the term 'agreement' had a technical

---

[2] 12 C. B. 801, 74 E. C. L. 801.

[3] This decision has been criticised in 1 Juridical Soc. Papers, 283. But its authority seems to have been generally accepted. Wood on Stat. Frauds, § 166; Addison on Contracts, 176; 1 Smith Lead. Cas. (8th Am. ed.), 1027, note to Mostyn *v.* Fabrigas. See also Scudder *v.* Union Nat. Bank, 91 U. S. 406; Hunt *v.* Jones, 12 R. I. 265; Downer *v.* Chesebrough, 36 Conn. 39.

[4] 5 East 10.

STATUTE OF FRAUDS.

meaning, and was not used in the loose or popular sense of undertaking, promise, or even in the sense of consent; but that it imported all the elements which are necessary to make a valid simple contract. It was accordingly held that the writing must contain evidence not only of the promise, but of the consideration which made it valid. The reasoning on which Lord Ellenborough placed this judgment is not satisfactory.

In the first place he was not justified in giving the word a technical meaning merely because Lord Hale, who died before the statute was passed, had been traditionally associated in some way with the act. Every line shows that the act was loosely and carelessly drawn. But if the word 'agreement' was to be treated as a term of art, nothing can be more certain than that it had never before been taken to have the meaning attributed to it in that decision.[5]

The word 'agreement' means no more than the meeting of minds, technically the concord or consensus. The fanciful derivation (*aggregatio mentium*), hit upon by the mediæval lawyers, comported well with this signification. By the universal understanding of mankind, proved by daily and hourly use, 'agreement' means a union of minds, a concurrence of views or intention. This union of minds may result in legal relations or not. If there be a consideration the law clothes the agreement with legal obligation, and this other element is an entirely distinct thing from the mere meeting of the minds. In other words, agreement, instead of including all the elements of a valid contract, if restricted to its technical meaning, implies only consensus and promise, the latter being the sole recognized vehicle of consensus. Every thing done or omitted by the compact of two or more persons is familiarly called an agreement by every one who knows the meaning of our speech.[6]

That the conclusion reached by the court in *Wain v. Warl-*

Chapter XIX

Writing must recite or show a consideration.

Criticism of this rule.

Meaning of 'agreement.'

---

[5] The language of Comyns to which his lordship here referred is taken from the argument of counsel in Reniger *v.* Fagossa, 1 Plowd. 1. It is merely to the effect that where an agreement is executory it must be certain in its terms before it can give rise to an action. See Comyn's Digest, *Agreement*.

[6] See Sage *v.* Wilcox, 6 Conn. 81.

ters ran entirely counter to fundamental English thought, is obvious from the havoc wrought in the field of simple contract by requiring the consideration as well as the promise to be put in writing. The decision was made in a case involving a parol guaranty, but of course extended to all contracts in section four. It necessarily had far-reaching effects and operated with much injustice, especially in the particular field of parol guaranty. It generally happens from the nature of this contract that the consideration is some matter tacitly implied in the relations or circumstances of the parties. It is a future giving of credit, or a continuance of credit already given; or it is the employment or continuance of a person in office. The consideration of a guaranty does not strike the parties as a thing naturally to be stated, like the price in the sale of goods or the wages in a contract of hiring. Hence, the parties to a guaranty content themselves with writing the undertaking agreed upon. This probably accounts for the large number of written guaranties in which the consideration has been omitted or challenged for insufficient statement. In most of them a valid consideration could have been proved had the statute permitted.

It may well be admitted that it is wise to require written evidence of the promise; for the fact that the promise was made and the extent of the obligation assumed are thereby put beyond question. There can be no additional safety secured by requiring the consideration to be also stated. In a system of law which admits that a barleycorn may be a sufficient consideration to support a release for any amount, or that the surrender of a piece of paper worthless for all purposes save possibly to light a cigar, may be sufficient to support a guaranty for ten thousand pounds, it seems wholly unwarranted to defeat a contract based upon consideration merely because the consideration is not stated in the writing.

Reasoning such as this has caused the majority of the American courts to reject the conclusion reached in *Wain v. Warlters*, and subsequently followed in other English cases,[7]

---

[7] Saunders *v.* Wakefield, 4 B. & Ald. 595, 6 E. C. L. 616;. Jenkins *v.* Reynolds, 3 Brod. & B. 14, 7 E. C. L. 328. For the prevailing rule

though in many of the states the question has been set at rest by a more careful wording of the statute.[8]

In England the rule which was laid down in *Wain v. Warlters* having been found to be altogether too rigorous, was relaxed by the Mercantile Law Amendment Act (1856),[1] so as to dispense with the necessity of putting the consideration in the memorandum in all contracts to answer for the debt, default, or miscarriage of another. This was the very class of cases to which the rule had been first applied. No inconvenience seems to have resulted from the requirement of a statement of the consideration in other contracts within the statute.

Rule abrogated by statute.

The Signing.

It is further required that the written agreement or note or memorandum be signed by the party to be charged or his agent. From this it results that the contract may be good without being signed by the party who seeks to enforce it. The situation may thus be presented of a contract being enforceable at the option of one party, but not at the instance of the other, a further reason going to show that contracts failing to comply with the statute are only unenforceable and not void. It will be observed that the statute does not require the memorandum to be subscribed by the party to be charged. It is accordingly settled that although the signature be at the beginning or at the middle of the memorandum, the contract is as binding as if the signature were at the foot, if it be manifest that the party meant to be bound by the contract bearing his name.[2]

Must be signed by party to be charged, or his agent.

Where signature must appear.

---

in America see D'Wolf v. Rabaud, 1 Pet. (U. S.) 501; How v. Kemball, 2 McLean (U. S.) 107; Sage v. Wilcox, 6 Conn. 81, and cases cited in Wood, Statute of Frauds, § 22, p. 61.

[8] Thus, in Virginia, the statute reads as Justice LeBlanc thought that the English statute should have read, "unless the promise or agreement upon which such action shall be brought, or some note or memorandum thereof, shall be in writing." In a number of the states it is expressly provided that the consideration need not be stated. 1 Stimson's Stat. Law, § 140 *et seq.*

[1] 19 & 20 Vict., c. 97, § 3.

[2] Schneider v. Norris, 2 M. & S. 286. Many of the American re-enactments of the statute require that the signature be *subscribed*, a provision which of course makes it necessary for the name to be at the foot of the document.

Mode of signing.

The signature need not be an actual subscription of the party's name. A mark or figure intended as a signature or adopted as such will suffice. It may of course be printed or stamped.[3]

[3] Saunderson *v.* Jackson, 2 B. & P. 238. See also Clason *v.* Bailey, 14 Johns. (N. Y.) 484.

CHAPTER XX.

THE STATUTE OF FRAUDS (CONTINUED).

Collateral Liability of Personal Representatives and of Guarantors and Sureties.

THE first two clauses of the statute are intended for the protection of those who promise to pay for benefits accruing to others or who undertake to answer for damages properly chargeable to some third person; in other words, to protect those who are connected with the transaction out of which liability arises, by means of their promise only.[1] The first clause applies to promises by representatives personally to pay claims primarily chargeable against the estates of their decedents. It will be seen that the situation here contemplated is really only one of the particular cases covered by the more general language of the second clause.

By law the executor or administrator is not liable in his personal capacity and cannot be compelled to pay anything out of his own pocket towards the satisfaction of claims against the estate he represents. But if, in order to save the credit of the deceased, or for other reasons, he chooses to promise, he may make himself personally liable, a consideration being of course necessary before liability can attach. Engagements of this kind are not common. It is no doubt proper that promises evincing an intention to assume such liability should be required to be in writing. The double capacity of the executor or administrator would be an easy source of confusion and misunderstanding, if merely verbal promises were sufficient to charge such person individually. The promise certainly ought to be clearly proved; and the statute wisely makes a written promise alone sufficient.

Before the second clause can apply, there must be a trans-

Chapter XX

Collateral liability.

The promise of the executor or administrator.

[1] Sutton v. Grey, (1894) 1 Q. B. 288.

action involving three parties — a creditor, a debtor, who is himself actually or prospectively liable to the creditor, and the guarantor or surety, who in consideration of some act or forbearance on the part of the creditor makes a promise to be liable for the debt, default, or miscarriage of the principal. The expression " debt, default, or miscarriage " is wide enough to include every species of obligation. Debt is self-explanatory. Default more particularly applies to failures to do acts imposed by covenants or promises; in other words, to such breaches of contract as cannot be remedied in an action of debt. Miscarriage is a somewhat awkward expression which applies to and includes all obligations arising from tortious acts as well as breaches of contract.[2]

It has been found exceedingly difficult to frame a statement that will serve to delimit the exact ground to which the second clause applies. What promises must be in writing under this clause? Perhaps the best clue is found in the term 'collateral liability.' Collateral liability is of two kinds, viz., that of the surety and that of the guarantor. There are different incidents to these two contracts, but they have one feature in common — that is to say, both the surety and guarantor are bound for another person.

Now it is certainly true that all guaranties are within the statute and must be in writing. The same may be said of all true contracts of suretyship; but there are some contracts which are commonly looked upon as engagements of suretyship which are not within the statute, and perplexing questions have arisen as to the application of the statute in regard to such promises. The guarantor always becomes liable by his own separate undertaking in which the principal does not join. It is usually entered into at a different time, either before or after the principal becomes liable, and is often founded upon an altogether different consideration from that which binds the principal. On the other hand, the surety is usually bound at the same time and his promise is supported by the same consideration as the promise of the principal. He is an original promisor and debtor from the beginning.

[2] Kirkham v. Marter, 2 B. & Ald. 613.

Now taking the expression 'collateral liability' as affording the best clue to the application of the second clause, we may lay down the rule that if the promise sued on is a promise to be collaterally responsible for any liability which has already attached or is to attach to another, or which the law imposes primarily upon another, the promise must be in writing.

This enables us to begin the process of exclusion. First, we must eliminate all cases in which the principal obligation is destroyed by the making of the new promise. Thus, suppose B is liable to A: e. g., owes him a debt or has violated a contract or has committed a tort. Now if C promises to pay A one pound in consideration that he release the debt or other cause of action against B, this promise of C is not within the statute and hence need not be in writing. Here the engagement of C is a wholly new contract based upon consideration of the complete satisfaction of the old cause of action against B. When C's promise becomes effective there is no other claim in existence to which it can be collateral. Hence the principle can be deduced that before the second clause of section four can apply, original or principal liability must be a continuing one.[3]

In *Read v. Nash* (1751),[4] it was held that a promise given in consideration that the plaintiff would dismiss a suit against B was an original and independent promise and not within the statute, although the act of the creditor did not amount to a destruction of the right of action, if any existed, against B. But in *Kirkham v. Marter* (1819),[5] where C's promise was to pay damage actually inflicted by B, provided the creditor would forego to sue the latter, the contract was held to be within the statute.

Again, it is plain that where the promise sued on embodies the only liability which can arise out of the original transaction, the statute does not apply; for such promise is original and independent and therefore cannot be collateral to any other liability. The decision in the leading case of *Birkmyr v.*

---

[3] *Goodman v. Chase*, 1 B. & Ald. 297; *Eden v. Chaffee*, 160 Mass. 225.
[4] 1 Wils. C. Pl. 305.
[5] 2 B. & Ald. 613.

Darnell (1705)⁶ was based on this principle. In this case it was said that if two come to a shop and goods are furnished to one, and the other says to the shopkeeper, " let him have the goods; I will be your paymaster or I will see you paid," this is an original undertaking and the promisor shall be treated as the actual purchaser. On the other hand, if the promisor says, " if he does not pay you, I will," this is a collateral undertaking and must be in writing. This rule has been reduced to greater certainty, though possibly not without some violence to principle, by holding that the credit must be extended solely to the promisor in order to keep the statute from applying. Therefore, if any credit at all is given to the purchaser, the promise must be in writing.⁷ In cases of this kind, where one party is said to come in aid to procure credit for another, it is possible for the tradesman to give credit to them both jointly. If this be done, both are liable as debtors and no writing is necessary.⁸

Promise to Indemnify.

It has been said that a promise to indemnify is not a collateral undertaking and therefore not within the statute. Thus, an oral promise by an indorser of a dishonored bill to reimburse a subsequent indorsee for the expenses of a suit, provided the latter will sue the acceptor, is good.⁹

This class of cases has given a great deal of trouble, for it often happens that two antagonistic elements are found in the transaction, one of which would seem to show that the undertaking is independent and therefore not within the statute, while the other would as clearly indicate that the statute applies. Thus, the giving by C to A of a promise to indemnify him for some act of his own may occur in a case where there is an implied obligation on the part of B also to in-

---

⁶ 1 Salk. 27.

⁷ Matson *v.* Wharam (1787), 2 T. R. 80. See Browne on Statute of Frauds, § 197.

⁸ Swift *v.* Pierce, 13 Allen (Mass.) 136; Gibbs *v.* Blanchard, 15 Mich. 292; Wainwright *v.* Straw, 15 Vt. 215; Matthews *v.* Milton, 4 Yerg. (Tenn.) 576.

⁹ Bullock *v.* Lloyd, 2 C. & P. 119, 12 E. C. L. 53. See generally, Thomas *v.* Cook, 8 B. & C. 728, 15 E. C. L. 333; Browne on Statute of Frauds, § 158 *et seq.*

STATUTE OF FRAUDS. 187

demnify him for the same act. As we have already seen, a promise to satisfy an obligation which is already valid as against another is almost necessarily within the statute. These two antagonistic factors have led to confusion and conflict.

Thus, in *Thomas v. Cook* (1828),[1] B was indebted to A; C, at the request of D, and upon the latter's special promise to save him harmless, became surety with B in a bond to A. Subsequently C became liable on the bond, and B, his principal, thereby became bound to reimburse him. C sued D upon the special promise made by the latter. It was held that he could recover. In *Green v. Cresswell* (1839)[2] a different conclusion was reached. But the later decision has been overruled in England,[3] and the prevailing rule both in that country and in America is in accordance with *Thomas v. Cook*.[4]

These decisions justify the conclusion that in order to be within the statute the special promise of the guarantor must create a new liability collateral to some liability already existing or intended to be raised, and that the new liability must be intended primarily to discharge that liability.

Another distinction to be noted is that the statute applies only to promises made to the creditor and does not extend to promises made by the third person to the debtor directly. Thus, if B is indebted to A and C contracts with B to pay off this obligation, the contract need not be in writing.[5] Such situation, though apparently within the language of the statute, certainly appears not to be within either its spirit or its purpose. If C contracts with B to pay off a debt owing by the latter, it must be upon a consideration moving from B to C, and such contract is no more likely to be subject to the danger legislated against than other simple contracts which are left out of the statute.

---

[1] 8 B. & C. 728, 15 E. C. L. 333.
[2] 10 Ad. & El. 453.
[3] Wildes *v.* Dudlow, L. R. 19 Eq. 198; Cripps *v.* Hartnoll, 2 B. & S. 697, 110 E. C. L. 697, on appeal 4 B. & S. 414, 116 E. C. L. 414.
[4] See Tighe *v.* Morrison, 116 N. Y. 263.
[5] Barker *v.* Bucklin, 2 Den. (N. Y.) 45. See Browne, Statute of Frauds, § 166*b*.

Chapter XX

Difficulty of application.

General principle.

Promise made to debtor by third person.

It will be seen from the foregoing remarks that the courts, especially in modern times, have exercised the greatest ingenuity in order to enable them to withdraw from the operation of this clause of the statute as many contracts as possible. It seems strange that it did not occur to the courts, when the interpretation of the statute was yet open, that the words "to answer for the debt, default, or miscarriage of another" contemplated only claims already in existence at the time the collateral promise is made. It will be noticed that all personal engagements by the representatives of a deceased person must necessarily be collateral to existing claims. Strong reasons may be advanced for believing that the succeeding clause contemplated the same situation. The reason of the statute certainly does not apply with as much force where the guaranty is given before the principal obligation is incurred as where the collateral promise is made afterwards; for the guaranty almost invariably draws the consideration, e. g., the credit, from the promisee.

Statute probably intended to apply only to promises collateral to existing liability.

Recognition of the distinction just stated would have made the clause in question vastly less radical than it actually proved to be. Lord Mansfield had the acumen to perceive that the statute did not apply to any case where the promise sued on induced the creation of the principal obligation.[6] Upon further consideration, however, this distinguished judge found that the law was already settled differently and that the rule was too firmly fixed to be shaken.[7] At a later day Buller, J., had occasion to lament that the question was no longer open for consideration.[8]

Opinion of Lord Mansfield.

An observation may, in conclusion, be made in regard to the general purpose and effect of this clause of the statute. That the collateral contract of guaranty or suretyship may well be subjected to restrictions all will admit; though as a matter of fact, communities living under the civil law seem not to have been impressed with this fact. In the ordinary

General observations on policy of the second clause of section 4.

---

[6] Mawbrey v. Cunningham, cited in Jones v. Cooper, 1 Cowp. 228.
[7] Jones v. Cooper, 1 Cowp. 227.
[8] Matson v. Wharam, 2 T. R. 80.

See language of Parker, C. J., in Perley v. Spring, 12 Mass. 297, afterwards disapproved in Cahill v. Bigelow, 18 Pick. (Mass.) 369.

simple contract where the promisor is bound by a good consideration and himself gets the benefit of the contract, if there be any (and of this he is the exclusive judge), there can be no sense in requiring written evidence. The thing delivered or act done or the counter-promise (in mutual promises) is generally capable of easy proof, and is not more likely to be bolstered up by perjury than any other cause of action. In suretyship and guaranty, on the other hand, the liability of the defendant is founded wholly upon the alleged promise, and he cannot always fully protect himself against a misrepresentation of language by an appeal to the facts out of which the main liability grew. He may be held merely upon proof that the sale was made on his credit or that he promised to pay if the purchaser should not. When the guaranty is given after the sale, a new consideration is indeed necessary, but it may consist of a real or pretended forbearance on the part of the vendor.

At a period when neither party could testify in court, and the facts could not therefore be thoroughly sifted in order to ascertain the truth of the respective claims of the plaintiff and defendant, and when large interests might depend upon the testimony of an apparently disinterested but really corrupt witness, this situation appealed powerfully to the minds of judges and legislators. Accordingly promises by which one person became obligated to answer for the debt of another were put within the protection of the statute. But though the idea underlying the enactment may have been a sound one, the unfortunate manner in which it was framed has led to such a vast amount of litigation that one must doubt whether the benefits resulting from it are at all commensurate with the price paid.

The fact that the courts have seen fit to take out of its operation so many cases where the danger of perjury is just as great as in the cases left within it, perhaps evinces a judicial feeling that the protection to public morality and individual honesty afforded by the statute is a fanciful and remote benefit; while, on the other hand, it is obvious that the enforcement of contracts honestly made is one of the immediate ends of the administration of law, and this whether the contract be written or not. On one occasion the late Sir George Jessel said: "If there is one thing which more than another public policy requires, it is that men of full age and competent understanding shall have the utmost liberty of contracting, and that their contracts, when entered into freely and voluntarily, shall be held sacred and shall be enforced by courts of justice. Therefore you have this paramount public policy to consider — that you are not lightly to interfere with this freedom of contract." [9]

Promises Supported by Consideration of Marriage.

The third clause in section four embraces "agreements made upon consideration of marriage," and, as we have already stated, this language is construed to mean all agreements, except agreements to marry, made upon consideration of marriage.[1] Agreements to marry are certainly as much within the evil legislated against as any form of contract can possibly be; but it must have been seen that to apply the statute to such mutual promises would virtually outlaw actions for breaches of the marriage promise. Two confiding lovers can hardly be expected to reduce their vows to writing with a view to its future use in a suit for damages.[2] Mutual promises of marriage were accordingly taken out of the operation of the statute by a decision in *Harrison v. Cage* (1697),[3] and other unreported contemporary decisions. These rulings were based upon the theory that the "statute intended only agreements to pay marriage portions." Lord Holt, it was said, had repeatedly held to this effect.[4]

Mutual promises of marriage held not to be within the statute.

Other bilateral agreements involving promise of marriage left within the statute.

Notwithstanding mutual promises to marry were thus taken out of the operation of the statute, the bilateral contract composed of a promise to marry given for a counter-promise

---

[9] Printing, etc., Registering Co. v. Sampson, L. R. 19 Eq. 462.

[1] Philpott v. Wallet, 3 Lev. 65; Harrison v. Cage, 1 Ld. Raym. 386.

[2] "It would be imputing to the legislature too great an absurdity to suppose that they had enacted that all our courtships, to be valid, must be in writing." Withers v. Richardson, 5 T. B. Mon. (Ky.) 94.

[3] 1 Ld. Raym. 386; Cork v. Baker, 1 Stra. 34; Short v. Stotts, 58 Ind. 29.

[4] Harrison v. Cage, 1 Ld. Raym. 388.

STATUTE OF FRAUDS.

to do some act other than to marry was left within its operation. This was illogical, for the two bilateral engagements have exactly the same character. To illustrate, contracts involving promises to marry may take one of the following forms: (*a*) A agrees to settle property on C if she marries him. She accordingly does so. Here A's promise is based upon the consideration of marriage and must be in writing. (*b*) A promises to marry C and in consideration thereof she promises to marry him (mutual promises to marry). Each promise is supported by the counter-promise, and the contract is not based upon consideration of actual marriage. Hence the contract is not within the statute and no writing is necessary.[5]

Again, (*c*) A, being interested in the marriage of B and C, promises the latter to pay her a sum of money, in return for which promise, or "in consideration" of which promise, she gives a counter-promise to A to the effect that she will marry B. In this case there is a perfect bilateral contract between A and C independent of any mutual promises to marry that may exist between B and C. The contract here supposed may also be made between the parties whose marriage is contemplated. Thus, A may promise to convey land to C, in return for her promise to marry him. Such a contract is a perfect bilateral engagement, yet it is not made up of mutual promises to marry, nor is it founded upon consideration of actual marriage.

Now, it is plain that as far as principle is concerned there can be no difference, under the wording of the statute, between bilateral contracts in forms (*b*) and (*c*). Both are within the statute or both out of it. If the early construction made in *Philpott v. Wallet*[6] had prevailed, both classes of engagements would have remained within the statute, while if the dictum of Lord Holt, reported in *Harrison v. Cage* (1697),[7] had been faithfully adhered to, both forms of the

Chapter XX

Illustrations.

Discussion.

---

[5] In the language of Prof. Bishop, "One's promise to marry another is not and cannot be in consideration of marriage, since until after the contract has been fulfilled, there is no marriage." Bishop on Marriage, etc., § 212.

[6] 3 Lev. 65.

[7] 1 Ld. Raym. 386. The proposition that "the statute intended

bilateral contract might have been taken out of its operation. This, however, did not happen. The courts did not perceive that all bilateral contracts are alike and that consequently a promise to pay money or settle property given for a promise to marry was exactly like a promise to marry given for a counter-promise to marry, in the respect that neither is based upon the consideration of marriage. The validity of the contract arises, as in all bilateral contracts, out of the mutuality of the promises.

Marriage usually made a condition in marriage contracts.

It will be observed that contracts in (c) do not often arise. Where promises to settle property or pay money are given to induce a marriage, the contract is usually and naturally put into the unilateral form, and the contract is very likely to show that the consummation of marriage is intended to be both the consideration and a condition of the promise. Wherever this happens the contract comes within (a), above mentioned, and, under all the authorities, is governed by the statute. The result has been that, in practice, no distinction has been drawn between contracts in (a) and (c), and mutual promises to marry thus form the only exception to the third clause of the fourth section of the statute.[8]

American rule.

In America very many, perhaps a majority, of the statutes adopting the English Statute of Frauds provide that every agreement, promise, or undertaking made upon consideration of marriage, except mutual promises to marry, must be in writing.[9] This language, of course, determines that contracts in (c) are within the statute. The fact that it has been thought proper to make an express exception in the case of mutual promises perhaps shows a feeling that, notwithstand-

only agreements to pay marriage portions" would, it seems, have excluded all forms of the bilateral contract from the operation of the statute, since the agreement to pay a marriage portion is usually, if not always, a unilateral promise based on the executed consideration of marriage.

[8] Montacute v. Maxwell (1720), 1 P. Wms. 618; De Beil v. Thomson, 3 Beav. 469; Coverdale v. Eastwood, L. R. 15 Eq. 121; Ungley v. Ungley, 5 Ch. D. 887; Brenner v. Brenner, 48 Ind. 263; Henry v. Henry, 27 Ohio St. 121; White v. Bigelow, 154 Mass. 593; Brown v. Conger, 8 Hun (N. Y.) 625; Matter of Willoughby, 11 Paige (N. Y.) 257; Adams v. Adams, 17 Oregon 247.

[9] Matter of Willoughby, 11 Paige (N. Y.) 257; Stimson's Am. Stat. Law, § 4140.

ing the English decisions to the contrary, mutual promises to marry are after all within the statute. This may be the correct view.

Chapter XX

Contracts for Sale of Land.

In regard to the fourth clause of the fourth section of the Statute of Frauds, which applies to contracts or sales of land, tenements, or hereditaments, or any interest therein, it may be observed that the law governing the sale and transfer of land belongs to the subject of conveyancing and will not be treated here. Generally, it may be said, the classification is here made along the line of division between real and personal property, one of the most fundamental seams known to the common law. Theoretically it would seem that here, at least, the lines of demarcation between the contracts required to be in writing and those not required so to be would be easy of determination. This language, however, opens the question of the boundary line between real and personal property, and it has proved a very debatable one. Into its details we shall not enter.

Line of classification.

Contracts Not Performable Within One Year.

The last clause in the fourth section of the statute applies to "contracts not to be performed within one year from the making thereof." In regard to this provision we have already observed the ingenuity exercised by the courts in limiting the application of it to the narrowest possible compass. As suggested by Lord Holt in *Smith v. Westall* (1697),[1] the obvious intention of the statute is to dispense with the necessity of trusting the memory of witnesses after the lapse of a year.

The clause is necessarily prospective. "Not to be performed within one year" is the criterion by which the necessity of a writing is to be judged. The court must consequently determine the validity of the contract at the time of the making of it and cannot suffer its validity to depend upon an uncertain or contingent event thereafter to happen. In *Peter v. Compton* (1692),[2] it was held that a contract to pay a sum

Clause prospective.

---

[1] 1 Ld. Raym. 317.   [2] Skin. 353.

of money upon marriage was good though the marriage did not take place for nine years. Lord Holt's dissent was untenable. It could not be permitted that a contract should remain suspended, subject to be rendered good or bad by retroaction, upon the happening of a contingency. If a contract not in writing is good when made, it is good until the right of action on it is barred by limitations. Conversely, if the agreement is clearly meant to last beyond the year, it is not taken out of the statute by the fact that it may be ended before the lapse of a year.[3]

Validity of contract determined at time it is made.

Sales of Goods.

The seventeenth section of the Statute of Frauds includes only one sort of contracts, viz., contracts for the sale of any goods, wares, or merchandise for the price of ten pounds or upwards; but this class of engagements is a large and important one.

Much trouble was experienced in applying this statute to contracts for making and providing goods not in existence or not complete at the time of the contract. It was often difficult to say whether such engagement was a sale of goods or a contract for work and labor. To solve this it was necessary to determine at what precise point of time the work and labor merged into the product. Lord Tenterden's Act was directed to this difficulty. This act provided that the statute should extend to "all contracts for the sale of goods of the value of ten pounds and upwards, notwithstanding the goods may be intended to be delivered at some future time, or may not, at the time of such contract, be actually made, procured, or provided, or fit or ready for delivery, or some act may be requisite for the making or completing thereof, or rendering the same fit for delivery."[4]

Contract for purchase of goods which are to be made to order.

Lord Tenterden's Act.

This enactment also changed the test from 'price' to the 'value' of the goods — an alteration evidently not in the direction of clearness. Price is determined by the terms of the sale; value may depend upon altogether different considera-

'Value.'

[3] Davey v. Shannon, 4 Ex. D. 81.
[4] 9 Geo. IV., c. 14.

STATUTE OF FRAUDS.

tions. The Sale of Goods Act re-enacted with some modifications the seventeenth section of the Statute of Frauds and embodied the substance of Lord Tenterden's Act.[5]

Chapter XX

The memorandum now required is a memorandum of the 'contract.' In the fourth section of the Statute of Frauds the term 'agreement' was interpreted to mean contract. In the seventeenth section 'bargain' was used, being evidently intended to convey the same import. In contracts of bargain and sale, the price, if agreed upon, must be put into the memorandum, for it is then a part of the contract. If the price is not fixed the law will determine the value of the goods upon a *quantum valebant*. If no consideration (price) is set forth in the contract, the law will presume a promise to pay the reasonable value and the agreement will be enforced; but if the proof shows that the parties did in fact agree upon a price, and the contract shows that such price is not stated in the written contract, it cannot be enforced.[6]

Memorandum.

Quantum valebant.

Place of Statute of Frauds in Modern Contract Law.

Having thus considered at some length the manner in which the Statute of Frauds has affected English contract law, we are impressed with the fact that this piece of legislative interference has contributed greatly to make the subject of simple parol contracts complex and difficult. This is no

Theoretical difficulties presented by Statute of Frauds.

---

[5] 56 & 57 Vict., c. 71, § 4. This enactment is as follows:

(1) A contract for the sale of any goods of the value of £10 or upwards shall not be enforceable by action unless the buyer shall accept part of the goods so sold, and actually receive the same, or give something in earnest to bind the contract, or in part payment, or unless some note or memorandum in writing of the contract be made and signed by the party to be charged or his agent in that behalf.

(2) The provisions of this section apply to every such contract, notwithstanding that the goods may be intended to be delivered at some future time, or may not at the time of such contract be actually made, procured, or provided, or fit or ready for delivery, or some act may be requisite for the making or completing thereof, or rendering the same fit for delivery.

(3) There is an acceptance of goods within the meaning of this section when the buyer does an act in relation to the goods which recognizes a pre-existing contract of sale, whether there be an acceptance in performance of the contract or not.

[6] Anson on Contracts, 73; Hoadly v. M'Laine, 10 Bing. 482, 25 E. C. L. 208; Ide v. Stanton, 15 Vt. 685.

doubt partly due to the unscientific classification adopted in the statute and the loose manner in which it was framed. Hardly a single historical or scientific line of cleavage in the whole field of contract law was followed. Even the distinction between real and personal property is a conception which belongs to the law of succession and not to the law of contracts.

Undoubtedly much of the difficulty encountered was inherent in the nature of the enactment and could not be escaped by any amount of legal acumen. The object aimed at was to prevent perjury. The method adopted was to put entirely beyond the aid of the law such transactions as seemed likely to be infected with it. It was inevitable that an enactment conceived from a point of view so far removed from the actual principles of contractual liability should cause difficulty in its application.

English contract law otherwise simple.

Apart from the confusion and difficulty introduced into our contract law by the Statute of Frauds, no subject could be simpler than the modern English law of simple contract, in which liability is based upon the elements of agreement, consideration, and promise. This simplicity was the result of a natural process of evolution. For ages the courts had carefully nurtured the expanding principles of contractual liability, moulding them to fit the needs of a slowly growing society. The Statute of Frauds was in its nature reactionary. It radically interfered with the lines of natural growth in contract law. It made form a necessary element in many of our most common transactions and thus ran counter to a deep principle of growth in this department of law.

Statute in a measure reactionary.

A temporary makeshift in evolution of contract law.

The Statute of Frauds is therefore essentially and necessarily, in some of its features at least, a temporary phenomenon in the evolution of contract law. Born of a desire to prevent the imposition of liability by means of perjured testimony, the need for it must decrease as the means of discovering and punishing perjury are increased. This danger has undoubtedly been greatly lessened by alterations made during the last fifty years in the law of evidence. Parties are now admitted as competent witnesses in their own cause, and, as observed by a master of modern contract law, "this must be a great obstacle to charging persons with contracts which they have never made; while, on the other hand, it must be acknowledged to give them a dangerous facility for getting rid of those which they have made. But, on the whole, by bringing the evidence nearer to the issue and more within the knowledge of the witness, it cannot fail to deter from perjury, inasmuch as it thereby aggravates its enormity and facilitates its detection. And so it may be expected to obviate much of the necessity which may be supposed formerly to have given rise to the statute. It would be a curious matter for reflection if perjury, which was formerly met by restrictions on evidence, should be found eventually to be more effectually prevented by the removal of restrictions."[7]

<small>Effect of statutes making parties competent as witnesses.</small>

These remarks suggest the conclusion that legislation like the Statute of Frauds possibly belongs only to that anomalous period in the evolution of English law, now past, when parties were incompetent to testify in their own behalf. This view is supported by the experience of those nations who live under the civil law. In the time of Justinian it was not essential that the terms of any agreement should be reduced to writing,[8] except in the case of a sale where the parties agreed that the contract should not be binding until reduced to writing.[9] At the same time, with few exceptions, the only grounds for excluding witnesses were mental incapacity and conviction of crime.[1] Is it possible that the English-speaking people are so much more deeply tainted with a proclivity for lying, that a policy so radically different must be pursued? Such suggestion is manifestly to be put aside.

<small>Roman law.</small>

The moment we distinctly realize that the object of judicial investigation is the discovery of truth, it becomes clear that the wholesale exclusion of witnesses because of antecedent incredibility due to interest, admits of no justification. Such exclusionary rules being abolished, it is obvious that it is no

---

[7] Statute of Frauds as It Affects the Law of Contracts, a paper read before the Juridical Society (1856) by S. M. Leake. See 1 Jur. Soc. Papers 289.

[8] C. 4, 21, 15; C. 4, 22, 1.
[9] See W. A. Hunter, Roman Law, 3d ed., 1054.
[1] *Ib.*, 1055, 1056.

Volume II

Abolition of exclusionary rules removes need for the statute.

longer necessary to outlaw agreements made in good faith and based upon sufficient consideration, merely because they are not in writing. The manner in which the courts have constantly limited the application of the Statute of Frauds, and this, too, prior to the abolition of incompetence for interest, shows in what direction legal sense leans.[2]

Criticism not applicable to laws of inheritance and sales.

It should be added, however, that these suggestions as to the Statute of Frauds have nothing to do with its bearing upon the law of testamentary succession, conveyancing, and possibly bargain and sale. These transactions involve the transmission of title to real or personal property, and they necessarily rest upon considerations of reason and policy very different from those which underlie the assumption of contractual liability by means of a promise based upon consideration.

[2] It is perhaps worth observing that in modern times the general diffusion of knowledge makes it much easier than formerly for the parties to a contract to put their engagement in writing. Notwithstanding this, the nations who derive their laws from the Roman system have been slow to make requirements as to the form of contracts Almost the only test is based, like the seventeenth section of our Statute of Frauds, upon the value of the thing which is the subject-matter of the contract. Thus, the French Code, §§ 1341-48, requires an instrument in writing when the subject-matter exceeds the sum or value of one hundred and fifty francs. The Italian Code fixes the limit at five hundred lire. Moreover, sales of real property, leases for more than nine years, grants of annuities, and compromises (§ 1314) must be written. Prussian law requires a writing where the value of the subject-matter exceeds fifty thalers. Landrecht, Pt. I, title 5, § 131. Among all these nations commercial contracts are specially excepted from provisions like the foregoing. See Pollock on Contracts, App. note E.

CHAPTER XXI

DUTIES IN THE NATURE OF DEBT.

WE now turn to the consideration of implied and quasi-contracts. Much confusion exists in the professional mind concerning the duties grouped under these heads. The reason for this is undoubtedly to be found in the fact that the subject has been approached from the wrong direction. The unsatisfactory state of the law in this field abundantly justifies us in taking a new cut.

The word 'contract' usually conveys to the modern mind the conception of an assumptual tie, that is, of obligation incurred by promise. This has been brought about by the extraordinary extension of assumpsit by means of the fiction of implied promise into fields where the remedy did not by nature belong. The conception of assumptual tie has thus overlaid the older conception of contractual duty which is embodied in the common-law debt. Inasmuch as this occultation of debt is due to procedural causes and is not at all implicated with fundamental principle, it follows that in order to ascertain the true basis of liability in the field where this anomalous extension of assumpsit has occurred, we must brush away the artificial superstructure and bring to light the conception which is here really at the root of legal growth. Viewed as a natural and necessary extension of the conception of contractual duty (debt), the so-called implied and quasi-contracts fall into an harmonious system; viewed as an extension of the conception of assumptual obligation, they are for the most part anomalous and in plainest violation of fundamental principle. Thus, not to cavil over the fact that in all implied and quasi-contracts the promise is merely a figment of the legal mind, we observe that in this field neither assumptual capacity on the part of the person on whom the duty is imposed nor his actual consent is a necessary condition to the creation of

Chapter XXI

Conception of assumptual tie.

Occultation of the conception of debt.

The quasi-contracts embody an extension of the conception of debt.

Early limit of duty to pay for benefit conferred.

the contract. This fact is alone sufficient to warn us of the futility of attempting to bring these duties into harmony with the theory which underlies assumpsit. Accordingly let us put aside all that we have thus far learned about the assumptual tie and transport ourselves to the world of simple legal duty in which our early contract law had its being.

That system of remedial law must be pronounced defective indeed where a plaintiff cannot obtain relief upon such facts as were involved in *Young v. Ashburnham* (1587).[1] There an innkeeper supplied lodging to a "gentleman of quality." The value of the accommodation was not agreed upon and therefore was not reduced to certainty; nor had the defendant made any express promise. Debt accordingly was declared not to be maintainable, and assumpsit upon a quantum count was as yet unknown.

The twofold extension of legal theory.

This defect in the law was soon remedied by a twofold development of legal theory. In the first place, the transaction contemplated was treated as raising a legal duty in the nature of a debt; and in the second place, a fictitious promise to satisfy this duty was implied by law. This enabled the plaintiff to maintain indebitatus assumpsit for the recovery of such compensation as he was reasonably entitled to. That the duty now enforced was *in consimili casu* with debt is obvious.[2]

---

[1] 3 Leon 161. "Upon the evidence given for the plaintiff, the case appeared to be this, that the said Young was an innholder in a great town in the county of Sussex, where the sessions used to be holden; and that the defendant was a gentleman of quality in the county there; and he, in going to the sessions, used to lodge in the house of said Young, and there took his lodging and his diet for himself, his servants, and horses; upon which the debt in demand grew; but the said Young was not at any price in certain with the defendant, nor was there ever any agreement made betwixt them for the same. It was said by Anderson, Chief Justice, that upon that matter, an action of debt did not lie. And therefore afterwards, the jury gave a verdict for the defendant."

[2] In course of time the duty to compensate for a benefit conferred in cases like the one referred to has been so far assimilated to the common-law debt, that the action of debt is permitted, in at least some jurisdictions, to be maintained upon the duty. Smith *v.* Lowell First Cong. Meetinghouse, 8 Pick. (Mass.) 178; Van Deusen *v.* Blum, 18 Pick. (Mass.) 229.

And it is a rule of pleading in modern times that a count in debt upon a *quantum meruit* can be

The principle underlying this extension of the conception of contractual liability may be stated as follows: Where the circumstances of any particular transaction show that a benefit has been conferred by one person on another, either in the form of service done or goods supplied, and it further appears that such benefit was conferred at the request of the person benefited, or with his consent, express or implied, the law will impose a duty to pay for such benefit. The duty is of a contractual nature in the same sense that the common-law debt is a contract, and indeed it would perhaps be well to say that it is a true debt.

Chapter XXI

Duty to pay for benefit conferred.

The law is here said to create or imply the contract on the facts of the case. One who procures another to labor for him, or who obtains supplies from a tradesman, must answer for the value of the benefit conferred. The transaction makes the contract. The situation here conceived is usually described in terminology peculiar to assumpsit. The act of employment or the acceptance of the tradesman's goods operates, it is said, as an assumpsit *per se*. In other words, a promise is implied by law. But this figment of legal reasoning, the implied promise, exists solely for procedural purposes and is wholly aside from the real ground of liability.

Contract implied on the facts of the case.

Take a very simple illustration of the implied contract, the situation, for instance, which arises where a person requests a livery keeper to furnish a coupé for his use, which is accordingly supplied. The reason why the law imposes a duty to pay for the use of the vehicle, notwithstanding no express promise to this effect is made, is obvious. The only inference that an intelligent mind can draw from this transaction is that the party furnishing the coupé expects to be paid, and the other, knowing this, gives consent to this condition by the very act of user.

Why the law imposes the duty.

The contract here evidently springs from the facts of the case. For this reason the books tell us duties of this kind are contracts implied as of fact. It is further pointed out that while the ordinary assumptual contract is proved by words

joined with a count upon a debt due by specialty. Union Cotton Manufactory *v.* Lobdell, 13 Johns. (N. Y.) 462.

of promise, the contract implied as of fact is proved by the conduct of the parties. From this very plain and manifest fact the conclusion has been erroneously drawn that the express assumptual contract and contracts or debts implied as of fact differ only in their mode of proof.[3] But this is a very grave mistake. The assumptual contract and the contractual duty imposed by law differ fundamentally in legal principle as well as in the mode of proving them. Nowhere do we find a more conspicuous illustration of the truth that things that are similar are not the same. In one case the duty springs from the obligation of promise; in the other the duty is imposed by law in the absence of promise.

The erroneous notion just referred to sometimes appears in the form of a proposition to the effect that in contracts implied as of fact the promise on which the action of assumpsit is permitted to be maintained is an inference of fact and is merely proved by circumstantial evidence.[4] But clearly the promise is an inference of law. This is indubitably shown by the fact that indebitatus is the only form of assumpsit which can be maintained upon the implied promise. If there is an actual promise proved either directly or by circumstantial evidence, special assumpsit is the proper remedy.

Thus if an express contract is made for the performance of service at a specified salary for a particular period, and after the termination of such period the service is continued with the consent of the employer, the law infers that the same contract is renewed for a like period and upon similar terms. The contract here proved is an express one though it is established purely by circumstantial evidence, and the plaintiff must sue in special assumpsit to recover compensation for the extra

---

[3] "The terms express contracts and contracts implied in law are used to indicate not a distinction in principles of contract, but a difference in the character of the evidence by which a simple contract is proved." Keener on Quasi-Contracts, 5.

"Both express and implied contracts are founded upon the actual agreement of the parties, the only distinction between them being as to the mode of proof or evidence by which they are substantiated." 2 Greenl. on Evid., § 102.

[4] "The promise is implied not as a matter of law, but as a matter of fact." Clark on Contracts, 753.

DUTIES IN THE NATURE OF DEBT.   203

service. He cannot recover on a *quantum meruit*, but is limited by the rate of payment fixed in the original contract.[5]

But though we can never say concerning transactions of the kind now under consideration that the promise is implied as of fact, it is perfectly proper to say that the contract or contractual duty arises from the facts of the case, or that the contract is implied as of fact, the idea being that the parties have shown an agreement (not a promise) by their conduct.[6]

We have so far assumed the coexistence of three factors — 1. The conferring of a benefit; 2. That the person on whom the duty to compensate is imposed has sufficient legal capacity to have bound himself by a promise if such had been given; and, 3. That he gives a legal assent to the conferring of the benefit. Thus, in the case where a coupé is supposed to be supplied, the hirer is of full legal status and by his request and actual conduct shows a consent to profit by the use of another's property. The presence of the two elements, consent and assumptual capacity, brings the duty in question into almost complete harmony with the theory of assumpsit and supplies the reason why such contracts are usually viewed as implied promises (assumpsits) rather than as debts.

But that we are on the right track in classifying them as debts, or duties in the nature of debt, rather than as assumpsits, becomes manifest when we proceed further; for nothing is better established than the principle that neither capacity nor consent on the part of the person on whom the duty is imposed is at all necessary as a prerequisite condition to the imposition of the duty.

Thus, infants, though they have no capacity to bind themselves by an express assumpsit, are nevertheless liable in indebitatus for a benefit conferred, provided it represents what

Chapter XXI

Essential elements in quasi-contract.

Assumptual capacity not essential.

Liability of infant for necessaries.

---

[5] Wallace *v.* Floyd, 29 Pa. St. 184; Taylor *v.* Lambertville, 43 N. J. Eq. 107; Lalande *v.* Aldrich, 41 La. Ann. 307.
[6] In the Six Carpenters Case ('1610), 8 Coke 147a, it was said concerning the case of the tailor who received goods to be made into a robe: "The putting of the cloth to the tailor to be made into a gown, is sufficient evidence to prove the said special contract, for the law implies it."

the law deems a necessary.[7] In such case, as is well known, the infant is not bound to pay the price that may have been agreed upon, where an agreement was in fact made. He can be held only for the actual and reasonable value of the service rendered or goods supplied.[8] Insane[9] and drunken persons are upon the same footing as infants in respect to their liability to compensate for necessaries. The law makes the contract for them, or at least imposes the legal duty on the particular facts of the case.

It is true that where an express promise to pay for necessaries is made by a person who knows what he is doing, as by an infant of discreet years, the courts have been accustomed to enforce the promise to pay, taking the amount agreed upon as being *prima facie* just.[1] But it is manifest that the duty enforced in these cases is imposed by law on the facts of the case and does not have its source in the obligation of the infant's promise. The practice mentioned is accordingly to be sanctioned only for reasons of convenience. The infant of discreet years who is supplied with necessaries, by the appropriation thereof may be said to evince an assent to the contract which the law makes for him. This cannot be said of very young children and of lunatics, for these are wholly devoid of power to give an assent upon which the law would predicate an assumptual obligation.

Not only will the law, as in the case of lunatics, impose a duty to compensate for necessaries without the affirmative assent of the debtor; it sometimes goes further and imposes a duty to compensate for articles furnished against the positive will of the person on whom the duty is laid. Thus a delinquent husband is bound to pay for necessaries furnished his wife,[2] and in some jurisdictions parents can likewise be held

---

[7] "The obligation of an infant to pay for necessaries actually furnished him does not seem to arise out of contract in the legal sense of the term, but out of a transaction of a quasi-contractual nature; for it may be imposed on an infant too young to understand the nature of a contract." Gregory v. Lee, 64 Conn. 407, 413; Trainer v. Trumbull, 141 Mass. 527.

[8] Earle v. Reed, 10 Met. (Mass.) 387; Trainer v. Trumbull, 141 Mass. 530.

[9] *In re* Rhodes, 44 Ch. D. 94, 107.

[1] Gay v. Ballou, 4 Wend. (N. Y.) 403.

[2] Read v. Legard, 6 Exch. 636.

for necessaries furnished to their children.³ The fact that the husband or parent is unaware that the necessaries are being supplied or that he knows of it and forbids it is wholly immaterial. Inasmuch as infancy is no impediment to the imposition of a contractual duty where the law sees fit to create it, the fact that a husband has not reached his majority is no defense when he is sued for necessaries furnished his wife.⁴

Chapter XXI

The reader will perceive that when viewed from the standpoint of legal duty, all of these cases make up a homogeneous mass of contractual duties in the nature of debt, and are not to be distinguished from each other, the principle of liability being the same in all of them. But when viewed from the standpoint of assumptual obligation they fall into two distinct classes, viz., the so-called implied contracts (contracts implied as of fact) and the quasi-contracts (contracts implied as of law). Implied contracts comprise duties imposed by law upon one person to compensate for a benefit conferred by another, where the circumstances indicate that the parties expected the benefit to be paid for, and where it also appears that the beneficiary had capacity to bind himself by an express promise if he had given one. The term 'quasi-contract' is restricted to those duties to pay money or to compensate for benefits conferred where capacity and assent to the imposition of the duty, or either of these elements, are wanting in the person on whom the duty is imposed. This division of debts and duties in the nature of debts into implied contracts and quasi-contracts is subject to criticism for the reason that, though conceived wholly from the standpoint of assumptual theory, it is nevertheless used for the purpose of dividing non-assumptual duties. Hence it is neither fruitful nor logical.

Implied contract and quasi-contract distinguished.

Criticism of this mode of division.

The result is that the line of classification in this branch of the law appears to be improperly drawn. No objection,

---

Husband liable for burial expenses of wife. Cunningham v. Reardon, 98 Mass. 538.

³ Gilley v. Gilley, 79 Me. 292; Van Valkinburgh v. Watson, 13 Johns. (N. Y.) 480. *Contra*, Kelley v. Davis, 49 N. H. 187.

⁴ Chapman v. Hughes, 61 Miss. 339. An infant husband is liable for debts of the wife contracted before marriage. Roach v. Quick, 9 Wend. (N. Y.) 238.

Volume II

Scope of 'quasi-contract.'

however, can be urged against the use of the term quasi-contract provided it is given the proper scope. When rightly used the term is a very satisfactory and even a happy expression. The conception which underlies it belongs to universal jurisprudence and the term itself is adopted from the Roman law.

Broadly speaking, the term quasi-contract is applicable to all contractual duties which are not enforceable by special assumpsit or by the action of debt. If the action of debt can be maintained on the duty, we have a true debt; if special assumpsit will lie, we have a perfect assumptual contract.

Judgments, Customary and Statutory Duties.

Recognition of this distinction makes it necessary to exclude from the category of quasi-contract some duties which have commonly been brought within it. This leads us to say a word here about judgments and about customary and statutory duties.

Debts of record.

In view of the almost complete occultation of the conception of debt in modern law, it is not surprising that debts of record (judgments and recognizances) should be classed as quasi-contracts. When we look at these duties from the standpoint of assumptual obligation, nothing is more obvious than the fact that they are not contracts. Consequently it is imagined that they must be called quasi-contracts. But in so doing there is a suppression of the class to which the duties really belong. Judgments are debts;[5] and as debts are and always have been called contracts (indeed they were the first contracts known to the law), there is no necessity for denying to judgments the right to be called contracts if we only remember that they are not the same kind of contract as that in which obligation results from promise.

The question whether judgments are contracts has frequently arisen in construing statutes. In *O'Brien v. Young* (1884),[6] it was held that a judgment was not a "contract or

---

[5] Morse *v.* Toppan, 3 Gray (Mass.) 412.
[6] 95 N. Y. 428.

obligation" within the meaning of a statute reducing the rate of interest. In *Gutta Percha, etc., Mfg. Co. v. Houston* (1888),[7] it was held in construing a statute that a judgment is a "contract express or implied." In *Louisiana v. New Orleans* (1883),[8] it was held that a judgment for damages for a tort is not a contract within the meaning of the clause in the federal constitution which forbids the enactment of laws impairing the obligation of a contract.

There are numerous other decisions in which judgments have been held not to be contracts within the meaning of particular statutes. But this is a mere question of interpretation. If it appear that the legislative mind meant to include only assumptual contracts, the statute must be given effect accordingly.[9] On the other hand, if it appear that the term contract is broadly used in the statute, it will be interpreted to include judgments.[1]

This all merely shows that the term contract has a narrow and a broad meaning and is for this reason somewhat ambiguous. To treat judgments as quasi-contracts merely because one conceives of the term contract in its narrow sense is incorrect. Yet this is often done, a circumstance which shows that the term quasi-contract is used as a general receptacle for contractual duties not easily placed elsewhere. One conclusive reason why the judgment cannot be treated as a quasi-contract is that it is not, generally speaking, actionable in indebitatus assumpsit. Debt is the only remedy upon a contract of record. Judgments are specialties.[2]

What has been said about the judgment is also applicable to statutory duties such as fines and penalties, and duties imposed by custom. These duties are clearly not of an assumptual nature and hence they are not contracts in the narrow

---

[7] 108 N. Y. 276.
[8] 109 U. S. 285.
[9] See Rae *v.* Hulbert, 17 Ill. 572; Smith *v.* Harrison, 33 Ala. 706; Wolffe *v.* Eberlein, 74 Ala. 99; Sheehan, etc., Transp. Co. *v.* Sims, 28 Mo. App. 64.
[1] Weaver *v.* Lapsley, 43 Ala. 224; Stuart *v.* Lander, 16 Cal. 372; Reed *v.* Eldredge, 27 Cal. 347; Henry *v.* Henry, 11 Ind. 236; Childs *v.* Harris Mfg. Co., 68 Wis. 231.
[2] Morse *v.* Toppan, 3 Gray (Mass.) 411.

sense.³ It has been customary to speak of these duties as quasi-contracts.⁴ But this is doubtful. They appear to be true debts. It so happens that indebitatus assumpsit is the usual remedy upon these duties, but this remedy is evidently here used merely as a substitute for the action of debt.

Elements of the true quasi-contract.

Upon examination of the nature of the true quasi-contracts it will be found that they have two elements in common. In the first place, the duty imposed is a duty to pay money (or to surrender chattels).⁵ In the second place the money or chattels in respect to the payment or surrender of which the duty is raised is conceived as being the equivalent of money or chattels wrongfully detained or wrongfully taken by the person on whom the duty is imposed.

Heritage from debt.

It will be perceived that both of these distinguishing marks of the quasi-contract are inherited from debt. The limitation that the duty must be one for the payment of money (or chattels) plainly comes from that source, and the conception of equivalence for benefit conferred or acquisition made has its root of course in the doctrine of *quid pro quo*. The gain of one being the loss of the other, the law imposes a duty to compensate on the person benefited. Otherwise there would be an unjust enrichment of one person at the expense of another, without any means of redress. This the law does not tolerate. No one, it is said, shall be allowed unjustly to enrich himself at the expense of another.⁶

Unjust enrichment.

The proposition that no one shall be allowed unjustly to enrich himself at the expense of another embodies the general principle underlying the true quasi-contracts, yet it must not be taken as a definitive statement of that principle. It is a

---

³ See Milford *v.* Com., 144 Mass. 64.

⁴ Pacific Mail Steamship Co. *v.* Joliffe, 2 Wall. (U. S.) 450.

⁵ The quasi-contractual duty to turn over chattels arises, for instance, where one tortiously converts the chaise of another by exchanging it for other chattels. An indebitatus count for chattels received to the plaintiff's use could be maintained in such case, and the plaintiff would be said thereby to waive the tort and sue on the contract. The count for *money* had and received can only be maintained where the property is converted into money or its equivalent.

⁶ 2 Harv. L. Rev. 64; Keener on Quasi-Contracts, 16.

maxim, and like most maxims it points a truth which it does not define. As a definition the maxim is a failure, since the word 'unjustly' is here used in the sense of unlawfully. The proposition in question is manifestly a *petitio principii*.[7] The difficulty arises from the fact that the quasi-contractual duty belongs to the highest category in the law, namely, that of pure legal wrong, and no logical definition of it can be framed.

<small>Chapter XXI</small>

Though the maxim to which we refer is defective in the respect just stated, it still has a very real value. Like other legal maxims, it serves as a convenient *memoria technica* and it points with unmistakable certainty to the important truth that the quasi-contractual duty will not be imposed on any person unless he has obtained the money, property, or service of another and is enriched thereby. It is merely another aspect of the principle inherited from the common-law debt, that the loss of one must be the gain of the other.[8]

<small>Value of the maxim.</small>

---

[7] See article by E. V. Abbot criticising Professor Keener's Treatise on Quasi-Contracts, 10 Harv. L. Rev. 221 *et seq.*

[8] *Doctrine of Unjust Enrichment in Roman Law.*—The idea underlying the doctrine of unjust enrichment in Roman law substantially coincides with the idea underlying the duties which are properly classed as quasi-contractual in English law. Accordingly it is worth while here to ascertain the situations where the Roman law imposed the duty to compensate for unjust enrichment. Such a duty arose (1) where the enrichment was said to be *sine causa;* (2) where the enrichment was said to be *ex injusta causa.*

1. There are three forms of enrichment *sine causa:*

a. The payment of money under a mistaken opinion that it is justly due gives rise to a duty to restore the amount so received. This is the *solutio indebiti.*

b. Another sort of enrichment *sine causa* is found in the *dare ob causam.* Here there is a transfer of property from one to another upon a future consideration which fails. Thus if property is transferred by A to B in anticipation of a future marriage to be consummated between them, and the marriage fails to occur by default of the transferee, there is, in the eye of the law, an unjust enrichment, and the party thus enriched is bound to restore the amount by which his estate has thus been increased. This form of unjust enrichment is known as the *dare ob causam.* In the *solutio indebiti* there is what, in common-law modes of speech, is denominated want of consideration. In the *dare ob causam* there is what we would call a failure of consideration.

c. The third form of enrichment *sine causa* is distinguishable from the other two by the fact that here the *dare,* or transfer, fails to take effect according to the intention of the parties. Thus, if A delivers money to B intending thereby to produce a legal result, as, for example, to make a loan to B, but B receives it thinking that a gift is intended, the amount so delivered can be recovered. A, not being able to sue upon a loan, can recover only upon the principle of unjust enrichment. The same principle applies where A, intending to make a loan to B, delivers to him money or property belonging to a stranger. In such case B does not become owner by the delivery, but is enriched by his consumption or use of the thing delivered, and he is therefore bound to compensate for the benefit. Generally speaking, the duty to compensate arises under this head wherever one person receives something which ought to have been received by another. Thus, if A converts a chattel belonging to B by selling the same, the owner, being no longer able to vindicate his ownership by an action *in rem*, is allowed to recover the amount realized by the sale. The right of action here recognized is identical with that enforced at common law by the common count for money had and received when used to recover the proceeds of a sale made by one guilty of a conversion.

2. There are three forms of enrichment *ex injusta causa*.

a. Theft. The possession of stolen property enriches the thief and makes him liable to compensate for the value of the goods appropriated or to restore the property itself.

b. *Dare ob turpem causam.* Where a transfer is made under circumstances which render its acceptance not only illegal but immoral, and contrary to public policy, the law imposes a duty to compensate upon the person so accepting the benefit. The payment of a ransom extorted by brigands is given as an illustration of this form of unjust enrichment; and presumably it would include all forms of duress. A party who himself participates in the purpose which infects a transaction with turpitude cannot, of course, recover. Thus, one who hires an assassin or gives money to corrupt a voter could not recover as for an unjust enrichment.

c. *Dare ex injusta causa.* Under this head are classed all cases not grouped under the preceding heads, where one person is enriched at the expense of another in a manner which the law regards as unjust; as where the *malæ fidei* possessor is enriched at the expense of the owner by fruits he has consumed. The two heads of unjust enrichment last mentioned seem to differ little.

The foregoing note is based on Sohm's Institutes of Roman Law, Ledlie's Trans. (2d ed.), pp. 423–426. See also Hunter, Roman Law (3d ed.), pp. 655–661.

Roman law also classed among quasi-contracts duties which arise from the creation of trusts and the performance of acts for another without previous request (*negotiorum gestio*). In English law, duties arising out of trusts are of exclusive equitable cognizance, and the duties incident to *negotiorum gestio*, so far as they are recognized at all, have been absorbed into agency and bailment, or are enforced by the action on the case where liability attaches for damage resulting from intermeddling with the property of another. Hence it is unnecessary to take account of such duties in this connection. It results, then, that the duty to compensate for unjust enrichment is the true analogue of the English quasi-contract.

CHAPTER XXII

DUTIES IN THE NATURE OF DEBT (CONTINUED).

Benefit Conferred under Mistake of Fact.

WE now proceed to point out particular situations where it can be properly said that the law imposes a quasi-contractual duty.[1] Perhaps the most conspicuous instance of such a duty is that which arises where money (or chattels) is paid under a mistake. Here the recipient is bound to refund an amount equal to that by which he is enriched.

The mistake which is here operative in giving rise to the duty to compensate may be of several varieties. Thus it may appear that the plaintiff paid the money in question under a mistaken opinion that it was really due;[2] or it may have been paid as consideration for a contract the subject-matter of which is, contrary to the belief of the contracting parties, nonexistent;[3] or, again, it may have been paid as consideration for the sale of property to which the seller has no title.[4] In all of these cases the person paying can recover the amount of the benefit conferred. So, the mistaken overpayment of a debt gives rise to the duty of returning so much as is **not** actually due.[5]

Chapter XXII

Types.

---

[1] In the treatment of the special classes or groups of quasi-contracts we have derived material assistance from the article by W. A. Martin on Implied or Quasi-Contracts, in 15 Am. and Eng. Encyc. of Law (2d ed.), pp. 1076–1118; and from Prof. Keener's Law of Quasi-Contracts (New York, 1893). The latter work was the first, as it is the fullest, treatise on the subject that has been written.

[2] *Recovery of Money Paid under Mistake as to Existence of Obligation.*—Chatfield *v.* Paxton, cited in Bilbie *v.* Lumley, 2 East 471, note *a;* Kelly *v.* Solari, 9 M. & W. 54; Mills *v.* Guardians of Poor, 3 Exch. 590; Stuart *v.* Sears, 119 Mass. 143; Rheel *v.* Hicks, 25 N. Y. 289.

[3] Martin *v.* Sitwell, 1 Show. 156; McDonald *v.* Lynch, 59 Mo. 350.

[4] Here it seems there must be such a state of facts as would entitle the plaintiff to sue for a breach of warranty of title. See Keener on Quasi-Contracts, 125.

[5] *Recovery of Overpayment* resulting from mistake in sale by

Where money paid under an alleged mistake as to the existence of a debt or other obligation is sought to be recovered, it must appear that the plaintiff really thought the money to be due.[6] If he knows a fact to exist which negatives liability, the payment is voluntary and cannot be recovered; and this is true although at the time of payment no proof of such fact was procurable but is subsequently obtained.[7] But it is held that mere suspicion on the part of the person paying that there is a good defense to the claim does not preclude him from recovering where the true state of facts is subsequently revealed.[8]

In order that a mistake may operate to raise a duty to refund, it must be a mistake as to a material fact, one that goes to the root of liability. If the mistake is as to a collateral matter, there can be no recovery.[9]

Where money is paid under a mistake the person making the payment, though moved to do so by a mistaken apprehension of the true state of fact, actually consents to the transfer of the money. Hence the payment is in a sense voluntary. All cases of recovery of money so paid are therefore in the nature of equitable exceptions to the general doctrine that payments voluntarily made cannot be recovered. Therefore the equity of the party suing to recover money paid under a mistake must be complete.

For this reason it is settled that recovery will not be allowed in any case unless the retention of the money by the

weight or measurement. Devaux v. Conolly, 8 C. B. 640, 65 E. C. L. 640; Billings v. McCoy, 5 Neb. 187; Devine v. Edwards, 101 Ill. 138.

Mistake in Account Rendered.— Townsend v. Crowdy, 8 C. B. N. S. 477, 98 E. C. L. 477.

[6] Windbiel v. Carroll, 16 Hun (N. Y.) 101.

[7] See National L. Ins. Co. v. Jones, 59 N. Y. 649; Frambers v. Risk, 2 Ill. App. 499.

[8] Chatfield v. Paxton, cited in Bilbie v. Lumley, 2 East 471, note a; Guild v. Baldridge, 2 Swan (Tenn.) 295.

[9] The drawee of a bill who had a right to insist upon a particular application of the proceeds paid the amount thereof to an indorsee under the mistaken impression that the proceeds were being applied in conformity with the prior understanding. But this was not in fact done. It was held that he could not recover, the mistake being one as to a collateral or future fact. Southwick v. Memphis First Nat. Bank, 84 N. Y. 420. See Dambmann v. Schulting, 75 N. Y. 55; Justh v. National Bank of Commonwealth, 56 N. Y. 478.

DUTIES IN THE NATURE OF DEBT. 213

defendant would be against conscience. In conformity with this doctrine it is held that money cannot be recovered where there was a moral obligation to support the claim, as where money is paid after bar of the statute of limitations has become effective.[1] "Money due in point of honor or conscience, though a man is not compellable to pay it, yet if paid, shall not be recovered back."[2]

For similar reasons, where recovery is allowed at all, it will be for only so much as under the particular facts the plaintiff ought in equity to recover. In other words, the action being equitable in its nature is subject to equitable defenses.[3] In conformity with this view the courts have sometimes refused to compel a defendant to refund money paid under a mistake where he has by virtue of the payment incurred a detriment and cannot be put *in statu quo*. This is particularly true where negligence or laches is imputable to the person who seeks to recover.[4] But the principle must be applied with an eye to the particular equity of each case, and no well-settled rule has yet been attained.[5]

It is determined upon good authority that a negligent payment does not estop one to recover where the other party will be in no worse plight or can be put *in statu quo*;[6] and *a fortiori* where the mistake is attributable to the defendant himself, recovery can be had although he has altered his position and cannot be restored to it.[7]

In the early part of the nineteenth century an important

Chapter XXII

Money paid upon moral obligation.

Equitable nature of the action.

Change of position by party receiving payment.

---

[1] See Moses *v.* Macferlan, 2 Burr. 1012.

[2] Farmer *v.* Arundel, 2 W. Bl. 824. See also Taylor *v.* Hare, 1 B. & P. N. R. 260.

[3] See Merchants' Nat. Bank *v.* National Bank of Commonwealth, 139 Mass. 513.

[4] Skyring *v.* Greenwood, 4 B. & C. 281, 10 E. C. L. 335; Smith *v.* Mercer, 6 Taunt. 76, 1 E. C. L. 312; Boas *v.* Updegrove, 5 Pa. St. 516. See also opinion of Sir James Mansfield in Brisbane *v.* Dacres, 5 Taunt. 162, 1 E. C. L. 51.

[5] Professor Keener submits that where legal title to money or property has by mistake passed to a defendant not responsible for the mistake, a recovery should not be allowed against him which would involve him in loss. This seems to be good law. See Keener on Quasi-Contracts, 65.

[6] Kelly *v.* Solari, 9 M. & W. 54; Appleton Bank *v.* McGilvray, 4 Gray (Mass.) 518.

[7] Union Bank *v.* U. S. Bank, 3 Mass. 74.

214   FOUNDATIONS OF LEGAL LIABILITY.

Money paid under mistake of law not recoverable. exception was ingrafted upon the doctrine that money paid under a mistake can be recovered. This exception originated in *Bilbie v. Lumley* (1802),[8] wherein Lord Ellenborough denied the right of an insurer to recover money voluntarily paid with knowledge of all material facts but in ignorance of the legal principle which rendered the policy invalid by reason of a concealment on the part of the assured. Since that day it has been accepted in nearly all common-law jurisdictions that money paid under a mistake of law cannot be recovered, provided there is no fraud or imposition and the money is paid with knowledge of the material facts.[9] In a few jurisdictions this doctrine has not been accepted,[1] and in all it has been more or less mitigated by qualifications.

Contrary doctrine.

Qualifications. Thus if there be a total failure of consideration relief will be given whether the mistake be one of law or of fact;[2] and where the mistake is one of foreign law,[3] or of domestic law made by a foreigner,[4] recovery can be had as if the mistake were one of fact. Likewise, money paid under a mistake of law to an officer of court, as to a trustee in bankruptcy, must be refunded.[5] So, also, where the mistake is one of private right, as where it concerns a question of ownership or the existence of legal obligation, it may be treated as a mistake of fact although it be implicated with and results from a mistake of law.[6]

---

[8] 2 East 469.
[9] Stevens v. Lynch, 12 East 38; Lowry v. Bourdieu, 2 Dougl. 468; Elliott v. Swartwout, 10 Pet. (U. S.) 137; U. S. Bank v. Daniel, 12 Pet. (U. S.) 33; Cahaba v. Burnett, 34 Ala. 400; State University v. Keller, 1 Ala. 406; Livermore v. Peru, 55 Me. 469; Camden v. Green, 54 N. J. L. 591; Vanderbeck v. Rochester, 122 N. Y. 285. See also 15 Am. and Eng. Encyc. of Law (2d ed.) 1102.
[1] Mansfield v. Lynch, 59 Conn. 320; Culbreath v. Culbreath, 7 Ga. 64; Ray v. State Bank, 3 B. Mon. (Ky.) 510; Underwood v. Brockman, 4 Dana (Ky.) 309, 29 Am. Dec. 407.

[2] Champlin v. Laytin, 6 Paige (N. Y.) 189.
[3] Norton v. Marden, 15 Me. 46; Haven v. Foster, 9 Pick. (Mass.) 112; Bentley v. Whittemore, 18 N. J. Eq. 366.
[4] Chillicothe Bank v. Dodge, 8 Barb. (N. Y.) 233.
[5] *Ex p.* James, L. R. 9 Ch. 609; *Ex p.* Simmonds, 16 Q. B. D. 308.
[6] For a discussion of the question as to when a mistake is one of fact and when of law, see Keener, Quasi-Contracts, 96 *et seq.* Compare the following: Wilde v. Baker, 14 Allen (Mass.) 349; Hubbard v. Martin, 8 Yerg. (Tenn.) 498; Birkhauser v. Schmitt, 45 Wis. 316.

Duty to Compensate for Chattels or Service Wrongfully Appropriated.

Chapter XXII

A second group of quasi-contractual duties is found in those cases where a plaintiff is allowed to waive the tort and sue on the contract. The doctrine here is that wherever a tortious act results in the enrichment of the tortfeasor at the expense of another, whether by the acquisition of property or of labor and service, the person from whom the property is taken or withheld, or the person who bestows the labor and service, may sue upon the duty to compensate which the law imposes upon the wrongdoer. In these cases it was originally necessary that there should be some specific thing passing from the person injured to the tortfeasor before the law would impose a duty to compensate. In other words, legal theory here clung to the original conception of *quid pro quo*. But just as in the early common law labor and service came to be conceived as a sufficient *quid pro quo* upon which to predicate a debt, so here it is now held that labor and service are sufficient to raise a quasi-contractual duty in the nature of debt.

Unjust enrichment from tortious act.

Original limitation upon right of recovery.

This extension of theory was first sanctioned in *Lightly v. Clouston* (1808),[7] where it was held that one who entices the apprentice of another, and induces such apprentice to work for him, may be sued by the master for the value of the services. The wrongful acquisition of service was thus treated as being *in consimili casu* with the wrongful acquisition of a *res*. In conformity with this view there is modern authority to the effect that one who is wrongfully required or compelled to labor for another can recover compensation by suing upon the quasi-contractual duty;[8] and where personalty is wrongfully used in a way that stops short of absolute appropriation, the owner can recover the value of its use.[9]

Extension of doctrine.

Enticement of apprentice.

Enforced service.

In all cases where the plaintiff is allowed to waive a tort and sue on the quasi-contractual duty he must use some form

Form of remedy where tort is waived

---

[7] 1 Taunt. 112. See Foster *v.* Stewart, 3 M. & S. 191; James *v.* Le Roy, 6 Johns. (N. Y.) 274.

[8] Patterson *v.* Prior, 18 Ind. 440.
[9] Fanson *v.* Linsley, 20 Kan. 235.

Conversion of chattel by sale.

of the action of indebitatus assumpsit. If the tortfeasor appropriates money he can be sued for money had and received;[1] and if by a sale he wrongfully converts chattels into money or its equivalent the same form of action is proper.[2]

If, however, the tortfeasor instead of selling the disseised chattels for money or its equivalent, retains them in his own hands and appropriates them to his individual use,[3] or if he exchanges them by barter for other goods,[4] the count for money had and received is plainly improper.

Conversion of chattel by appropriation without sale.

A clear perception of this fact together with the circumstance that the count for money had and received was the first and for a long time the only form of indebitatus which was used where the tort was permitted to be waived, led a number of the American courts to declare in the early part of the nineteenth century that no form of indebitatus will lie against a converter unless he sells the chattels and turns them into money or its equivalent, such being in the opinion of these courts the only situation where the law will impose a contractual duty upon the disseisor of chattels.[5] But by the weight of modern authority, the plaintiff may declare in indebitatus against any disseisor of chattels, using the count for goods sold and delivered, the sale of course being a fiction.[6] This is undoubtedly good law.

---

[1] Neate v. Harding, 6 Exch. 349; Clarke v. Shee, 1 Cowp. 197.

[2] Lamine v. Dorrell, 2 Ld. Raym. 1216. See 15 Am. and Eng. Encyc. of Law (2d ed.) 1113.

It has been held that selling under a contract for the future payment of money gives the person injured an immediate right to sue for money had and received, the purchaser's promise to pay being treated as the equivalent of money, as against the tortfeasor. Burton Lumber Co. v. Wilder, 108 Ala. 669. *Contra*, Miller v. Miller, 7 Pick. (Mass.) 134.

[3] Jones v. Hoar, 5 Pick. (Mass.) 285.

[4] Fuller v. Duren, 36 Ala. 73; Kidney v. Persons, 41 Vt. 386.

[5] The Massachusetts case, Jones v. Hoar, 5 Pick. (Mass.) 285, is leading authority for this view. But in that case it was admitted that the count upon fictitious sale for goods bargained and sold would lie against the tortfeasor or his representative where death had intervened and put an end to the right of action for the tort. See 5 Pick. (Mass.) 290.

[6] Abbott v. Blossom, 66 Barb. (N. Y.) 353; Logan v. Wallis, 76 N. Car. 416; Alsbrook v. Hathaway, 3 Sneed (Tenn.) 454.

For an enumeration of the authorities on the question see 15 Am. and Eng. Encyc. of Law (2d ed.) 1116.

On general principle it would seem the disseisor of real property might be held liable for use and occupation upon an implied contract to pay the reasonable value of the use of the premises; but this is not permitted. The explanation is to be found in the history of the action of indebitatus assumpsit. This action cannot at common law be used for the recovery of rent, since a debt for rent is considered to be of a higher nature than the ordinary simple debt upon which indebitatus assumpsit lies. It being accepted that indebitatus assumpsit would not lie for the recovery of rent due by contract, it would have been anomalous to permit the remedy to be used against a trespasser.

Chapter XXII

No implied contract to compensate for use and occupation.

By statute of 11 Geo. II, c. 19, § 14, an action on the case in the nature of assumpsit for use and occupation was permitted to be maintained for the recovery of rent where the demise was not by deed. This statutory action can be maintained only where the relation of landlord and tenant exists. In conformity with this enactment judicial decision both in England and America has in modern times been explicitly to the effect that the action for use and occupation cannot be maintained against a trespasser.[7]

In harmony with the doctrine underlying the entire subject of quasi-contract, it is always necessary, before the plaintiff can waive a tort and sue in contract, not only that the plaintiff himself should have suffered a detriment, but that a benefit should have accrued to the tortfeasor or his estate.[8] Furthermore, the action being of an equitable nature, only so much can be recovered as would be contrary to conscience for the defendant to retain.[9]

---

[7] Lloyd v. Hough, 1 How. (U. S.) 160; Smith v. Houston, 16 Ala. 111; Weaver v. Jones, 24 Ala. 420; Watson v. Brainard, 33 Vt. 88. See 15 Am. and Eng. Encyc. of Law (2d ed.) 1117, 1118.

For a more detailed account of the history of the action of use and occupation, see the paper on Assumpsit for Use and Occupation by Professor Ames, 2 Harv. L. Rev. 377; also Keener, Quasi-Contracts, 192.

[8] Phillips v. Homfray, 24 Ch. D. 439.

See also Webster v. Drinkwater, 5 Me. 319; Ford v. Caldwell, 3 Hill L. (S. Car.) 248.

[9] Western Assur. Co. v. Towle, 65 Wis. 247. In this case the in-

Election of remedies.

In the situation where the tort may be waived and suit brought upon the quasi-contract, the plaintiff is said to have an election of remedies;[1] and where either the delictual or contractual remedy has been chosen, the plaintiff cannot, it has been held, ordinarily lay it aside to try the other.[2] In a sense it is undoubtedly true that there is merely an election of remedy, for exactly the same state of facts must be shown in order to maintain either. But it should not escape observation that the respective remedies proceed upon different theories. In pursuing the contractual remedy (indebitatus assumpsit) the plaintiff sues upon a legal duty, in the nature of a debt, to compensate for benefit received by the defendant. In trespass and trover he sues upon the legal duty to compensate for damage done. A plaintiff who, according to the accepted formula, 'waives the tort' and sues upon the contractual duty may therefore more properly be said, in the language of Judge Nicholson, merely to waive damages for the conversion and to sue for the value of the property.[3]

Joint tort-feasors; effect of election by plaintiff.

The question of the effect of the election of remedy in cases of conversion becomes important where more than one person is concerned in the wrong. In Tennessee it has been held by a learned judge that the commencement of an action against one tortfeasor upon the quasi-contractual duty to compensate for goods wrongfully converted does not operate as a waiver of the right to proceed in tort against joint trespassers.[4] But in New York it has been held that the recovery of judgment in assumpsit against one of several joint tort-

---

sured fraudulently obtained payment of a policy of insurance as upon a complete loss. The company was permitted to recover only so much as was paid by it over and above the true loss, although the fraud vitiated the right of the insured to recover anything on the policy if he had been forced to sue thereon.

[1] Cooper v. Cooper, 147 Mass. 370.
[2] Thompson v. Howard, 31 Mich. 309; Conrow v. Little, 115 N. Y. 387; Equitable Co-operative Foundry Co. v. Hersee, 103 N. Y. 25.

Professor Keener, in a sound criticism of Thompson v. Howard, supra, shows conclusively to the mind of this writer that the bringing of an action either in contract or in tort ought not to constitute a binding election against the bringing of the other, where the action has been dismissed by the plaintiff. See Keener, Quasi-Contracts. 205 et seq.
[3] Kirkman v. Philips, 7 Heisk. (Tenn.) 222, 224.
[4] Huffman v. Hughlett, 11 Lea (Tenn.) 549.

feasors bars the right to sue the others for damages occasioned by the conversion. Thus, in *Terry v. Munger* (1890)[5] it appeared that three persons had been jointly guilty of wrongfully detaching and carrying away certain mill machinery belonging to the plaintiff. The latter thereupon sued two of them upon the implied contract to compensate for the machinery taken. This action, it will be noted, proceeded upon the idea of a fictitious sale. Subsequently, in an action *ex delicto* brought by the same plaintiff against the third tortfeasor, it was held that by electing to treat the conversion as a sale, the plaintiff was precluded from thereafter proceeding in tort. The fact that no satisfaction had been obtained as a result of the first proceeding was held to be immaterial.

Chapter XXII

[5] 121 N. Y. 101. Professor Keener criticises this decision with vital effect. See Keener on Quasi-Contracts, 210 *et seq.*

CHAPTER XXIII

DUTIES IN THE NATURE OF DEBT (CONTINUED).

Benefits Conferred under Unenforceable Contract.

Volume II

General principle.

A THIRD important group of quasi-contractual duties, or duties in the nature of debt, arises out of situations where the parties have entered into a binding assumptual contract which for one reason or another cannot be enforced. Here the legal duty is predicated upon the conferring of a benefit by one party to the contract upon the other. The rule is that if, in fulfilment or part fulfilment of the assumptual contract, one party confers a benefit on the other, the law will impose a duty to compensate therefor provided the contract made by the parties cannot be enforced, and provided equity and good conscience require that compensation should be made. The following situations are deserving of notice: 1. Where the original contract has been materially modified; 2. Where full performance has been prevented by the default of the defendant; 3. Where performance is prevented by the act of God or by a rule of law; 4. Where nonperformance is attributable to the default of the plaintiff.

Effect of special contract.

It is a general principle of law that where a special contract is made it is the exclusive source of legal rights and duties between the parties as regards the matters to which that contract pertains. An express contract excludes an implied one.[1] *Expressum facit cessare tacitum.* The duties now to be considered are therefore in the nature of exceptions to a general principle, and can only arise where the right of action upon the original contract is defective and has to be supplemented for equitable reasons.

[1] See opinion of Morton, J., in Olmstead *v.* Beale, 19 Pick. (Mass.) 528.

Original Contract Materially Modified.

Chapter XXIII

Where there is a contract to do a particular piece of work on an agreed plan at a specified price, and by mutual consent a deviation is made from the specifications, the party who does the work can recover on an implied contract where the original plan is so far abandoned that the original contract cannot be taken to cover the work in question.[2]

Contract modified by mutual consent.

It is also held that where a party employed to perform designated service for another performs such service defectively and not in strict accordance with the terms of the contract, he may recover on an implied contract for the benefit conferred, though he could not recover on the special contract.[3] But it is necessary that performance, though defective, should be finished.

Compensation for defective work.

Recovery is permitted in this situation on purely equitable grounds. The rule of strict law would be that one unable to recover on the special contract should not recover at all. But this would give an unconscionable advantage to the person benefited.[4] As the action is of an equitable character, the defendant is permitted to mitigate the recovery by the amount of damages which he has incurred by reason of the failure of the plaintiff to comply with the contract.[5]

Basis of the right of recovery.

Where by the terms of an express contract for personal service extending over a fixed period of time, either party is given a right to put an end to the contract at his pleasure, and such option is exercised, recovery may be had upon a *quantum meruit* for the service rendered.[6] But the amount of the recovery is governed by the contract.[6*]

Relation of service terminated at election of one.

---

[2] Wheeden v. Fiske, 50 N. H. 125; Hummer v. Lockwood, 3 Greene (Iowa) 90.

[3] Cooke v. Munstone, 1 B. & P. N. R. 351; Burn v. Miller, 4 Taunt. 745; Dermott v. Jones, 23 How. (U. S.) 220; Hawkins v. U. S., 96 U. S. 697.

[4] Pinches v. Swedish Evangelical Lutheran Church, 55 Conn. 183.

[5] Lucas v. Godwin, 3 Bing. N. Cas. 737, 32 E. C. L. 309; Escott v. White, 10 Bush (Ky.) 169; Corwin v. Wallace, 17 Iowa 374; Cullen v. Sears, 112 Mass. 299; Gallagher v. Sharpless, 134 Pa. St. 134.

[6] Fitzgerald v. Allen, 128 Mass. 234; Booth v. Ratcliffe, 107 N. Car. 6.

[6*] Patnote v. Saunders, 41 Vt. 66.

Full Performance Prevented by Default of Defendant.

Performance prevented.

Where one of two contracting parties in part fulfilment of the contract confers a benefit upon the other, as by the performance of service, he may recover in indebitatus the reasonable value of such benefit if the other party abandons the contract and thereby makes complete performance impossible or unnecessary.[7] The defendant himself being in default is not permitted to set up nonperformance of the special agreement as a defense.

Election of cause of action.

Inasmuch as a contracting party who prevents performance thereby violates the contract, the other, if he sees fit so to do, may treat the contract as still existing and sue in special assumpsit to recover damages for its breach.[8]

The election here, in addition to being an election between two different remedies, is also an election between two different and mutually exclusive causes of action. If suit is brought on the implied contract the plaintiff's recovery, though not limited by the terms of the contract, can be only for so much as represents the value of the benefit conferred or work done.[9]

Extent of recovery.

If, on the other hand, the plaintiff elects to sue for the breach of the special contract, his recovery may be prospective, and future benefit to be reaped from the contract can be taken into consideration.[1] But the amount of the recovery cannot be greater than the contract price. Inasmuch as both causes of action arise out of the same state of facts, a plaintiff who has sued in special assumpsit for the breach of the contract cannot subsequently sue in indebitatus upon the duty to compensate and *vice versa.*[2]

Repudiation based on violation of Statute of Frauds.

Where performance of a contract is rendered impossible by reason of a breach on the part of one, the right of the other to recover on the implied contract for such benefit as

---

[7] Goodman *v.* Pocock, 15 Q. B. 576, 69 E. C. L. 576; Prickett *v.* Badger, 1 C. B. N. S. 296, 87 E. C. L. 296; Chicago *v.* Tilley, 103 U. S. 146; Fitzgerald *v.* Allen, 128 Mass. 234.

[8] Derby *v.* Johnson, 21 Vt. 17.

[9] McCullough *v.* Baker, 47 Mo. 401; Ehrlich *v.* Ætna L. Ins. Co., 88 Mo. 249; Derby *v.* Johnson, 21 Vt. 17.

[1] Ream *v.* Watkins, 27 Mo. 516.

[2] Goodman *v.* Pocock, 15 Q. B. 576, 69 E. C. L. 576.

has been conferred and accepted under the terms of the contract is not affected by the fact that the contract was invalid under the Statute of Frauds and was repudiated by the defendant for that reason.³ This is a necessary corollary from the principle that contracts violative of the Statute of Frauds are only unenforceable and not wholly void.

<small>Chapter XXIII</small>

An exception to the rule that one party can recover compensation for a benefit conferred in part performance of a contract which the other repudiates is recognized in cases where the contract is infected with illegality and the benefit in question was conferred by the plaintiff in furtherance of its illegal purpose.⁴ In such case the plaintiff, being *in pari delicto,* is denied relief just as complainants who come with unclean hands are repelled in equity.

<small>Benefit conferred in furtherance of illegal purpose.</small>

But if the party rendering the service is not a privy to the unlawful design, nor otherwise *in pari delicto,* he may recover though the contract was illegal and void; and indeed, though the plaintiff has been a party to the illegal design the law permits recovery in cases where the illegal object has not yet been accomplished. This is done in order to encourage persons who enter upon illegal transactions, to resile before it is too late.⁵ The law is here said to afford room for repentance (*locus pœnitentiæ*).

<small>Innocent party may recover.</small>

<small>Locus pœnitentiæ.</small>

In conformity with this rule one who deposits money with a stakeholder on a wager may, after the wager is determined and before it has been paid over to the winner, recover it upon demand made on the stakeholder.⁶

<small>Money in hand of stakeholder.</small>

Performance Prevented by Act of God or Rule of Law.

It is settled that where complete performance of a contract for personal service is prevented by a visitation of Providence or by an inevitable accident or by an act of the law, the party

---

³ Cadman *v.* Markle, 76 Mich. 448; Wonsettler *v.* Lee, 40 Kan. 367; Wallace *v.* Long, 105 Ind. 522; Ellis *v.* Cary, 74 Wis. 176.

⁴ Embrey *v.* Jemison, 131 U. S. 336; Roundtree *v.* Smith, 108 U. S. 269; Gibbs *v.* Baltimore Gas Co.,
130 U. S. 396; Harvey *v.* Merrill, 150 Mass. 1.

⁵ Taylor *v.* Bowers, 1 Q. B. D. 291.

⁶ Hampden *v.* Walsh, 1 Q. B. D. 189; Lewis *v.* Bruton, 74 Ala. 317; Fisher *v.* Hildreth, 117 Mass. 558.

224   FOUNDATIONS OF LEGAL LIABILITY.

Volume II

Death.

Inevitable casualty.

Epidemic may excuse performance

thus withholden from performing, or his representative, can recover for a benefit conferred in part performance of the contract. Death and sickness and other inevitable casualties are occurrences which excuse full performance under this rule,[7] and it has even been held that danger of contracting a fatal epidemic is sufficient to excuse a failure to labor in a particular locality. In such case the employee can recover on a *quantum meruit* for the service elsewhere rendered.[8]

Contract abrogated by law.

If a contract during the course of performance is abrogated by legal authority, a party may recover for such work as has been done by him prior to the time when the contract is ended.[9] In such case the inability to perform is due to the act of the law.

Destruction of property pending performance.

If one is employed to do certain work upon the property of another, and pending the performance of the contract the property is destroyed by casualty and without the fault of either party, the person supplying the service can recover for so much work as was done prior to the destruction of the property, unless perhaps where the contract expressly provides that he shall receive nothing until all the work is done.[1] The propriety of these decisions cannot be questioned. In one aspect, to be sure, there is no unjust enrichment of the defendant, since the property about which the labor is

---

[7] Wolfe *v.* Howes, 20 N. Y. 197; Harrington *v.* Fall River Iron Works Co., 119 Mass. 82; Fuller *v.* Brown, 11 Met. (Mass.) 440; Leopold *v.* Salkey, 89 Ill. 412; Knight *v.* Bean, 22 Me. 531; Hillyard *v.* Crabtree, 11 Tex. 264.

But where a contract by its express terms is clearly indivisible, as where a sailor hired for a voyage took a promissory note for a certain sum which provided that he should continue and do his duty during the voyage, it was held, in the leading English case of Cutter *v.* Powell, 6 T. R. 320, that death did not excuse performance in such sense as to enable the legal representative of the sailor to recover for services performed prior to his death.

[8] Lakeman *v.* Pollard, 43 Me. 463. Where the event which disables a party from full performance is such as might have been foreseen at the time of the making of the contract, he is not excused from full performance and cannot recover on a *quantum meruit* for part performance. Jennings *v.* Lyons, 39 Wis. 554.

[9] Jones *v.* Judd, 4 N. Y. 411; M'Gowan *v.* Windham, 25 Conn. 86; Heine *v.* Meyer, 61 N. Y. 171; Kingsley *v.* Brooklyn, 78 N. Y. 216.

[1] Rawson *v.* Clark, 70 Ill. 656; Cleary *v.* Sohier, 120 Mass. 210; Whelan *v.* Ansonia Clock Co., 97 N. Y. 293; Cook *v.* McCabe, 53 Wis. 250. See Fildew *v.* Besley, 42 Mich. 100; Brumby *v.* Smith, 3 Ala. 123.

DUTIES IN THE NATURE OF DEBT.

employed is destroyed; but he gets the labor of the plaintiff, and must be said to be enriched to that extent.

Chapter XXIII

Nonperformance Attributable to Default of Plaintiff.

As the duty to compensate for a benefit conferred by the part performance of a contract is imposed solely for equitable reasons, it necessarily follows that upon principle one who has wilfully abandoned the fulfilment of an entire contract cannot recover on a *quantum meruit* for so much as he may have actually done in part performance thereof.[2]

No recovery where party abandons entire contract.

Thus, a servant who leaves the employment of his master before the termination of the period of the contract can recover nothing for the service rendered.[3] The same is true of a contractor who wilfully abandons work on a house before its completion.[4]

As the right of the defaulting party to be compensated is lost upon the abandonment of the contract by him, the situation is not changed by a subsequent offer on his part to complete the contract, which the other party refuses to permit.[5]

Subsequent offer to resume work.

Though the reasons for denying the right to recover on a *quantum meruit* by a plaintiff who is himself in default are unquestionably sound in point of theory, the rule sometimes operates with hardship and in a few states the courts have broken away from it. This departure was apparently first made in *Britton v. Turner* (1834),[6] where one who had contracted to labor for the period of a year was permitted to recover the value of services actually rendered though he had abandoned the contract without reasonable cause before his time was up. This conclusion was erroneously based on decisions already referred to, and which are apparently everywhere recognized as sound, to the effect that one who has completely performed a contract, but in a defective manner, may recover for the benefit conferred, although the defect

Anomalous rule.

---

[2] Hawkins *v.* Gilbert, 19 Ala. 54; Nesbitt *v.* Drew, 17 Ala. 379; Thayer *v.* Wadsworth, 19 Pick. (Mass.) 349. See also Sinclair *v.* Bowles, 9 B. & C. 92, 17 E. C. L. 140.

[3] St. Albans Steamboat Co. *v.* Wilkins, 8 Vt. 54.
[4] Malbon *v.* Birney, 11 Wis. 107.
[5] Lantry *v.* Parks, 8 Cow. (N. Y.) 63.
[6] 6 N. H. 481.

15

in performance is of such character as to preclude recovery on the special contract.

Distinction between complete but defective performance and unfinished performance.

In the case just referred to the court declared that it could see no difference between a failure to do the work properly and a failure to finish the term. Yet the distinction is a real and important one. A contracting party who without lawful excuse has failed to finish his job, whether it be for the construction of a house or for a term of personal service, has no standing in court. If he has finished the job, though his work be defectively done, he can recover what it is worth. Defective performance is an equitable defense. Nonperformance or only part performance is a complete legal defense. It must therefore be considered that the New Hampshire case just cited, and decisions which have followed it,[7] are anomalous. The doctrine in question has the appearance of being good equity, and no doubt it sometimes prevents hardship; but it is certainly bad law.

Repudiation of contract by infants.

Though it is impossible to reconcile this line of cases with sound theory, there are undoubtedly some situations where plaintiffs who have not completed the term of their contract may well be permitted to recover. Thus infants, as is everywhere recognized, may repudiate a contract at any time and recover for the benefit conferred by their partial performance.[8]

Qualification of general principle where contract is divisible.

Again, in order to preclude a plaintiff who has not completely performed on his part, from recovering for the benefit conferred by a partial performance, the contract must be entire and indivisible; as where one agrees to serve for a specified time and the wages are not to be paid until the end of the term. Where no time of payment is fixed by the parties, the law intends that the work shall be paid for when it has

---

[7] Pixler *v.* Nichols, 8 Iowa 106; McClay *v.* Hedge, 18 Iowa 66; Parcell *v.* McComber, 11 Neb. 209; School Dist. No. 46 *v.* Lund, 51 Kan. 731; Carroll *v.* Welch, 26 Tex. 149; Lee *v.* Ashbrook, 14 Mo. 379; Gregg *v.* Dunn, 38 Mo. App. 283.

Recoupment of Damages for Breach.— Where recovery is permitted under sanction of the doctrine in question the defendant is allowed to mitigate the recovery by the amount of damages which he may have sustained by the plaintiff's breach. Hartman *v.* Rogers, 69 Cal. 643; Duncan *v.* Baker, 21 Kan. 99.

[8] Dallas *v.* Hollingsworth, 3 Ind. 537; Wheatly *v.* Miscal, 5 Ind. 142; Moses *v.* Stevens. 2 Pick. (Mass.) 332; Judkins *v.* Walker, 17 Me. 38.

been accomplished.⁹ If the contract is severable or divisible in respect to the matter of compensation; as, for instance, where one agrees to serve for a year at wages payable weekly, monthly, or quarterly, one who renders service for only part of the period stipulated is generally permitted, it seems, to recover so much wages as has actually accrued subject of course to recoupment for damages caused by the breach.¹

Where a contract is within the Statute of Frauds, one who has partly performed the contract is not, by the weight of authority, permitted to repudiate it solely on that account and to sue on a *quantum meruit* for the benefit conferred by his part performance if the other person is not in default.² Contracts which violate the statute are not illegal but only unenforceable, and the courts are not inclined to put a premium on the breach of them. If the defendant is ready and willing to fulfil his part, the plaintiff must proceed to do likewise. Thus, if an oral contract is made for the purchase of land and the vendee pays part of the price down, he cannot repudiate the contract and recover the money, so long as the other is willing to convey.³

Chapter XXIII

Repudiation of contract which violates Statute of Frauds.

---

⁹ Stark *v.* Parker, 2 Pick. (Mass.) 267; Beach *v.* Mullin, 34 N. J. L. 343.

If nothing is said as to the time of payment and the term is definite the contract will be entire though the compensation be stated as so much per month or per piece. Davis *v.* Maxwell, 12 Met. (Mass.) 286; Lantry *v.* Parks, 8 Cow. (N. Y.) 63; Thayer *v.* Wadsworth, 19 Pick. (Mass.) 349.

¹ Davis *v.* Preston, 6 Ala. 83;

Chamblee *v.* Baker, 95 N. Car. 98; Matthews *v.* Jenkins, 80 Va. 463; La Coursier *v.* Russell, 82 Wis. 265.

² Ketchum *v.* Evertson, 13 Johns. (N. Y.) 359; Collier *v.* Coates, 17 Barb. (N. Y.) 471; Galvin *v.* Prentice, 45 N. Y. 162; Clark *v.* Terry, 25 Conn. 395. But see Crawford *v.* Parsons, 18 N. H. 293.

³ Plummer *v.* Bucknam, 55 Me. 105; Gray *v.* Gray, 2 J. J. Marsh. (Ky.) 21. See Kriger *v.* Leppel, 42 Minn. 6.

CHAPTER XXIV

DUTIES IN THE NATURE OF DEBT (CONTINUED).

Money Paid under Undue Pressure.

Involuntary payment of money under pressure.

Form of the count.

Money paid to obtain enlargement after illegal arrest.

A FOURTH important group of quasi-contractual duties is found in situations such as these, namely: where the money is paid under undue pressure and to prevent threatened injury to person or property, or in order to prevent irreparable damage to the business of the person paying; or where it is improperly and unlawfully exacted under compulsion of law; or is exacted as a condition precedent to the performance of a public duty. Here the law imposes a duty on the person who thus unrighteously acquires the money, to return it or to compensate therefor. The operative element in all these cases is found in the fact that the person paying the money does so involuntarily and the person receiving it has no right to retain the same. It follows that wherever this element is found the law imposes the duty to compensate or to surrender the money unrighteously acquired, whatever may be the facts of the case. Inasmuch as in situations of this kind the money is paid directly to the defendant, the count for money had and received to the plaintiff's use is properly used.

Where an innocent person is arrested on criminal process which authorizes the arrest of another person, and in order to obtain liberation he is compelled to pay into court money which under a statute is turned over to the person at whose instance the arrest was made, the person arrested can recover the money so paid by him.[1]

In general recovery can be had in any case where the person arrested pays money for his enlargement, provided it appears that the arrest was for an improper purpose and **without just cause, or for a just cause but without lawful**

[1] De Mesnil *v.* Dakin, L. R. 3 Q. B. 18.

authority, or for a just cause and under lawful authority but for an improper purpose.²

It has been held that money paid by an innocent person under a threat of immediate arrest upon a real or pretended warrant is recoverable as having been paid under undue pressure.³ But it has been declared that mere threats of criminal prosecution as distinguished from threats of immediate imprisonment are not enough to render payment involuntary in such sense as to permit of its recovery.⁴

The principle enounced in the case last referred to is supported by considerable authority, but that it is a stricter rule than in theory ought to be applied is clear. It was only reached by applying to the equitable count for money had and received the same principle that is applied where the defense of duress is pleaded at law in an action brought upon a contract. It is manifestly proper that a full measure of proof should always be required where it is sought to recover money previously paid away by a person *sui juris,* and this in order to prevent the improper repudiation of valid acts. But it is not necessary that the same rule should apply to the equitable action for money had and received as to an action at law on the contract.

The proper criterion here is not whether there has been sufficient duress to avoid a contract at law, but whether the defendant has unlawfully extracted money from a person who acts involuntarily. If the money is obtained by undue influence it can be recovered though there be no pretense of duress in the legal sense. Thus, it has been held that a married woman, who is induced by threats of the arrest of her husband to pay a debt due by him, can recover the money.⁵ So where an innocent aged person ignorant of the law is wrought upon by threats of prosecution and imprisonment and is thereby induced to pay an unjust claim, he can maintain an action to recover the money.⁶

Chapter XXIV

Money paid to escape unlawful arrest.

Undue pressure distinct from duress.

Proper criterion of the action for money paid under pressure.

² Richardson *v.* Duncan, 3 N. H. 508.
³ Foshay *v.* Ferguson, 5 Hill (N. Y.) 154; Taylor *v.* Jaques, 106 Mass. 291.
⁴ Harmon *v.* Harmon, 61 Me. 227.
⁵ Adams *v.* Irving Nat. Bank, 116 N. Y. 606.
⁶ Cribbs *v.* Sowle, 87 Mich. 340.

Money paid to prevent prosecution on well-grounded charge.

If the charge on which the threat of prosecution or imprisonment is based be well founded, one who pays the money cannot ordinarily recover, either because the money paid was due in point of fact or because by making the payment the plaintiff participates in compounding a felony and hence is *in pari delicto* with the other party.[7]

Money paid to get release of property.

That the undue pressure which makes a payment of money involuntary in such sense as to permit of its recovery from a person not entitled thereto, is an element different from the duress which is necessary to avoid a contract at law, is illustrated where money is paid to prevent the unlawful taking or detention of property. Here the person paying is permitted to recover although the unlawful seizure of property is not recognized as a species of legal duress.[8]

Thus one who pays money to prevent a wrongful distress,[9] or a wrongful taking of goods for harbor duties,[1] may recover the same. The right to recover in such cases is not affected by the circumstance that the wrongful seizure is made or threatened under the color of legal process.[2]

The general principle.

Generally it may be stated that whenever money is exacted by one person from another under compulsion, and as a condition prerequisite to the exercise of a legal right, the money can be recovered. In conformity with this doctrine one who, having the lawful custody of goods, unlawfully exacts the payment of a sum of money, or a sum in excess of that which is lawfully due, may be sued on the duty, which the law imposes, to surrender his unjust acquisition.[3]

On a similar principle one who is compelled to pay money

---

[7] Haynes *v.* Rudd, 102 N. Y. 372. See also Gotwalt *v.* Neal, 25 Md. 434.
But the mere execution of a mortgage is not equivalent to the payment of money and leaves the party room to withdraw from the contract upon recourse to equity. Schoener *v.* Lissauer, 107 N. Y. 111.

[8] Duress in the legal sense must be based on (1) fear of loss of life; (2) or of member; or on (3) fear of mayhem, or (4) imprisonment. 2 Bacon Abr. 156.

[9] Hills *v.* Street, 5 Bing. 37, 15 E. C. L. 358.

[1] Hooper *v.* Mayor, 56 L. J. 457.

[2] Preston *v.* Boston, 12 Pick. (Mass.) 7.

[3] Astley *v.* Reynolds, 2 Stra. 915; Chamberlain *v.* Reed, 13 Me. 357; Ashmole *v.* Wainwright, 2 Q. B. 837, 42 E. C. L. 938; Robertson *v.* Frank Bros. Co., 132 U. S. 17.

to prevent an unlawful and injurious interference with his business can recover the money so expended by him.[4] The law is not so unreasonable in these cases as to sanction the doctrine that the person upon whom the unlawful demand for money is made should refuse and thereby incur the penalty of an injury to his business which perhaps could not be fully redressed in any subsequent action for damages.

<small>Chapter XXIV</small>

<small>Money paid to secure immunity from interference with business.</small>

Money unlawfully exacted by a public officer as a condition precedent to the discharge of an official duty can be recovered by the person paying the same. Thus if a sheriff, as the condition of issuing a warrant, imposes a fee which is unlawful in whole or in part he is liable for the amount over and above the lawful charge.[5]

<small>Money exacted by officer</small>

As a general rule money paid in satisfaction of a claim for the recovery of which an action is pending cannot be recovered, though it should afterwards appear that the claim was in fact unfounded.[6] *A fortiori*, where judgment is actually obtained on the claim, a payment thereof is binding on the judgment debtor. But if after the judgment has been paid or satisfied under execution he should obtain a reversal, the money must be refunded to him.[7]

<small>Money paid in legal proceedings.</small>

<small>Reversal of judgment.</small>

The right to recover money paid upon a judgment subsequently reversed is not limited to parties of record. A third person who is so interested in the suit as to be estopped by the judgment stands upon the same footing as the judgment debtor.[8]

<small>Right of person not party to record.</small>

In *Moses v. Macferlan* (1760),[9] Lord Mansfield correctly expounded the equitable nature of the count for money had and received, but he nevertheless violated the principle stated above, namely, that money paid in satisfaction of a regular judgment cannot be recovered. It appeared in this case that the plaintiff Moses, the payee of a note, had indorsed the same

---

[4] Westlake *v.* St. Louis, 77 Mo. 47; Carew *v.* Rutherford, 106 Mass. 1; Swift, etc., Co. *v.* U. S., 111 U. S. 22.

[5] Dew *v.* Parsons, 2 B. & Ald. 562.

[6] Marriott *v.* Hampton, 7 T. R. 265.

[7] Clark *v.* Pinney, 6 Cow. (N. Y.) 297; Scholey *v.* Halsey, 72 N. Y. 578.

[8] Stevens *v.* Fitch, 11 Met. (Mass.) 248.

[9] 2 Burr. 1005.

to Macferlan in order that the latter might sue the maker. At the time of the transfer an independent special agreement was made to the effect that Moses should in no event be held liable on his indorsement. The defendant, however, in violation of this contract sued Moses and the other parties liable on the paper in a court of equity and recovered a judgment which Moses was ultimately compelled to pay. The latter then sued Macferlan in an action for money had and received, and was permitted to recover the money that had been paid to him under the prior judgment. The mistake in this decision was in allowing indebitatus to be maintained where special assumpsit would lie. In suing the plaintiff on the note the defendant had violated an express agreement, and that he thereby rendered himself liable in damages is clear. But there was certainly no ground upon which the law could predicate a duty to refund. The law will not imply a contract where there is an express assumpsit which covers the same ground.

Money Paid to the Defendant's Use.

A quasi-contract arises where money can be said to be paid by one person to the use of another. Here it is necessary for the plaintiff to show that the money was paid of necessity or in obedience to some legal or moral obligation. That the payment was gratuitous or voluntary is always a good defense. The idea here is that if money be expended by one person on behalf of another the law will impose a duty to compensate on the person thereby benefited, if on general principles of equity the money should have been paid in the first instance, in whole or in part, by him rather than by the plaintiff.

Thus, it has been held that the executor of an estate who pays an annuity to a legatee without retaining the tax, and who subsequently has to pay the same himself, can recover the money so expended from the legatee.[1] So where the plaintiff had deposited with the defendant as security for

---

[1] Hales v. Freeman, 1 Brod. & B. 391, 5 E. C. L. 131.

goods sold a bill accepted by himself, but for which he had received no value, and the defendant, after receiving payment of the goods, wrongfully sold and indorsed the bill to an innocent party whereby the plaintiff was compelled to take it up, it was held that he might recover of the defendant the amount so expended as having been paid to the defendant's use.[2]

The general doctrine that a plaintiff may recover money as having been paid to the use of another wherever upon equitable principle the money should, as between the parties, have been paid by the defendant, is further illustrated in *Brittain v. Lloyd* (1845),[3] where an auctioneer was allowed to recover the auction tax of the person whose land was sold at auction, although the statute imposed the tax on the auctioneer. The court proceeded on the idea that though the statute made the auctioneer personally liable yet the tax was a tax on the auction in respect of the property sold, and by requesting the auctioneer to sell, the owner impliedly contracted to indemnify him for the tax. Having placed the plaintiff in a position where he was obliged to pay the tax, the defendant was compelled to exonerate him. It follows from this decision that it is not necessary that the defendant should have been relieved from a liability by the payment.

Auction tax paid by auctioneer.

On its surface *Spencer v. Parry* (1835)[4] appears to be authority for a different doctrine, but it is not. In this case it was held that one who was compelled to pay taxes charged on his own land could not recover the same, in an action for money paid, from a lessee who had contracted to pay the tax. In this case the contract of indemnity was express and the proper remedy of the plaintiff was by an action of special assumpsit. This case does not therefore prove, as on its surface it might seem to do, that the money paid must have been used to satisfy a debt owing by the defendant.

The duty to compensate for money expended to the use of another is sometimes imposed under circumstances where

---

[2] Bleaden v. Charles, 7 Bing. 246, 20 E. C. L. 119.

[3] 14 M. & W. 762.

[4] 3 Ad. & El. 331, 30 E. C. L. 107.

to superficial observation there seems to have been no enrichment of the defendant, an element which, as we have already stated, is an absolute prerequisite to the imposition of a quasi-contractual duty. But a little thought will show that a party is unjustly enriched as well where his estate is exonerated, or where a claim is settled which he ought to have paid, as where property or money directly accrues to him.

<small>Money paid for dilapidations suffered by lessee.</small>

In *Moule v. Garrett* (1872),[5] the original lessee of certain premises was compelled to pay a sum of money by reason of dilapidations which had occurred during the tenancy of a remote assignee of the term. It was held that he could recover of such assignee the amount so expended, the tenant being under an implied contract to indemnify for breaches of the covenants of the original lease which were incurred during the continuance of his tenancy; and this duty, it was held, was not affected by any express covenants which the assignee may have made with his immediate assignor. In this case the element of unjust enrichment is to be found in the fact that the defendant was primarily in duty bound to repair, and his failure to do so, having resulted in the payment of money by the plaintiff, gave rise to a duty to compensate.

<small>Duty to compensate carrier for maintenance of horse.</small>

It has been held that where the owner of a horse wrongfully refuses to receive the same from a carrier, he is liable for money paid out by the latter for the keep of the horse by a liveryman to whom the animal is turned over.[6]

[5] L. R. 7 Exch. 101.
[6] Great Northern R. Co. *v.* Swaffield, L. R. 9 Exch. 132.

CHAPTER XXV

OBLIGATIONS IN THE NATURE OF ASSUMPSIT.

THE quasi-contracts with which we have dealt in the preceding chapters consist of duties in the nature of a debt. In all of them the element of *quid pro quo,* which is at the foundation of debt, is clearly visible. These duties do not conform in any fundamental particular with assumptual obligations, and hence they are not, properly speaking, quasi-assumpsits. To be sure, the expressions 'implied promise' and 'implied assumpsit' are often used in the cases dealing with these quasi-contractual duties; but these expressions merely have reference to that fiction of law whereby, for remedial purposes, these duties are held to give rise to promissory obligations.

So far, then, as appears at this stage, the ordinary quasi-contracts are all emanations from the conception of debt, and the conception of assumpsit seems not to be at the root of any of the quasi-contracts. It certainly would be strange if this barrenness of our law of assumpsit should prove to be real. The conception of debt is so rich in the development of quasi-debt, why, one asks, should not the conception of obligation derived from promise be equally fertile in throwing off a similar growth of genuine quasi-assumptual obligation? As may be readily guessed, this barrenness of assumptual law is apparent only.

By what is perhaps more a mere accident of legal development than anything else, our law concerning obligations in the nature of assumpsit has not been gathered together under one head, as has happened in the case of duties in the nature of debt. On the contrary, it is for the most part hidden away, as it were, in the interstices of tort law. We do not propose here to attempt to collect the material for any elaborate synthesis of this branch of the law of contract, but we shall briefly indicate the sources from which that material may be drawn.

The first question that arises is naturally this: What is the mark of the genuine quasi-assumptual obligation? What distinguishes the quasi-assumpsit from the ordinary quasi-contract, or duty in the nature of debt? The answer is this: In the ordinary quasi-contract we have to deal with a positive legal duty to pay or surrender a specific sum of money either definable in fact or reducible to certainty, or to turn over a measurable or ponderable quantity of chattels or their proceeds. In the quasi-assumptual obligation, on the other hand, we have to deal with positive obligations whereby a man is bound to do particular acts other than to pay money or chattels, or is bound to do his acts in a particular way, or is bound to warrant particular states of fact, or is bound to refrain from acting altogether.

Let us now cast an eye over the field of legal liability in order to discover where obligations of the latter type may be found. In the first place, it is obvious that sundry statutes create obligations of this kind. *Couch v. Steel* (1854)[1] supplies an instance. There a statute imposed a positive obligation on shipowners to keep an adequate supply of medicine on their ships. The statutes which require carriers to observe certain precautions in running trains or managing ships clearly create obligations of a quasi-assumptual nature. The obligation resting upon public officers to perform the functions of their office[2] furnishes another illustration of a true quasi-assumptual obligation deriving from statute. Violations of such obligations as those just mentioned are usually dealt with under the head of negligence.

There are a few obligations in the nature of assumpsit which exist merely by virtue of certain positive rules of law. These obligations supposedly have their source in custom and are imposed only upon persons who ply one of the common callings. Illustrations are found in that positive obligation imposed on the innkeeper by virtue of which he is bound to

---

[1] 3 El. & Bl. 402, 77 E. C. L. 402.
[2] Com. Dig., *Action upon the Case for Negligence* (A 1).

entertain all unobjectionable wayfarers,[3] and in that obligation which at one time rested on the smith to shoe the horses of all persons who desired his service.[4] The common carrier, it will be remembered, is also bound to convey for all the public alike.[5]

Chapter XXV

The whole subject of negligence is, in one aspect, reducible to the head of quasi-assumptual obligation, and in the first volume of this work the modern tendency to conceive of negligence as the breach of an implied obligation was remarked upon, the idea being that whenever a person assumes or undertakes to do a particular act or to pursue a particular course of conduct he is under an implied duty or obligation to do that act or to pursue that course of conduct with reasonable care and prudence.[6]

Duty to use care; negligence.

All that branch of the law of deceit which blossoms out into the law of warranty is very easily and very naturally referable to the head of quasi-assumpsit. The implied warranty of title in chattel sales and the implied warranty of quality and fitness, so far as such implied warranties are recognized, clearly belong among these obligations. This branch of the law has been dealt with in its proper place in the law of tort, and, as in regard to negligence, no more than a mere reference to the subject is here needed.[7]

Law of warranty.

Again, it occurs to us that those decisions which recognize the right of one who is a stranger to the consideration to recover on a contract made for his benefit, are properly referable to the head of quasi-assumpsit. The true assumptual obligation, upon common-law principles, arises only in favor of one from whom the consideration moves. But in those jurisdictions where the stranger is permitted to sue, the law clearly proceeds on the idea of enforcing an implied obligation in the nature of assumpsit. The principle by which this end is accomplished has already been considered in this volume, and the subject will not be here resumed.

Contract for benefit of third person.

Collen v. Wright (1857)[8] furnishes a singularly instruc-

---

[3] Keilw. 50, pl. 4.
[4] *Ib.*
[5] Jackson *v.* Rogers, 2 Show. 327.
[6] See vol. 1, p. 91 *et seq.*
[7] See vol. 1, pp. 374, 382–385, 407.
[8] 8 El. & Bl. 647, 92 E. C. L. 647, 7 El. & Bl. 301, 90 E. C. L. 301.

238 FOUNDATIONS OF LEGAL LIABILITY.

Volume II

Agent's implied warranty of authority.

tive illustration of the genuine quasi-assumptual obligation. It there appeared that one W, professing to act as agent for G, made an agreement with the plaintiff for the lease of a farm belonging to G and signed it " W, agent to G, lessor." W had no authority from G to let the premises in question, and G repudiated the lease. It was held that, by assuming to act as agent, W impliedly contracted that he had such authority as he pretended to have, and that in consequence he was liable in damages to the plaintiff for the breach of this implied warranty. The fact that the purported agent in good faith thought that he had authority was held not to affect his liability in the least.

Implied promise not to prevent performance.

Another illustration of the implied obligation in the nature of assumpsit, not so familiar as the one above referred to, is found in that obligation which the law sometimes imposes upon a party to a contract not to prevent the other party from performing his part of the agreement. The necessity for raising such an implied obligation arises out of the fact that in the bilateral contract, performance by one is sometimes a condition precedent to a right of recovery against the other. Where this is so, the party who, without violating his own side of the contract, succeeds in preventing the other from performing his part, will escape liability upon the contract itself. To prevent injustice in such situations the law allows the party injured to proceed against the other on the implied promise not to prevent performance.[9]

Exoneration of surety.

The obligation of the principal debtor to exonerate a surety who pays off the debt or obligation for which both are liable is a quasi-assumptual obligation. Originally the surety who had paid off his principal's debt had no remedy at law, and it was necessary for him to resort to equity for relief. In *Decker v. Pope* (1757),[1] however, it was ruled by Lord Mansfield, at Nisi Prius, that the surety could recover money so paid in indebitatus assumpsit.

This case was an action by the administrator *de bonis non* of a surety, who at the defendant's request had joined with another friend of the defendant in giving a bond for the

---

[9] 17 Harv. L. Rev. 46.   [1] 1 Selwyn N. P. (13th ed.) 91.

payment of the price of some goods that were sold to the defendant. The surety had subsequently been compelled to pay the money. Lord Mansfield directed the jury to find for the plaintiff, observing that "where a debtor desires another person to be bound with him or for him and the surety is afterwards obliged to pay the debt, this is a sufficient consideration to raise a promise in law and to charge the principal in an action for money paid to his use."[2] The law courts thus obtained concurrent jurisdiction with the court of equity over cases of exoneration where only a money judgment is sought by the surety against his principal.

Chapter XXV — Origin of doctrine.

The right of a surety who has paid off a secured debt to have contribution from his co-sureties rests upon the same footing as his right to enforce exoneration against the principal. Very naturally the right was first recognized in courts of equity and was thence imported into the courts of law.[3]

Contribution among sureties

In *Deering v. Winchelsea* (1787)[4] it was held that the right of contribution among sureties exists in cases where the obligations of the several sureties are evidenced by separate bonds as well as where they are bound by the same instruments. On similar grounds it has been determined that the right to have contribution exists though the sureties become such at different times and without each other's knowledge.[5]

Where two sureties are liable for a debt of their principal, one who pays it off cannot have contribution from the other surety if it appears that as between the two he was first liable.[6] In such case the sureties cannot be said to be co-sureties at all. As between themselves they are not equally, but only successively liable.

Successive suretyship.

A right similar to that of exoneration and contribution, if not in principle identical with it, is sometimes enforced in

---

[2] In Toussaint v. Martinnant (1787), 2 T. R. 100, Buller, J., speaking of the right of the surety to recover at law in such case, credited the innovation to Gould, J. But that was a mistake.

[3] 1 Pom. Eq. Jur., § 406.

[4] 2 B. & P. 270.

[5] Norton v. Coons, 6 N. Y. 33.

[6] Turner v. Davies, 2 Esp. 479; Craythorne v. Swinburne, 14 Ves. Jr. 160. In the former case it was held that where B, being a surety for A, requests C also to become surety for A, and C thereupon does so, B, after paying off the whole debt, cannot recover contribution from C.

240   FOUNDATIONS OF LEGAL LIABILITY.

Volume II

Contribution among persons jointly and severally liable.

relations which arise out of tort. Thus if one of several owners of a vehicle used in carrying passengers is compelled to satisfy damages incurred by the negligent act of their common employee, he may recover of his partners their aliquot part of the sum paid away by him.[7]

Exoneration as between principal and agent.

Again, where an agent is employed to do an act which is not clearly illegal or known by him to be so, and he incurs liability in the performance of the act, the law imposes on the principal a duty to compensate for such loss, damage, and expenditure as immediately and naturally result from the execution of the agency.[8] Contrariwise, it has been determined that an employer or principal who is mulcted in damages for the negligent act of an employee or agent can reimburse himself in an action on the obligation, which the law imposes on the actual wrongdoer, to make good the loss.[9]

The general principle to be laid down is that wherever the wrongful act of one person results in liability being imposed on another, the latter may have indemnity from the person actually guilty of the wrong.[1] In all cases of this kind the law proceeds in effect upon the idea that there is an implied obligation in the nature of an assumpsit arising out of the facts of the case, whereby the delinquent party is bound to reimburse to the extent of the liability which has been brought by him upon the other.

The implied assumpsit.

No contribution or exoneration among tortfeasors.

To the right of exoneration and contribution as incident to liability resulting from tort there is one important qualification in the rule, namely, that as between actual tortfeasors the law will not enforce contribution or indemnity at all. This doctrine was first formulated in *Merryweather v. Nixan* (1799),[2] where it appeared that in an action of tort judgment had been recovered by the plaintiff against two joint tortfeasors. All of the damages were then levied upon the goods of one of them. It was held that this person could not recover

---

[7] Pearson *v.* Skelton, 1 M. & W. 504; Wooley *v.* Batte, 2 C. & P. 417, 12 E. C. L. 198; Bailey *v.* Bussing, 28 Conn. 455.
[8] Moore *v.* Appleton, 26 Ala. 633.
[9] Smith *v.* Foran, 43 Conn. 244;
Grand Trunk R. Co. *v.* Latham, 63 Me. 177.
[1] Port Jervis *v.* Port Jervis First Nat. Bank, 96 N. Y. 550; Churchill *v.* Holt, 127 Mass. 165.
[2] 8 T. R. 186.

of his former codefendant the moiety which should in justice have been paid by him.

In dealing with this subject of contribution between tortfeasors it has generally been assumed that *Merryweather v. Nixan* states what may be termed the general principle, and that those cases in which recovery has been allowed by way of contribution or exoneration in tort relations embody qualifications of this general principle; but it now appears that this is not the correct view. The general principle is that which allows contribution, and the doctrine of *Merryweather v. Nixan* merely embodies a special exception, limited to cases where the party seeking contribution is *in pari delicto* with the other.[3]

In closing these observations upon the various obligations in the nature of assumpsit which have been referred to above, the writer may be permitted to suggest that those obligations which are dealt with in the preceding chapter under the head of "Money Paid to the Defendant's Use," may well be considered to belong not among duties in the nature of debts, as is there indicated, but among obligations in the nature of assumpsit. Still, they apparently conform in at least one important particular to the idea underlying the duty in the nature of debt, and may provisionally be permitted to remain where they have been placed.

The Equitable Estoppel.

The subject of equitable estoppel, or estoppel *in pais*, is referable to the head of obligations in the nature of assumpsit. It will suffice for the present purpose to deal briefly with that particular form of the estoppel *in pais* which arises from misconduct or misrepresentation on the part of the person against whom the estoppel is invoked.

This branch of the law is entirely modern. The principle underlying it was first clearly enunciated in *Pickard v. Sears*

---

[3] See article, Contribution Between Persons Jointly Charged for Negligence, T. W. Reath, 12 Harv. L. Rev. 176.

(1837).⁴ This was an action of trover. It appeared that the plaintiff was mortgagee and as such the owner of the legal title to certain machinery and other goods which were left by him in the possession and control of the mortgagor. A judgment was recovered against the mortgagor by a third party, and an execution issuing thereupon was levied by the sheriff upon the machinery and goods in question. The plaintiff, the mortgagee, knew of the levy, and even after he learned that a sale was in contemplation came upon the premises and consulted with the attorney of the execution creditor and with the mortgagor about the state of affairs and about the course to be taken. He gave the attorney no notice of the fact that he had any claim upon the goods, though he did intimate that he was a creditor to the extent of five hundred pounds. The sale was made and the defendant purchased the goods in total ignorance of the fact that the plaintiff had any interest in them. It was held that the plaintiff, having allowed the sale to take place without asserting his right, was estopped from subsequently asserting the same, and judgment was given for the defendant. Denman, C. J., said: "Where one by his words or conduct wilfully causes another to believe the existence of a certain state of things, and induces him to act on that belief, so as to alter his own previous position, the former is concluded from averring against the latter a different state of things as existing at the same time." ⁵

The principle thus laid down has been accepted in innumerable modern decisions. The following cases will give an idea of the extent and application of the doctrine. In *Gregg v. Wells* (1839)⁶ one G, the owner of the fittings of a public house, demised them to D, who thereupon became tenant of the house to a third party under an agreement which gave his landlord a lien on the fittings. G was present at the execution of this agreement. D afterwards sold the good will and fittings, without G's knowledge or assent, to W, who,

---

⁴ 6 Ad. & El. 469, 33 E. C. L. 115.

⁵ Substantially the same principle had previously been enunciated in America. Stephens *v.* Baird, (1828)

9 Cow. (N. Y.) 274. The facts in this case were similar to those in Dewey *v.* Field, 4 Met. (Mass.) 381.

⁶ 10 Ad. & El. 90, 37 E. C. L. 54.

being told by the landlord that D was his tenant, bought them bona fide in ignorance of G's title, and was accepted by the landlord as tenant. It was held that G could not maintain trover for the fittings against W.

Chapter XXV

Lord Denman, referring to *Pickard v. Sears,* observed that the principle of that case could be stated even more broadly than it was there laid down. "A party," said he, "who negligently or culpably stands by and allows another to contract on the faith and understanding of a fact which he can contradict cannot afterwards dispute that fact in the action against the person whom he has himself assisted in deceiving."

Negligent and culpable silence.

In *Dewey v. Field* (1842)[7] goods were attached as the property of A. B, knowing all the facts pertaining to his own title to the goods, gave the attaching officer a receipt therefor and promised to deliver them on demand. He gave no intimation that he claimed them as his own. When the goods were attached and the receipt given there were other sufficient goods of A which the officer could and would have taken, if B had claimed those which were attached. In an action against B on his receipt, it was held that he was estopped from asserting title in himself.

Failure to assert ownership in self.

In *M'Cance v. London, etc., R. Co.* (1861)[8] the principle in question was applied in the case of a shipper of horses who had knowingly undervalued his animals at the time of the shipment. It was held that the shipper was bound by the valuation, the horses having been accepted for transportation upon conditions which were to some extent determined by such valuation.

Undervaluation by shipper.

In *Dickerson v. Colgrove* (1879)[9] it was held that one who has an interest in real property is estopped from asserting that claim where he writes a letter expressly renouncing it and another purchases upon faith of such renunciation. Said Mr. Justice Swayne in this case: "The vital principle is that he who, by his language or conduct, leads another to do what he would not otherwise have done, shall not subject such person to loss or injury by disappointing the expectations upon which he acted. Such a change of position is sternly forbid-

Estoppel from renunciation of title to land.

[7] 4 Met. (Mass.) 381. [8] 7 H. & N. 477. [9] 100 U. S. 578.

den. It involves fraud and falsehood, and the law abhors both."

In *Bobbitt v. Shryer* (1880)[1] A, B, and C executed their joint note without anything on its face to indicate that any of them were sureties. A was really the principal and B signed the note as surety with the understanding that C, or some one else, should sign as a co-surety. The note with the names of A and B signed to it was presented to C by A, who stated to C that he and B wanted to renew a note and asked C to execute the note with them. This C did, believing that both A and B were principals. Subsequently B had to pay off the note and sought to enforce contribution from C. But it was held that, as against C, B was estopped from denying that he was a joint maker with A.[2]

The facts in *Simpson v. Moore* (1880)[3] were as follows: A note signed by three makers was given for the purchase price of land. The note was purchased by a third person on the faith of a statement made in their presence that the note was supported by a lien on the land and that there was no defense to it. It was held that the makers could not subsequently claim an abatement of the note by virtue of a particular contingency provided for in the deed, the purchaser of the note having had no notice of that provision when he took the same. Where a party to a note asserts that he has no defense to it and another purchases on the faith of this statement, the former cannot subsequently repudiate that statement and set up any defense which might have been in existence at the time the note was transferred.[4]

In *Gheen v. Osborne* (1872)[5] A appeared to be the owner of a lot with a frontage of twenty feet. His father owned the adjoining lot. A contracted by title bond to convey twenty-six feet to C. The father urged C to make the purchase and was himself a witness to the title bond. The purchaser did not know that the six-foot strip on one side of the lot belonged to the father and not to the son. He accordingly

---

[1] 70 Ind. 513.
[2] To the same effect, Melms *v.* Werdehoff, 14 Wis. 19; Keith *v.* Goodwin, 31 Vt. 268.
[3] 5 Lea (Tenn.) 372.
[4] Brooks *v.* Martin, 43 Ala. 360; Wilkinson *v.* Searcy, 74 Ala. 243.
[5] 11 Heisk. (Tenn.) 61.

OBLIGATIONS IN NATURE OF ASSUMPSIT.   245

paid part of the purchase money, took possession of the whole twenty-six feet, and erected a building thereon. It was held that the father could not subsequently assert title to the six feet in question.

In *Hope v. Lawrence* (1867)[6] a principal was held to be estopped from taking advantage of a violation of instructions on the part of his agent under the following circumstances: The defendants, as brokers, had purchased gold in the market for the plaintiff, and they had instructions to sell if the market should reach 217. The market for gold did on one occasion rise to that point and was steady. The brokers failed to sell and informed the plaintiff next day that they had not done so for the reason that the market looked strong. The plaintiff made no complaint of the violation of instructions, but determined to await the future development of the market. Gold shortly went down, and the brokers sold later at 207. It was held that the plaintiff by his acquiescence was estopped from subsequently holding the brokers liable for their violation of instructions in failing to sell on the high market.

In *Faxton v. Faxon* (1873),[7] it appeared that a mortgagee of land, after the death of the mortgagor and when the land was of little value, persuaded a son of the mortgagor, who was intending to remove to another region, to remain on the farm and take care of it, and to support the family of his deceased father, upon a promise that the mortgage should never be enforced. He remained upon the farm and cared for the family. It was held that after the farm had grown valuable under his tillage, the mortgagee was estopped from foreclosing the mortgage.

In *Carr v. London, etc., R. Co.* (1875),[8] the learned Brett, J., stated the general doctrine underlying this branch of estoppel in the following lucid propositions: (1) "If a man by his words or conduct wilfully endeavors to cause another to believe in a certain state of things which the first knows to be false, and if the second believes in such state of things and acts upon his belief, he who knowingly made the false statement is estopped from averring afterwards that such a state

Chapter XXV

Estoppel from acquiescence in unauthorized act of agent.

Mortgagee estopped from foreclosing.

Lord Esher's summary.

1. The wilful misrepresentation.

[6] 50 Barb. (N. Y.) 258.   [7] 28 Mich. 159.   [8] L. R. 10 C. P. 315-318.

of things did not in fact exist." (2) "If a man, either in express terms or by conduct, makes a representation to another of the existence of a certain state of facts which he intends to be acted upon in a certain way, and it be acted upon in that way, in the belief of the existence of such a state of facts, to the damage of him who so believes and acts, the first is estopped from denying the existence of such a state of facts." (3) "If a man, whatever his real meaning may be, so conducts himself that a reasonable man would take his conduct to mean a certain representation of facts, and that it was a true representation, and that the latter was intended to act upon it in a particular way, and he with such belief does act in that way to his damage, the first is estopped from denying that the facts were as represented." (4) "If, in the transaction itself which is in dispute, one has led another into the belief of a certain state of facts by conduct of culpable negligence calculated to have that result, and such culpable negligence has been the proximate cause of leading and has led the other to act by mistake upon such belief, to his prejudice, the second cannot be heard afterwards, as against the first, to show that the state of facts referred to did not exist."

It requires no great amount of critical insight to enable one to see that the law concerning estoppels *in pais* is a manifestation of implied warranty. The subject is therefore referable, as was stated above, to the head of obligations in the nature of assumpsit. One who makes a representation to another on the faith of which the latter acts is impliedly held to warrant the truth of the representation and is precluded or estopped from subsequently denying it. The equitable estoppel which arises from misrepresentation, as in the cases above referred to, is a sort of imperfect contract. It does not give rise to an affirmative right of action in a court of law, but is available only as a defense.

The law concerning equitable estoppel is analogous to that concerning deceit and is a sort of supplement to the latter branch of the law. This will be readily perceived by reference to the essential elements of the equitable estoppel. These are stated by Professor Bigelow to be as follows: (1) There

OBLIGATIONS IN NATURE OF ASSUMPSIT. 247

must have been a false representation or a concealment of material facts; (2) the representation must have been made with knowledge, actual or virtual, of the facts; (3) the party to whom it was made must have been ignorant, actually and permissibly, of the truth of the matter; (4) it must have been made with the intention, actual or virtual, that the other party should act upon it; and (5) the other party must have been induced to act upon it.⁹

Chapter XXV

Essentials of the estoppel.

Where these elements are present the law imposes an implied obligation by which the person making the representation is bound to warrant its truth. It will be noted that in the field of deceit liability is imposed because damage has already fallen upon the person who is deceived. In the field of estoppel the law interposes before the damage has fallen, and inhibits the person making the representation from taking a position which would result in the infliction of damage upon the person deceived.

Doctrine of estoppel forestalls damage.

As one might expect, the doctrine of equitable estoppel had its origin from those situations where an actual intention to mislead is entertained by the person making the representation. As was said by Denman, C. J., in *Pickard v. Sears* (1837),¹ "where one by his words or conduct *wilfully* causes another to believe the existence of a certain state of things and induces him to act," he is estopped. But the doctrine was not destined to be restricted to the bounds of intentional or wilful misrepresentation.

Intention in law of estoppel.

In *Freeman v. Cooke* (1848),² Parke, B., observed upon this point: "If, whatever a man's real intention may be, he so conducts himself that a reasonable man would take the representation to be true and believe that it was meant that he should act upon it, and did act upon it as true, the party making the representation would be equally precluded from contesting its truth; and conduct, by negligence or omission, where there is a duty cast upon a person by usage of trade or otherwise, to disclose the truth, may often have the same

When actual intent to mislead unnecessary.

⁹ Bigelow on Estoppel (4th ed.), 552.
¹ 6 Ad. & El. 474, 33 E. C. L. 115.
² 2 Exch. 663.

effect. As, for instance, a retiring partner omitting to inform his customers of the fact in the usual mode, that the continuing partners were no longer authorized to act as his agents, is bound by all contracts made by them with third persons on the faith of their being so authorized." [3]

A rather radical extension of the doctrine of estoppel by negligence is found in a class of cases of which *Birmingham First Nat. Bank v. Allen* (1893)[4] is the type. In this case it appeared that the plaintiff Allen was a depositor in the defendant bank. The business of attending to the bank account was intrusted by the plaintiff to his clerk, but the latter had no authority to draw a check upon the account. During the course of several months this clerk committed a series of forgeries and drew money from the bank in his employer's name. The plaintiff's passbook was regularly balanced each month, but the plaintiff did not examine the returned checks, and hence did not discover the forgeries in question for a considerable period. An action was then brought by the plaintiff to recover the money which the bank had paid away on the forged checks. It was held that the plaintiff owed the bank the legal duty of looking over the returned vouchers and that his failure to notify the bank of the forgeries, by which the clerk's peculations could have been ended, operated to estop the plaintiff from recovering for the money so paid away.[5] The plaintiff's silence when he should have known of the forgeries and given notice of them, was in effect a representation that the forged signatures were good and binding.

---

[3] To the same effect, Cornish *v.* Abington, 4 H. & N. 549; Preston *v.* Mann, 25 Conn. 118; Tiffany *v.* Anderson, 55 Iowa 405.
[4] 100 Ala. 476.
[5] To the same effect, Leather Manufacturer's Bank *v.* Morgan, 117 U. S. 115; De Feriet *v.* Bank of America, 23 La. Ann. 310; Dana *v.* National Bank of Republic, 132 Mass. 156; Weinstein *v.* National Bank, 69 Tex. 38. *Contra*, Weisser *v.* Denison, 10 N. Y. 69.

PART II

HISTORY AND THEORY OF THE LAW
OF BAILMENT

CHAPTER XXVI

THE EARLY LAW OF BAILMENT.

THE transactions by which personal property belonging to one man may rightly come into the possession of another are many and are as characteristic of the early stages of society as of our own. Implements of industry, tools of trade, domestic animals, the cattle (*catalla*) — or, if we soften the *c* and give the word a wider meaning than *catalla* once bore, the chattels — of the husbandman, play an important part in his life. Borrowing and lending, letting to hire, the doing of kindly turns for one's neighbor, the carrying of goods for pay, are transactions which give rise to legal relations, and any system of law must at a very early stage be prepared to solve the problems raised by them. The body of rules developed in the process of solving the questions raised by situations of this kind we know, in modern times, as the law of bailment.[1]

Chapter XXVI

Antiquity of the law of bailment.

The old French word *bailler*, from which *bailment* is derived, means *to deliver*, and the term itself points us to the most characteristic features of our modern bailment, viz., the necessity that the subject-matter of the transaction should be a deliverable thing and that, in pure bailments, there should be in fact a delivery of it by the bailor to the bailee with the intention of giving him possession. The problem presented for legal solution is, What are the duties and corresponding rights involved in transactions of this kind? The modern bailment is easily identified with the contract *re*, or real contract, of the early law.

Delivery.

Bailment identified with real contract.

We forego for the time any attempt to describe the various transactions which give rise to the relation of bailor and bailee, as it will be preferable to trace them as they arise in

---

[1] See article Possession, 12 Am. L. Rev. 697, by O. W. Holmes; 2 Poll. & Mait. Hist. Eng. Law, 2d ed., 176; Poll. & Wright, Essay on Possession, 161 *et seq.*

the course of legal history. At this juncture one observation will serve to bring out the most striking feature of the bailment, and, indeed, its distinguishing mark: In all bailments possession is severed from ownership. Under the theory of the common law, every bailee has true possession as distinguished from mere custody. The nature of the ownership inhering in the bailor may sometimes, especially in early law, become a matter of inquiry and it may sometimes appear to be almost non-existent; but there can never be any doubt that the bailee has true legal possession. It should further be observed that in all true bailments delivery is made with the consent of the owner, a circumstance which supplies one of the first requisites of a contractual relation. It is doubtless this circumstance which makes the physical custody of the bailee an instance of true legal possession.

Where a transaction of any kind results in a bailment, there can be no question but that the bailee ought to deliver up the object when the purpose of the bailment is accomplished. The bailee then owes the object to its owner. This, the first and most conspicuous duty of the bailee, was of course recognized in our early law almost before it reached the stage of articulate utterance. The proper action for the bailor to bring in order to enforce this duty was the action of debt in the *debet et detinet*.

We must not be misled, however, into the inference that the bailor could always, by the use of this form of action, extract the specific chattel from the hands of an obstinate debtor. In prosecuting his action the plaintiff was always required to state the value of the chattel sued for, and judgment was given in the alternative. If the defendant refused to surrender the chattel, only so much of the judgment as gave a moneyed decree could be enforced. There was no perfect action *in rem* by which the bailor could recover the actual thing itself when still existent.[2]

---

[2] Bracton, 102b; Bracton and Azo, 172: "It would seem at first sight," says he, "that the action in which a movable is demanded would be *in rem* as well as *in personam*, since a specific thing is demanded and the possessor is bound to restore that thing. But in truth it is merely *in personam*, for he from whom the thing is demanded is not

We surmise that this was merely an instance where legal machinery was defective. If the chattel was totally lost or destroyed no sort of remedy would bring it back to the owner, and if the bailee withdrew it or hid it, the object had to be treated as lost, and the most that the law could do was to compensate the owner in damages. Bracton seems to have had the idea that this inability of the owner to recover the thing actually bailed made the action of detinue a purely personal remedy. But it was in fact a proprietary or real action, being founded on the duty of the bailee to surrender the chattel bailed.

Chapter XXVI

Detinue defective.

It is characteristic of law in its early stages that it recognizes a broad duty and enforces it without regard to special circumstances which, in a later stage of legal development, are sufficient to excuse the delinquent. In English law the duty of the bailee to restore was rigorously enforced. Thus Glanvill, writing near the end of the twelfth century, after telling us that a debt arises when an object is lent gratuitously to a borrower to be made use of by him, says that the service being finished, the borrower is bound to restore the chattel without deterioration if it be in existence. But if the thing itself be destroyed, or has by any means been lost while in the custody of the borrower, he is absolutely bound to return a reasonable price.[3] It is well to observe that the principle here laid down is stated concerning gratuitous loans, and is not authority that other bailees were held to the same strict accountability. There can be little doubt, however, that strict accountability was the general rule of law.

Strictness of the early law of bailment.

Bracton, writing near the middle of the thirteenth cen-

---

absolutely bound to restore it, but is bound alternatively to restore it or its price. . . . Therefore, if a man vindicates his movable chattel as having been carried off for any cause or as having lent (*commodatum*), he must in his action define its price, and propound his claim thus: I, such an one, demand that such an one do restore to me such a thing of such a price; or, I complain that such an one detains from me or has robbed me of such a thing of such a price; otherwise no price being named, the vindication of a movable thing will fail." See also 2 Poll. & Mait. Hist. Eng. Law, 2d ed., 174 *et seq.*

[3] Glanvill, Bk. X., ch. 13.

Volume II

Tendency towards mitigation.

tury, evidently stated the law more favorably to bailees than the common law of that day justified. But what he said shows that men were becoming familiar with the idea that there are some circumstances which ought to excuse the bailee. Bracton, of course, borrowed largely from the Digests and Institutes of Justinian — in no department was he more directly influenced than here. But his effort to ingraft on our law the Roman distinctions as to the varying degrees of diligence due from bailees under different circumstances, was too premature to produce much impression.

Depositary.
Pledgee.
Commodatary.

Bracton would relieve the depositary, that is, the gratuitous bailee to keep, where he is not guilty of negligence amounting to a fraud (*dolus*); while the pledgee and bailee for hire are liable if they fail to show due diligence. The commodatary, or person who borrows an article to use and return, is held to the highest degree of diligence.[4]

---

[4] *Liability of Depositary.*—" He with whom a thing is deposited is bound *re* and is required to restore that which he received, especially if he is guilty of any fraud in connection therewith; but he is not held for fault of inattention or negligence, because whoever delivers a thing to be kept by a careless friend ought to blame himself and his own folly." Bracton, 99b.

Liability of Pledgee.—" A creditor who receives a pledge is bound *re* and must restore it; and, since a thing of this kind is given in pledge to the advantage of both, of the debtor as he obtains credit, of the creditor as the debt is thereby more secure, it suffices for him [creditor] to evince due (*exactam*) diligence in keeping the thing, and if he shows this and by accident it be lost he shall be free, nor shall he be hindered from collecting the debt." *Ib.*

Liability of Bailee for Hire.—" Whoever gives or promises compensation for the use of clothes or gold or silver or other ornament, or for the use of an animal, such custody is required of him as a very prudent householder shows in regard to his own things. If he shows this care and by any accident the thing is lost, he shall not be required to restore it. Nor is it enough for him to exercise such diligence as he exercises over his own things unless he shows such as is indicated above" (i. e., the diligence of a very prudent householder). Bracton, 62b. This language is quoted almost verbatim from the Institutes, and there is dispute over the meaning of the term *diligentissimus,* as used in this passage.

Liability of the Borrower of Chattel.—" Where one receives a thing to use [i. e., borrows], it is not enough that he shows such diligence in keeping it as he exhibits in caring for his own, if otherwise he could preserve it by greater diligence; but he is not held to answer for superior force or fortuitous accident unless his own negligence may have intervened." Bracton, 99b.

The original of the first, second,

It would be surprising indeed if principles drawn by Bracton bodily from the Institutes of Justinian were in harmony at all points with the law of England. We may be sure that Bracton did not state English law. He was, however, preparing the way for the amelioration of the harsh rule of the common law; but the actual recognition of the principles laid down by him was still far distant in the future.

Chapter XXVI

Bracton premature.

In conformity with the principle of strict liability which the early English law recognized, the bailee was held liable where his possession was invaded by a wrongdoer who destroyed or carried away the chattel bailed. In other words, robbery or theft from the bailee was not available by him as a defense. That such a rule should ever have prevailed is perhaps a little surprising, but that it constituted a beginning point in the law concerning the liability of the bailee seems to be sufficiently attested.[5]

Robbery or theft no defense for bailee.

The bailee was treated as a debtor. He owed the chattel or its value to the bailor, and the unpreventable loss of it was his misfortune. In other words, the early bailee of a specific chattel was held liable to the same extent as the borrower of money or consumable goods, returnable in like value or quantity, is held liable in modern law. The defense of unpreventable loss is really a defense *in pais;* that is, it derives its efficacy from equitable considerations. Naturally the admission of such a defense in a court of law requires time and a certain degree of maturity in legal conceptions. It belongs to a later stage than that in which the principle of naked legal liability is settled.

Unpreventable loss a sort of equitable defense.

While the principle of the absolute liability of the bailee as a debtor undoubtedly constitutes the point of departure in our early law of bailment, it was to be expected that when occasion arose efforts should be made to break away from it. The early precedents are few in number and by no means as clear as could be desired. In A. D. 1200, a plaintiff sued in

Hence not available in early law.

---

and fourth of the passages here quoted is to be found in note 8, p. 15, *ante.*

[5] Holmes, Common Law, 164 *et seq.* See 2 Poll. & Mait. Hist. Eng. Law, 2d ed., 170 *et seq.* But see Carrier's Liability, by J. H. Beale, 11 Harv. L. Rev. 159.

detinue for two charters delivered to the defendant for safe-keeping. The defendant pleaded that his house was burned by robbers and that at the same time they took the charters from his possession. On this admission that the charters had been lost out of his custody the plaintiff obtained judgment.[6]

Half a century later Bracton wrote his great book, and in a generation or two we apparently begin to see the ameliorating effects of his ideas. Britton, writing about A. D. 1287 and giving currency to Bracton's views, says that where anything is borrowed to be restored on a certain day, the debtor is bound to restore to the creditor the thing borrowed in as good condition, or better, than it was received, or else its value, unless by accident of fire, water, robbery, or larceny, restoration has become impossible; for, says he, "against such accidents no one ought to answer for things lost, unless they happened by his own fault or negligence."[7]

A few years later a case was decided in which this view is partially reflected. Detinue was brought for charters bailed for safe-keeping. The defendant tendered the charters with their seals cut off, which mutilation, he alleged, had been done by robbers. This was accepted as sufficient.[8] As will be perceived, the question whether unpreventable loss is a good defense for the bailee was not squarely presented, for the fact that the charters, though mutilated by cutting off their seals, were actually returned to the plaintiff, supplied a fair ground for evading the principle of the absolute responsibility of the bailee without materially qualifying it.

In *Bonion's Case* (1315)[9] the plaintiff brought detinue to recover certain seals, plate, and jewels which had been delivered to the defendant for keeping. The latter alleged that the plaintiff had delivered the jewels in a locked chest, the key to which was taken away by the plaintiff without giving information as to the contents. Subsequently robbers came by night and carried off the chest into the field, where they

[6] Select Civ. Pleas (Selden Soc.), pl. 8.
[7] Britton, 62.
[8] Record of Brinkburn Cartulary (1299), 105, cited by Messrs. Pollock and Maitland in 2 Hist. Eng. Law, 2d ed., 171, note.
[9] Y. B. 8 Edw. II. 275; Fitz. Abr., *Detinue*, pl. 59.

EARLY LAW OF BAILMENT. 257

forced the lock and abstracted the contents. At the same time the defendant was robbed of his own goods, a circumstance which was alleged in order to show that the defendant displayed at least as much care in guarding the chest as in keeping his own goods. The plaintiff replied that the jewels were delivered in a chest *not locked,* which was to be restored at the pleasure of the bailor. On this allegation issue was joined. In other words, the defendant was to be discharged provided he could make good the assertion that the jewels were delivered in a locked chest.

This decision is quite celebrated and has been cited many times in connection with the law of bailment. In his comment on *Southcote's Case,*[1] Lord Coke offers the explanation that where the valuables are delivered sealed and under key as alleged in the plea, the plaintiff does not trust the defendant with the goods, and so they are not in his possession in the sense necessary to perfect the bailment.[2] At a later day, Lord Holt said: "I cannot see the reason of that difference nor why the bailee should not be charged with goods in a chest as well as with goods out of a chest. For the bailee has as little power over them when they are out of a chest as to any benefit he might have by them, as when they are in a chest; and he has as great power to defend them in one case as in the other."[3] By this language Lord Holt meant to indicate that the bailee was not liable in any event where the chattels were lost by robbery from the bailee.

The distinction recognized in *Bonion's Case* is perhaps a rather specious one, but it served the end of justice, and sufficed to take the case out of the operation of the principle which made the bailee absolutely liable. Crude devices must sometimes be used in order to parry the effect of a general rule. When the work of demolition has gone far enough we

Chapter XXVI

Coke's explanation of Bonion's Case.

Criticism of Lord Holt.

---

[1] 4 Coke 84.
[2] The compiler of the table to the Y. B. of 8 Edw. II., in digesting Bonion's Case states the distinction thus: "If jewels be bailed to me and I put them into a casket and thieves rob me of them in the night time, I am answerable; not if they be delivered to me in a chest sealed up." Quoted by Sir Wm. Jones, Bailment, Am. ed. (1806), 45.
[3] Coggs v. Bernard, 2 Ld. Raym. 909.

Still later Sir William Jones, in his brilliant essay, echoing the criticism of Lord Holt, and with his

17

may feel inclined to smile at the ancient subterfuge. But it was helpful in its day.

Closely associated with the principle of the absolute liability of the bailee as debtor was the rule, at one time fully settled in the common law, that the bailee was the only proper person to bring an action against one who wrongfully dispossessed him.[4] In the early common law, and indeed in any primitive system, the concession of a right of action to the bailee almost necessarily involves a denial of such right to the bailor. The bailor cannot sue the third or strange hand which strips the bailee of his lawful possession.

The rule that the bailee must sue the tortfeasor has often been treated as a corollary from the general doctrine of the absolute liability of the bailee.[5] Sometimes theory inverts this relation and it is accordingly declared that the doctrine of absolute responsibility is derived from the rule which gives the suit to the bailee.[6] Apparently the two propositions were considered merely two different aspects of the same truth.[7]

---

mind on the various degrees of diligence required of bailees under varying circumstances, said: " I confess, however, that, anxiously as I wish on all occasions to see authorities respected and judgments holden sacred, Bonion's case appears to me wholly incomprehensible, for the defendant instead of having been grossly negligent seems to have used at least ordinary diligence; and, after all, the loss was occasioned by a burglary, for which no bailee can be responsible without a very special undertaking. The plea therefore in this case was good and the replication idle." Jones on Bailment, Am. ed. (1806), 44.

[4] 2 Poll. & Mait. Hist. Eng. Law, 2d ed., 172; Holmes, Common Law, 165 et seq.

[5] Thus Beaumanoir (1283) says that if a hired thing is stolen the suit belongs to the bailee because he is answerable to the owner. Beaum. XXXI. 16, quoted by Judge Holmes, Common Law, 167. This explanation is the one commonly given in the Year Books. Thus Brian, C. J., said in 1469, " If I bail certain goods to a man to keep and they are then taken away, he shall have a writ of trespass for the possession, for he is chargeable over to me." Y. B. 9 Edw. IV. 34, pl. 9. See also the authorities cited by Judge Holmes, Common Law, 170, 171.

[6] Judge Holmes makes an elaborate and ingenious argument to show that the principle of absolute liability of the bailee is derived from the rule which gives the right of suit against the third hand to the bailee only. See Common Law, 164 et seq; also his article on Possession, 12 Am. L. Rev. 688 et seq.

[7] On this point Messrs. Pollock and Maitland observe: " Perhaps we come nearest to historical truth if we say that between the two old rules there was no logical priority. The bailee had the action because he was liable and was liable because

The two rules at least belong to the same legal stratum and have their roots in the same idea.

During the fourteenth century we observe that the old rule of strict liability continues to show the signs of weakening which had been manifested in *Bonion's Case*. In 1354, Thorpe, B., said in the Exchequer, "if one bails me his goods to keep and I put them with my own and they are stolen, I shall not be charged."[8] And in the case where this suggestion was made, the plaintiff, suing to recover a pledge, in order to avoid the plea that the goods were stolen, was driven to reply by alleging a tender, which of course would have left the pledgee a wrongdoer and therefore liable as for a conversion.[9] This relaxation of the rule of strict liability took place in the law of pledge, and it was for a long time limited to that particular branch of bailment; but in the end, as we shall see, the innovation spread over most of the field.[1]

In the fifteenth century Cotesmere, J., stated the law clearly in these words: "If," said he, "I deliver goods to a man to keep for my use, and the goods by his negligence (*mesgard*) are stolen, he shall be charged at my instance for those goods; but if he be robbed of them it is excusable by the law."[2] But this was dictum, and we shall find that the just rule stated by him was not always applied.

Chapter XXVI

Relaxation in the law of pledge.

---

he had the action." 2 Hist. Eng. Law, 2d ed., 171.

[8] Y. B. 29 Ass. 163, pl. 28.

[9] See *Coggs v. Bernard*, 2 Ld. Raym. 909, where Lord Holt points out that after a lawful tender the pledgee who refuses to surrender the pledge is absolutely liable for all loss that may be suffered. He is a wrongdoer, and not a general bailee.

[1] St. Germain, writing on bailments about 1530, after stating certain distinctions according to which the bailee shall be charged or not, adds: "These diversities hold most commonly upon pledges, or where a man hireth goods of his neighbor to a certain day for certain money." Dial. II., ch. 38.

Coke, of course, had an explanation for this distinction, though it seems a rather artificial one. The pledgee, says he, "has a property in them and not a custody only." Southcote's Case, 4 Coke 83b.

[2] Y. B. 10 Hen. VI. 21, pl. 69.

As the substantive rule was weakened, so as to allow the bailee to escape liability in certain cases by showing that the chattels were taken from him by theft or robbery, it was necessary for the procedural counterpart of this doctrine to undergo revision also. Thus in 1373 it was declared that where goods are unlawfully taken from the bailee at will, the owner as well as the custodian may maintain an action of trespass; but it was observed by

260   FOUNDATIONS OF LEGAL LIABILITY.

Volume II

Action against jailer for escape.

Public enemy.

Alien enemy.

Near the middle of the same century the *Marshal's Case* (1455)³ arose. It is cited in all subsequent cases of bailment down to *Coggs v. Bernard* (1703),⁴ and is therefore worthy of careful notice. An action of debt was brought against the Marshal of the King's Bench as jailer, to recover for an escape. Jailers, it will be observed, were treated as ordinary bailees. The defendant pleaded that the enemies of the king broke into the prison and took off the prisoner against his will. The court intimated that if alien enemies like the French were to break into the prison, or give occasion for the prisoner to escape by burning the prison, the jailer would not be liable, leaving the inference that where the unlawful act is done by persons against whom redress could be had, as presumably would be the case against local rioters or traitors, the jailer must answer. Such was the view of Danby, J.; but Prisot, C. J., preferred to base the judgment against the defendant on the ground of negligence in guarding the prisoner, though the facts stated in the report of the case seem to negative the idea of negligence in fact. This judge also said that escape by accidental fire would be a defense for the jailer.

In subsequent decisions the *Marshal's Case* was taken as authority for the rule stated in 1488 as follows: "If goods are taken by a trespasser known to the bailee, he [the bailee] shall be charged by his bailor and shall have his own action against the trespasser." ⁵

Special proviso against absolute liability.

A distinction was always made in favor of a bailee where upon the delivery of the goods they were accepted with the special proviso that they were to be kept by the bailee with the same care as his own goods. Danby, J., once said that such a proviso was absolutely necessary to protect the bailee from the liability of an absolute debtor in any case.⁶ This dictum was undoubtedly too strong, but it shows how deeply the principle of the absolute liability of the bailee was rooted in the common law. Long afterwards, the learned Coke ad-

Persay, J., that he who first recovered should oust the other of his action. Y. B. 48 Edw. III. 20, pl. 8.
³ Y. B. 33 Hen. VI. 1, pl. 3.

⁴ 2 Ld. Raym. 909.
⁵ Y. B. 3 Hen. VII. 4, pl. 16. See also Holmes, Common Law, 178.
⁶ Y. B. 9 Edw. IV. 40, pl. 22.

monished the prospective bailee always to make a qualified acceptance; otherwise he may be charged in case of theft.[7]

Chapter XXVI

St. Germain, in the second dialogue of his quaint Doctor and Student, published in 1530, touches upon the liability of bailees. The fact that this book has always been held in high esteem for accuracy and learning, and the additional circumstance that it stands at the close of the year-book period, make it worth while for the reader to peruse what is there said in connection with the topic of the "chances that may happen to goods that a man hath in his keeping which be not his own"—a very happy definition of the bailment, by the way.

St. Germain on law of bailment.

The author's illustrations are taken from a little tract called the *Summa Rosella,* and the rule of milder liability for the bailee which the previous writer sanctioned evidently commended itself strongly to St. Germain. "If," says he, "a man lends another a horse and a house by chance falleth upon the horse, the bailee shall not be liable if the house was well built and fell by reason of a sudden tempest or other casualty. But if the house were like to fall, then it cannot be taken as a chance, but as the default of him that had the horse delivered to him."[8] But the borrower of a consumable thing, it is pointed out, is absolutely liable as debtor. Here the old principle remains unimpaired.[9] On the whole, St. Germain

Loss by tempest.

---

[7] Southcote's Case, 4 Coke 83*b*.
[8] Dial. II., ch. 38.
[9] "A man may have of another, by way of loan or borrowing, money, corn, wine, and such other things, where the same thing cannot be delivered if it be occupied, but another thing of like nature and like value must be delivered for it; and such things he that they be lent to, may by force of the loan use as his own, and therefore if they perish, it is at his jeopardy; and this is most properly called a loan." Dial. II., ch. 38.

St. Germain on Law of Bailment (*1530*).—In the following passage St. Germain treats on common-law principles certain other aspects of the law of bailment:

"Also a man may lend to another a horse, an ox, or a cart, or such other things as may be delivered again, and they by force of that loan may be used and occupied reasonably in such manner as they were borrowed for, or as it was agreed at the time of the loan that they should be occupied; and if such things be occupied otherwise than according to the intent of the loan and in that occupation they perish, in what wise soever they perish, so it be not in default of the owner, he that borrowed them shall be charged therewith in law and

gives us a concise and by no means a bad statement of the law of bailment in his day. Two hundred and thirty-five years later Blackstone had hardly anything more to say, and he did not say it nearly so well.[1]

Woodlife's Case (1596)[2] is notable as having developed some difference of opinion among the judges on the question of the liability of a factor. An action of account was brought against a factor for goods delivered to be sold. The defendant pleaded that he had been robbed of these goods along with conscience; and if he that borrowed them occupy them in such manner as they were lent for, and in that occupation they perish in default of him that they were lent to, then he shall answer for them; and if they perish not through his default, then he that owneth them shall bear the loss. Also if a man have goods to keep to a certain day, for a certain recompense for the keeping, he shall stand charged or not charged after, as default or no default shall be in him as before appeareth; and so it is if he have nothing for the keeping. But if he have for the keeping, and make a promise at the time of the delivery to redeliver them safe at his peril, then he shall be charged with all chances that may fall; but if he make that promise and have nothing for keeping, I think he is bound to no such casualties but that be wilful and his own default, for that is a nude or a naked promise, whereupon as I suppose no action lieth. Also, if a man find goods of another, if they be after hurt or lost by wilful negligence, he shall be charged to the owner; but if they be lost by other casualty, as if they be laid in a house that by chance is burned, or if he deliver them to another to keep, that runneth away with them, I think he is discharged. And these diversities hold most commonly upon pledges or where a man hireth goods of his neighbor to a certain day for certain money."

William Noy, Attorney-General and Privy Councillor to Chas. I., and author of the Grounds and Maxims of the English Laws, in treating of this subject a hundred years later, was content to adopt the language of St. Germain without any substantial alteration. See Noy's Maxims, ch. 43.

[1] 2 Bl. Com. 451. Blackstone got most of what little he had to say about contracts in general and about bailments in particular from Sir Henry Finch's Discourse on Law (1613). Any one who will take the trouble to glance at Finch's chapter on 'Bailments and Contracts' will see that Blackstone has perpetuated not only the form but the substance of the earlier writer's remarks — a circumstance which is to be regretted. Blackstone was less excusable in this, as when he wrote the subject had been illuminated by Lord Holt's opinion in Coggs v. Bernard, 2 Ld. Raym. 909. The author of the commentaries no doubt looked suspiciously on Holt's Roman learning.

[2] Owen 57. This case is somewhat differently reported in Moo. K. B. 462. Mosley v. Fosset, Moo. K. B. 543, shows that Fenner rather inclined to Popham's view on this question, thus dividing the court equally, Popham and Fenner being against applying the rule of strict liability and Clench and Gawdy favoring it.

other of his own goods and chattels. Gawdy, J., relied on the *Marshal's Case* and was of opinion that the plea was bad. Popham, J., however, said " it is a good plea before auditors, and there is a difference between carriers and other servants and factors, for carriers are paid for their carriage and take upon them safely to carry and deliver the things received."

Chapter XXVI

The first year of the seventeenth century gives us the still more notable case of *Southcott v. Bennett* (1601), or, as it is more frequently styled, *Southcote's Case*.[3] This decision is instructive because it is one of the last in which the ancient view that the bailor is liable as a debtor was fully accepted. It may be admitted that the decision was reactionary and the principle laid down in it was afterwards repudiated. This circumstance has caused *Southcote's Case* to be unduly discredited. In fact, the seed of dissent had already been sown, and apparently the decision was itself made possible only by the fact that Gawdy and Clench were the only judges present.

Southcote's Case.

The facts were as follows: Southcote sued the defendant, Bennett, in detinue for chattels delivered to him "to keep safely." The defendant pleaded robbery; replication that the alleged robber was one J. S., servant of the defendant. The bearing of the replication on the question of liability was not considered, being evidently looked upon as immaterial, and the court awarded judgment in favor of the plaintiff on the admission of delivery made in the plea. The use of the word 'safely' in the declaration would naturally lead us to infer that the court treated it as implying a warranty to keep safely at all events. Such is the construction placed upon the case in Jones on Bailments.[4] This view brings it into harmony with present conceptions; but by the judges who decided the case, the word 'safely' seems to have been treated

Bailment for safekeeping

---

[3] 4 Coke 83b, Cro. Eliz. 815. There is an excellent report of this case in a MS. volume of reports of 42-45 Eliz. now in Harvard Law School Library. The case has been edited from this MS. by Professor Beale and reprinted in 13 Harv. L. Rev. 43. It is the only report of the case which gives the argument of counsel.

[4] Am. ed. (1806), 47. Professor Beale also seems to lean towards this view. Carrier's Liability, 11 Harv. L. Rev. 162; Southcott *v.* Bennett, 13 Harv. L. Rev. 46.

Ancient doctrine applied.

as stating merely a conclusion of law and as adding nothing to the obligation implied by law upon delivery.

Coke, as appears from his report of the case, understood the decision in this latter sense, for he remarks that "to be kept and to be kept safe is all one." This was no mere conceit of his. If such had not already been the law, it was made the law of that case at least by the decision then rendered.[5] The conclusion is irresistible that *Southcote's Case* is

---

[5] *Mode of Declaring on the Duty to Keep.*— It must be admitted that the language "to be kept safe" is capable of being construed either as alleging a warranty in fact or as stating a legal conclusion. The latter seems to be the better view, though the language of Coke's Report is at some points not in harmony with it. In declaring on bailments it has always been customary to charge all bailees with the duty *salvo et secure* to keep and deliver. This is shown by the long series of precedents referred to in Ross *v.* Hill, 2 C. B. 877, 52 E. C. L. 877, where the undertaking charged in the declaration is *safely and securely* to convey the plaintiff and his luggage. Tindal, C. J., held that *safely and securely* meant no more than safely and securely with reference to the degree of care which under the circumstances the law requires of the defendant. "If it had appeared that the defendant was a common carrier his duty would have been to carry and deliver safely at all events, without excuse, unless prevented by the act of God or the queen's enemies. If, on the other hand, he had been a mere gratuitous bailee, then a less degree of care and caution would have been required of him than is required from a bailee for reward. The words 'safely and securely,' therefore, receive different interpretations with reference to the character in which the defendant is charged."

In Coggs *v.* Bernard, 2 Ld. Raym. 909, the declaration alleged that the defendant undertook safely and securely (*salvo et secure*) to transport and lay down goods in Water Lane. On this point Lord Holt says very positively that such an undertaking will not make the bailee liable at all events, as upon a warranty. "Nay, suppose the bailee undertakes safely and securely to keep the goods in express words; yet even that would not charge him with all sorts of neglect." The undertaking is evidently looked upon as an agreement to keep safely, subject to the liability fixed by law.

As appears from the manuscript report of Southcott *v.* Bennett, printed in 13 Harv. L. Rev. 43, Dodderidge argued for the defendant that in case of a general bailment the bailee would not be liable in case of robbery, and that a special undertaking to keep at his own peril was necessary to fix absolute liability upon him. Pynde, for plaintiff, insisted, on the contrary, that the bailee was absolutely liable in case of robbery, and that a special engagement to keep as his own was necessary in order to enable him to escape in such case. This view met the approval of the court.

On the whole, it clearly seems that injustice has been done to Lord Coke by later writers, who, in order to find a basis for the actual decision which would harmonize it with existing views, have interpreted the word 'safe' in the declaration as importing a warranty, a construction which leaves the conclusion of Coke that to keep and to

in entire harmony with the ancient view that a bailee is debtor for the thing bailed. Opinion may well differ about the propriety of the particular decision, for the time was now at hand when the old rule was to be discarded.[6]

<small>Chapter XXVI</small>

It will be observed that the unquestioned and unquestionable right of the bailor to sue in detinue was probably of itself sufficient in the minds of our early judges to fix absolute liability upon the bailee; for detinue, like its congener debt, lay only where the obligation on which the action was founded could be conceived as being in the nature of a debt. If the bailor happened to sue in some other form, as by bringing a writ of account or of trespass on the case, it was a much easier thing to relax the principle of absolute liability, and in connection with these actions, the relaxation first occurred.

<small>Ancient rule peculiar to action of detinue.</small>

As Professor Beale has pointed out,[7] if the bailor brought against his bailee the action of trespass on the case, it was necessary that the defendant should be shown to be guilty of negligence before he could be held, and all considerations going to rebut the charge of negligence were admissible in his favor. In *Williams v. Hide* (1628)[8] an action on the case was brought to recover damages for the loss of a gray gelding by the bailee. It appeared that the animal had been stolen without any negligence on the part of the bailee. It was held that he was not liable.

<small>Negligence on part of bailee essential in action on the case.</small>

Again, if the bailor brought the action of account, the defendant could show that the goods were lost without fault

---

keep safe are all one, without support.

Professor Beale, in 13 Harv. L. Rev. 46, cautions against attaching too much importance to Southcott *v.* Bennett. It was decided by only two judges in the absence of the others, at least one of whom (Popham) held a different view; and the report referred to by him recites that judgment was given for the plaintiff *nisi aliquod dicatur in contrario die veneris proximo*. We have no means of knowing what was the subsequent fate of the case.

[6] In Calye's Case, (1581) 8 Coke 32, it was declared that one who, not being a common innkeeper, lodges a guest upon the latter's request, is not liable for the goods of the guest stolen by the servant of the householder. So, the innkeeper himself was not liable where the guest requested the innkeeper to put the horse to pasture and it was subsequently stolen. This is certainly a rule of liability quite different from that recognized in Southcote's Case.

[7] Carrier's Liability: Its History, 11 Harv. L. Rev. 158.

[8] Palmer 548, W. Jones 179.

Volume II

Liability in account.

on his part, as, for instance, by robbery.[9] In *Vere v. Smith* (1661)[1] an action of account was brought against a bailee to whom certain money had been intrusted. The defendant pleaded that certain malefactors who were unknown to him entered his house and stole the money in question. The plea was adjudged to be good.[1*]

Detinue ceases to be used against bailee.

During the seventeenth century *Southcote's Case* was frequently cited, but the question of the liability of a bailee who had been robbed did not come up in any action of detinue. Detinue, the time-honored remedy of the bailor, had become, or like debt was fast becoming, unpopular. It could not be brought in the King's Bench by original writ. The defendant could wage his law. Furthermore, as Professor Ames has pointed out, if the bailor had paid in advance for the safekeeping of his property he could not recover the money in case of a failure on the part of the bailee to comply with his obligation.[2] Likewise, while the plaintiff in detinue might recover the chattel, he could not recover damages for deterioration resulting from a negligent omission on the part of the bailee.[2*]

It is therefore not surprising that the action on the case

---

[9] Fitz. Abr., *Accompt*, pl. III; Tanworth's Case, Y. B. 41 Edw. III. 3, pl. 8.

[1] 1 Vent. 121.

[1*] In the case where Danby, J., gave utterance to the dictum referred to above, to the effect that there should be a special acceptance if the bailee wished to escape absolute liability, the court held that robbery could not be pleaded in bar, but should be pleaded before the auditor of accounts. Y. B. 9 Edw. IV. 40, pl. 22.

Professor Beale is inclined to think that the principle of absolute liability was never fully recognized even in detinue prior to Southcote's Case. On this point we agree with Judge Holmes that Southcote's Case merely reflected the ancient theory and made no new law. See Common Law, 178 *et seq*. The bailee was debtor, and solely for that reason detinue could be maintained against him.

[2] History of Assumpsit, 2 Harv. L. Rev. 4, citing Statham's Abr., *Action on Case* ('1469).

[2*] In 1510 Moore, Serjeant, pointed out the distinction in this respect between detinue and case as follows: "If I bail goods to a man to keep safely and he undertakes to do this, for a reward or otherwise, and by reason of his negligence my goods perish [or are permitted to deteriorate], I shall then have an action on the case; for if I bring an action of detinue, as I may if I prefer, then I shall recover the thing as it is. And it is my own folly to bring such an action where I can have a better." Keilw. 160, pl. 2.

should have finally supplanted detinue as a remedy against the bailee. This naturally led to the rejection of the ancient principle of absolute liability. Upon this movement Lord Holt sheds some light at the beginning of the eighteenth century. There is no reason or justice, says he, in holding a bailee for accommodation liable without some default on his part. Speaking then of *Southcote's Case*, which declared the contrary rule, he said it had not been followed and that the practice during his own and Chief Justice Pemberton's time had been against it. This remark, be it remembered, was made in deciding a suit where the plaintiff had brought an action of trespass on the case. It was in the same connection that Powell, J., gave utterance to the memorable words: "Let us consider the reason of the case, for nothing is law that is not reason." [3]

Chapter XXVI

Adoption of case leads to final rejection of old doctrine.

In connection with the use of the action on the case as a remedy against the bailee, one thing is to be observed. The declaration nearly always contained the words *super se assumpsit* or their equivalent.[4] Where the action was against a bailee plying one of the common occupations, such as carrier or innkeeper, he was chargeable by common law without the use of this formula.[5]

Allegation of the assumpsit.

In the earlier cases this expression was clearly intended to bring out the fact that the defendant had entered upon the execution of the bailment; that is, had taken the chattel into

---

[3] Coggs v. Bernard, 2 Ld. Raym. 909.

[4] See Common Law, 183; 2 Harv. L. Rev. 4, 11 Harv L. Rev. 166.

[5] Y. B. 42 Edw. III. 11, pl. 13; Y. B. 46 Edw. III. 19, pl. 19; Rich v. Kneeland, Hob. 17, Cro. Jac. 330. In Symons v. Darknoll, Palmer 523, it appeared that the defendant was a lighterman, but it was not alleged that he was a common lighterman. It was said, "Although no promise be laid, the plaintiff should recover, and the failure to allege that the defendant was a common lighterman does no harm." Hyde, C. J., said: "Delivery makes the contract;" that is, delivery to a common carrier implies the undertaking on his part. The same principle was applied in Kenrig v. Eggleston (1648), Aleyn 93; Nicholls v. More (1661), 1 Sid. 36.

In Rogers v. Head, Cro. Jac. 262, the carrier agreed for reasonable compensation to transport goods from London to Southwark, and this was held sufficient to charge him for his failure to deliver, although the declaration omitted to allege that the defendant was a common carrier at the time the agreement was made.

Function of the formula super se assumpsit.

his custody upon his promise to do something therewith or to redeliver the chattel at the proper time. The allegation of the assumption or undertaking accordingly brought the case within the principle which made any one liable for damage to property by reason of his misfeasance or negligence in carrying the undertaking into effect. Prior to the development of special assumpsit as a contractual remedy, this was the only function which it was possible for the allegation *super se assumpsit* to serve, since the mere making of a promise imposed no legal duty whatever. The taking of the goods into custody with the understanding that they were to be used in a particular way, and the subsequent default, fixed upon the bailee the liability of a tortfeasor. The action sounded purely in tort.

Expression becomes ambiguous after advent of special assumpsit.

When, however, the modern action of assumpsit appeared and the contract of bailment was transferred to modern assumptual law, the expression *super se assumpsit* became, or appeared to become, ambiguous. No man could now infallibly tell whether the action sounded in tort or contract. If it was viewed as an action of tort all that was necessary to be shown was that the bailee entered upon possession and negligently suffered the goods to be damaged. If it was viewed as an action of contract a consideration for the assumpsit had to be shown. From this circumstance it becomes necessary for the student of our early legal history to analyze each case in which an assumpsit is alleged before he can determine whether the action is really in contract or in tort. The difficulty disappears only in the eighteenth century.

Carrier by sea.

The most interesting case in the seventeenth century bearing on the liability of the bailee is *Mors v. Slew* (1668),[7] which involved the question of the liability of a carrier by sea. It was twice debated in the King's Bench. Sir Matthew Hale presided at the hearing and delivered the opinion. It appeared that while a ship was lying at anchor in the Thames a number

---

[7] 2 Keb. 866, 3 Keb. 72, 112, 135, 2 Lev. 69, 1 Vent. 190, 238, 1 Mod. 85, T. Raym. 220. There is very little disagreement among the several reporters of this case, a circumstance worthy of notice during this period.

of robbers came on board under the pretense of impressing seamen. Having gained admission in this way, they forcibly took certain chests of money, for the loss of which an action on the case was brought against the master. The defendant was entirely blameless, as he had the ordinary number of watchmen requisite for the protection of the ship. The court accordingly inclined strongly to the defendant, but after full argument he was held liable. "The first reason wherefore the master is liable," said Lord Hale, "is because he takes a reward."

A few years later the distinction between the gratuitous bailment and the bailment for hire was further recognized in *Rex v. Hertford* (1681),[8] wherein Pemberton, C. J., held that one who accepts money to keep for accommodation only and without reward is not liable in case of robbery.[9]

---

[8] 2 Show. 172.
[9] This decision was in full conformity with the earlier case of Williams *v.* Hide, Palmer 548.

CHAPTER XXVII

MODERN LAW OF BAILMENT.

_{Volume II}

_{Negligence of gratuitous bailee.}

THE celebrated case of *Coggs v. Bernard* (1703)[1] raised the question of the liability of one who had undertaken to remove for the plaintiff certain casks of brandy. The declaration did not allege that the defendant was a common porter or a common carrier, nor that he was to be paid any compensation. It was simply alleged that he had undertaken safely and securely to take up and transport several hogsheads of brandy to a certain cellar in Water Lane, and that in so doing the defendant so negligently and improvidently put them down that, through lack of care, one of the casks was staved and the brandy lost.

After verdict for the plaintiff it was moved in arrest of judgment that the declaration was insufficient, there being no averment that the defendant was to have anything for his pains, nor any allegation that he was a common porter. If the defendant had been a common carrier, an agreement to pay a reasonable compensation would have been implied. The only question, then, raised by the motion was whether a consideration was necessary to fix liability on the bailee in this case. The fact that this point should have been so strongly pressed marks the culmination of a gradual change in the way of looking at the bailment. It was no longer looked upon as a real contract in which duty attaches under the law, without assistance from the conception of the obligation of promise.

_{Misfeasance.}

The absence of an assumptual consideration in the bailment declared upon now made it necessary to go back to fundamental principles and to place liability on the ground of a breach of primary legal duty. Said Powell, J.: "An action indeed will not lie for not doing the thing, for want of a sufficient consideration; but yet if the bailee will take the

[1] 2 Ld. Raym. 909.

goods into his custody, he shall be answerable for them; for the taking the goods into his custody is his own act." So Gould, J.: "Any man that undertakes to carry goods is liable to an action, be he a common carrier or whatever he is, if through his neglect they are lost or come to any damage." Behind these expressions was that unbroken line of precedents from the time of the earliest recorded decisions holding persons liable in trespass on the case for damage inflicted by reason of a misfeasance in carrying out an undertaking. The chief significance of the decision is then not to be found in the principle actually decided, for that was indeed old.

Chapter XXVII

The Classification of Bailments.

Lord Holt, however, took advantage of the opportunity presented in *Coggs v. Bernard* to examine the entire subject of bailments with some fulness. As a result he gave us our modern classification of bailments and stated with reasonable precision and substantial accuracy the various degrees of care which are required of the different bailees. Let us first examine his classification, which was based largely on the Roman law as laid down in Bracton. He distributes all bailments into six classes, namely:

Lord Holt's division.

1. *Depositum,* or the naked bailment of goods to be kept for the use of the bailor and without any compensation.

2. *Commodatum,* where goods or chattels are lent to the bailee for his temporary use and subject to be returned.

3. *Locatio rei,* where chattels are let to the bailee to be used for hire.

4. *Vadium* (pledge or pawn), where a chattel is delivered to be held as security for a debt.

5. *Locatio operis faciendi,* where goods are delivered to be carried or to have something done about them, for a reward paid to the bailee.

6. *Mandatum,* a delivery of goods to one who is to transport them or do something to them without compensation.[2]

---

[2] *Genesis of Lord Holt's Classification of Bailments.*— The Roman origin of this classification is very manifest. The Roman contracts *re,* or real contracts, were the *depositum,* the *commodatum,* the *pignus*

In his Essay on Bailments, first published in 1781, Sir William Jones departed somewhat from Lord Holt's classification and discussed the subject under the five heads — *Depositum, Mandatum, Commodatum, Pignus, Locatum*. The last was subdivided into the three following: (a) *locatio rei*, (b) *locatio operis faciendi*, (c) *locatio operis mercium vehendarum*. This is by no means a bad classification.

Late writers are inclined to follow the main lines of the classification marked out by Judge Story in his work on Bailments (1832). His primary division is threefold, viz.: I. Bailments in which the trust is exclusively for the benefit of the bailor or of a third person; II. Bailments in which the

Jones's classification.

Threefold classification of Story.

and the *mutuum*. The first three are transactions which we recognize at once as true bailments. These terms were accordingly adopted by Lord Holt as the names of his first, second, and fourth classes of bailments, and he used them in exactly the same sense they bore in the Roman law, merely substituting the word *vadium*, the equivalent of *pignus*, as the name of his fourth class. Of course in this Holt was following Bracton.

The fourth of the Roman real contracts (*mutuum*) is not a bailment, and of course was not classed by Lord Holt as such. It arises where an article consumable in use, like oil, wheat, or wine, is lent with the understanding that it is to be returned in like amount, kind, and quality. It cannot be treated as a bailment because under both the civil and common law there is a transmutation of ownership which is inconsistent with the fundamental conception of bailment. We call it a loan, but the two terms are not coextensive, as loan also includes the *commodatum*, which is a true bailment. This defect in English terminology attracted the attention of Gibbon. "The Latin language very happily expresses the fundamental difference between the *commodatum* and the *mutuum*, which our poverty is reduced to confound under the vague and common appellation of loan." Decline and Fall, ch. 44. In choosing the names to apply to his third and fifth classes of bailments Lord Holt appropriated the Roman word *locatio* as the significant term. Glanvill and Bracton had used the term *locatum* in the same sense, and we have already noticed the process by which the Roman consensual agreement was turned for English purposes into a contract *re*. Holt now perpetuated this perversion in English law for all time; for in using the term *locatio* as the name of a class of bailments he thereby restricted it to cases involving the delivery of a chattel.

As the name of his sixth and last class of bailments Lord Holt used the term *mandatum*. Like the *locatio*, the *mandatum* was a consensual agreement in Roman law and was not restricted to cases where the gratuitous commission involved the doing of something with or about a thing. The *mandatum*, it will be observed, was the Roman substitute for our contract of agency. The mandatary was a person authorized to do a thing for another, or one commissioned to act for him in a certain capacity without any remuneration. The *mandatum* was the agreement establishing this relation between the *mandator* and the *mandatarius*.

trust is exclusively for the benefit of the bailee; and III. Bailments in which the trust is for the benefit of both parties or for the benefit of one of them and a third party.

Here the criterion by which the different classes of bailments are discriminated from each other and by which the degree of care and diligence required of the different bailees is fixed, is the benefit accruing to the one or the other party to the transaction. Perhaps it represents a triumph of our peculiarly English doctrine of consideration. At any rate it is based on the fundamentally just notion that the risk should be with him who has the benefit.

The following scheme shows where the bailments enumerated by Lord Holt fall under such a classification as that made by Judge Story:

I. Bailments for Benefit of the Bailor.
  1. Gratuitous taking of a thing on deposit (*depositum*).
  2. Gratuitous performance of work on or about a thing, or the gratuitous carriage thereof (*mandatum*).

II. Bailments for Benefit of the Bailee.
  1. Gratuitous lending of a thing for temporary enjoyment (*commodatum*).
  2. ———.[3]

III. Bailments for Mutual Benefit.
  1. Putting a thing in a pledge or pawn (*pignus* or *vadium*).
  2. Putting a thing to hire for a reward paid by the bailee (*locatio rei*).
  3. Putting a thing in hands of a bailee to be worked upon by him for a reward paid by the bailor (*locatio operis faciendi*).
  4. Putting a thing in hands of a bailee to be kept for a reward paid by the bailor (*locatio custodiæ*).

---

[3] The gratuitous loan of a consumable thing (*mutuum*), a form of contract corresponding with the *commodatum*, not being a bailment, has no place in this classification. In other words, the *mutuum* has been lost as a separate form of engagement by the breaking up of the category of real contracts.

5. Putting a thing in charge of a bailee to be carried by him for a reward (*locatio operis mercium vehendarum*).

The first two classes of bailments are gratuitous. In bailments of the third class there is always a letting, putting, or placing (*locatio*) of the chattel in the hands of the bailee for a consideration.[4]

The Deposit.

We shall now briefly consider the rights and duties of the respective parties in connection with the several bailments.[5] The deposit, as we have seen, is a naked bailment of goods for custody. Being solely for the benefit of the bailor or of a third person indicated by him, the law requires only slight

---

[4] The term used in Roman law for the bailment for hire is *locatio-conductio*. The bailor is called the *locator*, the bailee the *conductor*. For convenience the term *locatio* is generally used instead of *locatio-conductio*.

The transaction can be looked at from the standpoint of either the bailor or bailee. In the former case the transaction is viewed as a putting out or letting for hire; in the latter as a receiving (conduction) for hire. Usually the transaction is viewed as a letting (location). But this is not very material. Uniformity, however, should be observed.

[5] *Provisions of the Mosaic Law Concerning Bailments.*— As prefatory to this consideration of the several bailments we may observe that the Mosaic law, as laid down in Exodus xxii. 7-15, throws some light upon the customs of the ancient Hebrews, in regard to bailments. These provisions, however, form nothing like a system and, so far as is apparent, exerted no influence upon the institutions of the Romans or of ourselves. It is worthy of note that the depositary, in case the goods or money was stolen out of his keeping, was a competent witness to prove that he had not "put his hand unto his neighbor's goods" (ver. 8). If the care of an ox, or sheep, or any beast was committed to another and it died or was hurt or driven away, no man seeing it, the keeper was not held responsible, if he could swear that he was not colluding (ver. 11); but if it was stolen from him he was required to make restitution to the owner (ver. 12). If it was torn in pieces and he could produce the mangled body in evidence, he was not to make it good (ver. 13).

Again, in case of loans, the borrower was held absolutely liable to make good the bailment in case it was hurt or died (ver. 14), but if the owner was with the hired thing, the hirer was not required to make the object good, as it was supposed to have come for the hire (ver. 15). Jacob looked upon Laban's requirement that he should answer absolutely for torn beasts and for beasts stolen by day or night (Gen. xxxi. 39) as a hardship; and it is manifest that Laban held him to a stricter accountability than was subsequently prescribed in the Mosaic law for bailees.

diligence of the bailee and makes him answerable only for so-called gross neglect. In this contract the bailee is held to the exercise of good faith, and consequently he must take reasonable care of the deposit. Lord Holt said that the depositary is not liable "if the goods are stole without any fault in him, neither will a common neglect make him chargeable; but he must be guilty of some gross neglect." [6] The ruling in *Southcote's Case* was opposed to this view, but Lord Holt declared that decision to be unsound and contrary to the prior decisions. At any rate no one has subsequently questioned the principle which was now laid down.

<small>Chapter XXVII</small>

A remark of Bracton quoted by Lord Holt caused him to infer that if the bailee uses the same degree of diligence in caring for the chattels bailed that he uses in caring for his own goods, then the bailee is not liable But this notion is incorrect and the true rule is now established to the effect that if the bailee uses the same care in regard to the property bailed that he bestows upon his own, this is only evidence tending to show that he is not guilty of gross negligence. It is merely "an argument of his honesty" and is not conclusive.[7]

<small>Diligence used in caring for one's own.</small>

In 1834 a noteworthy case involving this question arose. A coffee-house keeper, having undertaken to keep certain money for accommodation, put it, together with a larger sum of his own, into a cash box kept in the tap room. This room was left open on Sunday, but other parts of the house were not. On that day all the money so left in the cash box was stolen. It was held that the question whether or not the defendant was guilty of gross negligence in keeping the money

<small>Doorman v. Jenkins.</small>

---

[6] Coggs v. Bernard, 2 Ld. Raym. 909, 913.

[7] It is not sufficient to exempt a gratuitous bailee from liability, that he keeps goods deposited with him in the same manner as he keeps his own, though this degree of care will ordinarily repel the presumption of gross negligence. But there is no case that puts the duty of a bailee of this kind higher than this, namely, that he is bound to take the same care of the property intrusted to him as a reasonably prudent and careful man may fairly be expected to take of his own property of like description. See Giblin v. McMullen, L. R. 2 P. C. 317.

Tindal, C. J., once observed that to fix a standard of liability coextensive with the individual judgment would make it as variable as the foot of each individual. Vaughan v. Menlove (1837), 3 Bing. N. Cas. 468, 32 E. C. L. 208.

was properly left to the jury, and the court refused to disturb a verdict for the plaintiff.[8]

Special Deposit with Bank.

Liability of depositary for loss of special deposit.

Foster v. Essex Bank (1821),[9] and subsequent decisions recognizing the principle applied in this case, illustrate in a striking way the rule that the depositary is liable only for gross negligence. A large special deposit of gold was kept for safe-keeping in a bank upon the receipt of its cashier and with the knowledge of the president. The money was in a chest, the key to which was originally retained by the owner's agent; but subsequently the cashier received authority, from time to time, to open the chest and take from it certain sums of money on the owner's order. The cashier afterwards appropriated a large part of the money. Prior to the discovery of this dishonesty, the cashier had enjoyed a good reputation for honesty, and the bank directors were guilty of no negligence in having him in that responsible position. It was held that the bank was not liable.

Criticism.

So far as this decision rests upon the principle that the depositary is liable only for gross negligence it is sound law. In other respects the conclusion reached seems to be open to question. If such facts were now presented for the first time, the case would doubtless be solved upon consideration of the nature of the relation between the bank and its cashier. Was he, it would be asked, acting within the scope of his employment in receiving and protecting the special deposit?[1] If so, the bank was liable for his embezzlement, to the same extent

---

[8] Doorman v. Jenkins, 2 Ad. & El. 256, 29 E. C. L. 80.

[9] 17 Mass. 479, 9 Am. Dec. 168.

[1] The following observation of Chief Justice Parker in Foster v. Essex Bank, 17 Mass. 510, shows a misapprehension of the real point in issue: "We are then," said he, "to inquire whether in this case, when the gold was taken from the cask by the cashier and clerk, they were in the course of their official employment."

The true question is whether in receiving and in keeping the money in the bank the cashier was acting in the scope of his official power and duty. If so, the bank was liable for his violation of that duty. Of course the cashier does not act within the scope of his duty in the act of embezzlement. That is not the proper criterion. The act of embezzlement constitutes a breach of duty owing by the cashier in his representative capacity.

as if the fund had been misappropriated by the cashier to the use of the bank itself. But this question belongs to another department of law. It is possibly true that a depositary is not liable for a theft committed by a menial servant,[2] and Chief Justice Parker thought that the same rule should be applied to the cashier.

In reason it is clear that the depositary is liable where the servant, employee, or officer who commits the depredation is himself charged on behalf of the principal with the duty of oversight.[3] In fulfilling this duty the employee is a true representative or vice-principal. Notwithstanding *Foster v. Bank* is thus open to this grave criticism, it has been generally approved in America,[4] and the same principle has been declared in England.[5]

Chapter XXVII

Liability of depositary for act of servan' or agent.

[2] This rule is reasonable enough and is generally accepted as sound, but Finucane *v.* Small, 1 Esp. 315, which is usually cited as authority on this point, is worthless. The case went no further than Nisi Prius, and Lord Kenyon's opinion was based largely on the exploded proposition that a bailee who uses the same care in guarding the chattels bailed as in keeping his own goods is not liable for their loss. Besides, the bailment in that case was not gratuitous, the bailee being paid a reward, a circumstance which makes the decision of very little value on the question of the liability of the depositary.

In Clarke *v.* Earnshaw (1818), 1 Gow. 30, 5 E. C. L. 448, it was held that a watch maker with whom a chronometer was left for repairs was liable where his servant forced open the locked drawer in which the chronometer was kept overnight, and stole it. In this case, Dallas, C. J., remarked that the defendant was bound to protect the property against the depredation of those who were within. This case is contrary to Finucane *v.* Small, and is better authority.

[3] In the Supreme Court of the United States, Judge Field not long ago said that persons depositing valuable articles with banks for safe keeping have a right to expect that such measures will be taken as will ordinarily secure them from burglars outside and thieves within, and intimated that where the duties of an officer embrace supervision of the property, appropriation of the deposit by him will render the bank liable. Preston *v.* Prather, 137 U. S. 604. See also Gray *v.* Merriam, 148 Ill. 179.

[4] In a late case, the rule is stated in these words: "For a special deposit received by a bank through its cashier for gratuitous safe-keeping and return to the depositor on demand, the bank is not liable if the cashier, without its knowledge or consent, steals it or fraudulently appropriates it to his own use, provided the bank has exercised due diligence in selecting the cashier and in not keeping him in office after it knew or ought to have known that he was or had become untrustworthy. In stealing or clandestinely appropriating the deposit to his own use the cashier would not be acting in the bank's business or within the scope of his employment." Merchants Nat. Bank *v.* Guilmartin, 88 Ga. 797.

[5] Giblin *v.* McMullen, L. R. 2 P. C. 318, 38 L. J. P. C. 25.

The Finder of Lost Goods.

Finder a quasi-depositary.

Where the finder of lost goods takes them into his possession he becomes a quasi-depositary and is subjected to the same liability in respect to the duty of caring for the goods as if the owner had in the first instance given his consent to the creation of the relation of bailor and bailee. In truth, in the case of lost goods the consent of the owner that another shall take and hold them for his benefit is implied as a matter of fact.

Held to exercise of slight diligence only.

Inasmuch as a finder who takes possession of the chattel has no contract right to be compensated, he is a depositary and is held to the exercise of slight diligence only. But he must exhibit good faith and is liable for gross neglect. Though under no obligation in the first place to take the goods into his custody, he is properly held liable for the negligent keeping of them when he does accept the burden of possession.[6] The same rule applies when property is brought by involuntary means upon the land of a person other than its owner, as by the accident of flood or tempest. If the owner of the premises assumes the burden of possession he will be held to the liability of a depositary.

No right to use chattel for own benefit.

In conclusion it may be added that the depositary has no right to use for his own benefit the chattel deposited with him,[7] unless there be an express or implied consent on the part of the owner that he shall so use it. If a particular use is proper for the preservation of the bailment, this beneficial use will be impliedly authorized. If the chattel be inclosed in a sealed box or chest nothing short of express permission would suffice.

The Mandate.

The duty imposed on the bailee who undertakes for accommodation to transport a chattel or to do something with or about it gratuitously (*mandatum*), and who actually enters upon the performance of the mandate, is exactly the same as that imposed on the depositary. In the absence of special

---

[6] Isaack v. Clark, 2 Bulst. 306.   [7] Story on Bailments, §§ 89, 90.

contract both are bound to exercise slight diligence only, and are liable for nothing short of gross negligence, the reason in each case being the same, namely, that neither is to receive any reward for his service. Accordingly, whenever the liability of the mandatary is being considered cases involving the liability of the depositary are good authority, and *vice versa.* In the deposit, custody is the principal thing in the mind of the parties, and in the mandate, the service to be rendered or the labor to be performed in regard to the chattel bailed is the matter of chief concern.[8]

Sir William Jones imagined that there is a distinction between the degree of care required of a mandatary to transport goods and one engaged to do work upon them. The latter, he said, is bound to use a degree of diligence adequate to the proper performance of the work. It was clearly shown by Judge Story that this distinction does not exist,[9] and the notion in question is now abandoned.

The mandatary then is held to the exercise of slight diligence and must always exhibit good faith. His failure to comply with this requirement was characterized by Lord Holt as a species of fraud resembling the *dolus malus* of the civil law.[1]

Language importing that the actionable gross negligence of the mandatary is equivalent to fraud is also found in some modern cases. But all such expressions are misleading and they are not found in late decisions. In the English and American law fraud and gross negligence are by no means convertible terms. Fraud, in its more restricted meaning, implies mental advertence, and an act done in carrying out an

---

[8] 2 Kent Com. 569; Story on Bailment, § 164.

[9] Story on Bailments, § 177 *et seq.;* Moore *v.* Mourgue, 2 Cowp. 480; Shiells *v.* Blackburne, 1 H. Bl. 158; Nelson *v.* Macintosh, 1 Stark. 237, 2 E. C. L. 96.

[1] In the civil law, gross negligence was termed *magna culpa* or *lata culpa,* and was sometimes deemed equivalent to fraud or deceit. It has been often said by English judges that gross negligence approximates so nearly to *dolus malus* or positive misconduct as to be indistinguishable from it. It was put by Paulus for fraud and Ulpian assimilated it to fraud. Said the Digest: Magna negligentia culpa est, magna culpa dolus est. Lata culpa plane dolo comparabitur. Dig. 20, 16, 226; Dig. 11, 61, 1.

Volume II

Illustration.

intention to damage; while, on the other hand, gross negligence means only a very culpable degree of inadvertence.

Thus, to use an illustration given by Judge Story, if one, out of pure inadvertence, leaves a cask of jewels or purse of gold upon the table of a public room in an inn; or leaves a large package of bills in his greatcoat, the jury may well find him guilty of gross negligence without being able to charge him with actual fraud.[2]

Wickedness and knavery are never necessary to make out a case of gross negligence. When the older writers use the terms 'fraud' and 'deceit' as the equivalent of gross negligence, they merely mean that the act reprobated constitutes a sort of fraud in law. Had the view obtained that negligence is not gross unless it amounts to a fraud, as we now understand that term, the verdict against the defendant in *Doorman v. Jenkins* (1834)[3] could never have been allowed to stand.

Bailment made at request of bailee.

Writers on the civil law have suggested that a depositary or mandatary to whom a bailment is committed upon his own solicitation will be held to a stricter liability than other bailees in the same class.[4] In such case the bailment though gratuitous is not solely for the accommodation of the bailor, and it is reasonable to tighten the rule. The question has not arisen, or at least seems never to have been discussed on common-law principles. The circumstance that the chattel was intrusted to a bailee at his own instance would doubtless be given due weight by a jury in considering the question of the amount of diligence necessary to constitute good faith.

---

[2] Story on Bailments, § 22.
[3] 2 Ad. & El. 256, 29 E. C. L. 80.
[4] This idea is recognized in Louisiana, where it is provided that the liability of the depositary shall be rigorously enforced if the deposit has been made at his request. Code La. (1825), §§ 2908, 2909.

CHAPTER XXVIII

MODERN LAW OF BAILMENT (CONTINUED).

The Commodate.

CASES involving the question of the degree of care required of the commodatary seldom reach the courts, perhaps for the reason, suggested by one writer, that where honor does not hold the borrower to his duty, delicacy restrains the lender from pursuing legal remedies.[1]

It is essential to the commodate that the loan be made without reward and that the subject-matter of the loan should be personal property. Permission to use real property is considered a mere license.[2]

If the time during which the loan is to continue is not defined and cannot be inferred from the circumstances under which the loan is made, the owner can, under the common law, reclaim it at any time. Judge Story expressed the opinion that a loan for a definite period could also be terminated at the option of the bailor, as he considered it questionable whether there is such a consideration in this transaction as will make the bailment binding. The authorities are meagre and hardly in point. But there can be no doubt that, if a time for the termination of the loan is fixed, both parties will be bound by reason of their respective promises, provided they intend to enter into a contractual relation. The promise to keep the chattel for the agreed period is sufficient to support the counter-promise to allow the borrower to retain the chattel for the time stated.

The rule of diligence stated by Lord Holt as applicable to the commodatary has never been qualified. Such bailee is held to the exercise of the strictest care and is answerable for damage resulting from the least neglect. There must be no devia-

[1] Schouler on Bailments, § 65.
[2] Williams v. Jones, 3 H. & C. 256.

tion from the terms of the loan. For instance, if one lends another his horse to go to a designated place and the bailee travels to a different destination he will be liable for any accident happening to the animal while on such journey, for, perchance, the accident would not have befallen had he traveled to the place specified.[3]

For a similar reason the borrower of a yoke of oxen for the purpose of ploughing up a hedge is liable for injuries sustained by the cattle while drawing stones and rolling them on a boat.[4] It has been held that where a horse runs away and demolishes a borrowed sulky, the bailee may be held liable for the damage done thereto.[5] The gratuitous loan of a chattel is looked upon as a strictly personal favor and the borrower has no right to delegate the use.[6]

It is now established that loss by inevitable accident and by such catastrophes as cannot be provided against by human skill and foresight will relieve the commodatary,[7] and *a fortiori* all other bailees, of all liability for the thing bailed. Robbery is of course sufficient, unless the bailee by some culpable lack of foresight puts himself in a way to be robbed. This was a rule of the Roman law, and it made its way into English law with the obsolescence of the principle that the bailee is a debtor.

---

[3] Coggs v. Bernard, 2 Ld. Raym. 915.

So where one borrowed a mare to ride three miles in the country and in violation of the loan drove her in a carriage twelve miles, where she died during the night, judgment was given for her value, there being no proof to show that her death was due to natural causes. Kennedy v. Ashcraft, 4 Bush (Ky.) 530.

[4] Buchanan v. Smith, 10 Hun (N. Y.) 474.

[5] Casey v. Suter, 36 Md. 1.

[6] Bringloe v. Morrice, 1 Mod. 210, 3 Salk. 271. In this case the plaintiff lent the defendant a horse to ride at his pleasure. The borrower suffered his servant to ride the animal. It was held that this was unauthorized and that the master was liable for the immoderate riding of the servant. The court said: "The license is annexed to the person and cannot be communicated to another; for this riding is a matter of pleasure."

Scranton v. Baxter, 4 Sandf. (N. Y.) 5, is one of the few cases in which there is a discussion of the question of the liability of the commodatary. It is there said that the borrower of a chattel is bound to extraordinary diligence and is responsible for the slightest neglect; and that he must exercise all the care and diligence that the most careful persons are accustomed to use in their own affairs.

[7] Fortune v. Harris, 6 Jones L. (51 N. Car.) 532.

Pledge.

Chapter XXVIII

The species of bailment which goes by the name of pledge or pawn is one of the most common transactions known to the law. Its history begins with the earliest use of credit in primitive communities and it has, in several systems of law, a distinct history of its own. Lord Holt gives a very clear outline of the fundamental principles underlying it. We need only observe that he follows Bracton, who quotes the exact language of the Institutes in defining the measure of liability to which the pledgee is held. The care to be observed by the pledgee in respect of the property pledged is said by Bracton to be *exactam diligentiam*. Lord Holt uses 'true diligence' as the equivalent of this term. As we now say, the bailee is bound to take ordinary care and is answerable only for ordinary neglect. The fact that the bailment is beneficial to both parties makes it just that the risk of destruction or loss should be pretty equally balanced.

Antiquity of the pledge.

Pledgee held to exercise of ordinary care.

Lord Coke, in his report of *Southcote's Case*,[8] points out a distinction that had been recognized at an early day in favor of the pledgee, viz., that he has an actual interest or, as Coke calls it, "a property" in the goods pledged. Hence it was always an implied term in cases of pledging that the pledgee should hold the goods as his own. Consequently the pledgee, unlike the other bailees in the early common law was not held liable where the goods pledged were stolen. This explanation seems to be somewhat specious. But that the pledgee was one of the first bailees to be relieved of absolute liability as debtor is clear.[9]

The 'property' of the pledgee.

In modern times it is of course unquestioned that the pledgee is not liable if the pawn be lost by casualty or unavoidable accident, or by superior force, or perishes of intrinsic defect or infirmity unaccompanied by any negligence on his part.[1]

Pledgee not liable unless negligent.

Sir William Jones entertained the idea that the pledgee is responsible if the pledge be stolen, or taken from him clandes-

---

[8] 4 Coke 83.   [9] Y. B. 29 Ass. 163, pl. 28.   [1] 2 Kent Com. 570.

tinely, but not if it be robbed, or taken from him by violence. This conclusion was reached on the theory that the mere fact that the goods are furtively taken raises a presumption of negligence against the pledgee. But this view is not now accepted. The true rule is that the burden of proving negligence is on the plaintiff, and the existence of such element is a conclusion to be drawn by the jury or not, as it sees fit, upon all the facts and circumstances in proof.[2]

Letting for Hire.

The Roman law comprised three different agreements under the term *locatio-conductio:* the *locatio-conductio rei,* a contract whereby one party agrees to let another have the use of a thing for compensation; the *locatio-conductio operarum,* a contract whereby one party, such as a laborer, agrees to supply another with a certain amount of unskilled labor; and the *locatio-conductio opcris,* a contract whereby one party agrees to supply another with a finished article made from materials furnished by either.[3]

The English conception of bailment requires that in every case there shall be a chattel belonging to the bailor which the bailee is to use, or upon which he is to do work, or about which he is to be employed. We therefore eliminate at once all agreements for personal service to be rendered otherwise than upon or in connection with a chattel belonging to the bailor, which, for the purpose of this service, is delivered to the bailee and comes into his possession for hire.

The contract for the letting of a thing for hire places the owner, or locator as he is called in the civil law, under the obligation of allowing the hirer to use the chattel bailed in accordance with the terms of the bailment. The corollaries that follow from this primary duty on the part of the bailor have been worked out with some fulness in the civil law. For

---

[2] Story on Bailments, §§ 333-338. See also article by Judge Bennett, criticising Cass *v.* Boston, etc., R. Co., 14 Allen (Mass.) 448, published in American Law Review for January, 1871 (5 Am. L. Rev. 205).

[3] See Sohm, Inst., Ledlie's trans., 2d ed., 419.

example, it is stated by Pothier, in language which is true at common law also, that the bailor must deliver the chattel to the hirer; he must refrain from every obstruction to the use of it by the hirer during the period of the bailment; must do no act which shall deprive the hirer of the thing, must warrant the title and right of possession to the bailee to the extent of the bailment use; must ordinarily keep the thing in suitable order and repair for the purposes of the bailment; and finally, must, in most cases, warrant the thing free from any fault inconsistent with the proper use or enjoyment of it.[4]

Chapter XXVIII

Duty of bailor.

In stating the degree of care exacted of the bailee for hire, Lord Holt was misled by language which Bracton had adopted from the Institutes. Such bailee, we are told, is bound to the utmost diligence, such as the most careful householder uses in the conduct of his own affairs.[5] But this lan-

Care exacted of bailee for hire.

---

[4] Pothier, Contrat de Louage, n. 53–58.

[5] Coggs v. Bernard, 2 Ld. Raym. 916.

Diligence Required of Bailee for Hire.— The language of the Institutes which was appropriated by Bracton is as follows: " Ab eo custodia talis disideratur qualem diligentissimus paterfamilias suis rebus adhibeat. Quam si praestiterit et aliquo casu rem amiserit de restituenda ea non tenebitur." Just. Inst., Lib. III., tit. 24, § 5.

This text certainly imports on its face to require an unusual degree of care.

Heineccius says that the bailee for hire is liable for gross and ordinary negligence (*latam et levem*). Hein. Pandects, Lib. XIX., tit. 2, § 324.

Pothier says he is held only to common diligence and is answerable for slight neglect. Contrat de Louage, n. 77, 106, 107, 130, 139. See Civ. Code Louisiana, art. 2663, 2664.

The idea that the contract imports a high degree of diligence on the part of the bailee was adopted by Buller, Nisi Prius 72, who declares that the hirer is to take all imaginable care. Sir William Jones took much pains to show that these views are incorrect, and that the true rule of the common law is that the contract is one of mutual benefit and that therefore the bailee is liable only for ordinary neglect. This is doubtless also the meaning of Pothier in the passage cited above, if we do not put too much stress upon the expression 'slight negligence' (*faute legère*).

We must not forget that the use of terms implying degrees in negligence is misleading. The Digest of Justinian does not state the law in language similar to that of the Institutes, but only points to the rule that the hirer is liable for negligence without stating the degree. Dig. 50, 17, 1, 23; Dig. 13, 61, 5, 2. It is needless to say that the Institutes, being only a convenient manual or text for beginners, have never had the authority of the Digests. Sir Wm. Jones suggested that the term *diligentissimus* was possibly loosely used and that it was hardly to be taken as implying more than ordinary diligence. Pothier agrees with this view. The expression was used by the Roman writers in connection with the degree of

guage does not state the modern common-law rule, and it was probably not a general principle of law when Lord Holt wrote his opinion.

Ordinary diligence.

The general rule is that the bailee of a chattel for hire is to be held only to the exercise of ordinary diligence, and he is not liable for the inevitable loss or destruction of the chattel, nor for ordinary deterioration.[6] Any damage befalling a chattel while in the hands of a bailee without his misconduct, and while the chattel is employed in the use for which it was bailed, must accordingly be borne by the bailor.

Exceptional rule applying in case of departure from terms of bailment.

To this general rule there is certainly one striking exception. This is found in the rule that where the hirer of domestic animals, like horses, departs from the terms of the bailment in using them, he virtually becomes an insurer. Lord Holt said that if one lends a horse to go westward, and the bailee goes northward instead, he is chargeable in case of any accident. This rule is apparently applied where compensation is paid, as well as where the bailment is purely gratuitous.[7]

Driving horse beyond destination.

In *Wheelock v. Wheelwright* (1809),[8] it was said for the first time in this country that the hirer, by driving the horse beyond the place agreed upon, is guilty of a conversion. There the horse actually died while being driven out of the course for which the animal was hired. The statement that the bailee is, under such circumstances, guilty of a conversion

Conversion.

is based upon the idea that any deviation whatever from the terms of the contract of hiring involves an assumption of a right of property, or of dominion over the animal, such as constitutes an appropriation by the bailee, and casts upon him all the risks of an owner.[9] Hence it is no defense for the bailee

---

care necessary to be taken in removing a marble column from one place to another, and under these special circumstances it is manifest a very high degree of care would be necessary for the proper accomplishment of the design. See 2 Kent Com. 588.

[6] Story on Bailments, §§ 398, 399; 2 Kent Com. 586, 587.

[7] Disbrow *v*. Tenbroeck, 4 E. D. Smith (N. Y.) 397.

[8] 5 Mass. 104.

[9] Morton *v*. Gloster, 46 Me. 520; Rotch *v*. Hawes, 12 Pick. (Mass.) 136; Woodman *v*. Hubbard, 25 N. H. 67; Fish *v*. Ferris, 5 Duer (N. Y.) 49.

One who, after losing his way, discovers the mistake and then travels by what seems to be the best road home, is not liable for a conversion. Spooner *v*. Manchester, 133 Mass. 270.

that the horse succumbs by reason of inherent defects,[1] though such fact would go to mitigate the damage.[2]

This rule undoubtedly operates with some hardship, and considered merely as an application of the doctrine of conversion it is anomalous. To hold the bailee absolutely liable in such cases is one thing; to declare that he is guilty of a technical conversion is quite another. In truth we are here confronted with an unconscious reversion to the primitive doctrine which holds the bailee absolutely liable. Under a laxer rule, it may be urged, the owner would have difficulty in getting compensation for the extra service or use of the chattel bailed, and unscrupulous persons would be tempted to misstate the nature of the journey or other work to be undertaken. Considerations such as these undoubtedly account for the application of the rule of strict liability.

As an application of the doctrine of conversion the position assumed is clearly untenable, for the general principle underlying conversion is that where possession has a lawful inception no act will amount to a conversion unless it is of such character as conclusively to show an intention on the part of the bailee to hold adversely and to the exclusion of the rightful owner. Another circumstance which shows that the doctrine of conversion is not the true basis of the exceptional liability fastened upon the bailee in this situation is the fact that the rule in question cannot be invoked merely for the purpose of vesting the general property in the bailee, thus making him an unwilling purchaser of the animal. It is applied only in order to fix liability upon the bailee in case of actual loss. There is no case where a bailee, being willing and able to return the animal sound within a proper time, has been held liable in trover merely because he traveled in the wrong direction or went beyond the destination stated.

Judge Story suggested that the bailee should never be held liable for a conversion where he is merely guilty of some negligence or omission or violation of duty not conducing to

---

[1] Lucas v. Trumbull, 15 Gray (Mass.) 306.
[2] Wheelock v. Wheelwright, 5 (Mass.) 104.

288   FOUNDATIONS OF LEGAL LIABILITY.

Volume II

Mere deviation from contract not a conversion.

the loss.³ *Harvey v. Epes* (1855)⁴ was in line with that suggestion. In this case it was held that it is not *ipso facto* a conversion for a hirer of slaves to take them to work in a county other than the county specified in the contract of hiring, unless the destruction of the property is thereby occasioned or the act done with the intent to convert the property and thus destroy or defeat the interest of the owner.

In a still later case it has been held in Iowa that a mere deviation from the line of travel, or going beyond the point for which a team is hired, will not, without more, amount to a conversion of the property so as to render the bailee liable for all loss.⁵ These decisions are not in line with the weight of authority, but they reveal a consciousness that the theory of conversion is inadequate. If the rule of strict liability is to prevail its exceptional character must be recognized, and

Colorable hiring made with intent to convert.

it must be justified, if at all, by the peculiar nature of the trust involved in such a bailment. It may be added that a distinction can well be drawn between the case where possession is obtained upon a false statement by the hirer of his intended destination, and the case where he subsequently determines to depart from the course indicated. In the former instance it is reasonable to hold that there is no bailment at all, and hence the hirer is absolutely liable for all losses. A similar distinction is made in the criminal law of larceny, where it is held that a taking under the color of bailment with intent to convert is a larcenous trespass.

Procuring of Service.

The term *locatio operis*⁶ is applied to that bailment where compensation is given for labor and service done upon a

---

³ Story on Bailments, § 413. Mr. Schouler also observes that a technical misuse should not be visited with the heavy penalty attached to conversion unless there is an actual abuse of the terms of the hire. Bailments, § 140.

⁴ 12 Gratt. (Va.) 153.

⁵ Doolittle v. Shaw, 92 Iowa 348.

⁶ The expression *locatio operis* is generally used for the sake of brevity instead of *locatio operis faciendi causa*. The bailment for carriage, *locatio operis mercium vehendarum*, may be considered a form of this bailment, but it is treated separately because of the great importance attached to the contract for the carriage of goods in recent years. So the bailment

chattel or in connection with it; as, for instance, where cloth is delivered to a tailor to be made into clothes, or where a watch is left with a jeweler to be mended.

Chapter XXVIII

The chattel must be delivered to the artisan or workman for the purpose of doing the service or there is no bailment. Thus, workmen who make repairs on a ship in its owner's yard, or a mechanic who repairs a coach without taking it to his shop, are not bailees, and their rights and liabilities are determined by their contract. The true bailee acquires possession, and this circumstance puts him on a different plane; for he thereby acquires what is usually spoken of as a special property in the chattel, has an insurable interest therein, and is given a lien for his compensation.

Delivery of possession necessary.

In this bailment ordinary care and diligence are required of the bailee; though, of course, where an undertaking presupposes the possession of technical skill and knowledge, the bailee is held to the ordinary professional standard. If, while the bailment continues, the chattel is destroyed, or stolen, or perishes, without fault on the bailee's part, the loss, as in other hirings, falls upon the owner.

Ordinary care required.

Bailment for Custody.

Where deposits are made with the understanding, express or implied, that compensation is to be paid for the keeping, the transaction becomes a *locatio custodiæ*. St. Germain, in the passage which we have already quoted, expressed the opinion that there is no difference, as far as the duty of the bailee is concerned, between a keeping for hire and a gratuitous keeping, though it did appear to him that where something was paid, this would support a special promise to keep at the bailee's peril.[7] But the distinction between naked bailments and bailments for a reward became clear by Lord Holt's time. As in cases of hiring, the bailee is held to the exercise of the diligence of a prudent man.

Rule as to diligence required.

---

for custody, *locatio custodiæ*, might be considered a form of the *locatio operis*, since the bailee expends labor and care in keeping the chattel bailed; but it is more convenient to treat it as a separate bailment.

[7] Doctor & Stud., ch. 38. See *ante*, p. 262, note.

19

Agistor.

One of the oldest bailees for custody is the agistor of cattle (a term which includes all domestic quadrupeds). Agistors are not treated as persons plying a common calling, since they are at liberty to accept or refuse such animals as they please. They are, therefore, private keepers of quadrupeds for pasture, and must exercise ordinary care and prudence. Both the civil and the common law require that the agistor should have enough skill to be able to attend his duties properly, an implied warranty which enters into every bailment where the bailee really undertakes to act. The agistor did not, at common law, have a lien for his compensation unless by special agreement; but this protection is now given in a number of states by statute.[8]

Has no lien at common law.

Warehousemen.

Warehousemen, wharfingers, and forwarding merchants are also clearly mere bailees for custody. There is no difficulty about fixing their liability on general principles when their character as such bailees is once determined. These occupations, however, are usually plied in connection with the business of a common carrier, and it is often a question of difficulty to ascertain when a bailee ceases to be liable in one capacity and becomes liable in the other.

Grain elevator.

Distinction between bailment and sale.

The deposit of grain in elevators results in a rather complicated legal relation, and discussions of it have led to some fine distinctions between a bailment and a sale. It is an established test that, in the bailment, the identical thing is to be returned, though perhaps in an altered form. Title does not pass as by a sale. Accordingly where by the true construction of the contract, however complicated, the article is to be returned, either just as received, or when turned into other goods — as grain into meal, leather into shoes, lumber into boards, or wool into cloth — the transaction is a bailment. On the other hand, if the contract contemplates that the thing received shall not be specifically returned, but that its equivalent shall be surrendered in the same or in an altered form, or that it shall be paid for in money, at the option of the receiver, the transaction is not a bailment, but is analogous to the *mutuum* and constitutes a contract of sale or exchange.

[8] See Stimson's Am. Statute Law, § 4642.

Especially is this true where the receiver expressly reserves the right to dispose of the material delivered.[9]

In the particular case of deposits of grain in warehouses and elevators, it is customary for the grain to be mingled with that of other depositors. The warehouseman also buys and stores grain of his own with the common mass and has authority to sell from the common stock and buy other grain to replace that which is so sold, being of course under obligation to keep on hand a sufficient amount to meet outstanding receipts. In late years the courts are inclined to look upon this transaction as creating a tenancy in common in the commingled grain, rather than as constituting a bailment or sale. This theory seems to work out satisfactory results and is perhaps unobjectionable. But there is no difficulty in looking upon the owner of the elevator as a special bailee to keep, with power to change the bailor's original tenancy in severalty into a tenancy in common of a proportionately larger mass, and back again, and also with a continuous power of sale, substitution, and resale.[1]

In recent years the courts have been called upon to pass upon contracts made by safe-deposit companies. In the usual course of business these companies rent safes or boxes in their vaults to depositors. They usually engage to keep a guard over the vaults, but have no access in person to the boxes or their contents. The depositor himself, or his agent, places his property in the safe and removes it as he sees fit. It is clear that this is not a bailment. The company does not have possession and there is no delivery. The liability of the company must therefore be determined entirely by the contract and the usages of business incident to carrying it out.[2]

Chapter XXVIII

Grain owned by tenants in common.

Bailee with special authority.

Safe-deposit companies not bailees.

---

[9] This distinction seems to have been originally drawn in Ewing v. French, (1825) 1 Blackf. (Ind.) 354, where wheat was delivered to a miller to be exchanged for flour not necessarily to be ground from the wheat in question. It was held that the mill man was bound to supply the requisite amount of flour although the wheat was accidentally burned. This decision has been followed in a great number of cases. See Benj. on Sales, Bennett's ed., p. 6.

[1] See Grain Elevators, 6 Am. L. Rev. 450.

[2] See Peers v. Sampson, 4 Dowl. & R. 636, 16 E. C. L. 216; Roberts v. Stuyvesant Safe Deposit Co., 123 N. Y. 57; Jones v. Morgan, 90 N. Y. 4; Safe Deposit Co. v. Pollock, 85 Pa. St. 391.

Volume II

Officer in charge of public funds subject to same liability as bailee.

Judged by any test that may be suggested, officers who are intrusted with the custody of public funds are bailees. They have legal possession and are charged with the duty to keep for another. "They are nothing but bailees. To call them anything else, when they are expressly forbidden to touch or use the public money except as directed, would be an abuse of terms. But they are special bailees, subject to special obligations."[3] In England this seems to be accepted without question, and accordingly in that country treasurers and collectors of public funds are held not liable where money committed to their keeping is lost by irresistible force or by the act of God.[4]

This view is accepted in some American jurisdictions. Thus, in Colorado it has been declared that when an officer comes into the possession of public funds by virtue of his office, his liability, in the absence of legislative provision, is measured by the law of bailment.[5]

American doctrine.

By the weight of American authority, however, public officers who are intrusted with the keeping of public funds are absolutely liable where such funds are lost, without regard to the question of fault on the part of the officer. The prevailing American doctrine originated in *U. S. v. Prescott* (1845),[6] where a receiver of public funds was held liable though he had been robbed of the money without negligence on his part. For the defendant it was ably argued that he was in the position of a bailee for hire and should not be held to a higher degree of responsibility than such bailees. The court relied chiefly on the language of the bond — "should well, truly, and faithfully keep safely "— as evincing an intention to make the officer responsible absolutely. It was deemed sufficient that there was no condition in the bond holding him harmless in case of robbery or theft. The principle laid down

Officer absolutely liable.

---

[3] U. S. *v.* Thomas, 15 Wall. (U. S.) 347.

[4] See Walker *v.* British Guarantee Assoc., 18 Q. B. 277, 83 E. C. L. 277.

[5] Wilson *v.* People, 19 Colo. 199. This conforms with the view entertained by Judge Story of the liability of court officers into whose keeping money or specific chattels are committed. See Story on Bailments, § 620.

[6] 3 How. (U. S.) 578.

in this case has been adopted in the federal courts and in a number of the state courts.⁷ But the later cases show a tendency to relax the doctrine.⁸

Chapter XXVIII

⁷ U. S. v. Bryan, 82 Fed. Rep. 290; U. S. v. Zabriskie, 87 Fed. Rep. 714; Smythe v. U. S., 188 U. S. 156; Ramsay v. People, 197 Ill. 572; Hancock v. Hazzard, 12 Cush. (Mass.) 112; Perley v. Muskegon County, 32 Mich. 132; Adams v. Lee, 72 Miss. 281; New Providence Tp. v. McEachron, 33 N. J. L. 339, 35 N. J. L. 528; Tillinghast v. Merrill, 151 N. Y. 135; Cox v. Blair, 76 N. Car. 78. See, however, U. S. v. Thomas, 15 Wall. (U. S.) 337; U. S. v. Humason, 6 Sawy. (U. S.) 199.

These decisions, which fix absolute liability on the receiver of public funds, confront us with a very curious fact and with a still more curious paradox. The fact they prove is that here we have another reversion to that primitive theory in accordance with which the bailee is liable as debtor. The paradox is that these decisions, or at least some of them, are placed on the ground that the public officer is not a bailee at all. U. S. v. Prescott, 3 How. (U. S.) 578; Adams v. Lee, 72 Miss. 281. What is meant by this assertion is that his liability, in the opinion of these courts, is not the same as the liability of the ordinary bailee for custody, but is determined by considerations of public policy, by the tenor of his bond, or by statute.

The Alabama court has said that the collector is a bailee, or occupies a position analogous to that of a bailee, his liability as such being made greater than that of the ordinary bailee, on grounds of public policy. State v. Houston, 78 Ala. 576, 56 Am. Rep. 59.

⁸ Wilson v. People, 19 Colo. 199; State v. Lanier, 31 La. Ann. 423; Cumberland County v. Pennell, 69 Me. 357; Livingston v. Woods, 20 Mont. 91; York County v. Watson, 15 S. Car. 1.

Statutory expressions often put into bonds, such as "keep and pay over according to law," "faithfully keep the public money," "faithfully discharge the duties of the office," can very well be taken as a sufficient ground for enforcing a less rigorous rule than that which was applied in the Prescott case. See State v. Copeland, 96 Tenn. 296; Cumberland County v. Pennell, 69 Me. 357; State v. Houston, 78 Ala. 576; State v. Gramm, 7 Wyo. 329.

Where an officer lawfully deposits funds in a bank of good reputation and the money is lost by its failure, the officer and his bondsmen are not liable, under a statute requiring him to keep and pay over the funds according to law. State v. Copeland, 96 Tenn. 296.

CHAPTER XXIX

MODERN LAW OF BAILMENT (CONTINUED).

The Innkeeper.

Volume II

Innkeeper liable as insurer of guest's goods.

FOR the common-law principles governing the liability of the innkeeper it is not necessary to go further back than *Calye's Case* (1584),[1] where it was said that the innkeeper is bound in law to keep the goods and chattels of his guest in safety without any stealing or purloining. In other words, he is held virtually as an insurer of the safekeeping of the goods.[2] It has been said that the law makes innkeepers thus liable in view of the reward paid and by reason of the fact that the inn is a place appointed and allowed by law for the accommodation and security of travelers.[3]

Rule based on public policy.

But clearly we are here confronted with a rule grounded upon considerations of public policy.[4] Danger of collusion between the innkeeper and thieves, and the difficulty that would have been encountered by the plaintiff if he had been required to prove negligence, supplied sufficiently cogent reasons why strict liability should be enforced. Besides, the traveler, like the mediæval merchant, is here to-day and there to-morrow, a circumstance which makes it necessary to protect him by a hard and fast rule unless he is to be denied justice altogether.

It should be observed that from the earliest day the remedy used to enforce the liability of the innkeeper was the action

---

[1] 8 Coke 32.
[2] By the law of the land the common innkeeper is bound to warrant the goods of his guest. Sanders v. Spencer, 3 Dyer 266b.
At Rome extraordinary liability was fixed upon the innkeeper, as well as upon stablers and carriers by sea, by the pretorian edict: "Nautæ, caupones, stabularii, quod cujusque salvum fore receperint nisi restituent, in eos judicium dabo." Dig. 4, 9, 1, 1. Upon this Ulpian remarks: "Maximus utilitas est hujus edicti; quia necesse est plerumque eorum fidem sequi, et res custodiæ eorum committere." Dig. 4, 9, 1, 1.
[3] Bac. Abr., *Inns and Innkeepers* (C) 4.
[4] Pinkerton v. Woodward, 33 **Cal.** 557, 91 Am. Dec. 657.

294

on the case.[5] This fact is perhaps enough of itself to show that the exceptional liability of the innkeeper is not to be treated merely as a survival of the early conception of the bailee as a debtor. Still the rule harmonizes in a degree with that ancient notion.

Liability of innkeeper not a survival from early law of bailment.

In modern times great changes have supervened in the calling of innkeeping. The country is not, as in the mediæval ages, infested with robbers. The danger of collusion between them and the innkeeper would not therefore at this day appeal to the courts as a strong reason for fixing upon this personage any heavier liability than that imposed upon other bailees for hire. But other considerations remain and afford a sufficient ground for the retention of the rule by such courts as see fit to approve it. Yet in a number of jurisdictions the old doctrine has been relaxed. The result is that modern decisions in regard to the liability of the innkeeper are by no means harmonious.

In England it was declared, in *Dawson v. Chamney* (1843),[6] that the liability of the innkeeper is grounded on negligence. Accordingly where goods of a guest are lost or injured at an inn, the keeper, it was held, may show by way of defense that he exercised due diligence in caring for the chattels. In this view there is a mere presumption of negligence against the innkeeper which may be rebutted.

Liability of innkeeper supposed to be grounded on negligence.

This doctrine was, however, contrary to previous decisions and was subsequently repudiated by the judges of the Court of Exchequer in *Morgan v. Ravey* (1861),[7] which laid down the rule now accepted by the English courts. It was there

---

[5] See Brooke Abr., *Accion sur Case*, pls. 28, 41, 59; 1 Rolle Abr., *Action sur Case* (D), (E), (F). The writ is given in the Register. Reg. Brev. Orig. 105.

[6] 5 Q. B. 164, 48 E. C. L. 164.

[7] 6 H. & N. 265. See also Cashill v. Wright, 6 El. & Bl. 891, 88 E. C. L. 891; Kent v. Shuckard, 2 B. & Ad. 803, 22 E. C. L. 186; Oppenheim v. White Lion Hotel Co., L. R. 6 C. P. 515; Richmond v. Smith, 8 B. & C. 9, 15 E. C. L. 144.

That the innkeeper is not liable where the loss results from the negligent act of the guest himself was settled in *Sanders v. Spencer*, 3 Dyer 266b. There the host announced to his guest that he would not be responsible for the goods unless the guest should lock them up in a chamber. The latter left them in an outer court, where they were stolen. The innkeeper was discharged.

296   FOUNDATIONS OF LEGAL LIABILITY.

Volume II

Act of God; negligence of guest.

held that the innkeeper, though guilty of no negligence and though he is even diligent, is liable for the loss or injury of the money or goods of his guest, unless such loss results from the act of God or of the public enemy, or from the negligence of the guest himself.

In America there are some decisions which adopt the view advanced in *Dawson v. Chamney* (1843),[8] but by the weight of authority the innkeeper is, in the absence of statute, held to the liability of an insurer except as against the act of God, or of the public enemy, or as against the negligent act of the guest himself.[9]

Loss by accidental fire.

Some of the American courts, without entirely discarding the doctrine of strict liability, have added natural casualties, like fire, to the three exceptions generally recognized.[1] Loss by accidental fire is certainly not an unreasonable exception in itself, but the recognition of it, as the results show, inevitably leads to the demolition of the old rule of liability and to the adoption in its stead of the rule of *prima facie* liability sanctioned in *Dawson v. Chamney*.[2]

Writ against innkeeper.

It is worth observing that the departure from common-law doctrine indicated in *Dawson v. Chamney* was due to a false gloss on an expression found in the ancient writ against the innkeeper. In stating the duty imposed on innkeepers by the custom of the realm, the old writ declares that they are bound to keep by night and day, without subtraction or loss, such goods of their guests as are deposited in the inn.[3] Then follows a clause, *ita quod pro defectu dictorum hospitatorum vel serventium suorum hospitibus damnum non eveniat ullo modo*. The meaning of this language, as given by Fitzher-

[8] 5 Q. B. 164, 48 E. C. L. 164; Metcalf *v.* Hess, 14 Ill. 129; Hulbert *v.* Hartman, 79 Ill. App. 289; Laird *v.* Eichold, 10 Ind. 212, 71 Am. Dec. 323.
[9] Mateer *v.* Brown, 1 Cal. 221; Pinkerton *v.* Woodward, 33 Cal. 557, 91 Am. Dec. 657; O'Brien *v.* Vaill, 22 Fla. 627, 1 Am. St Rep. 219; Mason *v.* Thompson, 9 Pick. (Mass.) 280, 20 Am. Dec. 471;

Sibley *v.* Aldrich, 33 N. H. 553; Hulett *v.* Swift, 33 N. Y. 571, 88 Am. Dec. 405; Meacham *v.* Galloway, 102 Tenn. 415.
[1] Cutler *v.* Bonney, 30 Mich. 259; Merritt *v.* Claghorn, 23 Vt. 177; McDaniels *v.* Robinson, 26 Vt. 316.
[2] Johnson *v.* Chadbourn Finance Co., 89 Minn. 310.
[3] Reg. Brev. Orig., 105; Calye's Case, 8 Coke 32; Fitz. Nat. Brev 94 B.

bert, is merely this: "so that by the default of them, the innkeepers or their servants, no damage may come in any manner to the guests."[4]

In *Calye's Case,* which is largely a comment on this writ, it was observed in connection with this expression that "the innholder shall not be charged unless there be a default in him or his servants in the well and safe-keeping" of the chattels within the inn.[5] As clearly appears from the context, it was not intended by these words to qualify the liability of the innkeeper.[6] In other words, there is a default within the meaning of the writ when the goods are not duly forthcoming under the conditions prescribed by law, the term *defectus* being used merely to indicate the breach of legal duty.[7]

Apparently no other construction was placed upon this language until Story, two hundred and fifty years later, deliberately but nevertheless erroneously used the word 'negligence' as the equivalent of *defectus*.[8] The suggestion was plausible and its fruits are now visible in many quarters.[9]

The laxer doctrine advocated by this writer would, of course, have made no headway but for the social progress which has in modern times changed the relation between the innkeeper and his guest. As security in travel becomes greater it may seem wise to relax the rule declaring the innkeeper a virtual insurer.

Before dismissing the innkeeper entirely from our notice we may be permitted to ask a very pertinent question. Is he after all really a bailee? Modern writers treat him as a

---

[4] Fitz. Nat. Brev. 94 B.
[5] 8 Coke 33.
[6] Coke goes on to say, "for the innkeeper is bound in law to keep them safe without any stealing or purloining." 8 Coke 33.
[7] Mateer v. Brown, 1 Cal. 221; Sibley v. Aldrich, 33 N. H. 553, 66 Am. Dec. 745.
[8] Story on Bailments, § 470. Sir William Jones had previously contended that the innkeeper should only be held to the degree of care which a prudent man takes of his own property, but he cited no authority in support of the proposition and he acknowledges that the common-law authorities enounce a stricter rule. Jones on Bailments, Am. ed. (1806), 97.
[9] Denman, C. J., who decided Dawson v. Chamney, 5 Q. B. 164, 48 E. C. L. 164, was clearly misled by Story. In England the error was soon corrected, but in this country it still has currency.

bailee, and the question of his liability is everywhere discussed in terms of the law of bailment. That the innkeeper may become and often is actually a bailee in the full sense is certainly true. But there is a point at which he usually falls short of being a true bailee. This is on the critical point of possession. When the guest appears at the inn and takes with him into the room assigned to him his money and other personal belongings, who has the legal possession of those things? In whom would the right of action for their recovery be vested if they are carried away by a stranger? What reason or necessity is there for attributing possession, either actual or constructive, to the keeper of the hostelry in such case? If he has no possession he is not a bailee and is liable merely as innkeeper by the custom of the realm.[1]

The Bailment for Carriage.

In the bailment for carriage (*locatio operis mercium vehendarum*) the law discriminates between the common carrier and other carriers. The former is bound to answer for the goods committed to his care absolutely and upon all contingencies save where loss or damage results from the act of God or of the public enemy.

The nature of the liability of a person other than a common carrier who undertakes to convey chattels was quaintly stated by Lord Holt in the leading case: " Though a bailee is to have a reward for his management, yet he is only to do the best he can, and if he be robbed it is a good account." [2] In other words, the private agent, factor, or servant who is employed to carry for hire is held to the same degree of accountability for goods committed to him as other bailees.[3]

Perhaps the earliest specific statement concerning the lia-

---

[1] In Y. B. 42 Edw. III. 11, pl. 13, the defendant, an innkeeper, in a suit where a guest sought to charge him for money and goods taken from his room at the inn, excepted to the sufficiency of the plaintiff's writ and count because neither a delivery of the property to the innkeeper was alleged, nor was the innkeeper or his servants alleged to be guilty of appropriating the goods. But the plaintiff had judgment.

[2] Coggs v. Bernard, 2 Ld. Raym. 918.

[3] Story on Bailments, § 457.

bility of the common carrier to be found in our early writers is in St. Germain's Dialogue. "If a common carrier go by ways that be dangerous for robbing, or drive by night or in other inconvenient time, and be robbed; or if he overcharge a horse whereby he falleth into the water, or otherwise so that the stuff is hurt or impaired; he shall stand charged for his misdemeanor." [4]

<small>Chapter XXIX

Negligence in common carrier.</small>

This passage merely applies to the carrier the ancient principle of liability for damage to property resulting from the negligent misfeasance of an undertaking, and perhaps evinces no great legal acumen. From the language used it is a fair inference that the question of the liability of a carrier for a loss not attributable to his negligence had not then been considered by the courts of common law. This conclusion is amply borne out by the absence if any reference to such a case in the early authorities. No one, however, can doubt that if such question had arisen in an action of detinue, it would have been resolved in conformity with the ancient doctrine that the bailee must have the goods forthcoming or answer for their value.

Nay, such weighty considerations can be advanced in favor of the strict liability of the carrier, that when the time did come for the relaxation of the general rule of liability no one dreamed of relaxing it in favor of carriers, even though the plaintiff sued in case. Thus in *Woodlife's Case* (1596),[5] Popham, C. J., whose notions were apparently more advanced than those of his associates, defined the undertaking of the carrier by saying: "Carriers are paid for their carriage and take upon them safely to carry and deliver the things received." In other words, the common carrier is bound to deliver at all events. The same idea appears in *Southcote's Case* (1601),[6] where the distinction between the carrier's liability and that of merchandising factors was pointed out. During the suc-

<small>Principle of strict liability never relaxed in favor of carrier.</small>

<small>[4] Dial. II., ch. 38, near end. The writer adds: "And if he would percase refuse to convey it, unless promise were made unto him that he shall not be charged for no misdemeanor that should be in him, the promise were void, for it is against reason and against good manners."

[5] Moo. K. B. 462; Anonymous, Owen 57.

[6] 4 Coke 84.</small>

ceeding century a number of cases were decided in conformity with this strict view, and the same doctrine was applied to carriers by water as to carriers by land.[7]

Act of God and act of public enemy only exceptions.

On the whole, Lord Holt was fully justified in saying in his summary of the law of bailments, that "the law charges this person thus intrusted to carry goods against all events but acts of God and of the enemies of the king."[8] He says the rule is adopted from necessity and is founded on what we now speak of as considerations of public policy. In this he speaks truly. The policy and necessity of the thing fully accounts for the existence of the principle in his day and in our own. In the absence of such considerations, the law would certainly have shifted its ground here as in other bailments.

Present basis of doctrine found in policy and necessity.

The strict liability of the carrier is not, then, to be considered a mere perpetuation of the obsolete principle that the bailee is debtor, the efficacy of which was lost with the obsolescence of detinue, but it is an admirable illustration of a principle which has maintained itself because a new and better reason has been found for it and which has acquired a new significance and content in the ground where it now thrives.

Exceptions to Liability of Common Carrier.

The act of God and the act of the public enemy furnish two contingencies which were recognized by Lord Holt as affording a good defense to the common carrier. As suggested by Judge Holmes, the second of these defenses perhaps had its origin in the idea brought out in the *Marshal's Case*

Origin of exception arising from act of public enemy.

(1655),[9] to the effect that where the goods are taken or de-

---

[7] Rich *v.* Kneeland (1613), Cro. Jac. 330, Hob. 17; Symons *v.* Darknoll (1628), Palmer 523.

[8] Coggs *v.* Bernard, 2 Ld. Raym. 918. Proceeding, the learned judge says: "Though the force be never so great, as if an irresistible multitude of people should rob him, nevertheless he is chargeable. And this is a politic establishment, contrived by the policy of the law, for the safety of all persons, the necessity of whose affairs oblige them to trust these sorts of persons, that they may be safe in their ways of dealing; for else these carriers might have an opportunity of undoing all persons that had any dealings with them, by combining with thieves, etc., and yet doing it in such a clandestine manner as would not be possible to be discovered. And this is the reason the law is founded upon in that point."

[9] Y. B. 33 Hen. VI. 1, pl. 3. See Common Law, 201.

stroyed by a public enemy the carrier has no remedy over. But clearly the inability of a carrier to resist such force and the impossibility of guarding against it supplied a cogent reason why the exception should be recognized.

The term 'act of God' as descriptive of certain events not due to human agency and which constitute a defense to an action for the breach of a contract, had been used in *Mouse's Case* (1609),[1] in connection with a bailment of common carriage; but the idea was familiar in the law. It has been surmised that Lord Holt used the term 'act of God' in a sense broad enough to include all inevitable accidents, the *casus fortuitus* of the civil law.[2] The meaning of the term, however, had not then been made clear by adjudication, and indeed it was not clearly defined until within very recent years.

It is clear that the liability of the carrier, as stated by Lord Holt and subject to the two exceptions mentioned by him, is virtually that of an insurer. But the particular term was not used. Nearly three-quarters of a century later, Lord Mansfield had occasion to state the rule again. He did so in language that had been current since the days of Popham. "The common carrier," said he, "in respect of the premium he is to receive, runs the risk of them [i. e., the goods] and must make good the loss, though it happen without any fault in him; the reward making him answerable for their safe delivery."[3]

A few years later, in *Forward v. Pittard* (1785),[4] the same learned judge was called upon to examine more fully into the meaning of the term 'act of God.' It appeared that

---

[1] 12 Coke 63. Here the defendant pleaded that the goods in question had been thrown overboard in the midst of a tempest in order to save the lives of the passengers. This was held a good defense. "If the danger accrued only by the act of God, as by a tempest, no default being in the ferryman, everyone ought to bear his [own] loss." See also Bird v. Astcock, 2 Bulst. 280.

[2] See Carrier's Liability, by Prof. J. H. Beale, 11 Harv. L. Rev. 167.

In Amies v. Stevens, (1718) 1 Stra. 128, the carrier's boat was sunk by a sudden gust of wind as she passed through a bridge. The defendant was held not to be chargeable for the loss of goods on the boat. In this case the loss would now be attributed merely to accident, but it was treated as an act of God.

[3] Gibbon v. Paynton, (1769) 4 Burr. 2300.

[4] 1 T. R. 27.

goods in the hands of a common carrier had been destroyed by a fire which originated in premises adjoining the booth where the goods were stored. Negligence on the part of the carrier was therefore expressly negatived. Judgment, however, was given against him. The carrier, said Lord Mansfield, is in the nature of an insurer, and is liable for every accident except by the act of God or of the king's enemies.[5]

Mansfield's statement concerning 'act of God.'

While Lord Mansfield was the first to describe the engagement of the carrier as being in the nature of an insurance, the actual judgment rendered in this case embodied no greater innovation than was involved in giving a more definite and perhaps somewhat narrower meaning to the term 'act of God.'[7] Concerning this expression he said: "I consider [act of God] to mean something in opposition to the act of man; for everything is the act of God that happens by His permission; everything by His knowledge. But to pre-

---

[5] In Garside v. Trent, etc., Nav. Co. (1792), 4 T. R. 581, Lord Kenyon, adopting this expression of Lord Mansfield said: "He [the carrier] is held responsible as an insurer."

In declaring that common carriers are virtually insurers, Lord Mansfield brushed aside an ingenious argument which, if adopted, would have ingrafted upon the law of carriers the same error which Judge Story subsequently introduced into the law of innkeeping. The carrier, it was insisted, is liable only for loss occasioned by the negligence of himself or of his servants.

This argument was based on the circumstance that the old form of declaration against the carrier, like the writ against the innkeeper, in stating the duty of the carrier contained the clause, "Ita quod pro defectu dictorum communium portatorum seu serventium suorum, hujusmodi bona et catalla eis . . . deliberata non sint perdita, amissa, seu spoliata." See Forward v. Pittard, 1 T. R. 29. Upon this it was insisted that negligence on the part of the carrier must be proved. In other words, the defendant's attorney would have had the court declare that *defectus*, as used in the declaration, means negligence. But, as was pertinently said by counsel in reply, negligence in fact is not of the gist of such an action; or if negligence be considered essential "everything is negligence which the law does not excuse." 1 T. R. 32. Compare Dale v. Hall, 1 Wils. C. Pl. 282.

[7] In writing what has been said on the subject of the carrier's liability we have had in mind the contents of the critical and instructive article by Professor Beale on Carrier's Liability, 11 Harv. L. Rev. 158. We must add that we do not agree with his proposition that the strict liability of the common carrier is an anomaly which was introduced by Lord Mansfield in Forward v. Pittard, 1 T. R. 27. To our mind it is clearly, what Judge Holmes pronounced it to be, a survival from that period when all bailees were held strictly liable as debtors.

vent litigation, collusion, and the necessity of going into circumstances impossible to be unraveled, the law presumes against the carrier, unless he shows it was done by the king's enemies or by such act as could not happen by the intervention of man, as storms, lightning, and tempest." [8]

A most luminous discussion of the meaning of the term 'act of God' is found in the opinion of Lord Chief Justice Cockburn in *Nugent v. Smith* (1876).[9] Among other things his lordship said: "It is somewhat remarkable that previously to the present case no judicial exposition has occurred of the meaning of the term 'act of God,' as regards the degree of care to be applied by the carrier in order to entitle himself to the benefit of its protection. We must endeavor to lay down an intelligible rule.

"That a storm at sea is included in the term 'act of God' can admit of no doubt whatever. Storm and tempest have always been mentioned in dealing with this subject as among the instances of *vis major* coming under the denomination of 'act of God.' But it is equally true, as has already been pointed out, that it is not under all circumstances that inevitable accident arising from the so-called act of God will, any more than inevitable accident in general by the Roman and continental law, afford immunity to the carrier. This must depend on his ability to avert the effects of the *vis major*, and the degree of diligence which he is bound to apply to that end.

"It is at once obvious, as was pointed out by Lord Mansfield in *Forward v. Pittard* (1785), that all causes of inevitable accident — '*casus fortuitus*' — may be divided into two classes — those which are occasioned by the elementary forces of nature unconnected with the agency of man or other cause, and those which have their origin either in the whole or in part in the agency of man, whether in acts of commission or omission, of nonfeasance or of misfeasance, or in any other

---

[8] 1 T. R. 33.
In Trent Nav. Co. v. Wood, (1784) 3 Esp. 127, 4 Dougl. 287, 26 E. C. L. 358, Lord Mansfield had already defined the 'act of God' as being "natural and inevitable necessity, as winds and storms." "Robbery," said he, "is certainly very strong, but not a natural necessity."

[9] 1 C. P. D. 423.

cause independent of the agency of natural forces. It is obvious that it would be altogether incongruous to apply the term 'act of God' to the latter class of inevitable accident. It is equally clear that storm and tempest belong to the class to which the term 'act of God' is properly applicable.

"On the other hand, it must be admitted that it is not because an accident is occasioned by the agency of nature, and therefore by what may be termed the 'act of God,' that it necessarily follows that the carrier is entitled to immunity. The rain which fertilizes the earth and the wind which enables the ship to navigate the ocean are as much within the term 'act of God' as the rainfall which causes a river to burst its banks and carry destruction over a whole district, or the cyclone that drives a ship against a rock or sends it to the bottom. Yet the carrier who by the rule is entitled to protection in the latter case, would clearly not be able to claim it in case of damage occurring in the former. For here another principle comes into play. The carrier is bound to do his utmost to protect goods committed to his charge from loss or damage, and if he fails herein he becomes liable from the nature of his contract. In the one case he can protect the goods by proper care, in the other it is beyond his power to do so. If by his default in omitting to take the necessary care loss or damage ensues, he remains responsible, though the so-called act of God may have been the immediate cause of the mischief. If the ship is unseaworthy, and hence perishes from the storm which it otherwise would have weathered; if the carrier by undue deviation or delay exposes himself to the danger which he otherwise would have avoided; or if by his rashness he unnecessarily encounters it, as by putting to sea in a raging storm, the loss cannot be said to be due to the act of God alone, and the carrier cannot have the benefit of the exception. . . . In other words, all that can be required of the carrier is that he shall do all that is reasonably and practically possible to insure the safety of the goods. If he uses all the known means to which prudent and experienced carriers ordinarily have recourse, he does all that can be reasonably required of him; and if, under such circumstances, he is overpowered by storm or other natural agency, he is within the rule which gives immunity from the effects of such *vis major* as the act of God. I do not think that because some one may have discovered some more efficient method of securing the goods which has not become generally known, or because it cannot be proved that if the skill and ingenuity of engineers or others were directed to the subject something more efficient might not be produced, that the carrier can be made liable. I find no authority for saying that the *vis major* must be such as ' no amount of human care or skill could have resisted,' or the injury such as ' no human ability could have prevented,' and I think this construction of the rule erroneous."

In accordance with this reasoning it was held that a carrier by sea is not liable for the death of a horse while in course of transportation by sea, where the jury found that the injury which resulted in the animal's death was caused partly by the excessively rough weather and partly by the struggling incident to the fright of the animal, there being no negligence on the part of the carrier's servants.

Liability of carrier by sea.

In the early cases which distinguish between the liability of common carriers and others, the strict liability of the former is uniformly placed on the ground of the payment of a reward.[2] This would seem to indicate that all persons who received a reward for carriage were deemed common carriers and that only bailees for gratuitous carriage were excepted from the principle of strict liability.

But, as the modern decisions show, the payment of a reward is not the sole criterion by which the question is to be determined whether a bailee in a particular instance is a common carrier or not. Thus, while it is certainly true that the bailee for gratuitous carriage is not liable as an insurer,[3] the

Taking pay does not make a carrier a common carrier.

---

[2] "If one delivers goods to a common carrier to convey and the carrier is robbed of them, still he shall be charged, because he has hire for them and thus impliedly undertakes to deliver the goods turned over to him; and for this he shall answer the value of them if he be robbed." Woodleife v. Curties, 1 Rolle Abr. 2 (C), pl. 4. See also Anonymous, Owen 57, and Gibbon v. Paynton, 4 Burr. 2300. It will be remembered that the strict liability of the innkeeper was put on the same ground.

[3] Fay v. Steamer New World, 1

306   FOUNDATIONS OF LEGAL LIABILITY.

<small>Plying the calling makes the common carrier.</small>

mere fact that compensation is contracted for does not under the generally accepted view make the bailee a common carrier. To be a common carrier one must hold himself out as habitually plying the vocation. A casual engagement to carry does not make the bailee a common carrier.[4] But compensation coupled with the exercise of the common calling does make him such.

<small>An insurer without rights of insurer.</small>

It has been said that our law fixes upon the carrier the liability of an insurer without conceding to him the rights of an insurer.[5] In one respect this is true. The public calling of the carrier imposes on him a duty to carry for all who comply with such reasonable terms as he may impose, and he can arbitrarily reject none.[6] The insurer owes no such duty to the public and can choose his own risks. In respect to the matter of compensation the carrier can always reasonably protect himself by imposing a charge proportioned to the risk assumed, and there is no question but that he may also ordinarily limit his occupation to the carriage of particular kinds of chattels.

<small>Limiting the occupation.</small>

Postmasters.

<small>Postmaster a bailee.</small>

Postmasters, like innkeepers and common carriers, were originally and are now exceptional bailees, and had not the governmental authorities assumed to do the work of transporting mail, postmasters would no doubt have been subjected to the same degree of liability as other common carriers of goods. Indeed, in 1699 Lord Holt showed an inclination to hold the postmaster-general liable for exchequer bills lost while in the custody of the employees of a post office. He was, however, overruled by the three other judges, who held that inasmuch as the postmaster-general is the head of a department of the government he is not liable for money lost in the mails. Nor does the fact that he has the appointment of the employees in the department alter the rule.[7]

<small>Exempt from liability by reason of official privilege.</small>

Cal. 348; Pender v. Robbins, 6 Jones L. (51 N. Car.) 207.
[4] Ingate v. Christie, 3 C. & K. 61; Nugent v. Smith, 1 C. P. D. 27; Fish v. Chapman, 2 Ga. 349, 46 Am. Dec. 393.

[5] 11 Harv. L. Rev. 168.
[6] Garton v. Bristol, etc., R. Co., 1 B. & S. 112, 101 E. C. L. 112.
[7] Lane v. Cotton, 1 Ld. Raym. 646. Lord Holt's argument in this case is worth noting. He referred

MODERN LAW OF BAILMENT.   307

At a later day the question of the liability of the postmaster-general came before Lord Mansfield in the case of *Whitfield v. Le Despencer* (1778),[8] and, after a careful examination of the entire ground anew, the conclusion reached by the majority in the previous case was reaffirmed.

In America the postal department has always been a part of the public service and its officials are mere public officers. It has therefore always been conceded that neither the head of the department nor any officer not himself a misdemeanant is liable for losses incurred in transporting mail. The remuneration paid is so small as, in most cases, to make the department merely a gratuitous bailee.[9]

Chapter XXIX

Gratuitous nature of the bailment.

to the rule enforced in the Marshal's Case and to the rule which makes the sheriff liable where goods, taken on a *levari facias* or *extendi facias,* are rescued; also to the liability of the jailer where a debtor condemned for a trespass *vi et armis* escapes. He further added, "There is no difference between this case of the postmaster-general and the jailer, sheriff, etc.; for he ought safely to keep the letters delivered to him, as the others ought safely to keep their prisoners, or goods taken in execution." 1 Ld. Raym. 651.

[8] 2 Cowp. 754.
[9] See Sawyer *v.* Corse, 17 Gratt. (Va.) 230.

CHAPTER XXX

OWNERSHIP AND POSSESSION.

Volume II

Severance of ownership and possession.

AS was stated at the beginning of this discussion, the distinguishing feature of the true bailment is found in the severance of the possession of a chattel from the ownership. This point is made manifest in the better definitions of bailment. "The bailment consists," says Professor Parker, "of the delivery of something of a personal nature by one party to another, to be held according to the purpose or object of the delivery, and to be returned or delivered over when that purpose is accomplished."[1] Says Professor Hammond, "a bailment may be said to exist whenever the possession of a chattel is lawfully severed from its ownership or from any right derived from and representing ownership."[2]

Definitions of bailment.

That delivery to the bailee does vest legal possession in him has always been recognized in the common law. It is

[1] From MSS. of Prof. Joel A. Parker, adopted in Bouv. L. Dict., s. v. *Bailment,* and in Schouler on Bailments, § 2.

[2] Synopsis of Bailments (unpublished). The last clause in this definition includes cases of subbailment, a feature not covered by the definitions of other writers.

It is perhaps worthy of at least passing notice that during a long period of time the bailment was spoken of in the common-law courts and by common-law writers as a trust. That every bailment involves an intrusting of property by one person to another is literally true and must always remain so. This, of course, is the true significance of language in which the bailment is called a trust, but sometimes it superficially appears to have a deeper meaning.

Blackstone, in treating of trusts, expressly states that in addition to the particular species of trusts cognizable in equity alone, "there are other trusts which are cognizable in a court of law, as deposits and all manner of bailments." 3 Bl. Com. 432. In another connection the same writer defines bailment as the delivery of goods in trust, upon a contract express or implied, that the trust shall be faithfully executed by the bailee. 2 Bl. Com. 451.

Sir William Jones says that the bailment is a delivery of goods in trust on a contract, expressed or implied, that the trust shall be duly executed. Jones on Bailments, Am. ed. (1806), 125.

Chancellor Kent and Judge Story both substantially adopted the language of Blackstone. See 2 Kent Com. 558; Story on Bailments, § 2.

for this reason that the bailee has a right of action against one who tortiously deprives him of the chattel. In our earliest law it was the bailee who entered upon pursuit and prosecuted the thief in the *actio furti*. At a later day he usually brought detinue against the trespasser, and his undoubted right to do so was, as we have seen, assigned as a reason for his absolute liability to the owner.

Chapter XXX

Possessory right of bailee.

Inasmuch as the bailee has undoubted possession no dishonest or wrongful act done by him during the continuance of the bailment can constitute trespass or theft. It was once considered that the completion of the purpose or term of the bailment might divest possession. This view was not in harmony with the early cases and has been declared unsound.[3]

End of term or of purpose of the bailment.

The possession of a bailee does not cease until he has redelivered the thing at its destination or transferred his possession to another. There are some exceptions to this rule. For instance, where a person gains possession by color of bailment with intent to convert and defraud, there is no real bailment; and again, where the bailee determines the bailment by some act inconsistent with the bailment, as by breaking bulk, his subsequent conversion of the goods will be larceny.[4]

When possession of bailee ceases.

Colorable bailment.

The doctrine that by a breaking of the bulk the possession of the bailee is terminated so as to make him liable for theft was clearly stated in 1473 by one of the judges in the Star Chamber in a case where a carrier who had been engaged to transport certain bales of goods to Southampton took them to another place and broke open the bales. Said Choke, J.: "I think that where a man has goods in his possession by reason of a bailment he cannot take them feloniously, being in possession; but still it seems here that it is felony, for the things which were within the bales were not bailed to him: only the

Breaking bulk.

---

[3] Rex. *v.* Banks, (1821) R. & R. C. C. 441, overruling the doctrine laid down in 2 East P. C. 690. Here the prisoner borrowed a horse for a special journey, and after the time for the bailment was ended sold the horse. The court held that unless the felonious intent existed when the possession was obtained, there was no larceny.

[4] 3 Co. Inst. 107; Kelynge P. C. 81, 82; 2 East P. C. 695, 696; 1 Hale P. C. 504; 4 Bl. Com. 230.

310 FOUNDATIONS OF LEGAL LIABILITY.

Volume II

bales as an entire thing were bailed to carry. In which case if he had given the bales or sold them, it is not felony, but when he broke them and took out of them what was within he did that without warrant; as if one bailed a tun of wine to carry, if the bailee sell the tun, it is not felony nor trespass, but if he take some out it is felony. So is it if I bail the key of my chamber to one to guard my chamber, and he takes my goods within this chamber, it is felony, for they were not bailed to him." [5]

Larcenous conversion.

In making the conversion larcenous where bulk is broken the law has evidently, as said by Lord Campbell in a modern case, resorted to some astuteness in order to protect the bailor.[6] After the breaking, it is not material whether the whole or only a part of the goods be converted. In either case it is larceny. But, as is well settled, a conversion of the whole package of goods without a breaking of bulk is not a larcenous taking. In explanation of this East says: "Up to the moment of [the bailee's] parting with the whole package his possession is lawful, and he has no unlawful possession afterwards whereby to constitute a new taking, unless he break the package, or sever part of the commodity from the rest while it continues in his possession." [7]

The general principle that the bailee has legal possession

[5] Y. B. 13 Edw. IV. 9, pl. 5. The report of this case is translated in Pollock and Wright on Possession, 134-136. After having been considered in the Star Chamber the question was argued in the Exchequer Chamber, and by the opinion of the majority of the judges the defendant was declared guilty of felony. But it was explicitly stated that where goods are bailed the bailee cannot take them feloniously. The idea underlying the case seems to be that by carrying the goods to an entirely different place from that agreed upon, and by opening the bales, the bailee showed an intention to convert from the beginning. Hence there was no bailment. But in later years Choke's opinion, to the effect that the mere breaking of bulk is sufficient to terminate the bailment, was accepted. East puts this rule on the ground that "the privity of the contract is determined by the act of breaking the package, which makes him a trespasser." 2 East P. C. 697.

[6] Reg. v. Poyser, 2 Den. C. C. 233. Cases from the last century applying the rule that a conversion after a breaking of bulk is larcenous are very numerous. Rex v. Madox (1805), R. & R. C. C. 92; Rex v. Brazier (1817), R. & R. C. C. 337; Rex v. Fletcher ('1831), 4 C. & P. 545, 19 E. C. L. 519; Rex v. Jones (1835), 7 C. & P. 151, 32 E. C. L. 474; Reg. v. Cornish (1854), Dears. 425.

[7] 2 East P. C. 696.

is so thoroughly grounded in the common law that the bailor can sometimes be prosecuted for larceny in taking his own chattels from his bailee.[8] For instance, it has been determined that if one who commits money to a servant to carry to a certain place, afterwards waylays and robs him in order to charge the hundred, he is guilty of a felony.[9] The act of the master in committing the money to his servant to carry is a temporary renunciation of any claim of possession in himself.

<small>Chapter XXX</small>

<small>Possession of bailee good as against bailor.</small>

It is obvious that the recognition by the criminal as well as civil courts of the principle that the bailee has full legal possession of the chattel bailed leaves the bailor without adequate protection against the fraudulent acts of the bailee. In modern times this defect has been remedied by legislation which began in England after the miscarriage of justice which occurred in *Rex v. Walsh* (1812),[1] where a broker escaped punishment after having fraudulently converted bank notes committed to him for investment.

<small>Embezzlement by bailee made criminal by statute.</small>

Special Property of the Bailee.

Having now seen that the bailee undoubtedly has possession at common law, it becomes necessary to inquire whether he has any more extensive interest. Undoubtedly there are frequently found in the old decisions and in the old text writers statements to the effect that the bailee has a property in the chattel bailed, or at least a special property.[2] But it is apparent that the possessory right of the bailee sufficiently accounts for all or nearly all of the phenomena presented by the de-

---

[8] Y. B. 13 Edw. IV. 10a, pl. 5 (Nedham, J.); 2 Russ. on Crimes, 283n; Vin. Abr., *Trespass*, 589; *ib., Trover*, 685, 689; Poll. & Wright, Possession, 165.

[9] 2 East P. C. 558.

[1] 2 Leach C. C. 1054, 4 Taunt. 258.

[2] A property right is attributed to the bailee in Y. B. 21 Hen. VII. 14, pl. 23.

Blackstone, after giving illustrations of the several bailments, says: "In all these instances there is a special qualified property transferred from the bailor to the bailee, together with the possession. It is not an absolute property, because of his contract for restitution; the bailor having still left in him the right to a chose in action, grounded upon such contract. And on account of this qualified property of the bailee, he may (as well as the bailor) maintain an action against such as injure or take away these chattels." 2 Bl. Com. 452.

312   FOUNDATIONS OF LEGAL LIABILITY.

cisions touching his interest. Hence it seems to be unnecessary to attribute to bailees generally any property right at all. The persistence, however, of the expression 'special property' as indicative of the bailee's interest makes it necessary to examine into the subject further.

At the outset it is plain that there may well be a distinction between gratuitous bailments, such as deposits, mandates, and loans on the one hand, and bailments for hire on the other. It may be conceded that the bailee for hire, especially the pledgee, has a higher interest than the gratuitous bailee. But if by the term 'special property' is meant something in the nature of an estate carved out of the general ownership or property right in a thing, the depositary, mandatary, and commodatary certainly did not have such property. The interest commensurate with the legal remedies accorded to these bailees is possession only.

Recent investigation has given to possessory rights much greater recognition than was formerly accorded to them. Thus Sir Frederick Pollock tells us truly, that possession in law is a substantive right or interest which exists and has legal incidents and advantages apart from the true owner's title. Hence it is itself a kind of title, and it is a natural development of the law that a possessor should be able to deal with his apparent interest in the fashion of an owner, and that as regards every one not having a better title those acts should be valid.[3] When possession is understood in this light, it certainly becomes unnecessary to suppose the existence of an

---

[3] Pollock & Wright on Possession, 19. Again, the same writer lays down the principle that possession is equivalent to title as against a wrongdoer, and that this is a substantive rule of law not affected by forms of action. *Ib.*, 91. Further, "possession confers more than a personal right against wrongdoers; it confers a qualified right to possess, a right in the nature of property which is valid as against every one who cannot show a prior and a better right. Having reached this point the law cannot stop at protecting and assisting the possessor himself. It must protect those who stand in his place by succession or purchase. . . . The qualified right which arises from possession must therefore be a transmissible right. . . . Hence the rule that possession is a root of title is not only an actual but a necessary part of our system." *Ib.*, 93.

OWNERSHIP AND POSSESSION. 313

actual property right in the gratuitous bailee to account for the consideration given to him by our law.

Some countenance has been given to the idea that gratuitous bailees have a special property in the bailment by the circumstance that trover can be maintained by such bailee against one who interferes with his possession and converts the property. But this is not a conclusive test. Trover, to be sure, is often founded on a property right, but not exclusively so. It is clear that a remedy which is founded exclusively on the right of property, like replevin, will not lie at the instance of the gratuitous bailee. In other words, he has no real property, general or special.[4]

The nature of the interest acquired by the depositary was discussed in *Hartop v. Hoare* (1736),[5] where jewels were deposited in a sealed packet with a jeweler for safe-keeping. The jeweler broke the seal and then pledged the jewels for an advancement of three hundred pounds. It was held, upon the authority of Coke's interpretation of *Bonion's Case*, that the jeweler had the mere custody, as the owner had not intrusted him with the goods. From this it necessarily followed that the bailee had no interest which he could transmit, and that the original owner could maintain trover against the pledgee who refused to surrender the jewels without the repayment of his advancement.

As to pledgees, the opinion that they have a special property in the goods pledged is an old one. Coke referred to it in *Southcote's Case*, and the fact that pledgees have such an interest in the bailment was sufficient to relieve the pledgee from any higher degree of diligence in caring for the pledge than he exhibited in keeping his own goods.

Chapter XXX

Trover by bailee.

Replevin not maintainable by gratuitous bailee.

When trover maintainable by owner.

Special property ascribed to pledgee.

---

[4] Waterman v. Robinson, 5 Mass. 303. In this case Parsons, C. J., said that trover may be maintained by him who has the possession, but replevin can be maintained only by him who has the property, either general or special. The plaintiff "had no interest in the goods, but merely had the care of them for safe-keeping. If his possession was violated he might maintain trespass or trover, but he had no special property by which he could maintain replevin; in which the question is not of possession, but of property; although possession may be *prima facie* evidence of property."

[5] 3 Atk. 44.

Special property ascribed to bailee for definite term.

Likewise there is little difficulty in ascribing a special property to all bailees to whom things are let for hire and to bailees employed to perform service on things for hire. In an old case where a horse had been let to one for two days, and the bailor, suspecting that the bailee was about to abscond with the horse, forcibly retook the animal, the court, in giving judgment for the plaintiff in a suit for damages arising out of the assault connected with the taking, said the plaintiff had a special property good for the two days against all the world.[6]

Illusory nature of this special property.

This special property of the bailee for hire is not, however, of a definite nature, and the more it is examined the more shadowy it appears. Thus, in *Lilley v. Barnsley* (1844),[7] it was held that, where goods are bailed for the purpose of having work done upon them, the bailor can countermand the order and have the goods back with the work incomplete, on the payment of the reasonable value of the work done. Of course the bailee can recover damages for the breach of the contract, but he cannot hold the chattels bailed in order to secure this claim. This is a practical denial of any special property in the bailee. It puts the bailee in such cases on a lower plane than that of an agent where the agency is coupled with an interest.

Right of Bailee as Against Stranger.

Possession is property as against stranger.

While it thus appears that the special property often attributed to the bailee is hardly more than the right of possession when properly understood, there is one aspect in which the law undoubtedly considers the bailee in exactly the same light as if he were an owner. This is when the question arises between the bailee and a stranger. As against such person the bailee is treated as owner. But even here we seem merely to be confronted with another aspect of the right of possession, for, as the formula generally runs, "as between bailee and stranger, possession gives title;"[8] or, as put by

---

[6] Lee v. Atkinson, Yelv. 172.
See also Eaton v. Lynde, 15 Mass. 242; Wilbraham v. Snow, 2 Saund. 47, and note.

[7] 2 M. & Rob. 548.

[8] See language of Collins, M. R., in The Winkfield, (1902) P. 60.

Lord Campbell, "the person who has possession has the property."⁹

In *Rooth v. Wilson* (1817),¹ it appeared that a horse had been sent to one B to pasture for accommodation. B turned the animal into a pasture on a dark night and it fell over into an adjacent field by reason of a defective fence and was killed. B then sued the adjacent proprietor, whose duty it was to maintain the fence. It was held that B, by reason of his negligence in turning the horse into an insecure pasture to which it was not accustomed, was liable to the owner for the value of the horse, and that the existence of this liability gave him a right to sue the adjacent proprietor for damages to the full value of the horse.

Claridge v. South Staffordshire Tramway Co. (1892),² presented the following state of facts: A horse was put into the hands of an auctioneer and the owner gave the auctioneer permission to use the animal until sold. While being so used the horse was injured by the negligence of a tramway company. It was held in the Queen's Bench Division that, under the circumstances of the case, the bailee was not liable to the owner, and that consequently the bailee had no such interest as would sustain an action for damages by him. This right of action, it was said, belonged to the owner.

This case differed from *Rooth v. Wilson* solely in respect of the fact that whereas in the earlier case the bailee was liable to the bailor because of his own negligence, in the later case no such liability existed. In deciding the later case the court proceeded on the idea that the bailee's right of action was merely a consequence of his liability to the bailor. But this was a mistake. The bailee's right of action is a consequence of the violation of his possessory interest, which interest is, as against a stranger, equivalent to actual ownership.

In *The Winkfield*,³ substantially the same question came before the Court of Appeal and *Claridge v. South Staffordshire Tramway Co.* was overruled, it being held by all the

---

⁹ Jefferies v. Great Western R. Co., 5 El. & Bl. 806, 85 E. C. L. 806.
¹ 1 B. & Ald. 59.
² 1 Q. B. 422.
³ (1902) P. 42.

Chapter XXX

Bailee's action against stranger supposed to depend on his responsibility to owner.

Repudiation of this notion.

judges that in an action against a stranger for the loss of goods caused by his negligence, the bailee in possession can recover the value of the goods, though he himself has a good defense as against an action by the bailor to recover for the loss of the chattels.

<small>Bailee's right of action a corollary from his possession.</small>

The opinion of Collins, M. R., in this case is rich in historical matter and withal exceedingly instructive. Among other things he said: " I am of opinion that Claridge's case was wrongly decided, and that the law is that in an action against a stranger for loss of goods caused by his negligence, the bailee in possession can recover the value of the goods, although he would have had a good answer to an action by the bailor for damages for the loss of the thing bailed. It seems to me that the position, that possession is good against a wrongdoer and that the latter cannot set up the *jus tertii* unless he claims under it, is well established in our law, and really concludes this case against the respondents. As I shall show presently, a long series of authorities establishes this in actions of trover and trespass at the suit of a possessor. And the principle being the same, it follows that he can equally recover the whole value of the goods in an action on the case for their loss through the tortious conduct of the defendant. I

<small>Wrongdoer cannot set up want of title in bailee.</small>

think it involves this also, that the wrongdoer who is not defending under the title of the bailor is quite unconcerned with what the rights are between the bailor and bailee, and must treat the possessor as the owner of the goods for all purposes, quite irrespective of the rights and obligations as between him and the bailor. I think this position is well established in our law, though it may be that reasons for its existence have been given in some of the cases which are not quite satisfactory. I think also that the obligation of the bailee to the bailor to account for what he has received in respect of the destruction or conversion of the thing bailed has been admitted so often in decided cases that it cannot now be questioned; and further, I think it can be shown that the right of the bailee to recover cannot be rested on the ground suggested in some of the cases, viz., that he was liable over to the bailor for the loss of the goods converted or destroyed. It cannot be denied that since the case of *Armory v. Delamirie*,[4] not to mention earlier cases from the year books onward, a mere finder may recover against a wrongdoer the full value of the thing converted. That decision involves the principle that as between possessor and wrongdoer the presumption of law is, in the words of Lord Campbell in *Jefferies v. Great Western R. Co*,,[5] 'that the person who has possession has the property.' "[6]

<small>Chapter XXX</small>

Again, the same learned judge observed: " The root principle of the whole discussion is that, as against a wrongdoer, possession is title. The chattel that has been converted or damaged is deemed to be the chattel of the possessor and of no other, and therefore its loss or deterioration is his loss, and to him, if he demands it, it must be recouped. His obligation to account to the bailor is really not *ad rem* in the discussion. It only comes in after [the bailee] has carried his legal position to its logical consequence against a wrongdoer. . . . As between bailee and stranger, possession gives title — that is, not a limited interest, but absolute and complete ownership, and he is entitled to receive back a complete equivalent for the whole loss or deterioration of the thing itself. As between bailor and bailee the real interests of each must be inquired into, and as the bailee has to account for the thing bailed, so he must account for that which has become its equivalent and now represents it. What he has received above his own interest he has received to the use of his bailor. The wrongdoer, having once paid full damages to the bailee, has an answer to any action by the bailor."[7]

<small>As against wrongdoer possession is title.</small>

<small>Bailee who recovers of stranger must account to bailor.</small>

Conceding to the bailee a right of possession which in certain conditions partakes of the nature of a special property, it remains for us to refer for a moment to the interest of the bailor. Generally speaking, he is said to have the ownership. In our early law it sometimes seems that the bailor in delivering the chattel to the bailee has parted with every interest

<small>The bailor is owner.</small>

---

[4] 1 Stra. 505.
[5] 5 El. & Bl. 806, 85 E. C. L. 806.
[6] Collins, M. R., in The Winkfield, (1902) P. 54, 55.
[7] *Ib.*, 60, 61.

that the law will take notice of, since the possessory remedies go along with the possession, and the bailee consequently becomes the necessary actor against all wrongdoers. But however defective legal machinery may have once been as regards the enforcement of the bailor's rights against third persons, legal theory has never denied that the bailor is the general owner. Bracton, Glanvill, and the author of the Mirrour, all understood that while the bailee may have possession and with it the right to enforce the possessory remedies, the bailor undoubtedly has the *dominium,* or ownership. Indeed, without this concession the bailor could not have maintained detinue against the bailee, for that action is founded on property. At any rate before the end of the middle ages the bailor was said to have the general property,[8] this particular expression being chosen, of course, to distinguish his interest from the special property attributed to the bailee.

In conclusion a word may be added concerning the forces which have operated to bring the English law of bailment to its present maturity. The circumstance that the writers who have contributed most to the literature of the subject have had a strong predilection for the civil law has given to our law of bailment a decidedly foreign appearance. The names given to the various bailments are mostly of Roman origin, and the subject has been constantly overlaid by learning drawn from that source.

Notwithstanding this, the internal growth of the law of bailment has been almost purely English. Beneath a superficial layer of the learning of civil law the current of English instinct has been constant and steady. Considering the manner in which our law of bailment has been handled by the text writers, it is certainly not surprising that the impression should generally prevail that this branch of law is deeply marked by principles drawn from the civil law. But, as was shown by Lord Cockburn in *Nugent v. Smith* (1876),[9] this is not so. Our law of bailments is English law, glossed over, it may be,

---

[8] See 2 Poll. & Mait. Hist. Eng. Law, 2d ed., 177.
[9] 1 C. P. D. 423.

with a coating of Roman terms and framed in a form resembling that of the foreign system; but still it is of truly English origin, somewhat tediously and unsystematically wrought out by the builders of the common law.

Chapter XXX

PART III

HISTORY AND PRINCIPLES OF THE LAW OF BILLS AND NOTES

CHAPTER XXXI

BILLS AND NOTES.

WE believe that no more instructive chapter in legal history could be written than that which would tell in an adequate way the story of the development of mercantile law. In the following pages we shall trace as best we may the main outlines of the history of the most important branch of mercantile law, namely, the law of bills and notes. It is more than strange, and much to be regretted, that heretofore no serious attempt has been made in this direction. A suggestive article or a few pages here and there in legal literature and a few luminous and instructive opinions are all that one who undertakes to sketch the history of bills and notes in English law has for his guidance.[1] Many able expounders this branch of the law has certainly had, and this fact makes the absence of a work written on historical lines in this field still more conspicuous. This poverty is more keenly felt when we consider the comparative richness of the literature bearing upon the history of commercial paper in the continental states of Europe. The result of our labors will show that legal science has much to gain in this field from a thorough examination of the foundations of liability and from a patient study of the actual growth of the law. In the effort to grasp the body of existing law in its entirety — a feat that has now become impossible — English

---

[1] The most valuable historical discussion to be found in any of the reports is a contribution from the pen of Judge William Cranch, printed as an Appendix (Note A) to the first volume of his reports of Cases Argued and Decided in the Supreme Court of the United States. It is particularly helpful in the period preceding the enactment of 3 & 4 Anne, c. 9, and we wish here to acknowledge our special indebtedness to it. The conclusion which the writer draws, as applied to the particular case, is erroneous, but this does not impair the value of the paper in other aspects. Lord Cockburn's opinion in Goodwin v. Robarts, L. R. 10 Exch. 337, also contains much that is valuable to the student in this department of legal history.

and American lawyers have so far failed to realize the truth that if we are to interpret the present aright we must approach it through the avenues of the past.

The Lex Mercatoria.

Notwithstanding the fact that the law of bills and notes is in a sense very modern, it is necessary for us first to obtain a clear conception of the ancient law merchant (*lex mercatoria*), for the law of bills and notes is one of its offshoots.

In England, from the earliest times the merchant, like the priest and the Jew, enjoyed a sort of immunity from the law administered in the king's court. When the common law was passing through its first formative stages we find that, side by side with the custom of the king's court, which was the common law of England, there existed an indefinite mass of independent usages known as the *lex mercatoria,* or custom of merchants.

The customs, laws, and usages which went under the general name *lex mercatoria* were administered in special courts, and this contributed to stamp an independent character upon it. But very little, if any, of this body of law was concerned with bills of exchange, for the use of these instruments was limited and their transferability was not recognized. The *lex mercatoria* was, however, undoubtedly the matrix from which modern mercantile law has sprung. Admiralty and insurance law, as well as the law of commercial paper, have their genesis in this source.

In the course of ages the special courts in which the *lex mercatoria* was administered dwindled into insignificance, and the common-law courts then undertook to administer this body of law. The *lex mercatoria* was thereby assimilated into the common law. The process was highly beneficial to both elements. The custom of merchants has gained in certainty, consistency, and uniformity. Above all, it has within certain limits obtained the sanction of law and become fully binding. On the other hand, the common law has been broadened and its conceptions, especially in the field of contract law, greatly modified. As we proceed we shall perceive that the interplay between the custom of merchants and the common law has produced highly specialized results. Here legal development has reached a degree of finality not to be found elsewhere. The bill of exchange is the best illustration. This instrument is an ambulatory contract circulating like money, and in a large degree it performs the functions of money. It has aptly been termed a "courier without luggage." Being backed by the needs of the commercial world, it has triumphed in many successive encounters with common-law principle.

Chapter XXXI
Broadening effect of interplay.

It is sometimes difficult to tell whether a particular rule found in the existing body of mercantile law is a pure commercial custom sanctioned by law, or a common-law principle merely applied to new transactions. In most cases it will perhaps be found to be a result of the quickening of the common law along certain lines by a recognition of commercial needs; for the common law is by no means so inelastic as is sometimes supposed.

Even in early times the English people showed the greatest liberality in dealing with traders and merchants from foreign lands. Provision was made in Magna Carta for the advancement of trade and encouragement of commerce. By section 41 of that instrument all merchants were guaranteed the right safely to enter and dwell in England and to travel therein and depart without being harassed by unjust exactions. Even in case of war they were to be held without damage to person or property until it should be known how English merchants were treated in the hostile state. If the English merchants were then found to be safeguarded in such country, the foreign merchants were to be safe in England.

Foreign merchant in medieval England.

It was clearly the interest of the king to encourage the foreign traders. They had ready money. They were able to pay for the privileges enjoyed by them and they were not so quick to cry out against impositions as the local traders and burghers. Like the Jews, they consequently looked upon the king as their protector. Nor was the baronage hostile to them. The merchants were able to lend money to the noblemen, and as they turned money into the royal exchequer,

King protects the traders.

they thereby relieved the demand for taxes upon the various estates of the realm.

At one point, however, the merchants were subjected from time to time to much annoyance. They could get concessions from the king, including the privilege of trading in the various cities of the realm, but the cities in which they had to do their trading held charters which in many cases gave them the right to regulate the activities of the foreign merchants. The local traders were, of course, jealous of the foreigners and were constantly insisting that their stay be limited to the customary forty days. It was also insisted that the foreign merchant must abide with a responsible burgher, and that he must not sell in secret, by retail, or to other foreigners.[2]

From time to time the king had to intervene in behalf of his protégés, the merchants. The Statute of Acton Burnell *de mercatoribus*[3] was framed for the purpose of giving to them a speedy process for collecting their debts by means of an attachment. Doubtless the chief reason for this favor towards the foreign merchants is found in the fact that it proved easier to squeeze foreigners bringing their wares into the kingdom than subjects of the realm taking merchandise to the continent. The former needed the king's protection against the local hostility of the king's subjects and were willing to submit to the payment of tolls which might, under other circumstances, have struck them as exorbitant.

In 1303, Edward I granted the *Carta Mercatoria*. This charter as well as subsequent legislation tended to accentuate the line of demarcation between merchants and other sorts of men. If the local merchants as a class had been more keenly alive to their political position, they might, like the clergy, have attained the position of a separate estate. Edward I called the merchants together in 1303 in a way that indicates the political importance of their position. Edward III followed the same policy. These gatherings, however, were almost purely for the purpose of raising revenue, and the English

---

[2] 2 Poll. & Mait. Hist. Eng. Law, 2d ed., 465.
[3] 13 Edw. I., c. 3.

merchants wisely in the end cast in their political lot with the commons.⁴

> Chapter XXXI

By the *Carta Mercatoria*, which was merely a grant of privileges and which consequently had not the full force of a statute, as well as by statutes passed in the reign of Edward III,⁵ the right of having their causes judged by a jury *de mediatate linguæ*, composed wholly or in part of aliens, was secured to the foreign merchants. They seem at this period also to have vindicated the right, which had previously been denied them, of leasing houses and defending their possession by the action of trespass.⁶

> Foreign merchants acquire privileges.

The striking thing about the merchant during the mediæval period is the fact that he was treated as a privileged person and not subject to the common law. His disputes arose in connection with commercial transactions. Special courts existed for his accommodation, especially in connection with the fairs and markets. Such causes as were not heard in these courts fell under the jurisdiction of the local communal courts or of courts provided by statute. He could hardly get a hearing in the king's courts at all.

> Merchants not subject to common-law jurisdiction.

This immunity from the jurisdiction of the common-law courts really had notable advantages. He could not sue in the king's courts, but he was under the personal protection of the sovereign, and the chancery, as a last resort, was open to him. Here his grievances were judged according to the universal law, or law of nature.⁷

> Equity court open to merchant.

The courts attached to the mediæval fairs were, like all early local courts, popular. That is to say, the suitors (not litigants), who knew the customs, themselves declared the law and gave judgment. The courts of the fair were generally called courts of Piepoudres (court of the dusty feet) and were established to settle such matters as arose at the fairs. They were courts of record. Blackstone in his account of the English courts begins with this as the lowest and most expeditious.⁸

> Piepoudres Court.

⁴ 2 Stubbs, Const. Hist., 200–203.
⁵ 27 Edw. III., stat. 2, c. 8; 28 Edw. III., c. 13.
⁶ Y. B. 32 Hen. VI. 23, pl. 5.
⁷ Y. B. 13 Edw. IV. 9, pl. 5.
⁸ 3 Bl. Com. 32.

Volume II

Same principles applied in all trading cities.

The merchant traders traveling from fair to fair might form part of a court at St. Ives to-day and in a few weeks they might be found in one of the European marts forming a part of the market court there. It would be preposterous to imagine that courts so constituted should enforce one principle at Bristol and another at Ypres. The same questions were constantly arising and they were doubtless decided the same way in all places, whether at Lyons, Antwerp, Winchester, or St. Ives, to which places the merchants flocked from afar at the season of the fairs.

Need of merchant for speedy justice.

The most pressing need felt by merchants in the transaction of their business was speedy justice. Mercantile men must be about their business. Quick justice they must have rather than unerring justice. They feel that it is better to lose by the application of a swift and certain rule than to win after long and uncertain delay. In a report on the customs of Newcastle-upon-Tyne drawn up in the reign of Henry II, it is declared that if a dispute arises between a burgher and a merchant it must be decided (in the local courts, of course) before the third ebb of the tide.[9]

Characteristic features of law merchant.

Separate courts and speedy administration of justice according to the universal custom of merchants were therefore the features which distinguished the administration of the law merchant during the middle ages. The most instructive glimpses which we get of the transactions of these courts from a legal point of view are to be found in the rolls of the courts held at the fairs. In the Select Pleas of Manorial Courts, published in 1888 by the Selden Society, Professor Maitland has supplied us with valuable material for forming an idea of the things that came up for settlement in the piepoudres courts in the reign of Edward I.

The learned editor characterizes the law merchant of this period as follows: "In Edward I's day the *lex mercatoria* was already conceived as a body differing in some respects

---

[9] Stubbs, Sel. Char. 112: "Inter burgensem et mercatorem si placitum oriatur, finiatur ante tertiam refluxionem maris." Bracton notices the same necessity for swift justice in disputes among merchants, "qui celerem habere debent justiciam." Bracton, 334a.

from the common law. Within certain limits it was for the merchants themselves to declare the law. In Edward II's day two merchants fell out about a point of pure law raised in the court of the Fair of St. Ives, and the case was brought before the King's Bench; twelve merchants were summoned from each of four towns — London, Lincoln, Winchester, and Northampton — to testify to the law.¹ How large a body of doctrine there was bearing the name 'law merchant' is hard for us to say. Probably in some respects it took a more liberal and modern view of contractual obligations than that which was taken by the common law." ²

As an illustration of this greater liberality in the matter of contracts, Professor Maitland refers to a suit upon an instrument payable to B or bearer.³ It is to be observed, however, that the action in that case was brought by B, and not by a transferee by indorsement or delivery. The record recites a *quid pro quo,* namely, the wine for the purchase price of which the obligation was given, and the form of the complaint is purely in debt. Consequently this case cannot be taken as conclusive proof that the law merchant was one whit in advance of the common law in its theory of contract. This action indeed was no more than an ordinary plea of debt in the court of the Fair. Those words in the obligation which made the money payable to any representative of the creditor who produced the paper were not taken as imparting the quality of transferability to the contract in such sense as would authorize a mere bearer to maintain a suit for the money. They merely authorized the debtor to make payment to any one who produced the instrument.⁴ The idea that a bearer, as such, could maintain an action upon a contract made between

---

¹ Plac. Abbrev. 321.
² Select Pleas Manorial Courts, 132.
³ B. complains of W. T. and R. W., the peers, parceners, and commoners of one R. D., for that the said W. T. and R. W., along with the said R. D., by force and unjustly detain from him £8 of silver of a sum of £8, 10s., which they were bound to pay to the said B. or any on his behalf bearing a certain obligatory writing made between them for wines which the said B. had sold to the said R. D., etc. Select Pleas Manorial Courts, 152.
⁴ Lord Holt took this view of the import of the phrase 'or bearer,' in Horton *v.* Coggs (1689), 3 Lev. 299.

two other persons had not yet dawned upon the judges in any court of justice. Nor as yet had commercial usage sufficiently sanctioned such a doctrine to make such position in any wise tenable.

Differences between law merchant and common law.

There are, however, undoubtedly points at which the law merchant during this period differed from the common law in regard to contracts. These differences were largely of a formal and procedural character. Thus, the production of the tally was sufficient proof of a merchant's debt, and the defendant could not wage his law. Again, the payment of the earnest was sufficient to make a mercantile bargain binding. This advance over the common-law theory of contract was accomplished by the *Carta Mercatoria* (1303). This was a healthy innovation.[4*]

Wager of law.

The earnest.

Law merchant distinct from common law.

Whatever may have been the distinguishing features of the law merchant, it was conceived as a system of rules known especially among merchants, and they were supposed to conform to its usages. The merchants themselves were the suitors in their courts and they themselves declared the law. These rules were not looked upon as purely English law. The differences were no doubt less than was supposed, and many of the commercial usages enforced in the merchants' courts which were supposed to conflict with the common law could doubtless be reconciled with common-law principle. Even in modern times we are aware how the separate existence of courts of equity and of common law has given rise to similar confusion, and we frequently find the chancellors declaring a certain principle to be the rule in equity, taking it for granted that the common-law principle is different, whereas, in fact, the particular rule declared may be good common law also.

Universality of the law merchant.

Different courts, different judges, and different modes of procedure certainly contribute much to magnify slight differences of substantive principle and at the same time to make obscure more important points of real resemblance. Above all other features the universality of the law merchant marked

[4*] See *ante*, p. 6.

it off with distinctness from the common law. Indeed the law merchant is and always has been a sort of private international law. It springs from the usages of merchants throughout Christendom. In this respect it is analogous to the *jus gentium* of the Roman law.[5]

Chapter XXXI

Just as the Roman lawyer identified the *jus gentium* with the *lex naturæ*, or universal idea of justice, so the English judges identified the law merchant with the universal law of nature. Thus, the chancellor in 1473, in the great suit between a foreign merchant and a carrier who broke bulk, said in the Star Chamber: "This suit is brought by an alien merchant who has come here under safe-conduct and he is not required to sue according to the law of the land and await the trial of twelve men and other solemnities of the law of the land, but he can sue here and it shall be determined according to the law of nature in chancery; and he can sue there from hour to hour and from day to day for the expedition of merchants. . . . And this shall be *secundum legem naturæ*, which is called by some the law merchant, which is law universal throughout the world."[6] Lord Mansfield, in *Luke v. Lyde* (1756),[7] speaking of the maritime law used similar words: "[It] is not the law of a particular country, but the general law of nations." Again, said he, quoting the well-known language of Cicero: "*Non erit alia lex Romæ, alia Athenis; alia nunc, alia posthac; sed et apud omnes gentes, una eademque lex obtinebit.*"[8]

Identified with universal law of nature.

We cannot pause longer to consider the ancient *lex mercatoria* as administered in special courts. We have little accurate knowledge of the body of rules so administered. The reason for this is that the records of the local courts which enforced it are lost or inaccessible; and again, but few cases involving the law merchant came up for decision in the king's courts.

The most interesting fact in the history of the *lex merca-*

---

[5] See article, Jus Gentium and Law Merchant, by W. W. Howe, 41 Am. L. Reg. N. S. 375.
[6] Y. B. 13 Edw. IV. 9, pl. 5.
[7] 2 Burr. 887.

[8] "There shall not be one law at Rome, another at Athens; one now, another hereafter; but among all nations one and the same law shall prevail."

332   FOUNDATIONS OF LEGAL LIABILITY.

toria was its dissolution as a separate body of legal principle and its final absorption in the common law. The first symptom of its breaking up is seen in the gradual decay and extinction of the local courts. The concentration of the foreign trade in the staple cities which resulted from the legislation of Edward III resulted in the local-fair courts becoming more and more unimportant. The same concentration of business in a few places gave occasion for the transfer of jurisdiction over controversies between merchants and others to the Court of Admiralty.

Admiralty courts administer mercantile law.

During the time of the Tudors this court claimed a wide jurisdiction. In fact it drew to itself practically all cases in any way dependent upon the principles of the law merchant. It comprised all mercantile and shipping cases. All contracts made abroad, foreign bills of exchange, charter parties, insurance, average, freight, questions arising out of negligent navigation, breaches of warranty of seaworthiness, as well as torts committed on the sea and matters of salvage, were all litigated in the Admiralty Court. It was in fact during the sixteenth century the great organ through which the principles of the law merchant were declared.

Contest between Admiralty and common-law courts.

But scarcely had the Admiralty Court attained to this position when the common-law judges began to look with envious eyes at the wide and rich field which the development of commerce brought within the jurisdiction of the admiral. Accordingly in the reign of Elizabeth the common-law judges began war upon him. The most effective instrument was found to be the writ of prohibition, and this weapon was accordingly used with vital effect. Coke was raised to the bench in 1606 and took the lead in the contest. As was once said by Buller, Coke seemed to have not only a jealousy, but a positive enmity against the admiralty jurisdiction.[o]

Waning of Admiralty.

Notwithstanding the fact that the procedure of the Admiralty Court was vastly better adapted to the settlement of controversies over which that court had acquired jurisdiction, political events told heavily against it in the contest. The common-law judges were in closer touch with the revolu-

[o] Smart *v.* Wolff (1789), 3 T. R. 348.

tionary forces. The result of the Civil War and the establishment of the Commonwealth insured the victory of the common law over its rival. The jurisdiction of the Admiralty Court was thereby reduced to a low ebb. Much of the lost ground has been recovered to this court by modern legislation. The point here to be noted is that the common-law judges under the leadership of Coke wrested from the admiralty general jurisdiction over commercial causes. The extent of the victory could not at the time be fully appreciated, for English commerce was destined to expand beyond the most sanguine expectations.

<small>Chapter XXXI</small>

<small>Commercial causes fall to common-law courts.</small>

The transfer of commercial contracts from the admiralty to the common-law courts certainly meant a slower and more laborious development for the mercantile law. The common law was destined to follow along the same lines of development as had been pursued in the system which it had defeated, "with tardy steps, perhaps unconsciously, certainly without acknowledgment." Questions pertaining to bills of exchange, bills of lading, general average, and insurance, which had already been solved in the admiralty courts had to be worked out by the common law anew.[1] The transfer of jurisdiction certainly also meant inconvenience and delay to litigants. In the end these difficulties were in a measure compensated by the expansion and elasticity which the common law gained as a result of its appropriation of the new field. The non-traversable fiction as to the place of making contracts was introduced, and assisted the common law in digesting the causes of which it deprived its rival. Prynne, who contended manfully in favor of the losing forces, spoke contemptuously of "the new strange poetical fiction" and of "the imaginary sign-posts in Cheapside," by which the common-law courts got jurisdiction over contracts made in foreign countries.[2]

<small>Development of mercantile law retarded.</small>

<small>Common law gains in elasticity.</small>

It is to be observed that as a result of the decay of the local courts throughout the country, the common-law courts obtained jurisdiction over the internal trade much sooner than

---

[1] 1 Holdsworth, Hist. Eng. Law, 326.
[2] Prynne, Animadversions, 95, 97.

they did over the mercantile contracts wrested from the admiralty. The internal trade of the country was well in the hands of the common-law courts by the end of the reign of Elizabeth (1603). The contest with the admiralty continued for a half century later.

As long as the law merchant was administered in special courts it remained a body of law for a particular class of men. As the common-law courts began to administer it, this characteristic disappeared and the law merchant became, in the new forum, a body of rules applicable to particular classes of transactions. Statutes, as for instance, the bankruptcy laws, would sometimes make differences between traders and others, but in general the common-law courts applied the same rules to dealings between all men. By the end of the seventeenth century the law merchant was practically absorbed into the legal system of the country.

A few of the particular rules which were doubtless adopted from the law merchant can be mentioned. The English rule that there is no warranty of title in the sale of personalty,[3] and that a sale in market overt will pass title to goods though the seller has none, were probably derived from this source. The right of partners to have an accounting with each other likewise comes from the law merchant. At common law joint tenants held subject to the right of survivorship. The law merchant gave a right for an accounting by the representatives of a deceased partner against the survivor.[4]

---

[3] Morley *v.* Attenborough, 3 Exch. 500.

[4] "If two merchants be partners in merchandises, one shall have an action of account against the other, *secundum legem mercatoriam.* Reg. Brev., 135; F. N. B. 117 D. And yet by the rule of the common law if two men be jointly possessed of other goods which are no merchandise, the one cannot bring an action of account against the other; if one of the merchants die, the executor may bring his account against the survivor for his moiety. Reg. f. 135, F. N. B. 117. But if it were a copartnership for other goods, it would survive *per jus accrescendi* according to the rules of the common law." East-India Co. *v.* Sandys (1684), 10 How. St. Tr. 525.

CHAPTER XXXII

BILLS AND NOTES (CONTINUED).

Early History of Bills of Exchange.

THE exact date and place of the appearance of the bill of exchange as a modern instrument of commerce cannot be determined, but it is pretty well settled that the event belongs to the thirteenth century, and it is settled beyond question that the Italian bankers and money-changers of North Italy were the first to use it extensively.[1] These men, known generally in England as Lombards, formed a guild, and its members established themselves in the various cities of the Netherlands, England, France, Germany, and in all Mediterranean states where commerce began to flourish. From these different places they corresponded with one another, and doubtless before the beginning of the thirteenth

Chapter XXXII

Origin of bill of exchange.

---

[1] Von Reumont tells us that bills of exchange are first met with in the dealings between England and Italy in 1199 and that these transactions were conducted by Florentines. Lorenzo de Medici, by Von Reumont, Bk. 2, ch. 4. But it is hardly probable that the date when these instruments were first used can be exactly fixed. It was not far from the beginning of the thirteenth century.

Says Mr. Reddie in Historical View of Laws of Maritime Commerce (1841): "The precise era of that most useful invention does not appear to have been exactly ascertained; but that it originated . . . in the usages and customs observed and in the regulations adopted at fairs, from considerations of general security and convenience, there is every reason to believe. And after it was once established upon a small scale, the utility and convenience of the invention behooved gradually to lead to its more extensive adoption, particularly in foreign and maritime commerce. Indeed, it seems probable that bills of exchange, such, or nearly such, as we have at present, first came into general use in the course of the extended commerce carried on by the maritime cities of Italy, and of the south of France and Spain, under their comparatively free and well-administered governments. Weber, in his Ricerche sull' Origine e sulla Natura del Contratto di Cambrio, published at Venice in 1810, states positively that such documents were in use at Venice in 1171; and a law of Venice, of 1272, clearly designates bills of exchange. The unpublished statute of Avignon, of 1243, contains a paragraph entitled De Litteris Cambii.

century commenced the custom of receiving money in one place to be paid out by an order upon their correspondents in another. The merchants who traveled from country to country to trade and attend the various marts and fairs were thus saved the expense and risk of transporting money in specie.

The Florentine money-changers are said to have been incorporated before 1204. About the same time we find them established in England, where they did business for Henry III. Here they conducted the money transactions of the Papal chair in conjunction with the bankers of Siena. The operations of these capitalists — for they soon waxed rich — were confined to no place or country. They acquired notoriety as usurers and incurred popular dislike. In the middle of the fourteenth century the Florentine bankers suffered irremediable damage from the repudiation by Edward III, of debts to the extent of several hundred thousand marks owing to the Bardi and Peruzzi.

Lending, exchanging, and transmitting money constituted the chief business of these exchangers. One of the earliest known statutes bearing on the conduct of trade was drawn up at Florence in 1280 by a commission of five members of the great houses.[2] In 1307, Peter's pence was sent from England to the Pope through these exchangers. Charges, amounting it is said to five or six per cent, were made upon such transactions, and the large profits to be obtained attracted many wealthy and even noble families to engage in the business. There are said to have been eighty such houses in

A statute of Marseilles, dated 1253, presents evident traces of them; and a transaction of this description is attested by a document of 1256, relative to England."

German scholars have of late years accumulated, notably in the Zeitschrift fuer das gesammte Handelsrecht, an abundance of material for the study of the early history of bills of exchange upon the continent. Other authorities in the same field are the following: Martens, Versuch einer historischen Entwickelung des Wahren Ursprungs des Wechselrechts (Goettingen, 1797); Biener, Wechselrechtliche Abhandlungen ('Leipzig, 1859); Endemann, Studien in der Romanisch Kanonistischen Wirthschaft- und Rechtslehre, (Berlin, 1874). Some of the materials are sifted and discussed by Prof. Edward Jenks, Early History of Negotiable Instruments, 9 L. Quar. Rev. 70.

[2] Statuto dell' Universita della Mercatanzia.

Florence at the middle of the fourteenth century. The Florentine family of Medici had sixteen houses established in as many large cities of Europe and the Levant. Presently the merchants of the Hanseatic League in Northern Europe made similar arrangements for the convenience of trade.

Chapter XXXII

Early examples of bills of exchange are found in a bill dated at Milan in 1325, payable in five months at Lucca; one dated at Bruges, 1304, and payable at Barcelona. Another is dated at Bologna in 1381 and payable in Venice. The Italian origin of the modern bill is attested by the fact that these early instruments are in the Italian language, whether drawn between Italian cities or not. The first writers who treat of bills are Italians, and the Italian language furnishes most of the technical terms connected with bills of exchange in the various languages of Europe.[3] An Italian writer, Pegoletti, in a work on mercantile usage (*Practica della Mercatura*), attributed by Martens to the early part of the fourteenth century, makes references to bills of exchange, but does not treat them with any detail. They are barely referred to in an English statute of the year 1381.[4]

Early bills.

Early references to bills.

A Piacenza ordinance of 1391 compelled the *campsores,* or money-changers, to give written acknowledgments of the money left with them on deposit and gave a speedy remedy upon such certificates.[5] Of course these certificates were not transferable by indorsement. An ordinance passed at about the same date (1394) by the magistrates of Barcelona deals with the form and acceptance of letters of exchange. The drawee, it is provided, must answer within twenty-four hours whether he will accept or not, and must further indorse on the document his decision and the date of presentation. If he did not comply with this rule he was deemed to have accepted.

Ordinances of Piacenza and Barcelona.

An interesting phase of mercantile business analogous in many respects to the business of exchanging money is found in the operations of the earliest of the modern banks of deposit. Venice claims the honor of having been the city

Banks of deposit.

---

[3] See Yeats, Growth and Vicissitudes of Commerce, Appendix F.
[4] 5 Rich. II. stat. 1, c. 2.
[5] 9 L. Quar. Rev. 71.

Volume II — *Checks not transferable from hand to hand.*

where the first of the modern banks of deposit was established. The Bank of Venice was in operation in the first half of the fourteenth century and it probably has a still greater antiquity. According to some writers a similar institution was established at Barcelona about 1349. The Bank of Genoa was founded in 1407. Depositors in these institutions issued orders or checks on the funds to their credit for payments to be made by the bank to other persons. Such persons on surrendering these assignments to the bankers received the money called for, or the sum was credited to them on the books of the bank. There is no evidence to show that these orders were made payable to order or bearer or that they were transferable from one to another.

Specimens of the bill.

Let us now examine the early bill of exchange and see what it was like and what were the legal relations which resulted from it. Below may be seen two early specimens.[6] The most striking feature of these documents is that they contain no words which would authorize payment to any

---

[6] The following belongs to the year 1339, and is one of the earliest specimens known. It is drawn by Barna of Lucca on Bartolo Casini and Company, of Pisi, payable to Landuccio Busdraghi and Company of Lucca. Tancredi Bonaguinta and Company seem to be the remitters. It reads thus: "Al nome di Dio amen. Bartalo e compagni: Barna da Lucha e compagni salute. Di Vignone. Pagherete per questa lettera a di XX di novembre 339 a Landuccio Busdraghi e compagni da Luca fiorini trecento dodici e tre quarti d' oro per cambio di fiorini trecento d' oro, che questo di della fatta n'avemo da Tancredi Bonaguinta e compagni, a raxione di IIII e quarto per C alloro vantaggio, e ponete a nostro conto e regione. Fatta di V d' ottobre 339.— Francesco Falconetti ci a mandate a paghare per voi a gli Acciaiuoli scudi CCXXX d' oro." 22 Zeitschrift fuer Handelsrecht, 8.

Another example is from the year 1404. It is as follows: "Al nome di Dio amen. A di 18 Maggiore, 1404. Pagate per questa prima di cambio ad usanza a Piero Gilberto et a Piero di Scorpo scuti mille de Felippo e soldi 10 Barcelonesi per scuto, i quali scuti mille sono per cambio, che (. . .) con Giovanni Colombo a grossi 22 di 9. scuto; et pagate a nostro conto et Christo vi guardi.—Antonio Quarti Sal. de Bruggias." The draft is addressed to "Francisco de Prato et Comp. à Barcelona." 22 Zeitschrift fuer Handelsrecht, 7.

Stripped of its verbiage this is an order, drawn by Antonio of Bruges on Francisco of Barcelona, to pay the sum stated, with interest, to Peter Gilbert and Peter Scorpo, and to charge the same to the account of the drawer. The drawee's name appears only on the outside of the order.

other person whatever than the payee named in them. The expressions 'to order' and 'to bearer' which are so prominent in the modern bill of exchange, and indeed necessary to make it transferable, are conspicuously absent. Another feature also worthy of notice is the fact that in both cases the receipt of the money paid by the remitter to the drawer for the bill is acknowledged on the face of the draft. In other words, it recites a good consideration, or value received of the person purchasing the bill.

It will be further observed that each bill has four parties. There is the remitter or purchaser of the bill, who pays the money and gets the draft. Malynes speaks of this party as the deliverer (i. e., of the money). Then there is the drawer, who issues the draft and receives value therefor. He is called by Malynes the taker (i. e., of the money). The drawee is the person on whom the bill is drawn. If it is a time draft and is presented to the drawee, he becomes liable as acceptor if he signifies an intention to pay it at maturity. Lastly, there is the payee, or person in whose favor the bill of exchange or draft is drawn. He must, of course, appear and get the money in person, for the instrument does not authorize payment to any one else. If the drawee, or acceptor, undertakes to pay to any one else as agent or servant of the payee the risk is upon him, the drawee; for the mere production of the bill would be no protection. This necessarily follows from the non-negotiable character of the bills in question.

The legal relations which may result from transactions accomplished by these bills are not complex, but it was sometimes found difficult to state them in common-law terms, even after the development of assumpsit had made simple promises binding in English law. Let us examine these relations for a moment with the eye of a person who looks at them from the standpoint of the common-law practitioner.

We first observe that the remitter pays a consideration for the bill. In return he gets an order on the drawee. The issuing of the order by the drawer necessarily implies not only a representation, but a promise amounting to a warranty, that

Chapter XXXII

Not negotiable.

Value received.

Parties to the bill.
1. Remitter.
2. Drawer.
3. Drawee.
4. Payee.

Legal relations of parties.

Remitter v. drawer.

the instrument shall be paid according to its tenor. If the drawee refuses to pay it, then evidently the remitter, who parted with his money for a worthless bill, is entitled to recover of the drawer. This he can do, according to the state of development in this branch of the law, either by suing upon the dishonored instrument or by suing for the money paid out by him for the instrument.

<small>Payee v. acceptor.</small>

The rights of the payee are also to be considered. If the bill be accepted and subsequently dishonored by nonpayment, he undoubtedly has a right of action against the acceptor. Acceptance is *per se* a promise to pay the note, and while a consideration for this promise does not always lie on the surface, still one is not difficult to find. Thus, if the drawee has funds of the drawer, he is to this extent debtor; and since the middle of the sixteenth century it has been a well-recognized principle at common law that 'being indebted,' or the legal duty to pay a debt, is a sufficient consideration to support a promise to pay the whole or a part of it in a certain way and at a certain time. If the drawee is not a debtor to the drawer, then there is a bilateral contract. By accepting, the drawee becomes bound to pay and the drawer becomes bound to reimburse him. The only anomalous feature of the engagement, so far as common-law principles of contract are concerned, consists in the fact that the consideration for the promise to pay to the payee moves from the drawer, and at common law the person from whom the consideration moves is the only one who can sue on a promise. Now permitting the payee himself to sue the acceptor is a step in advance, to be sure, but it was a necessary step, and that it was taken was certainly due to the stimulus of the custom of merchants and the necessities of trade.

<small>Immaturity of English contract law.</small>

But we are anticipating. In the fifteenth century, when the instruments above referred to were drawn, the common law lacked much of being ready for the questions which might arise upon them. The action of assumpsit as a remedy upon the unilateral contract was not mature until about 1505, and the bilateral engagement was not recognized until about seventy years later. The action of debt no doubt would have been equal to some of the situations, but the fact that law merchant was administered in its particular courts kept cases involving rights growing out of bills and notes from coming into the king's courts as yet. Doubtless an even more potent reason why the common law was not appealed to is found in the fact that the credit of the English merchants was so highly esteemed and so carefully guarded that the bills were practically always paid. We therefore find no decisions on rights arising from bills of exchange in any of the common-law courts during either the fifteenth or sixteenth centuries; but as we shall see, these contracts were known to the common-law practitioners and they could, after assumpsit had become a well-known remedy, state a proper case at common law upon them.

No early decisions on rights growing out of bills.

The judicial archives of other countries are more fortunate than our own. For instance, we have record of a case decided at Bruges in 1448 of this kind: One Cerruche bought a bill of the Ricys of Avignon for 450 florins, drawn by the Ricys on Marian Rau, of Bruges, payable to Bernard Camby. Cerruche was therefore the remitter or purchaser of the bill, the Ricys were the drawers, Rau the drawee, and Camby the payee. The drawees paid it, but, possibly failing to take it up, the payee, Camby, contrived to have it protested. It accordingly went back on the drawers, the Ricys, who paid it again. Action was brought by an assignee of Marian Rau, the drawee, against Camby to recover the amount paid by him to the latter. The plaintiff failed, for the reason that he ought to have sued in the name of Marian Rau.[7]

Spinula v. Camby.

In this case, it will be observed, protest was recognized as being a sufficient and proper means of charging the drawer upon a dishonored bill, and it was further assumed that the protested instrument was sufficient authority to the drawer to pay. Consequently the drawee, who had paid the instrument according to its tenor, but who had failed to take it up and thereby given opportunity for it to be protested, was com-

Effect of protest.

---

[7] Spinula v. Camby, reported in 22-24: see Early Hist. Neg. Inst., 22 Zeitschrift fuer Handelsrecht, 9 L. Quar. Rev. 75.

pelled to look to the payee, Camby, to reimburse him. His right of action against the latter was obviously based, not upon the instrument, but upon the legal duty of the defendant to return the money paid to him. This right was therefore merely a chose in action, and Spinula, who claimed as mere assignee of the right of action, could not recover. This result is exactly the same that would have followed from the application of common-law principle.

This case, it should be noted, did not in any way involve the question of the transferability of the bill, for the suit was not upon the instrument at all. If a similar problem had been presented to the English courts of common law at this period (1448), the plaintiff would have failed for the same reason. Nay, even if Rau had himself sued to recover the money paid to Camby he would doubtless also have failed. The English courts were then willing to admit that debt would lie upon a promise given for any *quid pro quo* actually delivered or performed,[8] but they could hardly have held that the legal duty to refund money paid for a consideration that has failed would support debt. It was indeed nearly two hundred years before general assumpsit for money had and received came into common use for the purpose of recovering money thus paid.

No such question, however, came before the courts of common law during the fifteenth century. If controversies of this kind arose the parties would discreetly arbitrate the cause or the plaintiff resorted to the chancellor or admiral. In the course of long experience a piece of wisdom sunk deep into the minds of those who dealt in bills of exchange, to the effect that the less they had to do with the common law the better it would be for them.

[8] Y. B. 37 Hen. VI. 8, pl. 18.

CHAPTER XXXIII

BILLS AND NOTES (CONTINUED).

Adaptation of Bills to Common-law Theory.

THE first evidence we have of an effort on the part of the men versed in the common law to apply its principles to disputes arising out of bills of exchange is found in the old books on pleading, especially in Rastell's Entries, the first edition of which appeared in the latter part of the sixteenth century. The author or compiler of this work gives some forms of declaration suited to such suits. He gathered his material, as is indicated in the preface, from four old books of precedents then existing. At the time he wrote, the action of assumpsit, or action on the case upon a promise, was nearly a hundred years old and it had been in common use for about sixty years. Just about this time, too, the bilateral contract, based upon mutual promises, was recognized. Nothing is said in any of his forms about duty attaching by the custom of merchants.

The declaration printed below [1] is evidently adapted to the

Chapter XXXIII

Declarations in special assumpsit.

[1] "A complains of B, etc., 'for that whereas the said A, by a certain I. C., his sufficient attorney, factor, and deputy in this behalf, on such a day and year at L. at the special instance and request of the said B, had delivered to the said B by the hands of the said I. C. to the proper use of the said B £110 8s. 4d, lawful money of England; for which said £110 8s. 4d, so to the said B delivered, he, the said B, then and there to the said I. C. (then being the sufficient attorney, factor, and deputy of said A in this behalf) faithfully promised and undertook, that a certain John of G. well and faithfully would content and pay to Reginald S. (on such a day and year, and always afterwards, hitherto the sufficient deputy, factor, and attorney of the said A in this behalf), 433 2-3 ducats on a certain day in the declaration mentioned. And if the aforesaid John of G. should not pay and content the said Reginald S. the said 443 2-3 ducats, at the time above limited, that then the said B would well and faithfully pay and content the said A £110 8s. 4d, lawful money of England, with all damages and interest thereof, whenever he should be thereunto by the said A requested.' It then avers that the said 443 2-3 ducats were of the value

Custom of merchants applies only to foreign bills.

case of an action by the remitter, or purchaser, of a bill of exchange, against the drawer, upon the dishonor of the bill by the drawee. It is to be inferred from the circumstance that pounds sterling were to be exchanged for ducats, that the bill was drawn upon a foreign city, but this is not expressly stated. Only foreign bills were at this time known to the custom of merchants. The declaration in question is so replete with allegations of promise, consideration, agency, etc., that it requires some inspection before we perceive that the transaction in question really involved a bill of exchange. I. C. purchased a bill of exchange of B, who drew the bill upon John of G. in favor of and payable to R. S. The drawee dishonored the bill, and the drawer, having been requested to pay, refused to do so. Thereupon suit was brought by the remitter against the drawer.

The drawer's promise.

It will be seen from an inspection of the declaration that the whole transaction is minutely anatomized and fully stated in terms of the common-law assumpsit. A promise on the part of the drawer to pay in case of the failure of the drawee to pay, is stated in express terms. This allegation would doubtless be satisfied by mere proof of the purchase of the bill, as the law would probably have implied such a promise from the mere selling of the bill. If so, this would have been, by a few years, the earliest implied assumpsit ever

of £110 8s. 4d, lawful money of England, that John of G. had not paid the ducats to Reginald S., and that if he had paid them 'to the said R., I. B., and their associates, or to either of them, then the said 443 2-3 ducats would have come to the benefit and profit of the said A. Yet the said B contriving the aforesaid A of the said £110 8s. 4d, and of the damages and interest thereof, falsely and subtly to deceive and defraud, the same or any part thereof, to the said A, although often thereunto required, according to his promise and undertaking aforesaid, had not paid or in any manner contented, whereby the said A, not only the profit and gain which he, the said A, with the said £110 8s. 4d, in lawfully bargaining and carrying on commerce might have acquired, hath lost; but also the said A in his credit towards diverse subjects of our Lord the King (especially towards R. H. and I. A., to whom the said A was indebted in the sum of £110 8s. 4d, and to whom the said A had promised to pay the same £110 8s. 4d, at a day now past, in the hope of a faithful performance of the promise and undertaking aforesaid) is much injured, to his damage,'" etc. Rastell's Entries, 10a. Here reproduced from 1 Cranch (U. S.), Appendix, 375.

recognized at common law. Likewise the allegations that I. C. was the factor of A in purchasing the bill, and his agent for the purpose of receiving the promise from B; that B was the agent of John of G. for the purpose of binding the latter to pay R. S., and that R. S. was in some sort of privity with the plaintiff, may or may not have corresponded with the actual facts. Such of these statements as were material or necessary to make the drawer liable would doubtless be implied in any transaction by bill of exchange. At any rate, there can be no question that the declaration states a good common-law cause of action by a remitter against the drawer.

The same writer gives us two other forms of declaration adapted to the purpose of enforcing liability on bills of exchange. Both are actions brought by the payee, who in one case sues the acceptor, or one who had promised to accept; in the other he sues the drawer. The declaration against the acceptor or person promising to accept is quite well worth examination.[2]

Chapter XXXIII

Payee v. acceptor.

[2] This declaration sets forth that whereas the plaintiff, on June 10, 1585, at Rochelle, in France, by the "hands of a certain T. S., then the factor of the plaintiff, at the request of a certain R. W., then the factor of the defendant, delivered and paid to said R. W., to the use of the defendant, as much ready money as amounted to 1,400 French crowns, of the money of France, in parts beyond seas, at the rate of 5s. 11d, lawful money of England, for each French crown. And thereupon the said R. W., at Rochelle aforesaid, then delivered to said T. S. three bills of exchange, viz., first, second, and third; in the first of which bills of exchange the said R. W. requested the defendant to pay to the plaintiff at L., £414 3s. 4d, lawful money of England, at the end of thirty days next after sight of that bill of exchange (the second and third bills of exchange to the plaintiff not paid). It then set forth the tenor of the second and third bills, and then avers that the defendant, on the day and year first aforesaid, at the city of E., in the county of the said city, in consideration thereof undertook, and to the plaintiff then and there faithfully promised, that he, the defendant, well and faithfully would pay to the plaintiff, to the plaintiff's use, at the city of E. aforesaid, in the county of the said city, by way of exchange, according to the usage of merchants, the aforesaid £414 3s. 4d, lawful money of England, at the end of thirty days next after sight of any of the bills of exchange aforesaid; and the plaintiff in fact saith, that afterwards, viz., on the 1st of September, in the year aforesaid, at, etc., the first of the said bills came to the sight of, and was then and there shown to, the defendant, yet the defendant, not regarding, etc., but contriving, etc., did not pay the said £414 3s. 4d, etc., at the end of the thirty days, etc. Whereby the defendant lost the benefit of trading with said £414 3s. 4d, etc., to his damage £600."

346   FOUNDATIONS OF LEGAL LIABILITY.

Volume II

This declaration apparently gets no assistance from any idea of duty imposed by the custom of merchants, and the date supposed puts the transaction at the very close of the sixteenth century. We find four parties to this bill of exchange: (1) T. S., the remitter or purchaser of the bill; (2) R. W., the drawer; (3) the drawee or acceptor, who is the defendant in the action; and (4) the payee, who is the plaintiff.

Allegation of agency as between remitter and payee.

The duty of the acceptor is alleged to arise from a promise (acceptance) in fact made by him to pay the bill. This promise is supported by the consideration of the payment of value by the remitter to the drawer. The difficulty that arises from the fact that the consideration does not move from the promise is evaded by the allegation of a relation of agency between the remitter and the payee; and no doubt in the early cases this allegation corresponded with the facts. As may be seen from *Vanheath v. Turner* (1622),[3] persons engaged in the business of exchange in this period were not only what we would call correspondents of each other, but actual partners, forming an association or *communitas*, and liable on each other's contracts. If the allegation of agency, however, were true to the full extent, it would seem that the drawer should be able to bind the drawee without the latter's actual acceptance, which in the ordinary course of business he cannot do. One who is agent in fact can bind his principal without the latter's acceptance.[4] At any rate the allegation of agency soon became a non-traversable fiction. This fiction

Fiction of factorage.

Rastell's Entries, 338a. Here reproduced from 1 Cranch (U. S.), Appendix, 377.

In Browne's Vade Mecum, published some time after Rastell, we find a similar common-law declaration in an action by the payee against the acceptor of a bill of exchange. The instrument here sued on apparently belongs to about the same period as the one referred to by Rastell. Vade Mecum, 2d ed. (1695), 12.

[3] Winch, 24.

[4] Malynes says, "If a known servant do take up moneys beyond the seas upon his master, and give his bill of exchange for it upon the said master, the master is liable to pay the same, although he did not accept the bill of exchange; for it is understood, that by his credit (and not by the servant's credit) the money hath been taken up, so that until he make a publick declaration, denouncing his servant to the brokers of exchanges and otherwise, the master is to pay all by the custom of merchants to be kept inviolable." Lex Mercatoria, 272.

BILLS AND NOTES. 347

of factorage or implied agency will be seen to furnish a clue to the apparent anomaly of allowing the payee to sue at law upon a promise made to him upon a consideration furnished by another. This is one of the striking features of the law of bills and notes.

Chapter XXXIII

The first reported common-law decision in a suit upon a bill of exchange is *Martin v. Boure* (1602),[5] a case which was decided in the Exchequer Chamber. No legal principles of importance were involved in the case, but it is instructive. The declaration is worked up in an exceedingly laborious fashion and was evidently modeled after the forms given by Rastell. It is framed purely in assumpsit and contains no word concerning liability incurred under the custom of merchants. The facts were of the following character: Harris, being in Aleppo, drew on his debtor Saltar, who lived in England, for a sum of money, through Boure. Boure transmitted the draft to Martin, and the latter presented the same to the drawee, Saltar. Saltar took up the draft and paid the money. In order to transmit it to Aleppo, Martin then issued a bill of exchange on Boure payable to Harris. Boure failed to pay, whereby Martin became liable and, having paid the bill, sued Boure on the latter's acceptance. The suit was therefore that of drawee against acceptor.

Earliest report of action upon bill.

By referring to the pleadings in this case the reader will perceive that it was doubtless always possible, yet often exceedingly difficult, to frame a good declaration in assumpsit on a transaction by exchange. That some lawyers failed in this feat Malynes (1622) has recorded.

Difficulty incident to use of special assumpsit.

Custom of Merchants a Source of Legal Duty.

Up to this time it had apparently not occurred to any one that a custom prevailing between merchants could originate a legal duty. In 1542, an effort had been made to get the benefit of "a custom between merchants throughout the whole realm," but the plea was held bad on the ground that a custom through the whole realm was common law. A custom to be good as such had to be localized,[6] and a custom

Custom of merchants not pleadable at law

[5] Cro. Jac. 6.   [6] Brooke Abr., *Customes*, pl. 59.

prevailing only among a certain class was bad even though general throughout the realm.

At the period to which we have now come, however, that is to say, at the beginning of the seventeenth century, the common-law judges were putting forth great efforts to strip rival courts of their jurisdiction. The work done by Coke in waging war upon the admiralty has already been referred to. The part played by him in the contest with the Chancery Court was equally conspicuous but less successful. To the active and fertile minds of those who sympathized with this movement, it must have seemed a good piece of legal strategy to put forth the claim that the law merchant was a part of the common law. It proved to be a timely claim, and it marked an important advance in legal theory. The common law was destined to increase, its rivals to decrease.

Acting upon this idea the common-law judges appropriated the law merchant, or at least that part of it which dealt with bills of exchange. This event happened in the first decade of the seventeenth century. One who reads the declaration in *Martin v. Bourc* (1602),[7] cannot wonder that some better mode of pleading was shortly discovered. The very next case arising upon a bill of exchange is *Oaste v. Taylor* (1612),[8] and upon reference to pleadings in that case the

---

[7] Cro. Jac. 6.

[8] Cro. Jac. 306. The declaration is in assumpsit by David Oaste, merchant-stranger against William Taylor, a merchant: "for that whereas by the custom of London, between merchants trafficking from London into the parts beyond the seas, if any merchant commorant in London, and trafficking beyond seas, direct his bill of exchange, *bona fide*, and without covin, to another merchant, commorant beyond seas, and trafficking betwixt London and the parts beyond seas; upon such a merchant's accepting a bill, and subscribing it according to the use of merchants, it hath the force of a promise, to compel him to pay it at the day appointed by the bill; and alledgeth, *in facto*, that William Kenton, being a merchant, trafficking betwixt London and Middleburgh beyond the seas, and commorant in London, directed his bill of exchange to the defendant, commorant in Middleburgh, and trafficking between London and Middleburgh, requiring him to pay £355 Flemish at the usance of four months to the plaintiff, being a merchant; and that the defendant accepted thereof, *secundum usum mercatorum*, and subscribed it, and had not paid it; whereupon, etc., after verdict, upon non assumpsit pleaded, and found for the plaintiff, it was moved in arrest of judgment, because the defendant is not averred to be a merchant at the time of the bill accepted."

reader will see what lengthy recitals could be pared off upon acceptance of the idea of duty arising from a custom of merchants. This simplicity of pleading has since prevailed in declaring on these contracts. In *Hussey v. Jacobs* (1696),[9] for instance, there is a simple declaration " upon the custom of merchants, by which, if a bill of exchange is drawn upon a person and he accepts it, he is liable to pay it."

Chapter XXXIII

While the earlier actions on bills were purely in assumpsit, when the notion of duty arising from the custom of merchants was accepted, the action immediately ceased to be in pure assumpsit and became a special action on the case in the nature of an action of assumpsit. Of course assumpsit is a branch of case, but it should be remembered that when we declare on the custom of merchants and state facts to bring the transaction within the principle of that custom we are declaring in case. The reports seem to take little notice of the distinction, and the action on a bill is usually spoken of as assumpsit. It is a very special form of assumpsit.

Nature of the action on the bill.

The idea that the law merchant is a part of the common law and that it is one of the functions of the common-law courts to declare and enforce it at once became widely current and was universally accepted. In *Vanheath v. Turner* (1622),[1] it was urged in the argument that " the custom of merchants is a part of the common law of this kingdom, of which the judges ought to take notice, and if any doubt arise about these customs, the judges may send for the merchants to know their custom, as they may send for the civilians to know their law." In Coke's Commentary on Littleton (1628), this writer observed that the *lex mercatoria* is a part of the law of the realm.[2] In other words, he considered it an integral part of the common law of England.

Custom of merchants a part of the common law.

Three features of these customs of merchants, as thus adopted and sanctioned by the common law, are to be observed as peculiar. Although the judges claimed that the customs of merchants were a part of the common law they did not profess to have judicial knowledge of them. Conse-

Judicial notice.

---

[9] 1 Comyns, 4.   [1] Winch. 24.   [2] Co. Litt. 182a.

quently, it was necessary for those customs to be specifically alleged in the pleadings and subsequently to be proved by persons who knew them. "Although we must in general take notice of the law of merchants, yet all their customs we cannot know but by information." [3]

Custom good only among merchants.

Again, the customs were good only between merchant and merchant, and at that time only foreign bills were recognized as being within the custom. In *Eaglechild's Case* (1631),[4] it was said to have been previously ruled in the King's Bench that a declaration upon the custom of merchants could only be maintained between parties who were actually merchants, and that if they were not such, the plaintiff must declare in assumpsit.

Custom comes to apply to all bills.

This doctrine, however, could not stand. The law merchant was soon extended to all contracts of a certain class and became a general rule for all bills of exchange regardless of the persons who were concerned in the transaction. *Woodward v. Rowe* (1666)[5] marks the acceptance of this principle. In this case an action was brought by an indorsee against the drawer. The plaintiff declared that by the custom and law of the realm, if any man draws a bill upon another and the latter refuses to pay for value received by the drawer, the latter shall himself be required to pay the same. It was argued for the defendant that this allegation was bad inasmuch as the plaintiff declared upon a general rule of law, and that no such principle was known to the common law. If such rule existed, it existed, so it was urged, only by virtue of the custom of merchants and was good only among this class of persons. But it was declared by the court that by the common law a man may resort to him that received the money if he to whom the bill was directed refused to pay it. It was further held that the law merchant was part of the law of the land, and that "the custom is good enough generally for any man without naming him merchant."

Fiction of agency.

Furthermore, in this case the fiction of agency between the remitter and payee was recognized by the whole court, "for

---

[3] Anonymous (1668), Hardres 485. [4] Hetley 167. [5] 2 Keb. 105, 132.

they will intend that he of whom the value is said to be received by the defendant was the plaintiff's servant."

The process by which the common law and the law merchant of bills were gradually identified and amalgamated can be plainly seen in many decisions during the latter half of the seventeenth century. In *Anonymous* (1668),[6] it was said that a mercantile custom being once proved and established becomes a part of the law of the land and the court will then take judicial notice of it. In *Carter v. Downish* (1668),[7] Pollexfen, C. J., said: "as to the law of merchants, I think we are bound to take notice of it." In *Mogadara v. Holt* (1690),[8] Lord Holt held that "the law of merchants is *jus gentium* and part of the common law, and ought to be judicially noticed when set forth in pleading."

In *Williams v. Williams* (1692),[9] the plaintiff declared upon a general custom throughout England. It was insisted for the defendant that this was bad; that if liability is based upon custom it ought to be localized, e. g. as a custom of the merchants of London, or of some other particular place, from which a venue might arise to try it; and that, on the other hand, if liability was based upon a common-law principle, it was erroneous to plead it as a custom (*per consuetudinem Angliæ*), for then the court would judicially know it. The objection was overruled on the ground that "the custom of merchants concerning bills of exchange is part of the common law of which the judges will take notice. And so 'tis needless to set forth the custom specially, it being sufficient to say that such a person, *secundum usum et consuetudinem mercatorum*, drew the bill."[1] Consequently erroneous or immaterial allegations of special customs or allegations contrary to settled law are treated as surplusage.[2]

Near the close of the seventeenth century, Treby, C. J., summing up the stages through which the law as to bills of

Courts begin to take judicial notice of the custom.

---

[6] Hardres 485.
[7] 1 Show. 127.
[8] 1 Show. 318.
[9] Carth. 270.
[1] See to the same effect, Hodges v. Steward, (1691) 12 Mod. 37; 1 Salk. 125; Pinkney v. Hall, (1697) 1 Ld. Raym. 175; Bromwich v. Loyd, (1696) 2 Lutw. 1585.
[2] Mogadara v. Holt, 1 Show. 318; Hawkins v. Cardy, 1 Ld. Raym. 360.

Practice of pleading the custom abandoned.

exchange had passed, observed that at that time (1698) it was not necessary for the plaintiff to allege any custom, since it would be judicially noticed. This was contrary to the previous practice, and the reporter punctuates this suggestion of the chief justice by observing that it was denied by none of the other judges. The practice of specially pleading the custom was slowly abandoned.[3]

Brownloe's precedents.

The books of precedents published during the seventeenth century are equally instructive of the manner in which legal theory in actions upon bills shifted towards the idea of legal duty as resulting from the custom of merchants. At the same time we can trace the assimilation of the law merchant into the body of the common law. Brownloe gives us a declaration by a payee against an acceptor. There is no statement of agency as between the plaintiff and the remitter, but the drawee (acceptor) is alleged to be the factor of the drawer.[4] In another precedent, in which the payee sues the drawer, the remitter is said to be the plaintiff's factor; but no such relation is stated as between drawer and drawee.[5] In both cases, the custom relied on is one between English merchants and foreigners. In still another precedent the relation of agency is alleged to have existed between drawer and drawee and between remitter and payee.[6] This precedent seems to have been taken from a case decided in 1607.

Vade Mecum.

The Vade Mecum supplies us with other illustrations of pleadings in actions on bills. We here find forms for the declaration by a payee against an acceptor,[7] by a payee against the drawer,[8] and by a remitter against a drawer.[9] These pleadings are so framed as to be good at common law, but in some of them the custom is alleged. In the declaration by a remitter against the drawer, it is alleged that the drawer 'undertook' that he would pay the plaintiff the sum advanced if the drawee should not accept or pay the bill accord-

---

[3] Bromwich v. Loyd, 2 Lutw. 1585.
[4] 1 Brownloe, Declarations, 267.
[5] Ib., 269.
[6] 2 Brownloe, Declarations, 58.
[7] Vade Mecum, 12, 16.
[8] Ib., 19.
[9] Ib., 21.

ing to its tenor. The declaration then alleged a protest for nonacceptance and notice to the defendant. The word 'undertook' is here plainly used to state the legal effect of the drawing of the bill, and not as an allegation of an express promise to that effect.

Chapter XXXIII

The Vade Mecum and Brownloe's book of declarations both appear to be decidedly behind the contemporary decisions of the courts. All the authorities taken together conclusively show that by the time of the accession of William and Mary, it was everywhere admitted that the law merchant, as a body of rules applicable to bills of exchange, was a part of the common law of England, and there was no longer any room for caviling upon the point. *Bromwich v. Loyd* (1696)[1] may well be taken as marking the complete acceptance of this idea.

Final assimilation of the law merchant.

The custom of merchants and the common law of the realm henceforth are one. The only difficulty is to ascertain it. When a custom hitherto unrecognized is alleged to exist, the judges will consult with the merchants or allow them to be produced as witnesses to prove its existence. Holt and Mansfield followed this course. It is done yet. But when a general usage has once been ascertained and judicially established, it is thereupon labeled as a rule of the law merchant. Thenceforth the judges are bound to know and recognize it as binding.[2]

Proof of the custom.

[1] 2 Lutw. 1585.
[2] Brandao *v.* Barnet, 12 Cl. & F. 787, 805.

CHAPTER XXXIV

BILLS AND NOTES (CONTINUED).

The Early Bill of Exchange Not Transferable.

IN tracing the course by which the custom of merchants gained recognition as a source of legal duty, we have covered practically the whole of the seventeenth century (1603–95). It now becomes necessary to begin again near the same point of departure and trace the gradual recognition of the transferability of bills of exchange. Hitherto we have observed no traces of a custom to make bills of exchange payable to order or to bearer. Just when this custom originated cannot be stated with certainty. It embodied a happy thought. That the bill of exchange should become negotiable was indispensable to growing commerce. Hartmann, a late German writer on bills of exchange, states that the first known instance of the indorsement of these instruments occurs in the Neapolitan Pragmàtica of 1607. Savary is said by the French writer M. Nougier to have assigned it to a later date, to wit, 1620.[1] In England the law of bills was at this time somewhat less advanced than on the continent, and we have good evidence that bills were never, in England, made payable to order or bearer until after 1622.

In that year Malynes published his treatise on the *Lex Mercatoria*. This book shows evidences of wide personal observation and has always been accepted as a reliable source of information on the subjects which it treats. The writer's learning is not inconsiderable, and he displays that cosmopolitan temper which has always been characteristic of those versed in the law merchant. Some things said by him have been misconstrued because of a failure to discriminate between his bills of exchange and bills obligatory, or bills of

[1] See Goodwin *v.* Robarts, L. R. 10 Exch. 348.

debt, these being what we now call promissory notes. There is really little room for confusion when we keep clearly in mind what he is talking about.

Chapter XXXIV

The only bill of exchange known to Malynes was, of course, the bill drawn between different countries — the foreign bill. No other bill was within the custom of merchants.[2] He tells us that the merchant who went abroad to buy goods might go armed with ready money or letters of credit; or he might, if he had money in banks "at Amsterdam, or other place where banks are kept," go to the bank and assign so much of his deposit to his creditor. From this it is manifest that checks were not at that period transferable.[3]

Assignment of deposit.

Again, the merchant might pay for his purchases by giving a bill of exchange drawn upon some other place.[4] Malynes says that these instruments "subsist merely by a reverend custom"; that they are of "noble nature, excelling all other dealings between merchants, and are not subject to any prescription by law or otherwise." By this he means that they originated in the usage of merchants, that they had not then obtained the full sanction of the law, and that they were protected only by the jealousy with which the merchants

---

[2] It seems that in France to this day, as when Malynes wrote, a bill drawn upon a person in the same city as the drawer is not a good bill. "The place where the bill is drawn must be so far distant from the place where it is payable that there may be a possible rate of exchange between the two." M. D. Chalmers, in Introduction to Digest of Bills, Notes, and Cheques, 41.

[3] Malynes, Lex Mercatoria, 71. All references herein to this work are to the edition of 1686.

In ch. 20, page 95, on Banks and Bankers, we have the following description of the mode in which deposits were assigned or made over by the banks from one person to another: "As for example, Peter hath 2,000 ducats in bank, John hath 3,000, and William 4,000, and so consequently others more or less. Peter hath occasion to pay unto John a thousand ducats; he goeth to the bankers at the appointed hours (which are certain both in the forenoon and afternoon) and requireth them to pay 1,000 ducats to John; whereupon they presently make Peter debtor for one thousand ducats, and John creditor for the same sum; so that Peter having assigned unto John 1,000 ducats hath now no more but one thousand ducats in bank, where he had two thousand before; and John hath four thousand ducats in the same bank, where he had but 3,000 before. And so in the same manner of assignation, John doth pay unto William, and William unto others without that any money is touched, but remains still in the banker's hand, which within a short time after the erection of the bank, amounteth unto many millions."

[4] Malynes, Lex Mercatoria, 70.

356   FOUNDATIONS OF LEGAL LIABILITY.

Volume II

Bills not payable to order.

guarded their personal credit. But the common law was coming to their support more rapidly than Malynes knew. He gives us some specimens of these instruments which are worth examining.[5] The forms given by Malynes do not contain the words 'or order,' and we are expressly cautioned that the bill should not be made payable "to the bearer or bringer thereof." [6] This, the writer thinks, might result in situations derogatory to "the nobleness of the bill, which every merchant is bound to maintain." Thus, if the bill were produced by one claiming under a thief, or even by the thief himself, the party would apparently be bound to pay the instrument according to its tenor; yet it seemed hard for the owner to lose his money in this way. The situation was too difficult for the legal conceptions of that day. Besides, to make the bill payable to the bearer would, it was supposed, detract from the simplicity of the contract, which was one of its strongest features.

Bill payable to bringer.

The explicit admonition of Malynes against the insertion, in the bill, of words making it payable to the bearer or bringer was evidently directed against a habit of some frequency. In West's Symboleography (1622) we find a form of bill which

---

[5] 1. "Laus Deo. 24th August, 1622, in London — £500 34ss. 6d. At usance pay by this my first Bill of Exchange to A. B. the sum of five hundred pounds sterling, at thirty-four shillings and six pence Flemish, for every pound sterling currant money in merchandise, for the value hereof received by me of C. D., and put it to account as per advice. A Dio, etc. G. M." On the back is indorsed, "To my loving friend Master W. C., Merchant at Amsterdam, Pa. [*pagate,* pay]."

2. "Laus Deo. 20th of September, 1622, in Amsterdam — £100 at 33ss. 6d. At usance pay this my first Bill of Exchange unto W. M. the sum of one hundred pounds lawful money of England, for the value here by me received of D. H. Make him good payment, and put it to your account. God keep you. Subscribed, W. C." On the back side is indorsed, "To my loving friend Master G. M., Merchant at London, Pa." Malynes, Lex Mercatoria, 270.

The meaning of the term 'usance' in the early bill is explained in the following passage by West (1622): "Bills of Exchange are commonly directed, and to be answered in foure maners, viz.: (1) At sight, which is upon shew of the Bill. (2) At halfe usance, which is at the end of halfe a moneth after the date of the Bill. (3) At usance, which is at the end of a moneth after the date of the Bill. (4) At double usance, which is at the end of two moneths after the date of the Bill." West, Symboleography, *Merchants' Affairs,* § 660.

[6] Malynes, Lex Mercatoria, 270.

contains the words "or the bringer hereof."[7] A generation later Marius does not deny the validity of a bill made payable to bearer, but he discountenances the practice of making it so payable as being dangerous to the rights of the person who is intended to get the benefit of the instrument.[8]

Malynes says again and again that the great corner stone of commercial engagements is credit. "The credit of merchants is so delicate and tender that it must be cared for as the apple of a man's eie."[9] "Faith or trust is to be kept between merchants without quillets or titles of law."[1] "Such is the sincerity and *candor animi* among merchants of all nations beyond the seas in the observation of plain dealing concerning bills obligatory, that no man dare presume to question his own hand."[2]

While Malynes clearly shows that bills of exchange were not transferable by custom in his day, he goes to some pains to explain a plan devised to accomplish the desired end. He notes that in England merchants had already begun to circulate bills of debt, taking care at each negotiation to go to the maker and have a new bill made out payable to the new taker. He observes that this proceeding is accompanied by some risk, as the new payee loses recourse against the person transferring the note. He also tells us that the foreign merchants were accustomed to transfer these bills of debt by mutual understanding before they were issued. In this case the original makers would make the instrument payable to the last person in the chain.[3]

Chapter XXXIV

Circulation of bills of debt.

---

[7] "Laus Deo, in London 26 Junij, 1598. At double usaunce, I pray you pay by this my first bill of exchange, my second and third not being paied unto R. P. merchant, or the bringer hereof, the summe of one hundred pounds Flemmish mony, currant in H. for merchandizes, and is for the very value thereof here by me received of the said R. P. At the day I pray you make him good payment. And thus God keepe you. Per me A. B." Symboleography, § 660.

[8] Marius, Advice, 13.
[9] Malynes, Lex Mercatoria, 76.
[1] *Ib.*, 68.
[2] *Ib.*, 74.
[3] This transaction is illustrated as follows: "Suppose that A. B., the clothier, selleth to C. D., the merchant, one pack of clothes for the sum of one hundred pounds payable at six months, and doth condition with him to make him a bill in the name of such a man as he shall nominate unto him; A. B., the clothier, buyeth of D. E., the gen-

Negotiation of bills of exchange prior to issuance.

The foreign merchants, Malynes further tells us, have still another custom whereby bills of exchange may be negotiated and transferred before they are made. Thus, P applies to J and gives one hundred pounds for a bill of exchange on X. P wishes to transfer the bill to W, W to N, and N to F. They accordingly repair together to the drawer, J, who issues the bill payable to the last transferee, F. This bill will recite value received " of P for W for N upon the account of F." The advantage derived from this cumbersome and inconvenient mode of transfer is found in the fact that each of the transferees in this chain became liable to the subsequent parties. The document recites value received by each of them on the account of the payee, and each thus becomes a new drawer.

Recourse on prior parties.

Consequently, if the bill was not honored by the drawee, and the drawer also refused to pay it, the holder could have recourse upon the others *seriatim,* beginning with the party in immediate juxtaposition.[4]

Bearing in mind the difficulty encountered by the common-law practitioner in stating a good cause of action in assumpsit upon a simple bill of exchange, as shown in *Martin v. Boure* (1602),[5] there is little wonder that an action of assumpsit which was brought in a case of this kind on the advice of merchants was unsuccessful. " This course of dealing is altogether strange to the common law of England," is the melancholy comment of Malynes in recording such a failure.[6] The merchants accordingly remained shy of the common-law courts. " The right dealing merchant doth not care how little he hath to do in the common law or things of that nature." [7]

tleman, so much wool as amounteth to one hundred pounds, and doth intend to deliver him the bill of C. D., the merchant, in full payment of his wools, and to cause the same to be made in his (this gentleman's) name; but D. E., the said gentleman, caused him to make the bill payable to E. G., the mercer, and the mercer is contented with the like condition to accept thereof; but he caused the same to be made payable to C. D., the merchant, of whom he buyeth his velvets and silks; and so in payment of them he delivered him (by an intermissive time) his own bill, which he first should have made to the clothier." Malynes, Lex Mercatoria, 71.
[4] Malynes, Lex Mercatoria, 271, 274.
[5] Cro. Jac. 6.
[6] Malynes, Lex Mercatoria, 271.
[7] Marius, Preface to Advice Concerning Bills of Exchange.

So great was the need for a recognition of the negotiability of bills of exchange that merchants were compelled in many cases to resort to the issuance of bills and letters of credit in blank, to be filled up for the proper party by their agent in the distant marts. This placed them at the mercy of the parties trusted, and was accompanied by risk; but "honest and plain dealing was used among the merchants," and they took the risk in order to effectuate their purpose.[8]

From what has been said it appears that when Malynes wrote, bills of exchange were not, generally speaking, transferable in England by indorsement or delivery, either as a matter of custom or of law. On the continent a clumsy substitute for this quality had been found in the practice of transferring before delivery.

The only legal questions that could arise at that time upon bills of exchange were such as arose between parties to the original bill, the remitter or purchaser of the bill, the drawer, the drawee (acceptor, if the bill was accepted), and the payee. Even within these limits there were mercantile customs which defined the liability of the various parties with some clearness. Malynes states the substance of these succinctly in his Twelve Observations.

These customs were, says he, to be kept and maintained as carefully and as seriously as the Romans did their law of the Twelve Tables. What sanction did they possess? We suspect from the persistent way in which he insists on their observance that the writer felt that he was appealing to business sense and business integrity. He does not in terms hold over the business man who might violate them the prospect of liability being fixed upon him by law.

The Bill of Exchange Becomes Transferable.

John Marius published in 1651 a small treatise concerning bills of exchange. It was republished about 1670 with some emendations and additions. In the preface to this edition he says his work is the fruit of twenty-four years' experience as

---

[8] Malynes, Lex Mercatoria, 272, 77.

a notary public in the Royal Exchange of London. About the extent and accuracy of his observation and the soundness of the opinions given by him there can be no question. His little book is called "Advice Concerning Bills of Exchange" and was not intended as a legal treatise. Its value is greater than if it had been confined to the legal questions already decided in that day. It is written by a practical man and was intended for the use of persons actually engaged in negotiating bills of exchange. He gave good advice, and where his instructions were followed it is safe to say that a party's rights would be protected.[9]

It is to be inferred from his preface that the usage and practice concerning bills of exchange were substantially the same in 1651 and 1670, and whatever advances in theory his treatise shows over Malynes's earlier essay (1622) belongs to the period between 1622 and 1651 rather than to the period from 1651 to 1670. This inference is corroborated by what we learn from other sources.

Words of negotiability appear in the bill.

The striking feature of the bill of exchange in Marius's pages is that words of negotiability have been inserted. He gives us a dozen specimens, all dated 1654. Each contains the words 'to A or order' or 'to A or assigns.' The idea seems to be that 'or assigns' should be used if the rights consequent upon transfer are likely to be questioned in England. The other phrase belongs to bills going into foreign parts or drawn in a foreign language.

The inland bill.

Another equally striking feature is that the custom of merchants now includes bills drawn in England upon another city within the realm. Marius describes himself as a notary of twenty-four years' standing for both inland and outland bills. In 1608 John Trenchant had observed in his Arithmetic, printed at Lyons, that real exchange could only take place between cities subject to different lords. Neither does Malynes give recognition to inland bills. Marius takes some pains to vindicate their right to be placed upon the same footing as foreign bills. "A bill of exchange which shall be made for moneys taken up at Edinborough, York, Bristol, Exon, Ply-

[9] See comments of Parke, B., in Whitehead *v.* Walker, 9 M. & W. 514.

mouth, Dover, or any other part of England or Scotland, and payable at London, is in all things as effectual and binding as any bill of exchange made beyond the seas and payable here in England. . . . The inland and outland bills ought to be esteemed of equal worth and the custom of merchants on both equally observed." [1]

<small>Chapter XXXIV</small>

Both classes of bills being made payable to order or assigns, they were now transferable by indorsement, or, as he calls it in both cases, by assignment. He gives the following illustration of assignment by two successive holders: "Pay the contents on the other side hereof to Mr. Humfrey N., or assigns, value of Mr. Joseph B., Rotterdam, 4 Oct. 1654. Roger C." The second indorsement is briefer: "Pay the contents hereof to Mr. John D. [Signed] Humfrey N." [2]

<small>Form of the indorsement.</small>

He carefully states the effect of an indorsement in blank. It was sufficient to pass the title and authorized the holder to write a special indorsement to himself or a receipt in full over the signature.[3]

<small>Indorsement in blank.</small>

The effect of the absence of words of negotiability is stated in these terms: "If the bill be made payable positively to such a man, and not to such a man or his assigns, or order, then an assignment on the bill will not serve the turn, but the money in the strictness of the letter must be immediately paid to such a man in person, and he must be known to be the same man mentioned in the bill of exchange, that so the money may not be paid to a wrong party, and so the acceptor forced to pay it twice. And if the bill be made payable positively to such a man as hath been said, such a man's name written on the back side of the bill in blank, is no sufficient warrant for another man to come (as in his name) to receive the money, but the man himself, to whom the bill is payable, must appear in person."

<small>The non-negotiable bill.</small>

It could hardly have escaped observation that a payee, or subsequent indorsee, who wrote the full or abbreviated indorsement on the back of a bill of exchange was in effect and in fact drawing a new bill. Marius, however, says nothing about the indorser's liability. This is certainly a little strange.

<small>Liability of indorser.</small>

---

[1] Marius, Advice, 2.   [2] *Ib.*, 9.   [3] *Ib.*, 30.

A few years later the courts advanced the idea that the indorser, like the drawer, guarantees the bill,[4] and there was already, at least on the continent, mercantile sanction for this liability.

[4] See Claxton *v.* Swift, (1685) 3 Mod. 87, in Exchequer, 1 Lutw. 878; Hodges *v.* Steward (1691), 1 Salk. 125.

CHAPTER XXXV

BILLS AND NOTES (CONTINUED).

The Promissory Note.

WITHOUT going more fully into the state of the law of bills of exchange when Marius wrote, we must pause at this juncture to trace the incorporation of the promissory note, or, as it was then called, the bill of debt, into the custom of merchants. That this instrument was so incorporated into the usage of the commercial world about the middle of the century is undeniable. The courts recognized this fact in a number of cases. Lord Holt, however, in *Clerke v. Martin* (1702),[1] stubbornly set himself against giving the sanction of law to this usage, and he for a time prevailed.

In some respects the law concerning bills of debt, or promissory notes, has developed faster than the law pertaining to bills of exchange. Bills of debt were undoubtedly the first ambulatory contracts. A bill obligatory payable to A or any person in his behalf producing the instrument has already been noted as supplying a foundation for an action of debt in the Fair of St. Ives (1275). In Edward I's day obligations or bonds of indebtedness regularly contain promises to pay the creditor " or his attorney producing these letters." [2] This

---

[1] 2 Ld. Raym. 757.
[2] 2 Poll. & Mait. Hist. Eng. Law, 2d ed., 227. From these authors we borrow this note: "The clause '*vel suo certo attornato* [*vel nuntio*] *has litteras deferenti*' is quite common. The only English instance that we have seen of a clause which differs from this is in Select Pleas in Manorial Courts, 152, where in 1275 a merchant of Bordeaux sues on a bond which contains a promise to pay to him '*vel cuicunque de suis scriptum obligatorium portanti.*' But here the person who demands the debt can apparently be required to show that he is a partner or the like (*de suis*) of the creditor named in the bond. For the history of such clauses, see Brunner, Forschungen, 524; Heusler, Institutionen, I., 211; Jenks, Early History of Negotiable Instruments, 9 L. Quar. Rev. 70. Appar-

form of engagement is doubtless of Italian origin and was introduced into England by the cautious Lombard money lender.[3]

Bearer taking as agent.

It will be observed that the idea of representation as embodied in obligations payable to the bearer as agent, is much more easily adjusted to contract law than that of succession in title to a chose in action by alienation or assignment. This latter conception was wholly foreign to English contract law until the seventeenth century.

Ambulatory bill of debt not limited to use among merchants.

Another point to be noted is that this idea of representation by attorney or bearer, so far as it is developed at all, finds its place in the general body of law, and its recognition is not restricted to the usage of a particular class of men (merchants) nor to dealings of a certain character. Bearing this in mind, we shall be prepared to understand, even though we may not accept, the idea that bills of debt, so far as legal rights growing out of them can have recognition, are common-law contracts and that the king's court needs no assistance from the principles of the law merchant to enable it to deal satisfactorily with them. So it seemed to Lord Holt.

Value of the bill of debt as a circulating credit.

Such indeed would have been the case but for events that transpired during the seventeenth century. It was then that the commercial world took up the unsealed evidence of indebtedness and began to apply it constantly to the uses of trade. It was found to answer a need. It resembled the bill of exchange in its simplicity and in its unilateral character. It was thus well fitted to serve as a circulating credit. By this means it acquired the character of a mercantile contract. It became transferable, at least abroad, even sooner than the bill of exchange, and thus obtained the sanction of the custom of merchants. The attempt of Lord Holt to strip it of its mercantile character and return it to the category of a pure common-law contract was reactionary and proved fruitless.

ently Bracton, 41b, knew these mercantile documents under the name *missibilia.*"

[3] Dr. Brunner has collected materials illustrating the growth of this form of contract with much fulness. His matter is drawn largely from Lombard sources and illustrates nearly every sort of contract, as gifts, sales, leases, bonds, and even wills. See 9 L. Quar. Rev. 78, 85.

As we have previously seen, Malynes tells us that in his time bills obligatory were already on the continent being made payable to bearer, and that when so made they could be "set over by tradition [i. e., delivery] only." Such transference of a bill obligatory was called a *rescounter in payment;* and while this custom did not prevail in England and was not then recognized as valid by the common law, its convenience was apparent and English lawyers and merchants hoped some day to see an act of Parliament that would establish a like course in England.[4] Malynes even suggested that the custom might be adopted without the aid of a statute by merely treating the bearer as attorney in fact.[5]

<small>Chapter XXXV</small>
<small>Bill of debt negotiable by delivery.</small>

Prevailing opinion, however, in England did not sanction this advanced idea, and those who used bills of debt resorted to the cumbersome plan, already noticed, by which the instrument was re-executed in favor of the would-be transferee. Malynes timidly suggested that in England bills obligatory made payable to a party, his heirs, executors, or assigns, might be transferred by assignment. He does not tell us to what court the assignee could resort to have his rights protected. He certainly could not sue on it in his own name in a court of common law.

<small>This usage not known in England.</small>

The form of the bill obligatory, or promissory note, as given by Malynes is somewhat redundant.[6] It conforms to the state of the law merchant in that day by showing the following facts, not now deemed requisite to be stated, viz., (1) that the transaction was between merchants; (2) that one of them was a foreigner; (3) that it grew out of a mercantile

<small>Form of the promissory note.</small>

---

[4] Malynes, Lex Mercatoria, 71.
[5] *Ib.,* 73.
[6] "I, A. B., merchant of Amsterdam, do acknowledge by these presents to be truely indebted to the honest C. D., English merchant dwelling in Middleborough, in the sum of five hundred pounds currant money for merchandise, which is for commodities received of him for my contentment, which sum of five hundred pounds as aforesaid, I do promise to pay unto the said C. D. (or the bringer hereof) within six months next after the date of these presents. In witness whereof I have subscribed the same at Amsterdam the 10 of July 1622, *stilo novo."* Malynes, Lex Mercatoria, 74.

In substance this is merely a somewhat wordy promissory note: Six months after date I promise to pay to C. D. or bearer £500, value received. Amsterdam, this July 10, 1622. A. B.

transaction; and (4) that it was supported by a good consideration. Later the first three of these recitals became immaterial and the fourth is now presumed as a matter of law; but the question of the actual presence of consideration is of course open to inquiry. Malynes tells us that in some lands, as in the Netherlands, it was customary to affix a seal, but this was not essential to the validity of the obligation. Furthermore, delivery was always presumed in favor of the bill and did not have to be proved as in case of deeds.

Seal not necessary.

Delivery presumed.

The same writer directs attention to one principle of the law merchant applicable to bills of debt which was more favorable to the debtor than the rule of common law. If several sign as principal parties, each is absolved upon payment of his *pro rata* share, unless all are expressly bound *in solidum* or unless the *exceptio divisionis* is inserted.

Joint makers liable pro rata.

What the author deems an eccentricity of the common law causes him to shake his head. It is the rule that "if one do release one of his debtors by way of acquittance that is bound with others unto him, they are all released and acquitted thereby, though there were never so little paid for the debt." Thereupon he tells a doleful story of a merchant stranger who, after he had accepted a trifling composition from an insolvent party, found to his dismay that he had thereby lost recourse on the other joint purchasers. Finally, we are told, a bill thirty years old was dead by the civil law; and the law merchant in conformity with this rule likewise treated such a bill as of no effect.[7]

Release of one releases all.

It will thus be perceived that in 1622 the bill obligatory, as a commercial engagement, had found scant recognition in the custom of English merchants and occupied a comparatively insignificant position in the English law of contract. There was never a time, of course, when such a promissory note would not support an action of debt. If it were under seal, no proof of *quid pro quo* was necessary. It was then an obligation in itself and only delivery had to be proved. If not under seal, it was good evidence of a debt if the plaintiff proved a *quid pro quo*. After assumpsit was developed, this

Bill of debt as a common-law contract.

[7] Malynes, Lex Mercatoria, 75, 76.

action would lie upon such a promise, provided there was a consideration. But neither debt nor assumpsit could be maintained by any other person than the promisee, i. e., the person who furnished the *quid pro quo* or from whom the consideration moved. It had no qualities as a mercantile contract. As it was not generally made payable to bearer, at least in England, an assignee would get no legal title and could not sue upon it in his own name. Such rights as were vouchsafed to him in equity he got as representative of the assignor and as standing in his shoes. At best he could stand on no higher ground than the ancient attorney producing the creditor's evidence of indebtedness.

Chapter XXXV

Rights of assignee.

The causes which finally brought the bill obligatory prominently into commercial use were largely political and economic. Just before the outbreak of the Civil War, Charles I forcibly borrowed £200,000 of the merchants of London. There being no banks of deposit in those days, they had been accustomed to lodge their money in the king's mint in the Tower of London for safe-keeping. It is needless to say that after Charles took advantage of the merchants to force this compulsory loan from them, this repository was not trusted any more.

About 1645 the custom came into vogue of making deposits with the goldsmiths, who plied the vocation of dealing in bullion, coin, and plate. The needs of business were such that the goldsmiths soon became actively engaged in banking and in the lending of money. They induced deposits by paying a small per cent, and thereby accumulated large sums which they loaned out to necessitous merchants and others of good credit, usually at a high rate of interest. They also began to discount bills and advance money to Cromwell on the public revenues. They were patronized by Charles II in the same way, anticipating all the revenues and taking every parliamentary grant into pawn as soon as it was given. Their business was very active and extensive, but in 1667 their credit was much impaired by a run occasioned by the panic resulting from the successes of the Dutch at sea. In 1672 the

London goldsmiths engage in banking.

Exchequer was closed. The goldsmiths were thus cut off from resorting thither for the weekly revenue coming to them from the government. Consequently they failed for nearly a million and a half sterling, which sum they had advanced to the king. Ten thousand families are said to have been ruined or greatly injured by this catastrophe.

The period of the brief career of the goldsmiths in the business of banking marks the introduction of bills obligatory extensively into English commerce. They issued their notes as evidence of money deposited, and these instruments were frequently denominated 'goldsmiths' notes.' So far as may be judged, the inland bill of exchange and the bill obligatory or note of hand came into use at approximately the same time. A careful writer assumes 1645 as a safe conjecture.[8] But in *Buller v. Crips* (1703),[9] Lord Holt, on good hearsay, said that promissory notes had then been in use only about thirty years. In the same case he also said that he himself remembered when inland bills were first successfully sued on.[1]

Taking the middle of the fifteenth century as about the date of the introduction of both of these instruments, let us

---

[8] See 1 Cranch (U. S.), Appendix, 386.

[9] 6 Mod. 29.

[1] "Holt, Chief Justice: 'I remember when actions upon inland bills of exchange did first begin; and there they laid a particular custom between London and Bristol; and it was an action against the acceptor; the defendant's counsel would put them to prove the custom; at which Hale, Chief Justice, who tried it, laughed, and said, they had a hopeful case of it. And in my Lord North's time it was said, that the custom in that case was part of the common law of England; and these actions since became frequent, as the trade of the nation did increase and all the difference between foreign bills and inland bills is, that foreign bills must be protested before a public notary before the drawer can be charged, but inland bills need no protest; and the notes in question are only an invention of the goldsmiths in Lombard street, who had a mind to make a law to bind all those that did deal with them.' . . . At another day Holt, Chief Justice, declared, that he had 'desired to speak with two of the most famous merchants in London, to be informed of the mighty ill consequences that it was pretended would ensue by obstructing this course; and that they had told him it was very frequent with them to make such notes, and that they looked upon them as bills of exchange, and that they had been used for a matter of thirty years, and that not only notes, but bonds for money, were transferred frequently, and indorsed as bills of exchange.'" Buller *v.* Crips, 6 Mod. 29.

examine some of the decisions made upon them. At the outset we are confronted with a verbal difficulty which causes confusion. The term 'bill' or 'bill of exchange' is used indifferently for true inland bills of exchange and also for the bill obligatory or promissory note. Sometimes both bills and notes are called 'notes' and sometimes both instruments are spoken of as 'bills or notes.' Terminology was not here cleared up until after the Statute of 3 and 4 Anne, chapter 9.[2]

<small>Chapter XXXV
Confusion of bills and notes.</small>

This indifference as to the term to be applied to inland bills and promissory notes coincided with another point of resemblance. The law concerning both was the same. "They both came into use at the same time, were of equal benefit to commerce, depended upon the same principle, and were supported by the same law."[3]

Let us glance at the cases to see whether this statement be true; for it imports that whatever qualities the law merchant could impart had now attached to the promissory note. In other words, the usage of merchants had taken up a common-law contract, and imparted to it new qualities; and now that the common law had absorbed the law merchant we may reasonably expect to see the unsealed writing obligatory, or bill of debt, shine with a light borrowed from the principles of universal law (*jus gentium*) embodied in the law merchant.

What seems to be the first reported case upon an inland bill is *Edgar v. Chut* (1663),[4] where the payee obtained judgment against the drawer of a bill dishonored by nonacceptance. It was drawn by one in Norfolk upon a party in London. The question whether such an inland bill was within the custom of merchants was not even raised, and we may infer that it was not debatable, doubtless having already been settled.

<small>Inland bill held to be within custom of merchants.</small>

The point actually debated was whether it was necessary

---

[2] In Grant *v.* Vaughan, 3 Burr. 1525, Lord Mansfield remarked upon this difficulty, saying that in all the cases in King William III.'s time, "there is a great confusion; for, without searching the record, one cannot tell whether they arose on promissory notes or inland bills of exchange. The reporters do not express themselves with sufficient precision, but use the words 'notes' and 'bills' promiscuously."

[3] 1 Cranch (U. S.), Appendix, 386.

[4] 1 Keb. 592, 636.

that the drawer and payee should actually be merchants, and it was held that it was sufficient that the procurer (remitter) of the bill was a trader or that the drawee was a merchant. The instrument in this case was called a bill of exchange. The term 'inland bill' was not used, it seems, until a few years later.[5]

Inland bill of equal validity with foreign bill.

In *Woodward v. Rowe* (1666),[6] the declaration shows that any bill drawn in the country was considered as good as when one of the parties was a foreigner; and it was also there held that the custom extended to all persons regardless of whether they are merchants or traders or not. Indeed, the local inland bill of exchange was never questioned in an English court, being recognized from its first appearance as having equal validity with the foreign bill.[7]

Sealed note.

Cases recognizing the commercial character of the bill of debt, bill obligatory, or true promissory note, are later than those on inland bills. In the first case involving such a contract, the obligation happened to be under seal. In modern times putting a promise to pay money under seal, makes it a specialty and takes it out of the custom of merchants altogether; but as we shall presently see, the nature of the instrument to which transferability was being now attached by the custom of merchants was not understood, and later opinion inclined to the view that they were all specialties alike. Consequently the presence of a seal caused no comment in *Shelden v. Hentley* (1681),[8] where an action was brought by the bearer upon a sealed note payable to bearer. The point actually insisted on was that the obligation was void for indefiniteness of the description of the party to take as grantee. "There was no person named in the deed to take by it." It was, however, held that delivery to any one made definite the party who was to take, and that this was good. *Traditio facit chartam loqui.*

This case marks a definite advance in legal theory, since the bearer was here regarded as being the party with whom

---

[5] Baker *v.* Hill, (1676) 3 Keb. 627. This, however, may have been an action on a promissory note.
[6] 2 Keb. 105, 132.
[7] In Anonymous (1668), Hardres 485, no distinction was drawn between the inland and foreign bill.
[8] 2 Show. 161.

the contract was made. He was not treated as an attorney or representative, nor as taking by mere assignment an estate that had been vested in another. He is within the express terms of the original contract. He takes his title by purchase and directly from the grantor. This is truly the heart of the principle of negotiability. The transferee is the party with whom the promisor is in contractual relation. Long afterwards Judge Story will put this view of the contract payable to bearer, in the following words: "The note is an original promise by the maker to pay any person who shall become the bearer; it is therefore payable to any person who successively holds the note *bona fide*, not by virtue of any assignment of the promise, but by an original and direct promise moving from the maker to the bearer." [9]

Chapter XXXV. Bearer takes as successor in title and as nominee under the contract.

In *Shelden v. Hentley* (1681),[1] one of the judges plainly said that it was the law merchant which gave validity to this bond and that it could not be good as a pure common-law obligation under seal. He illustrated this by saying that if a man bind himself at common law to pay to ———— and seal it, the subsequent insertion of his name by a holder would not make it valid.

In *Norfolk v. Howard* (1682)[2] assumpsit was brought upon an unsealed promissory note. The plaintiff failed because unable to prove demand. In *Hinton's Case* (1682),[3] in an action upon a note it was held that the bearer who sues must prove that it came to him for a consideration, " for if it came to a bearer by a casualty or knavery, he shall not have the benefit of it." In the same case, Pemberton, C. J., said that bankers' notes, when made payable to bearer, passed from hand to hand by delivery without indorsement.

Bearer of note must show that he is holder for value.

Horton v. Coggs (1689)[4] was an important case upon a promissory note, but the instrument there sued upon is improperly called a bill of exchange in some of the reports. The action was brought by a bearer who declared properly

---

[9] Bullard v. Bell (1817), 1 Mason (U. S.) 243. See Reed v. Ingraham (1799), 3 Dall. (Pa.) 505; Thompson v. Perrine (1882), 106 U. S. 593.

[1] 2 Show. 161.
[2] 2 Show. 235.
[3] *Ib.*
[4] 3 Lev. 299.

372   FOUNDATIONS OF LEGAL LIABILITY.

Volume II

Note payable to bearer held not to be negotiable.

upon the custom of merchants.[5] In the course of the decision it was said that the maker had already paid the debt to the original holder before notice of the transfer. The supposed hardship of requiring the debtor to pay twice had its effect, and the judges held that the words 'to bearer' are too general and that the custom of making obligations so payable was not valid. This practically destroyed the negotiability of notes payable to bearer. It will be remembered that notes alone were at this period made payable to bearer. Bills of exchange were seldom drawn in this form. Marius cautioned against the practice and Malynes had said that such bills were not used. The decision in question therefore deprived promissory notes of a feature which by custom they had practically enjoyed alone.

In *Hodges v. Steward* (1691),[6] a bill was drawn by the defendant upon himself, payable to another or bearer. The payee indorsed it, and the indorsee, as such indorsee and not as bearer, brought suit against the drawer. The plaintiff recovered for technical reasons, but it was thought by the court that the indorsee could not recover as indorsee upon a note thus payable to bearer.

---

[5] "If any merchant, or other person merchandizing in London, makes a note in writing under his hand, and thereby promises to pay any sum of money therein mentioned to the person therein named, or to the bearer; and if the person named in the note, to whom by the note it is promised to be paid, shall assign or deliver it to another person to receive it to his own use, and he carries it to the drawer of the note, and requests him to pay it to him that brings it, that then the person who makes the note is chargeable to pay it to the bearer; and that the defendant being a goldsmith made such a note," etc. Horton v. Coggs, 3 Lev. 299.

[6] 1 Salk. 125, 12 Mod. 36.

CHAPTER XXXVI

BILLS AND NOTES (CONTINUED).

Marius on Bills of Exchange.

AT this juncture we must notice the following points concerning bills of exchange, which Marius thought worth dwelling upon in his well-known book of Advice (1670). ^{Chapter XXXVI}

In his day it was not fully settled that the drawer was discharged by a failure of the holder to present a time draft for acceptance prior to its maturity. According to the custom of merchants in England, it was the duty of the holder to present it with convenient speed and demand acceptance of the bill, in order that the drawer might, in the event it was dishonored by nonacceptance, take steps to protect himself accordingly. Marius argues strongly in favor of this custom. Even in cases where substantial justice does not seem to require such presentation, considerations of general policy are conclusive. The bill of exchange concerns others besides the holder and drawer, and the rights of these are to be respected.[1] ^{Presentment for acceptance.}

In regard to the acceptance he observes that by the custom of London the three days of respite (grace) were not allowed. The bill should be presented at once, and if acceptance is refused it should forthwith be protested the same day. There was, however, a custom to allow the drawee four and twenty hours to consider whether he should accept, if request for this allowance were made.[2] ^{When presentment to be made.}

Again there were some who thought that the acceptor was freed from liability upon protest for nonpayment. To this proposition the author answered with an emphatic No. " True, by protesting the drawer is liable to make satisfaction, but the party which accepted the bill is so far thereby from being ^{Protest for nonpayment does not discharge acceptor.}

[1] Marius, Advice, 12.   [2] *Ib.*, 15.

freed (by protesting for nonpayment) that he is thereby made more liable, or at least liable to pay more, than he was before the protest was made," i. e., more by reason of the damages, costs, and interest.[3]

Acceptance.

If a bill was drawn upon two it was necessary for both to accept, and if only one accepted, the instrument was to be protested for want of due acceptance. If it was drawn upon two in the alternative, acceptance by one was enough. A verbal acceptance was sufficient, and any words importing a direct promise to accept or pay were treated as a good acceptance. Thus, " Call for it to-morrow and you shall have it accepted " was sufficient. If the drawee accepted for part, the holder,

Qualified acceptance.

in order to preserve a right of recourse against the drawer for the balance, was required to protest for want of due acceptance.[4]

Likewise where the acceptance was to pay at a time different from that stated in the bill, the holder could protest for want of due acceptance and could then also take the benefit of the acceptance actually made. This operated to split the contractual duties of the drawer and drawee apart, each being liable upon the instrument at separate dates. So where the drawee, without authority, altered the time mentioned in the draft, protest was to be made for nonacceptance. The drawee was nevertheless, curiously enough, held liable. By acceptance he acknowledged himself debtor, and his alteration was treated as an unauthorized spoliation.[5]

Acceptance and payment for honor.

Acceptance for honor and payment for honor were recognized as a proper mode of intervention by an agent or friend,[6] and three days of grace were allowed by the custom of London before protest could properly be made for nonpayment.[7] An acceptance once given could not be revoked.[8]

Grace.

---

[3] Marius, Advice, 13.
[4] Ib., 16, 17.
[5] Ib., 21.
[6] Ib., 21, 30, 31.
[7] Ib., 23.
[8] "It happened one day," says Marius, "that a young merchant, though a middle-aged man, came to me, and told me, he had a few hours ago accepted a bill of exchange, and delivered it back to the party to whom it was payable, but that just now he had received letters of advice, that the party for whose account the money was drawn, namely, the drawer of the bill, was failed of his credit, and therefore the acceptor would (if he

Marius also notices the right to protest for better security, where the party accepting became insolvent or unduly absented himself from the Exchange before the bill became due. "One string being cracked you must seek to get a new one, so that you may still have two strings to your bow." [9]

Chapter XXXVI

Protest for better security.

At one point we remark a wide divergence between the custom of merchants and the doctrine subsequently accepted by the courts of common law. In modern times the doctrine has prevailed that suit cannot be maintained at common law upon a lost bill or note.[1] Some such doctrine had doubtless been mooted in Marius's day, or he had at least seen unfair dealings arising out of the loss or destruction of such an instrument. He accordingly exhibits unusual warmth in controverting the idea that the party liable could escape by reason of such a mishap.[2] The most that can be required, says he, is that the party to whom the bill is payable should give bond or other reasonable writing to indemnify the party liable against the contingency of being subsequently sued by a holder in due course.[3]

The lost bill or note.

The common-law judges did not sanction this requirement of the custom of merchants. They doubtless would have done

could) un-accept the bill, or make void his acceptance thereof, and desired me to advise him how he ought to do it: To whom I made answer merrily, Sir, pray go to the party that hath your accepted bill, and tell him as much as you have told me (if he know it not already), and if he will give you leave to cancel your acceptance of the bill (which he ought not to do), then you may be free from your engagement; but for my part I know no other way, for if you cannot recall your word in such case, much less can you make void your deed without mutual consent; but the truth is, a bill of exchange being once accepted, that acceptance cannot be recalled, but the acceptor stands liable to the payment, and must make it good if he be able." Marius, Advice, 20.

[9] Marius, Advice, 27. The duty to protest for want of better security is stated in these terms: "You must then presently upon such report cause demand to be made by a notary for better security, and in fault thereof, cause protest to be made for want of better security, and send away that protest by the very next post, that so upon receipt thereof by your friend which sent you the bill, he may procure security to be given by the party which drew the bill."
[1] Pierson v. Hutchinson, 2 Campb. 211; Davis v. Dodd, 4 Taunt. 602; Hansard v. Robinson, 7 B. & C. 90, 14 E. C. L. 20; Ramuz v. Crowe, 11 Jur. 715; Moses v. Trice, 21 Gratt. (Va.) 556. Compare Lazell v. Lazell, 12 Vt. 443, 36 Am. Dec. 353.
[2] Marius, Advice, 19.
[3] Ib., 22.

376   FOUNDATIONS OF LEGAL LIABILITY.

Courts refuse to sanction suit upon lost bill.

so had the difficulty been one of frequent occurrence and had not the court of equity been a more convenient forum for adjusting the terms of the bond of indemnity.[4] In late years statutes have provided ways for getting over the supposed legal difficulty involved in suits upon lost instruments,[5] and a few courts of law have not hesitated to adopt the rule stated by Marius on this point.[6]

A perusal of this book of Marius shows that in his day the law of bills and notes had arrived at a considerable degree of maturity. He outlines the subject in a lucid, accurate way, and nearly all he wrote has been accepted as good law in modern times. Though he expressly stated that he was not writing for lawyers, he was evidently versed in all current legal doctrines pertinent to the subject. He observes that the proper form of proceeding against the acceptor of a bill is by an action on the case upon the custom.[7] This point had lately been passed upon by the courts in several cases.[8]

Liability of Indorser.

The principle that the indorser of a bill of exchange may be held liable thereon when the paper is dishonored was apparently not generally accepted as a part of the custom of merchants when Marius published the second edition of his book (1670). It was shortly accepted, however, by the law courts. This event is worthy of more than passing notice.

In *Claxton v. Swift* (1685),[9] the chief justice thought the liability of the indorser might be deduced from principles of equity. The indorser is chargeable because, if he make an indorsement upon a bad bill, it is equity and good conscience that the indorsee may resort to him to make it good.

Indorser liable on equitable grounds.

In Sir Bartholomew Shower's report of this case we find

---

[4] See Hansard v. Robinson, 7 B. & C. 90, 14 E. C. L. 20; Tercese v. Geray, Finch 301; Walmsley v. Child, 1 Ves. 341; Savannah Nat. Bank v. Haskins, 101 Mass. 370.
[5] See 17 & 18 Vict., c. 125, § 87.
[6] Bridgeford v. Masonville Mfg. Co., 34 Conn. 546; Union Bank v. Warren, 4 Sneed (Tenn.) 167.
[7] Marius, Advice, 13.
[8] Anonymous (1668), Hardres, 485; Brown v. London, 1 Vent. 152; Cramlington v. Evans, 2 Vent. 307.
[9] 3 Mod. 86, 2 Show. 494.

the able argument made by himself in favor of charging the
indorser after the drawer had been successfully sued, but without satisfaction of the judgment. Among other things, in
the course of this argument, it was said:

"The necessity of trade and commerce, and the usefulness
and convenience of transferring money by bills of exchange,
has introduced the same; and the civil law allowing them in
other nations has occasioned their approbation here; and
amongst them the rule is, *ubi literæ excambii non habuerunt
effectum, duret prima obligatio;* and I think the same rule
ought to hold with us. This and every indorsement is as a
new bill of exchange, and has all the requisites and parties that
a bill has, . . . and a man that has a bill indorsed has,
as it were, two bills for the same sum: and it is most true this
action is not joint, and cannot be brought both against the
drawer and indorser, for that the assumptions are at several
times, and upon distinct considerations." All of the judges,
however, except the chief justice, concurred in giving judgment for the defendant; but this decision was subsequently
reversed in the Exchequer Chamber. The point for which
Shower contended was thus accepted as law.[1]

The reason assigned for fixing liability upon the indorser
is that by writing the indorsement he virtually and in fact
draws a new bill. It will be perceived that this reasoning
applies to the indorsement of a bill not containing words of
negotiability as well as to those made payable to order or
bearer. Accordingly if a bill or note is made payable to B,
without more, and B indorses this instrument to C, the latter,
upon nonpayment of the bill, can sue his indorser, though of
course he has no right of action against the party primarily
liable, for the reason that the contract is not transferable by its
terms.[2]

The case of *Williams v. Williams* (1692)[3] illustrates this.
There a note payable to one W, but not containing the word
'order' or 'bearer,' was twice transferred and the final holder

---

[1] Claxton *v.* Swift, 1 Lutw. 878, 882b.
[2] Hodges *v.* Steward, (1691) 1 Salk. 125.
[3] Carth. 269.

378 FOUNDATIONS OF LEGAL LIABILITY.

obtained judgment against the payee as indorser.[4] The same principle was applied in *Hill v. Lewis* (1693),[5] Lord Holt saying that goldsmiths' notes were governed by the same laws and customs as bills of exchange, and that so long as they continued in circulation each indorser became liable as a new drawer.

In this case it was also held that if the holder fails to present the paper in a reasonable time and meanwhile the maker becomes insolvent, the indorser is discharged. What constitutes reasonable time was not determined, but the jury were instructed that they should be governed on this question by the usage of merchants. It will be observed the liability thus fixed on the indorser is one of conditional warranty. The holder is therefore in duty bound first to resort to the party primarily liable and get the money from him if he can.[6] But the law does not require that the holder should first exhaust legal remedies against the party primarily liable. Malynes had made this clear long before Holt's day.[7]

Rapid Development of the Law of Commercial Paper.

The cases just considered bring us into the reign of William and Mary. With the advent of these sovereigns the law concerning negotiable instruments entered upon a period of remarkable growth. This was due to the expansion of trade and to the fact that the common-law courts had now definitely taken complete control of this branch of the law and were thereafter to guide its development. Lord Holt soon became Chief Justice of the King's Bench and he was destined to exert a powerful and salutary influence in this field. Though radically reactionary in dealing with promissory notes, in other respects he displayed much learning and judgment in deciding rights arising out of commercial transactions, and the law of bills is greatly indebted to him. Let us now follow the course

---

[4] "The last indorsee may bring an action against any of the indorsers, because every indorsement is a new bill and implies a warranty that the money shall be paid." Williams *v.* Field, 3 Salk. 68.

[5] 1 Salk. 132.

[6] See language of Lord Holt in the case of Hill *v.* Lewis, (1693) 1 Salk. 133.

[7] Malynes, Lex Mercatoria, 273.

of events prior to the passage of 3 and 4 Anne, chapter 9. It is much to be regretted that the reporters on whom we rely during this period have, with a few notable exceptions, done their work poorly. Even when reporting the same case they often so far differ among themselves that it is impossible to ascertain the points actually decided. Lord Raymond's reports are by far the most satisfactory, and those of Sir Bartholomew Shower are next in accuracy to his.

We have already seen that in *Horton v. Coggs* (1689)[8] the right of the bearer to sue the maker of a promissory note payable to bearer was denied. In *Hodges v. Steward* (1691)[9] the same rule was applied to bills of exchange. It was said: There is a difference between a bill payable to J. S., or bearer, and a bill payable to J. S. or order; "for a bill payable to J. S. or bearer is not assignable by the contract so as to enable the indorsee to bring an action, if the drawer refuse to pay, because there is no such authority given to the party by the first contract, and the effect of it is only to discharge the drawee if he pays it to the bearer, though he comes to it by trover, theft, or otherwise. But when the bill is payable to J. S. or order, there an express power is given to the party to assign, and the indorsee may maintain an action."

In *Pearson v. Garrett* (1693)[1] we see traces of the expiring principle that in order to be within the law merchant a note or bill must originate in trading. This was assigned as one reason for holding the declaration in that case to be bad, but the note in question was subject to a contingency, and judgment was given for the defendant on this ground. In *Bromwich v. Loyd* (1696),[2] the old notion was completely dissipated.[3]

The law merchant had now been adopted by the law courts,

---

[8] 3 Lev. 299.
[9] 1 Salk. 125.
[1] Comb. 227, 4 Mod. 242.
[2] 2 Lutw. 1582.
[3] Other cases decided upon bills and notes during this period which may be consulted to advantage are: Nicholson v. Sedgewick, 1 Ld. Raym. 180, 3 Salk. 67; Lambert v. Oakes, 1 Ld. Raym 443, 1 Salk. 127, 12 Mod. 244, Holt 118; Starke v. Cheesman, Carth. 509; Carter v. Palmer, 12 Mod. 380; Woolvil v. Young, 5 Mod. 367; Pinkney v. Hall, 1 Ld. Raym. 175; Hawkins v. Cardy, 1 Ld. Raym. 360; Jordan v. Barloe, 3 Salk. 67.

and foreign bills, inland bills, and promissory notes were equally within the custom. The expression 'or bearer' when put in a promissory note did not have the effect of imparting negotiability to the contract. As a matter of custom it was seemingly universal to insert the words 'or order' in bills of exchange. Notes were perhaps in most cases drawn payable merely to a particular person.

Protest of inland bill.

The inland bill did not have to be protested. Consequently the drawer could not be held liable for interest and damages in case of dishonor.[4] To remedy this defect an act was passed by the Parliament, providing that inland bills reciting value received could be protested upon dishonor by nonpayment after acceptance and the drawer thereby held liable for all damages, costs, and interest.[5]

This statute was defective in respect of the fact that before the holder could get the benefit of it, actual acceptance was necessary. This was remedied by a provision in 3 and 4 Anne, chapter 9, permitting the same course to be pursued in case of nonacceptance. Inland bills were thus placed on the same footing, as to the amount of damages recoverable by the holder, as the foreign bill.

---

[4] Borough v. Perkins, 1 Salk. 131; Brough v. Parkings, 2 Ld. Raym. 992; Bacon Abr., *Merchant and Merchandise*, (M) Inland Bills.

[5] 9 & 10 Will. III., c. 17. This act, though it authorized the protest of an inland bill in order to enable the holder to recover interest and damages, did not take away the common-law right of action on an unprotested inland bill. Thus, in Brough v. Parkings, 2 Ld. Raym. 993, Lord Holt says: "A protest on a foreign bill is part of the custom, but on an inland bill no protest was necessary by the common law, but by this statute. But this statute does not destroy or take away the party's action, where there is no protest, nor is the want of a protest any bar of the action; but the act seems only to take away from the plaintiff his interest or damages, where he has not made a protest, or to give the drawer a remedy against him by way of action for the costs and damages."

CHAPTER XXXVII

BILLS AND NOTES (CONTINUED).

Is the Bill of Exchange a Specialty?

THE bill of exchange and promissory note having now (1696) attained a prominent position in the eye of both merchant and lawyer, we must take account of a view which presently became current regarding the nature of these instruments.

<small>Chapter XXXVII</small>

Lord Holt thought that the bill was a specialty; that the law merchant, from which the bill derived its binding force, was a body of legal rules wholly *sui generis* and fundamentally antagonistic to common-law principle. The chief consequence of this view was the proposition that a bill of exchange is good without a consideration. That the bill does bear some resemblance to the common-law specialty is no doubt true; but the differences are equally striking. Lord Holt also erred in assuming that the custom of merchants, as a matter of fact, imposed duty regardless of the presence or absence of consideration.

<small>Opinion of Holt.</small>

The law merchant, it has always been said, is a kind of international private law. It is universal law, a part of the *jus gentium*. If this be true, it does not belong to any particular system of jurisprudence more than to any other. It is the product of the interaction of the habits and usages of merchants the world over. Notwithstanding this character has been universally conceded to it, the fact nevertheless remains that the law of commercial paper was developed more rapidly in the continental states of Europe, especially during its formative period, than in England; and English judges have too often been accustomed to look upon it as a pure product of the civil law.

<small>Law merchant not pure product of civil law.</small>

Now one of the features of the civil law pertaining to con-

Volume II

Consideration.

tracts which strikes the English lawyer as most peculiar is the absence of the requirement of consideration. English judges have accordingly sometimes reasoned that, inasmuch as the law merchant is a product of the civil law and inasmuch as the civil law does not require a consideration, therefore the bill of exchange is good without a consideration. But this is not the case.

Consideration must be recited.

All of the early bills of exchange show on their face that they arise out of commercial transactions and they recite in some form the fact that value has been given for them.[1] This was not peculiar to early English bills. The custom of merchants did not give any validity in any country to an instrument which failed to show value. Malynes says: "The civil law and the law merchant do require that the bill shall declare for what the debt groweth, either for merchandise or for money or any other lawful consideration."[2]

Consideration presumed.

In England, since 1840, the actual recital of value received is deemed unnecessary, as the law will now raise the presumption of a consideration;[3] but this is a rule which pertains purely to a matter of pleading, and the defendant can always impeach a bill by showing that no consideration has ever been given for it. The English law seems, upon this point, to have been further relaxed than elsewhere. In France, it seems, even to this day, the bill must state that value has been received for it, and a false statement of the consideration avoids the bill in the hands of all parties with notice.[4]

Marius in one or two connections loosely speaks of the bill as a specialty, but it is clear that he fully appreciated the difference between it and the true common-law specialty.[5] The manner of declaring upon bills contributed somewhat to give currency to the erroneous notion that the bill is a specialty. The early declaration stated the custom and the facts

---

[1] Note the words in the form of the bill of exchange as found in West's Symboleography, § 660: "for the very value thereof here by me received of the said R. P." The forms given by Malynes contain substantially the same language.

[2] Malynes, Lex Mercatoria, 74.

[3] Hatch v. Trayes, 11 Ad. & El. 702, 39 E. C. L. 207.

[4] M. D. Chalmers, in Introduction to Digest of Bills, Notes, and Cheques, p. xi.

[5] Marius, Advice, 1.

which brought the case within it. The obligation was derived from the law merchant. As no consideration was stated it superficially appeared that none was necessary to be proved. It escaped observation that every commercial transaction by bill or note necessarily involved this element. The custom required its presence, though no reference was made to it in the pleadings. There are decisions, too, in this period which possibly indicate that a consideration was deemed necessary as a matter of law before the plaintiff could recover. Thus, in *Hinton's Case* (1683),[6] Pemberton, C. J., required the bearer of a promissory note to prove that he had given value, "for if he had come by it by knavery or trickery he should not have the benefit of it."

However, by this time the doctrine was being accepted by at least some of the judges, that while common-law contracts require a consideration, contracts within the custom of merchants do not. Thus, in *Cramlington v. Evans* (1689),[7] Lord Holt said: "If the drawer mention 'for value received,' then he is chargeable at common law; but if no such mention, then you must come upon the custom of merchants only." It soon became firmly fixed in the mind of this judge that all instruments subject to the law merchant are specialties and that no consideration need be recited in them or is in any way necessary to make them valid. This was generally accepted as the correct view, and to bring an instrument within the protection of the law merchant was an artifice which made such instrument equal with any bond and good without a consideration.[8]

Promissory Note Not Within the Law Merchant.

This brings us to the point of view occupied by the judges when they decided that the law merchant was to be limited strictly to cases clearly within the custom. Up to this point we have seen the principles of the law merchant constantly extended; but now, when the courts were confronted by the

[6] 2 Show. 235. Compare Anonymous, ('1696) 1 Comyns 43.
[7] 1 Show. 5.
[8] Pearson v. Garrett. (1693) Comb. 227.

fact that they were recognizing a new specialty, a contract that seemed to be good without a consideration, Lord Holt thought that this attitude should be changed.

Accordingly, when the opportunity presented itself in *Clerke v. Martin* (1702),[9] he began his assault upon promissory notes. The plaintiff in this case, suing on such an instrument, declared upon the custom of merchants and did not, of course, allege a consideration. *Horton v. Coggs* (1689),[1] had denied negotiability to a note payable to bearer, and this supplied an entering wedge. Holt, we are told, was *totis viribus* against the action, saying, "that the maintaining of these actions upon such notes was an innovation upon the rules of the common law; and that it amounted to a new sort of specialty unknown to the common law, and invented in Lombard street, which attempted, in these matters of bills of exchange, to give laws to Westminster Hall." He further said "that continuing to declare upon these notes upon the custom of merchants proceeded upon obstinacy and opinionativeness, since he had always expressed his opinion against them." Gould, J., modestly suggested that he did not remember it had ever been adjudged that a note in which the subscriber promised to pay to J. S. or bearer was not a bill of exchange; but against the imperious force of character displayed by the chief justice no opposition could stand. Judgment was therefore given for the defendant.

Subsequent decisions confirmed this doctrine. In *Potter v. Pearson* (1703)[2] a particular custom to the effect "that if a merchant signed a note promising to pay J. S. or order, etc., he became obliged by the custom to pay it," was declared void, "since it binds a man to pay money without any consideration." If the assumption had been true that such a promise to pay did subject the promisor to liability regardless of consideration, this ruling would have been sound. In *Cutting v. Williams* (1702)[3] Lord Holt tells us that the idea of promissory notes not being within the custom of merchants was original with him. "He had proposed it to all the judges and

[9] 2 Ld. Raym. 757, 1 Salk. 129.
[1] 3 Lev. 299.
[2] 2 Ld. Raym. 759.
[3] 7 Mod. 155.

they were of the opinion that a declaration upon the custom of merchants upon a note subscribed by the defendant to the plaintiff for so much money was void, for it tended to make a note amount to a specialty."

In *Buller v. Crips* (1703)[4] the question was debated again with the same result. Holt, C. J., said: "To allow such a note to carry a lien [i. e., obligation] with it, were to turn a piece of paper, which is in law but evidence of a parol contract, into a specialty; and besides, to empower one to assign that to another which he could not have himself." As said by counsel in *Grant v. Vaughan* (1764),[5] Lord Holt was truly peevish on the question of the negotiability of notes.[6]

Statute of 3 and 4 Anne Makes Notes Negotiable.

The result of this victory of Lord Holt was that where the holder sued the maker, he had to declare at common law in special or indebitatus assumpsit, and, upon alleging and proving a sufficient consideration, could give the note in evidence of the promise. The merchants of London thought that "mighty ill consequences" would result from the subversion of the usage concerning notes, and Parliament thought so too, for the Statute of 3 and 4 Anne, chapter 9, overruled the principle for which the chief justice had so persistently contended. This enactment placed promissory notes upon the same footing as inland bills.[7] The statute was called forth by the decisions we have just reviewed, and the universal opinion

[4] 6 Mod. 29. This was a suit by an indorsee against the maker, and not by the payee, as were the other cases. Lord Holt admitted that if the indorsee had sued the payee, his indorser, he could have maintained the action, for the indorser was the drawer of a new bill.
[5] 3 Burr. 1520.
[6] See Lord Kenyon's remarks in Brown *v.* Harraden, 4 T. R. 151, and those of Lord Hardwicke in Walmsley *v.* Child, 1 Ves. 346; also Mansfield's observations in Grant *v.* Vaughan, 1 W. Bl. 487.
[7] The statute is drawn with much prolixity. In substance it declares that where a note in writing is made and signed by any person whereby such person promises to pay to any other person, or to order or to bearer, any sum of money, said sum of money shall be taken and construed to be due and payable, and such note shall be assignable or indorsable over in the same manner as inland bills according to the custom of merchants. Stat. 3 & 4 Anne, c. 9. The statute is printed in Bacon's Abridgment, *Merchant and Merchandise* (M).

now is that it was merely declaratory of the common law and had no other effect than to overrule erroneous decisions.[8]

Inasmuch as the statute settled the law as to promissory notes it became a new point of departure in the history of these instruments and practically removed all necessity for the subsequent examination by English judges of the cases on promissory notes prior to its passage. The real merit of the question raised by Lord Holt has therefore been seldom investigated, and we consequently find many judicial dicta in modern times which take it for granted that Holt's position was correct and that, by common law, promissory notes were not negotiable. Any competent person who examines the decisions will see that this assumption is incorrect. Lord Holt's ruling was reactionary and was adopted by him and his fellow judges solely in order to escape the consequences of the doctrine then accepted, but afterwards repudiated, that contracts subject to the law merchant are specialties and require no consideration.

Effect of Statute on Notes Not Containing Words of Negotiability.

There is one point, however, where the law of notes was not left upon the same footing as the law of bills. This resulted from a judicial construction placed upon the language used in describing the instruments which were by the statute made transferable, viz., " shall promise to pay to any other person or persons, body politic and corporate, his, her, or their order or unto bearer." This language is perhaps somewhat ambiguous, inasmuch as it fails to make clear whether the act was intended to be applied to three kinds of notes — notes payable ' to A,' notes payable ' to A or order,' and notes payable ' to A or bearer '; or whether it was intended to be applied to two classes only — those payable to ' A or order '

---

[8] To the effect that the statute was declaratory only and did not change the law, see 1 Cranch (U. S.), Appendix, 408; Goodwin v. Robarts, L. R. 10 Exch. 350; Story on Promissory Notes, 7th ed., 10, note: 3 Kent Com. 73. The statute itself, in its preamble, purports merely to brush away difficulties created by decisions.

and those payable to 'A or bearer.' If the idea that the statute was merely intended to put notes on the same footing as bills had been faithfully adhered to, it would undoubtedly have been held that the statute applied only to notes containing words of negotiability. But this view was not adopted. In *Burchell v. Slocock* (1728)[9] it was held that a note payable to A simply, and not containing words of negotiability, was within the meaning of the statute. In *Moore v. Paine* (1736)[1] Lord Hardwicke, in response to an objection that the note sued on was not within the statute because payable to the plaintiff and not to his order, said that this objection had been often overruled. By judicial construction the statute was thus made to introduce something of an anomaly into the law of promissory notes, making such instruments fully transferable although lacking words of negotiability.[2]

It should be added that the English Bill of Exchange Act (1882) extended this principle to bills of exchange, while the American Negotiable Instruments Law deprived notes of the benefit of the statute of Anne on this point. The result is that in England both bills and notes payable to particular persons, without the addition of the expression 'to order' or 'bearer,' are negotiable in the fullest sense, while in America they are not.[3]

Chapter XXXVII

Notes made negotiable though words of negotiability absent.

Distinction between English and American law.

Bills and Notes Not Specialty Contracts.

The Statute of 3 and 4 Anne having placed the promissory note on the same footing in regard to negotiability as the bill of exchange, it followed that if Lord Holt was right in thinking the bill of exchange to be a specialty the note had now

---

[9] 2 Ld. Raym. 1545.
[1] Lee t. Hardw. 288.
[2] Goshen, etc., Turnpike-Road Co. v. Hurtin, 9 Johns. (N. Y.) 217; Leonard v. Mason, 1 Wend. (N. Y.) 522; Leidy v. Tammany, 9 Watts (Pa.) 353.
In Smith v. Kendall, 6 T. R. 123, it was held that a note payable to A, without adding the words 'order' or 'bearer,' was entitled to grace. The same was taken for granted in Tindal v. Brown, 1 T. R. 167. The decision in May v. Cooper, Fortescue 376, was overruled. In Backus v. Danforth, 10 Conn. 297, a note not containing words of negotiability was declared not to be entitled to grace.
[3] Bills of Exchange Act (1882), § 3 (1), and § 83 ('1); Am. Neg. Inst. Law, § 1.

truly become a specialty also. The question did not arise until *Brown v. Marsh* (1721),[4] wherein it was insisted that the promissory note is valid though shown not to be founded on a consideration. Two of the judges accepted this doctrine, basing their opinion on the language of the statute, which on its face appeared to create the duty to pay, merely upon the execution of the note. The lord chancellor and the other two judges, however, were of a different opinion. According to them the note is only a simple contract, " and notwithstanding the statute says that the money shall be due and payable by virtue of the note, that only makes the note itself evidence of the consideration. . . . Though the note itself be evidence of a consideration, yet it is not conclusve evidence, but turns the proof on the defendant to show that there was no consideration given."

It thus appears that the Statute of 3 and 4 Anne was interpreted like the earlier Statute of Frauds. Both expressly give validity to written contracts fulfilling certain requirements as to form, but neither dispenses in any degree with the necessity for the common-law element of consideration. The prevailing opinion in this case found favor at once,[5] and its soundness was never afterwards questioned.

It will be observed that the point debated in *Brown v. Marsh* was whether the statute of Anne had turned the note into a specialty, and the question whether the bill of exchange is a specialty was not touched upon. The question naturally arises, What has become of the view entertained by Lord Holt and his contemporaries as to the nature of the bill of exchange? Is it still to be considered a specialty contract? To this we answer, No. Lord Holt was in error in saying that a bill of exchange is a specialty, and after he and his contemporaries were dead the notion to which he had given currency gradually disappeared. It was simply dissipated like

---

[4] Gilb. Eq. 154.
[5] See *Jefferies v. Austin*, (1725) 1 Stra. 674. In this case Eyre, the Chief Justice of the Common Bench, gave judgment in favor of a defendant upon a plea of want of consideration. It was clearly understood that in such case the burden of proof was on the defendant.

a mist. In *Pillans v. Van Mierop* (1765)[6] Lord Mansfield undertook to resurrect that doctrine, but it did not again become current. The dictum of the House of Lords in *Rann v. Hughes* (1797)[7] was sufficient to put a final quietus upon it.[8]

While bills of exchange are not specialty contracts and hence must be supported by a consideration, there are two points at which the law in regard to consideration in bills of exchange is peculiar. The burden of showing the want of it is on the defendant, and it is not material who furnishes the consideration for the bill in any particular case, provided it moves from the holder who brings suit or from some person in privity with him.[9] The exceptional rule which imposes the burden of proof on the defendant is apparently of a purely procedural character. The other exception embodies an innovation of substance and was rendered possible by reason of the fact that the action on the case was used as the remedy on the bill instead of special assumpsit. Both rules were evidently adopted merely to promote the currency of the instrument.

Burden of proof as to consideration.

From whom must the consideration move?

Note Given for Precedent Debt Treated as a Conditional Payment.

The rule that a note or bill given for a precedent debt operates only as a conditional payment of the debt originated in Lord Holt's time. In *Ward v. Evans* (1702)[1] a demand note made by a third party payable to bearer was delivered by the debtor to his creditor in part payment of a debt. The maker became insolvent before the note could be conveniently presented and the creditor was permitted to recover on the

---

[6] 3 Burr. 1665.

[7] 7 T. R. 346, note *a*.

[8] We note that Professor Ames, in 2 Cases on Bills and Notes, 872, says that the bill of exchange is a specialty. With all respect due to the scholarship of this writer we are bound to say that this view is out of harmony with modern notions and has not been judicially entertained in any quarter for more than a hundred years.

[9] "Though the plaintiff gave no value, the bill by indorsement is transferred to him, and he has the right to sue on the bill if any intermediate party is a holder for value." Parke, B., in *Oulds v. Harrison*, 10 Exch. 572.

The payee may sue the drawer or maker although the consideration moves from a third person. *Munroe v. Bordier*, 8 C. B. 862, 65 E. C. L. 862; *Horn v. Fuller*, 6 N. H. 511.

[1] 2 Ld. Raym. 928.

Note as conditional payment of precedent debt.

original debt. Lord Holt said: "I am of opinion . . . that the acceptance of such a note is not actual payment. I agree that taking a note for goods sold is a payment because it was part of the original contract, but paper is no payment where there is a precedent debt. For, when such a note is given in payment, it is always intended to be taken under this condition, to be payment if the money be paid thereon in convenient time. . . . But if the party who takes the note keep it by him for several days, without demanding it, and the person who ought to pay it becomes insolvent, he that received it must bear the loss, because he prevented the other person from receiving the money, by detaining the note in his custody."[2]

Implied term of common-law contract.

This doctrine has generally been followed.[3] The principle in question was laid down at a time when a promissory note, such as was transferred in this case, was being treated as a pure common-law contract and when it was held that the bearer could not sue upon it under the principles of the law merchant. The condition here ingrafted upon the transaction was therefore treated as an implied term of the common-law contract. After the statute of Anne changed the status of notes the same rule was followed, and in later years it has been applied where debts are paid by means of bills of exchange[4] and checks,[5] as well as by notes. It is also applied where the debtor indorses or transfers by delivery, as well as where he makes the note or draws the bill.[6] Against Holt's

---

[2] There was an earlier recognition of the same principle by Pemberton, C. J., in Vernon v. Boverie, (1682) 2 Show. 296.

[3] Lumley v. Musgrave, 4 Bing. N. Cas. 9, 33 E. C. L. 265; Lyman v. U. S. Bank, 12 How. (U. S.) 225; Mooring v. Mobile Marine Dock, etc., Ins. Co., 27 Ala. 254; Bill v. Porter, 9 Conn. 23; Edwards v. Trulock, 37 Iowa 244.

The bill or note given in payment of a pre-existing debt operates, of course, as absolute payment if there is an express agreement that it is taken as payment and at the risk of the creditor. Maxwell v. Day, 45 Ind. 509.

In some of the American states it is held that the acceptance of a promissory note or bill of exchange is presumptively a satisfaction, but the presumption may be rebutted by proof that it was accepted as conditional payment.

[4] League v. Waring, 85 Pa. St. 244.

[5] McIntyre v. Kennedy, 29 Pa. St. 448.

[6] Peter v. Beverly, 10 Pet. (U. S.) 532; League v. Waring, 85 Pa. St. 244; Nightingale v. Chafee, 11 R. I. 609.

position it was asserted that it was the custom of merchants to consider the note or bill as absolute payment. Such usage may have been at the point of maturing into a custom, but *Ward v. Evans* settled the law the other way.

In *Garnet v. Clarke* (1709)[7] Lord Holt declared that a note signed by A and payable to B on account of N was not within the Statute of 3 and 4 Anne and consequently could be sued on only as a common-law contract. This opinion proceeded upon a narrow construction of the statute, and a few years later the contrary was held in a case which foreshadowed the modern rule that a negotiable instrument need not recite 'value received.'[8]

Chapter XXXVII

Note given for debt of another.

Recital of Value Received.

As we have already shown, a recital of 'value received' is found in all the early specimens of bills. The goldsmith's note, however, seems to have contained no such statement. This was one of the grounds of Lord Holt's objection to it. Now when the statute of Anne expressly brought notes within the law merchant, there could thereafter be no question but that a promissory note not containing a recital of 'value received' was good. This principle being accepted as applicable to the note, it was but natural that the same view should in the end prevail in regard to the bill of exchange. In *Josceline v. Lassere* (1714)[9] Chief Justice Parker, afterwards Lord Macclesfield, and Eyre, J., agreed upon this; but the term 'value received' continued to be nearly always inserted in the bill as a matter of fact. Consequently the question whether the omission of such recital is fatal to a bill of exchange did not arise for decision until Lord Denman's time. In *Hatch v. Trayes* (1840)[1] it was said that the words 'value received,' when inserted in a bill, express only what the law must imply from the nature of the instrument and the relation of the

Recital of value made unnecessary in note by statute of Anne.

Recital becomes unnecessary in the bill.

---

[7] 11 Mod. 226.

[8] Poplewell *v.* Wilson, (1719) 1 Stra. 264. The note in this case recited that it was in part payment of the debt of a third person, and did not contain a recital of value received. Nevertheless it was held to be a promissory note within the meaning of the statute.

[9] Fortescue 281.

[1] 11 Ad. & El. 702, 39 E. C. L. 207.

parties apparent upon it; and it therefore makes no difference whether the words be or be not inserted.

Note payable on contingency.

In *Colehan v. Cooke* (1742)[2] it was decided upon principles applicable to bills of exchange that a note payable upon a contingency is not negotiable, but that a note will be negotiable if made payable on an event which is bound to happen, though the time of the happening be uncertain. In *Carlos v. Fancourt* (1794)[3] a note payable out of a particular fund was held not to be within the statute. These decisions are important as settling the principle that the statute of Anne merely puts notes on the same footing as bills.

Note payable out of particular fund.

In the latter case Lord Kenyon said that in *Jenney v. Herle* (1723)[4] it was decided that a bill not payable at all events could not be considered a bill of exchange; "there is no difference in this respect between promissory notes and bills of exchange, for both are *in pari ratione*. If we were to render this point in the least doubtful, we should shake the foundation of that which has been considered as clear law since the time of Lord Holt."

[2] Willes 393.   [3] 5 T. R. 482.   [4] 2 Ld. Raym. 1361.

CHAPTER XXXVIII

BILLS AND NOTES (CONTINUED).

FROM what has been said in the preceding chapter the reader will perceive that the decisive epoch in the history of the law of bills and notes is found in the period of William and Mary, William III, and Anne. It was then that the common-law courts took fully in hand the work of shaping the development of this branch of the law. Most of the work of adjustment was done by or under the influence of Lord Holt, whose career as chief justice extended over the whole critical period (1689–1710).[1] During the succeeding half century comparatively little was added to the law of the subject, and we may well pass without more to the period of Lord Mansfield.

The Innocent Purchaser.

One of the first subjects pertaining to the law of bills which it was Lord Mansfield's fortune to illuminate by his learning and independence of mind was that of the rights of the innocent purchaser. In *Miller v. Race* (1758)[2] the question was raised whether trover could be maintained against the innocent purchaser of a stolen bank note. The defendant had received the note as money in the usual course of business and had no knowledge of any defect in the title of the person from whom he received it. The bill in question was identified, and it was insisted that the property in the note could not be divested out of the owner by the theft or subsequent transfer.

---

[1] A glance at the reports covering this period will show how exceedingly rich they are in cases pertaining to bills and notes. The cases reported by Sir Bartholomew Shower (1678–95), by Lutwyche (1682–1704), Carthew (1686–1701), Lord Raymond (1694–1734), Salkeld (1689–1712), Comyns (1695–1714), Strange (1715–47), and those found in the Modern Reports are the most instructive.

[2] 1 Burr. 452.

394   FOUNDATIONS OF LEGAL LIABILITY.

<small>Volume II</small>

To this the chief justice replied: "It has been quaintly said 'the reason why money cannot be followed is because it has no ear-mark,' but this is not true. The true reason is upon account of the currency of it. It cannot be recovered after it has passed in currency. So in case of money stolen, the true owner cannot recover it after it has been paid away fairly and honestly upon a valuable and *bona fide* consideration; but before money has passed in currency, an action may be brought for the money itself." Taking the note in the due course of trade vests the property in the purchaser, and his title cannot be defeated by showing that the transferor had none.

<small>The bill payable to bearer.</small>

Grant v. Vaughan (1764)[3] presented another question as to the rights of the innocent purchaser. An inland bill of exchange was made payable to bearer. It was lost and the finder sold to the plaintiff, who took it for value in due course of trade. The circumstance that the bill had been drawn payable to bearer, a feature which had always been characteristic of notes rather than of bills of exchange, was remarked upon as unusual, but the bill was held to be good. The plaintiff was allowed to recover. The view taken of the term 'bearer' in the bill was the same that had been entertained in *Shelden v. Hentley* (1681),[4] namely, that it is a description of the person to whom the promise is made and that when the instrument comes to one's hand, in due course of trade, it is a contract with him. Said Wilmot, J.: "This is a negotiable note, and the action may be brought in the name of the bearer. 'Bearer' is *descriptio personæ*, and a person may take by that description as well as by any other. In the nature of the contract there is no impropriety in his doing so. It is a contract to pay the bearer or the person to whom he shall deliver it (whether it be a note or a bill of exchange); and it is repugnant to the contract that the drawer should object that the bearer has no right to demand payment from him.[4*]

<small>Blank indorsement of bill payable to order.</small>

In *Peacock v. Rhodes* (1781)[5] the same doctrine was extended to a stolen bill of exchange payable to order and bearing an indorsement in blank. Lord Mansfield said: "The

[3] 3 Burr. 1516.
[4] 2 Show. 161.
[4*] 3 Burr. 1527.
[5] 2 Dougl. 633.

holder of a bill of exchange, or promissory note, is not to be considered in the light of an assignee of the payee. An assignee must take the thing assigned, subject to all the equity to which the original party was subject. If this rule applied to bills and promissory notes, it would stop their currency. The law is settled, that a holder, coming fairly by a bill or note, has nothing to do with the transaction between the original parties; unless, perhaps, in the single case (which is a hard one, but has been determined) of a note for money won at play. I see no difference between a note indorsed blank and one payable to bearer. They both go by delivery, and possession proves property in both cases. The question of *mala fides* was for the consideration of the jury. The circumstances that the buyer and also the drawers were strangers to the plaintiff, and that he took the bill for goods on which he had a profit, were grounds of suspicion, very fit for their consideration. But they have considered them, and have found it was received in the course of trade, and therefore the case is clear."

Chapter XXXVIII

Holder not a mere assignee.

Good faith of purchaser a question for the jury.

From the foregoing cases it clearly appears that the innocent purchaser is protected by the currency of the bill. The promisor is in direct contractual relation with the ultimate holder. The bearer holds title by succession rather than derivation. The same view was clearly put at a still later day by Judge Story in words which we have already quoted.[6] The money is due to the bearer, not by virtue of any assignment of the promise, but by an original and direct promise moving from the maker to the bearer. It is obvious that, under this view, the maker can have no right to set up defenses available against prior holders.[7]

The Currency of the Bill.

The decisions above noted point to one of the most characteristic features of the English law of bills. The object of giving currency to the bill and of making it a substitute for

---

[6] Bullard v. Bell (1817), 1 Mason (U. S.) 243.

[7] See Negotiability and Estoppel, by J. S. Ewart, 16 L. Quar. Rev. 143, 144.

money has been kept steadily in view by the English and American courts. Mr. M. D. Chalmers has contrasted this feature of the English law of bills with the French law on the same subject, in the following words: "The English theory," says he, "may be called the banking or currency theory, as opposed to the French or mercantile theory. A bill of exchange in its origin was an instrument by which a trade debt due in one place was transferred in another. This theory the French law keeps steadily in view. In England bills have developed into a perfectly flexible paper currency. In France a bill represents a trade transaction; in England it is merely an instrument of credit. English law gives full play to the system of accommodation paper; French law endeavors to stamp it out."[8]

The same author truthfully points out that while the French law on this subject reached an earlier maturity, it has

---

[8] Chalmers, in Bills of Exchange, 5th ed., Introduction, lvii (Benjamin's ed. xi). This writer gives the following illustrations of the differences referred to: "In England it is no longer necessary to express on a bill that value has been given, for the law raises a presumption to that effect. In France the nature of the value must be expressed, and a false statement of value avoids the bill in the hands of all parties with notice. In England a bill may now be drawn and payable in the same place (formerly it was otherwise). In France the place where a bill is drawn must be so far distant from the place where it is payable, that there may be a possible rate of exchange between the two. A false statement of places, so as to evade this rule, avoids the bill in the hands of the holder with notice. As French lawyers put it, a bill of exchange necessarily presupposes a contract of exchange. In England (since 1765) a bill may be drawn payable to bearer, though formerly it was otherwise. In France it must be payable to order; if it were not so, it is clear that the rule requiring the consideration to be expressed would be an absurdity. In England a bill originally payable to order becomes payable to bearer when indorsed in blank. In France an indorsement in blank merely operates as a procuration. An indorsement, to operate as a negotiation, must be an indorsement to order, and must state the consideration; in short, it must conform to the conditions of an original draft. In England, if a bill be refused acceptance, a right of action at once accrues to the holder. This is a logical consequence of the currency theory. In France no cause of action arises unless the bill is again dishonored at maturity; the holder in the meantime is only entitled to demand security from the drawer and indorsers. In England a sharp distinction is drawn between current and overdue bills. In France no such distinction is drawn. In England no protest is required in the case of an inland bill, notice of dishonor alone being sufficient. In France every dishonored bill must be protested."

subsequently suffered from arrested development. English and French law were substantially the same when Beawes wrote (*cir.* 1750). Since then the English law, not being crystallized by codification, has continued to develop along lines marked out by the needs of the mercantile world, while the French law remains practically at the point of evolution which had then been reached.

<small>Chapter XXXVIII</small>

<small>Arrested development of French law of bills.</small>

Lord Mansfield's genius for dispersing the mists of confusion which sometimes accumulate over a subject is shown to its best advantage in *Heylyn v. Adamson* (1758).[9] Owing to the early habit of calling promissory notes bills of exchange, and of speaking of the maker as a drawer, it had happened that language and principles applicable only to notes had been improperly applied to bills of exchange. This had introduced confusion. For instance, the notion was widely current that the drawer of a bill of exchange, even after acceptance, remained primarily liable, and that in a suit against an indorser it was necessary for the holder to show a demand upon the drawer made within reasonable time. How this confusion arose was now clearly shown by Lord Mansfield, and the true distinction between bills of exchange and promissory notes was clearly expounded for the first time.

<small>After acceptance drawer no longer primarily liable.</small>

Edie v. East India Co. (1761)[1] is of almost equal importance. It had been usual from the time the courts first accepted the law merchant as a part of the common law, to allow proof to be introduced as to the usage of merchants and bankers on the particular point involved. It was now held that the finding of a custom contrary to decided law cannot stand and that witnesses ought never to be examined upon a point already settled. The proper function of commercial usage in building up the edifice of the commercial law was thus made clear. Usage can suggest, initiate, and tentatively sanction a new principle, but when the courts have adopted that principle no contrary custom can avail to change it. This contributed much to give firmness and consistency to the law

<small>Custom contrary to settled rule of law invalid.</small>

[9] 2 Burr. 669.   [1] 2 Burr. 1216.

of bills and notes. Prior to the decision in question, the evidence in such cases had too often been jumbled together and left to the jury as a whole. The consequence was that general principles were not readily worked out, and the law of negotiable instruments was in considerable confusion.²

In that case it was said by Wilmot, J.: "There may indeed be some questions depending upon customs amongst merchants, where, if there be a doubt about the custom, it may be fit and proper to take the opinion of merchants thereupon. Yet that is only where the law remains doubtful; and even there the custom must be proved by facts, not by opinion only, and it must also be subject to the control of law." ³

The concrete point decided in *Edie v. East India Co.* is also quite important and worthy of note. A bill being drawn payable to order was specially indorsed "pay to A," without adding the words "or order." The question was raised whether the omission of these words destroyed the negotiability of the note. It was held that it did not and that the note could still be transferred indefinitely. Lord Mansfield said that a draft payable to order is in its origin a bill of exchange and is negotiable. It belongs to the payee and he can use it as best suits his convenience. It is his property. He may assign it as such to whom he pleases. "Direction to pay 'to such a one,' is a direction to pay 'to him or his order,' for he assigns his whole property in it." Denison, J., added: "Where a bill is originally made payable 'to A or order,' it is of course and in its very essence negotiable from hand to hand." In other words, a special indorsement to a

---

² See observations of Buller, J., in Lickbarrow v. Mason, (1787) 2 T. R. 73. He said that within the preceding thirty years the commercial law had taken a very different turn from what it had been before; that Lord Hardwicke himself was proceeding with great caution, not establishing any general principle, but decreeing on all the circumstances put together. "Before that period we find that, in courts of law, all the evidence in mercantile cases was thrown together; they were left generally to a jury; and they produced no established principle. From that time, we all know, the great study has been to find some certain general principles, which shall be known to all mankind, not only to rule the particular case then under consideration, but to serve as a guide for the future."

³ Edie v. East India Co., 2 Burr. 1228.

particular person does not terminate the negotiability of the bill.

In the case just referred to is also to be found the first recognition of the restrictive indorsement. An indorsement is said to be restrictive when it prohibits the further negotiation of the instrument, as ' pay to A only '; when it constitutes the indorsee the agent of the indorser, as ' pay A for collection only '; or when it vests title in the indorsee in trust for or to the use of another.⁴ Wilmot, J., in the same case intimated that such indorsements would be given effect. They do not destroy the actual transferability of the paper, but all subsequent indorsees acquire only the title of the first indorsee under the restrictive indorsement.⁵

In *Ancher v. Bank of England* (1781)⁶ the doctrine announced by Wilmot, J., was accepted. The reasons for its recognition were fully stated later by Lord Tenterden in *Sigourney v. Lloyd* (1828),⁷ and his reasoning was subsequently approved on appeal in the Exchequer Chamber.¹

The Promise to Accept.

Another important case decided while Mansfield was chief justice is found in *Pillans v. Van Mierop* (1765).² It appeared in this case that one White, a merchant of Ireland, desired to draw upon the plaintiffs, merchants in Rotterdam, and offered them credit upon Van Mierop & Hopkins, a house in London. The plaintiffs honored White's draft and then wrote to Van Mierop & Hopkins, desiring to know whether they would accept such bills as the plaintiffs would, in about a month, draw upon them on White's credit. Van Mierop &

---

⁴ Neg. Inst. Law, § 36; N. Y. Act, § 66.
⁵ Neg. Inst. Law, § 37.
⁶ 2 Dougl. 637.
⁷ 8 B. & C. 622, 15 E. C. L. 319, 3 M. & R. 58.
¹ Lloyd v. Sigourney, 5 Bing. 525, 15 E. C. L. 527, 3 M. & P. 229, 3 Y. & J. 220. Lord Tenterden said that restrictive indorsements were then of frequent use. They do not, said he, prevent the indorsee from receiving the money when due, but they do prevent a failing man from disposing of the bill before it becomes due and from pledging it to relieve himself from his own debts at the expense of another. He added that so far from prejudicing the interest of commerce the recognition of this principle would, in his opinion, on the contrary, advance it.
² 3 Burr. 1663.

400 FOUNDATIONS OF LEGAL LIABILITY.

Hopkins notified them that they would honor the drafts. White, however, presently failed and Van Mierop & Hopkins notified the plaintiffs of this fact and forbade them to draw. The plaintiffs nevertheless drew the bills. Thereupon the defendants, Van Mierop & Hopkins, refused to honor the drafts and suit was brought against them. The jury found for the defendants, but the verdict was set aside.

Criticism. Three reasons were assigned for giving judgment in favor of the plaintiffs: (1) that a bill of exchange is good without a consideration; (2) that there was a consideration in fact in that case; and (3) that a promise to accept is the same as an acceptance. The first of these reasons is utterly exploded. But even if it were true that a bill of exchange is good without a consideration, that would afford no ground for holding the defendants in this case unless by their promise to accept they had become a party to the bill. The second reason assigned for the decision goes upon the idea that when the promise to accept was given, the plaintiffs were thereby lulled into a sense of security and might have been thus prevented from getting further security or from resorting to White before his failure. This detriment to the plaintiffs, it was thought, could be treated as a consideration for the defendants' promise to accept.[3] But this is apparently untenable.

It remains to consider the third reason assigned for the decision. Is there any principle of the law merchant by virtue of which a mere promise to accept, not good as a common-law assumpsit, can be treated as an actual acceptance?

The promise to accept. That a promise to accept when supported by a sufficient consideration is binding is clear. But such a promise derives its validity from common-law principles, and the party promising is not liable on the bill. In refusing to accept the bill he refuses to become liable on the bill and can be held only for the breach of his promise to accept. In case of an actual acceptance liability attaches by virtue of the law merchant and the party is bound on the bill. Now there has always been a tendency among merchants to confuse the common-law promise to accept with actual acceptance. This is no doubt

[3] Wilmot, J., in Pillans *v.* Van Mierop, 3 Burr. 1672.

BILLS AND NOTES. 401

partly due to the circumstance that by the custom of merchants verbal acceptances were valid.[4] It never entered the mind of any tradesman that it is anomalous to make one liable on a bill whose name does not appear upon it.

Chapter XXXVIII

Verbal acceptance valid.

The rule being thus settled that a verbal acceptance, which is merely a verbal promise to pay the bill at its maturity, is binding, it is easy to go further and say that a simple promise to accept a bill in the future is good. Marius said that words importing a promise to accept operate as an actual acceptance. "Call on me to-morrow and you shall have it accepted" was, in his opinion, enough.[5] The same principle is recognized by others.[6] None of the writers on the *Lex Mercatoria* seem to mean more than this — that a promise to accept a bill already drawn and then actually presented is an acceptance of that bill.

Qualification.

Now in *Pillans v. Van Microp* (1765)[7] the principle above referred to was pressed so far as to sustain an action on a voluntary promise to accept a bill not then drawn, and this too where the party giving the promise subsequently withdrew it before it was acted on. This was a mistake, and Lord Mansfield himself, in *Pierson v. Dunlop* (1777),[8] qualified the doctrine of the previous case, saying that the promise to accept is not an acceptance unless it is accompanied by circumstances which induce a third person to take the bill by indorsement. In *Johnson v. Collings* (1800),[9] it was held that a mere promise to accept an undrawn bill does not amount to an acceptance after the bill is drawn.[1] Since this decision the English courts have not countenanced the idea that a man can be made liable on a bill when he refuses to accept it, merely because he may have promised, before the bill was drawn, to accept it.

Virtual Acceptance.

In America, however, the doctrine of virtual acceptance, as it is called, has been extensively applied.[2] Thus, if A

---

[4] Jarvis *v.* Wilson, 46 Conn. 90; Dull *v.* Bricker, 76 Pa. St. 255.
[5] Marius, Advice, 16.
[6] See Molloy, Lib. 2, c. 10, § 20.
[7] 3 Burr. 1663.
[8] 2 Cowp. 571.

[9] 1 East 98.
[1] To the same effect, Bank of Ireland *v.* Archer, (1843) 11 M. & W. 383.
[2] Coolidge *v.* Payson, 2 Wheat. (U. S.) 66; Wildes *v.* Savage, 1

promises to accept a bill to be drawn by B, and the latter, acting upon the faith of this promise, draws a bill in conformity with the authority and puts it into circulation, A's promise is treated as a virtual acceptance of that bill.

It is to be observed that in such a case B incurs a legal detriment not only in going to the trouble of drawing the bill, but in taking the risk of damage to his credit and of liability for costs in the event it is dishonored. Hence the promise of A to accept the bill is supported by a good consideration and the promise is binding as a common-law assumpsit. Furthermore, in no case can a virtual acceptance be given effect unless the promise is supported by a consideration.

The conditions usually required to be fulfilled by the American courts before there is held to be a virtual acceptance are three, namely: (1) that the contemplated drawee shall, in the letter describing the bill to be drawn, promise to accept it; (2) that the bill shall be drawn in a reasonable time after the letter is written; and (3) that the holder shall take the bill upon the faith of the promise.[3]

The doctrine of virtual acceptance is subject to criticism in respect to the fact that it results from a confusion of a common-law liability with liability under the law merchant. When a man contracts to accept a bill but afterwards refuses to do so, he is liable for his breach of contract, but he is not, strictly speaking, liable on the bill.

The American doctrine of virtual acceptance, moreover, is not without certain advantages. In England the modern cases have kept the two sorts of liability distinct, and the trouble there experienced in working out a satisfactory theory by which to protect those who advance money on the bill is illustrated in *In re Agra, etc., Bank* (1867),[4] where a bill was negotiated on the faith of a letter of credit given by a bank to the drawer. The letter[5] was unquestionably a general

---

Story (U. S.) 27; Gates *v.* Parker, 43 Me. 544; Central Sav. Bank *v.* Richards, 109 Mass. 413; Johnson *v.* Clark, 39 N. Y. 216.

[3] 2 Ames, Cases on Bills and Notes, 788.

[4] L. R. 2 Ch. 391.

[5] It was in the following terms: "No. 394. You are hereby authorized to draw upon this bank at six months' sight, to the extent of £15,000 sterling, and such drafts I

BILLS AND NOTES. 403

offer, and when it was acted upon by any bank to which it was presented a binding contract resulted. In order to protect such a bank the English court was compelled to treat this contract right as being negotiable to the extent of cutting off all equities existing between the bank and its customers. Where such a contract is treated as an acceptance, as is done by the majority of the American courts, no difficulty is experienced in reaching this end at once.[6]

Chapter XXXVIII

Bill Payable to Fictitious Party.

In *Minet v. Gibson* (1789)[7] an important step was taken looking towards the protection of innocent purchasers and the establishment of the currency theory on a still firmer basis. This case presented for consideration the question of the negotiability of a bill drawn in favor of a fictitious payee, indorsed in the name of such fictitious party by the drawer, accepted with knowledge, and subsequently transferred for value to an innocent party by the drawer. A divided court held that such a bill could be treated as payable to bearer, and it was suggested that an action might also be maintained by the holder against the acceptor as upon a bill payable to the order of the drawer. There was undoubtedly some previous authority supporting the view that a bill payable to a fictitious party is, or may be treated as, payable to bearer, but the decision to a certain degree ignores the tenor of the instrument. Lord Chief Baron Eyre dissented, and delivered what has sometimes been thought to be an unanswerable argument against the negotiability of such an instrument. The majority was against him. Lord Mansfield had given paramount weight to the character of the bill as a circulating medium, and had

Treated as payable to bearer.

---

undertake duly to honor on presentation. This credit will remain in force for twelve months from this date, and parties negotiating bills under it are requested to indorse particulars on the back hereof. The bills must specify that they are drawn under credit, No. 394, of the 31st of October. 1865."

"It is worth observing that the doctrine of virtual acceptance is embodied in the American Negotiable Instruments Law, though the term virtual acceptance is not there used. See Neg. Inst. Law, § 135; N. Y. Act, § 223.

[7] 3 T. R. 481, on appeal in House of Lords, Gibson v. Minet (1791), 1 H. Bl. 569, 625.

404   FOUNDATIONS OF LEGAL LIABILITY.

Volume II

thrown around innocent holders the highest possible degree of protection. In so doing he struck the keynote of the future.

Exchequer bill.

In *Wookey v. Pole* (1820),[8] the exchequer bill was for the first time declared to rest upon the same footing as notes of the Bank of England and to pass by delivery so long as the blank is not filled.

During the first years of the nineteenth century the question as to what is necessary to constitute a *bona fide* holder was *Bona fide holder.* much discussed, and as decisions on this important point at first showed much vacillation, it will be well to notice them.

Lord Mansfield long ago said that " where money or notes are paid *bona fide* and upon a valuable consideration, they never shall be brought back by the true owner; but where they come *mala fide* into a person's hands, they are in the nature of specific property, and if their identity can be traced and ascertained, the party has a right to recover."[9] The *Notice of defect.* question therefore often arises, to be determined on the particular facts of each case, what circumstances are sufficient to fix notice upon a purchaser and deprive him of the complete protection which is thrown around innocent purchasers for value.

In *Lawson v. Weston* (1801)[1] it appeared that a bill for five hundred pounds had been lost or stolen after having been accepted by the drawee and indorsed by the payee. The person who found, or stole, the bill took it to the plaintiffs, who discounted it in the usual course of their business. The person presenting the bill was not known to the plaintiffs, but the bill had been drawn in their neighborhood and the signatures of the several parties were recognized by the plaintiffs as genuine. It was held that the plaintiffs could recover on *Purchaser not bound to inquire into antecedents of paper.* this bill against the acceptor. It was insisted for the defendant that a banker or other person to whom a bill of this value is presented by a stranger to be discounted should be required to use diligence to inquire into the circumstances, as well re-

[8] 4 B. & Ald. 1, 6 E. C. L. 365.   [1] 4 Esp. 56.
[9] Clarke *v.* Shee, 1 Cowp. 197.

specting the bill as of the person who offers it for discount. But this contention was put aside, Lord Kenyon observing that the adoption of this principle would tend to paralyze the circulation of all the paper in the country and with it all the commerce. But he added that if there had been any fraud on the part of the plaintiffs or if they had not paid value the result would have been different. Indeed, in *Solomons v. Bank of England* (1791),[2] the same learned judge had held that where the circumstances are such as to lead to the inference that at the time a bill was taken in negotiation the party taking it knew or ought to have known that the transaction was tainted with fraud, he could not recover.

In *Gill v. Cubitt* (1824),[3] the Court of King's Bench assumed a decidedly reactionary attitude. The facts were as follows: A properly indorsed bill of exchange was fraudulently abstracted from a letter while in transit. The next morning the bill was presented for discount to the plaintiff, a bill broker in London, by a person having a respectable appearance and whose features were familiar to the broker, but whose name was unknown. He desired that the bill might be discounted, but this was at first refused by the broker, because the acceptor was unknown to him. The person who brought the bill then said that a few days before he had brought other bills to the office, and that if inquiry was made it would be found that the parties whose names were on the bill were highly respectable. He then quitted the office and left the bill, and upon inquiry the broker was satisfied with the names of the acceptors. The stranger returned after a lapse of two hours and indorsed the bill in the name of Charles Taylor, and received the full value for it, the usual discount and a commission of two shillings being deducted. The broker did not ask the name of the person who brought the bill, or his address, or whether he brought it on his own account or otherwise, or how he came by the bill. It was the practice in the broker's office not to make any inquiries about the drawer or other parties to a bill, provided the acceptor was good.

[2] 13 East 135, note.   [3] 3 B. & C. 466, 10 E. C. L. 154.

In an action brought by the broker against the acceptors of the bill, Abbott, C. J., told the jury that there were two questions for their consideration; first, whether the plaintiff, the broker, had given value for the bill, of which there could be no doubt; and, secondly, whether he took it under circumstances which ought to have excited the suspicion of a prudent and careful man. If they thought he had taken the bill under such circumstances, then, notwithstanding he had given the full value for it, they ought to find a verdict for the defendant. Then the chief justice, after stating the evidence and commenting upon the practice in the plaintiff's office of discounting bills for any persons whose features were known to him, but whose names and abode were unknown, without asking any questions, asked the jury what they would think if a board were affixed over an office with this notice, "Bills discounted for persons whose features are known, and no questions asked."

The plaintiff moved for a new trial on the ground of misdirection, and it was insisted that the case had been put too strongly to the jury. The court, however, was of the opinion that although the trial judge may have been too emphatic, the jury had drawn the right inference, and the motion was denied. The court expressed its disapproval of *Lawson v. Weston* (1801),[4] and in effect overruled that decision.

Gill v. Cubitt at once became the refuge of parties seeking to impeach the transfer of bills, and though the decision was followed for a while,[5] its doctrine did not long remain unquestioned. In *Crook v. Jadis* (1834),[6] Lord Denman rejected the idea that in order to constitute an innocent purchaser one must use due caution and must not take the bill under circumstances which ought to excite the suspicion of a prudent man. Instead of this he laid down the doctrine that it requires gross negligence to deprive a purchaser of the rights of a *bona fide* holder. The other judges approved of the departure.

[4] 4 Esp. 56.
[5] Down v. Halling, 4 B. & C. 330, 10 E. C. L. 347; Snow v. Peacock, 3 Bing. 408; Beckwith v. Corral, 4 Bing. 444, 13 E. C. L. 44.
[6] 5 B. & Ad. 909, 27 E. C. L. 234.

The new rule, however, proved to be only a temporary makeshift. It was applied in *Backhouse v. Harrison* (1834),[7] but in *Goodman v. Harvey* (1836),[8] Lord Denman said: "We are all of the opinion that gross negligence only would not be a sufficient answer where the party has given a consideration for the bill. Gross negligence may be evidence of *mala fides*, but it is not the same thing. We have shaken off the last remnant of the contrary doctrine. Where the bill has passed to the plaintiff without any proof of bad faith in him, there is no objection to his title."

In *Jones v. Gordon* (1877),[9] Lord Blackburn said in the House of Lords: "If value be given for a bill of exchange, it is not enough to show that there was carelessness, negligence, or foolishness in not suspecting that the bill was wrong when there were circumstances which might have led a man to suspect that. All these are matters which tend to show that there was dishonesty in not doing it, but they do not in themselves make a defense to an action upon a bill of exchange. . . . It is necessary to show that the person who gave value for the bill, whether the value be great or small, was affected with notice that there was something wrong about it when he took it. I do not think it is necessary that he should have notice of what the particular wrong was. If a man, knowing that a bill was in the hands of a person who had no right to it, should happen to think that perhaps the man had stolen it, when if he had known the real truth he would have found, not that the man had stolen it, but that he had obtained it by false pretenses, I think that would not make any difference if he knew that there was something wrong about it and took it. If he takes it in that way he takes it at his peril. But then I think that such evidence of carelessness or blindness as I have referred to may with other evidence be good evidence upon the question which, I take it, is the real one, whether he did know that there was something wrong in it."

[7] 5 B. & Ad. 1098, 27 E. C. L. 276.
[8] 4 Ad. & El. 870, 31 E. C. L. 212. To the same effect, Uther v. Rich, 10 Ad. & El. 784, 37 E. C. L. 232; Arbouin v. Anderson, 1 Q. B. 498, 41 E. C. L. 642; May v. Chapman, 16 M. & W. 355.
[9] 2 App. Cas. 628.

In America early cases are to be found following the doctrine of *Gill v. Cubitt*, but it is repudiated by the great weight of authority in both federal and state jurisdictions.[1]

Once valid always negotiable.

One of the most effective steps taken in order to protect the rights of the innocent holder is found in the decision that an innocent purchaser can transmit a good and perfect title to one who has knowledge of a defect in the origin of the instrument, though the transferee may not have given value. It is obvious that if C be a purchaser for value, he has good title and may dispose of the instrument in any lawful manner he sees fit. To require him to go out and seek a buyer or transferee who has no knowledge of the pre-existing defects would impose unnecessary hardship on him and often cripple the circulation of commercial paper. Once valid, always negotiable until dishonored at maturity, is the rule.[2]

---

[1] Swift *v.* Tyson, 16 Pet. (U. S.) 1; Goodman *v.* Simonds 20 How. (U. S.) 343; Shaw *v.* Railroad Co., 101 U. S. 564; Clark *v.* Evans, (C. C. A.) 66 Fed. Rep. 263; Credit Co. *v.* Howe Mach. Co., 54 Conn. 357; Matthews *v.* Poythress, 4 Ga. 287; Comstock *v.* Hannah, 76 Ill. 530; Mann *v.* Springfield Second Nat. Bank, 30 Kan. 412; Maitland *v.* Citizens Nat. Bank, 40 Md. 540; Lee *v.* Whitney, 149 Mass. 447; International Trust Co. *v.* Wilson, 161 Mass. 80; Bottomley *v.* Goldsmith, 36 Mich. 27; Hamilton *v.* Marks, 63 Mo. 167; Rublee *v.* Davis, 33 Neb. 779; Merriam *v.* Rockwood, 47 N. H. 81; National Bank of Republic *v.* Young, 41 N. J. Eq. 531; Magee *v.* Badger, 34 N. Y. 247; Chapman *v.* Rose, 56 N. Y. 140; Phelan *v.* Moss, 67 Pa. St. 59; Parkersburg First Nat. Bank *v.* Johns, 22 W. Va. 520.

[2] May *v.* Chapman, (1847) 16 M. & W. 355; Masters *v.* Ibberson, (1849) 8 C. B. 100, 65 E. C. L. 100; Marion County *v.* Clark, 94 U. S. 286; Byles on Bills (5th Am. ed.) 118; Story on Notes, § 196; Story on Bills, § 220.

CHAPTER XXXIX

BILLS AND NOTES (CONTINUED).

Common-Law Principles Ingrafted upon the Law Merchant.

FROM what has been said it appears that the modern law of bills and notes, as well as other branches of commercial law, is a product of the interplay of mercantile custom and common-law principle. It is naturally to be expected that the finished result should be a body of doctrine quite different from that which either factor would have produced without assistance from the other. In the preceding chapters we have dealt with features of the law merchant in which the impress of mercantile custom is most manifest. In this chapter we propose to consider certain principles which are of purely common-law origin. Here, we shall perceive, the common-law doctrine has, so to speak, been ingrafted on the principles of the law merchant.

<small>Chapter XXXIX</small>

<small>Law of bills and notes a product of interplay between custom and law.</small>

The virtual acceptance, already dealt with, furnishes an obvious instance. Here a common-law promise to accept is treated to all intents and purposes as an acceptance under the law merchant. The common-law contract has thus become attached as a sort of parasite to the mercantile contract.

<small>Virtual acceptance.</small>

The requirement of a consideration is sometimes thought to afford an instance where a common-law principle has been forced upon the law merchant by the common-law courts. But this is not exactly true; for, as we have already seen, the requirement of a consideration originally inhered in the bill of exchange under the custom of merchants. Mercantile usage both in England and abroad required that the bill should issue from a mercantile transaction and be given for value received, usually in merchandise. The common law, however, undoubtedly supplied a congenial atmosphere where this feature of the law merchant could attain full recognition, and

<small>Requirement of consideration.</small>

Liability of purported agent.

the principle in question was therefore duly cherished and maintained by the English courts when they came to sanction the principles of the law merchant.[1]

The Negotiable Instruments Law supplies us with the following instance where a common-law liability has been ingrafted upon the law merchant. Section 20 of that law provides that a person who adds to his signature words indicating that he acts as agent for another shall be personally liable on the instrument, if he be not in fact authorized to bind his principal.[2] Thus if A, without authority, signs as 'A, agent for B,' or 'B by A,' he is liable to the same extent as if he had signed as 'A' only. The instrument is thus given an effect contrary to its tenor. The innovation embodied in this section of the statute has been subjected to criticism,[3] but the

---

[1] Notwithstanding the incontrovertible fact that there must always be a consideration moving from some one in the chain of persons through whom title to a bill is derived before such instrument can be enforced, it is nevertheless true that by a rule prevailing in some foreign countries and erroneously adopted in England, a bill or note could formerly be there discharged by parol and without any consideration being given for such discharge. The law was so declared in Foster v. Dawber (1851), 6 Exch. 839, where the Court of Exchequer accepted the civil-law doctrine of renunciation as applicable to bills and notes, and held that the writing of a receipt in full upon a promissory note operated as a discharge of the note, when so intended, and this though nothing was paid, nor the instrument itself surrendered.

The decision in question has never been expressly overruled in England, but its doctrine is now abrogated by the Bills of Exchange Act, § 62, which requires that a renunciation, unaccompanied by a surrender of the instrument, must be in writing in order to be effective. In America, Foster v. Dawber has had no following whatever.

Parke, B., delivered the opinion in Foster v. Dawber, and he found some support in a loose and doubtful suggestion in Byles on Bills. His language shows an erroneous conception of the law merchant and of the manner in which its principles have become a part of the common law. Said he: "No person is liable on a bill of exchange except through the law merchant; and probably, the law merchant being introduced into this country, and differing very much from the simplicity of the common law, at the same time was introduced that rule quoted from Pailliet as prevailing in foreign countries, viz., that there may be a release and discharge from a debt by express words, although unaccompanied by satisfaction or by any solemn instrument. Such appears to be the law of France."

Here the law merchant is viewed as a finished product of foreign jurisprudence transplanted into England and there maintained as a separate body of law regardless of common-law doctrine.

[2] Neg. Inst. Law, § 20; N. Y. Act, § 39.

[3] The Negotiable Instruments Law, J. B. Ames, 14 Harv. L. Rev. 247.

rule conforms with the provision of the modern German Exchange Law on this point and meets with pretty general approval.[4]

Another instance where a common-law liability has been ingrafted upon the law merchant is found in section 137 of the same enactment. This section provides that "where a drawee to whom a bill is delivered for acceptance destroys the same, or refuses within twenty-four hours after such delivery, or within such other period as the holder may allow, to return the bill accepted or not accepted to the holder, he will be deemed to have accepted the same."[5] One who destroys a bill or improperly detains it from the owner thereby converts it, and to hold him liable as for an acceptance plainly has the effect of turning a common-law liability into a liability under the law merchant.

The wisdom and propriety of inserting this provision in the Negotiable Instruments Law have been questioned,[6] but with this we are not concerned. The provision in question goes on the idea that the retention of a bill operates at least as a constructive acceptance. This notion was originally suggested by Lord Ellenborough in *Harvey v. Martin* (1808)[7] and in *Jeune v. Ward* (1818),[8] but the other judges did not favor its adoption. Accordingly the doctrine that a drawee accepts a bill merely by retaining it did not gain currency prior to the enactment of the present law.

Warranties Incident to Transfer of Commercial Paper.

The most important common-law liability which has been attached to the bill in the manner above indicated is a liability imported, we may say, from the law of sales. This is found in the rule that the transferor of a bill or note, in addition to the liability which he incurs by virtue of the law merchant, warrants certain things to his transferee and to persons into whose hands the instrument may subsequently come.

[4] The Negotiable Instruments Law, Chas. L. McKeehan, 41 Am. L. Reg. N. S. 462, 465.
[5] Neg. Inst. Law, § 137; N. Y. Act, § 225.
[6] The Negotiable Instruments Law, J. B. Ames, 14 Harv. L. Rev. 245.
[7] 1 Campb. 425, note.
[8] 1 B. & Ald. 653.

<small>Volume II</small>

From the first recognition of the transferability of bills and notes, indorsement has operated both as a transfer of title and as a conditional engagement or contract on the part of the indorser that he will pay the instrument in case of its dishonor. This conditional liability was placed upon the indorser because he was viewed as a new drawer. From the nature of this conditional undertaking of the indorser certain necessary corollaries follow. For instance, just as the acceptor is precluded from denying the existence of the drawer, the genuineness of his signature, and his capacity and authority to draw the bill, as well as the existence of the payee and his then capacity to indorse;[9] and just as the drawer is precluded from denying to the holder in due course the existence of the payee and his then capacity to indorse;[1] so the indorser is not permitted to deny the genuineness and regularity of the drawer's signature, nor the genuineness of any previous indorsement, nor that the instrument was a valid bill at the time of the transfer, nor that his own title was good and effective.[2]

<small>Undertaking of (1) acceptor, (2) drawer, (3) indorser.</small>

The reason for these holdings is found in the principle that the indorser cannot set up defenses inconsistent with his promise of indemnity. He is obligated to pay if the paper is dishonored, and the courts have not permitted this obligation to be undermined. The English courts have been inclined to treat the rules referred to as arising upon the principles of estoppel. We accordingly find them using such expressions as 'the indorser is precluded from denying,' 'estop the indorser to deny,' or 'the indorser admits.' This is also the language used in the English Bill of Exchange Act.[3] In America the term 'warranty' has come into use in this connec-

<small>Estoppel of indorser.</small>

<small>Warranty of indorser.</small>

<small>[9] Cooper v. Meyer, (1830) 10 B. & C. 468, 21 E. C. L. 116; Sanderson v. Collman, (1842) 4 M. & G. 209, 43 E. C. L. 115; Drayton v. Dale, (1823) 2 B. & C. 293, 9 E. C. L. 91; 41 Am. L. Reg. N. S. 562.
[1] Collis v. Emett, (1790) 1 H. Bl. 313; Phillips v. Im Thurn, (1865) 18 C. B. N. S. 694, 114 E. C. L. 694.

[2] Ex p. Clarke, 3 Bro. C. C. 238; Thicknesse v. Bromilow, 2 Cromp. & J. 425; Macgregor v. Rhodes, 6 El. & Bl. 266, 88 E. C. L. 266; Burchfield v. Moore, 3 El. & Bl. 683, 77 E. C. L. 683, 23 L. J. Q. B. 261. See The Negotiable Instruments Law, by C. L. McKeehan, 41 Am. L. Reg. N. S. 563.
[3] §§ 54, 55.</small>

tion, and is used in the American Negotiable Instruments Law to express the same idea.

Thus far, it will be perceived, the liability of the transferor can be said to be derived strictly from the principles of the law merchant. The transferor becomes liable, under the law merchant, however, only by virtue of the fact that his name is written on the back of the paper. If a note payable to bearer is transferred by delivery only, the law merchant attaches no liability whatever to the transferor. Such paper may circulate indefinitely without carrying any marks to show through whose hands it has passed, and no liability can arise under the law merchant unless the person upon whom liability is sought to be imposed is in some way a party to the bill.

We now come to consider the position of the transferor when the transfer is viewed in the light of a sale of chattels. The common law has much to say concerning liability growing out of this aspect of the transaction. Here the word warranty has a familiar sound. The implied warranty of the title of the vendor has long been familiar. In America our law recognizes the implied warranty that a thing sold is what it purports to be. In England the same end is reached by holding that it is a condition of the principal contract that the thing delivered shall, in essence and in substance, be the thing which was contracted for.[4]

That the common-law principles worked out in the law of sales should be applied to sales of negotiable paper was both inevitable and logical. The Negotiable Instruments Law shows how the two streams of doctrine, one emerging directly from the law merchant and the other from the common law of sales, have blended and become fused together into one harmonious body of principle in a most remarkable way.

Observe the language of the statute on this point, here slightly transposed: "Every indorser who indorses without qualification, engages that on due presentment the instrument shall be accepted or paid, or both, as the case may be, according to its tenor, and that if it be dishonored and the necessary proceedings on dishonor be duly taken, he will pay

[4] Meyer v. Richards, 163 U. S. 385.

414   FOUNDATIONS OF LEGAL LIABILITY.

the amount thereof to the holder or to any subsequent indorser who may be compelled to pay it."[5] This is a perfectly clear statement of the duty originally imposed by the custom of merchants and sanctioned by the courts.

But the undertaking of the indorser who indorses without qualification is further defined thus: "[He] warrants, to all subsequent holders in due course, 1. That the instrument is genuine and in all respects what it purports to be; 2. That he has a good title to it; 3. That all prior parties had capacity to contract, and that the instrument is at the time of his indorsement valid and subsisting."[6] Certainly one of these warranties (i. e., that as to the capacity of prior parties), and possibly others, may be drawn from the general principle underlying the liability of the indorser; but they all have the distinct flavor of the common-law principles applicable to sales, and are couched in language drawn from that source.

It will be seen that the undertakings or warranties of the indorser, whether derived from the law merchant or from the principles of sale, are completely ingrafted upon the instrument and pass with it to all subsequent holders in due course. In strict common-law theory the warranty of the seller of a bill, like the warranty of a vendor of a chattel, would inure only to the benefit of his immediate indorsee as vendee.

The warranty of the transferor by delivery of a bill payable to bearer and of an indorser without recourse is stated in the Negotiable Instruments Law as follows: "Every person negotiating an instrument by delivery or by a qualified indorsement, warrants — 1. That the instrument is genuine and in all respects what it purports to be; 2. That he has a good title to it; 3. That all prior parties had capacity to contract; 4. That he has no knowledge of any fact which would impair the validity of the instrument or render it valueless. But when the negotiation is by delivery only, the warranty extends in favor of no holder other than the immediate transferee."[7] The liability of such a transferor is manifestly deduced wholly

---

[5] Neg. Inst. Law, § 66, final paragraph.
[6] This is the combined effect of language in §§ 65, 66 (N. Y. Act, §§ 115, 116).
[7] Neg. Inst. Law, § 65.

from common-law principles of sale applied with due regard to the particular circumstances involved and with an eye to the needs of the commercial community.

It will be observed that when the transfer is by delivery only, the warranty does not extend to all subsequent holders, but only to the immediate vendee. The anomaly of having one whose name is not on the instrument, held liable to remote holders in an action upon the bill, is thus avoided.

Chapter XXXIX

Warranty inures to immediate vendee only.

On the other hand, the indorser without recourse may be held liable by any holder on the common-law warranty. This apparently lands us in a dilemma. The indorser without recourse by the express terms of his contract cannot be made liable on his indorsement under the principles of the law merchant. But the statute makes him liable on his warranty at the suit of any holder. Here, then, common law and mercantile theory cannot fuse; and the statute operates to modify the legal effect of the indorsement without recourse in a very material degree.

Distinctions.

A further distinction between the warranty of the ordinary indorser and that of the transferor by delivery or by qualified indorsement is to be noted. The former absolutely undertakes and warrants that the instrument is valid and subsisting at the time of his indorsement; the latter only warrants that he has no knowledge of any defect that would impair its value or render it worthless. In other words, as against the transferor by delivery and as against the indorser without recourse notice of any defect must be proved.[8]

Conclusion.

In the preceding pages we have sketched the process by which the law merchant, at first sanctioned only by the usages of a particular class of men, finally obtained the approval of

[8] There are some authorities which favor the distinction here indicated, but the propriety of introducing the distinction into the statute has been questioned. Crawford's Neg. Inst. Law, § 115, note: The Negotiable Instruments Law, 41 Am. L. Reg. N. S. 569. See generally, Challiss v. McCrum, 22 Kan. 157; Meyer v. Richards, 163 U. S. 385; Watson v. Chesire, 18 Iowa 202; Littauer v. Goldman, 72 N. Y. 506; Daskam v. Ullman, 74 Wis. 474.

the English courts and thereby became a part of the common law. The growth of the law of bills and notes is thus highly instructive. It furnishes us in very modern times with an illustration of the way in which the common law has been created. We are here able to behold the special custom in the very process of becoming a part of the 'law of the realm,' which, as the judges used to be fond of saying, is the common law.

Nothing is more characteristic of common law than the manner in which the special custom of merchants, having now attained to maturity, was dealt with by lawyers and judges; for no sooner had the law merchant been fully recognized as a part of the general law than the courts proceeded to clothe it with the fiction of antecedent immortality. Though the exact period when the most important mercantile usages originated and were sanctioned by the courts can be pointed out, nothing is more familiar in the older declarations on bills than allegations of immemorial usage approved by the courts for a time beyond which the memory of man runneth not to the contrary.[9] Such conceits no longer engage the attention of even the pleader, and in the latest decisions, such as *Bechuanaland Exploration Co. v. London Trading Bank* (1898),[1] it is rightly declared that usage originating within the memory of living persons can operate to create a valid custom under the principles of the law merchant.

The law merchant is often conceived as a body of substantive legal principle entirely distinct from the common law and antagonistic to it. This is a mistake. The modern law merchant differs, to be sure, from the great mass of common-law rules in important particulars. It originated in the special customs of a particular class of men. Its principles have an ascertainable origin within historic times. Furthermore, the customs which have obtained the sanction of law are concerned with a particular class of transactions. Such are the features which distinguish the law merchant from the body of the common law; but we must not think of the relation as being one of antagonism. Commercial law is now as much

[9] See Chitty on Bills, 559. [1] 2 Q. B. 658.

a part of the common law as any other element in its make-up, and it is not to be regarded, as it sometimes is, as a fully developed body of extraneous law imported into England and there subsisting as an anomalous mass in a more or less independent state.

In *Goodwin v. Robarts* (1875),[2] Cockburn, C. J., gave the following account of the manner in which the principles of the law merchant were judicially approved and developed in the English courts: " It [the law merchant] " said he, " is neither more nor less than the usages of merchants and traders in the different departments of trade, ratified by the decisions of courts of law, which, upon such usages being proved before them, have adopted them as settled law with a view to the interests of trade and the public convenience, the court proceeding herein on the well-known principle of law that, with reference to transactions in the different departments of trade, courts of law, in giving effect to the contracts and dealings of the parties, will assume that the latter have dealt with one another on the footing of any custom or usage prevailing generally in the particular department. By this process, what before was usage only, unsanctioned by legal decision, has become ingrafted upon, or incorporated into, the common law, and may thus be said to form part of it." [3]

In studying the development of this branch of the law the student will be impressed with the fact that the term 'law merchant' is rather vague and deceptive. In the common use of the term it is taken to import a fact that is not strictly true, namely, that the body of law to which it refers is something which has a separate and distinct existence and that it rests upon foundations entirely different from those which support other branches of common-law doctrine. There is no law merchant in any such sense. To say of a particular rule that it is derived from the law merchant is too often accepted as sufficient to put an end to inquiry. But this of itself explains nothing. The expression, however, is useful and instructive if it is taken only as pointing to a body of legal

[2] L. R. 10 Exch. 357.
[3] To the same effect see Cudahy Packing Co. v. State Nat. Bank, (C. C. A.) 134 Fed. Rep. 542 *et seq.*

principle which has peculiar sources and peculiar characteristics and is applicable to particular kinds of transactions.[4]

[4] See What Is the Law Merchant, by F. M. Burdick, 2 Columbia L. Rev. 470; also, What Is the Law Merchant, by J. S. Ewart, 3 Columbia L. Rev. 135.

In these articles the reader will find an interesting discussion of the question whether there is really after all such a thing as a law merchant. Professor Burdick contends that there is, or at least was. Mr. Ewart contends, on the other hand, that there is not and never was a law merchant in the sense of a definite, definable, and independent body of legal truth.

CHAPTER XL

TRANSFERABLE SECURITIES.

As we find points at which common-law doctrine has modified the pure law merchant as applicable to bills and notes, so we find points at which the law merchant has modified the common-law principles applicable to contracts analogous to bills and notes, but not within their accepted description. This brings us to the subject of non-negotiable contracts. In observing the phenomena met with in this field, the reader will soon learn to be on his guard against dogmatism. There is certainly no branch of the law where actual facts are of more value. The whole field is characterized by continuous growth.

Chapter XL

Law merchant as modificative of common-law principle.

Transferable Bonds, Coupons, and Debentures.

The gradual recognition of the negotiable character of transferable bonds, coupons, and debentures in England can best be traced in a few of the leading decisions made during the last century. In *Glyn v. Baker* (1811),[1] it appeared that sealed bonds of the East India Company were made payable to a specified person, his executors, administrators, or assigns, by indorsement. In a suit for the conversion of such bonds, it was held that they were not negotiable and that consequently the rightful owner of them might recover their value in an action for money had and received against an innocent purchaser for value. In this case there was no evidence that the bonds in question were accustomably transferable from hand to hand in fact, and the question whether instruments not strictly within the law merchant could acquire transferability by modern usage so as to protect innocent purchasers was not squarely raised.

Sealed bonds payable to assigns.

[1] 13 East 509.

420   FOUNDATIONS OF LEGAL LIABILITY.

Bonds payable to holder.

In *Gorgier v. Mieville* (1824),² it appeared that bonds of the King of Prussia were marketed in England, in which he declared himself and his successors bound " to every person who should for the time being be the holder of the bond " for the payment of the principal and interest in a certain manner. One of the bonds had been deposited by the plaintiff with A & Co., to hold the same for plaintiff's benefit. The depositary, in violation of the trust, pledged the bond to the defendants. In this case it was shown in proof that foreign bonds such as these were sold in the market and passed from hand to hand daily, like exchequer bills, at a variable price according to the state of the market. Upon these facts Abbott, C. J., said the bonds in question were precisely analogous to a bank note payable to bearer, or to a bill of exchange indorsed in blank, and that being of the same description, they were subject to the same rule of law. Whoever was the holder of the bond, therefore, had the power to give a perfect title to an innocent purchaser for value.

Foreign bonds passing from hand to hand.

In *Atty.-Gen. v. Bouwens* (1838),³ the transferable character of foreign bonds which pass from hand to hand by delivery only was further recognized. In *Partridge v. Bank of England* (1846),⁴ the question was as to the negotiability of dividend warrants issued by the Bank of England. It was pleaded and proved that, according to the usage and custom of bankers and merchants used and approved in London for sixty years, all such dividend warrants were transferable by delivery only, and without indorsement, and that the *bona fide* holder of every such warrant was, according to such custom, entitled to receive payment of the money on demand. Such was the custom, although the warrants were not in terms made payable to bearer. The negotiable character of such warrants was denied. The custom relied on was local, and the plea of innocent purchase was defective. Tindal, C. J., was careful to state that it by no means followed from the decision then made that mercantile usage might not in some cases be allowed to operate.

Dividend warrants of Bank of England.

² 3 B. & C. 45, 10 E. C. L. 16.   ⁴ 9 Q. B. 396, 58 E. C. L. 396.
³ 4 M. & W. 171.

Some important suggestions as to the manner in which the law merchant is incorporated into common law were made in *Brandao v. Barnett* (1846).[5] In this case, speaking of the bankers' lien, Lord Campbell said: "When a general usage has been judicially ascertained and established, it becomes a part of the law merchant which courts of justice are bound to know and recognize. . . . Justice could not be administered if evidence were required to be given *toties quoties* to support such usages, and issue might be joined upon them in each particular case." By the term 'law merchant' is evidently here meant the mass of rules which the common-law courts recognize as applicable in general to mercantile transactions. It was accordingly held that the custom giving bankers a general lien was to be judicially noticed and was a part of the law merchant in the sense indicated.

Chapter XL

Bankers' lien.

In *Lang v. Smyth* (1831),[6] Neapolitan bonds with attached coupons payable to bearer were pledged without authority to an innocent purchaser. It appeared that the coupons were never circulated or transferred without the bonds. These obligations were such that it might now seem proper for the court upon the face of the instrument to instruct the jury that they were negotiable; but as they were foreign securities and their status had never been established, and as no evidence was furnished as to their status in the country of their origin, the jury was allowed to determine whether they were by usage transferable in fact. The jury found that they were not, and this was held fatal to their negotiability. The conclusion to be drawn from this case is that although an instrument may contain nothing on its face inconsistent with the character of negotiability, still if it be not accustomably transferable, it will not be treated by the courts as a negotiable instrument.

Negotiability of foreign securities left to jury.

It will be noted that the securities involved in the cases of *Gorgier v. Mieville* and *Atty.-Gen. v. Bouwens* were foreign. There is apparently nothing inconsistent with sound principle in recognizing a right which is given to the holder of a foreign instrument by the law of the country in which it was made

[5] 12 Cl. & F. 787.   [6] 7 Bing. 284, 20 E. C. L. 130.

and in which it is to be discharged. Whether the same principles are applicable in an English court in passing upon English securities is an entirely different question, and was squarely presented for the first time in *Crouch v. Credit Foncier* (1873).⁷

In this case an English joint stock company had issued debentures expressed to be payable to bearer, which, from the conditions contained in the debentures, could not be held to be promissory notes. One of the debentures had been stolen and had been purchased by the plaintiff without knowledge of the theft. The company, having had notice of the robbery, refused to pay the amount due on the debenture to the plaintiff, and thereupon the action was brought by him as holder of the debenture to recover the amount, and was defended in the name of the company by the person from whom it had been stolen.

The question was, therefore, whether the plaintiff, who had taken the debenture for value without notice of the theft, was entitled in his own name and for his own benefit to recover the money secured by the instrument. The judgment of the Court of Queen's Bench was delivered by Blackburn, J. His learned opinion is instructive, but the conclusion reached was reactionary. This judgment, as we shall hereafter see, has since been many times examined in the higher English courts with great thoroughness, and it is now in effect overruled. The position taken by this learned judge is that the law merchant as a body of legal rules applicable to certain classes of contracts is a closed book, and that no amount of modern usage can avail to bring within the English law merchant any other contracts than those which were in it by ancient custom. Statutes may do so, but not commercial usage. Those who view the law merchant as a perfectly independent body of law altogether separate from the common law and totally irreconcilable with it are likely to approve this decision.¹ Those who perceive that the law merchant and the common law have become amalgamated and that the

---

⁷ L. R. 8 Q. B. 374.
¹ See Law Merchant and Transferable Debentures, by F. A. Bosanquet, 15 L. Quar. Rev. 130.

two have thus produced a new mass of rules of different complexion from that originally borne by either, are likely to pronounce it unsound.[2]

Lord Blackburn's conclusions did not remain long unchallenged. In *Goodwin v. Robarts* (1875),[3] government scrip, binding the authorities issuing it to deliver bonds of a specified denomination in exchange therefor upon compliance with certain conditions, was held to be transferable in accordance with commercial usage, and the title of an innocent purchaser was declared to be perfect though he obtained it from one who negotiated it unlawfully. The judgment of the Court of Exchequer Chamber was rendered by Lord Cockburn. The previous decision in *Crouch v. Credit Foncier* (1873),[4] and the great ability with which the case for the plaintiff was presented, made necessary an exhaustive examination of the history of the law of bills and notes. This examination was made by his lordship and the results presented in a masterly way. In the end it was shown that modern commercial usage can give negotiability to new forms of obligation. Lord Cockburn's opinion was thus irreconcilable with the doctrine of *Crouch v. Credit Foncier*, and though on appeal the House of Lords was able to decide *Goodwin v. Robarts*[5] on the ground of estoppel, Lord Blackburn's decision in the earlier case was virtually left without support.

Accordingly, in *Bechuanaland Exploration Co. v. London Trading Bank* (1898)[6] the Court of the Queen's Bench, after reviewing the decisions, declared that conditional debentures payable to bearer pass by delivery and that an indefeasible title will vest in an innocent purchaser, where, by commercial usage, they are treated as transferable by delivery. The opinion of Kennedy, J., in this case is a notable one. The American courts, it is to be added, long ago reached the same conclusion now reached in England as to the transferability of bonds and coupons.[7]

---

[2] See Negotiability of Debentures to Bearer and Growth of the Law Merchant, by F. B. Palmer, 15 L. Quar. Rev. 245.
[3] L. R. 10 Exch. 76.
[4] L. R. 8 Q. B. 374.
[5] 1 App. Cas. 476.
[6] 2 Q. B. 658.
[7] White v. Vermont, etc., R. Co., (1858) 21 How. (U. S.) 575;

Volume II

Common law modified by law merchant.

It is worth observing that the courts are accustomed to discuss the problem presented by securities other than bills, notes, and checks from the standpoint indicated in the inquiry whether such securities have by custom come within the law merchant and are thus subject to its rules. Perhaps additional light might be shed upon the subject if we should view the problem from the point indicated in such a question as this: How far has the influence of mercantile principle been felt in English contract law outside the field of those contracts, such as bills, notes, and checks, which are admittedly within the law merchant in its narrowest scope? It is plain that the pure common-law doctrines of contract have been measurably modified throughout the whole field of mercantile transactions by the attraction and influence of the law merchant. Such principles as that underlying *Bechuanaland Exploration Co. v. London Trading Bank* should be viewed as common-law doctrine modified by the law merchant rather than as a pure mercantile principle extended by usage to a contract manifestly not within the law merchant. The result of the interplay between the two forces is equally conspicuous whichever way we view it.[8] As the law merchant as now applicable to negotiable instruments has a quite different texture from that which

Gelpke v. Dubuque, 1 Wall. (U. S.) 175; Vermilye v. Adams Express Co., 21 Wall. (U. S.) 138.

[8] A recent contribution of much value to the student of English Contract Law is found in Negotiability and Estoppel, by J. S. Ewart. It forms part of his work on Estoppel by Misrepresentation, but is also published in 16 L. Quar. Rev. 135. This writer shows that classification and terminology in the field of mercantile law has, in course of time, become defective. The term 'negotiability,' which is used in a double sense, is peculiarly misleading. He shows further that the so-called negotiable instruments, viz., bills, notes, and checks, instead of being characterized by the possession of features peculiar to themselves, share all their qualities with other contracts to a greater or less extent.

Consideration of this situation leads him to suggest that a new category must be framed which will include with bills and notes all the forms of obligation possessing the feature used by him as the basis of classification. He fixes upon 'ambulatory intent' as the proper criterion. Says he: "The 'negotiable instrument' category was originally formed to meet the case of a single sort of document. The essentially distinguishing characteristic of such instrument was not observed. Other documents, therefore, which had that characteristic, but were dissimilar from bills of exchange in other immaterial respects, were denied admission to the category. Nevertheless, upon one ground or another

it would have had but for the influence of common-law principles, so the common-law principles applicable to mercantile contracts which are not by nature negotiable are very different from what they would have been but for the influence of ideas which have their root in the doctrines of the law merchant.

various classes of documents were eventually admitted. Now we see that ambulatory intent was the true distinguishing characteristic, and the category must be rectified accordingly." 16 L. Quar. Rev. 143.

The principle to which he appeals to support the qualities which the law fixes upon the ambulatory contract is that of estoppel. We cannot go into the arguments which are used to support this view. Historically they appear to be defective, but as an interpretation of the past in the light of maturing knowledge the suggestions of Mr. Ewart are well worthy of attention.

PART IV

THE HISTORY AND THEORY OF THE
LAW OF REPRESENTATION

CHAPTER XLI

THE LAW OF REPRESENTATION.

General Observations.

THAT one person may do an act and the legal consequences of it be visited upon another is a proposition that must at first appear unnatural and unjust. It will appear less so when approached from the direction in which legal evolution has gradually worked towards it and defined the situations in which the result indicated may happen. Viewed from this point, we perceive that the recognition of the principle of representation is only an extension of the fundamental conception of responsibility for one's own acts. Both in morals and in law one is responsible for the thing which he brings to pass, whether he employs an inanimate object to effectuate his purpose or sets in operation the infinitely more complicated chain of causation which results from the employment of another moral agent.

It is manifest that one can never be legally responsible for the act of another with which he is in no way connected. It would indeed be a stigma on human society if its life and its thought gave countenance to such a proposition, and it would be a still graver reflection upon the sanity and soundness of the legal system which could, in whatever disguise, impose liability upon one who is altogether unconnected with the chain of causation resulting in the injury. Properly interpreted, the law of agency rests upon as sound a basis of common sense and is as much in harmony with fundamental notions of justice as any other branch of the common law. Certain historical difficulties in which the subject is involved have caused at least one learned investigator to adopt a different conclusion.[1] We shall endeavor to clear away some of the difficulty

[1] See Agency, by O. W. Holmes, Jr., 5 Harv. L. Rev. 14.

Volume II

Agency.
1. Principal and agent.
2. Master and servant.

and to indicate at least the direction in which is to be found the solution of the supposed anomalies of the law of agency.

At the outset we observe that the term 'agency' is properly used to cover the whole field of representation in both contract and tort. Unfortunately the term 'agent,' which ought in theory to be coextensive with 'agency,' is given a narrower sense, being used to indicate the representative in the field of contract. The other branch of agency is covered by the law pertaining to the relation of master and servant. As has been observed, it would be better if usage permitted us to speak of the whole field as 'law of representation,' and to use 'agency' and 'service' respectively to cover the ground in contract and in tort. As usage now is, 'agency' is the general term, and its two branches are indicated by the terms 'principal and agent' and 'master and servant.'[2]

[2] Huffcutt on Agency, 2d ed., 10, note 5.

If one person becomes the representative of another for the purpose of bringing the principal into a legal contractual relation with a third person, he is termed an agent. If employed to perform service subject to the direction and control of the principal, he is a servant. We thus see that the sole distinction between the servant and agent is found in the business about which they are respectively employed. Historically and as a matter of legal principle, agents are merely a particular class of servants. Such diversity as exists between the law applicable to them results from the different circumstances to which it is applied. Blackstone and Woodeson both classify agents as a sort of servants. 2 Bl. Com. 427; 1 Woodeson's Lectures, [469].

And before the beginning of the nineteenth century it had occurred to no one to treat agency as a separate branch of the law. Two facts sufficiently account for the splitting asunder, during the last century, of the law of master and servant from that of principal and agent. One was the enormous importance attained by the latter as a branch of contracts. This was due to commercial growth. The other circumstance is found in the fact that the law of master and servant, owing to its peculiar origin, had become inseparably associated with the law of domestic relations. In modern times the law pertaining to master and servant has lost nearly all traces of its origin in status, and rights which were once determined by the social relation of parties are now determined upon the basis of contract or consent. Nevertheless, even to our own day, the title 'Master and Servant' holds its place among the Domestic Relations, though not without some vigorous protest from various quarters. See Schouler on Domestic Relations, §§ 454 *et seq.*

While the law of service has thus been nominally kept within the bounds of the law of domestic relations, it was impossible that agency in the field of contracts should ever be treated as belonging to the same department of law. Modern con-

REPRESENTATION.   431

The law of agency affords a striking illustration of a branch of law which begins, or appears to begin, in one fundamental conception and ends in a totally different conception. Agency begins, or appears to begin, in the conception of status. In modern times, subject to certain qualifications hereafter to be stated, it rests upon no other foundation than consent. As will be seen further on, the idea of representation, so far as it found recognition in the early law of status, was probably not an illustration of true representation at all. But at all events, whatever recognition was given to the idea of representation or agency in early law is found in the law of status, and the idea found no countenance, or next to none, in any other quarter.

<small>Chapter XLI</small>

<small>Early law of agency implicated with statu</small>

The fact that agency in its origin thus had one basis and in modern times has another, causes confusion. One who has mastered the early conception is likely to bring it with him into modern law. It is therefore not surprising that when a person so indoctrinated looks upon the modern decisions, all should seem to be in confusion. We must remember not to put the new wine into old bottles. In law, as in other departments of knowledge, vehicles of thought may become antiquated and require new adjustment in order to meet changing conceptions. The continuity of the common law and the perdurance of its legal principles is one of its most striking features. Breaks in this continuity, however, do sometimes occur, and we must not lose their significance.

<small>Modern law of agency rests on different basis.</small>

Perhaps the most striking of all breaks in the continuity of legal doctrine is found in the general history of contract. There, as we have seen, liability is at first conceived as arising from the pure legal duty incident to the contract *re*. As legal development proceeds the conception of the obligation of promise appears, and upon this new notion modern contract law mainly but not exclusively rests.

In the field of representation we observe a similar but less tract law is only four hundred years old, and long before existing conceptions of agency were formed, the law of status as a root of legal principle had become inert. We consequently find that agency in contract is free from every vestige of status, being based on agreement.

striking transition. At first a duty is imposed by law upon the head of the household to answer for the doings of his dependents, because of the manner in which the family is organized and because of its peculiar relation to the community at large. In modern society, we find that responsibility for acts done by another still flows from relationship, but this relationship springs not, as in former times, from social condition or status, but from the consent of the parties entering into the relation. By this change of basis, the law of representation or agency was started upon its modern career. The transition was gradual and is an illustration of that march of human society from status to contract, to which Professor Maine has directed attention.[3]

Let us first put away the notion that agency itself is a contract. It is a relation; and though this relation may result from contract, and though contractual rights often flow from it, agency does not necessarily originate in contract. It must, however, originate in agreement. Agency, in every case, involves the consent of the principal, actually given or implied as a matter of fact. The so-called cases of agency by necessity, in which the consent of the principal is implied as a matter of law, bear the same relation to the law of agency that the quasi-contract bears to true contracts. Hence these cases need not be taken into account in defining the scope of agency proper.

In addition to the consent of the principal, it is necessary that the representative should also consent. This mutual consent of the principal and agent may find expression in several ways. Thus, (1) A, the principal, authorizes B to do the act x in A's behalf without compensation. B thereupon does the act x. The doing of this act, if it is done in pursuance of the authority, is sufficient evidence of B's consent to act as representative of A. (2) A authorizes B to do the act x in his behalf without compensation, and B signifies his consent by giving a promise to do such act. Here the relation of principal and representative exists as before. In both these

[3] Ancient Law, 164, 165.

situations the parties are not contractually bound, and the position of neither party can be legally affected unless and until the authority is acted upon. This follows from the requirement of a consideration to support a simple promise. (3) A authorizes B to do the act *x* and at the same time promises to pay him for the service. B signifies his assent by giving a counter-promise or by doing the act in question in acceptance of the offer made by A. Only in this situation are the parties bound by contract to each other.

Agency associated with contractual relation.

We may accordingly say of agency that it is a relation resulting from the consent of two persons, in which one, called the principal or master, authorizes another to act in his behalf, and the other consents to do so. The representative is called the agent or servant. If the agency be gratuitous, it must be acted upon before either party's rights are affected. If the agreement is supported by a consideration both parties are bound from the time the agreement is made.

Definition of agency.

The following language from the opinion of Judge Taft, in *Central Trust Co. v. Bridges* (1893),[4] shows a clear perception of the distinction between contract and agency. Said he: "An agency is created — authority is actually conferred — very much as a contract is made, i. e., by an agreement between the principal and agent that such a relation shall exist. The minds of the parties must meet in establishing the agency. The principal must intend that the agent shall act for him, and the agent must intend to accept the authority and act on it, and the intention of the parties must find expression either in words or conduct between them."

Agency and contract distinguished.

Principle of Representation Not Found in Roman Law.

Bearing in mind that consensus, or agreement, is the true goal to which the law of representation is destined to travel, let us begin in early law and trace the growth of this idea. We must turn for a moment to the Roman law. Here we find the law of status highly developed and at the same time there is hardly a trace of the notion of true representation.

Agency undeveloped in Roman law.

[4] 57 Fed. Rep. 753, 764.

The perfect type of agency implies three things: (1) That the authority of the agent is derived from the consent of the principal; (2) that the agent can neither sue nor be sued in respect to the contract which he makes for his principal; and (3) that the principal alone can sue or be sued.[5]

Law of status excludes agency.

The early Roman law had no place for such an idea. The formal nature of the transactions which the early law recognized as productive of legal relations required that each party should take part in the legal ceremony and that each should do the necessary act or recite the necessary words in person before he could acquire rights or become liable. Besides, the organization of the family was such that there was little room for the conception of agency and as little necessity for it. The *paterfamilias* was the family's corporate head and the *patria potestas* exercised by him was such as to merge into his person all the legal rights which pertained to his dependents. Everything acquired by the slave and son belonged to the *paterfamilias*. Their acquisitions passed by operation of law to the master or father regardless of the question whether the slave or son acted in his own name or in that of his superior, and regardless of whether there was any actual authority to act or not. Consequently this is not a true instance of representation. It was a consequence of the legal relation of the parties.

Master of ship a true representative.

In a few cases, however, agency was recognized in Roman law. The master of a ship (*exercitor*) was able to bind the owner, and this whether the master of the ship was a slave, son, or free person. A situation can hardly be imagined where the necessity of recognizing the power to bind the owner or principal could be greater than where a ship is in charge of a master and in a country remote from its owner. The pretor accordingly recognized the power of the master of the ship to charge the owner for supplies as a sort of agency *ex vi necessitatis*.

The institor.

Another point at which the rigor of the early Roman law was relaxed so as to admit the principle of representation was where the owner committed the business of buying and selling

[5] Hunter, Roman Law, 3d ed., 609.

REPRESENTATION. 435

to the management of his slave or of a free person. Here the master was held liable upon such contracts of his *institor*, or manager, as were within the scope of the business intrusted to him.[6]

Under the pressure of commercial necessity, the Roman law thus advanced somewhat towards a realization of the idea that what one does through another may be imputed to him as his own act. Savigny contended that the principle of representation gained wide recognition, even in classical times, in the field of the consensual contracts, but this has been refuted. Aside from an exception found in the law of property (possession), free persons could not generally act or acquire for another.[7]

There were, to be sure, certain forms of engagement recognized by the Roman law which afforded clumsy and inadequate substitutes for a comprehensive law of agency. Thus, if a creditor wished to authorize another to collect a debt for him, the would-be representative was joined as a correal creditor in the stipulation. Being thus a joint promisee at the inception of the debt, the representative was entitled to proceed on his own account against the debtor. Such a representative was called an *adstipulator*. If it was desired to associate another with the debtor in order that the principal debtor might absolve the debt through such representative, he was joined as *adpromissor* in the creation of the debt.[8]

The contract of *mandatum*, within its limited sphere, to a certain extent furnished a means of attaining the end that would have been reached by a recognition of the principle of agency. This engagement is the gratuitous undertaking by which the mandatary promises to fulfil a commission or do some act for the mandator. But the compass of the mandate is narrow and it fell conspicuously short of the conception of true agency.[9]

In the Roman contract of *societas*, or partnership, one

---

[6] See Sohm, Inst., Ledlie's trans., 2d ed., § 88.
[7] Hunter, Roman Law, 3d ed., 621, 622.
[8] Sohm, Inst., Ledlie's trans., 2d ed., § 80.
[9] Hunter, Roman Law, 3d ed., 485 *et seq.*

would expect to find at least the germs of a theory of representation. But in this we are disappointed, and we find instead a most striking illustration of that absence of agency which characterizes every department of ancient law. In the law of *societas,* the rights and duties of the partners *inter sese* were declared with some fulness. But here the Roman law stopped. One of the partners had no implied power, as partner, to bind the other even in matters strictly within the scope of the partnership enterprise. Whatever authority as agent one of the partners might exercise was derived from other sources than the contract of partnership itself.[1]

Such doctrines of agency as found lodgment in the Roman law were of pretorian origin, and in accordance with the tradition of innovations made by them, the pretors never advanced far beyond the original lines. Freemen were allowed to act as agents in the capacity of *exercitor* (master of ship) and *institor,* but beyond that the pretor did not go. " His measures seem to have been sufficient for the public wants, and Justinian found no occasion to introduce one of those glittering generalizations of which he was so fond, and by a stroke of the pen convert the contract of mandate into a true agency." [2]

It has sometimes been supposed that the liability imposed by the Roman law upon carriers and innkeepers (*nautœ, caupones, stabularii*) when their servants lost or destroyed the goods committed to them, is an instance of the application of the principle of representation, but this is not so. The law, as worked out by the pretor, imposed a positive duty upon the carriers and innkeepers, founded upon considerations of public policy, and they were held liable for goods committed to their custody regardless of the party by whose default the goods were lost. As in modern English law, carriers and innkeepers were substantially insurers.

Associated with the almost total absence of any true theory of representation in Roman law we find a corresponding development of the law of status, which is at the same time both a cause and compensation for the absence of agency. Into

[1] Hunter, Roman Law, 3d ed., 521.   [2] Hunter, Roman Law, 3d ed., 623.

this matter we shall not here enter. Roman and Germanic law, of which latter the English law is a branch, both afford abundant proof of the truth of the assertion that human society begins in status and ends in contract or agreement. As the one increases in importance, the other wanes.

Representation in Old English Law.

The law concerning representation, in the old Germanic law, in so far as it concerns the responsibility of the master or lord for the tortious acts of the members of his household, has been clearly stated by Dr. Brunner. This scholar tells us that according to Germanic law the head of the house was held responsible for the acts of the free and half-free persons attached to the household as well as for the acts of his bondsmen. The landless freeman who associated himself with a household became so far dependent that the head of the establishment was answerable for him. For the wrongful acts of bondsmen, this writer adds, the housemaster was fully responsible to the third person. He had to represent the wrongdoer as a party to the suit and had to make satisfaction for him.[3]

The early English law fully recognized this principle of vicarious responsibility. Professors Pollock and Maitland, in their account of early English law, make the following statement: "If we go back far enough we shall see a measure of responsibility far severer than that which we now apply to masters or employers, applied to some superiors. A man was absolutely liable for the acts of his slaves — though some penal consequences he might be able to escape by a noxal surrender — and a householder was in all probability liable for what was done by the free members of his household. A lord, on the other hand, could not be charged with the acts of his free 'men,' his tenants or retainers who formed no part of his family. The most that could be expected of him was that he should produce them in court, so that they might

---

[3] 2 Brunner, Deutsche Rechtsgeschichte (1892), § 93. A translation of this passage is given by Professor Wigmore in 7 Harv. L. Rev. 330.

'stand to right,' if any one accused them. Already in the dim age that lies behind the Norman Conquest we seem to see the lords reducing their liability. In Cnut's day they would, if they could, ignore the difference between their slaves and the numerous free but very dependent tenants who would soon be called *villani*."[4]

"*Omne damnum quod servus fecerit, dominus emendet,*" say the old laws.[5] The *Lex Salica* declares that the master shall pay one-half of the wergeld and, for the other, surrender the slave.[6] Gradually the principle of the vicarious responsibility of the lord faded away, as the slaves became free; and by turning them over to the courts the master was completely discharged. In this way was the primitive rule by which the master or lord was held strictly liable for the acts of his servants and retainers abandoned.

The curious institution of frank-pledge doubtless had its origin partly in social and legal conditions of this kind. The lords from an early day had striven to escape from the personal duty of producing retainers guilty of wrongs. They divided their men into groups and made all members a sort of collective bail for the forthcoming of any member who might be charged. The lords were then allowed to substitute the responsibility of the frank-pledge for their own. The kings were not always consenting to this, and from time to time we see enactments placing upon the broad and responsible shoulders of the lord the duty of producing wrongdoers. Thus, William I said, "All who have servants are to be their pledges. If any such is accused, the masters are to bring him before the hundred for trial. If in the meantime he flees, the master shall pay the money due."[7] But the frank-pledge was already an established institution, and such regulations

---

[4] 2 Poll. & Mait. Hist. Eng. Law, 529. Compare Holmes, Common Law, 17 *et seq.;* 7 Harv. L. Rev. 330 *et seq.*

[5] Lex Angl. et Wer., c. 16, 59.

[6] Lex Sal. 35, 1; 35, 5. Compare Laws of Ine, 74, cited by Prof. J. H. Wigmore: "If a Wessex slave slay an Englishman, then shall he who owns him deliver him up to the lord and his kindred or give sixty shillings for his life." See also 1 Thorpe, Ancient Laws, 27, 29. Leges Henrici Primi, LXX., § 5.

[7] Leges Will. I., c. 52.

as the foregoing were in the nature of statutory extensions of it.⁸

Professor Wigmore has pointed out that, as the responsibility of the lord for the torts and crimes of his man was relaxed, he was allowed to complete his own exoneration by swearing that he did not participate in the deed ⁹— a limitation which shows by implication that a master who connived at a tort or abetted its commission could not escape.

At the end of the twelfth century every trace of the lord's vicarious responsibility for the crimes of his retainers had disappeared.¹ Slavery had gone or was fast disappearing. Villenage had taken its place and the legal personality of the villein was not merged in the *persona* of the lord as the slave's had been. The lord could no longer be held as a natural and legal bail for his retainer. The institution of frank-pledge among unattached free men and villeins was universal.

The liability of the lord to respond in civil damages for the torts of his men passed away more slowly than his responsibility for the criminal penalty. Professor Wigmore says this took place in the thirteenth century, and the evidence produced by him shows that during that period (1201-1300) the lord was still sometimes held civilly liable, while the appearance of the new test (consent or participation) and its gradual substitution for the older vicarious liability for the criminal penalty is apparent.²

In the proceedings of the Fair of St. Ives (1275) we find an interesting illustration of the manner in which the mercantile law dealt with a piece of rascality that came up before the tribunal of the fair. A servant who acted as salesman in a booth was convicted of having sold cloth by a false measure. His employer paid a fine of forty shillings for him. The

---

⁸ Compare the statute of William the Conqueror requiring all free men to be in frank-pledge. "Omnis homo qui voluerit se teneri pro libero sit in plegio, ut plegius teneat illum ad justicium si quid offenderit." Stubbs, Sel. Char., 84.

⁹ 7 Harv. L. Rev. 332.

¹ 2 Poll. & Mait. Hist. Eng. Law, 529.

² See 7 Harv. L. Rev. 332, 335; Select Pleas in Manorial Courts, 8, where there is record of a fine assessed against a mother for her son's trespass in cutting wood.

servant alleged that his master supplied him with a false ell, but this was denied. We cannot say from the record, whether the merchant paid the fine assessed against the servant merely in order to get the servant out of the trouble, or whether he paid the fine for the reason that he, as master, was responsible for the act of his servant.[3]

Agency in time of Bracton. Bracton's pages are almost barren of matter that would throw light upon the liability of masters or principals for the acts of their servants. His language in regard to disseisins indicates that the lord who disavowed the disseisin of his servant was not liable for the legal penalty, provided he paid the actual damage.[4]

Messrs. Pollock and Maitland, in dealing with the subject of the master's liability during the time of Bracton and in the subsequent century, point out that the difficulty in holding the master for the trespass of the servant resulted largely from the absence of any remedy by which the civil liability could be enforced. The only action capable of being used was the action of trespass *vi et armis*. This remedy was penal and criminal in its nature, and the principle that the master could not be held criminally responsible was already grounded in the law. The statute of Westminster II, as if voicing a principle of universal law, recites that one person shall not be punished for the act of another.[5]

Conception of status loses vitality. It is possible, say these writers, that the current morality of the day would have sanctioned a stricter application of the theory of the vicarious responsibility of the master. The remedies available in the king's courts were not, however, adapted to the purpose, and as the local courts lost their importance all idea of holding a man liable for damage done by another merely because the tortfeasor was of his household (*mainpast*) disappeared. In this way status lost its vitality as a root of legal liability. Henceforth no one was to be held answerable for an act unless he himself could be brought into some sort of connection with the wrong.

[3] Select Pleas in Manorial Courts, 140, 153, 154.
[4] Bracton, 204*b*, 171*a*, 172*b*, 158*b*; 2 Poll. & Mait. Hist. Eng. Law, 531.
[5] "Quia quis pro alieno facto non est puniendus." West. II., c. 35.

In connection with the passing away of this phase of the ancient law one aspect of the conception of status should be noticed. It is a favorite fiction with the civilians that the father and those subject to his power bear the same legal character. The legal being of the son and the slave is merged in that of the *paterfamilias*. So far as agency is admitted at all, the civilians incline to the view that the *persona* of the agent is identified with that of the principal; but it was, of course, perceived by the civilians that this is a pure fiction. "*Eadem est persona domini et procuratoris; eadem, inquam, non rei veritate, sed fictione.*" [6]

Chapter XLI

Fiction of identity of legal personæ.

This conception identifies the person of the father with that of the dependent. This 'unity of person' is an altogether unnecessary and confusing attempt at explanation.[7] The true theory is to be found not in the identification of the persons of the principal and agent, but in identifying the acts of the agent with the acts of his principal. The phrase always used by the English judges gives the correct point of view. "What is done by the deputy is done by the principal, and it is the act of the principal."[8] So said Lord Holt. Lord Mansfield said: "For all civil purposes the act of the sheriff's bailiff is the act of the sheriff."[9] About the same time Blackstone said: "The wrong done by the servant is looked upon in law as the wrong of the master himself."[1]

Legal identification of acts of principal and agent.

---

[6] Dig. 44, 2, 4, note to Elzevir edition.
 Again, *cum et natura pater et filius eadem esse persona pene intelligantur*, for by nature the father and son are understood to be practically the same person. Cod. 6, 26, 11.

[7] The identification theory has been ably put forward by Judge Holmes to account for the English law of agency. 4 Harv. L. Rev. 345; 5 Harv. L. Rev. 1; but it has not been able to withstand criticism. The facts to support it are meagre and contrary to the weight of the proof. Professor Wigmore contributed much towards undermining it, and Messrs. Pollock and Maitland also reject it. See Responsibility for Tortious Acts, 7 Harv. L. Rev. 315, 383, *passim;* 2 Poll. & Mait. Hist. Eng. Law, 532.

[8] Lane *v.* Cotton, 1 Salk. 17, 18.

[9] Ackworth *v.* Kempe, 1 Dougl. 40.

[1] 1 Bl. Com. 432.
 Judge Holmes has found some traces of the Roman identification fiction in English sources. West, for instance, in his Symboleography, speaks of status and agency as a bond by which the two parties are feigned in law to be one. The passage is evidently based upon the corresponding Roman expressions. See Agency, 4 Harv. L. Rev. 352; also 7 Harv. L. Rev. 399, note.

CHAPTER XLII

REPRESENTATION (CONTINUED).

Responsibility for Commanded Acts.

<small>Master responsible only for commanded acts.</small>

THE vicarious principle by which the lord or master was in early times held absolutely responsible for the tortious acts of his retainer or servant having passed away, there followed a period of some hundreds of years during which the accepted doctrine was that the master could not be held responsible unless he had consented to the wrongful act or had actually commanded it. The following authorities show how this idea manifested itself during the fourteenth and fifteenth centuries.[1]

<small>Parent not liable for unauthorized trespass of son.</small>

In a case from 1302 it appeared that a certain lad was being brought up in the home of his mother, doubtless a widow. He committed a trespass upon the woodland of a neighbor and an action was brought against her for the trespass. It did not appear that the mother was a party to the injury or consented to the commission of it. It was held that she was not responsible for the trespass.[2]

In another case from the same period the facts appeared to be these: One Hugo was charged with abduction. The jury found that the act of abduction was done by certain retainers of Hugo without his consent. Hugo was thereupon acquitted.[3]

<small>Wife agent of husband.</small>

In 1305 a husband was held liable upon principles of agency for a disseisin effected by his wife, " as the deed of the wife is the deed of the husband." [4]

---

[1] In treating of the subject of responsibility of the master for the tortious acts of his servant we have derived much assistance from the able article on Responsibility for Tortious Acts, by Professor Wigmore, 7 Harv. L. Rev. 384 *et seq.* To this writer we are indebted for reference to the authorities here cited.
[2] Y. B. 30 & 31 Edw. I. (Rolls ed.), 202, 203.
[3] Y. B. 30 & 31 Edw. I. (Rolls ed.), 532.
[4] Y. B. 32 & 33 Edw. I. (Rolls ed.), 474.

In a statute of 27 Edward III we find legislative recognition of the principle that a merchant is not to be held liable for the trespass of his servant unless the act be done by the procurement or command of the master, or unless the act is done in the course of the business in which the servant is employed.[5] This provision was inserted for the encouragement and for the protection of the foreign merchants, but the principle embodied in it was already recognized and its application was not restricted to mercantile transactions.

The case of *Beaulieu v. Finglam* (1401)[6] is interesting as showing that exceptional liability was recognized in connection with the dangerous element fire. It was held in that case that the owner of premises was liable to an adjacent proprietor for damage occasioned by a fire originating in the negligence of a servant. It was said, by way of dictum, that the same liability existed in case of a fire started by a guest; but a hundred years later the author of the Doctor and Student said that this point had never been actually decided to be law in England.[7] The strict liability enforced in *Beaulieu v. Finglam* was apparently not a survival from the old principle of vicarious responsibility attaching by reason of status, but was rather a reminiscence of the liability imposed upon property for injury issuing from it, examples of which are not wanting even in modern times. At any rate the liability was exceptional and was recognized as such.

In a case from 1431 we find some suggestions worth noting. An action was brought for selling bad wine. The defendant pleaded that the wine was sold by his servant and not by himself. Martin, J., said that where, by one's covin and commandment, a servant sells bad wine an action will lie at the suit of the buyer, for it is the master's own selling. In other words, the act of the servant done at the instance of his master is the master's act. The selling of bad wine was within the principle of law which made the seller of unwholesome food and drink liable in an action of deceit. But generally speaking there was no warranty of soundness in sales, and in that

[5] 27 Edw. III. 2, c. 19.   [7] Dial. II., ch. 42.
[6] Y. B. 2 Hen. IV. 18, pl. 6.

444   FOUNDATIONS OF LEGAL LIABILITY.

Absence of particular command relieves master.

case it was said that if a servant who is also a merchant goes to market with an unsound horse and sells it, no action of deceit can be maintained by the buyer. A sufficient explanation of this might be found in the general absence of the principle of warranty just referred to. Martin, J., gave another, to wit, "for you did not order him to sell the thing to the other, nor to any particular person." [8]

In working out the idea that the master is responsible for the commanded acts of his servant, the first thought of the English judges was that there must be a command to do the particular act. Whatever particular act the master sets his servant to do, defining its character and naming the very person with whom the servant is to deal, that act is within the principle of representation, and none other is. The doctrine of particular, as distinguished from general, command which Martin, J., recognized in the case just referred to was subsequently accepted.

Rolle's summary of law as to fraudulent sale by servant.

Rolle sums up the law on this point as reflected in the old authorities thus: "If a servant who is a merchant sells a diseased horse or other merchandise to one at a fair, no action lies against the master for a deceit if he has not commanded the servant to sell to some one in particular. But if the servant by the command and covin of the master sells to a particular man an action lies against the master if the goods be worthless, for it is his sale." [9]

Immunity of Servant Acting at Instance of Master.

Master alone liable for commanded act of servant.

The principle having been accepted that the master is only liable for such acts as are done by his servant or agent at his particular instance and command, a corollary was drawn from this principle, to the effect that all the legal consequences of a commanded act attach to the master. Having once fulfilled instructions, the servant sinks out of sight. He cannot sue, nor, on the other hand, can he be sued. Accordingly in 1472, Choke, J., said: "If a man takes upon himself to cure me of a certain malady, and he gives medicine by which I am im-

---

[8] Y. B. 9 Hen. VI. 53, pl. 37.   [9] 1 Rolle Abr., 94 (S), pls. 1, 2.

paired, I shall have an action on my case against him; but if, having undertaken as before, he commands his servant to administer the medicine to me whereby I am injured, I shall have no action against the servant, but against the master. So if one undertakes to shoe my horse and commits it to a servant, who lames him, the action lies against the master." [1]

This was in a way an entirely logical conclusion. If the act of the servant is the act of the master, in other words, if the principle of representation is fully recognized, only the master is liable. The idea fitted in with social conditions then existing, in virtue of which the servant was much more dependent than now. Just emerging from a condition of true servitude, he was considered bound to obey his master save in the commission of crime. Every servant was, both socially and legally, bound to " do the precept of his master in all that is legal;" [2] and it was just that acts done at the behest of his superior should be treated as privileged.

In course of time the servant came to be viewed more and more as a free agent, and when the master's liability was extended beyond the limits of particular command, the courts were ready to hold the servant also responsible for his act, at least when it amounted to a tort. As long, however, as the doctrine of particular command was strictly adhered to, the servant was no more considered liable for damages resulting from his negligence in the conduct of the master's business than the agent who brings parties into contractual relation is personally liable to-day. Even Blackstone says with Choke, J.: " If a smith's servant lames a horse while he is shoeing him, an action lies against the master, but not against the servant." [3] But Blackstone is here repeating language which has long ceased to represent the true state of the law.

The individual liability of the servant for a positive misfeasance in the execution of his master's command was recognized at an early day. Thus, in 1505, this language was used: " If I command my servant to make distress for my

---

[1] Y. B. 11 Edw. IV. 6, pl. 10.
[2] Rede, C. J., in Y. B. 21 Hen. VII. 22, pl. 14 (incorrectly numbered 21 in Maynard ed.).
[3] 1 Bl. Com. 431.

rent, which he does, and brings the distress to me, whereupon I kill the beasts or do other unlawful thing with them, the servant is excused. But where I command my servant to take lawful distress and he rides [the beasts] down, in this case he shall be punished and I am excused; because when I command a lawful act and the servant acts contrary to instructions, he is guilty of a tort. As I did not consent to this it is reasonable that he should be punished instead of me."[4]

To the judges and lawyers of the sixteenth century it seemed contrary to principle that both master and servant should be liable where the servant negligently does a lawful act commanded by the master, as in the case of a smith's servant driving a nail into the quick of a horse's foot. So much has legal theory now changed that writers on this subject are ready to postulate liability on the part of the actual wrongdoer as a starting point in discussion. Thus, says Sir Frederick Pollock: "Whoever commits a wrong is liable for it himself. It is no excuse that he was acting as an agent or servant on behalf and for the benefit of another. But that other may also well be liable, and in many cases a man is held answerable for wrongs not committed by himself."[5]

The foregoing cases sufficiently exhibit the law of representation in tort as exemplified in the decisions found in the year books. The cases showing a recognition of agency in the creation of the contractual relation are necessarily much more meagre. Debt was practically the only remedy available upon simple contracts, as assumpsit was barely coming into use. Such references to agency in contract as are found accordingly bear upon the creation of debts. It was, of course, always necessary that there should be *quid pro quo* before the law would create a debt. If the servant acted in the scope of his authority (this phrase, however, was not used), the master was bound, if the *quid pro quo* accrued to him as a benefit in consequence of his servant's act. This was so even though the master did not authorize or command the particular act. If he did command the servant to procure the

---

[4] Rede, C. J., in Y. B. 21 Hen. VII. 23, pl. 14.
[5] Torts, 6th ed., 72.

article which constituted the *quid pro quo*, then he was liable under the doctrine of particular command whether any benefit accrued to him or not. Thus, Brooke says that if a man sends his servant to buy certain goods, or his factor or attorney to buy merchandise for him, and he buys, the master shall be charged though the goods never come to his hands and though the master has no notice of it, and the master cannot countermand it without giving notice to the servant, attorney, or factor.[6]

<small>Chapter XLII</small>

<small>Buying of goods by servant.</small>

Again, "if a bailiff pawns an ox for corn which comes to the master's use and agrees that, if he does not pay for the corn by a certain day, the pawnee shall keep the ox, the master cannot retake the ox, if the money is not paid." Conversely, if the buyer, surveyor, or clerk of the market buys stuff to the use of the king, debt lies not against him; for the king is the debtor, and the seller must look to him.[7]

An interesting case involving the question of the liability of a principal on a contract made by his bailiff comes from 1353. The plaintiff sued a writ of trespass for the wrongful taking of a horse and a beef under the following circumstances: The defendant W, it appeared, had left his affairs in the hands of his bailiff. The latter thereupon sold the animals in question to the plaintiff, receiving money for one and grain for the other. Thereafter W returned, repudiated the sale, and retook the horse and the beef. It appeared that the grain which had been received in payment "came to the profit of W;" that is to say, was devoted by the bailiff to W's use. As to the money, it did not appear whether W had received the benefit of it or not. The jurors were asked to find whether the bailiff was known to be the bailiff of the defendant. They answered, Yes, and said that he had sold other beeves of the defendant in the market. They were further requested to find whether the bailiff had a special authority to make the sale in question. To this inquiry the jurors answered that he had no such authority. Upon these findings it was held that the

<small>Power of bailiff to bind principal.</small>

---

[6] Brooke Abr., *Contract*, pl. 24, citing Pigot and Fairfax, JJ., in Y. B. 8 Edw. IV. 11. pl. 9.

[7] Brooke Abr., *Contract*, pl. 39; Y. B. 11 Hen. IV. 28. pl. 53.

Volume II

Implied authority.

St. Germain on law of agency.

plaintiff could recover his damages of W for the wrongful recaption of both the horse and the beef. In other words, W was bound by the sale which was made by his bailiff while acting within the scope of his ostensible authority.[8]

This case clearly gives recognition to the idea that an agent may bind his principal by any act within the scope of his authority, and that authority may be implied from circumstantial evidence. That is, the master is bound where he holds the agent out as having authority or permits him to occupy a position to which authority naturally attaches. There is no evidence, however, that this principle had as yet received any recognition save in the particular case where the agent was a bailiff, an office whose functions were exceptionally well understood in mediæval times. As for other agents, the general rule then and for a long period thereafter was that the master was not liable unless he either commanded the particular act or ratified it by accepting the benefit of it.

St. Germain's Second Dialogue of Doctor and Student (1530) stands at the close of the year-book period and contains a suggestive summary of the law of representation as then understood. It is worth perusal. The author begins by stating the principles of representation as embodied in the early conception of family status. His authority here is a little tract called Summa Angelica, written by a civilian. He attributes the responsibility of the master to a real or fictitious negligence in failing to appoint honest persons or in failing properly to discipline those who are dependent on him. This explanation is ancient, but is of course entirely adequate.

The second part of the discourse traces the growth of the notion of master's liability as found in the English statutes beginning with Westminster II. There are several of these enactments. They relate to public officers and their deputies, and it is hardly probable that such provisions exercised much influence in familiarizing the public with the principle that the employer must answer for acts done by servants in the furtherance of his business.

[8] Y. B. 27 Ass. 133, pl. 5.

One idea advanced by St. Germain is worth noting: "where the superior is charged by the default of him that is under him, he in whose default his superior is so charged, is bound in conscience to restore him that is so charged through his default." The use of the phrase "in conscience" points to the fact that the master's remedy was supposed to be in the court of equity. The right had not been recognized at law.

Chapter XLII

Servant's duty to exonerate master.

The writer of the Dialogue then gives the substance of the law of agency as administered in the law courts. He recognizes that in debt the master is liable on contracts of which he authorizes the making, and is also liable for goods which come to his use by his assent, whether the purchase be authorized or not. Liability for torts done at the master's particular command is also noted, as well as the exceptional liability of innkeepers and persons who suffer damage to be done to others by fire. The chapter furnishes a correct synopsis of the law as it is reflected in the year books.[9]

During the next century and a half (*cir.* 1531–1689) little or no advance in legal theory is to be observed. *Waltham v. Mulgar* (1606)[1] and *Southern v. How* (1618)[2] are the most important cases. In both the doctrine of particular command was strictly applied in favor of the master. In the first case

Doctrine of particular command still applied.

---

[9] Dial. II., c. 42.

"First, for trespass of battery, or wrongful entry into lands or tenements, ne yet for felony or murther, the master shall not be charged for his servant, unless he did it by his commandment.

"Also, if a servant borrow money in his master's name, the master shall not be charged with it unless it come to his use, and that by his assent. And the same law is, if a servant make a contract in his master's name, the contract shall not bind his master, unless it were by his master's commandment, or that it came to the master's use by his assent. But if a man sends his servant to a fair or market to buy for him certain things, though he command him not to buy them of no man in certain and the servant doth according, the master shall be charged, but if the servant in that case buy them in his own name, not speaking of his master, the master shall not be charged, unless the things bought come to his use.

"Also, if a man send his servant to the market with a thing which he knoweth to be defective, to be sold to a certain man, and he selleth it to him, there an action lieth against the master: but if the master biddeth him not to sell it to any person in certain, but generally to whom he can, and he selleth it according, there lieth no action of disceit against the master." *Ib.*

[1] Moo. K. B. 776.
[2] 2 Rolle, 5, 26.

29

450   FOUNDATIONS OF LEGAL LIABILITY.

Volume II

Departure from course of duty.

it was held that the owner of a privateer commissioned to prey upon the enemy's commerce was not liable where the crew fell upon the ship of a friendly nation. Popham, C. J., said that the crew were sent upon a lawful errand and that by departing from the line of their duty and doing an illegal act, they themselves became liable and the master was not bound. But, added he, " if the master sends his servant to do an illegal act, he shall answer if the servant mistakes in its performance. . . . So if one sends his servant to market to buy or sell, and he robs or slays by the way, the master shall not answer; but if he sends him to commit an assault and he kills, or, by mistake, attacks and kills another instead, the master is a murderer."

Fraudulent sale.

In the other case the court applied the rule of particular command, holding that the vendor of a counterfeit jewel is not liable where he sells the jewel through another, unless he commands his representative to sell to a particular person as distinguished from giving him general instructions to sell. Counsel for the plaintiff argued forcibly but ineffectually in favor of the liability. " Though the servant pursues not his master's command in all points, but varies from it in some little things for the better accomplishment of his master's command, this should not change the case, for when one commands a thing to be done he impliedly commands all means to be used for the accomplishment of the act." [3]

Noy's Maxims.

William Noy, who wrote his book on The Grounds and Maxims of the English Laws, near the beginning of the Civil War, has a chapter on Agency, chiefly noticeable as indicating that the law had not then materially changed.[4]

Michael v. Alestree (1677) [5] is generally looked upon as marking the beginning of the modern conception of the liability of masters for their servants' torts. Its importance has probably been overestimated, but it does show a certain broadening of conception. A servant undertook to train ungovernable horses in Lincoln Inn Fields and a bystander was in-

---

[3] 2 Rolle, 27.   [4] Noy's Maxims, c. 44, 110-112.
[5] 2 Lev. 172, 3 Keb. 650.

jured. The master was absent, but was held liable. The idea underlying the decision is that one is guilty of negligence who undertakes to train wild horses in public grounds, and that the master in this case was responsible for the act of his servant in taking the horse to that place.

Chapter XLII

Master responsible for negligent act of servant.

If the doctrine of particular command had been strictly applied the master, so far as appears from the report of this case, would have escaped. The court avoided the difficulty by indulging the presumption that the master had given commands for the training of the horse in that place. "It shall be intended the master sent the servant to train the horses there." [6]

A most interesting point about the case is found in the fact that master and servant were joined as defendants. Both were held liable. Thereafter the idea that only the master, and not the servant, is liable for damages occasioned by the latter's negligence found no recognition.

Master and servant both liable.

The revolution of 1688 marked the advent of a new epoch in the law pertaining to agency. Lord Holt came to the bench as chief justice in 1689, and he was largely instrumental in producing the change which now supervened. The inadequacy of the particular-command test of liability had become fully apparent. Social, industrial, and commercial development required that the law as to the master's responsibility should be put on a broader basis, and that his liability for his servant's acts should be much extended.

The language of Lord Holt in *Turberville v. Stampe* (1698) [7] marks a notable advance. Said he: "Though I am not bound by the act of a stranger in any case, yet if my servant doth anything prejudicial to another, it shall bind me, where it may be presumed that he acts by my authority, being about my business;" or, as his language is elsewhere reported, "If the defendant's servant kindled the fire in the way of husbandry and proper for his employment, though he had no express command, yet the master shall be liable, . . . for it

Presumption of authority from course of employment.

[6] 2 Lev. 172.   [7] Comb. 459.

shall be intended that the servant had authority from his master, it being for his master's benefit.

In other words, where the master sets his servant about the prosecution of a particular enterprise he necessarily authorizes the doing of all acts which are reasonably necessary in accomplishing the end aimed at. Consequently if the servant, acting in furtherance of his master's business, inflicts damage, the master is responsible therefor. This doctrine contains the essence of the modern law pertaining to the liability of the master. According to the language here used the law raises a presumption that all acts done in furtherance of the master's affairs are done by his authority.

The very fact that we here find a substantive doctrine parading in the garb of a legal presumption puts us on notice that we have found a rule of law which is likely at some time in its career to play havoc with facts. To the mind of Lord Holt, upon the facts of the case before him, it must have appeared that the presumption was one of fact only. It is logical to say that, as the whole comprises all its parts, so the authorization of an end *per se*, authorizes the use of all means necessary to accomplish that end. It is impossible that such a presumption of fact and of logic should remain such. It ripens in time into the irrebuttable presumption, or rule of positive law. If social needs require it and the rule itself squares with the judicial sense of justice, this is sure to happen. If, in *Turberville v. Stampe*, the master had given his servant general authority to clean up his field, but had specially cautioned him against the use of fire, Lord Holt could hardly have been so sure of reaching the same conclusion. The fact that kindling the fire was forbidden would probably have been received as rebutting the presumption that the act was authorized.

But in course of time the logical presumption of fact ripens into a positive rule of law, and this cuts off all inquiry as to whether the master did in fact authorize the particular act which results in damage. Where it is established that the general authority is given and that the particular act is done in the course of carrying the general authority into effect,

⁸ Turberville *v.* Stampe, 1 Ld. Raym. 264.

proof is irrelevant which tends to show that the master did not consent to the particular act complained of or that he actually forbade it. This is the goal which has finally been reached. The presumption of fact and of logic has become a positive rule of law; and the question now is merely whether a particular act is done by the servant in the course of his employment. Difficult questions of fact arise even upon this point, and fine distinctions sometimes have to be drawn; but the problem is no longer complicated by the presence of particular instructions limiting the general authority.[9] From this time on the decisions involving representation all go upon the doctrine laid down in *Turberville v. Stampe,* whether the question arises in contract or tort.[1]

<small>Chapter XLII</small>

There is no substantial difference between the test as formulated in contract and tort. When speaking in the language of the books on master and servant we say that the master is liable for any act of the servant done in the course of his employment and in furtherance of it. When speaking in accepted terms of the law of principal and agent, we say the principal is bound by any contract which the agent makes while acting in the scope of his apparent authority. Both statements amount to the same. In every case the first and fundamental question is, What has the principal set his representative to doing? What end does he intend for him to accomplish? What means are proper to be used in executing the purpose?

<small>Course of employment.</small>

<small>Scope of apparent authority.</small>

The circumstance that the expansion which we have noted in the doctrine applicable to masters in the field of tort did not take place until near the end of the seventeenth century, when the courts were now confronted with the necessity of settling the rule in contract law, would naturally lead one to infer

<small>Kinship between law of service and law of agency.</small>

---

[9] See Gregory *v.* Piper, 9 B. & C. 591, 17 E. C. L. 454; Croft *v.* Alison, 4 B. & Ald. 590, 6 E. C. L. 614; M'Manus *v.* Crickett, 1 East 106.

[1] See generally, Boucher *v.* Lawson (1743), Lee t. Hardw. 85, 94; Seignior *v.* Wolmer, Godb. 361; Southby *v.* Wiseman, 3 Keb. 625; Lane *v.* Cotton, 12 Mod. 488, 489;

Bolton *v.* Hillersden, 1 Ld. Raym. 224, 3 Salk. 234, Holt K. B. 641, Comb. 450; Middleton *v.* Fowler, 1 Salk. 282; Boson *v.* Sandford, 2 Salk. 440, 3 Mod. 321; Jones *v.* Hart, 2 Salk. 441; Hern *v.* Nichols, 1 Salk. 289; Armory *v.* Delamirie, 1 Stra. 505.

Volume II

Common basis of law concerning agents and servants.

that the growth of contract law probably exerted some influence upon the law of master and servant in the field of tort. This cannot be asserted. Such influence as was exerted apparently came from the other direction, and principles first laid down as controlling in the relation of master and servant were afterwards accepted in the relation of principal and agent. The two branches of law are intimately connected and there has never been a time when cases on master and servant were not cited as authority in the law of principal and agent, and *vice versa*.[2]

Blackstone's statement of law of master and servant.

Blackstone states the liability of the master in terms which, as the decisions show, precisely reflect the law as understood in his day. "The master," says he, "is answerable for the act of his servant, if done by his command, either expressly given or implied; *nam qui facit per alium facit per se.*" Thus, "if the drawer at a tavern sells a man bad wine, whereby his health is injured, he may bring an action against the master; for although the master did not expressly order the servant to sell it to that person in particular, yet his permitting him to draw and sell it at all is impliedly a general command."[3]

---

[2] See article, Agent and Servant Essentially Identical, by C. C. Allen, 28 Am. L. Rev. 9.

[3] 1 Bl. Com. 429.

Again, says he: "In the same manner, whatever a servant is permitted to do in the usual course of his business is equivalent to a general command. If I pay money to a banker's servant, the banker is answerable for it; if I pay it to a clergyman's or a physician's servant, whose usual business it is not to receive money for his master, and he embezzles it, I must pay it over again. If a steward lets a lease of a farm, without the owner's knowledge, the owner must stand to the bargain; for this is the steward's business. A wife, a friend, a relation, that use to transact business for a man, are *quoad hoc* his servants, and the principal must answer for their conduct: for the law implies that they act under a general command; and without such a doctrine as this no mutual intercourse between man and man could subsist with any tolerable convenience. If I usually deal with a tradesman by myself, or constantly pay him ready money, I am not answerable for what my servant takes up upon trust; for here is no implied order to the tradesman to trust my servant; but if I usually send him upon trust, or sometimes on trust and sometimes with ready money, I am answerable for all he takes up; for the tradesman cannot possibly distinguish when he comes by my order, and when upon his own authority. If a servant, lastly, by his negligence, does any damage to a stranger, the master shall answer for his neglect. . . . But in

From Blackstone's language it appears that he had in mind some such principle as the following: A master is liable for the consequences of all authorized acts. Acts are authorized within the meaning of the law where the master commands the particular act in question or where the act is such an act as may reasonably be done and is in fact done in order to carry out the master's general instructions or to accomplish a commanded act. Again, a general command may be inferred from conduct or usage.

these cases the damage must be done while he is actually employed in the master's service; otherwise the servant shall answer for his own misbehavior." 1 Bl. Com. 430, 431.

CHAPTER XLIII

REPRESENTATION IN RELATION OF MASTER AND SERVANT.

Volume II

IN tracing the law of representation subsequent to Blackstone, it will be advisable to pursue the course actually taken by the text-writers and separate contract and tort from each other. Let us accordingly first take up the development of the doctrine of the master's responsibility for wrongs done by his servant.

During the nineteenth century the wording of the test by which the liability of the master is to be determined underwent a change. The expression 'command and consent, express or implied' was completely supplanted by the 'scope or course of employment.'[1]

Master liable for acts of servant done in course of employment.

This change in the phraseology of the test marked the ripening of the previous presumption of fact into the positive rule of law. The master now becomes absolutely liable for all acts done in the course of employment, even though there be contrary private instructions and the act itself be plainly against the master's interest.

Liability for act incident to performance of commanded act.

Of course the old theory of authority and implied consent will still suffice for many cases. Thus, in *Gregory v. Piper* (1829),[2] a master set his servant to piling rubbish close to his neighbor's wall. He gave explicit directions to the servant not to touch the wall. The work, however, was of such nature that it was reasonably to be expected that the rubbish, if placed according to instructions, would shear down and press against the wall in question. The servant followed orders and, though he used reasonable care, the material fell against the neighbor's wall. It was held that this act was a tres-

---

[1] See Bolingbroke *v.* Local Board, L. R. 9 C. P. 577; Sleath *v.* Wilson, 9 C. & P. 607, 38 E. C. L. 249; Cornfoot *v.* Fowke, 6 M. & W. 358; Sharrod *v.* London, etc., R. Co., 4 Exch. 581.
[2] 9 B. & C. 591, 17 E. C. L. 454.

pass on the part of the master. A man is responsible for the results naturally to be expected in carrying out his commands, and the fact that the servant was instructed not to touch the wall, and that if he had used great and extraordinary care in piling the material it would not have fallen, does not relieve the master of liability. The master must be taken to foresee and consent to all acts necessary to accomplish his object, and though he forbade the wall to be touched, still, in the language of Blackstone, he must be said to have given an implied consent thereto, or, in effect, to have commanded it. Such a case is clearly within the principle laid down by Lord Holt and his immediate successors.

Chapter XLIII

Private instructions inconsistent with general authority irrelevant.

Let us now consider such a case as was presented in *Limpus v. London General Omnibus Co.* (1862),[3] where the driver of an omnibus had received printed instructions not to race with or obstruct other omnibuses. He violated instructions by pulling across the road in front of a rival omnibus, and caused it to be upset. It was held that his employers were liable provided he did the act in the course of his employment and in the supposed interest of his employers.

It will be perceived that cases of this kind, and they are now innumerable, embody a marked advance in legal theory. All that can be said of the act is that it is done in furtherance of the master's business. It is not in fact for the master's benefit, and it would be an abuse of terms to say that the master's consent is to be implied either in fact or in law, for the act is contrary to positive orders. The court, in this case, said that the driver was employed not only to drive the omnibus, but also to drive it effectively and to get as much money as he could for his master. This involved rivalry with other like vehicles. Consequently driving across the road to impede, and thus get before, a rival was consistent with the servant's employment. Willes, J., added, concerning the company's instructions: "The law is not so futile as to allow a master, by giving secret instructions to his servant, to discharge himself from liability."

The negligent act of servant done while about his master's business.

In holding the master liable in cases of this kind, the law

[3] 1 H. & C. 526.

visits upon him the consequences of acts which he has neither done nor approved. Nor can it be said that the case is covered by the axiomatic principle that the authorization of an end shall be taken to include all acts reasonably necessary to effectuate that end; for an employer cannot be held to contemplate the misdoing of his servant as a probable consequence of employing him. Nevertheless he must answer for the damage. In cases of this kind, the reason given by Lord Holt in *Turberville v. Stampe*,[4] namely, "that it shall be intended that the servant had authority from his master, it being for his master's benefit," will not hold, for the act in question involves the master in heavy personal loss, apart from the claims of parties injured.

Let us endeavor to ascertain the basis on which the rule in question rests. It is commonly considered an anomaly in the law of master and servant. As previously indicated, in adopting the rule that the master is liable for all acts done by the servant in the course of his employment, the courts have merely turned what to Holt and Blackstone was simply a presumption of fact and of reason into a positive rule or presumption of law. This of course forced the abandonment of consent as a test, and caused the term 'course of employment' to be used instead. This, however, throws no light upon the rationale of the rule in question, nor does it give us any assistance in arriving at the considerations which made it possible for the courts to reach the conclusion indicated.

Many reasons have been assigned by different writers for holding a master liable for damage resulting from the negligent act of his servant. Nearly all of them have been criticised and declared inadequate. Let us examine them.

The most hoary reason is that long ago advanced by the civilians, namely, that the master is liable because, as the event shows, he has employed an incompetent servant.[5] Now it

---

[4] 1 Ld. Raym. 264.
[5] Just. Inst., Bk. IV., tit. V., § 3. "The master of a ship, of an inn or a stable is liable for any damage through fraud or theft, occurring in the ship, inn, or stable. . . . as he is so far in fault in employing bad persons as his servants, that he

may well be conceded that the master should be liable if he employs a person of known incompetency; or, in case of especial hazard, if he employs one of doubtful skill. But as is well known, no amount of care in choosing a servant will relieve the master. "If A's coachman, being in one instance careless or drunk, in driving his master's carriage in his service runs over B, and B sustains an injury, A cannot excuse himself from answering for it because he had taken all imaginable care in selecting him for his servant, or because he had had the best of characters with him from his last employer, or because such misconduct in a long course of years had never happened before."[6]

Chapter XLIII

Negligence of master in employing incompetent servant.

Consequently care in choosing the servant does not furnish the proper criterion of the master's liability. Nevertheless language has been used numberless times to this effect, a circumstance which merely shows that men have been at a loss to account for the rule in question. Bentham and Austin repeat, as a reason for holding the master liable, that his breach of duty consists in having employed a careless servant.[7] Indeed it is found current in all ages. St. Germain gives it prominence, saying it is the master's fault to choose dishonest servants.[8]

Currency of this theory.

Even in modern times, eminent and learned judges have indulged the fancy that the reason for the master's liability is his employment of an incompetent person. Lord Kenyon voiced it in *M'Manus v. Crickett* (1800),[9] and Parke, B., did the same in *Sharrod v. London, etc., R. Co.* (1849).[1] The most that can be said of this explanation is that it offers sufficient reason for holding the master liable in some cases; that is, where he actually selects a person of known incompetence or is negligent in choosing him. It cannot explain the cases where this element is not present, and these cases, it may be observed, are by far the most numerous.

Inadequacy of the idea.

---

seems to be bound *quasi ex maleficio."*

[6] Coleridge, J., in Dansey *v.* Richardson (1854), 3 El. & Bl. 161, 77 E. C. L. 161.

[7] 1 Austin, Lectures on Jurisprudence, Campbell's ed., 513.
[8] Dial. II., c. 42.
[9] 1 East 106.
[1] 4 Exch. 580, 585.

Desire to reach person of financial responsibility.

In dealing with the subject of the liability of the master for the unauthorized torts of his servant, Messrs. Pollock and Maitland suggest that the desire of reaching a person financially responsible has perhaps unconsciously caused the courts to hold the master for the servant's tort done in the course of employment. "No law except a fanciful law of nature has ever been able to ignore the economic stratification of society, while the existence of large classes of men 'from whom no right can be had' has raised difficult problems for politics and for jurisprudence ever since the days of Æthelstan." [2] Professor Pollock has elsewhere given expression to the same individual opinion,[3] and in a modified form this reason has met with approval in other quarters. Thus, a late writer finds the reason and cause for the rule in the sentimental sympathy which we instinctively feel for injured persons, and the consequent desire to enforce reparation from some responsible person. According to this view, the master falls a victim to the desire for vengeance and reparation, because he is connected in our imagination, but not in fact, with the injury done.[4] Such considerations may perhaps modify our notion of the justice of holding the master liable, but could not, of course, have any direct effect on legal theory. As judicial reasoning it is without any real value.

Still another theory was advanced a number of years ago by Judge O. W. Holmes. He endeavored to show that the

---

[2] 2 Poll. & Mait. Hist. Eng. Law, 2d ed., 533.

[3] "A wrong without a remedy is, in theory at least, odious to the law; but in many cases the law cannot prevent the remedy from being only nominal. It may compel wrongdoers to pay if they can, but it cannot make them solvent; and it must now and then happen that an injured person has no better comfort at his hands than a right of action against a man of straw. To the popular mind a remedy not substantial is no remedy at all, and a result of this kind is not only unsatisfying (as it must be to every honest man), but unintelligible. Hence there is a natural endeavor to fix responsibility on some one who can pay. In the case of injury suffered through a servant's negligence, the servant, generally speaking, cannot pay, and the master can; and the feeling that compensation ought to be had somewhere, jumps at the master's liability." Poll., Essays in Jurisprudence, 118.

[4] See article, Why Is a Master Liable for the Tort of His Servant, by F. W. Hackett, 7 Harv. L. Rev. 107.

master's liability for the negligent tort of his servant results from the application of the ancient fiction of identity of person as between master and servant.[5] As we shall presently see, this view contains an important element of truth, but in the form in which the theory in question was propounded it appears to be untenable.[6]

Chapter XLIII

Theory of legal identity of master and servant.

In *Duncan v. Findlater* (1839)[7] Lord Brougham, seeking for the true rationale of the master's liability, used the following language: "I am liable for what is done for me and under my orders by the man I employ, for I may turn him off from that employ when I please; and the reason that I am liable is this, that by employing him I set the whole thing in motion; and what he does, being done for my benefit and under my direction, I am responsible for the consequences of doing it."

Other suggestions.

Power of discharge.

The suggestion that the right to discharge the employee may be a reason for holding the master, is clearly no explanation save in those cases where the master finds his servant to be incompetent and fails to discharge him; nor is the power to control any reason or explanation, save where the servant acts under express and distinct instructions. Neither does Lord Brougham's final expression, "being done for my benefit and under my direction," serve any better purpose. The other reason assigned, "setting the whole thing in motion," seems to come much nearer reaching the true ground of the rule.

Setting thing in motion.

Lord Cranworth once used language in this connection which has been quoted with approval, but he states legal effects rather than reasons. Says he: "If a servant, in driving his master's carriage along the highway carelessly, runs over a bystander, or if a gamekeeper, employed to kill game, carelessly fires at a hare so as to shoot a person passing on the ground, or if a workman employed by a builder in building a house negligently throws a stone or brick from a scaffold, and so hurts a passer-by — in all these cases (and instances might be multiplied indefinitely) the person injured has a right to

---

[5] See article, Agency, 4 Harv. L. Rev. 345; 5 Harv. L. Rev. 1.
[6] See article, Responsibility for Tortious Acts, 7 Harv. L. Rev. 404, note.
[7] 6 Cl. & F. 910.

treat the wrongful or careless act as the act of the master. *Qui facit per alium, facit per se.* If the master himself had driven his carriage improperly, or fired carelessly, or negligently thrown a stone or brick, he would have been directly responsible; and the law does not permit him to escape liability because the act complained of was not committed with his own hand. He is considered, and reasonably considered, as bound to guarantee third persons against all hurt arising from the carelessness of himself or of those acting under his orders." [8]

In a case which much stirred the law on the subject of the master's liability for the acts of his servant Chief Justice Shaw said: "This rule is obviously founded on the great principle of social duty that every man in the management of his own affairs, whether by himself or by his agents or servants, shall so conduct them as not to injure another; and if he does not, and another thereby sustains damage, he shall answer for it." [9] In this view it is immaterial whether the default be the act of the master or the act of his servant. The master is liable because he sets the whole thing in motion.

As said by Lord Cranworth, in the case above referred to, "third persons cannot, or at all events may not, know whether the particular injury complained of was the act of the master or the act of his servant. A person sustaining injury by any of the modes suggested has a right to say: 'I was no party to your carriage being driven along the road, to your shooting near the public highway, or to your being engaged to build a house. If you choose to do or cause to be done any of these acts, it is to you and not to your servants I must look for redress, if mischief happens to me as their consequence.' A large portion of the ordinary acts of life are attended with some risks to third parties, and no one has a right to involve others in risks, without their own consent." [1]

Professor Pollock states the theory of the master's liability in language very similar to that used by Chief Justice Shaw. Says this writer: "I am answerable for the wrongs of my

---

[8] Barton's Hill Coal Co. *v.* Reid, 4 Jur. N. S. 769, 3 Macq. H. L. 266.
[9] Farwell *v.* Boston, etc., R. Corp., 4 Met. (Mass.) 49.
[1] Barton's Hill Coal Co. *v.* Reid, 4 Jur. N. S. 767.

servant or agent, not because he is authorized by me or personally represents me, but because he is about my affairs, and I am bound to see that my affairs are conducted with due regard to the safety of others."[2] It will be observed that this statement, if pressed to its logical consequences, places 'my affairs' in the category of distinct legal entities, but in fact the expression 'my affairs' is only a vague abstraction which does not really help to elucidate the principle involved. The proposition in question seems to have been framed particularly with an eye to that class of cases where 'things' are controlled or managed by servants and consequently where physical forces are to set in operation.

Chapter XLIII
Pollock's theory.
Implied obligation incident to conduct of one's affairs.

The assertion contained in Professor Pollock's statement, to the effect that the master is not represented by the servant, is true in one aspect and untrue in another aspect. There is no personal representation in the sense of an identification of the legal person of the servant with that of his master, but there is representation in the sense that the servant acts for the master and the act of the servant is the act of the master. To take the law of master and servant entirely out of the law of agency or of representation in this latter sense would be clearly improper.

With diffidence we must submit that none of the several theories yet advanced by legal writers are adequate fully to explain the principle by which the master is held liable for the acts of his servant. Instead of attempting to work out a new theory where so many have failed, let us cast an eye around and try to see what the trouble is. It will be at once manifest, we think, that the difficulty here encountered is due to the fact that writers on legal theory have been trying to explain a principle which the law accepts as axiomatic. Axiomatic truth in law as elsewhere must be accepted as fundamental and unexplainable. The axiom with which we here have to deal is embodied in the statement reiterated by our courts

Law of representation founded upon axiomatic truth.

---

[2] Poll. on Torts 6th ed., 77.
A full presentation of Professor Pollock's views on the subject will be found in the essay on Employers'
Liability, in Essays in Jurisprudence and Ethics (London, 1882), 114 *et seq.*

time and again, that the act of the servant is the act of the master. This is a true legal axiom, because the common law proceeds upon it and treats it as a fundamental principle. "*Qui facit per alium, per se ipsum facere videtur,*" said Hengham, J., six hundred years ago,³ and modern theory is unable to resolve the doctrine of agency into any simpler principle. We merely abridge the maxim somewhat and say, *qui facit per alium, facit per se.*

But it is said that the statement that the acts of the servant are the acts of the master is a question-begging proposition.⁴ But if the statement be really axiomatic this is not a just criticism, for all axiomatic truth is more or less of the same character. A fundamental principle cannot be explained by reference to a higher principle, for *ex hypothesi* there is no higher principle into which it can be resolved. Every ultimate truth closes the circle of reasoning, as it were, and this necessarily involves a sort of *petitio principii* if one only analyzes it.

Being axiomatic, it is impossible to reduce the principle of the legal identity of the acts of the servant and of the master to any simpler terms. All we can do is to show that the application given to the principle fits in with present social and industrial conditions and that it embodies such a conception of justice as we have now attained. If we say that where the master sets in motion a chain of causes, using for this purpose the hands and the mind of another free agent, he is responsible for all acts done by his representative in the conduct of the principal's business, we are merely stating the axiom in another form. All attempts to get nearer to ultimate legal truth or to resolve the axiom into simpler elements will prove futile.

If the reader will now once more direct his attention to the propositions in which Chief Justice Shaw and Professor Pollock have formulated the theory of the master's liability it will be perceived that in both statements there is a tacit assumption of the entire equivalence of the acts of the servant

---

³ Fitz. Abr., *Annuitie*, pl. 51.
⁴ Pollock, Essays in Jurisprudence, 117.

with the acts of the master. In other words, they both postulate the truth of the axiom *qui facit per alium, facit per se.* This is in fact the circumstance that gives the statements in question the large amount of truth which they undoubtedly contain.

Chapter XLIII

Said Littledale, J., in *Laugher v. Pointer* (1826) :[5] "Servants represent the master himself, and their acts stand upon the same footing as his own;" and in a modern case now considered leading and classical authority, Willes, J., said: "In all these cases [where the master is held liable for the tort of his servant] it may be said . . . the master has not authorized the act. It is true he has not authorized the particular act, but he has put the agent in his place to do that class of acts, and he must be answerable for the manner in which the agent has conducted himself in doing the business which it was the act of the master to place him in."[6]

Judicial recognition of this principle.

In order to make it fully apparent that our law treats the principle that the act of the servant is the act of the master as an axiomatic truth, we should perhaps refer to a few more decisions. One of the earliest cases is *Smith v. Shephard* (1599),[7] where it is said, "the driving of the servant is the driving of the master." The legal equivalence of the act of the servant and that of his master could not be more forcibly expressed. In *Ward v. Evans* (1704)[8] Lord Holt observed that "acquiescence . . . will make the act of the servant the act of the master." In *Middleton v. Fowler* (1699,)[9] the same judge said: "When he acts in the execution of the authority given by the master, the act of the servant is the act of the master." Again, "the act of the servant is the act of the master where he acts by authority of the master."[1] This language was used in a case where the act complained of was

Holt's recognition of the principle of equivalence.

---

[5] 5 B. & C. 547, 553, 12 E. C. L. 311.
[6] Barwick *v.* English Joint Stock Bank, (1867) L. R. 2 Exch. 266. Compare language of Field, J., in Barnard *v.* Coffin, 141 Mass. 37, 55 Am. Rep. 443: "The defendants [principals] are liable to the plaintiff for the acts of Ochs [their agent] in the same manner as if those acts were their own."
[7] Cro. Eliz. 710.
[8] 2 Salk. 442.
[9] 1 Salk. 282.
[1] Jones *v.* Hart, 2 Salk. 441, Holt K. B. 642.

30

FOUNDATIONS OF LEGAL LIABILITY.

Volume II

negligence on the part of the servant in driving over a boy in the streets. In *Lane v. Cotton* (1699)[2] he used this language: "What is done by the deputy is done by the principal, and it is the act of the principal." The idea underlying all these utterances, it will be perceived, is that of the identification of the act of the agent as the act of his principal. The idea is not that of an identification of the legal *personæ* of the principal and agent.[3]

Blackstone's statement.

Blackstone expressly places the master's liability on the principle of the legal equivalence of the servant's and master's act. "The reason for this is still uniform and the same; that the wrong done by the servant is looked upon in law as the wrong of the master himself."[4] The same idea was expressed by Lord Mansfield in *Ackworth v. Kempe* (1778),[5] where he says that, "for all civil purposes, the act of the sheriff's bailiff is the act of the sheriff."

In the very late decisions we do not find the particular formula always repeated, but it is involved in all cases where the master is held for the authorized or unauthorized act of the servant. Thus, in *Dansey v. Richardson* (1854)[6] Lord Coleridge said that the master "is to answer for the act [of his servant] as if it were his own," and that the quality of the act is not altered by the fact that it is done by the servant instead of the master.

Intrusting to manage.

One of the reasons frequently assigned for the equivalence of the act of the servant and that of the master is that the master puts it in the servant's power to mismanage by intrusting him with the business; but mismanagement can hardly be considered as a natural consequence of intrusting one to manage. "Setting the whole thing in motion" gives better insight into the reason for the master's liability and would be perfectly satisfactory if the servants were machines instead of moral agents. In Bacon's Abridgment we find some in-

---

[2] 1 Salk. 17, 18.
[3] There is a bare trace of the idea of the identification of legal *personæ* in the particular relation of sheriff and deputy. See Blackstone, J., in Saunderson *v.* Baker, 3 Wils. C. Pl. 317. But the idea is altogether artificial and superfluous even in this relation.
[4] 1 Bl. Com. 432.
[5] Dougl. 42.
[6] 3 El. & Bl. 161, 77 E. C. L. 161.

structive suggestions: "The reason why the acts of the servant are, in many instances, esteemed the acts of the master, arises from the relation between a master and servant; for as in strictness everybody ought to transact his own affairs, and it is by the favor and indulgence of the law that he can delegate the power of acting for him to another, it is highly reasonable that he should answer for such substitute, at least *civiliter;* and that his acts, being pursuant to the authority given him, should be deemed acts of the master." [7]

As one can readily see, this is merely an elaborate expansion of the thesis, the acts of servants are the acts of the master because it is highly reasonable that this should be so. What court has ever said that a man ought to transact his own affairs? Since human intercourse first began men have been employing others to do things. The decalogue contains no 'ought not' in the matter of having servants, but it does recognize the master's responsibility for their doings.

One of the necessary implications of the fundamental axiom of agency is that the act of the servant, before being imputable to the master as his, must be done by the servant in the capacity of servant. In modern decisions the term 'course of employment' is used to indicate this, but 'scope of employment' is often used as an equivalent. The use of the word 'scope' should probably be avoided, as it is more appropriate in contracts, being used in the expression 'scope of authority.' 'Scope' has sometimes been supposed to have a narrower signification than 'course,' [8] but the two words are commonly treated as synonymous.[9]

It being settled that the servant's acts as servant are to be imputed to the master, the problem in every case involving the master's liability is greatly simplified. What consequences would attach had the master done the act or been guilty of the alleged omission himself? Was the act in question really the act of the servant as servant? These are the questions to

Chapter XLIII

Bacon's theory.

Criticism.

Course or scope of employment.

Responsibility flows from the legal relation.

[7] Bac. Abr., *Master and Servant,* Bouv. ed., 535.
[8] Hale on Torts, 144-147.
[9] See Aycrigg *v.* New York, etc., R. Co., 30 N. J. L. 460; Bolingbroke *v.* Local Board. L. R. 9 C. P. 575.

be answered. The relation of master and servant being established, the master's connection with the act is sufficiently shown, and the question whether he gave particular consent or gave an implied consent or adopted the act in question as his own, or even forbade it, is irrelevant.

The relation originates in consent.

It may appear that the conclusion here reached is antagonistic to the proposition advanced at the beginning of this discussion of the law of representation, to the effect that the law of representation is based upon no other foundation than that of consent. We should remember, however, that in a broader sense the master does consent. Responsibility always attaches to him by virtue of the relation of master and servant or of principal and agent. In every case this relation itself originates in real consent.

By voluntarily entering into the relation the master assumes the burden which the law places upon him by virtue of the relation. But further than this we cannot go. We cannot say that the master consents to the doing of particular

Consent to the particular act not necessary.

unlawful and forbidden acts, though he is liable for their consequences. By the common law a woman's personalty vests in her husband upon marriage. Can she be said to consent to this legal transfer? Hardly, though she does consent to marry. Her consent is irrelevant when we come to consider the legal consequences of marriage. Likewise the master's consent is irrelevant when we come to consider the consequences of employment.

The proper criterion by which to determine whether in a given case the relation of master and servant exists is found

Criterion of the relation of master and servant.

in the right of the master to order and control the other in the performance of the work. A master is one who not only prescribes to the workman the end of his work, but directs, or at any moment may direct, the means also; or, as it has been put, " retains the power of controlling the work." [1]

What constitutes a departure on the part of the servant from the course of his employment such as will destroy the

---

[1] Pollock on Torts, 6th ed., 78, citing language of Crompton, J., in Sadler v. Henlock, 4 El. & Bl. 570, 578, 82 E. C. L. 570, 578.

relation of the master and servant *pro hac vice,* and thus relieve the master of responsibility, has been considered in a number of cases, not all of which are entirely consistent with each other.² The problem has been made harder by being implicated with a question of remedy.²*

In *Croft v. Alison* (1821),³ it was said: "If a servant driving a carriage, in order to effect some purpose of his own wantonly strike the horses of another person, and produce the accident, the master will not be liable. But if, in order to perform his master's orders, he strikes but injudiciously, and in order to extricate himself from a difficulty, that will be negligent and careless conduct for which the master will be liable, being an act done in pursuance of the servant's employment." As the master was held liable in that case, this language was dictum so far as it undertook to declare the circumstances under which the master would be relieved, and the modern cases hardly bear out the distinction there made.

If the driving be the driving of the master, and the act of striking with the whip be considered an incident in the driving, as it doubtless would to-day, the mental attitude of the driver would not be a sufficient basis on which to predicate a departure from the course of employment. Of course the intention of the servant is always relevant on the question of departure. If it appears that the servant thought himself to be acting in furtherance of his master's business, this would be strong evidence that he was acting in the course of his employment, but it could not be conclusive. Professor Pollock has the following instructive paragraph: "Not every deviation of the servant from the strict execution of duty, nor every disregard of particular instructions, will be such an interruption of the course of employment as to determine or suspend the master's responsibility. But where there is not merely deviation, but a total departure from the course of the master's business, so that the servant may be said to be 'on a frolic of

---

² M'Manus *v.* Crickett (1800), 1 East 106; Gregory *v.* Piper (1829), 9 B. & C. 591, 17 E. C. L. 454; Sleath *v.* Wilson (1839), 9 C. & P. 607, 38 E. C. L. 249; Williams *v.* Jones (1865), 3 H. & C. 602.

²* See vol. 3, *Trespass on Case.*

³ 4 B. & Ald. 590, 6 E. C. L. 614.

470   FOUNDATIONS OF LEGAL LIABILITY.

Volume II

Quitting sight of employment.

his own,'[4] the master is no longer answerable for the servant's conduct."[5]

The modern law on this subject largely has its roots in Lord Kenyon's saying, in *M'Manus v. Crickett* (1800):[6] "When a servant quits sight of the object for which he is employed, and, without having in view his master's orders, pursues that which his own malice suggests, he no longer acts in pursuance of the authority given him, . . . and his master will not be answerable for such act." It is, however, the quitting sight of his business which relieves the master, and the spirit in which it is done, when known, is only one circumstance from which the departure may be inferred. It is needless to say that mere excess or abuse of authority will not of itself constitute a departure.[7]

Fellow-servant doctrine.

The modern decisions have placed two limitations upon the liability of the master which deserve notice. The fellow-servant doctrine relieves the master from liability where the person injured is a fellow servant of the tortfeasor. Some difficulty has been encountered in finding the proper basis for the rule.

Assumption of risk by employee.

The reasoning in *Farwell v. Boston, etc., R. Co.* (1842)[8] is generally accepted as sound on this branch of the law both in England and America. The court there proceeded on the idea that those entering a common employment take the ordinary risks into consideration in fixing the compensation to be paid, and consequently it was thought unreasonable to insert another term into the agreement, by which the master should be compelled to undertake that the servant should suffer no damage by the negligence of his fellow laborers.

It should be borne in mind that the situations of the servant and that of a third person are different. To the latter the master must answer because he has "set a thing in motion" over which the outsider has no right of control or interference.

---

[4] Parke, B., in Joel *v.* Morrison, (1834) 6 C. & P. 503, 25 E. C. L. 512.
[5] Pollock on Torts, 84.
[6] 1 East 106.
[7] Bailey *v.* Manchester, etc., R. Co., L. R. 7 C. P. 415; Seymour *v.* Greenwood, 7 H. & N. 355.
[8] 4 Met. (Mass.) 49.

By giving his service to his employer, the servant, on the other hand, makes the business his own and assists in its prosecution. Consequently, so far as any duty is imposed by law on the master by virtue of his position as conductor of the enterprise, the reasoning now fails, and in law both master and his servant are in exactly the same position. The former cannot, therefore, be liable to the latter for injury occasioned by the negligence of a fellow worker. Other reasons have been advanced, but the foregoing seems the most satisfactory, and as the courts in all jurisdictions have reached the same conclusion, there can be no doubt of the general soundness of the position assumed.[9]

<small>Chapter XLIII</small>

<small>Servant makes the business of the master his own.</small>

The other limitation on the master's liability is found in those cases where an independent contractor is employed. Here the person who lets the contract is not liable for the torts of the servants employed by the contractor. The reason is obvious. The conductor, or one who lets the contract, has no control over employees of the contractor, and hence is not treated as their master. He is only concerned with the finished product of the labor, and the contractor, both in fact and in theory, is the master of those whom he employs. Simple as this appears, the principle in question was violated in proba-

<small>Independent contractor not a servant.</small>

---

[9] See also Murray v. South Carolina R. Co., (1841) 1 McMull. L. (S. Car.) 385; Priestley v. Fowler, (1837) 3 M. & W. 1; The Petrel, (1893) P. 320; Wilson v. Merry, (1868) L. R. 1 Sc. & D. 326; Tunney v. Midland R. Co., L. R. 1 C. P. 296.
There is a discussion of the rationale of the fellow-servant doctrine in Essays in Jurisprudence and Ethics, by Sir F. Pollock, pp. 128 *et seq*. In closing his essay he gives this parting shot at the identification theory: "If we attended more to verbal consistency than to real convenience, we might say that, every servant being 'identified' with his master, and the master identified with his servants, fellow servants are identified with one another, and one of them cannot sue another for anything done or omitted in the course of their employment any more than he can sue himself. It is perhaps fortunate that this particular conceit has never occurred to the courts: as it is, we may harmlessly suggest it as an illustration of the danger that constantly attends the use of metaphorical language. Even in strictly legal reasoning and when the subject-matter and the terms are familiar, a vigilant check should always be kept upon language of this kind. In considering the wider analogies of legal rules, and still more in discussing the policy, in other words, the convenience and justice of the law, the only safe way is to discard it altogether."

bly the first case presenting facts of this kind.[1] But that case was soon discredited, and the law is now well settled that the man who has immediate control or the right of control over the work is the master.[2]

---

[1] Bush v. Steinman, (1799) 1 B. & P. 404.

[2] Reedie v. London, etc., R. Co., 4 Exch. 244; Hilliard v. Richardson, 3 Gray (Mass.) 349; Pendlebury v. Greenlagh, 1 Q. B. D. 36.

CHAPTER XLIV

REPRESENTATION IN CONTRACT LAW.

THE relation of principal and agent is necessarily of more limited scope than that of master and servant, for the agent is employed for the sole purpose either of bringing his principal into contractual relations with third persons or of transacting business such as involves the exercise of the power to contract. Within its narrower limits, however, the law of principal and agent substantially reproduces the phenomena found in the law of master and servant. The same apparent anomalies confront us in one field as in the other. But the law of principal and agent has some difficulties of its own.

Chapter XLIV

Function of the agent.

In the field of contract, as in tort, we find the principle of the equivalence of the acts of the agent and those of his principal fully recognized. This is of course to be expected, and we find language to this effect from the earliest times. Thus, in *Drope v. Theyar* (1625),[1] it is said: "My servant makes a contract, or buys goods to my use; I am liable and it is my act."[2] The attorney's act has always been said to be the act of his client, since he is "put in the place" of his principal.[3] It is needless to repeat that the identification here observed is one of acts and not of legal *personæ*.

Principle of equivalence.

As was at first the case in the relation of master and servant, so in the relation of principal and agent, we find the doctrine recognized that normally the agent is a representative merely, and that consequently, after he has performed his function of bringing his principal and the third party into

Legal consequences of agent's act attach to principal.

---

[1] Popham 179.
[2] Compare Y. B. 8 Edw. IV. 11b, pl. 9.
[3] Bracton says of the attorney: "fere in omnibus personam domini representat." Bracton, 342a.

Coke uses language to the same effect, saying, "he [the principal] appoints the attorney to be in his place and represent his person." Combes' Case, 9 Coke 76b.

contractual relations, he disappears, all the legal consequences of his act being visited upon the principal. But of course there is nothing in the relation of the parties inconsistent with the power of the agent to subject himself to liability if he sees fit, the principal still remaining bound. It will also be seen that where one acts for an undisclosed principal the situation is peculiar, and the representative, having played the part of a principal, will be held as such if the other party chooses to hold him.

Authority. The existence of the relation of principal and agent implies authority. This term, more nearly than any other, gives us the key to agency in contract law. It occupies substantially the same position in contracts that 'employment' does in torts. The giving of authority is a grant of power, and *Consent.* necessarily involves the consent of the principal, without which agency cannot arise.

As a general principle it is immaterial what form the grant of authority takes. All that is necessary is that the principal should give his consent for the agent to represent him. To *Form of the authority.* this principle there is one ancient and well-recognized exception: authority to execute a sealed obligation or deed must also be under seal. The reason for this is to be found in the *The seal.* peculiar character of the formal sealed contract in English law rather than in any peculiarity of the law of agency.[4] Where, however, the law does not require a particular contract to be under seal, a sealed instrument executed by an agent whose authority is in parol merely, will be given effect simply as a parol contract, and this although the instrument be executed in the name of the agent, provided the principal ratifies.[5]

Again, it is to be observed, if a deed be executed by an

---

[4] Berkeley v. Hardy, (1826) 5 B. & C. 355, 11 E. C. L. 251; White v. Cuyler, 6 T. R. 176; Williams v. Walsby, 4 Esp. 220; Steiglitz v. Egginton, Holt 141, 3 E. C. L. 63.
[5] Hunter v. Parker, (1840) 7 M. & W. 322, 344.
Authority to execute an instrument under seal must itself be under seal; but where an agent, under a parol authority, executes a contract under seal in the name of his principal, it is binding on the latter as a simple contract. Worrall v. Munn, 5 N. Y. 229. See also Ingraham v. Edwards, 64 Ill. 526; Tapley v. Butterfield, 1 Met. ('Mass.) 515.

agent in the presence of the principal and under his immediate instructions, oral authority is sufficient; for the signature of the agent is there treated as if it were made by the principal himself.[6]

Right to Delegate.

A well-known principle in the law of agency is embodied in the maxim *delegata potestas non potest delegari* — delegated authority cannot be delegated; or, as it is sometimes otherwise expressed, *delegatus non potest delegare* — an agent cannot delegate. The reason for this rule is that in creating an agency the principal necessarily reposes a personal confidence in his agent, and it is to be supposed that the principal expects the agent to carry out the mandate in person.

The nature of the business, however, is often such as to make it impossible, impracticable, or inconvenient for the agent to perform the mandate or commission in person, in which case it is of course necessary for him to commit the doing of the work to his own agents or servants. Still, in strictness the only privity which the law recognizes is that between the principal and his immediate agent. The servants of the latter are not brought into contractual relations with the principal and are liable only to their immediate master. This rule is usually expressed by saying that agents may ordinarily delegate the performance of purely ministerial acts, which require no exercise of discretion on the part of the agent. Thus, it is held that one having authority to sign the name of another to a subscription paper may procure a third person to make the signature. In such case the agent is not delegating authority, but only performing an authorized act through his own servant instead of doing it himself. He may as well sign by the fingers of another person as by the pen of another person. If the signing is the act of the agent's will it is an effectual doing by him of the authorized act.

On the other hand, where the doing of the delegated act

---

[6] Jansen *v.* McCahill, 22 Cal. 563; Gardner *v.* Gardner, 5 Cush. (Mass.) 483; Rex *v.* Longnor, 4 B. & Ad. 647, 24 E. C. L. 131; McMurtry *v.* Brown, 6 Neb. 368; Ball *v.* Dunsterville, 4 T. R. 313.

Act of discretion cannot be delegated. requires judgment or discretion, it can be performed only by the agent in person. Thus, an arbitrator cannot delegate his function, but, having heard and decided as arbitrator, he can have another person draw up his award and put his name to it instead of doing it himself.[7]

Complete delegation. Under certain circumstances, the agent may substitute another instead of himself, in such a way as to create a privity between the principal and the new agent. Where the delegation is complete, the delegating agent is no longer bound to answer for the acts of the person to whom the execution of the agency is thus delegated. The latter must answer to the principal for his own acts in discharge of the commission. Before authority can be thus delegated it is necessary that the power so to delegate should be granted by the principal in the first place, or the circumstances must be such as to raise a presumption of consent on his part. The nature of the business in question or the usual practice of men engaged in the performance of like duties may be sufficient to raise such a presumption.

Special authority to delegate.

Appointment of substitute. In a modern leading case, Thesiger, L. J., stated the law on this point as follows: "As a general rule, no doubt, the maxim *delegatus non potest delegare* applies so as to prevent an agent from establishing the relationship of principal and agent between his own principal and a third person; but this maxim, when analyzed, merely imports that an agent cannot, without authority from his principal, devolve upon another obligations to the principal which he has himself undertaken personally to fulfil; and that, inasmuch as confidence in the particular person employed is at the root of the contract of agency, such authority cannot be implied as an ordinary incident in the contract. But the exigencies of business do from time to time render necessary the carrying out of the instructions of a principal by a person other than the agent originally instructed for the purpose; and where that is the case, the reason of the thing requires that the rule should be relaxed, so as on the one hand to enable the agent to appoint what

[7] Norwich University *v.* Denny, 47 Vt. 13; Grady *v.* American Cent. Ins. Co., 60 Mo. 116.

has been termed a 'sub-agent' or 'substitute' (the latter of which designations, although it does not exactly denote the legal relationship of the parties, we adopt for want of a better and for the sake of brevity), and, on the other hand, to constitute, in the interest and for the protection of the principal, a direct privity of contract between him and such 'substitute'; and we are of opinion that an authority to the effect referred to may and should be implied where, from the conduct of the parties to the original contract of agency, the usage of trade, or the nature of the particular business which is the subject of the agency, it may be reasonably presumed that the parties to the contract of agency originally intended that such authority should exist, or where in the course of the employment unforeseen emergencies arise which impose upon the agent the necessity of employing a substitute; and that when such authority exists and is duly exercised, privity of contract arises between the principal and the substitute, and the latter becomes as responsible to the former for the due discharge of the duties which his employment casts upon him, as if he had been appointed agent by the principal himself." [8]

Chapter XLIV

Usage of trade.

Unforeseen emergency.

It is sometimes a little hard to say whether the third person to whom the doing of an act is committed by an agent is merely a servant of the agent or becomes *pro hac vice* agent of the principal himself.[9] The presumption ordinarily is that he is servant of the agent merely; and contractual privity with the principal will not be inferred unless there be authority, express or implied, for its creation.

Undisclosed Principal.

Inasmuch as the essence of agency is found in the existence of the relation of principal and agent, that is, in the existence of authority, it becomes a matter of no moment, so far as legal consequences are concerned, whether the third person with whom the agent deals knows of the agency or not. For instance, if A constitutes B his agent for the pur-

[8] De Bussche *v.* Alt, 8 Ch. D. 286.
[9] Barnard *v.* Coffin, 141 Mass. 37.

pose of buying stock, and B in his own name purchases stock of C, the latter, upon discovering that B was acting as agent of A, can sue A as principal if he so chooses to do. This brings us to the subject of undisclosed principal, in regard to which the law has been considered anomalous. It certainly does seem somewhat strange that a contracting party should acquire a right of action against one who is not within the compass of his imagination at the time the contract is made, and still stranger perhaps that he should be subjected to liability at the suit of such person. But both branches of the rule clearly have the same basis, and both are equally consistent with theory and reason.

One of the earliest cases on the subject is *Gurratt v. Cullum* (1712),[1] where two factors sold goods for an undisclosed principal. Before collecting the debt the factors became bankrupt, and it was held by the court that the money due from the purchaser of the goods belonged not to the factors, but to their principal, the original owner of the property, and that consequently the assignee in bankruptcy, on collecting the debt, was bound to turn it over to the seller of the goods, and could not require him merely to prove his claim in bankruptcy.

In *Scrimshire v. Alderton* (1743)[2] a *del credere* factor sold oats to a purchaser without informing either seller or buyer of the identity of the other. The factor failed, and the seller, having ascertained who was the purchaser of his lot of oats, gave him notice not to pay the factor. He nevertheless did so, and the seller thereupon sued him. The court was clearly of the opinion that the plaintiff was entitled to recover, and directed the jury that the factor's sale, by a general rule of law, created a contract between the owner and buyer. It is interesting to observe the difficulty, however, which was encountered in getting the rule recognized, for in that case the first jury, though directed to find for the plaintiff, stubbornly refused to do so. They were sent out three times to reconsider, but found for the defendant each time.

[1] Referred to by Willes, J., in Scott v. Surman, Willes 405.
[2] 2 Stra. 1183.

Being discharged and a new trial granted, another special jury likewise found for the defendant, giving as their reason that "they thought from the circumstances no credit was given as between the owner and buyer, and that the latter was answerable to the factor only, and he only to the owner."

<small>Chapter XLIV</small>

The leading cases on the subject of the liability of an undisclosed principal are *Paterson v. Gandasequi* (1812),[3] *Addison v. Gandasequi* (1812),[4] and *Thomson v. Davenport* (1829).[5] These cases together comprise most of the law on the subject.[6]

<small>Leading authorities.</small>

That a contractual relation is established between an undisclosed principal and the party with whom his agent deals, necessarily results from the principle which, as we have already seen, lies at the foundation of agency — *the act of the agent is the act of the principal*. In some cases it is impossible to give full effect to this doctrine without doing injustice, and the courts in applying it always take into consideration the actual situation of the parties at the time they are respectively affected with notice of the identity of the other. Consequently, where the buyer has a personal debt against the factor and deals with him as a principal, and the real principal afterwards intervenes and sues for the purchase price, the buyer can set off his debt against the price of the goods.[7] In such a case the owner, having permitted the factor to deal with the goods as his own, is clearly estopped to assert his rights as owner to the detriment of one who buys on the faith of title being in the factor.[8]

<small>Qualification.</small>

It is to be observed that the party who contracts with another as principal, and subsequently ascertains that the person with whom he dealt was really acting as agent for another, is allowed to elect as between the principal and agent and may hold either, but not both, upon the contract made with him.

<small>Election of party dealing with agent of undisclosed principal.</small>

---

[3] 15 East 62.
[4] 4 Taunt. 574.
[5] 9 B. & C. 78, 17 E. C. L. 335.
[6] See 2 Smith Lead. Cas., 8th Am. ed., 386 *et seq.*
[7] Rabone *v.* Williams, 7 T. R. 356, note; George *v.* Clagett, (1797) 7 T. R. 355.

[8] Baring *v.* Corrie, (1818) 2 B. & Ald. 137; Cooke *v.* Eshelby, (1887) 12 App. Cas. 271, 56 L. J. Q. B. 505; Moore *v.* Clementson, 2 Campb. 22; Kaltenbach *v.* Lewis, 10 App. Cas. 617.

He can sue the principal because, on the facts of the case, the contract is in legal effect made with him, the act of the agent being attributed to his principal. He can sue the agent because the latter, having acted as a principal, is estopped to deny that he acted in such capacity. The two positions are inconsistent, and having once elected to hold the principal or agent, the contracting party cannot subsequently enforce the contract against the other.[9]

Contract in writing. It is further to be observed in this connection that where an agent acting as such contracts in his own name in writing, the other party may sue either principal or agent unless the contract itself or the circumstances connected with it show an intention to look solely to the agent. Thus, in *Calder v. Dobell* (1871),[1] in a transaction between two cotton brokers, the 'bought' and 'sold' notes recited no other names than those of the two brokers. The seller was informed that the purchasing broker was acting for a particular buyer whose name was not inserted in the memorandum. It was held that the vendor could sue the principal. Said Blackburn, J., in the Exchequer Chamber: "I apprehend that where a man is acting as agent, the principal is not the less bound because the contract is so drawn as to make the agent also liable. There are many cases where, although a man is acting for another, he is not contracting for another. . . . Contracts are frequently made by masters of ships (charter parties and other contracts); nobody ever doubted that the owners might sue and be sued upon them."[2]

Power of Agent Acting within Scope of Apparent Authority.

As in the relation of master and servant we found that the master is liable for all damages occasioned by the wrongful acts of his servant done in the course of employment, so in the relation of principal and agent we find that the principal

---

[9] Curtis *v.* Williamson, L. R. 10 Q. B. 57; Watteau *v.* Fenwick, (1893) 1 Q. B. 346; Priestly *v.* Fernie, 3 H. & C. 977; Kingsley *v.* Davis, 104 Mass. 178.

[1] L. R. 6 C. P. 486.
[2] Compare Higgins *v.* Senior, 8 M. & W. 834, 845; Huntington *v.* Knox, 7 Cush. (Mass.) 371; Nicoll *v.* Burke, 78 N. Y. 581.

is bound by all acts of his agent done while acting in the scope of his actual or apparent authority. It follows that the principal may sometimes be held where the agent's conduct is in violation of specific private instructions from the principal or is actually fraudulent. The following cases sufficiently illustrate this:

Chapter XLIV

Act violative of specific instructions.

In *Whitehead v. Tuckett* (1812)[3] it appeared that Sill & Co. were sugar brokers in Liverpool, and as such from time to time bought and sold great quantities of sugar for the defendant, Tuckett, who was a wholesale grocer of Bristol. Sill & Co. usually bought and paid for the sugar in their own name, and in like manner resold and received the purchase money in their own name. They did not draw upon the defendant for the particular amount of each purchase, nor remit to him the particular bill received in payment of each sale; but there was a general account running between them. Sill & Co. never had general authority to buy for the defendant, but in each instance received directions for so doing; but when the markets were low they had sometimes an unlimited authority as to quantity or price. Prior to the transaction out of which the controversy arose, Sill & Co. had not a general authority to sell at their discretion, but received from the defendant directions to sell on each occasion, and were limited as to price. Upon the occasion in question letters had been written by the defendant, Tuckett, authorizing Sill & Co. to dispose of certain sugars provided they could get a designated price. The brokers sold, but violated instructions by selling at a lower price than their principal had named. It was held that the principal was bound by the sale.

Broker selling at lower price than that authorized by principal.

In *Edmunds v. Bushell* (1865)[4] one A had employed B to manage his business and to carry it on in the name of 'B. & Co.' The drawing and accepting of commercial paper was a matter ordinarily incident to the conduct of the particular business, but it was specially agreed and understood between A and B that the latter should not draw or accept bills. He did, however, on one occasion accept a bill in the name

Acceptance of bill by manager of business.

[3] 15 East 400. [4] L. R. 1 Q. B. 97.

31

of 'B & Co.,' and it was held that A was bound by the acceptance, the bill having come into the hands of one who was ignorant of the fact that B had no right to accept.

In *Bentley v. Doggett* (1881)[5] the facts were as follows: The defendant Doggett was a wholesale merchant in the city of Chicago, and as such employed a traveling salesman whose business it was to go from place to place with samples and make sales. In order to do this it was necessary for the salesman to have the use of a carriage and team. Upon the occasion in question the salesman hired an outfit and pledged the credit of his principal for the hire. It was held that the principal was bound although there was an agreement between him and the salesman that the latter should have no authority to pledge the principal's credit.

In *Planters' Rice-Mill Co. v. Merchants' Nat. Bank* (1887)[6] it appeared that the defendant rice-mill company was engaged in receiving and storing rice, issuing therefor its transferable receipts. The officer whose duty it was to issue such receipts, on the occasion in question fraudulently issued a receipt for a quantity of rice which had not been in fact received. The receipt was made out to one S, an accomplice, who took the receipt and pledged it as collateral for a loan of money. It was held that the rice-mill company was bound by the act of its agent in issuing the bogus receipt, the same being in the hands of an innocent purchaser for value.

Batavia Bank v. New York, etc., R. Co. (1887)[7] was a case where the local freight agent of a railroad company, having authority to issue bills of lading for goods received for transportation, fraudulently issued a bill of lading without having received the goods. This bill of lading got into the hands of an innocent holder for value. It was held that the railroad company was liable on such bogus bill of lading.

In *Corn Exch. Bank v. American Dock, etc., Co.* (1896)[8] the facts were the same as in the preceding case, except that the officer of the warehouse company who issued the bogus receipts made the same out in favor of himself. It appeared that he had authority to issue receipts to third persons for

[5] 51 Wis. 224.   [6] 78 Ga. 574.   [7] 106 N. Y. 195.   [8] 149 N. Y. 174.

goods stored by them, but it did not appear that he had actual authority to make out receipts for goods stored by himself. It was held that an innocent pledgee for value of the receipts could recover provided it could be shown that the warehouse company had impliedly authorized the officer to make out receipts for goods deposited by himself; but not otherwise.

Chapter XLIV

Bogus receipts in name of fraudulent officer.

Furthermore, it was held in one of the cases which grew out of this particular piece of rascality, that implied authority was shown by proof that the company's directors, after having knowledge of the fact that the officer in question had been certifying receipts in his own favor, acquiesced in the practice.[9]

Substantially the same difficulty has been encountered in explaining the principle underlying cases like these as has been experienced in the effort to account for the responsibility of the master for the tortious and unauthorized acts of his servant done in the course of employment. In fact, the same principle is involved in both situations. Here, as there, we must be content to plant ourselves directly on the axiom of agency, *qui facit per alium, facit per se*. The further one allows himself to wander away from this rock the more confused will everything appear. So far as the agent acts within the apparent scope of his authority, the law attributes his act to the principal as the principal's own act. This does not involve any arbitrary assumption or legal fiction; it is merely a positive rule of law which is incapable of being reduced to any simpler terms. We do not pretend that the axiom of agency upon ultimate analysis really explains anything. It is merely a fact or phenomenon in the science of law. The explanation of agency, so far as it has any explanation, is to be found in the fundamental cognitions of the mind.

Theory underlying responsibility of principal for fraudulent act of servant.

Principle of legal equivalence involved.

It was formerly supposed that the power of the agent to bind his principal by acts in violation of his positive instruc-

Classification of agents.

[9] Hanover Nat. Bank *v.* American Dock, etc., Co., (1896) 148 N. Y. 612. See also New York Nat. Banking Assoc. Bank *v.* American Dock, etc., Co., 143 N. Y. 559.

tions, or in excess of his actual authority, if one chooses to put it that way, is confined to general agents; and for the purpose of this distinction, all agents have been classed as general or special. The general agent is one authorized to act for his principal in all matters concerning a particular business or employment of a particular nature. The special agent is one who is authorized to act for the principal in a single transaction. The general agency is created by power given to do acts of a class, the special agency by power given to do individual acts only.[1]

In regard to the power of the general and special agents to bind their principal by unauthorized acts, Judge Story states the distinction as follows: "In the former case [general agency] the principal will be bound by the acts of his agent within the scope of the general authority conferred on him, although he violates by those acts his private instructions and directions, which are given to him by the principal, limiting, qualifying, suspending or prohibiting the exercise of such authority under particular circumstances. In the latter class [special agency] if the agent exceeds the special and limited authority conferred on him, the principal is not bound by his acts, but they become merely nullities, so far as he is concerned, unless indeed he has held him out as possessing a more enlarged authority."[2]

It is obvious that this distinction cannot be very helpful in critical cases. It certainly states the law correctly as regards general agents, but it is no less true that an agent who is authorized to do only one particular act and who is thus a special agent can bind his principal by acts done in violation of instructions. Thus, if a person sends an agent or servant to effect a sale of his horse, the servant can bind his master by a warranty of soundness, although the principal expressly tells his agent not to warrant. In such a case, Willes, J., said that the power of warranty arose out of the general character of the transaction in question, and that any person dealing with the agent had a right to assume it. It was an

[1] Butler v. Maples, 9 Wall. (U. S.) 776.
[2] Story on Agency, § 126.

ostensible authority and could not be negatived by showing a secret understanding between the owner and his servant not to warrant.³

The power of the agent to bind by unauthorized acts evidently does not depend upon any distinction as to whether the agency is general or special, but depends merely upon the question whether the powers which the agent assumes to exercise are such usual and necessary powers as would be implied in the absence of indications to the contrary. As the greater includes the less, so the grant of a principal power *ex vi termini* includes all that is accessory to it, and secret limitations are, as against third persons acting in ignorance of them, invalid because repugnant to the principal power.

As a matter of construction merely, it is obvious that authority to do a particular act or class of acts includes the power of doing all things necessary and proper for carrying the power granted into effect. There is nothing peculiar to the law of agency at this point. Even the most formal grant of power must be construed according to this rule or it would prove entirely nugatory.⁴

In determining what acts are reasonably necessary and proper in order to accomplish an authorized end, the nature of the business and usages of the business world in connection therewith are to be considered; and the agent can always follow approved custom unless the contrary is expressly declared.⁵

It is often said that the ground on which the principal is held liable for the acts of an agent which are within the scope of his apparent authority, but beyond the limits of the authority actually given, is that of estoppel. If one man puts another man in a responsible position and thus holds him out to the world as having authority to do a certain act, and other

---

³ Howard *v.* Sheward, L. R. 2 C. P. 150; Oliphant on Horses, 3d ed., 124 *et seq.*

⁴ Valentine *v.* Piper, 22 Pick. (Mass.) 85; Schultz *v.* Griffin, 121 N. Y. 294.

⁵ Sutton *v.* Tatham, 10 Ad. & El. 27, 37 E. C. L. 25. See generally, Pole *v.* Leask, 28 Beav. 562; Bayliffe *v.* Butterworth, 1 Exch. 425; Cawthon *v.* Lusk, 97 Ala. 674; Peters *v.* Farnsworth, 15 Vt. 155.

men relying upon this appearance of authority have dealings with the agent, the principal is estopped from denying that the agent had such authority as he appeared to have.

In *Reynell v. Lewis* (1846),[6] Pollock, C. B., used this language: " Agency may be created by the immediate act of the party, that is, by really giving the authority to the agent, or representing to him that he is to have it, or by constituting that relation to which the law attaches agency; or it may be created by the representation of the defendant to the plaintiff, that the party making the contract is the agent of the defendant, or that such relation exists as to constitute him such; and if the plaintiff really makes the contract on the faith of the defendant's representation, the defendant is bound; he is estopped from disputing the truth of it with respect to that contract; and the representation of an authority is, *quoad hoc*, precisely the same as a real authority given by the defendant to the supposed agent. This representation may be made directly to the plaintiff, or made publicly so that it may be inferred to have reached him, and may be made by words or conduct."

The New York cases are very explicit in putting the liability of the principal, in cases like those we are now considering, on the ground of estoppel.[7] And there can be no doubt that wherever the circumstances are such as to raise an estoppel *in pais* against the principal, he is liable.

But as a philosophic explanation the estoppel theory clearly appears to be defective. It must always be borne in mind that the law of principal and agent is merely a branch of the broader doctrine of master and servant, and a common principle underlies both. In addition to being too narrow to have any claims to being considered an inclusive theory, the estoppel theory, so far as it has truth, appears to furnish only a roundabout approach to an end which is more directly reached by appealing at once to the axiom of agency.[8]

---

[6] 15 M. & W. 527, 528.
[7] Batavia Bank *v.* New York, etc., R. Co., 106 N. Y. 195. See A Misapplication of the Doctrine of Estoppel, by T. D. Kenneson, 5 Columbia L. Rev. 261.
[8] The estoppel theory has been lately pressed very much to the

Ratification.

<small>Chapter XLIV</small>

No subject connected with agency has given rise to more theoretical difficulties than that of ratification. Where an act is done by one person ostensibly acting as the agent of another, the latter may, upon being informed of the unauthorized act, assent to it and thereby adopt it as his own. This branch of the law of agency is old. In the civil law the principle underlying ratification was embodied in the maxim *omnis ratihabitio retrotrahitur, et mandato comparatur* — every ratification relates back and is analogous to prior authority. Lord Coke expressed it by changing the word *comparatur* to *æquiparatur,* doubtless without intending substantially to change the meaning of the maxim. <small>Ratification equivalent to prior authority.</small>

As in every case of relation, a fiction is involved. The act of ratification operates with the same effect as previous authority, and the relation of principal and agent is treated as existing *ab initio.* The fact that ratification can be given effect only by means of a fiction is sufficient to operate as a caution against applying the fiction literally, to the sacrifice of justice and common sense We accordingly find several exceptions which reason and necessity have combined to ingraft on the doctrine of ratification. Thus, it is said, ratification is impossible if the rights of strangers have meanwhile intervened.[9] <small>Fiction of relation. Qualifications. Rights of stranger.</small>

Again, ratification cannot be given effect where the act in question must as a matter of law be valid and effective at the time it is done or not at all. Thus, where an unauthorized <small>No ratification of act which must be valid *when done.*</small>

---

front by Mr. J. S. Ewart, who thinks he finds in this theory the complete explanation of the liability of the principal for the unauthorized acts of agents; but legal students do not generally agree on this point with Mr. Ewart. For his side of the matter see Ewart on Estoppel, ch. 26; Estoppel by Assisted Misrepresentation, 35 Am. L. Rev. 707; Estoppel, Principal and Agent, 16 Harv. L. Rev. 186; Agency by Estoppel, 5 Columbia L. Rev. 354; Estoppel by Assisted Representation, 5 Columbia L. Rev. 456.

On the other side, see Agency by Estoppel, W. W. Cook, 5 Columbia L. Rev. 36; Estoppel as Applied to Agency, 16 Harv. L. Rev. 324; Misapplication of Doctrine of Estoppel, T. D. Kenneson, 5 Columbia L. Rev. 261. See also 13 Green Bag, 50.

[9] Bird *v.* Brown, 4 Exch. 786; Pollock *v.* Cohen, 32 Ohio St. 514.

488 FOUNDATIONS OF LEGAL LIABILITY.

Rescission. notice to quit is given and the person receiving the notice is thus required to act, but fails or refuses to do so, the person in whose behalf notice is given cannot afterwards ratify and give validity to the ineffective notice.[1] It is also recognized that ratification cannot take place where the assumed agent and the other party have mutually rescinded the unauthorized transaction before ratification is attempted.[2]

The first of these limitations on the right of ostensible principal to ratify is obviously necessary to protect innocent parties. The ostensible principal can have nothing at stake until he does in fact ratify with knowledge, and it is just that he should be denied the right to intervene if others are to be injured thereby. The second limitation rests upon the very sensible ground that a person cannot be required to act upon an uncertainty. The notice must be effective when given or it is no notice. The third limitation rests upon the ground that that which can bind can unbind. An agent who is in fact unauthorized has as much right to rescind as he has to make the contract in the first instance, and the opposite party must not always be kept in uncertainty.

Right of third party to retreat before ratification. Another question has arisen in connection with the right of the ostensible principal to ratify, about which the decisions are in conflict. Suppose the person who deals with the ostensible agent for any reason repudiates the contract and notifies the assumed agent or ostensible principal of his withdrawal from the contract before ratification has taken place; can the principal nevertheless ratify and hold the third party to the contract regardless of his attempted withdrawal from it? To this different answers are given.

In *Dodge v. Hopkins* (1861)[3] it was held that, as the assent of the principal was not involved in the original transaction with the agent, the contract with the ostensible agent was of no effect. Its imperfection could only be cured by consent of the third party afterwards concurring with that of the principal at the time of the ratification. Consequently the

---

[1] Right *v.* Cuthell, 5 East 491.
[2] Walter *v.* James, L. R. 6 Exch. 124.
[3] 14 Wis. 630.

third party was there allowed to retreat from the contract at any time before ratification.

In *Bolton v. Lambert* (1889)[4] the English Court of Chancery reached a different conclusion. It was there held in effect that, by reason of the doctrine of relation, the original transaction, though not binding on the ostensible principal until ratification, did conditionally bind the third person from the beginning. Neither of these opposite views has met with general favor, and various lines of reasoning have been suggested as affording a proper basis for the solution of the difficulty.[5]

Conflict of authority.

Another branch of this subject of ratification in regard to which there is some conflict is found in the rule that the assumed agent must act as agent; that is, he must pretend to be agent for somebody. The mere fact that he has in his mind a particular person who is expected to ratify his conduct, and for whose benefit he acts, is not enough. This doctrine finds continuous expression in the reasoning of the courts and in the language of the text writers from the earliest times.

Agent must assume to act for another.

---

[4] 41 Ch. D. 295.
[5] See article, Problem as to Ratification, by Professor Wambaugh, 9 Harv. L. Rev. 60, also 5 Am. St. Rep. 109, note, 24 Am. L. Rev. 580, 25 Am. L. Rev. 74, 5 L. Quar. Rev. 440; Fry on Spec. Perform. (3d ed.) 711-713.

Perhaps the best-considered statement of the principle by which cases of this kind should be governed is that in which Professor Wambaugh embodies his theory, viz., "that the original transaction does not finally bind either the principal or the adverse party; that there can be no contract unless and until both parties actually or impliedly express simultaneous assent; that the assent expressed by the adverse party at the time of the original transaction must be considered as continuing until withdrawn; that the only effect of the assent expressed by the unauthorized agent is to meet the expressed assent of the adverse party with an expression which may ultimately be adopted by the assumed principal, and which, meanwhile, prevents the expressed assent of the adverse party from expiring by lapse; that before ratification the expressed assent of the adverse party may be withdrawn; that the withdrawal must be communicated either to the unauthorized agent or to the assumed principal; that ratification cannot be effective unless it precedes such communication; and that, subject to these limitations and to the general rule forbidding the doctrine of relation to be so applied as to work injustice, ratification relates back and causes the original transaction to be efficient as of its original date." A Problem as to Ratification, 9 Harv. L. Rev. 70, 71.

Strangely enough, the point here in question appears not to have arisen, or at least it was not actually decided until in very recent times.

Contract not capable of ratification where there is no assumption of agency.

In *Keighley v. Durant* (1901)[6] one Roberts made a contract for the purchase of corn in his own name, but, as he afterwards claimed, intending it to be for the joint account of himself and another. He did not, however, reveal such intention to the seller. Afterwards the person for whom he intended to act agreed to the transaction, but, in a suit subsequently brought by the seller against both Roberts and the ratifying principal, it was held that such a contract was not capable of ratification. In the Queen's Bench Division [7] the majority of the court adjudged the ratification good, but Smith, L. J., dissented and in an elaborate opinion went over the history of the whole subject. His reasoning was accepted as unanswerable in the House of Lords, when the case was afterwards taken on appeal to that court, and the decision of the Queen's Bench was accordingly unanimously reversed by this body.[8]

In the House of Lords, Lord Macnaghten, among other things, said: "If Tindal, C. J.'s, statement of the law [in *Wilson v. Tumman*] is accurate, it would seem to exclude the case of a person who may intend to act for another, but at the same time keeps his intention locked up in his own breast; for it cannot be said that a person who so conducts himself does assume to act for anybody but himself. But ought the doctrine of ratification to be extended to such a case? On principle I should say certainly not. It is, I think, a well-established principle in English law that civil obligations are not to be created by, or founded upon, undisclosed intentions. That is a very old principle." [9]

---

[6] A. C. 240.

[7] *Durant v. Roberts*, ('1900) 1 Q. B. 629.

[8] The opinion is too lengthy for insertion. The reader will do well to consult it. His Honor cited the following cases among others: *Saunderson v. Griffiths*, 5 B. & C. 909, 12 E. C. L. 404; *Bobbett v. Pinkett*, (1876) 1 Ex. D. 368; *Vere v. Ashby*, 10 B. & C. 288, 21 E. C. L. 79; *Wilson v. Tumman*, 6 M. & G. 236, 46 E. C. L. 236; *Watson v. Swann*, 11 C. B. N. S. 756, 103 E. C. L. 756.

[9] *Keighley v. Durant*, (1901) A. C. 247.

Death.

Inasmuch as agency is ordinarily a relation and not a contract, the death of either party terminates the relation and all rights incident to it except so far as the agency has already been executed. Even where the agency is made irrevocable during life by clothing it in the form of a perfect contract, it will ordinarily be taken as an implied term in the contract that it is to terminate on the death of either party. Apparently the application of the maxim that the acts of the servant are the acts of the master would also result in the same conclusion; for how can an act be attributed to a dead man?

Death terminates agency.

The doctrine that death terminates the agency is not pressed to its full consequences; for, under certain circumstances, an agent may execute his authority notwithstanding the death of the person from whom his authority is derived. It is well known that a provision in articles of partnership providing for the continuance of the business after the death of either member will be given effect, and will prevent such death from operating as a dissolution. But the agreement to this effect must be clearly expressed and will not be inferred.[1]

Effect of contract provision.

The continuance of agency after death is most frequently discussed in those cases where the agency is said to be coupled with an interest. Here the agency does not terminate upon the death of either the principal or the agent, and may be subsequently executed. It is to be observed that in England the term 'coupled with an interest' is used of all agencies which are irrevocable by the act of either party during life, irrevocability being due in such cases to the fact that both parties are bound to each other by a contract securing some benefit to the agent aside from his right to compensation. In America 'agency coupled with an interest' has a narrower signification, being limited to those agencies where an estate or interest in the property to be dealt with is vested in the agent for his protection or for the benefit of some third per-

Agency coupled with interest.

---

[1] Kirkman *v.* Booth, 11 Beav. 273; Exchange Bank *v.* Tracy, 77 Mo. 594; Alexander *v.* Lewis, 47 Tex. 481; Edwards *v.* Thomas, 66 Mo 468.

son. In this country we accordingly distinguish agencies with an interest from other irrevocable contracts of agency. Only in the former class of cases can the power be executed after the death of the principal.[2]

<small>Agency imports relation of confidence.</small>
Only one other feature of the relation of principal and agent need be here referred to, and this observation applies also to the relation of master and servant. The relation is one of confidence, and no agent has any right to retain acquisitions made by him during the course of his service. In the case of the servant this principle was perhaps originally derived from the law of status; but it is now in both cases based upon the necessary confidence reposed in the agent and from the situation of the respective parties. Consequently, <small>Liability of agent to account for profits.</small> any profit which an agent makes out of the business intrusted to him over and above the compensation agreed upon belongs to the principal and must be accounted for to him by the agent.[3] Though this doctrine originated in the court of equity and is most frequently applied there, the principle is fully recognized in the courts of law.[4]

[2] Hunt *v.* Rousmanier, 8 Wheat. (U. S.) 174; Knapp *v.* Alvord, 10 Paige (N. Y.) 205.
  See Watson *v.* King, 4 Campb. 272; Smart *v.* Sandars, 5 C. B. 895, 57 E. C. L. 895.
[3] Tyrrell *v.* London Bank, (1862) 10 H. L. Cas. 26, 2 Eng. Rul. Cas. 496; Kimber *v.* Barber, L. R. 8 Ch. 56; Parker *v.* McKenna, L. R. 10 Ch. 96; 2 Pomeroy Eq. Jur. 386; Mechem on Agency, § 469.
[4] Morison *v.* Thompson, L. R. 9 Q. B. 480; Salford *v.* Lever, ('1891) 1 Q. B. 168.

APPENDIX

THE NEGOTIABLE INSTRUMENTS LAW

THE NEGOTIABLE INSTRUMENTS LAW.

PRELIMINARY OBSERVATIONS.

The Origin of the Statute.

Judge M. D. Chalmers published his Digest of the English Law of Bills, Notes, and Cheques in 1878. In form it was modeled after the Indian Codes. In substance it was a statement, in succinct and orderly paragraphs, of the results of the decided cases. The general propositions were framed by the author and illustrated, so far as practicable, by reference to actual decisions. The writer, however, in order to complete the symmetry of his work, did not confine himself to the binding decisions of the English courts, but, where there was no expression from that source on a particular point, consulted the decisions of foreign tribunals and the works of foreign jurists, as well as usages of merchants and bankers.

The skill with which Judge Chalmers performed his task attracted much favorable notice, and accordingly soon afterwards the Institute of Bankers and Associated Chambers of Commerce procured his services in framing a bill. In doing this, he strove to reproduce, as exactly as possible, " the existing law, whether it seemed good, bad, or indifferent in its effect." The bill was then introduced in Parliament, and was passed after certain amendments had been incorporated, on the advice of a select committee of merchants, bankers, and lawyers, to whom the bill was referred.

The English Bills of Exchange Act (1882) is therefore substantially a codification of existing law. It has given great satisfaction in England and in her self-governing colonies, in all of which it has been adopted. The very small number of cases involving bills and notes which have reached the higher courts since its passage show that the act has contributed much to the removal of doubt and controversy.

The favor with which this piece of parliamentary legislation was received in England stimulated efforts to the same end in America, and in 1895 the American Commissioners on the Uniformity of Legislation [1] instructed their Committee on Commercial Law to have the American Laws of Bills and Notes put into the form of a code. The matter was referred to a subcommittee composed of Messrs. Lyman D. Brewster, Henry C. Wilcox, and Frank Bergen. These gentlemen procured Mr. J. J. Crawford of New York City to draft the law. The result of his labor was submitted to the commissioners at Saratoga in 1896. They carefully went over the bill and made a few changes, chiefly such as the draftsman had not felt at liberty, on his own authority, to make. As thus amended the draft was approved by the conference and submitted to the legislature of a number of the states. New York first enacted it into law,[2] and more than twenty of the American states have since followed this example.[3]

In the years that have elapsed since it went into force few

---

[1] An account of the genesis of the American Negotiable Instruments Law will be found in an article by Hon. Amasa M. Eaton, 2 Mich. L. Rev. 260. The Commissioners on Uniformity of Legislation are composed of a body of men appointed by the governors of several states under the authority of acts passed by the respective legislatures of such states. New York state was the first to authorize the appointment of such commissioners (1890). As a body the commissioners are distinct from the American Bar Association, but the passage of laws by the several states authorizing the appointment of the commissioners was due to the efforts of the bar association. The Commissioners on the Uniformity of Legislation have accordingly inherited the labors of the association's Committee on Uniform State Laws. The commissioners are accustomed to meet at the place appointed for the annual convention of the association, and only a few days prior to the time when the latter convenes. The two bodies are therefore in harmony with each other, and so far as possible collaborate to the same end.

[2] New York Laws of 1897, ch. 612. Took effect May 19, 1897.

[3] Prior to January 1, 1906, the Negotiable Instruments Law had become effective in the following thirty jurisdictions: Arizona, Colorado, Connecticut, District of Columbia, Florida, Idaho, Iowa, Kansas, Kentucky, Louisiana, Maryland, Massachusetts, Michigan, Missouri, Montana, Nebraska, New Jersey, New York, North Carolina, North Dakota, Ohio, Oregon, Pennsylvania, Rhode Island, Tennessee, Utah, Virginia, Washington, Wisconsin, Wyoming.

cases have arisen which involve the construction of its language — a circumstance which is doubtless to be taken as a favorable commentary on its clearness and precision, as well as upon the good judgment used in framing it. Mr. Crawford benefited by the labors of Judge Chalmers, but any one who will take the pains to compare the two acts will see that in form, style, and language the American act is simpler, less technical, and more easily intelligible than its English precursor. It is indoubtedly, as Mr. Arthur Cohen has said, " a very important and ably framed code." [4] The language of the act is so precise and the whole piece of work is generally so consistent with itself, that little comment or explanation is necessary. In the following pages the reader will find some subjects treated which could not well be dealt with in the body of this work.

We also direct the reader's attention, at the proper points, to some searching extrajudicial interpretation to which the act has been subjected. This criticism was set afoot by Professor Ames of Harvard University, who, in a paper published in 1900,[5] pointed out what he conceived to be certain defects in the act. Hon. Lyman D. Brewster, one of the subcommittee who procured the law to be framed, soon replied to Professor Ames's criticisms.[6] Others have done likewise.[7] On the whole, the literature pertaining to bills and notes has been substantially enriched by the papers which have been called forth in this controversy.

---

[4] See Ames-Brewster, Negotiable Instruments Law 82.

[5] The Negotiable Instruments Law, 14 Harv. L. Rev. 240, 442.

[6] A Defense of the Negotiable Instruments Law, 10 Yale L. J. 84.

[7] See article, Negotiable Instruments Law, by J. L. Farrell in the Brief of Phi Delta Phi, vol. 3, p. 131, and the very excellent papers by Charles L. McKeehan on the Negotiable Instruments Law published in 41 Am. L. Reg. N. S. 437, 499, 561; also the additional paper from Judge Brewster in 15 Harv. L. Rev. 26. The Ames-Brewster papers are published separately, with the text of the act, by the Harvard Law Review, Cambridge, Mass. Mr. Farrell has a still later paper on the same subject in Brief of Phi Delta Phi for First Quarter 1904, vol. 5, p. 1.

Amasa M. Eaton also contributes to the literature of the subject in 11 Mich. L. Rev. 260 (Jan. 1904). See also Necessary Amendments, by Professor Ames, 16 Harv. L. Rev. 255.

General Principle of Construction.

The Negotiable Instruments Law is an organic whole, covering so far as practicable all the rights and duties incident to the creation, transfer, and discharge of negotiable instruments. It therefore supplies an excellent opportunity for the application of the rule of interpretation that all parts of an act are to be construed together and in furtherance of the legislative intent.

The Court of Appeals of the District of Columbia, in the recent case of *Wirt v. Stubblefield* (1900),[8] had occasion to discuss this aspect of the act. The question to be determined was whether the passage of the Negotiable Instruments Law had impliedly repealed the English statutes making void all bills and notes given for a gambling consideration. In an opinion which is highly instructive the court held that inasmuch as the act was intended to cover the whole subject as far as it could be done by statute, all partial and local acts repugnant to it were of necessity repealed by implication.

Among other things it was said: "We know the origin and history of the Act of Congress. We know it is largely derived, in its form and provisions, from the English Act upon the subject; and we know, moreover, that the great and leading object of the act, not only with Congress, but with the large number of the principal commercial states of the Union that have adopted it, has been to establish a uniform system of law to govern negotiable instruments wherever they might circulate or be negotiated. It was not only uniformity of rules and principles that was designed, but to embody in a codified form, as fully as possible, all the law upon the subject, to avoid conflict of decisions, and the effect of mere local laws and usages that have heretofore prevailed. The great object sought to be accomplished by the enactment of the statute was to free the negotiable instrument, as far as possible, from all latent or local infirmities that would otherwise inhere in it, to the prejudice and disappointment of inno-

[8] 17 App. Cas. (D. C.) 283.

cent holders, as against all the parties to the instrument professedly bound thereby. This clearly could not be effected so long as the instrument was rendered absolutely null and void by local statute, as against the original maker or acceptor; as is the case by the operation, indeed, by the express provision, of the statutes of Charles and Anne." [9]

"It is difficult to conceive, if we bear in mind the object and policy intended to be promoted by, as well as the entire scope and express provisions of, the Negotiable Instruments Law, that the framers of that act ever intended to save and preserve unrepealed, as part of the law governing negotiable instruments, the old English statutes against gaming. On the contrary, it was most clearly among the objects and purposes of that act, to get rid of all such impediments and hindrances to the circulation of negotiable instruments as had been created by those old statutes, and to embody the entire law upon the subject, as far as practicable, into one well-digested and consistent act. It is true, as a general rule, that where there are two acts on the same subject, the rule is to give effect to both, if it can consistently be done. 'But if the two are repugnant in any of their provisions, the latter act, without any repealing clause, operates to the extent of a repugnancy as a repeal of the first; and even where two acts are not in express terms repugnant, yet if the latter act covers the whole subject of the first, and embraces new provisions, plainly showing that it was intended as a substitute for the first act, it will operate as a repeal of that act.' [1] It is quite clear that the Act of Congress was intended to cover the whole subject of negotiable instruments as far as it could be done by statute; and therefore to exclude the operation and effect of former statutes like those of Charles and Anne."

[9] 16 Car. 2, ch. 7; 9 Anne, ch. 14. (U. S.) 636; U. S. v. Tynen, 11
[1] Daviess v. Fairbairn, 3 How. Wall. (U. S.) 88, 92.

TITLE I

NEGOTIABLE INSTRUMENTS IN GENERAL.

ARTICLE I

FORM AND INTERPRETATION.

SECTION 1. An instrument to be negotiable must conform to the following requirements: —
1. It must be in writing and signed by the maker or drawer;
2. Must contain an unconditional promise or order to pay a sum certain in money;
3. Must be payable on demand, or at a fixed or determinable future time;
4. Must be payable to order or to bearer; and,
5. Where the instrument is addressed to a drawee, he must be named or otherwise indicated therein with reasonable certainty.

The title of the act, as well as its substance, shows that its provisions were intended to apply only to those instruments which conform to the requirements mentioned in § 1.[3] The schedule of definitions does not define the word 'negotiable,' but in § 30 negotiation is defined as such a transfer of an instrument as constitutes the transferee a holder of the paper. It is apparent that negotiable in § 1 is used in this primary sense — transferable.

If an instrument is transferable under the principles of the law merchant, the indorsee or bearer, as the case may be, acquires legal title and may sue on the instrument in his own name. This feature, as said by Strong, J., in *Shaw v. Railroad Co.* (1879),[4] is the essence of negotiability.

Negotiability, however, commonly imports certain other qualities in addition to mere transferability. Thus, the holder

---

[3] The references in this Appendix are to the act as recommended for passage by the Committee on Commercial Law of the Commissioners on Uniformity of Legislation, and as sectionized by that committee. Most of the states have followed the form of division here adopted. In some of them, however, the general provisions found in title IV, §§ 190–197, are transferred to the beginning of the act, thus altering the numbers of the sections throughout. In a few states where title IV is so transferred, the subdivisions of that title are left unnumbered.

[4] 101 U. S. 557.

in due course takes the paper free from all personal defenses or equities, as they are often called, of the party bound, and obtains a perfect title though the previous holder may have had none.

It is a rule that, if an instrument is negotiable by its original terms, it will remain transferable at will until discharged, unless some holder stops its further transfer by making a restrictive indorsement. Overdue paper therefore still remains transferable (§ 47), though the circumstance that the paper is dishonored puts the holder on inquiry and affects him with notice of all defects in the title of the person from whom he obtained it.[5]

Subsection 1.—It is of course essential that the contract be in writing — a term which by statutory definition includes printed matter and matter which is written with a pencil.[6] It is not required that the signature of the maker or drawer be *subscribed,* and inasmuch as § 10 expressly declares that the instrument need not follow the exact language of the act where the intention to conform to its substance clearly appears, it follows that a note in the form "I, A. B., promise to pay," or a bill in the form "I, A. B., request you to pay," would be good.[7]

Subsection 4.—By this provision the instrument must be payable to order or to bearer.[8] If words of negotiability are

---

[5] Deuters v. Townsend, 5 B. & S. 613, 117 E. C. L. 613. Compare § 7.

[6] Reed v. Roark, 14 Tex. 329, 65 Am. Dec. 127, 4 Am. and Eng. Encyc. of Law, 2d ed., 81.

[7] Taylor v. Dobbins, 1 Stra. 399; Saunderson v. Jackson, 2 B. & P. 238.

[8] See Westberg v. Chicago Lumber, etc., Co., 117 Wis. 589.

Though the statute requires that the bill or note in order to be negotiable shall be made payable to order or to bearer, § 10 provides that the instrument need not conform exactly to the language of the act. Hence under this act, as heretofore, a bill or note payable to " A or assigns " may be a good negotiable instrument under the act, provided it appears from the nature and tenor of the instrument that it was intended to be a negotiable instrument. See Zander v. New York Security, etc., Co., 178 N. Y. 208; Brainerd v. New York, etc., R. Co., 25 N. Y. 496; Citizens Sav. Bank v. Greenburgh, 173 N. Y. 215.

It has been held that a certificate of deposit which declares the certificate to be assignable only on the books of the company is not a negotiable instrument within the meaning of this act, and the addition of the words 'or assigns' does not change the nature of the instrument. Zander v. New York Security, etc., Co., 178 N. Y. 208.

omitted, the act does not apply and the law applicable to the instrument must be found elsewhere. The rights growing out of such paper must therefore be determined by the principles of the law merchant (see § 196) as adopted by the common-law courts.

By the very terms of the contract a promise or order to pay to A does not authorize payment to C, and such third person cannot acquire title to the paper so as to entitle him to sue the maker or acceptor in his own name. By 3 and 4 Anne, chapter 9, this basal principle was abrogated so far as notes are concerned, and a note drawn payable 'to A' was thereby put on the same footing as regards transferability as a bill or note drawn payable to 'A or order.' The same innovation was made in the law of bills by the English Bills of Exchange Act (1882).

In some of the American states the statute of Anne has been applied as part of the local law, and in others enactments similar to it have been passed. The passage of the Negotiable Instruments Law repeals all such legislation and thereby relegates paper not containing words of negotiability to its prior status. It would have been better if the authors of the Negotiable Instruments Law had copied the English Bills of Exchange Act and had dispensed with the necessity of the words order or bearer altogether. In regard to bills of exchange the question is of very little moment, for these instruments belong almost entirely to the transactions of the mercantile world, and are usually drawn by persons who know the requisites of a bill. Promissory notes, however, are in constant use among untechnical people and words of negotiability are often omitted by mere oversight. Wherever this is done, the rights of the parties are to be decided upon the principles of the law merchant applicable at common law to them.

The law in regard to the instrument lacking words of negotiability is not very well defined. One point that can be taken as established is that the bill or note lacking words of negotiability is a good mercantile contract. It is within the principles of the law merchant. Mr. Chitty tells us with perfect truth that a bill is good as a mercantile contract though not payable to order or bearer,[9] and the same is true of the promissory note. Originally, as we have seen, all bills and notes were made payable to particular parties and lacked words of negotiability, yet they were none the less subject to the rules of the law merchant. The difficult point about the instrument which lacks words of negotiability is to determine its qualities as a mercantile contract.

In the first place let us consider its disability. The bill or note lacking words of negotiability cannot be so transferred as to vest in the transferee that indefeasible title which cuts off the defenses of the maker, drawer, or acceptor. The person who acquires such an instrument is as against the original maker a mere assignee. Still, in one aspect the bill or note payable to a particular person is fully transferable. Thus an indorser of such paper can be held liable on his indorsement because his indorsement amounts to the drawing of a new bill.[1]

We may say, then, that as against the person actually indorsing the paper, a bill or note lacking words of negotiability is to all intents and purposes a negotiable instrument. But this holds good only as against such person. Thus, the assignee of a bill or note not payable to order or bearer can sue the acceptor or maker at common law only, and the suit must be brought in the name of the assignor to the use of the assignee. The actual plaintiff in such case cannot sue in his own name because the contract contains no words binding the acceptor or maker to pay the money to him.[2] In other words, negotiation is not authorized by the instrument.

Among the mercantile features which the bill or note lacking words of negotiability does possess is that quality by which it is entitled to days of grace. The weight of authority

---

[9] Chitty on Bills, 159. See also Story on Bills, §60; Arnold v. Sprague, 34 Vt. 402; Mehlberg v. Fisher, 24 Wis. 607; Corbett v. Clark, 45 Wis. 403.

[1] Hill v. Lewis, 1 Salk. 132;

Hodges v. Steward, 1 Salk. 125; Williams v. Williams, Carth. 269.

[2] Gerard v. La Coste, 1 Dall. (Pa.) 194; Reed v. Murphy, 1 Ga. 236.

is to this effect, though there are some decisions to the contrary.[3]

Again, it is settled that an instrument in the form of a bill of exchange which lacks words of negotiability, but which is in other respects a perfect bill, imports a consideration.[4] The promissory note has also been generally held to import a consideration, though it be not payable to order or bearer.[5]

This rule has been supposed to follow, as regards notes, from the Statute of 3 and 4 Anne, or from other local statutes in conformity with its provisions. It is certainly true that under that statute no doubt could reasonably be entertained on this point. But now that the statute of Anne is being repealed in America by the Negotiable Instruments Law, the question arises whether, apart from statute, a note not containing words of negotiability imports a consideration.

In theory the note ought to be held to be on precisely the same footing at this point as the bill, but there seems to be a general impression to the contrary. Thus in *Deyo v. Thompson* (1900),[6] it was held that inasmuch as the statute of Anne is now repealed, a note not payable to order or bearer no longer imports a consideration in the state of New York.[7]

We cannot avoid the conclusion that this is a mistake. The question resolves itself into the old debate which gave so much trouble in the closing years of the seventeenth century, and about which Lord Holt was so obstinately opinionated. Is the promissory note, apart from the statute of Anne, within

---

[3] Smith *v.* Kendall, 6 T. R. 123; Miller *v.* Biddle, 13 L. T. N. S. 334; Reed *v.* Murphy, 1 Ga. 236; Duncan *v.* Maryland Sav. Inst., 10 Gill & J. (Md.) 299. *Contra,* Backus *v.* Danforth, 10 Conn. 297; Bristol *v.* Warner, 19 Conn. 7.

[4] Josselyn *v.* Lacier, 10 Mod. 294; Louisville, etc., R. Co. *v.* Caldwell, 98 Ind. 245; Coursin *v.* Ledlie, 31 Pa. St. 506; Averett *v.* Booker, 15 Gratt. (Va.) 163.

[5] Cowan *v.* Hallack, 9 Colo. 572; Mitchell *v.* Rome R. Co., 17 Ga. 574; Stacker *v.* Hewitt, 2 Ill. 207; Durland *v.* Pitcairn, 51 Ind. 426;

Caples *v.* Branham, 20 Mo. 244, 64 Am. Dec. 183; Glasscock *v.* Glasscock, 66 Mo. 627; Carnwright *v.* Gray, 127 N. Y. 98, 24 Am. St. Rep. 424; Goshen, etc., Turnpike Road Co. *v.* Hurtin, 9 Johns. (N. Y.) 217, 6 Am. Dec. 273; Hegeman *v.* Moon, 131 N. Y. 462; Arnold *v.* Sprague, 34 Vt. 402; Peasley *v.* Boatwright, 2 Leigh (Va.) 196.

[6] 53 N. Y. App. Div. 9.

[7] Compare Edgerton *v.* Edgerton, 8 Conn. 6; Bristol *v.* Warner, 19 Conn. 7; Bircleback *v.* Wilkins, 22 Pa. St. 26; Courtney *v.* Doyle, 10 Allen (Mass.) 122.

the principles of the law merchant? If Lord Holt was right in saying that it was not, then it must now be said that the note lacking words of negotiability does not import a consideration. If he was wrong, as in our judgment he unquestionably was, then such a note does import a consideration.

Sec. 2. The sum payable is a sum certain within the meaning of this act, although it is to be paid,—
1. With interest; or
2. By stated instalments; or
3. By stated instalments, with a provision that upon default in payment of any instalment or of interest the whole shall become due; or
4. With exchange, whether at a fixed rate or at the current rate; or
5. With costs of collection or an attorney's fee, in case payment shall not be made at maturity.

Subsection 5.—This clause settles a point upon which the authorities were hopelessly in conflict. In California, Dakota, Michigan, Minnesota, Missouri, North Carolina, North Dakota, Pennsylvania, South Carolina, South Dakota, and Wisconsin it has been decided that such a provision in a note destroys its character as a negotiable instrument. In the federal courts and in Alabama, Arkansas, Georgia, Illinois, Iowa, Kansas, Kentucky, Louisiana, Montana, Oregon, Tennessee, and Washington it was held not to affect negotiability. The different courts have assigned various reasons for this, some holding that the stipulation for fees is valid and enforceable, others that the stipulation is invalid, but the instrument good.

Probably the best reason for holding the provision good and not destructive of the negotiability of the note is that the stipulation is of no effect as long as the instrument is negotiable in the full sense. It does not operate until the note is dishonored. Said Judge McAlister of Tennessee: " The amount to be paid is certain during the currency of the note as a negotiable instrument, and it only becomes uncertain after it ceases to be negotiable by the default of the maker in its payment." [8]

[8] Oppenheimer *v.* Farmers', etc., Bank, 97 Tenn. 33. See cases cited in 4 Am. and Eng. Encyc. of Law, 2d ed., 99-102.

Sec. 3. An unqualified order or promise to pay is unconditional within the meaning of this act, though coupled with —
1. An indication of a particular fund out of which reimbursement is to be made, or a particular account to be debited with the amount; or
2. A statement of the transaction which gives rise to the instrument.

But an order or promise to pay out of a particular fund is not unconditional.

Subsection 2.—That a mere statement of the transaction out of which a note arises, or of the executed consideration for which it was given, does not affect its negotiability is perfectly clear, unless the statement of the transaction or consideration itself shows that the promise to pay is conditional upon some other event.[9] If the consideration recited is executory and the promise to pay is dependent upon the performance of the consideration, then the note is not negotiable. Thus, in *Jarvis v. Wilkins* (1841),[1] a note in these words, " I undertake to pay R. the sum of six pounds for a suit of clothes ordered by P.," was held not negotiable, since, in the view of Lord Abinger, it appeared that the promise was made in contemplation of a sale to be afterwards made, and was a written undertaking to pay if the plaintiff would supply the clothes.[2]

Again, if a note shows that it was given as collateral security, such a statement of the transaction out of which the note arises shows a qualified or conditional promise, and consequently the note is not negotiable.[3]

The clause in question was inserted, Mr. Crawford tells us, to remove all doubts as to the negotiability of a note which recites that it is given for the purchase price of a chattel, title to which is retained in the seller until the purchase money is paid. These contracts have become very common, and while the great weight of professional and judicial au-

[9] See 4 Am. and Eng. Encyc. of Law, 2d ed., 89.
[1] 7 M. & W. 410.
[2] Compare Drury *v.* Macaulay, 16 M. & W. 146, and Drawn *v.* Cherry, 14 La. Ann. 705, where the note recited that it was given in consideration that the payee should assist in a prosecution.
[3] See The Negotiable Instruments Law, 41 Am. L. Reg. N. S. 442; A Defense of the Negotiable Instruments Law, 10 Yale L. J. 87.

thority supports their negotiability, a few courts — Massachusetts, Kansas, and Minnesota — have held that such recitals destroy the negotiability of the note. In Massachusetts, this holding is placed upon the ground that the promise is conditional, inasmuch as, if it be not paid at maturity, the seller may rescind and take back the chattel, in which event the purchaser is no longer liable on the note.[4] Where this view is entertained it is clear that the courts may, even after the enactment of the Negotiable Instruments Law, follow their previous rulings without violating the literal meaning of this particular provision of the statute.[5] Possibly § 5, subs. 4, might be considered persuasive of the negotiability of such a note, though that provision was evidently not framed with a direct view to this situation.

Sec. 4. An instrument is payable at a determinable future time, within the meaning of this act, which is expressed to be payable,—
1. At a fixed period after date or sight; or
2. On or before a fixed or determinable future time specified therein; or
3. On or at a fixed period after the occurrence of a specified event, which is certain to happen, though the time of happening be uncertain.

An instrument payable upon a contingency is not negotiable, and the happening of the event does not cure the defect.

Subsections 1–3.— *Colehan v. Cooke* (1742)[6] and *Carlos v. Fancourt* (1794)[7] are the leading cases on these clauses. In the former case the maker of a note promised to pay ten days after the death of his father. It was held that the event which determined the time of payment was certain to happen, and consequently that the fact that it was not known when the death would occur did not destroy the negotiability of the note. The case was decided on authority and custom rather than strict reason. Lord Chief Justice Willes referred to the fact that bills of exchange commonly called *billæ nundinales,* payable at particular fairs, had always been held good; for though the fairs were not held upon any fixed date, yet

---
[4] Sloan v. McCarty, 134 Mass. 245.
[5] See 14 Harv. L. Rev. 244; 41 Am. L. Reg. N. S. 443, 444.
[6] Willes 393.   [7] 5 T. R. 482.

it was certain that they would be held. His lordship said that the notion had once been entertained that the negotiability of a bill would be destroyed by making it payable at an unusual or unreasonable period in the future (e. g., seven months, according to one writer), but that this notion had never gained any countenance and that there was no limit of time fixed within which the bill or note must be payable. If distance of time constituted no impediment, the bill, reasoned he, would be good if the event which determines the time of payment is certain to happen at some time.

It has been held that a bill or note payable when a certain person becomes of age or marries, or upon the arrival of a ship, is not negotiable, as neither event may ever happen.[8]

Sec. 5. An instrument which contains an order or promise to do any act in addition to the payment of money is not negotiable. But the negotiable character of an instrument otherwise negotiable is not affected by a provision which —
1. Authorizes the sale of collateral securities in case the instrument be not paid at maturity; or
2. Authorizes a confession of judgment if the instrument be not paid at maturity;[9] or
3. Waives the benefit of any law intended for the advantage or protection of the obligor;[1] or
4. Gives the holder an election to require something to be done in lieu of payment of money.

But nothing in this section shall validate any provision or stipulation otherwise illegal.

Subsection 4.—In illustration of this subsection Mr. Crawford refers to notes which give the holder the right to elect to take stock in a corporation instead of requiring the payment of money.[2] It may possibly be also invoked to sustain the validity of notes which give the vendor of a chattel upon

---

[8] Pearson v. Garrett, 4 Mod. 242; Palmer v. Pratt, 2 Bing. 185, 9 E. C. L. 373; Coolidge v. Ruggles, 15 Mass. 387; Goss v. Nelson, 1 Burr. 226.

[9] A note containing authority for the holder to put it in judgment at any time whether due or not is not negotiable. Wisconsin Freewill Baptists v. Babler, 115 Wis. 289.

[1] This clause is evidently framed with a view to provisions in notes waiving the benefit of exemptions. Of course it does not operate to give effect to a waiver of exemption in a state where such a waiver is contrary to existing law.

[2] Crawford, The Negotiable Instruments Law, 2d ed., 15, note (c), citing Hodges v. Shuler, 22 N. Y. 114.

conditional sale the right to reclaim the chattel in case of the nonpayment of the note.

Sec. 6. The validity and negotiable character of an instrument are not affected by the fact that —
1. It is not dated; or
2. Does not specify the value given, or that any value has been given therefor; or
3. Does not specify the place where it is drawn or the place where it is payable; or
4. Bears a seal; or
5. Designates a particular kind of current money in which payment is to be made.

But nothing in this section shall alter or repeal any statute requiring in certain cases the nature of the consideration to be stated in the instrument.

Subsection 5.—The question of the negotiability of notes payable in currency, current funds, current notes, bank notes, etc., has arisen with great frequency in America. It cannot be said that the expression 'current money' here used in the statute is of much assistance, each court being left to its own resources in determining what sorts of currency can pass as money.[3]

The saving clause at the end of this section has in view the continuance in force of statutes such as those which require notes given for patent rights to recite the fact that the note was given for a patent right.

Sec. 7. An instrument is payable on demand: —
1. Where it is expressed to be payable on demand, or at sight, or on presentation; or
2. In which no time for payment is expressed.
Where an instrument is issued, accepted, or indorsed when overdue, it is, as regards the person so issuing, accepting, or indorsing it, payable on demand.

Subsection 1.— This provision assimilates sight and demand paper. Under the law as it previously stood instruments payable at sight were entitled to grace, while instruments payable upon demand were not.[4]

---

[3] The cases on this point will be found assorted in 4 Am. and Eng. Encyc. of Law. 2d ed., 103-107.

[4] Daniel on Neg. Inst., § 617. See Mass. Laws 1899, c. 130, restoring grace to sight drafts.

Subsection 2.—A note in the form "I promise to pay to the order of A, two thousand dollars at his office, N. Y. City," is payable on demand, and the contrary cannot be shown by parol evidence.[5]

Sec. 8. The instrument is payable to order where it is drawn payable to the order of a specified person or to him or his order. It may be drawn payable to the order of —
1. A payee who is not maker, drawer, or drawee; or
2. The drawer or maker; or
3. The drawee; or
4. Two or more payees jointly; or
5. One or some of several payees; or
6. The holder of an office for the time being.

Where the instrument is payable to order the payee must be named or otherwise indicated therein with reasonable certainty.

Subsection 2.—A bill or note payable to the drawer or maker is incomplete and inoperative until indorsed by him.[6]

Subsections 5 and 6.— These two clauses respectively nullify *Blanckenhagen v. Blundell* (1819),[7] *Cowie v. Stirling* (1856),[8] and similar cases. In the first of these it was decided that a note cannot be negotiable if made payable " to A or to B and C, or to his or their order." In the second it was held that a note is not negotiable if made payable " to the secretary for the time being " of a certain corporation, or to his order. In *Yates v. Nash* (1860),[9] a note payable " to the treasurer for the time being " of a particular institution was held not negotiable. The idea underlying these decisions is that the payee must be ascertained at the time of the execution or the acceptance of the note or bill.

Sec. 9. The instrument is payable to bearer —
1. When it is expressed to be so payable; or
2. When it is payable to a person named therein or bearer; or
3. When it is payable to the order of a fictitious or non-existing person, and such fact was known to the person making it so payable; or

[5] McLeod *v.* Hunter, (Supm. Ct. Tr. T.) 29 Misc. (N. Y.) 558, 49 N. Y. App. Div. 131.
[6] Pettyjohn *v.* National Exch. Bank, 101 Va. 111.
[7] 2 B. & Ald. 417.
[8] 6 El. & Bl. 333, 88 E. C. L. 333.
[9] 8 C. B. N. S. 581, 98 E. C. L. 581.

4. When the name of the payee does not purport to be the name of any person; or
5. When the only or last indorsement is an indorsement in blank.

Subsection 1.—When an instrument is, by its original terms, made payable to bearer, it remains negotiable by delivery, notwithstanding a special indorsement is subsequently placed upon it. For the effect of such special indorsement, see § 40.

Subsection 3.—The corresponding clause of the English Bills of Exchange Act is in these words: " Where the payee is a fictitious or nonexisting person the bill may be treated as payable to bearer." [1] The meaning of this language in the English statute was considered by the House of Lords in *Bank of England v. Vagliano* (1891).[2] This is by far the most important decision that has been rendered upon any aspect of the statute since it was enacted.

It appeared in this case that a real firm, Petridi & Co., was accustomed to draw upon Vagliano Bros. A clerk of the latter fraudulently drew a bill upon his employers in the name of Petridi & Co., and payable to Petridi & Co. Vagliano Bros. accepted the bill, and the clerk, having gotten it into his possession, indorsed it in the name of Petridi & Co., and procured it to be discounted at the defendant bank. Vagliano Bros., the drawees, accepted on the supposition, of course, that the bill was genuine, and did not know that Petridi & Co. had no interest in it and were intended, by the person who actually drew the bill, to have no interest in it at any time. It was held that Petridi & Co. was a fictitious or nonexisting person, within the meaning of the act, and that the bill was to be treated as payable to bearer in favor of the innocent purchaser. In other words, the expression "fictitious or nonexisting person," as used in the statute, includes a real person who is not intended to have any interest in the proceeds of the bill or note.

In *Clutton v. Attenborough* [3] a similar fraud was perpe-

---

[1] English Bills of Exchange Act (1882), § 7, subs 3.
[2] (1891) A. C. 107, reversing (1889) 23 Q. B. D. 243, (1888) 22 Q. B. D. 103.
[3] (1895) 2 Q. B. 306, 707.

trated by a clerk who fraudulently represented that work had been done by one George Brett, who in fact had no existence. The plaintiffs made out a check payable to George Brett and the clerk cashed it. The loss was held to fall upon the firm drawing the check and not upon the bank, as it was payable to a fictitious person. George Brett was no less fictitious by reason of the fact that the plaintiffs thought him a real person.

Now it will be seen that the American Act, § 9, subs. 3, is less radical than the corresponding provision in the English law; for under its provisions the bill is to be treated as payable to bearer, only when the fact of the fictitious character of the payee is known to the person making the instrument so payable. The American Act in this respect embodies the decision in *Shipman v. State Bank* (1891),[4] where a clerk drew checks, some payable to fictitious persons, as in *Clutton v. Attenborough,* and some payable to persons not intended to have any interest in the checks or their proceeds. He induced his employer, Shipman, to sign the checks, by representing that the payees were real persons entitled to the sums indicated in the checks. The clerk then indorsed the checks in the name of the fictitious payees and persons not having any interest in them, and cashed them at the defendant bank. It was held that the bank must bear the loss — a result different from that reached in *Clutton v. Attenborough.*

Whether the Negotiable Instruments Law fixes liability on an acceptor where the facts are the same as those involved in the case of *Bank of England v. Vagliano,*[5] is perhaps debatable. The section we are considering states that the bill is payable to bearer if the party making the bill payable to the fictitious person has knowledge of the fictitious character of the payee. In cases of genuine bills, the drawer is the person who makes the bill within the meaning of the language of § 9, subs. 3. Where, however, the paper is fabricated there is no drawer, and neither the nominal drawer nor the fabricator can be treated as the person *making* the instru-

[4] 126 N. Y. 318.   [5] (1891) A. C. 107.

ment *payable to* the fictitious payee. If the instrument has any vitality at all it is derived from acceptance by the drawee. It would seem therefore that, in such case, the acceptor must be treated as the person *making* the bill. Consequently, if the acceptor accepts in ignorance of the fact that the payee named in the bill is fictitious or not intended to have an interest in the proceeds, the paper cannot be treated as payable to bearer. In other words, a case involving facts like those of *Bank of England v. Vagliano* would be decided against the bank and not in its favor as under the English Bills of Exchange Act. The principle of *Shipman v. State Bank, ante,* is apparently good law, not only as applicable to cases involving its particular facts, but also in cases involving facts like those appearing in the Vagliano case. In the latter case it was the acceptor, in the former the drawer, who was ignorant of the fictitious character of the payee. Both are the persons who make the paper within the meaning of the language in § 9, subs. 3.

The English Act uses the words "may be treated as payable to bearer." The effect of these words was discussed in the Vagliano case, but not settled. The American Act uses the words "is payable to bearer" and thus removes all doubt. It will be observed that as a consequence of the wording of the American Act, the bill or note payable to the order of a fictitious or nonexisting person is payable to bearer without being indorsed.[6] This is the only instance where a note payable to order can be negotiated by mere delivery without any indorsement. "Surely," says Judge Brewster, "it is more logical to hold that a note which purports to be payable to a person, when there is no such person and the maker knows it, must have been intended to be payable to bearer, than to hold that somebody must assume the name of such fictitious person and make a false indorsement in order to give title to the note."[7] As a matter of fact it must nearly always happen that the maker or the person to whom he delivers the instrument

[6] This conforms to the doctrine of *Plets v. Johnson,* 3 Hill (N. Y.) 112; *Central Bank v. Lang,* 1 Bosw. (N. Y.) 203; *Irving Nat. Bank v. Alley,* 79 N. Y. 536; *Shipman v. Bank of State of New York,* 126 N. Y. 318.

[7] A Defense of the Negotiable Instruments Law, 10 Yale L. J. 89.

will indorse it in the name of the fictitious payee; otherwise no one would discount it.

It has been suggested that § 9, subs. 3, may have the effect of making notes payable to the order of unincorporated associations or to the order of the estates of deceased persons payable to bearer. This view finds some support in *Lewisohn v. Kent, etc., Co.* (1895),[8] but is repudiated by all the writers who have examined the question.[1]

Subsection 4.— This clause evidently refers to such instruments as checks payable to "cash," "exchange," etc.[2]

Subsection 5.— The blank indorsement of a bill payable to order originally merely operated as an authority to any holder to fill out a special indorsement to himself above the blank signature, or to write a receipt above the same.[3] By the time of Lord Mansfield this formality was dispensed with, and paper indorsed in blank became, in fact and in legal effect, payable to bearer.

In *Smith v. Clarke* (1794)[4] the following case arose: A bill payable to order was indorsed in blank by the payee. It thus became payable to any bearer. A subsequent holder, C, for instance, indorsed it specially to D. D then transferred by delivery to E, who sued upon the bill. The first indorsement was in blank, the second a special indorsement. Obviously D could not claim under the special indorsement, because he held by delivery. Lord Kenyon, however, held at Nisi Prius that the bill remained payable to bearer as long as the first indorsement remained in blank and was not filled out. Consequently E, though he obtained the instrument from D, was allowed to sue in his own name and strike out the indorsement to D as being unnecessary to his (plaintiff's) title. He was thus allowed to maintain suit as bearer under the blank indorsement. This decision was followed in both England

---

[8] 87 Hun (N. Y.) 257.
[1] See Crawford, Neg. Inst. Law, § 29; 14 Harv. L. Rev. 443, note; Shaw v. Smith, 150 Mass. 166; Peltier v. Babillion, 45 Mich. 384; Chalmers, Bills, 5th ed., 23, 24; 41 Am. L. Reg. N. S. 451.

[2] Crawford, The Negotiable Instruments Law, 2d ed., § 28, note (c).
[3] Marius, Advice, 30.
[4] Peake N. P. (ed. 1795) 225.

and America,[5] but was thought to run counter to the sense of the mercantile community, and accordingly the English Bills of Exchange Act changed the law. This step was followed by the American codifier, and the doctrine of *Smith v. Clarke* was thus overruled by legislation.

It must be borne in mind that § 9, subs. 5, applies only to instruments originally payable to order. It was at one time supposed by Professor Ames that § 40 contradicts § 9, subs. 5, and nullifies it; but, as pointed out by Mr. John L. Farrell and Prof. C. L. McKeehan, this latter section refers only to bills originally made payable to bearer.[6] There can be no possible doubt as to the soundness of this interpretation.

Sec. 10. The instrument need not follow the language of this act, but any terms are sufficient which clearly indicate an intention to confoim to the requirements hereof.

Sec. 11. Where the instrument or an acceptance of any indorsement thereon is dated, such date is deemed prima facie to be the true date of the making, drawing, acceptance, or indorsement as the case may be.

Sec. 12. The instrument is not invalid for the reason only that it is ante-dated or post-dated, provided this is not done for an illegal or fraudulent purpose. The person to whom an instrument so dated is delivered acquires the title thereto as of the date of delivery.

Sec. 13. Where an instrument expressed to be payable at a fixed period after date is issued undated, or where the acceptance of an instrument payable at a fixed period after sight is undated, any holder may insert therein the true date of issue or acceptance, and the instrument shall be payable accordingly. The insertion of a wrong date does not avoid the instrument in the hands of a subsequent holder in due course; but as to him, the date so inserted is to be regarded as the true date.

Sec. 14. Where the instrument is wanting in any material particular, the person in possession thereof has a prima facie authority to complete it by filling up the blanks therein. And a signature on a blank paper delivered by the person making the signature in order that the paper may be converted into a negotiable instrument operates as a prima facie authority to fill it up as such for any amount. In order, however, that any such instrument when completed may be enforced against any person who became a party thereto prior to its

---

[5] Walker *v.* Macdonald, 2 Exch. 527; Habersham *v.* Lehman, 63 Ga. 383; Johnson *v.* Mitchell, 50 Tex. 212; Mitchell *v.* Fuller, 15 Pa. St. 268.

[6] Brief of Phi Delta Phi, vol. 3, p. 142; 42 Am. L. Reg. N. S. 461.

completion, it must be filled up strictly in accordance with the authority given and within a reasonable time. But if any such instrument, after completion, is negotiated to a holder in due course, it is valid and effectual for all purposes in his hands, and he may enforce it as if it had been filled up strictly in accordance with the authority given and within a reasonable time.

Under § 13 any holder has lawful authority to insert the true date. Under § 14 he has *prima facie* authority to insert any date, but if he inserts an incorrect date or one not in conformity with his actual authority, none but an innocent purchaser can recover on it as against any person whose name was on the instrument before its completion.

Section 14 gives *prima facie* authority to one having possession of an incomplete instrument to fill it out; and even a signature on blank paper actually delivered with the intention that it be converted into a negotiable instrument may likewise be filled out, and will be good in the hands of an innocent holder, although the actual authority be transcended or violated.

Under the rule heretofore prevailing in America, one who issues an incomplete instrument thereby gives implied authority to any holder to complete it by filling in the blanks, and a transfer thereof to a *bona fide* purchaser will bind the maker according to the terms of the completed instrument, although the blanks be filled contrary to an express understanding.[7]

In England, however, a qualification of this general and extensive liability is recognized in the case where the purchaser takes the paper before the blank or blanks have been filled. In this instance notice of the unfilled blank is there treated as notice of a possible limitation on the holder's authority, and the taker must at his peril ascertain the extent of the authority actually conferred. Such is the effect of the Bills of Exchange Act, § 20, and the rule there declared is in conformity with the prior decisions of the English courts.[8]

The American codifiers adopted substantially the language of the English statute, and have thereby changed the law.

[7] Frank *v.* Lilienfeld, 33 Gratt. (Va.) 377.

[8] Awde *v.* Dixon, 6 Exch. 869; Hatch *v.* Searles, 2 Smale & G. 147.

Thus it will be seen that by virtue of the last sentence in § 14 an originally incomplete instrument to be fully effectual in the hands of an innocent purchaser must be negotiated *after completion*. Consequently one who takes a bill or note containing a blank must now, since the enactment of the Negotiable Instruments Law, be at the pains to ascertain the real authority of the person intrusted with the paper.[1]

Sec. 15. Where an incomplete instrument has not been delivered it will not, if completed and negotiated, without authority, be a valid contract in the hands of any holder, as against any person whose signature was placed thereon before delivery.

By this section even the innocent holder is not protected if it is shown that the incomplete instrument was never in fact delivered. The instrument is then treated, in effect, as a forgery.

Sec. 16. Every contract on a negotiable instrument is incomplete and revocable until delivery of the instrument for the purpose of giving effect thereto. As between immediate parties, and as regards a remote party other than a holder in due course, the delivery, in order to be effectual, must be made either by or under the authority of the party making, drawing, accepting, or indorsing, as the case may be; and in such case the delivery may be shown to have been conditional, or for a special purpose only, and not for the purpose of transferring the property in the instrument. But where the instrument is in the hands of a holder in due course, a valid delivery thereof by all parties prior to him so as to make them liable to him is conclusively presumed. And where the instrument is no longer in the possession of a party whose signature appears thereon, a valid and intentional delivery by him is presumed until the contrary is proved.

This section adopts an innovation first introduced in the German Bill of Exchange Act, which has met with favor. By virtue of this section, one who has signed but not delivered a completed instrument is liable on it to an innocent purchaser though it should be lost or stolen from him.[2]

---

[1] Guerrant *v.* Guerrant (1902), 7 Va. L. Reg. 639. See Boston Steel, etc., Co. *v.* Steuer, 183 Mass. 140.

[2] Greeser *v.* Sugarman (Supm. Ct. App. T.), 37 Misc. (N. Y.) 799. Delivery of a duly indorsed and negotiable certified check is conclusively presumed in favor of an innocent holder. Poess *v.* Twelfth Ward Bank (Supm. Ct. App. T.), 43 Misc. (N. Y.) 45.

Sec. 17. Where the language of the instrument is ambiguous or there are omissions therein, the following rules of construction apply: —

1. Where the sum payable is expressed in words and also in figures and there is a discrepancy between the two, the sum denoted by the words is the sum payable; but if the words are ambiguous or uncertain, reference may be had to the figures to fix the amount;
2. Where the instrument provides for the payment of interest, without specifying the date from which interest is to run, the interest runs from the date of the instrument, and if the instrument is undated, from the issue thereof;
3. Where the instrument is not dated, it will be considered to be dated as of the time it was issued;
4. Where there is a conflict between the written and printed provisions of the instrument, the written provisions prevail;
5. Where the instrument is so ambiguous that there is doubt whether it is a bill or note, the holder may treat it as either at his election;
6. Where a signature is so placed upon the instrument that it is not clear in what capacity the person making the same intended to sign, he is to be deemed an indorser;
7. Where an instrument containing the words, "I promise to pay," is signed by two or more persons, they are deemed to be jointly and severally liable thereon.

Sec. 18. No person is liable on the instrument whose signature does not appear thereon, except as herein otherwise expressly provided. But one who signs in a trade or assumed name will be liable to the same extent as if he had signed in his own name.

Sec. 19. The signature of any party may be made by a duly authorized agent. No particular form of appointment is necessary for this purpose; and the authority of the agent may be established as in other cases of agency.

Sec. 20. Where the instrument contains or a person adds to his signature words indicating that he signs for or on behalf of a principal, or in a representative capacity, he is not liable on the instrument if he was duly authorized but the mere addition of words describing him as an agent, or as filling a representative character,[3] without disclosing his principal, does not exempt him from personal liability.

To make one whose signature shows that he intends to bind another, and not himself, personally liable on the instrument in the event that he should afterwards appear to have been unauthorized to bind his principal, is an innovation, but is capable of being upheld upon considerations of practical

---

[3] As to the effect of adding the word 'trustee' to the signature of the maker of a note, see **Megowan** v. Peterson, 173 N. Y. 1.

utility. Professor Ames vigorously insists that this section should be amended by striking out the words, "if he was duly authorized." [4] Other writers defend it with equal vigor.[5] The section conforms to the rule declared in the German Exchange Act, Art. 95.

Sec. 21. A signature by "procuration" operates as notice that the agent has but a limited authority to sign, and the principal is bound only in case the agent in so signing acted within the actual limits of his authority.

Sec. 22. The indorsement or assignment of the instrument by a corporation [6] or by an infant passes the property therein, notwithstanding that from want of capacity the corporation or infant may incur no liability thereon.

The corresponding section of the English Act declares that indorsement by an infant or corporation having no power to incur liability on the instrument entitles the holder to receive payment of the bill and to enforce it against any other party thereto. The American Act says that the indorsement passes the property. Both mean the same thing. The question as to whether the infant may avoid the transfer and recover the note or its proceeds is left untouched. No doubt the infant or his representative may do so, but this is a question of common law with which the statute has nothing to do. "Passes the property therein" means vests the legal title in the indorsee so as to enable him to sue.[7]

Sec. 23. When a signature is forged or made without the authority of the person whose signature it purports to be, it is wholly inoperative, and no right to retain the instrument, or to give a discharge therefor, or to enforce payment thereof against any party thereto, can be acquired through or under such signature, unless the party, against whom it is sought to enforce such right, is precluded from setting up the forgery [8] or want of authority.

---

[4] 16 Harv. L. Rev. 256.
[5] 2 Mich. L. Rev. 272, 273; 41 Am. L. Reg. N. S. 462, 465.
[6] Indorsement *ultra vires* by a corporation transfers the property. Willard *v.* Crook, 21 App. Cas. (D. C.) 237.
[7] See Ames-Brewster Neg. Inst. Law, 36, 53, 54, and 41 Am. L. Reg. N. S. 499, 500.
[8] A party whose name is forged ratifies the signature by saying, when asked concerning its genuineness, "That is my name." Central Nat. Bank *v.* Copp, 184 Mass. 328.

This is a correct statement of a general principle on which all authorities agree. But there is a line of cases covered by it in which the authorities are not harmonious. The conflict existed before the Negotiable Instruments Law was framed, and the comments made by several writers on the case of *Tolman v. American Nat. Bank* (1901),[9] decided in Rhode Island since the law went into force in that state, show that the conflict is likely to continue.

The controversy is over the question as to what facts are sufficient to preclude a party from setting up the forgery or want of authority. Thus, suppose A represents himself to B as being a certain other person of financial responsibility, say X, of the town of N. On the faith of this representation and believing that the person before him is in fact X, B draws his check payable to X and delivers it to A, who indorses the same in the name of X and cashes it at the bank. Is B precluded from setting up the forgery of X's name by A, merely because he was himself deceived as to the person to whom the check was delivered? In such a case, it will be observed, B and the bank are both deceived in the same way and to the same extent, namely, as to the identity of A. The weight of authority is certainly in favor of imposing the loss upon B, either because he intended the money to be paid to the party to whom he delivered the paper, or because of his being estopped by his own negligence.[1]

In the case last above referred to,[2] Stiness, C. J., who was one of the commissioners passing upon the Negotiable Instruments Law before it was approved, took a different view of the law and held that the bank must bear the loss in such a case. He was of the opinion that upon legal principle the bank was liable and that the decisions to the contrary are fallacious; but he also stated that to his mind the Negotiable Instruments Law (§ 23) clearly covered the case, and that as a matter of statutory construction the bank is liable.

[9] 22 R. I. 462.
[1] See note to Land Title, etc., Co. v. Northwestern Nat. Bank, 196 Pa. St. 230, where the authorities are cited.
[2] *Tolman v. American Nat. Bank* (1901), 22 R. I. 462.

Nevertheless, the question as to what circumstances *preclude* the maker or drawer still remains, and the conclusion in *Tolman v. Bank* has been severely criticised.[3]

The word 'precluded,' as used in § 23, seems to bear and even necessitate more latitude of construction than a technical word like 'estop,' and circumstances which do not contain all the elements of estoppel may well be considered as precluding the maker or drawer. Certainly the courts which have heretofore held the drawer or maker liable can hardly be expected to overrule their former decisions upon the authority of § 23. In *Hoffman v. American Exch. Nat. Bank*[4] the Nebraska court declined to follow the reasoning of the Rhode Island case; but the Negotiable Instruments Law is not in force in Nebraska.

ARTICLE II

CONSIDERATION.[5]

Sec. 24. Every negotiable instrument is deemed prima facie to have been issued for a valuable consideration; and every person whose signature appears thereon to have become a party thereto for value.[6]

Sec. 25. Value is any consideration sufficient to support a simple contract. An antecedent or pre-existing debt[7] constitutes value; and is deemed such whether the instrument is payable on demand or at a future time.

The provision that an antecedent or pre-existing debt constitutes value determines a point on which the authorities have

---

[3] See Ames-Brewster Neg. Inst. Law, 83; 41 Am. L. Reg. 502. Amasa M. Eaton argues strongly in favor of the correctness of the conclusion of Stiness, C. J., in that case. See 2 Mich. L. Rev. 287, 289.

[4] (Neb. 1901) 96 N. W. Rep. 112.

[5] The whole of this article conforms to modern theory in requiring that there shall be a consideration before liability can arise out of any transaction concerning a bill or note. The idea that the bill is a specialty and good without a consideration has not been judicially countenanced in any quarter for more than a hundred years. See *ante*, p. 388.

[6] Bringman v. Von Glahn ('1902), 71 N. Y. App. Div. 537; Monticello Bank v. Dooly, 113 Wis. 590.

[7] Boston Steel, etc., Co. v. Steuer, 183 Mass. 140; J. H. Mohlman Co. v. McKane, 60 N. Y. App. Div. 546; Brooks v. Sullivan, 129 N. Car. 190. But the holder of the note must give up the debt either wholly or qualifiedly in order to constitute consideration. Roseman v. Mahony, 86 N. Y. App. Div. 377.

been in conflict since the time of the controversy between Chancellor Kent and Judge Story. The rule declared above is in conformity with the doctrine laid down by Judge Story in *Swift v. Tyson* (1842).[8] Such is the manifest meaning of the language of § 25, and it is to be accepted as abolishing the contrary doctrine of *Coddington v. Bay* (1822).[9] The statute says in effect, and almost in so many words, that the existence of a debt is sufficient consideration for the instrument. It is not necessary that it be given in satisfaction of the debt or in consideration of forbearance. It is enough if it be given merely as collateral security.[1]

Sec. 26. Where value has at any time been given for the instrument, the holder is deemed a holder for value in respect to all parties who became such prior to that time.

Sec. 27. Where the holder has a lien on the instrument, arising either from contract or by implication of law, he is deemed a holder for value to the extent of his lien.

Sec. 28. Absence or failure of consideration is matter of defense as against any person not a holder in due course; and partial failure of consideration is a defense pro tanto, whether the failure is an ascertained and liquidated amount or otherwise.

Sec. 29. An accommodation party is one who has signed the instrument as maker, drawer, acceptor, or indorser, without receiving value therefor, and for the purpose of lending his name to some other person. Such a person is liable on the instrument to a holder for value, notwithstanding such holder at the time of taking the instrument knew him to be only an accommodation party.[2]

Mr. Arthur Cohen, eminent as an authority on the English law of negotiable instruments, interprets the phrase "without receiving value therefor," in the definition of an accommodation party, as meaning 'without receiving any value for the bill,' and not 'without receiving any consideration for lending

---

[8] 16 Pet. (U. S.) 1.

[9] 20 Johns. ('N. Y.) 637. See Brewster *v.* Shrader (Supm. Ct. Spec. T.), 26 Misc. (N. Y.) 480.

[1] Payne *v.* Zell, 98 Va. 294.

[2] Willard *v.* Crook, 21 App. Cas. (D. C.) 237.

An accommodation maker being primarily liable is not released by an extension of time by the payee to the indorser. See § 192. National Citizens' Bank *v.* Toplitz, 81 N. Y. App. Div. 593.

In New York, a transferee who receives a note at a discount of 40 per cent is not an innocent purchaser, and the contract being infected with usury, he cannot enforce it against an accommodation maker even to the extent of the money paid by him. Strickland *v.* Henry, 66 N. Y. App. Div. 23.

his name.' Consequently, under this construction, one who receives a commission or is paid value for lending his name is an accommodation party. This brings the definition into conformity with the conceptions of lawyers and business men. It follows that the criticism of Professor Ames [3] on this definition appears not to be well taken.[4]

ARTICLE III

NEGOTIATION.

Sec. 30. An instrument is negotiated when it is transferred from one person to another in such manner as to constitute the transferee the holder thereof. If payable to bearer it is negotiated by delivery; if payable to order it is negotiated by the indorsement of the holder completed by delivery.[5]

Sec. 31. The indorsement must be written on the instrument itself or upon a paper attached thereto. The signature of the indorser, without additional words, is a sufficient indorsement.

Though this section (31) says that the mere writing of the name of the indorser without additional words is a sufficient indorsement, no attempt was made to state what effect is to be given to particular words like 'assign,' 'guarantee,' etc., which are sometimes used. In some jurisdictions one who writes upon a note "I assign this note to A" is liable as an indorser. In a number of states such assignee gets a title free from equities available against the assignor. In some, the assignee takes subject to such defenses. Likewise the authorities are not agreed on the question whether words of indorsement expressly guaranteeing the payment of the note have the effect of making the guarantor liable as an indorser, and there is also difference of opinion as to whether the assignee in such case takes subject to equities.[6]

---

[3] 14 Harv. L. Rev. 241.
[4] See 41 Am. L. Reg. N. S. 510; Ames-Brewster Neg. Inst. Law, 81.
[5] As to the rights acquired by a transferee, by delivery only and without indorsement, of a check payable to order, see Meuer v. Phenix Nat. Bank ('Supm. Ct. Tr. T.), 42 Misc. (N. Y.) 341, where it is held that title passes, but the transferee takes subject to equitable defenses.
[6] For the authorities, see 4 Am. and Eng. Encyc. of Law, 256 et seq., and Daniel on Neg. Inst., §§ 688 et seq. As Professor Ames has point-

Sec. 32. The indorsement must be an indorsement of the entire instrument. An indorsement, which purports to transfer to the indorsee a part only of the amount payable, or which purports to transfer the instrument to two or more indorsees severally, does not operate as a negotiation of the instrument. But where the instrument has been paid in part, it may be indorsed as to the residue.

The reason why a partial indorsement is invalid is that, if recognized, it would subject the acceptor or maker to suit at the instance of different persons and thereby split the cause of action. In *Hawkins v. Cardy* (1698),[7] Lord Holt held a declaration bad on demurrer which alleged a mercantile custom recognizing such partial indorsement. It was said, " a man cannot apportion such personal contract, for he cannot make one liable to two actions, where by contract he is liable to but one."

Sec. 33. An indorsement may be either special or in blank; and it may also be either restrictive or qualified, or conditional.

Sec. 34. A special indorsement specifies the person to whom, or to whose order, the instrument is to be payable; and the indorsement of such indorsee is necessary to the further negotiation of the instrument. An indorsement in blank specifies no indorsee, and an instrument so indorsed is payable to bearer, and may be negotiated by delivery.

An indorsement ' pay to A ' is the same in legal effect as ' pay to A or order.' This was settled in Lord Mansfield's day.[8] If the instrument is made payable to order in its body, its negotiation is not restricted by an indorsement to pay to a particular person without more. Observe that the words, " the indorsement of such indorsee is necessary to the further negotiation of the instrument," applies only to instruments originally payable to order. Where it is originally payable to bearer, § 40, *post,* applies.

The second sentence in § 34 must be construed *in pari materia* with § 9, subs. 5, and cannot be given full effect according to the literal meaning of the words, " is payable to bearer and may be negotiated by delivery." If the instru-

---

ed out, the codifier here missed an excellent opportunity to unify the law. Ames-Brewster Neg. Inst. Law, 64, 65.

[7] 1 Ld. Raym. 360.
[8] Edie *v.* East-India Co., 2 Burr. 1216. See also Leavitt *v.* Putnam, 3 N. Y. 494.

ment be originally payable to order, the blank indorsement must be the only or last indorsement in order that the instrument can be transferred by delivery. If the blank indorsement be followed by a special indorsement and none other, then the instrument can only be negotiated by indorsement and ceases to be transferable by delivery (§ 9, subs. 5). By § 40 an instrument originally payable to bearer is transferable by delivery, though specially indorsed, and a blank indorsement does not add to its transferability.[9]

Sec. 35. The holder may convert a blank indorsement into a special indorsement by writing over the signature of the indorser in blank any contract consistent with the character of the indorsement.
Sec. 36. An indorsement is restrictive, which either,—
1. Prohibits the further negotiation of the instrument; or
2. Constitutes the indorsee the agent of the indorser; or
3. Vests the title in the indorsee in trust for or to the use of some other person.
But the mere absence of words implying power to negotiate does not make an indorsement restrictive.[1]
Sec. 37. A restrictive indorsement confers upon the indorsee the right,—
1. To receive payment of the instrument;
2. To bring any action thereon that the indorser could bring;
3. To transfer his rights as such indorsee, where the form of the indorsement authorizes him to do so.
But all subsequent indorsees acquire only the title of the first indorsee under the restrictive indorsement.

The last section seems to effect only a procedural change. The indorsee by restrictive indorsement, as 'for collection,' is allowed to sue in his own name.[2] Subsection 2 in this section is permissive. It declares that the indorsee shall have the right to bring any action that his indorser might have brought. The effect of this language is that the full legal title is vested

---

[9] The whole of § 34 therefore properly applies only to paper originally payable to order. It has no application at all to paper originally payable to bearer, for the indorsement of such paper is elsewhere treated in the statute.

[1] Professor Ames criticises the phraseology of subsections 2 and 3 of this section, but Judge Brewster and Mr. McKeehan seem to have fully met his objections. Ames-Brewster Neg. Inst. Law, 34, 51; 41 Am. L. Reg. N. S. 572, 573. The final clause of this section embodies the principle of Edie v East-India Co., 2 Burr. 1216, also recognized in § 34.

[2] 41 Am. L. Reg. N. S. 513.

in the indorsee, at least so far as remedial rights are concerned. He occupies exactly the same position in the law as any other indorsee.

It was inferred by Professor Ames that the language used in subs. 2 denies, by implication, the right of an indorsee by restrictive indorsement to sue his indorser in all cases, since it merely gives the right to maintain such suits as the indorser could have brought. Suppose, for instance, that A, the holder of a note payable to his order, sells it to B and is about to indorse it to him, but, at B's request, indorses it to X in trust for B, instead of to B directly. At maturity the maker is insolvent, but A is solvent. Can X sue A? If we interpret the language of the statute literally, he cannot. A cannot sue himself, and if X is to be allowed to sue only in those cases where the indorser could sue, and not otherwise, then X cannot hold A liable on his indorsement.

Such construction causes the statute to violate justice and is altogether contrary to principle. When the legal title is put into an indorsee under the principles of the law merchant, it necessarily follows that he can sue his immediate indorser. In the case above supposed, if A, the person making the restrictive indorsement to X, is himself a holder by indorsement, he has the undoubted right to look to his immediate indorser if the paper be dishonored. Now when he indorses restrictively to X, the latter gets full legal title and has the same undoubted right to look to *his* immediate indorser. This is the meaning of § 37, subs. 2. The rights of X and A are put upon the same footing. A holds, we may suppose, as a regular indorsee; X holds as an indorsee by restrictive indorsement. Both can look to all indorsers alike, and the language used is evidently not intended to deprive X of his right to proceed against his own immediate indorser in the case supposed.[3]

Sec. 38. A qualified indorsement constitutes the indorser a mere assignor of the title to the instrument. It may be made by adding to the indorser's signature the words "without recourse," or any

---

[3] See Brief of Phi Delta Phi, vol. 3, pp. 140, 141; 41 Am. L. Reg. N. S. 514, 515. See Ames-Brewster Neg. Inst. Law, 76, 37.

words of similar import. Such an indorsement does not impair the negotiable character of the instrument.

Sec. 39. Where an indorsement is conditional, a party required to pay the instrument may disregard the condition, and make payment to the indorsee or his transferee, whether the condition has been fulfilled or not. But any person to whom an instrument so indorsed is negotiated, will hold the same, or the proceeds thereof, subject to the rights of the person indorsing conditionally.

There are very few cases in which rights arising under conditional indorsement are discussed. In the sole English case involving such an indorsement, a bill after being indorsed on condition was afterwards accepted and then passed through several successive hands. It was finally paid before the condition was fulfilled, and it was held that the acceptor must pay again to the payee.[4] This was hard on the acceptor. Accordingly the English Act, which is followed in the Negotiable Instruments Law, changed the doctrine announced in that case and permits a bill or note to be paid regardless of any condition embodied in the indorsement. The rights of the party for whose benefit the condition is inserted are sufficiently protected in the closing sentence.[5]

Sec. 40. Where an instrument, payable to bearer, is indorsed specially, it may nevertheless be further negotiated by delivery; but the person indorsing specially is liable as indorser to only such holders as make title through his indorsement.

This section must be interpreted as if it read, " where an instrument, *originally* payable to bearer," etc.; otherwise it will be found repugnant to § 9, subs. 5, and § 34. The doctrine of *Smith v. Clarke* (1794) [6] is overruled by § 9, subs. 5. That case involved a note originally payable to order. Section 40 apparently does not, as Professor Ames insists, restore the doctrine of *Smith v. Clarke*. It only recognizes the rule that a note originally payable to bearer is transferable by delivery, though specially indorsed. Mr. Farrell was, it seems, the first to point out the distinction.[7] His reasoning has been adopted and followed by Mr. McKeehan.[8]

---

[4] Robertson v. Kensington, 4 Taunt. 30.
[5] See Daniel on Neg. Inst., § 697; Crawford, Neg. Inst. Law, § 69n.
[6] Peake N. P. (ed. 1795) 225.
[7] See Brief of Phi Delta Phi, vol. 3, pp. 141, 142.
[8] 41 Am. L. Reg. N. S. 454-461.

Sec. 41. Where an instrument is payable to the order of two or more payees or indorsees who are not partners, all must indorse, unless the one indorsing has authority to indorse for the others.

Sec. 42. Where an instrument is drawn or indorsed to a person as "Cashier" or other fiscal officer of a bank or corporation, it is deemed prima facie to be payable to the bank or corporation of which he is such officer, and may be negotiated by either the indorsement of the bank or corporation, or the indorsement of the officer.

By § 42 a rule formerly recognized as applicable to cashiers of banks is extended to all the fiscal officers of corporations, e. g., treasurers of building and loan societies and secretaries of trust companies when charged with fiscal duties.

Sec. 43. Where the name of a payee or indorsee is wrongly designated or misspelled, he may indorse the instrument as therein described, adding, if he think fit, his proper signature.

Sec. 44. Where any person is under obligation to indorse in a representative capacity, he may indorse in such terms as to negative personal liability.

Sec. 45. Except where an indorsement bears date after the maturity of the instrument, every negotiation is deemed prima facie to have been effected before the instrument was overdue.

Sec. 46. Except where the contrary appears, every indorsement is presumed prima facie to have been made at the place where the instrument is dated.

Sec. 47. An instrument negotiable in its origin continues to be negotiable until it has been restrictively indorsed or discharged by payment or otherwise.

The fact that paper is past due brings into operation an altogether different set of rules by which to determine the liability of those who indorse after maturity, but it in no way affects the transferability of the instrument so far as the right to sue is concerned.

Sec. 48. The holder may at any time strike out any indorsement which is not necessary to his title. The indorser whose indorsement is struck out, and all indorsers subsequent to him, are thereby relieved from liability on the instrument.

See Ames-Brewster Neg. Inst. Law, 37, 63, 64. See also article Negotiable Instruments Law, 2 Mich. L. Rev. 274, in which Amasa M. Eaton expresses the opinion that the interpretation above given is correct. For a *résumé* of Professor Ames's argument see 16 Harv. L. Rev. 256.

To be construed with regard to § 40 and § 9, subs. 5. Where an instrument is originally payable to bearer, a holder can always sue as bearer and any special indorsement on the instrument may be stricken out as unnecessary to his title. Where the instrument is originally payable to order, no holder by delivery merely can sue in his own name unless the last indorsement is in blank.

Sec. 49. Where the holder of an instrument payable to his order transfers it for value without indorsing it, the transfer vests in the transferee such title as the transferor had therein, and the transferee acquires, in addition, the right to have the indorsement of the transferor. But for the purpose of determining whether the transferee is a holder in due course, the negotiation takes effect as of the time when the indorsement is actually made.

Sec. 50. Where an instrument is negotiated back to a prior party, such party may, subject to the provisions of this act, reissue and further negotiate the same. But he is not entitled to enforce payment thereof against any intervening party to whom he was personally liable.

The right to have the indorsement of the transferor actually placed upon the instrument can only be enforced by a bill in equity for specific performance. This court would adequately protect the indorser by requiring him to make only such indorsement as he ought to make. Section 49 does not require any particular kind of indorsement. What it does require is an indorsement that will transfer full legal title and place upon the transferor such liability as he is bound in equity or by contract to assume.[9]

ARTICLE IV

RIGHTS OF THE HOLDER.

Sec. 51. The holder of a negotiable instrument may sue thereon in his own name; and payment to him in due course discharges the instrument.

Sec. 52. A holder in due course is a holder who has taken the instrument under the following conditions: —

1. That it is complete and regular upon its face;

---

[9] See 41 Am. L. Reg. N. S. 516; Ames-Brewster Neg. Inst. Law, 39, 54.

2. That he became the holder of it before it was overdue, and without notice that it had been previously dishonored, if such was the fact;
3. That he took it in good faith and for value;[1]
4. That at the time it was negotiated to him he had no notice of any infirmity in the instrument or defect in the title of the person negotiating it.[2]

Sec. 53. Where an instrument payable on demand is negotiated an unreasonable length of time after its issue, the holder is not deemed a holder in due course.

Sec. 54. Where the transferee receives notice of any infirmity in the instrument or defect in the title of the person negotiating the same before he has paid the full amount agreed to be paid therefor, he will be deemed a holder in due course only to the extent of the amount theretofore paid by him.

Sec. 55. The title of a person who negotiates an instrument is defective within the meaning of this act when he obtained the instrument, or any signature thereto, by fraud, duress, or force and fear, or other unlawful means, or for an illegal consideration, or when he negotiates it in breach of faith, or under such circumstances as amount to a fraud.

Where a genuine signature is obtained to a bill or note by duress, the question whether it is absolutely void and unenforceable in the hands of all parties is unsettled. The Negotiable Instruments Law does not undertake to solve this problem. Section 57, *post,* merely states that a holder in due course may enforce the instrument for its full amount against all parties liable thereon. The question as to who are or may be liable is left to be determined by law.

In England it seems to have been fully accepted in the decisions and by the text writers, that duress is no defense

---

[1] The title of an indorsee is defective when the consideration for the indorsement is unlawful, or where the indorsement is procured by unlawful means; and an acceptor of a bill or maker of a note who has knowledge that the indorsee's title is defective has no right to pay the money to him. Drinkall *v.* Movius State Bank, 11 N. Dak. 10.

Where the indorsee takes the note at a usurious discount of 40 per cent he is not a holder for value. Strickland *v.* Henry (1901), 66 N. Y. App. Div. 23.

Bad faith on the part of the indorsee is not shown by the mere fact that the note was taken at a large discount, where it appeared that the payee was in need of money and the note was payable three months later at a remote place inaccessible during half the year. McNamara *v.* Jose, 28 Wash. 461.

[2] M. Groh's Sons Co. *v.* Schneider (Supm. Ct. App. T.), 34 Misc. (N Y.) 195.

against an innocent purchaser.³ And the wording of the English Bills of Exchange Act, § 30, subs. 2, is such as to settle the question in that country beyond all doubt.

To enforce the payment of a bill or note at anybody's instance as against one who is compelled to sign it contrary to his will is, however, utterly at variance with fundamental conceptions of contract law, and American authorities have shown a tendency to hold such an instrument absolutely void in the hands of all parties. Mr. Daniel takes this position, and there are numerous decisions containing strong dicta to the same effect.⁴

Sec. 56. To constitute notice of an infirmity in the instrument or defect in the title of the person negotiating the same, the person to whom it is negotiated must have had actual knowledge of the infirmity or defect, or knowledge of such facts that his action in taking the instrument amounted to bad faith.⁵

Sec. 57. A holder in due course holds the instrument free from any defect of title of prior parties, and free from defenses available to prior parties among themselves, and may enforce payment of the instrument for the full amount thereof against all parties liable thereon.⁶

Sec. 58. In the hands of any holder other than a holder in due course, a negotiable instrument is subject to the same defenses as if it were non-negotiable But a holder who derives his title through a holder in due course, and who is not himself a party to any fraud or illegality affecting the instrument, has all the rights of such former holder in respect of all parties prior to the latter.⁷

---

³ Duncan v. Scott, 1 Campb. 100. Byles on Bills (Sharswood's ed.) 220; Bayley on Bills, 318.

⁴ See Daniel on Neg. Inst., §§ 857, 858; Loomis v. Ruck, 56 N. Y. 465; Magoon v. Reber, 76 Wis. 392.

⁵ This provision adopts the doctrine of Goodman v. Harvey, 4 Ad. & El. 870, 31 E. C. L. 212, and subsequent cases overruling Gill v. Cubitt, 3 B. & C. 466, 10 E. C. L. 154. See also Goetting v. Day (Supm. Ct. App. T.), 87 N. Y. Supp. 510; Black v. Westminster First Nat. Bank, 96 Md. 399; Valley Sav. Bank v. Mercer, 97 Md. 458.

The use of a wrong name on partnership paper affects an indorsee with notice of an irregularity in the creation of the instrument, as where "Iba & Green" is used instead of "Empire Garden." Lucker v. Iba, 54 N. Y. App. Div. 566.

⁶ A gambling consideration does not vitiate a note in the hands of an innocent purchaser. Wirt v. Stubblefield, 17 App. Cas. (D. C.) 283.

⁷ Bryan v. Harr, 21 App. Cas. (D. C.) 190.

A party who takes a partnership note knowing its proceeds are to be applied to the individual liability of one partner is not an inno-

Sec. 59. Every holder is deemed prima facie to be a holder in due course; but when it is shown that the title of any person who has negotiated the instrument was defective, the burden is on the holder to prove that he or some person under whom he claims acquired the title as holder in due course. But the last-mentioned rule does not apply in favor of a party who became bound on the instrument prior to the acquisition of such defective title.

ARTICLE V

LIABILITIES OF PARTIES.

Sec. 60. The maker of a negotiable instrument by making it engages that he will pay it according to its tenor, and admits the existence of the payee and his then capacity to indorse.[8]

Sec. 61. The drawer by drawing this instrument admits the existence of the payee and his then capacity to indorse; and engages that on due presentment the instrument will be accepted or paid, or both, according to its tenor, and that if it be dishonored, and the necessary proceedings on dishonor be duly taken, he will pay the amount thereof to the holder, or to any subsequent indorser who may be compelled to pay it. But the drawer may insert in the instrument an express stipulation negativing or limiting his own liability to the holder.

Sec. 62. The acceptor by accepting the instrument engages that he will pay it according to the tenor of his acceptance; and admits,—
  1. The existence of the drawer, the genuineness of his signature, and his capacity and authority to draw the instrument; and
  2. The existence of the payee and his then capacity to indorse.

Sec. 63. A person placing his signature upon an instrument otherwise than as maker, drawer or acceptor, is deemed to be an indorser, unless he clearly indicates by appropriate words his intention to be bound in some other capacity.

Sec. 64. Where a person, not otherwise a party to an instrument,

---

cent purchaser as against the other member of the firm. Lucker v. Iba, 54 N. Y. App. Div. 566.

Where a note is subject to any valid defense as against the payee, the latter cannot get a better right by selling to an innocent purchaser and by afterwards buying the instrument back. Andrews v. Robertson, 111 Wis. 334.

A person with knowledge of equities, but who claims title under a *bona fide* purchaser, is fully protected as against all defenses available between the original parties. Jennings v. Carlucci, 87 N. Y. Supp. 475.

[8] Under this section the innocent purchaser of a note payable to a foreign corporation which has not complied with local laws can recover as against the maker, for its capacity to indorse cannot be questioned by him. McMann v. Walker, 31 Colo. 261.

So it is no defense that the indorsement was *ultra vires*. Willard v. Crook, 21 App. Cas. (D. C.) 237.

places thereon his signature in blank before delivery, he is liable as indorser, in accordance with the following rules: —
  1. If the instrument is payable to the order of a third person, he is liable to the payee and to all subsequent parties.
  2. If the instrument is payable to the order of the maker or drawer, or is payable to bearer, he is liable to all parties subsequent to the maker or drawer.
  3. If he signs for the accommodation of the payee, he is liable to all parties subsequent to the payee.

This last section states the law applicable to anomalous indorsements, which was formerly in the greatest confusion. This confusion the statute almost completely clears away, fixing upon all indorsers the liability which the law attaches to regular indorsers. One who indorses before delivery is no longer liable as guarantor or maker, as he was in many jurisdictions prior to the enactment of the Negotiable Instruments Law.

Professor Ames points out what he conceives to be a defect in the language of § 64, subs. 2. He supposes a case like this: A draws a bill payable to himself upon B. B accepts, and gets C to indorse the bill for his accommodation. It is then handed back to A, who negotiates to X. At maturity the bill is not paid and A is compelled to take it up. In this case C indorses for the accommodation of the acceptor, B, as in *Matthews v. Bloxsome*,[9] and is manifestly intended to be liable to the payee, A. Professor Ames thinks that by the statute he is not liable. How this follows is not clear. True, the statute says that C shall be liable to parties subsequent to the drawer, and of course he is not liable to the drawer. This means to the drawer as drawer. C is liable to the payee, for the payee is a party subsequent to the drawer. The fact that the drawer is at the same time the payee does not make the anomalous indorser less liable to the payee. The payee is not a party to a bill until it is delivered to him. The anomalous indorser who indorses before delivery to the payee is liable to the payee, because such payee is a subsequent party.[1]

In order for this section to apply, the irregular indorsement must be made before the instrument is delivered. Conse-

[9] 33 L. J. Q. B. 209.
[1] See 41 Am. L. Reg. N. S. 520, 522.

quently where the indorsement is made after delivery the payee cannot recover against the irregular indorser unless he alleges and proves that the indorsement was made for the purpose of lending credit and with the intent to charge the indorser to the payee.[2]

Sec. 65. Every person negotiating an instrument by delivery or by a qualified indorsement, warrants,—
1. That the instrument is genuine and in all respects what it purports to be;
2. That he has a good title to it;
3. That all prior parties had capacity to contract;
4. That he has no knowledge of any fact which would impair the validity of the instrument or render it valueless.

But when the negotiation is by delivery only, the warranty extends in favor of no holder other than the immediate transferee.

The provisions of subdivision three of this section do not apply to persons negotiating public or corporation securities, other than bills and notes.

The liability of the transferor is of a composite character. He transmits title under the principles and subject to the conditions of the law merchant, and at the same time he is usually the vendor of a chattel. It would be anomalous under principles of the pure law merchant, to fix any liability whatever on one who indorses without recourse or who transfers by delivery merely. The contract of the former negatives liability, and the other is not a party to the bill. The law of sales, however, imposes certain warranties upon such transferor; and it will be observed that this warranty runs with the instrument where the transferor's name is put upon it. Where the transfer is by delivery only, the transferor cannot be held liable on his warranty by a remote party. The liability of the indorser who indorses without qualification is also of the same composite character, and for the same reason. The subject here touched upon has been considered in the body of this work.

Professor Ames criticises subs. 3 and 4 of § 65, pointing out that while a transferor of an instrument void for coverture or voidable for infancy is made liable as a warrantor though

[2] Kohn *v.* Consolidated Butter, etc., Co., 30 Misc. (N. Y.) 725.

ignorant of the lack of capacity (subs. 3), the transferor of an instrument void for usury is made liable as a warrantor only in case he has knowledge of the defect (subs. 4).[3]

The reason for the distinction is stated by Mr. Eaton as follows: " Usury is the result of conduct between the parties of which an indorser is not presumed to have knowledge. Coverture, infancy, or other disability affects the competency of the parties to make any contract. An indorser is presumed to warrant the genuineness and competent character of previous parties, but not the result of their conduct unless he is aware of it and it was illegal."[4]

Sec. 66. Every indorser who indorses without qualification, warrants to all subsequent holders in due course:
1. The matters and things mentioned in subdivisions one, two, and three of the next preceding section; and
2. That the instrument is at the time of his indorsement valid and subsisting.[5]

And, in addition, he engages that on due presentment, it shall be accepted or paid, or both, as the case may be, according to its tenor, and that if it be dishonored, and the necessary proceedings on dishonor be duly taken, he will pay the amount thereof to the holder, or to any subsequent indorser who may be compelled to pay it.

Sec. 67. Where a person places his indorsement on an instrument negotiable by delivery he incurs all the liabilities of an indorser.

Sec. 68 As respects one another, indorsers are liable prima facie in the order in which they indorse; but evidence is admissible to show that as between or among themselves they have agreed otherwise. Joint payees or joint indorsees who indorse are deemed to indorse jointly and severally.

Before the Negotiable Instruments Law was enacted, joint makers, joint drawers, and joint indorsers were liable only jointly, save where statutes had made joint contracts joint and several. By the Negotiable Instruments Law this rule is changed; for by it joint payees who indorse and joint indorsers who indorse are deemed to indorse jointly and severally. The change is commended by some, but disapproved by Pro-

---

[3] See 16 Harv. L. Rev. 257; Littauer v. Goldman, 72 N. Y. 506.
[4] 2 Mich. L. Rev. 276.
[5] Packard v. Windholz, 88 N. Y. App. Div. 365, affirming 40 Misc. (N. Y.) 347.

fessor Ames. Still others wonder why the same principle was not extended to joint makers and drawers.[6]

Sec. 69. Where a broker or other agent negotiates an instrument without indorsement, he incurs all the liabilities prescribed by section sixty-five of this act, unless he discloses the name of his principal, and the fact that he is acting only as agent.

ARTICLE VI

PRESENTMENT FOR PAYMENT.

Sec. 70. Presentment for payment is not necessary in order to charge the person primarily liable on the instrument; but if the instrument is, by its terms, payable at a special place, and he is able and willing to pay it there at maturity, such ability and willingness are equivalent to a tender of payment upon his part. But except as herein otherwise provided, presentment for payment is necessary in order to charge the drawer and indorsers.

This section was evidently framed to apply to bills and notes, but as its words are general it is applicable to certificates of deposit, as Professor Ames has shown. It thus changes the law in a number of states.[7]

Sec. 71. Where the instrument is not payable on demand, presentment must be made on the day it falls due. Where it is payable on demand, presentment must be made within a reasonable time after its issue except that in the case of a bill of exchange, presentment for payment will be sufficient if made within a reasonable time after the last negotiation thereof.

Sec. 72. Presentment for payment, to be sufficient, must be made,
1. By the holder, or by some person authorized to receive payment on his behalf;
2. At a reasonable hour on a business day;
3. At a proper place as herein defined;
4. To the person primarily liable on the instrument, or if he is absent or inaccessible, to any person found at the place where the presentment is made.

Sec. 73. Presentment for payment is made at the proper place,—
1. Where a place of payment is specified in the instrument and it is there presented;

[6] See Ames-Brewster Neg. Inst. Law, 41, 56, 81; 41 Am. L. Reg. N. S. 570.

[7] See Ames-Brewster Neg. Inst. Law, 42.

2. Where no place of payment is specified, but the address of the person to make payment is given in the instrument and it is there presented;
3. Where no place of payment is specified and no address is given and the instrument is presented at the usual place of business or residence of the person to make payment;
4. In any other case if presented to the person to make payment wherever he can be found, or if presented at his last known place of business or residence.

Sec. 74. The instrument must be exhibited to the person from whom payment is demanded, and when it is paid must be delivered up to the party paying it.

Sec. 75. Where the instrument is payable at a bank, presentment for payment must be made during banking hours, unless the person to make payment has no funds there to meet it at any time during the day, in which case presentment at any hour before the bank is closed on that day is sufficient.[8]

Sec. 76. Where the person primarily liable on the instrument is dead, and no place of payment is specified, presentment for payment must be made to his personal representative if such there be, and if, with the exercise of reasonable diligence, he can be found.

Sec. 77. Where the persons primarily liable on the instrument are liable as partners, and no place of payment is specified, presentment for payment may be made to any one of them, even though there has been a dissolution of the firm.

Sec. 78. Where there are several persons, not partners, primarily liable on the instrument, and no place of payment is specified, presentment must be made to them all.

Sec. 79. Presentment for payment is not required in order to charge the drawer where he has no right to expect or require that the drawee or acceptor will pay the instrument.

Sec. 80. Presentment for payment is not required in order to charge an indorser where the instrument was made or accepted for his accommodation and he has no reason to expect that the instrument will be paid if presented.

Sec. 81. Delay in making presentment for payment is excused when the delay is caused by circumstances beyond the control of the holder, and not imputable to his default, misconduct, or negligence. When the cause of delay ceases to operate, presentment must be made with reasonable diligence.

Sec. 82. Presentment for payment is dispensed with:—
1. Where after the exercise of reasonable diligence presentment as required by this act cannot be made;

---

[8] Where a note is payable at a bank the maker has until the close of banking hours in which to make payment, and the holder has no authority to protest for nonpayment upon a demand made at an earlier hour, where the maker subsequently, before the close of banking hours, deposits funds to pay the note. German-American Bank v. Milliman, 31 Misc. (N. Y.) 87.

2. Where the drawee is a fictitious person;
3. By waiver of presentment, express or implied.[9]

Sec. 83. The instrument is dishonored by non-payment when,—
1. It is duly presented for payment and payment is refused or cannot be obtained; or
2. Presentment is excused and the instrument is overdue and unpaid.

Sec. 84. Subject to the provisions of this act, when the instrument is dishonored by non-payment, an immediate right of recourse to all parties secondarily liable thereon accrues to the holder.

Sec. 85. Every negotiable instrument is payable at the time fixed therein without grace. When the day of maturity falls upon Sunday, or a holiday, the instrument is payable on the next succeeding business day. Instruments falling due on Saturday are to be presented for payment on the next succeeding business day, except that instruments payable on demand may, at the option of the holder, be presented for payment before twelve o'clock noon on Saturday when that entire day is not a holiday.

Sec. 86. Where the instrument is payable at a fixed period after date, after sight, or after the happening of a specified event, the time of payment is determined by excluding the day from which the time is to begin to run, and by including the date of payment.[1]

Sec. 87. Where the instrument is made payable at a bank it is equivalent to an order to the bank to pay the same for the account of the principal debtor thereon.[2]

Sec. 88. Payment is made in due course when it is made at or after the maturity of the instrument to the holder thereof in good faith and without notice that his title is defective.

ARTICLE VII

NOTICE OF DISHONOR.

Sec. 89. Except as herein otherwise provided, when a negotiable instrument has been dishonored by non-acceptance or non-payment, notice of dishonor must be given to the drawer and to each indorser,

[9] Presentment of a note is waived by any words or any act of an indorser which misleads the holder and causes him to omit due presentment. Thus, where one partner indorses firm paper and before maturity the firm becomes insolvent, and after consultation between the holder and indorser an assignment is made by the partnership, presentment of the note is impliedly waived. *In re* Swift, 106 Fed. Rep. 65.

[1] The abolition of days of grace seems to meet with general favor. In Massachusetts, grace has been restored to sight drafts. Laws 1899, c. 130. See Crawford, Neg. Inst. Law, 2d ed., 149.

[2] This is the New York rule, and changes the law in some of the states. See e. g., Grissom *v.* Commercial Nat. Bank, 87 Tenn. 350.

and any drawer or indorser to whom such notice is not given is discharged.

By combining this section and § 185 it is seen that a literal interpretation of the meaning of the language used would lead to the conclusion that the drawer of a check is discharged by a failure to give notice of its dishonor. If such be the effect of the language, the law is thereby changed, as the rule has heretofore been that the drawer of a check who is not given notice of dishonor is discharged only to the extent of his actual damage.[3] This is the same penalty as that imposed by § 186 upon the holder who fails to present his check within a reasonable time. The language used in § 89 is taken from the English Bills of Exchange Act, and it was clearly an oversight upon the part of the draftsmen of both acts that the language used should be broad enough to apply to the drawer of a check. Professor Ames justly criticises §§ 89 and 135 on this point. Judge Brewster says that "since the only penalty for delay in presentment is the loss occasioned by delay (§ 186), and not a discharge, the natural inference therefrom would be that the same exceptional exemption as to checks would continue in case of nonpayment, namely, that the only penalty would be the loss occasioned by the delay, and not any absolute discharge."[4] This is straining inference pretty far. How the courts will get out of the dilemma remains to be seen.

It is possibly a case where the broader legislative intent may be given effect contrary to the apparent meaning of the language used. Everybody knows what the law in regard to the dishonor of checks has been. The statute is a codification of existing law, and presumably no changes, other than such as were plainly meant to follow, were intended. Here is apparently a covert change in the law, effected by bringing together, under a clause of general reference, parts of the act which are remote from each other. If given literal effect, the result approaches to absurdity. No such thing was intended.

The weight of nonjudicial opinion, however, seems to be to the effect that under these sections the drawer of a check

---

[3] Daniel on Neg. Inst., § 1587.
[4] Ames-Brewster Neg. Inst. Law, 79.

is wholly discharged upon failure to give notice of dishonor. It has been suggested that in such case the holder might sue at common law on the original consideration; but how this could be done when the right of action on the paper has been lost by the negligence of the holder is not clear. The general rule is that the failure to notify a party entitled to notice discharges the debt as well as liability on the paper.[5]

Sec. 90. The notice may be given by or on behalf of the holder, or by or on behalf of any party to the instrument who might be compelled to pay it to the holder, and who upon taking it up would have a right to reimbursement from the party to whom the notice is given.[6]

Sec. 91. Notice of dishonor may be given by an agent either in his own name or in the name of any party entitled to give notice, whether that party be his principal or not.

Sec. 92. Where notice is given by or on behalf of the holder, it inures for the benefit of all subsequent holders and all prior parties who have a right of recourse against the party to whom it is given.

Sec. 93. Where notice is given by or on behalf of a party entitled to give notice, it inures for the benefit of the holder and all parties subsequent to the party to whom notice is given.

Sec. 94. Where the instrument has been dishonored in the hands of an agent, he may either himself give notice to the parties liable thereon, or he may give notice to his principal. If he give notice to his principal, he must do so within the same time as if he were the holder, and the principal upon the receipt of such notice has himself the same time for giving notice as if the agent had been an independent holder.

Sec. 95. A written notice need not be signed, and an insufficient written notice may be supplemented and validated by verbal communication. A misdescription of the instrument does not vitiate the notice unless the party to whom the notice is given is in fact misled thereby.

Sec. 96. The notice may be in writing or merely oral and may be given in any terms which sufficiently identify the instrument, and indicate that it has been dishonored by non-acceptance or non-payment. It may in all cases be given by delivering it personally or through the mails.[7]

---

[5] Daniel on Neg. Inst., § 971.

[6] This section is in conformity with Chapman v. Keane, 3 Ad. & El. 193, 30 E. C. L. 69, which overruled previous decisions to the effect that only one who was holder at the time could give a valid notice. Tindal v. Brown, 1 T. R. 167.

[7] A certificate of a notary showing presentment and protest of a certain note, and that the notice of protest "of the before-mentioned note" (a copy of which appeared in the certificate) was served on the indorsers by depositing copies of the notice addressed to them in

Sec. 97. Notice of dishonor may be given either to the party himself or to his agent in that behalf.

Sec. 98. When any party is dead, and his death is known to the party giving notice, the notice must be given to a personal representative, if there be one, and if with reasonable diligence he can be found. If there be no personal representative, notice may be sent to the last residence or last place of business of the deceased.

Sec. 99. Where the parties to be notified are partners, notice to any one partner is notice to the firm, even though there has been a dissolution.

Sec. 100. Notice to joint parties who are not partners must be given to each of them, unless one of them has authority to receive such notice for the others.

Sec. 101. Where a party has been adjudged a bankrupt or an insolvent, or has made an assignment for the benefit of creditors, notice may be given either to the party himself or to his trustee or assignee.

Sec. 102. Notice may be given as soon as the instrument is dishonored; and unless delay is excused as hereinafter provided, must be given within the times fixed by this act.

Sec. 103. Where the person giving and the person to receive notice reside in the same place, notice must be given within the following times: —

1. If given at the place of business of the person to receive notice, it must be given before the close of business hours on the day following.
2. If given at his residence, it must be given before the usual hours of rest on the day following.
3. If sent by mail, it must be deposited in the post-office in time to reach him in usual course on the day following.

Sec. 104. Where the person giving and the person to receive notice reside in different places, the notice must be given within the following times: —

1. If sent by mail, it must be deposited in the post-office in time to go by mail the day following the day of dishonor, or if there be no mail at a convenient hour on that day, by the next mail thereafter.
2. If given otherwise than through the post-office, then within the time that notice would have been received in due course of mail, if it had been deposited in the post-office within the time specified in the last subdivision.

Sec. 105. Where notice of dishonor is duly addressed and deposited in the post-office, the sender is deemed to have given due notice, notwithstanding any miscarriage in the mails.[8]

Sec. 106. Notice is deemed to have been deposited in the post-office

---

the postoffice, is sufficient. Richmond Second Nat. Bank *v.* Smith, 118 Wis. 18.

[8] State Bank *v.* Soloman, 84 N. Y. Supp. 976.

when deposited in any branch post-office or in any letter box under the control of the post-office department.

Sec. 107. Where a party receives notice of dishonor, he has, after the receipt of such notice, the same time for giving notice to antecedent parties that the holder has after the dishonor.

Sec. 108. Where a party has added an address to his signature, notice of dishonor must be sent to that address; but if he has not given such address, then the notice must be sent as follows: —

1. Either to the post-office nearest to his place of residence, or to the post-office where he is accustomed to receive his letters;[9] or
2. If he live in one place, and have his place of business in another, notice may be sent to either place; or
3. If he is sojourning in another place, notice may be sent to the place where he is so sojourning.

But where the notice is actually received by the party within the time specified in this act, it will be sufficient, though not sent in accordance with the requirements of this section.

Sec. 109. Notice of dishonor may be waived, either before the time of giving notice has arrived, or after the omission to give due notice, and the waiver may be express or implied.[1]

Sec. 110. Where the waiver is embodied in the instrument itself, it is binding upon all parties; but where it is written above the signature of an indorser, it binds him only.

Sec. 111. A waiver of protest, whether in the case of a foreign bill of exchange or other negotiable instrument, is deemed to be a waiver not only of a formal protest, but also of presentment and notice of dishonor.

Sec. 112. Notice of dishonor is dispensed with when, after the

---

[9] Philip, etc., Ebling Brewing Co. v. Reinheimer, 32 Misc. (N. Y.) 594.

Where no address is given on the paper and neither the residence, former residence, place of sojourn, nor accustomed postoffice of the party is known, proof must be given of actual diligence in trying to ascertain the proper address. It is not sufficient for a notary giving notice in New York city merely to address the notice at haphazard to "Clarence Hartman, New York City, N. Y." Fonseca v. Hartman, 84 N. Y. Supp. 131.

[1] A promise by an indorser to pay a dishonored note made with the knowledge that notice has not been given operates as a waiver of want of notice. Schwartz v. Wilmer, 90 Md. 137.

A firm gave a note which was indorsed by one of the partners. Shortly before its maturity the indorser consulted the holder with reference to the making of an assignment by the firm and the partners for the benefit of creditors, stating their insolvency and that neither he nor the firm would be able to pay the note at maturity. As a result of the conference an assignment was made before the date of the maturity of the note. It was held that there was an implied waiver of presentment which also excused notice to the indorser of nonpayment. In re Swift, 106 Fed. Rep. 65.

exercise of reasonable diligence, it cannot be given to or does not reach the parties sought to be charged.

Sec. 113. Delay in giving notice of dishonor is excused when the delay is caused by circumstances beyond the control of the holder, and not imputable to his default, misconduct, or negligence. When the cause of delay ceases to operate, notice must be given with reasonable diligence.

Sec. 114. Notice of dishonor is not required to be given to the drawer in either of the following cases: —
1. Where the drawer and drawee are the same person;
2. When the drawee is a fictitious person or a person not having capacity to contract;
3. When the drawer is the person to whom the instrument is presented for payment;
4. Where the drawer has no right to expect or require that the drawee or acceptor will honor the instrument;
5. Where the drawer has countermanded payment.

Sec. 115. Notice of dishonor is not required to be given to an indorser in either of the following cases: —
1. Where the drawee is a fictitious person or a person not having capacity to contract, and the indorser was aware of the fact at the time he indorsed the instrument;
2. Where the indorser is the person to whom the instrument is presented for payment;
3. Where the instrument was made or accepted for his accommodation.

Sec. 116. Where due notice of dishonor by non-acceptance has been given, notice of a subsequent dishonor by non-payment is not necessary, unless in the meantime the instrument has been accepted.

Sec. 117. An omission to give notice of dishonor by non-acceptance does not prejudice the rights of a holder in due course subsequent to the omission.

Sec. 118. Where any negotiable instrument has been dishonored it may be protested for non-acceptance or non-payment, as the case may be; but protest is not required except in the case of foreign bills of exchange.

ARTICLE VIII

DISCHARGE OF NEGOTIABLE INSTRUMENTS.

Sec. 119. A negotiable instrument is discharged: —
1. By payment in due course by or on behalf of the principal debtor;[2]
2. By payment in due course by the party accommodated, where the instrument is made or accepted for accommodation;

[2] Where a certified check had been discharged by payment in due course to an indorsee and the latter had after that time refunded the

3. By the intentional cancellation thereof by the holder;
4. By any other act which will discharge a simple contract for the payment of money;
5. When the principal debtor becomes the holder of the instrument at or after maturity in his own right.[3]

Subsection 4.— This clause has caused some comment. Professor Ames puts this case: The maker of a note delivers to the payee before maturity a horse in satisfaction of the debt evidenced by the note, but fails to take up the note. The payee then negotiates the note to an innocent holder. Professor Ames argues that as the note is discharged by the language of subsection 4, it cannot be enforced against the maker.

This does not follow. That the contract is discharged as between the parties by such a transaction as that imagined is good law and is in exact conformity with the language of the statute. But it has never been held that discharged paper cannot be negotiated anew before maturity. If the holder of a note, after receiving satisfaction, subsequently indorses to an innocent purchaser, he thereby draws a new bill upon which the acceptance of the maker is already written. Just as putting an incomplete bill into the hands of another party operates as authority to fill it out (§ 14); and just as a delivery is conclusively presumed in favor of the *bona fide* holder of a completed bill (§ 16); so, in this case, the maker of the note is estopped from setting up the previous discharge as against a *bona fide* holder.[4]

Sec. 120. A person secondarily liable on the instrument is discharged: —
1. By any act which discharges the instrument;
2. By the intentional cancellation of his signature by the holder;

money under a threat of suit, it was held that an action would not lie against the bank on its acceptance or certification to recover the money so refunded. Poess *v.* Twelfth Ward Bank, 43 Misc. (N. Y.) 45.

[3] A note is discharged where it is surrendered by an indorsee to the maker with the intention of discharging it upon payment of part only of the money, and this even though the maker promises at the time to pay the balance due on the debt. In such case the maker becomes a holder of the instrument in his own right within the meaning of subsection 5. Schwartzman *v.* Post, 94 N. Y. App. Div. 475.

[4] See Ames-Brewster Neg. Inst. Law, 42, 57; 41 Am. L. Reg. N. S. 572; Brief of Phi Delta Phi, vol. 3, p. 153; Crawford, Neg. Inst. Law, § 200, note (d); 16 Harv. L. Rev. 258; 2 Mich. L. Rev. 276.

3. By the discharge of a prior party;
4. By a valid tender of payment made by a prior party;
5. By a release of the principal debtor, unless the holder's **right** of recourse against the party secondarily liable is expressly reserved;[5]
6. By any agreement binding upon the holder to extend the time of payment, or to postpone the holder's right to enforce the instrument, unless made with the assent of the party secondarily liable, or unless the right of recourse against such party is expressly reserved.

Subsection 3.— This clause does not explicitly state whether it applies only to acts of the holder which operate as discharges or whether it includes discharges resulting from the operation of law, e. g., bankruptcy. Inasmuch as the other clauses refer to acts *inter partes,* Judge Brewster insists that subsection 3 also applies only to such acts.[6] This view is doubtless the correct one, as it is a reasonable construction and avoids certain mischievous consequences that, as Professor Ames has pointed out, would be likely to follow from a different interpretation.[7]

Sec. 121. Where the instrument is paid by a party secondarily liable thereon, it is not discharged;[8] but the party so paying it is remitted to his former rights as regards all prior parties, and he may strike out his own and all subsequent indorsements, and again negotiate the instrument, except:—
 1. Where it is payable to the order of a third person, and has been paid by the drawer; and

---

[5] See 2 Mich. L. Rev. 280; Brief of Phi Delta Phi, vol. 5, pp. 14, 15; 41 Am. L. Reg. N. S. 578; 16 Harv. L. Rev. 259. Mr. Farrell points out that "the principal debtor" is not necessarily the same as "party primarily liable." The party primarily liable is the one who on the face of the instrument is absolutely required to pay the same, while the term "principal debtor" is peculiar to the law of suretyship and such person may be one who is only secondarily liable on the paper. Brief of Phi Delta Phi, vol. 5, p. 14.

[6] See 41 Am. L. Reg. N. S. 575 et seq.

[7] See Ames-Brewster Neg. Inst. Law, 42, 57; 2 Mich. L. Rev. 277; 16 Harv. L. Rev. 659. It is not to be doubted that a discharge of the person primarily liable by virtue of the statute of limitations discharges an indorser. Shutts *v.* Fingar, 100 N. Y. 539. But in this case the discharge results from the negligent omission of the creditor and not solely from the act of law. 2 Mich. L. Rev. 279; Brief of the Phi Delta Phi, vol. 5, p. 13.

[8] Twelfth Ward Bank *v.* Brooks, 63 N. Y. App. Div. 220.

2. Where it was made or accepted for accommodation, and has been paid by the party accommodated.

Sec. 122. The holder may expressly renounce his rights against any party to the instrument, before, at, or after its maturity. An absolute and unconditional renunciation of his rights against the principal debtor made at or after the maturity of the instrument discharges the instrument. But a renunciation does not affect the rights of a holder in due course without notice. A renunciation must be in writing, unless the instrument is delivered up to the person primarily liable thereon.

Sec. 123. A cancellation made unintentionally, or under a mistake or without the authority of the holder, is inoperative; but where an instrument or any signature thereon appears to have been cancelled the burden of proof lies on the party who alleges that the cancellation was made unintentionally, or under a mistake or without authority.

Sec. 124. Where a negotiable instrument is materially altered without the assent of all parties liable thereon, it is avoided, except as against a party who has himself made, authorized, or assented to the alteration, and subsequent indorsers.

But when an instrument has been materially altered and is in the hands of a holder in due course, not a party to the alteration, he may enforce payment thereof according to its original tenor.

What is the meaning of the word 'altered' in this section? In England it means 'changed'; in America it has a narrower import and has become so thoroughly identified with this acquired meaning that the presence of the word in this section has caused confusion. It has long been established in England that a material change in a bill or note avoids it regardless of whether the change was made by the holder or a stranger. The Bills of Exchange Act, § 64, perpetuates the English rule, but, to some extent, saves the right of innocent holders by providing that they may enforce the instrument according to its original tenor where the alteration is not apparent.

The American Negotiable Instruments Law, § 124, is almost a verbal copy of the English statute on this point. The question therefore arises whether the word 'alteration' is here used in the same sense that it bears in the statute from which this section was copied. Judge Brewster says that the codifiers intended to change the American rule and thus secure uniformity, and that in order to secure this uniformity they adopted the language found in the English statute. In *Jeffrey v. Rosenfeld* (1901),[9] in a considered dictum, it was suggested that, notwithstanding the similarity between the wording of the American and English sections, it was not unreasonable to suppose that it was the intention of the framers of the American Act that § 124 should be construed according to the law of this country rather than that of England. The clear weight of nonjudicial opinion is, however, to the effect that the word 'altered,' in § 124, is to be accepted in its primary signification, and that the American doctrine is accordingly abolished.[1] Between the two views there seems to be little reason for preference; but it is to be hoped the various American courts will arrive at the same conclusion, whatever it may be.

Sec. 125. Any alteration which changes: —
1. The date;
2. The sum payable, either for principal or interest;
3. The time or place of payment;
4. The number or the relations of the parties;[2]
5. The medium or currency in which payment is to be made;
Or which adds a place of payment where no place of payment is specified, or any other change or addition which alters the effect of the instrument in any respect, is a material alteration.

TITLE II

BILLS OF EXCHANGE.

ARTICLE I

FORM AND INTERPRETATION.

Sec. 126. A bill of exchange is an unconditional order in writing addressed by one person to another, signed by the person giving it, requiring the person to whom it is addressed to pay on demand or at a fixed or determinable future time a sum certain in money to order or to bearer.

[9] 179 Mass. 506.
[1] See Norton on Bills (Tiffany's ed.), 248; Ames-Brewster Neg. Inst. Law, 83, 85; 41 Am. L. Reg. N. S. 580, 582.

[2] Changing name of payee in an incomplete note is a material alteration. Hoffman *v.* Planters Nat. Bank, 99 Va. 480.

Sec. 127. A bill of itself does not operate as an assignment of the funds in the hands of the drawee available for the payment thereof, and the drawee is not liable on the bill unless and until he accepts the same.

Sec. 128. A bill may be addressed to two or more drawees jointly, whether they are partners or not; but not to two or more drawees in the alternative or in succession.[3]

Sec. 129. An inland bill of exchange is a bill which is, or on its face purports to be, both drawn and payable within this state. Any other bill is a foreign bill. Unless the contrary appears on the face of the bill, the holder may treat it as an inland bill.

Sec. 130. Where, in a bill, drawer and drawee are the same person, or where the drawee is a fictitious person, or a person not having capacity to contract, the holder may treat the instrument, at his option, either as a bill of exchange or a promissory note.

Sec. 131. The drawer of a bill and any indorser may insert thereon the name of a person to whom the holder may resort in case of need; that is to say, in case the bill is dishonored by non-acceptance or non-payment. Such person is called the referee in case of need. It is in the option of the holder to resort to the referee in case of need or not, as he may see fit.

ARTICLE II

ACCEPTANCE.

Sec. 132. The acceptance of a bill is the signification by the drawee of his assent to the order of the drawer. The acceptance must be in writing and signed by the drawee. It must not express that the drawee will perform his promise by any other means than the payment of money.

The statute requires that the acceptance be in writing, thus doing away with oral acceptances which had been recognized as good by mercantile custom and sanctioned by the courts. Further, the acceptance must be signed by the drawee, but it will be sufficient if the drawee merely write his name on the bill, as such name constitutes the required signature and of itself includes and imports acceptance. The acceptance is not required, as by the English Bills of Exchange Act, to be written on the bill.

In England the Mercantile Law Amendment Act (1856)[4]

---

[3] The provision that bills may not be drawn upon two or more persons in the alternative or in succession changes the law. Daniel on Neg. Inst., § 488.

[4] 19 & 20 Vict., c. 60, § 11; c. 97, § 6.

required that the acceptance be on the bill itself and signed by the drawee. In *Hindhaugh v. Blakey* (1878) [5] the Court of Common Pleas held that the signature of the acceptor alone was not enough. This decision came as a surprise, and immediately caused the passage of a statute [5*] to the effect that the signature of the drawee should be sufficient. This act was, said Lord Selborne, in *Steele v. McKinlay* (1880),[6] a clear legislative declaration that the decision in *Hindhaugh v. Blakey* was erroneous. The Bills of Exchange Act sums up the previous legislation on this point without change.

Sec. 133. The holder of a bill presenting the same for acceptance may require that the acceptance be written on the bill, and, if such request is refused, may treat the bill as dishonored.

Sec. 134. Where an acceptance is written on a paper other than the bill itself, it does not bind the acceptor except in favor of a person to whom it is shown and who, on the faith thereof, receives the bill for value.

Sec. 135. An unconditional promise in writing to accept a bill before it is drawn is deemed an actual acceptance in favor of every person who, upon the faith thereof, receives the bill for value.

The last section embodies the results of the American doctrine of virtual acceptance. It will be seen that the virtual acceptance, as here defined, is really a common-law promise to accept supported by a consideration.

Sec. 136. The drawee is allowed twenty-four hours after presentment, in which to decide whether or not he will accept the bill; but the acceptance, if given, dates as of the day of presentation.

Sec. 137. Where a drawee to whom a bill is delivered for acceptance destroys the same, or refuses [7] within twenty-four hours after such delivery, or within such other period as the holder may allow, to return the bill accepted or non-accepted to the holder, he will be deemed to have accepted the same.

The latter provision changes the law. The drawee who refuses to return a bill is of course guilty of conversion. Section 137 is adopted from a statute of New York which has

[5] 3 C. P. D. 136.
[5*] 41 Vict., c. 13.
[6] 5 App. Cas. 754.
[7] To make the drawee liable as acceptor under this section the detention must be shown to be wrongful. There must be a refusal to surrender, not a mere neglect to return the instrument. *Westberg v. Chicago Lumber, etc., Co.*, 117 Wis. 589.

been enacted in several states. It is supposed to supply a convenient working rule and to give the holder some advantage in the matter of procedure. The idea that the destruction of a bill operates as an acceptance is, however, unnecessary and illogical.[8]

Concerning this section Mr. Cohen says: "It would seem to imply that if the bill be destroyed or not returned accepted within a reasonable time, notice of dishonor need not be given to the drawer. This is not, in my opinion, the law, and ought not to be law. [9]

Though the statute makes the drawee who destroys the note liable as acceptor, it does not take away the common-law right of action for conversion. Consequently, it is submitted, "if the drawee should throw the bill in the fire" the payee could elect to sue at once for the conversion or could treat the drawee as an acceptor, in which case he could not have a remedy until after dishonor for nonpayment.

Sec. 138. A bill may be accepted before it has been signed by the drawer, or while otherwise incomplete, or when it is overdue, or after it has been dishonored by a previous refusal to accept, or by nonpayment. But when a bill payable after sight is dishonored by non-acceptance and the drawee subsequently accepts it, the holder, in the absence of any different agreement, is entitled to have the bill accepted as of the date of the first presentment.

Sec. 139. An acceptance is either general or qualified. A general acceptance assents without qualification to the order of the drawer. A qualified acceptance in express terms varies the effect of the bill as drawn.

Sec. 140. An acceptance to pay at a particular place is a general acceptance, unless it expressly states that the bill is to be paid there only and not elsewhere.

Sec. 141. An acceptance is qualified, which is: —
  1. Conditional, that is to say, which makes payment by the acceptor dependent on the fulfilment of a condition therein stated;
  2. Partial, that is to say, an acceptance to pay part only of the amount for which the bill is drawn;
  3. Local, that is to say, an acceptance to pay only at a particular place;

---

[8] See Ames-Brewster Neg. Inst. Law, 34, 51; 41 Am. L. Reg. N. S. 582 *et seq.*

[9] Ames-Brewster Neg. Inst. Law 81.

4. Qualified as to time;
5. The acceptance of some one or more of the drawees, but not of all.

Sec. 142. The holder may refuse to take a qualified acceptance, and if he does not obtain an unqualified acceptance, he may treat the bill as dishonored by non-acceptance. Where a qualified acceptance is taken, the drawer and indorsers are discharged from liability on the bill, unless they have expressly or impliedly authorized the holder to take a qualified acceptance, or subsequently assent thereto. When the drawer or an indorser receives notice of a qualified acceptance, he must, within a reasonable time, express his dissent to the holder, or he will be deemed to have assented thereto.

ARTICLE III

PRESENTMENT FOR ACCEPTANCE.

Sec. 143. Presentment for acceptance must be made: —
1. Where the bill is payable after sight, or in any other case, where presentment for acceptance is necessary in order to fix the maturity of the instrument; or
2. Where the bill expressly stipulates that it shall be presented for acceptance; or
3. Where the bill is drawn payable elsewhere than at the residence or place of business of the drawee.

In no other case is presentment for acceptance necessary in order to render any party to the bill liable.

Sec. 144. Except as herein otherwise provided, the holder of a bill which is required by the next preceding section to be presented for acceptance must either present it for acceptance or negotiate it within a reasonable time. If he fail to do so, the drawer and all indorsers are discharged.

Sec. 145. Presentment for acceptance must be made by or on behalf of the holder at a reasonable hour, on a business day and before the bill is overdue, to the drawee or some person authorized to accept or refuse acceptance on his behalf; and —
1. Where a bill is addressed to two or more drawees who are not partners, presentment must be made to them all, unless one has authority to accept or refuse acceptance for all, in which case presentment may be made to him only;
2. Where the drawee is dead, presentment may be made to his personal representative;
3. Where the drawee has been adjudged a bankrupt or an insolvent or has made an assignment for the benefit of creditors, presentment may be made to him or to his trustee or assignee.

Sec. 146. A bill may be presented for acceptance on any day on which negotiable instruments may be presented for payment under the provisions of sections seventy-two and eighty-five of this act. When Saturday is not otherwise a holiday, presentment for acceptance may be made before twelve o'clock, noon, on that day.

Sec. 147. Where the holder of a bill drawn payable elsewhere than at the place of business or the residence of the drawee has not time with the exercise of reasonable diligence to present the bill for acceptance before presenting it for payment on the day that it falls due, the delay caused by presenting the bill for acceptance before presenting it for payment is excused, and does not discharge the drawers and indorsers.

Sec. 148. Presentment for acceptance is excused, and a bill may be treated as dishonored by non-acceptance, in either of the following cases: —

1. Where the drawee is dead, or has absconded, or is a fictitious person or a person not having capacity to contract by bill;
2. Where, after the exercise of reasonable diligence, presentment cannot be made;
3. Where, although presentment has been irregular, acceptance has been refused on some other ground.

Sec. 149. A bill is dishonored by non-acceptance: —

1. When it is duly presented for acceptance, and such an acceptance as is prescribed by this act is refused or cannot be obtained; or
2. When presentment for acceptance is excused, and the bill is not accepted.

Sec. 150. Where a bill is duly presented for acceptance and is not accepted within the prescribed time, the person presenting it must treat the bill as dishonored by non-acceptance or he loses the right of recourse against the drawer and indorsers.

Sec. 151. When a bill is dishonored by non-acceptance, an immediate right of recourse against the drawers and indorsers accrues to the holder, and no presentment for payment is necessary.[1]

ARTICLE IV

PROTEST.

Sec. 152. Where a foreign bill appearing on its face to be such is dishonored by non-acceptance, it must be duly protested for non-acceptance, and where such a bill which has not previously been dishonored by non-acceptance is dishonored by non-payment, it must be duly protested for non-payment. If it is not so protested, the drawer and indorsers are discharged. Where a bill does not appear on its

---

[1] See Ballingalls v. Gloster, 3 East 481; Evans v. Gee, 11 Pet. (U. S.) 80; Weldon v. Buck, 4 Johns. (N. Y.) 144; Exeter Bank v. Gordon, 8 N. H. 66; Lenox v. Cook, 8 Mass. 460. Compare § 157. See also 4 Am. and Eng. Encyc. of Law (2d ed.) 379.

face to be a foreign bill, protest thereof in case of dishonor is unnecessary.

Sec. 153. The protest must be annexed to the bill, or must contain a copy thereof, and must be under the hand and seal of the notary making it, and must specify,—
1. The time and place of presentment;
2. The fact that presentment was made and the manner thereof;
3. The cause or reason for protesting the bill;
4. The demand made and the answer given, if any, or the fact that the drawee or acceptor could not be found.

Sec. 154. Protest may be made by,—
1. A notary public; or
2. By any respectable resident of the place where the bill is dishonored, in the presence of two or more credible witnesses.

Sec. 155. When a bill is protested, such protest must be made on the day of its dishonor, unless delay is excused as herein provided. When a bill has been duly noted, the protest may be subsequently extended as of the date of the noting.

Sec. 156. A bill must be protested at the place where it is dishonored, except that when a bill drawn payable at the place of business, or residence of some person other than the drawee, has been dishonored by non-acceptance, it must be protested for non-payment at the place where it is expressed to be payable, and no further presentment for payment to, or demand on, the drawee is necessary.

Sec. 157. A bill which has been protested for non-acceptance may be subsequently protested for non-payment.

It is a well-known rule of law that, as recognized in § 151, an immediate right of action accrues upon protest for nonacceptance. Section 157 recognizes that a bill already protested for nonacceptance may be again protested for nonpayment. There was some authority for this before the statute. *Campbell v. French* (1795)[2] is usually cited to this point, but in that case there was an express agreement that the bills should be protested for nonpayment. The authorities are not clear as to what effect is to be given to a protest for nonpayment such as is permitted to be made under § 157. It is obvious that after the drawer and indorsers are released by failure to protest or give notice of protest for nonacceptance, no new right of action can be called into being by protesting for nonpayment. In *Rogers v. Stephens* (1788)[3] it was held that protest for nonpayment must be supplemented by proof of protest for nonacceptance, and that it is not sufficient

[2] 6 T. R. 200.   [3] 2 T. R. 713.

merely to show that the instrument was noted for nonacceptance.[4] But it has been held that foreign bills of exchange which have been refused acceptance and subsequently protested for nonpayment may be given in evidence without any accompanying protest for nonacceptance.[5]

Sec. 158. Where the acceptor has been adjudged a bankrupt or an insolvent, or has made an assignment for the benefit of creditors, before the bill matures, the holder may cause the bill to be protested for better security against the drawer and indorsers.

Sec. 159. Protest is dispensed with by any circumstances which would dispense with notice of dishonor. Delay in noting or protesting is excused when delay is caused by circumstances beyond the control of the holder and not imputable to his default, misconduct, or negligence. When the cause of delay ceases to operate, the bill must be noted or protested with reasonable diligence.

Sec. 160. When a bill is lost or destroyed or is wrongly detained from the person entitled to hold it, protest may be made on a copy or written particulars thereof.

ARTICLE V

ACCEPTANCE FOR HONOR.

Sec. 161. Where a bill of exchange has been protested for dishonor by non-acceptance or protested for better security, and is not overdue, any person not being a party already liable thereon may, with the consent of the holder, intervene and accept the bill supra protest for the honor of any party liable thereon, or for the honor of the person for whose account the bill is drawn. The acceptance for honor may be for part only of the sum for which the bill is drawn; and where there has been an acceptance for honor for one party, there may be a further acceptance by a different person for the honor of another party.

Sec. 162. An acceptance for honor supra protest must be in writing, and indicate that it is an acceptance for honor, and must be signed by the acceptor for honor.

Sec. 163. Where an acceptance for honor does not expressly state for whose honor it is made, it is deemed to be an acceptance for the honor of the drawer.

Sec. 164. The acceptor for honor is liable to the holder and to all parties to the bill subsequent to the party for whose honor he has accepted.

[4] See Thompson v. Cumming, 2 Leigh (Va.) 321.

[5] Clarke v. Russell, 3 Dall. (U. S.) 425; Brown v. Barry, 3 Dall. (U. S.) 365.

Sec. 165. The acceptor for honor, by such acceptance engages that he will on due presentment pay the bill according to the terms of his acceptance, provided it shall not have been paid by the drawee, and provided also, that it shall have been duly presented for payment and protested for non-payment and notice of dishonor given to him.

Sec. 166. Where a bill payable after sight is accepted for honor, its maturity is calculated from the date of the noting for non-acceptance and not from the date of the acceptance for honor.[6]

Sec. 167 Where a dishonored bill has been accepted for honor supra protest or contains a reference in case of need, it must be protested for non-payment before it is presented for payment to the acceptor for honor or referee in case of need.

Sec. 168. Presentment for payment to the acceptor for honor must be made as follows:—

1. If it is to be presented in the place where the protest for non-payment was made, it must be presented not later than the day following its maturity.
2. If it is to be presented in some other place than the place where it was protested, then it must be forwarded within the time specified in section one hundred and four.

Sec. 169. The provisions of section eighty-one apply where there is delay in making presentment to the acceptor for honor or referee in case of need.

Sec. 170. When the bill is dishonored by the acceptor for honor it must be protested for non-payment by him.

ARTICLE VI

PAYMENT FOR HONOR.

Sec. 171. Where a bill has been protested for non-payment, any person may intervene and pay it supra protest for the honor of any person liable thereon or for the honor of the person for whose account it was drawn.

Sec. 172. The payment for honor supra protest in order to operate as such and not as a mere voluntary payment must be attested by a notarial act of honor, which may be appended to the protest or form an extension to it.

Sec. 173. The notarial act of honor must be founded on a declaration made by the payer for honor or by his agent in that behalf declaring his intention to pay the bill for honor and for whose honor he pays.

Sec. 174. Where two or more persons offer to pay a bill for the honor of different parties, the person whose payment will discharge most parties to the bill is to be given the preference.

Sec. 175. Where a bill has been paid for honor, all parties subse-

---

[6] This section abolishes the rule declared in Williams *v.* Germaine, 7 B. & C. 468, 14 E. C. L. 84.

quent to the party for whose honor it is paid are discharged, but the payer for honor is subrogated for, and succeeds to, both the rights and duties of the holder as regards the party for whose honor he pays and all parties liable to the latter.

This is the rule laid down in *Ex p. Lambert* (1806).[7] Professor Ames criticises it and says that the rule stated in *In re Overend* (1868)[8] is better. In this latter case, which overruled the former, it was held that the payer for honor is subrogated to the rights of the holder as against the party for whose honor he pays, and all parties *prior to* the latter instead of *liable to*. Under this latter rule one who paid for the honor of the drawer could maintain an action against an accommodation acceptor. But inasmuch as an acceptor who accepts for the accommodation of the drawer is not *liable to* the drawer, under the rule declared in § 175, the payer for the honor of the drawer cannot now sue such acceptor. The English Bills of Exchange Act embodied the rule of *Ex p. Lambert,* and the few American cases in point have followed it.[9] The draftsman of the English Act, as Professor Ames says, may have inadvertently adopted the earlier rule, though it had been overruled by *In re Overend*. Mr. Crawford followed the wording of the English Act, and as between the two rules there seems to be little ground for preference. The payer for honor and the accommodation acceptor are on about the same footing so far as equitable considerations are concerned. Each acts in order to favor the drawer. Each looks to the drawer for reimbursement, and it seems not unreasonable to give the payer for honor a right of action only against the person for whose credit he intervenes and those liable to him.[1]

Sec. 176. Where the holder of a bill refuses to receive payment supra protest, he loses his right of recourse against any party who would have been discharged by such payment.

Sec. 177. The payer for honor, on paying to the holder the amount of the bill and the notarial expenses incidental to its dishonor, is entitled to receive both the bill itself and the protest.

[7] 13 Ves. Jr. 179.
[8] L. R. 6 Eq. 344.
[9] Gazzam *v.* Armstrong, 3 Dana (Ky.) 554; McDowell *v.* Cook, 6 Smed. & M. (Miss.) 420.

[1] See Ames-Brewster Neg. Inst. Law 44, 58; 41 Am. L. Reg. N. S. 585, 586.

ARTICLE VII

BILLS IN A SET.

Sec. 178. Where a bill is drawn in a set, each part of the set being numbered and containing a reference to the other parts, the whole of the parts constitutes one bill.

Sec. 179. Where two or more parts of a set are negotiated to different holders in due course, the holder whose title first accrues is as between such holders the true owner of the bill. But nothing in this section affects the rights of a person who in due course accepts or pays the part first presented to him.

Sec. 180. Where the holder of a set indorses two or more parts to different persons he is liable on every such part, and every indorser subsequent to him is liable on the part he has himself indorsed, as if such parts were separate bills.

Sec. 181. The acceptance may be written on any part and it must be written on one part only. If the drawee accepts more than one part, and such accepted parts are negotiated to different holders in due course, he is liable on every such part as if it were a separate bill.

Sec. 182. When the acceptor of a bill drawn in a set pays it without requiring the part bearing his acceptance to be delivered up to him, and that part at maturity is outstanding in the hands of a holder in due course, he is liable to the holder thereon.

Sec. 183. Except as herein otherwise provided, where any one part of a bill drawn in a set is discharged by payment or otherwise the whole bill is discharged.

TITLE III

PROMISSORY NOTES AND CHECKS.

ARTICLE I

Sec. 184. A negotiable promissory note within the meaning of this act is an unconditional promise in writing made by one person to another, signed by the maker, engaging to pay on demand, or at a fixed or determinable future time, a sum certain in money to order or to bearer. Where a note is drawn to the maker's own order, it is not complete until indorsed by him.

Sec. 185. A check is a bill of exchange drawn on a bank payable on demand. Except as herein otherwise provided, the provisions of this act applicable to a bill of exchange payable on demand apply to a check.[2]

[2] See observations on § 89, *ante*.

Sec. 186. A check must be presented for payment within a reasonable time after its issue, or the drawer will be discharged from liability thereon to the extent of the loss caused by the delay.

Sec. 187. Where a check is certified by the bank on which it is drawn, the certification is equivalent to an acceptance.

Sec. 188. Where the holder of a check procures it to be accepted or certified the drawer and all indorsers are discharged from liability thereon.

Sec. 189. A check of itself does not operate as an assignment of any part of the funds to the credit of the drawer with the bank, and the bank is not liable to the holder, unless and until it accepts or certifies the check.

TITLE IV

GENERAL PROVISIONS.

ARTICLE I

Sec. 190. This act shall be known as the Negotiable Instruments Law.

Sec. 191. In this act, unless the context otherwise requires,—

"Acceptance" means an acceptance completed by delivery or notification.

"Action" includes counter-claim and set-off.

"Bank" includes any person or association of persons carrying on the business of banking, whether incorporated or not.

"Bearer" means the person in possession of a bill or note which is payable to bearer.

"Bill" means bill of exchange, and "note" means negotiable promissory note.

"Delivery" means transfer of possession, actual or constructive, from one person to another.

"Holder" means the payee or indorsee of a bill or note, who is in possession of it, or the bearer thereof.

"Indorsement" means an indorsement completed by delivery.[3]

"Instrument" means negotiable instrument.

"Issue" means the first delivery of the instrument, complete in form, to a person who takes it as a holder.

"Person" includes a body of persons, whether incorporated or not.

"Value" means valuable consideration.

"Written" includes printed, and "writing" includes print.

---

[3] Indorsement means an indorsement completed by delivery. But possession of paper properly indorsed is sufficient evidence of title, and no proof of delivery is required. New Haven Mfg. Co. v. New Haven Pulp, etc., Co., 76 Conn. 126; Louisville Coal Min. Co. v International Trust Co., 18 Colo. App. 345.

Sec. 192. The person "primarily" liable on an instrument is the person who by the terms of the instrument is absolutely required to pay the same. All other parties are "secondarily" liable.

Sec. 193. In determining what is a "reasonable time" or an "unreasonable time," regard is to be had to the nature of the instrument, the usage of trade or business (if any) with respect to such instruments, and the facts of the particular case.[4]

Sec. 194. Where the day, or the last day, for doing any act herein required or permitted to be done falls on Sunday or on a holiday, the act may be done on the next succeeding secular or business day.

Sec. 195. The provisions of this act do not apply to negotiable instruments made and delivered prior to the passage hereof.

Sec. 196. In any case not provided for in this act the rules of the law merchant shall govern.

[4] In Massachusetts demand must be made within sixty days on a demand note in order to hold an indorser, this term being the result of long usage, sanctioned for a great many years by statutes which are now repealed by the Negotiable Instruments Law. Merritt v. Jackson, 181 Mass. 69.

www.ingramcontent.com/pod-product-compliance
Lightning Source LLC
Chambersburg PA
CBHW020623220526
45464CB00001B/2